Higher Education in Ireland, 1922–2016

John Walsh

Higher Education in Ireland, 1922–2016

Politics, Policy and Power—A History of Higher Education in the Irish State

palgrave
macmillan

John Walsh
Cultures Academic Values and Education
   Research Centre, School of Education
Trinity College Dublin
Dublin, Ireland

ISBN 978-1-137-44672-5   ISBN 978-1-137-44673-2   (eBook)
https://doi.org/10.1057/978-1-137-44673-2

Library of Congress Control Number: 2018950503

This Palgrave Macmillan imprint is published by the registered company Springer Nature Limited
The registered company address is: The Campus, 4 Crinan Street, London, N1 9XW, United Kingdom

Acknowledgements

This book would not have happened without the support and assistance of a great many people. I am very grateful to Dr. Mairéad Finn and Rebecca Flynn for their assistance with the research at different stages of the study. I would like to thank fellow researchers, colleagues and friends who generously shared information from their own research or pointed me towards relevant documents, including Dr. Aidan Seery, Dr. Ann Nolan, Dr. Michelle Share, Prof Selina McCoy, Dr. Delma Byrne, Prof Andrew Loxley, Dr. Rory McDaid, Dr. Eavan O'Brien, Dr. Shane Martin, Dr. Ludovic Highman, Clodagh Byrne, Colm Mac Gearailt and Andrew Gibson.

This study drew upon an extensive range of archival and library sources and I would like to thank the staff of the National Archives, the National Library of Ireland, the Dublin Diocesan Archives, the National University of Ireland, the Higher Education Authority, Queen's University, Belfast, UCD Archives department and the Library of Trinity College Dublin. I am grateful too for the assistance of staff and activists with the Irish Federation of University Teachers and the Teachers Union of Ireland.

I greatly appreciate the co-operation of the former public represent-atives, civil servants and academics, who acted as expert 'witnesses' on policy or institutional developments in which they were involved: some of these interviewees are identified below and others have maintained anonymity in line with appropriate ethical guidelines, but all have my profound thanks. Rosaleen Rogers of Audiotrans supplied the tran-scripts of the interviews with her usual speed and professionalism.

This book benefited greatly from the support of the editors at Palgrave Macmillan; Laura Aldridge, Rebecca Wyde and Eleanor Christie, who showed exemplary patience and dedication and always offered helpful advice. The insightful comments by the Palgrave reviewers were invaluable and helped to make this a better book. I am grateful to Jananee Murugan and the production team for assistance in copy-editing and Julitta Clancy for producing the index in such a comprehensive and professional way. I wish to thank Nora Thornton in the National Photographic Archive and Berni Metcalfe and Glenn Dunne in the National Library for their assistance in sourcing the illustrations for the book.

I wish to acknowledge the interest and advice of colleagues in the Centre for Cultures Academic Values and Education and the School of Education, Trinity College Dublin. I greatly appreciated the support of colleagues on the M.Ed. team as the book was being written, Dr. Maija Salokangas, Keara Eades and Catherine Minet. I also benefited from the support of successive Heads of School in completing the study, Prof Michael Grenfell, Prof Carmel O'Sullivan, Prof Andrew Loxley and Prof Damian Murchan.

I am particularly grateful to friends and family who have also lived with this book over the last four years. Siobhán and Kevin offered advice, support and sometimes essential technical assistance. Above all I owe a debt of gratitude to my parents, John and Maura, who as always were constantly encouraging and supportive.

October 2018   John Walsh

Contents

List of Figures

Introduction

The scope of higher education is subject to conflicting interpretations and change over time. Higher level courses at degree and postgraduate level were almost exclusively the preserve of the universities in the early twentieth century. Primary teacher education in Ireland was envisaged as a post second level endeavour from the 1920s, but not explicitly linked to university qualifications until forty years later. Technical schools operated by Vocational Education Committees (VECs) in Dublin and Cork would not typically have been considered higher level institutions in the early 1900s, but several developed into colleges of technology within a reconfigured non-university sector from the 1960s. Post-compulsory further education and training was originally associated with the second-level sector and developed as a distinct sector in its own right only in the last two decades.[1] This study explores the emergence of the modern higher education system in the Irish state, tracing its origins from a fragmented tertiary space including traditional universities, teacher training colleges and technical schools in the early twentieth century to the complex, massified and diverse system of the twenty first century.

Burton Clark in a seminal analysis of forces of coordination in higher education, identified the state, academic oligarchy and the market as the three main elements within a 'triangle of coordination', which he envisaged as a continuum shaped by different forms of integration and influence within distinct national systems.[2] Clark's triangular model identified the dominant forms of integration in North America and Europe based on a cross-national comparison in the late twentieth century.[3] Yet this analysis risks understating other 'forces of coordination', often rooted in international organisation or ideology. As Marginson and Rhoades point out, the Catholic Church was 'a powerful example of global influence on the structural and ideological underpinnings of higher education.'[4] This applies with particular force to Ireland, where the rejection of neutral or 'godless' university colleges in the mid to late 1800s was a key inflection point in the triumph of ultramontane Catholicism. Higher education in Ireland evolved in a distinctive political and cultural context shaped by conflicting religious and national allegiances.

Hazelkorn et al suggest that Irish higher education remained 'essentially a self-referential system' in the twentieth century.[5] While this captures the persistence of established structures, institutions and practices up to the late 1900s, it understates the power of international forces and ideologies over a wider historical timeframe. Conceptualisations of the university and higher education in Ireland were shaped by ideologies with an international reach, including ultramontane Catholicism, postwar social and Christian democracy and theories of human capital formation rooted in liberal economics. Cultural and political nationalism also framed the context in which higher education institutions functioned in the early to mid-twentieth century. More recently, the emergence of globalisation has exerted a profound influence on higher education systems in the developed world, contributing to a reappraisal of policy, curriculum frameworks and institutional structures in Ireland. As Vaira notes, powerful supranational agencies such as the Organisation for Co-operation and Development in Europe (OECD) serve as 'institutional carriers' which promote and disseminate 'the wider rationalised myths' of globalisation, establish the legitimacy of policies and institutional behaviours and define the context in which HEIs (and national systems) operate in the contemporary world.[6] The interface between the state, academic institutions and other key institutional actors, including the churches, Irish language organisations, employers and trade unions, is the major focus of the study. Exploring the interplay between HEIs, domestic political, religious and business elites and supranational organisations such as the OECD and European Union, is essential to understanding the evolution of the modern Irish HE system. The study's focus on the influence of ideology and the role of supranational organisations in mediating dominant discourses is also intended to avoid the perils of 'methodological nationalism'[7] and the familiar trap of using Britain (or England) as the chief reference point.

There is no detailed academic study of higher education (HE) in the modern Irish state from a historical perspective. As White noted in 2001, while research on education has greatly expanded over the past generation, the history of higher education has attracted relatively little scholarly analysis, particularly in comparison with other developed countries.[8] Many of the texts on the history of Irish education, including Ó Buachalla (1988) and Mulcahy and O'Sullivan (1989) date from the 1980s and their access to state papers on education was restricted by the thirty-year rule.[9] John Coolahan's excellent (and recently updated) survey of the history and contemporary structure of education in Ireland has a broad focus encompassing primary, second level and higher education from 1800 to the present day.[10] Clancy (1989) and Ó Buachalla (1992) explore the massification and diversification of Irish higher education between the 1960s and the 1980s.[11] Tony White's work considered the transformation of the higher education system between 1960 and 2000, informed mainly by official publications and other published literature. Denis O'Sullivan (2005) explored the cultural politics underpinning Irish education as a whole, seeking to locate the transformation of the educational sector within a theoretical framework.[12] More recently, the historical development and current direction of teacher education in independent Ireland is explored by O'Donoghue, Harford and O'Doherty, in a detailed exposition informed by a range of secondary sources, while Richard Thorn has published a study on the evolution of the Regional Technical Colleges from their foundation to the contemporary period.[13]

While higher education in Ireland attracted relatively little historical analysis until the early 2000s, there is an increasingly extensive literature on contemporary higher education policy. Patrick Clancy's detailed analysis of Irish higher education is the most recent major work in the field, considering the contemporary higher education system in a comparative context.[14] Access and participation at higher level have been the subject of in-depth scholarly exploration since the 1970s (including successive HEA studies led by Clancy, a number of studies commissioned by the ESRI and most recently an edited volume by Loxley, Fleming and Finnegan) and this book has benefited greatly from their detailed engagement with the subject.[15] Loxley et al also presented a detailed overview of policy and curriculum developments linked to various thematic areas, while O'Connor undertook an in-depth analysis of gender in higher education management.[16] I have tried to avoid replicating the work or analysis of others, while drawing upon the growing body of literature in the field of higher education.

The book is informed principally by archival sources (particularly the departmental papers in the National Archives), many of which were not previously available or were not exploited for a study of higher education. The research also draws upon official publications, parliamentary debates and national newspapers. I have used extensively the reports of the Public Accounts Committee, which contain a wealth of data on education, particularly for the earlier chapters of the book. The records of the Catholic archdiocese of Dublin proved invaluable, particularly the voluminous McQuaid papers, in deciphering the close relationship between the bishops, their academic allies and public officials up to the 1970s. The book draws on a range of institutional records, including the minutes and correspondence files of the senate of the National University of Ireland and minutes and correspondence of the Board of TCD. Although the study is based principally on documentary research, I have also conducted a number of interviews, which were useful in understanding contemporary developments where government papers or other archival records are not yet available.[17]

The focus of the book is the history of higher education in independent Ireland from the creation of the Irish Free State until the end of the economic crisis triggered by the 'Great Recession'. As this study has a historical focus, it does not set out to offer a comprehensive exploration of academic practice, pedagogy or culture in contemporary higher education.[18] Higher education in Northern Ireland is outside the scope of this book, as it forms a distinctive educational sector requiring examination in its own right, shaped by the policies of the British state, the regional priorities of the Stormont administration (1922–72) and the community division in Northern Ireland. While further education as a whole is not the main focus of this work, important aspects of FE, including the development of a national framework for apprenticeship and the emergence of post Leaving Certificate courses, are closely interrelated with the history of higher education.

The study is structured primarily in a chronological format, including a brief analysis of the historical context in the early twentieth century; the ideological underpinnings of Irish universities; the emergence of the Irish Universities Act, 1908 and the position of women in higher education. The earlier Chapters (2–5) reflect on the university-dominated sector up to the 1950s, the under-researched sphere of higher technical education and the close alliance between the state and the major churches in the training of primary teachers. Chapters 7–8 present an in-depth analysis of the transformation of the higher educational sector through diversification, expansion and massification in the second half of the twentieth century. The final chapter takes a more explicitly thematic approach to contemporary policy developments in the early 2000s, exploring internationalisation, teaching and learning, research, the rise of managerialism, access, gender, private higher education, financial sustainability and the impact of economic crisis. The closing discussion of the Hunt Report and ensuing contemporary initiatives gives an introduction informed by a historical perspective to an ongoing and still fluid process of policy and structural change.

The book considers how the exercise of power at local, national and international level impinged on the mission, purpose and values of higher education and on the creation and expansion of a distinctive higher education system. The transformation in public and political understandings of the role of higher education is considered, charting the gradual and sometimes tortuous evolution from traditionalist conceptions of the academy as a repository for cultural and religious value formation to the re-positioning of higher education as a vital factor in the knowledge based economy. This study explores policy, structural and institutional change in Irish higher education, suggesting that the emergence of the modern higher education system in Ireland was profoundly influenced by ideologies and trends which owed much to a wider European and international context.

Notes

1. FE has recently began to attract more scholarly analysis, notably by Rory O'Sullivan, "From 'Cinderella' to the 'Fourth Pillar' of the Irish Education System—A Critical Analysis of the Evolution of Further Education and Training in Ireland" (Ph.D. diss., TCD, 2018).
2. Burton Clark, *The Higher Education System Academic Organisation in Cross-National Perspective* (Berkeley: University of California Press, 1983), 142–3.
3. Ibid., 143–5.
4. Simon Marginson and Gary Rhoades, 'Beyond Nation States, Markets and Systems of Higher Education: A Glonacal Agency Heuristic,' *Higher Education* 43 (2002): 288.
5. Ellen Hazelkorn, Andrew Gibson, and Siobhán Harkin, 'From Massification to Globalisation: Reflections on the Transformation of Irish Higher Education,' in *The State in Transition: Essays in Honour of John Horgan*, ed. Kevin Rafter and Mark O'Brien (Dublin: New Island, 2015), 256.
6. Massimiliano Vaira, 'Globalisation and Higher Education: A Framework for Analysis,' *Higher Education* 48 (2004): 488.
7. Clancy, *Irish Higher Education: A Comparative Perspective* (Dublin: IPA, 2015), 2.
8. Tony White, *Investing in People: Higher Education in Ireland from 1960 to 2000* (Dublin: IPA, 2001), vii.
9. Séamus Ó Buachalla, *Education Policy in Twentieth Century Ireland* (Dublin: Wolfhound, 1988).
10. John Coolahan, *Towards the Era of Lifelong Learning A History of Irish Education, 1800-2016* (Dublin: IPA, 2017).

11. Patrick Clancy, 'The Evolution of Policy in Third-Level Education,' in *Irish Educational Policy: Process and Substance*, ed. D. G. Mulcahy and Denis O'Sullivan (Dublin: IPA, 1989), 99–132; Séamus Ó Buachalla, 'Self-Regulation and the Emergence of the Evaluative State: Trends in Irish Higher Education Policy, 1987–92', *European Journal of Education* 27, no.1/2 (1992): 69–78.

12. Denis O'Sullivan, *Cultural Politics and Irish Education Since the 1950s: Policy, Paradigms and Power* (Dublin: IPA, 2005).

13. Tom O'Donoghue, Judith Harford, and Teresa O'Doherty, *Teacher Preparation in Ireland: History, Policy and Future Directions* (Emerald: 2017); Richard Thorn, *No Artificial Limits: Ireland's Regional Technical Colleges* (Dublin: IPA, 2018)—Richard Thorn's valuable study was published after the submission of the current study so the author did not have the opportunity to consult it in detail.

14. Patrick Clancy, *Irish Higher Education: A Comparative Perspective* (Dublin: IPA, 2015).

15. Patrick Clancy, *Who Goes to College? A Second National Survey of Participation in Higher Education* (Dublin: HEA, 1988); Ted Fleming, Andrew Loxley, and Fergal Finnegan, *Access and Participation in Irish Higher Education* (London: Palgrave, 2017).

16. Andrew Loxley, Aidan Seery, and John Walsh, *Higher Education in Ireland: Practices, Policies and Possibilities* (Basingstoke: Palgrave Macmillan, 2014).

17. The interviews fall into two distinct categories. A number of interviews were conducted with recent participants in the policy-making process who discussed their recollections on the basis of anonymity and confidentiality. These interviews have been anonymised and these interviewees are identified only by pseudonym (Interviewee A): The data has been kept confidential and is being used only for the purpose of this study. Interviews were also conducted with former policy-makers and academics, where anonymity could not be guaranteed or was not sought by interviewees. All interviews were conducted in line with the approval given to this project by the School of Education Research Ethics Committee.

18. For such analysis, see Andrew Loxley, Aidan Seery, and John Walsh, *Higher Education in Ireland: Practices, Policies and Possibilities* (Basingstoke: Palgrave Macmillan, 2014); Coolahan, *Towards the Era of Lifelong Learning*; O'Donoghue, Harford, and O'Doherty, *Teacher Preparation in Ireland: History, Policy and Future Directions*, on teacher education.

1

Ideas of the University

The history of higher education in Ireland is inseparable from wider debates around competing ideas of the university and more broadly of the purpose of higher level learning. John Henry Newman first expressed his famous ideal of a liberal university education in Dublin, in a series of lectures entitled *Discourses on the Scope and Nature of University education*. Newman's first series of lectures were delivered in May–June 1852 at the invitation of Paul Cullen, the newly appointed archbishop of Dublin and a leading proponent of ultramontane Catholicism, who sought an articulate critique of secular higher education. The *Discourses* offered a broad vision of university education, informed by a striking mixture of Oxbridge academic tradition and Catholic religious conviction:

> That it is a place of *teaching* universal knowledge. This implies that its object is, on the one hand, intellectual, not moral; and on the other, that it is the diffusion and extension of knowledge rather than the advancement. If its object were scientific and philosophical discovery, I do not see why a University should have students; if religious training, I do not see how it can be the seat of literature and science.[1]

© The Author(s) 2018
J. Walsh, *Higher Education in Ireland, 1922–2016*,
https://doi.org/10.1057/978-1-137-44673-2_1

Newman conceptualised the university as a place for intellectual formation and the cultivation of knowledge rather than training for the
professions or vocational preparation for a useful function in society. Teaching rather than scientific research or 'discovery' was at the
core of his vision of education. Moreover, his *Discourses* enunciated a
distinctive humanist ideal of the purpose of university education:
'Knowledge is capable of being its own end. Such is the constitution
of the human mind, that any kind of knowledge, if it be really such, is
its own reward'.[2] Among Newman's distinctive contributions to educational thought was to combine this broad conceptualisation of liberal
education, influenced by the example of Oxford in the mid nineteenth
century, with a defence of the importance of religion within the programme of studies.[3] Newman advanced a subtle argument that while
the university was not a centre of religious training, its essential function in teaching 'universal knowledge' required the teaching of theology
and the separation of religion from secular disciplines was nothing less
than the undermining of university education itself: 'Religious Truth is
not only a portion, but a condition of general knowledge. To blot it out
is nothing short, if I may so speak, of unravelling the web of University
Teaching'.[4] Newman's ideal was at odds with and in many respects a
response to influential political and educational developments in his
own time, notably the increasing emphasis on a more utilitarian model
of higher education, associated with the foundation of the University
of London in 1836 and the Queen's Colleges in Ireland in the 1840s,
which involved the application of learning in a secular context to the
practical and scientific challenges of an industrialised society.[5]

An equally distinctive and perhaps more influential vision of the university was offered by Wilhelm Von Humboldt's memorandum on the
organisation of 'intellectual institutions' in Germany in 1810.[6] Higher
intellectual institutions, such as the university, had as their task 'the cultivation of science and scholarship (Wissenschaft) in the broadest sense'.[7]
Von Humboldt envisaged the complementary activities of research and
teaching in the service of knowledge as the fundamental attributes of
a university: 'At the higher level...both teacher and student have their
justification in the common pursuit of knowledge. The teacher's performance depends on the students' presence and interest – without this

science and scholarship could not grow.'[8] The function of the state was to supply the organisational framework and resources for the practice of scholarship while preserving the autonomy of the intellectual life of the university: 'The state must understand that intellectual work will go on infinitely better if it does not intrude.'[9] The Humboldtian ideal did not exclude state intervention in the university, but urged that it be kept to a necessary minimum and should avoid interference with the intellectual activity of the university where its intrusion could only be prejudicial.[10] As Neave notes, this vision of autonomy was not always compatible with the increasing vocational demands for professional training in administration and business during the nineteenth century.[11] Yet Humboldt's ideal influenced the development of the research-oriented university in Germany, which combined a high level of state support and initiative with professorial power and autonomy.[12] Moreover, Humboldt's characterisation of teaching and research as the central, complementary purposes of the university has had a long-term resonance in shaping both scholarly understandings and institutional organisation of the university in Europe up to the contemporary period.

The Humboldtian ideal of autonomy was not universally accepted in Irish political discourse, where freedom was interpreted in the light of conflicting political or religious allegiances. Sir James Graham, who spearheaded legislation to create the Queen's Colleges as home secretary in 1845, insisted that the crown should retain the power to appoint and remove professors, ostensibly to protect students from proselytising: 'security must be taken that …opportunities are not seized of making these lectures the vehicle of any peculiar religious tenets.'[13] The majority of the British political elite adopted the principle of non-denominational education in Ireland from the mid nineteenth century, with the logical implication of no state endowment for denominational education at higher level. This conversion by the British government occurred just as Catholic opinion in Ireland, led by the Catholic bishops, moved firmly in the opposite direction. Cardinal Cullen, who condemned the 'godless colleges' precisely because of their secular, non-denominational status, was remarkably similar to Graham in his demands of any university serving Catholic students. The bishops would require the necessary power to exclude 'bad books and bad professors' to protect their co-religionists from proselytising by Protestant denominations or the equally baleful influence of 'the new sect, of Secularists...'.[14]

A distinctively Anglo-Saxon model of the academy, characterised by the absence of formal state regulation and a traditional perception of universities as corporations in a 'semi-private relationship' with the state, was also influential in the development of universities in Ireland.[15] Trinity College Dublin, the oldest university in Ireland which was established in 1592 under an Elizabethan charter, was obliged to secure the assent of the crown in relation to the appointment of its provost and amendments to the college statutes from 1637.[16] Yet under the statutes the provost and senior fellows enjoyed a high level of autonomy in managing the affairs of the college and their autonomy was respected by governments throughout the 1800s. The presidents of the Queen's Colleges were appointed by the government, but enjoyed considerable freedom in their academic affairs within the loose structure of the Royal University (1881–1909). The Irish Universities Act, 1908, gave considerable autonomy to the newly reconstituted National University of Ireland and Queen's University, Belfast, vesting authority in university senates which following a five year transition period were mainly elected by academics, graduates and professional interests, rather than nominated by the government.

The 'Irish University Question'

The development of the major universities on the island of Ireland was linked to religious and political divisions rooted in historical conflicts which cast a long shadow well into the twentieth century. Trinity College maintained a monopoly of posts and offices for an Anglican elite until the late nineteenth century: while all religious tests for posts and offices outside its Divinity School were abolished by Fawcett's Act in 1873, the college remained closely associated with the Protestant ruling class and was a bastion of unionism up to the first world war.[17] The debate over university education was entangled with the wider constitutional struggle over the union during the late nineteenth century.[18] A number of reforming initiatives for university education, embarked on with varying degrees of conviction by British ministers, failed in the face of the incompatible demands of conflicting political and religious forces. The most famous initiative was taken by William Gladstone, who proposed a grand plan for a single federal university in Ireland in 1873.[19] The Prime Minister succeeded in uniting a remarkable range of mutually hostile interests, spanning the ideological spectrum from Trinity College to Cardinal Cullen, against the legislation, which was defeated by three votes in the House of Commons in March 1873: the dramatic defeat decisively undermined Gladstone's government.[20] Arthur Balfour, the leading architect of constructive unionism, almost a quarter of a century later proposed two new universities in Ireland, one in Dublin for the Catholic majority and the other in Belfast for Protestants, while leaving TCD untouched.[21] But despite the advice of the Conservative *Spectator* that the 'Tory-Orange opposition is noisy but not formidable', the Conservative government backed away from legislation in the face of vehement unionist resistance.[22] Successive governments set up commissions of enquiry into university education, the Robertson commission (1901–03) and Fry commission (1906–07), but neither was able to achieve consensus even among their own members.[23]

A more modest initiative by Benjamin Disraeli's government in 1879 was successful in establishing the Royal University, as a degree awarding institution overseeing competitive examinations but not requiring attendance at any college institutions (with the exceptions of schools of medicine).[24] The 'Royal' allowed differing denominations to compete for the same examinations within a common institutional framework and opened up university qualifications to women for the first time.[25] Almost a quarter of the Royal University's 2173 graduates were women by 1900,[26] ensuring that university education in Ireland was no longer a male preserve. Its loose institutional structures facilitated a high level of autonomy among a diverse conglomeration of educational institutions, including the three Queen's Colleges and University College Dublin (UCD), administered by the Jesuits on behalf of the bishops. Moody points to the 'great and timely stimulus to higher education in

Ireland' given by the examining university at a pivotal time following the introduction of state support for intermediate schools in 1878.[27] Yet the Royal University was unloved by almost all the contending parties in late nineteenth century Ireland. William Walsh, archbishop of Dublin (1885–1921) expressed the view of most parties in arguing that 'The new University, then, was universally regarded as a temporary expedient...'[28]

The election of a Liberal government in 1906 and appointment of Augustine Birrell as chief secretary in January 1907 paved the way for the resolution of the 'Irish university question'. Birrell quietly dropped the venerable plan for reconstituting the University of Dublin within a great federal institution, instead adopting the more limited scheme originally floated by Balfour as the template for his universities bill.[29] Birrell collaborated closely with Walsh in drafting the legislation.[30] Birrell dispatched an outline of the scheme to Walsh on 31 December 1907, commenting that 'It is Your Grace will at once perceive a Skeleton – but anatomy in such matters is of the first importance'.[31] The legislation accommodated denominational realities rather than seeking to challenge them: 'two Universities Belfast Dublin – on the same Constitutional lines – with Governing Bodies which will reflect and represent the prevalent character of the place in which they are situated, the graduates of the University and so on'.[32] Birrell's initiative left the existing University of Dublin intact, while establishing two new universities in Ireland, both formally non-denominational, but with a federal institution based in Dublin to offer higher education acceptable to Catholics and a single university in Belfast, mainly to serve the Presbyterian community in Ulster.

Birrell urged Walsh to sound out his fellow bishops by ascertaining 'general views and suggestions – so as to avoid as many Rocks of offence as possible'.[33] Birrell accepted that it was impossible to legislate on university education in Ireland without taking account of ecclesiastical power. This would be a lesson closely followed by his successors in Irish governments until the late twentieth century. Walsh supported the scheme, warning Birrell that the new federal university should be as well financed as Trinity College and the reconstituted Queen's University:

As I have already said to you, I think it a very good scheme…better than any other kind of scheme I can think of, excepting of course one that would give us equality with TCD…Are we Catholics to get as much as the two great Protestant Colleges and Universities will get? If so, we have equality in one most substantial point…[34]

The bishops collectively accepted the federal framework of the university and the absence of religious tests, but set out as a key condition inclusion of the Catholic seminary at St. Patrick's College, Maynooth within the new federal university.[35]

The universities Bill provided for the dissolution of the Royal University; the reconstitution of Queen's College, Belfast as a separate university and the establishment of a new federal university based in Dublin, incorporating the Jesuit college at University College, Dublin (UCD) and the Queen's Colleges in Cork and Galway as its constituent colleges. The new universities were established as non-denominational institutions financed by the state, with 'no test whatever of religious belief' relating to professors, students or graduates and a strict prohibition on any religious preference.[36] County and borough councils were empowered to provide scholarships supporting students to attend the new universities, funded by local government rates, provided that no scholarship was 'subject to or conditional upon any religious qualification'.[37] The other defining principle of the Bill was that in contrast to the Royal University the new institutions would be teaching universities, requiring attendance at lectures as a condition for examination and graduation. The legislation ensured recognition for graduates of the Royal University as graduates of one of the new universities and credit to students for previous courses and examinations.[38]

The legislation delegated a great deal of authority to separate statutory commissions in Dublin and Belfast, which were given the crucial task of preparing the university statutes and making the first academic appointments for a seven year period.[39] The commissions were representative of local political and religious elites. Walsh was nominated to the Dublin commission, which was headed by Sir Christopher Palles, the first Catholic chief baron of the Irish exchequer and a close ally of the archbishop; the commission also included Denis Coffey, president of UCD from 1909, two nationalist MPs and the presidents of the colleges in Cork and Galway.[40] Crucially, a clause providing for 'affiliation' of recognised colleges was included in the Bill, to facilitate the incorporation of St Patrick's College, Maynooth and Magee College, an institution founded in 1865 in Derry for the training of Presbyterian ministers, within the new universities based in Dublin and Belfast respectively, although neither college was named.[41]

Birrell openly acknowledged that the Bill was designed to recognise cultural and denominational realities in Ireland:

> The most anybody can say is that we are planting one University on what, I suppose, may be called Protestant soil, although there are many Roman Catholics in Ulster, and the other on what may be called Roman Catholic soil, although there are many Protestants in Dublin and Cork, and some even in Galway…There is no originality about this scheme - anybody who likes may claim it as his own.[42]

The universities Bill was passed by the House of Commons with cross-party support in July 1908 by a decisive margin of 207 to 19, facing concerted opposition only from the Ulster unionist MPs.[43] Birrell's achievement was recognised by MPs of various persuasions, with the Conservative MP Samuel Butcher joking that he 'had to unite in his own person the views of a Roman prelate and a Nonconformist minister'.[44] The collaboration between Walsh and Birrell was fundamental to the success of the universities bill. The educational experiment initiated in the early 1900s signalled a pragmatic accommodation in university education between the British political elite and the Catholic bishops.

'Nobody's Ideal'

The verdict of historians on the Irish Universities Act has been varied. T. W. Moody commented that the educational settlement of 1908–10 foreshadowed the partition of Ireland little more than a decade later.[45] FSL Lyons followed a similar interpretation, suggesting that the settlement marked a defeat for the concept of 'mixed' education at higher level at least in the southern part of the island.[46] Coolahan, however, noted that while the solution reached in 1908 was in gestation for a long period 'it proved remarkably durable', surviving for three quarters of a century without serious alteration.[47] The prospect of 'neutral' higher education free of denominational influence was bleak in the early 1900s, due to the sharp cultural and religious cleavages in Irish society, the denominational basis of primary and intermediate education and the incompatible objectives of the major political forces on the island.

Timothy Healy's famous comment in July 1908 that 'The Bill is nobody's ideal' was essentially accurate but also explained why the universities settlement proved enduring.[48] The universities act reflected a historic compromise between an increasingly powerful nationalist political community in Ireland and the dominant forces within the British state, albeit one which was restricted to higher education. The university settlement was the least divisive solution in an Ireland deeply marked by religious and political conflict and the only one which could command support from the most influential forces in nationalist Ireland, established institutions such as Trinity College and the British political elite.

The NUI was firmly under the control of Catholic, nationalist elites and conflict within the senate largely took the form of generational or political differences among these elites. The new federal university met long-term Catholic demands and also offered a framework for the pursuit of cultural nationalist aspirations. The university in Belfast won rapid acceptance despite the early hostility of unionist politicians to the legislation, not least due to the shrewd decision to adopt the name of the Queen's University of Belfast, which appealed to the loyalty of local elites and graduates to the original Queen's College dissolved on the foundation of the Royal University.[49]

The first senate of the NUI was dominated by lay, professional, upper middle class Catholics, with a strong representation of lawyers, the medical profession and public representatives. Although it contained a number of Protestant nominees, the composition of the governing body reflected the predominantly Catholic cultural and ideological milieu which shaped the foundation of the new university. The proportion of Catholic clergy (4 out of 39) was relatively small, but carried considerable weight—two archbishops, Walsh and John Healy, archbishop of Tuam, were nominated to the senate by the crown, as was William Delany S. J., the outgoing president of UCD.[50] The NUI senate, in contrast to the Royal University where nominations had been reserved to the Crown, was allowed to elect the first Chancellor, with successors being selected by Convocation which included the senate, academic staff and graduates of the university.[51] Walsh was elected unanimously as Chancellor on 18 December 1908.[52] The archbishop's prestige, position and long-term advocacy for Catholic higher education made him the inevitable choice.[53] While the senate's decision was made with the support of its Protestant members, Walsh's election indicated the predominantly Catholic nature of the new federal university.

The first senate of Queen's was largely drawn from the Protestant social and commercial elite in the north-east of Ireland, offering representation to commercial, medical and local government bodies, as well as local magistrates and graduates of Queen's college.[54] The senate was a predominantly unionist body, although the crown appointed five Catholic members and it also included liberal mavericks such as W. J. Pirrie, a Liberal peer and the Rev. J. B. Armour of Ballymoney.[55] The majority of the senate were external members from the professions, politics or the Belfast commercial elite. The governing body was designed, like its federal counterpart in Dublin, to reflect its local cultural and religious milieu. The Presbyterian General Assembly accepted the new university despite its earlier opposition to the legislation.[56] The 'affiliation' clause offered an avenue for recognition of Magee by Queen's University and two representatives of the college, including its president, J. R. Leebody, were appointed to the senate. The college authorities, however, instead succeeded in making an agreement with TCD in 1909, which allowed students in Magee to secure a university degree, by pursuing most of the arts course in Magee, but attending four academic terms in Trinity and undertaking the degree examinations.[57] Magee maintained its affiliation to Trinity until 1968, forging a distinctive linkage between the University of Dublin and Ulster Presbyterianism.

UCD had 656 matriculated students in 1910–11, with over half pursuing courses in the Medical Faculty; most of the remainder were undertaking Arts courses, including Law.[58] Queen's University was broadly comparable to UCD in its size, boasting an enrolment of 620 full-time students in 1909–10.[59] Queen's also had a strong tradition of part-time participation, mainly through an extensive programme of university extension lectures by the Workers' Educational Association; there were over 200 part-time students attending afternoon and evening classes in 1910–11.[60] The largest proportion of students were Presbyterian, accounting for between 40 and 50% of the student body in its first decade as an independent university.[61] But Queen's also attracted a significant proportion of Catholic students: in 1915–16 Catholics accounted for over 25% of the total student body, surpassing the number of Church of Ireland students up to the early 1920s.[62]

Catholicism was an important unifying feature of the early NUI. The Catholic primate, Cardinal Michael Logue, alluded to the calculation made by the bishops in accepting the NUI, at St Mary's College, Dundalk, on 6 June 1911:

> They gave us what they hoped to be a pagan University, but, please God, let it be a Catholic University…turn loose upon it a lot of fine, young Irish Catholics, and they will soon make it a Christian institution.[63]

He sounded the same note in an address at Maynooth on 25 June 1912, expressing the confidence of most bishops that the cultural and religious setting in which the new institution operated would prevail over formal rules and prohibitions: '…they have dropped that Pagan bantling down in the midst of us, and, please God, if we can, we will baptise it and make it Christian.'[64]

Logue's confidence was justified. The NUI offered higher education in an institutional setting pervaded by the dominant Catholic religious milieu which produced its leaders and the large majority of its staff and students. UCD inherited its name, religious tradition and a substantial section of its staff from the Jesuit college on St. Stephen's Green.

About three-quarters of the professors appointed by the Dublin commission had been members of the faculty or former students in
University College, St. Stephen's Green or the Cecilia St. medical
school.[65] The transfer of students from the Jesuit college, Cecilia St.
and the Catholic women's university colleges made up the largest proportion of UCD's student population, while most first year entrants
were drawn from Catholic secondary schools.[66]

Both of the former Queen's Colleges in Cork and Galway experienced a far-reaching and relatively rapid process of 'Catholicisation',
which was well advanced before the foundation of the Irish state.
UCC president Bertram Windle, a convert to Catholicism whose zeal-
ous devotion to his adopted faith was recognised when he was made a
Knight of St. Gregory by Pope Pius X, exerted profound influence on
the college in its transition to the NUI. He assured Walsh in 1908 of
his determination to transform the college into a bastion of the Catholic
faith: 'I look upon this university as one of the greatest – I think the
greatest – opportunity that I have ever had and I hope to build up a
College here in Cork which will be a centre of Catholic influence for
the South of Ireland'.[67] Alexander Anderson, an eminent physicist and
native of Coleraine, was the sole leader of a Queen's College to continue
well into the early years of the Irish state, serving as president for thirty
five years (1899–1934).[68] The college's governing body consisted mainly
of lay Catholic notables and clergy by 1913 and Fr John Hynes BD, a
dominant figure on the governing body, was appointed as registrar in
1916.[69] UCG's student population was drawn almost entirely from the
overwhelmingly Catholic counties of Connacht and as the smallest and
least well financed of the colleges it was particularly dependent on the
financial support which it received from local county councils, making
UCG highly responsive to its regional cultural and religious context.[70]

The de facto Catholic tone and character of the university was reinforced by the admission of Maynooth. The senate agreed in February
1910 to approve St. Patrick's College, Maynooth as a recognised college of the university within the faculties of arts, philosophy and Celtic
Studies for an initial four year period.[71] This decision, which allowed
clerical students in Maynooth to secure university degrees, was later

renewed indefinitely. Maynooth functioned both as a seminary and a recognised college of the NUI, offering secular courses of study in arts and science to clerical students as well as theological training for the priesthood. The most balanced verdict on the new university was given by Samuel Butcher, a member of the first senate but essentially a sympathetic outsider, who identified the aim of the act as 'a University which should be Catholic in tone and spirit and yet academic in principles'.[72] This was an apt description of the NUI well into the second half of the twentieth century.

The NUI from the outset was profoundly affected by the political and popular movement for Gaelicisation. The Gaelic League enjoyed its most striking success less than a year after the inauguration of the new university, when the NUI senate agreed by majority vote in June 1910 to introduce Irish as an essential subject for matriculation within three years.[73] McCartney argued that 'essential Irish' was imposed by nationalist UCD representatives, over the opposition of the Cork and Galway members,[74] a complaint certainly voiced at the time by Windle. But while the UCD representatives were in favour of 'essential Irish', the outcome of the debate was not primarily due to the superior clout of the largest college in the NUI. The advocates of 'essential Irish' commanded the big battalions, in the form of the overwhelming support of county and borough councils, whose support was necessary for the establishment of local authority scholarship schemes.[75] Although two college presidents and several bishops opposed 'essential Irish', the Gaelic League succeeded in mobilising a national movement for compulsory Irish which overcame substantial academic and clerical opposition within the senate.[76]

The first world war and the 1916 Rising which ultimately created the conditions for the collapse of the union transformed the political context in which Irish universities had functioned. The revolutionary era between 1914 and 1922 saw a generational and ideological transition in the leadership of the NUI. The leading Catholic office-holders who had led the university at its foundation gave way to a more assertively nationalist leadership openly hostile to the British connection. Bertram Windle resigned as president of UCC in 1919, following the failure of his ill-fated campaign to create an independent university of Munster, which aroused fierce opposition in UCC, the NUI senate and from Sinn Féin MPs in Munster.[77] Delany was re-appointed to the first elected senate, but ceased to be active in university affairs during the war.[78] Walsh remained an influential Chancellor until his death in 1921, although he was unable to attend any meetings of the senate between October 1917 and his death in April 1921.[79]

The eclipse of constitutional nationalism during the 1918 general election was played out in the NUI graduate constituency, where Eoin MacNéill, the Sinn Féin candidate, decisively defeated Arthur Conway, running as a Home Ruler: MacNéill took his seat as an abstentionist MP in the First Dáil in January 1919.[80] The ascendancy of Sinn Féin led to the nomination of Eamon de Valera, the leader of the revolutionary government established by the First Dáil, as Chancellor in succession to Walsh. De Valera recognised the propaganda value of his nomination: '...actual election at the time might be of public value and of help to our Cause'.[81] When he was elected unopposed as Chancellor on 20 July 1921, de Valera was keen to underline its political significance in his telegram of acceptance: '...the conferring of this honour on the head of state indicates the path Ireland desires to tread'.[82]

The collapse of the union destroyed the traditional political architecture in which Trinity College had enjoyed a privileged position. Cautious accommodation to radically changing conditions became the hallmark of the college's leadership during the 1920s. The provost, J. H. Bernard (1919–27), publicly supported a home rule settlement in October 1919, along the lines of the abortive report of the Irish Convention; Bernard was attempting to avoid a worse outcome, namely a separate Irish republic on a partitioned island.[83] Bernard also sought to secure financial assistance from Westminster before a home rule settlement was implemented. A Royal Commission, headed by Sir Archibald Geikie, recommended in November 1920 an annual subsidy of £49,000 for the college, along with a generous capital allocation of £113,000.[84] Lloyd George's coalition included a legal guarantee of a state grant of £30,000 annually to Trinity in clause 64 of the Government of Ireland Act, 1920.[85] But the home rule legislation was defunct outside Northern Ireland from the moment of its adoption. Only Trinity's four parliamentary representatives attended the first meeting of the Parliament of Southern Ireland in July 1921.[86] Bernard appealed directly to Lloyd George in October 1921, warning that 'Trinity College Dublin is the centre of loyalty and allegiance to the King in this country and the gravest dissatisfaction will be caused among loyalists all over Ireland if we are left without the State aid which was pledged to us by an Act of Parliament.'[87] The interests of the college were intertwined with the embattled southern unionists, who might inspire sympathy in Westminster but whose power was increasingly a thing of the past.

The college's leadership was pragmatic in accepting the Anglo-Irish Treaty in December 1921, although it established a self-governing Irish state which went well beyond home rule. The Board of TCD approved a resolution supporting the new constitutional settlement on 10 December 1921 by a margin of nine votes to three: 'The true interest of Trinity College can only be furthered by Irish peace; and in the building up of happier conditions in Ireland the Board of Trinity College believes that Trinity men should take an active and supportive part.'[88] Despite the contested vote, the Board's statement was a striking gesture by an institution which had been a bastion of unionism barely a decade earlier and represented a key moment in the gradual accommodation by the college's leadership to a new Irish state.

Yet a decade of upheaval and revolution did not change fundamentally the institutional framework established by the universities legislation or provoke any further re-appraisal of the relationship between academic institutions, the state and the churches established in the early years of the twentieth century. The key rupture with the federal, all-Ireland university system had already occurred with the creation of two new universities in place of the pre-1909 Royal University. The institutional pattern of university education in Ireland until the late twentieth century was established by the settlement adopted in 1908–09.

Halfway Revolution

The enduring strength of restrictive Victorian social attitudes, dictating a separate and lesser place for women in society, remained a formidable barrier to female participation in higher education until the early 1900s. The success of women's university colleges in Dublin and Belfast in presenting students for the Royal University examinations during the late 1800s testified to the ability of women students to compete effectively with their male counterparts and helped to discredit the institutional inequalities imposed on them. But the campaign by the Irish Association of Women Graduates and Candidate Graduates (IAWG) founded in 1902 was crucial in winning public support for equal female participation at university level. The feminist movement faced resistance not only from bastions of the Anglo-Irish establishment and representatives of the increasingly influential Catholic lay and clerical elite, but from the women's colleges.

Institutional resistance proved strong enough to block any progress towards equal participation until the early 1900s. Although an increasing proportion of junior fellows and professors in TCD favoured a more liberal approach at the time of the college's tercentenary in 1892, George Salmon, the provost, was implacably opposed and the status quo was upheld by the majority of elderly senior fellows.[89] The Jesuit leadership of UCD was equally reluctant to admit women students. Delany allowed attendance by women students at 'public' lectures in the early 1900s, but refused to open UCD to women on a basis of equality with men, arguing that the college lacked the space and facilities to admit women. While this was no mere pretext, as the college on Stephen's Green was overcrowded, Delany was firmly opposed to co-education, which was inconsistent with the Victorian social propriety that he shared with many contemporaries.[90] Delany's intransigence provoked protests by students and a public clash with the college's registrar, Francis Sheehy-Skeffington, a leading supporter of female suffrage, whose wife Hanna was an IAWG activist. Sheehy Skeffington resigned as registrar in 1905, drawing greater publicity for the women graduates' campaign.[91] Delany's opposition blocked the formal admission of women students to UCD until the reconstitution of the college in 1909.

Opposition to inclusion of women in co-educational settings was not restricted to male upholders of the status quo. A key fissure emerged among female educational activists on whether women should continue to attend women's colleges (endowed and affiliated to universities) or be admitted to co-educational universities on an equal basis with men.[92] Separate provision for women emerged as the main bone of contention between leading educators in the women's colleges and a new generation of feminists in the IAWG, many of them graduates of the colleges. Feminist activists such as Alice Oldham, Mary Hayden and Agnes O'Farrelly clashed with the representatives of the women's colleges, both Protestant and Catholic, in their evidence before the Robertson Commission. The report of the Commission was a victory for the IAWG: referencing their submission, the commissioners concluded that 'the Degrees of the reconstituted University should be open to women on the same terms as to men…attendance at lectures should be required from all candidates – without distinction of sex…'[93]

Yet this proved indecisive as the commission's report had no immediate impact. Henrietta White, the principal of Alexandra College, addressed a renewed appeal to the Fry Commission in favour of the affiliation of separate women's colleges to the university[94]: similar arguments were advanced by early pioneers of women's education, including the formidable Margaret Byers, founder of Victoria College, Belfast.[95] This prospect was unacceptable to the IAWG, compromising as it did the principle of equal participation by men and women.[96] But it was an attractive halfway house that appealed to most of the male commissioners. The report of the Fry Commission in 1907 was ambivalent, supporting female participation but leaving open the possibility that it could be achieved through recognition of the women's colleges by an existing university.[97]

Yet the momentum towards the inclusion of women in university education ultimately proved too great to be derailed either by the persistence of Victorian attitudes among male elites or the reservations of the women's colleges. Most universities in England and Scotland either provided for entry of women without discrimination or at least for a system of examinations for female students by the end of the nineteenth century, although neither Oxford nor Cambridge allowed women to take university degrees. A gradual generational transition among the senior fellows in Trinity paved the way for change, as leading support-ers of female participation, including Anthony Traill and J. P. Mahaffy, became members of the Board when opponents were removed by death or retirement. The Board of Trinity College decided by a major-ity vote in 1902 to admit women students and award them degrees, despite Salmon's opposition; the King's letter giving force to the stat-utory change was issued in December 1903, allowing the entry of the first women students in 1904.[98] The feminist movement also gained support from a new generation of cultural and political nationalists. The demand from the Irish parliamentary party and nationalist opinion in Ireland for a 'democratic' university institution reinforced the pressure on Birrell to ensure admission on an equal basis for women.

The Irish Universities Act completed the gradual opening up of higher education to women, ensuring that the new universities would be open to men and women without legal discrimination. The legis-lation established equality of rights at entry level for women students and graduates, eliminating formal restrictions linked to gender. The act also provided for at least one of the government's four nominees in each university senate to be female—the first legislative requirement relating to gender equality in higher education in Ireland. Mary Hayden was nominated as the sole female member of the first senate of the NUI, while Margaret Byers and Mary Hutton became members of the senate of Queen's University, Belfast (ironically considering Byers' previous opposition to co-education).[99] The Universities Act was the culmination of a generation of incremental progress and resistance, in which the women's colleges (despite their reservations about the ultimate settle-ment) and the feminist movement played a crucial part.

While the legislation conceded the principle of female participation, a battle continued over the form that such participation might take, with the women's colleges and a number of prominent churchmen and lay Catholics ranged against the feminists of the IAWG. The religious orders managing the Catholic women's colleges embarked on a struggle for recognition by the NUI. At first the women's colleges applied for recognition to offer 'approved courses of study' sanctioned by the university, but this application was rejected in December

1909 by the Chancellor, based on legal advice that such recognition could be given only to students pursuing courses in either constituent or recognised colleges.[100] Then Loreto College, St. Stephen's Green and St. Mary's college in Eccles St., sought to secure the status of recognised colleges under the Universities Act. This manoeuvre was firmly opposed by the IAWG, which warned the senate that it was 'undesirable to recognise any Courses of Lectures for women students for the Arts Degrees of the University other than those delivered in the Lecture Halls of the Colleges named in the Charter...'[101] The women's colleges enjoyed influential supporters, notably Delany and a number of Catholic bishops, although Walsh stayed aloof from the fray. The governing body of UCD first rejected affiliation for the women's colleges, but reversed itself in 1911 to offer partial recognition to Loreto College for a three year period.[102] This recommendation drew a counter-blast from the IAWG, which argued in July 1911 that recognition of non-endowed private colleges would lead to a 'lowering of the prestige of the National University' and deprive women of the high standard of education offered in the university colleges.[103] The NUI Board of Studies expressed bemusement at the application, noting that 'they were unable to understand the exact relations between the proposed College and the secondary instruction admittedly given in the same locality...': the board requested the senate to secure a legal opinion on the status of women's colleges which offered both intermediate and higher education.[104] This provided a way out of the impasse, as the opinion of legal counsel was unfavourable and the senate decided on 30 October 1912 to reject the applications by the women's colleges on legal grounds.[105] The decision confirmed the triumph of the IAWG in securing equal access to university education regardless of gender.

While the settlement established legal equality in terms of admission to university education in Ireland, it did not transform the character of the colleges, which remained small, elite institutions dominated by men. Only 67 students in UCD were women in 1910–11, just over 10% of the student body.[106] Trinity admitted 47 female students in 1904 and women made up 15% of the student body by 1914.[107] Queen's had the highest enrolment of women among its full time cohort of any Irish university, with 132 female students making up over 21% of the student population in 1909–10, reflecting an earlier acceptance of women students than any other college on the island.[108]

Legislative reform transformed the statutory framework but could not change established traditions, cultures and professional networks which strongly favoured men, particularly in academic appointments. The Dublin commissioners appointed a small but exceptionally active and articulate cohort of women to academic posts. Four women were appointed to the teaching staff of UCD, including Mary Hayden as first lecturer and soon afterwards professor in modern Irish history, Mary Macken as professor of German and Maria Degani as professor in Italian and Spanish.[109] The commission defied local opinion by appointing Degani, a graduate of the University of Padova who was one of the few non-Irish nominees. This was the most contentious appointment by the commissioners, provoking critical commentary in newspapers and even a resolution by Monaghan county council questioning the propriety of the decision.[110] Degani suffered from the dual liability in the eyes of her critics that she was both female and a foreigner.

The commissioners achieved a genuine, albeit limited, advance in female participation within the academic body. There were three female professors out of 45 in UCD by 1916, with a fourth, Agnes O'Farrelly, serving as a lecturer in Irish language and later as professor of modern Irish poetry.[111] Yet this represented less than 7% of senior appointments in UCD. A similar pattern prevailed in UCC, where two of the first 20 professors were women—Mary Ryan, professor of Romance Languages and Elizabeth O'Sullivan in education.[112] Trinity was equally tentative in appointing female academics. Constantia Maxwell became the first woman lecturer in 1909 on her appointment as assistant in history: Maxwell enjoyed an outstanding academic career, culminating in her elevation to the Lecky chair of history in 1945.[113] Women who secured academic appointments in the early twentieth century were usually exceptionally gifted and frequently active in other professional fields. Both Hayden and O'Farrelly served as members of the governing body in UCD, while Hayden was also a member of the NUI senate. The first woman professor in Trinity, Dr. Frances Moran, Reid professor in the school of law from 1925, was a pioneer in several areas: a qualified barrister, Moran was the first female senior counsel in Ireland or England

and ended her career as Regius professor of law in TCD.[114] The university settlement was a halfway revolution in terms of female participation: it established formal equality of rights in terms of the entry of women and co-education at university level, both bitterly contested in the late nineteenth century. The reforms of the early 1900s also facilitated some upward mobility, particularly by a small minority of talented and determined women. But established structures of power and privilege remained intact, which militated strongly against equality of opportunity for women.

Notes

1. John Henry Newman, *Discourses on the Scope and Nature of University Education: Addressed to the Catholics of Dublin* (Dublin: 1852), ix.
2. Ibid., 103.
3. Fergal McGrath, *Newman's University: Idea and Reality* (Dublin: 1951), 133.
4. Newman, *Discourses*, 70–1.
5. Coolahan, *History of Irish Ecolucation*, 113.
6. Wilhelm Von Humboldt, 'On the Spirit and the Organisational Framework of Intellectual Institutions in Berlin,' *Minerva: A Review of Science, Learning and Policy*, 8, no. 2 (April 1970): 243.
7. Ibid., 242–3.
8. Ibid., 243.
9. Ibid., 244.
10. Ibid., 244–49.
11. Guy Neave, 'The Changing Boundary Between the State and Higher Education,' *European Journal of Education* 17, no. 2 (1982): 231–41.
12. Harold Pekin, 'The Historical Perspective,' in *Perspectives on Higher Education*, ed. Burton Clark (Berkeley: California University Press, 1984), 36–7.
13. Hansard, House of Commons 80, 9 May 1845, col. 356: the Queen's Colleges were established in Belfast, Cork and Galway and brought within the framework of the Queen's University from 1849.
14. William J. Rigney, 'Bartholomew Woodlock and the Catholic University of Ireland 1861–79' (Ph.D. diss., UCD, 1995), 389–9.

15. Neave, 'State and Higher Education,' 231–41.
16. John V. Luce, *Trinity College Dublin the First 400 Years* (Dublin: TCD, 1992), 18–19.
17. R. B. McDowell and D. A. Webb, *Trinity College Dublin 1592–1952: An Academic History* (Cambridge: Cambridge University Press, 1982), 254; Tomás Irish, *Trinity in War and Revolution 1912–23* (Dublin: RIA, 2015), 12.
18. FSL Lyons, *Ireland Since the Famine* (London: Fontana, 1973), 96–7.
19. Gladstone, *University Education in Ireland, Speech by W.E. Gladstone,* 13 February 1873, 13–15 (DDA *Cullen Papers,* 45/6/1/5). William Ewart Gladstone began his career as a Conservative minister; having joined the Liberal party, he was Chancellor of the Exchequer in governments led by Palmerston and Russell (1859–66). Gladstone served four terms as Prime Minister (1868–74; 1880–85, 1886 and 1892–94).
20. Hansard House of Commons Debates, vol. 214, 11 March 1873, col. 1865–68.
21. Morrissey, *Towards a National University William J. Delany S.J.* (Dublin: Wolfhound, 1983), p. 169: Arthur James Balfour was Chief Secretary in Ireland (1886–91); Leader of the House of Commons (1895–1902) and Prime Minister (1902–05). Balfour later served as foreign secretary in Lloyd George's wartime coalition government and was the author of the Balfour Declaration.
22. *Spectator,* 'The Government and Mr Balfour's University Scheme,' 4 February 1899.
23. *Royal Commission on University education in Ireland, Final Report* (Dublin: His Majesty's Stationery Office, 1903), 60–62; *Royal Commission on Trinity College Dublin and the University of Dublin* (Dublin: His Majesty's Stationery Office, 1906), 3.
24. Aine Hyland and Kenneth Milne, *Irish Educational Documents 2* (Dublin: CICE, 1992), 338–9.
25. T. W. Moody, 'The Irish University Question of the Nineteenth Century,' *History* 43 (1958): 103.
26. John Coolahan, 'From Royal University to National University,' in *The National University of Ireland 1908–2008 Centenary Essays,* ed. Tom Dunne et al. (Dublin: UCD Press, 2008), 5.
27. Moody, 'Irish University Question,' 103.
28. William Walsh, *Memorandum on the Irish University Question* (Dublin: 1887), 73.

29. Léon Ó Broin, *The Chief Secretary: Augustine Birrell in Ireland* (London: Chatto & Windus, 1969), 24–26.
30. Birrell to Walsh, 31 December 1907 (DDA NUI/14); Hyland and Milne, *Irish Educational Documents* 2, 358.
31. Birrell to Walsh, 31 December 1907 (DDA NUI/14).
32. Birrell to Walsh, 20 January 1908 (DDA NUI/14).
33. Birrell to Walsh, 20 January 1908.
34. Walsh to Birrell, 6 January 1908 (DDA NUI/14).
35. Walsh to Birrell, 23 January 1908 (DDA NUI/14).
36. *Irish Universities Act* (London: 1908), 3.
37. Ibid., 10.
38. Ibid., 12.
39. *Irish Universities Act*, 4.
40. Birrell to Walsh, 20 May 1908 (DDA NUI 14).
41. Birrell to Walsh, 29 March 1908.
42. Hansard, House of Commons Debates 187, 31 March 1908, col. 353–4.
43. Hansard, House of Commons Debates 188, 11 May 1908, col. 867; Hansard, HC Debates 193, 25 July 1908, col. 661.
44. Ibid., col. 646.
45. T. W. Moody, 'The Irish University Question of the Nineteenth Century,' *History* 43 (1958): 91–109.
46. Lyons, *Ireland Since the Famine*, 98.
47. Coolahan, *Towards the Era of Lifelong Learning*, 86.
48. Timothy Healy was a long serving conservative nationalist MP; a leading anti-Parnellite in 1890, Healy maintained a close alliance with the Catholic bishops.
49. T. W. Moody and J. C. Beckett, *Queen's Belfast 1845–1949: The History of a University*, vol. 1 (London, 1959), 389–90.
50. NUI, Senate Minutes, vol. 1, 18 December 1908, 1.
51. *Irish Universities Act*, 28.
52. NUI, Senate Minutes, vol. 1, 18 December 1908, 1.
53. Dáire Keogh, 'William J. Walsh,' in *The National University of Ireland 1908–2008 Centenary Essays*, ed. Dunne et al. (UCD Press, Dublin), 126.
54. *Charter of the Queen's University of Belfast*, Section 6, 9, *Irish Universities Act*, 20.
55. *Charter of the Queen's University of Belfast*, Section 6, 9.

56. Moody and Beckett, *Queen's Belfast 1845–1949*, 89–90.

57. 'Re-arrangement of the Magee College Scheme', 2 July 1910 (MUN V/5/20).

58. Denis Coffey, *Number of Students 1910–11* (DDA NUI 2/23).

59. Queen's University Senate, Minutes, 14 October 1910, *Statistics of Session 1909–10*: this total includes both matriculated and non-matriculated students. There was a small number of non-matriculated students (only 12 in 1909–10, but marginally higher in 1 912–13).

60. Queen's University Senate, Minutes, *Appendix to the Vice-Chancellor's Report, Statistics of Session 1910–11*, 15 November 1911.

61. Queen's University Senate, Minutes, 22 November 1916, *The Vice-Chancellor's Report for the Year 1915–16*, 216–7; *Statistics of Session 1915–16*, 237; information is drawn mainly from reports by the deans of residence for each denomination.

62. Ibid.

63. *Irish Times*, 'Cardinal Logue and the National University,' 8 June 1911.

64. *Irish Times*, 'Cardinal Logue and the National University: "A Pagan Bantling,"' 25 June 1912.

65. Donal McCartney, *UCD: The History of University College Dublin* (Dublin: Gill and Macmillan, 1999), 33–4.

66. Ibid.

67. Windle to Walsh, 29 December 1908 (DDA NUI 13).

68. Tadhg Foley, ed., *From Queen's College to National University, Essays on the Academic History of UCG/UCG/NUI, Galway* (Dublin: Four Courts Press, 1999), 298.

69. Séamus Mac Mathúna, 'National University of Ireland, Galway,' in *National University of Ireland Centenary Essays*, ed. Tom Dunne, John Coolahan, Maurice Manning and Gearóid Ó Tuathaigh (Dublin: UCD Press, 2008), 64.

70. Ibid., 64–5.

71. NUI, Senate Minutes, vol. 1, 23 February 1910, 61.

72. Hansard, HC Debates 193, 25 July 1908, col. 646.

73. NUI, Senate Minutes, vol. 1, 23 June 1910, 119–20.

74. McCartney, *UCD*, 40.

75. *Deputation by General Council of County Councils to the NUI*, 6 (DDA NUI 2/23); NUI, Senate Minutes, 11 November 1909, 22.
76. NUI, Senate Minutes, vol. 1, 23 June 1910, 119–20.
77. John A. Murphy, *The College a History of Queen's/University College Cork, 1845–1995* (Cork: Cork University Press, 1995), 213.
78. Thomas J. Morrissey, *Towards a National University William Delany S.J.* (Dublin: Wolfhound, 1983), 369.
79. NUI, Senate Minutes, vol. 6–7, 12 October 1917–11 March 1921.
80. *Irish Times*, 'The Elections: National University,' 24 December 1918.
81. Eamon de Valera Papers, 'My Selection as Chancellor' (UCD Archives P150/93).
82. Ibid.; Eamon de Valera Papers, De Valera to Cox, 20 July 1921 (UCDA P150/93).
83. *Irish Times*, 'The Provost and Home Rule,' 23 October 1919.
84. *Memorandum*, 11 April 1923, 2 (MUN V 6/6/15).
85. Note by J. H. Bernard, 2 November 1920 (MUN V 6/5/115); Bernard to Hamar Greenwood, 24 January 1921 (MUN V 6/5/116).
86. *Irish Times*, 'The Southern Irish Parliament: Today's Adjourned Meeting,' 13 July 1921.
87. Bernard to Lloyd George, 24 October 1921 (MUN V 6/5/116).
88. Board Minutes, 10 December 1921 (MUN V/5/22).
89. R. B. McDowell and D. A. Webb, *Trinity College Dublin 1592–1952 an Academic History* (Cambridge: Cambridge University Press, 1982), 345–6.
90. Morrissey, *Towards a National University*, 279–80.
91. Ibid., 280–1; Senia Paseta, 'Achieving Equality: Women and the Foundation of the University,' in *The National University of Ireland 1908–2008 Centenary Essays*, ed. Tom Dunne et al. (Dublin: UCD Press, 2008), 28.
92. Judith Harford, 'Women and the Irish University Question,' in *Have Women Made a Difference? Women in Irish Universities, 1850–2010*, ed. Judith Harford and Claire Rush (Oxford: Peter Lang, 2010), 16–17.
93. *Royal Commission on University Education in Ireland, Final Report*, 49–50.
94. *Royal Commission on Trinity College Dublin and the University of Dublin, Appendix to the First Report, Statements and Returns Furnished*

to the Commissioners in July and August 1906 (Dublin: His Majesty's Stationery Office, 1903), 134–36.

95. *Belfast Newsletter*, 'Margaret Byers: Pioneer of Education for Ulster Girls,' 29 February 2012.

96. *Royal Commission on Trinity College Dublin and the University of Dublin*, 129–33.

97. Harford, 'Women and the Irish University Question,' 20–1.

98. McDowell and Webb, *Trinity College Dublin*, 348–9.

99. *Irish Universities Act*, 20; *Belfast Newsletter*, 'Margaret Byers: Pioneer of Education for Ulster Girls,' 29 February 2012.

100. Palles to Walsh, 19 December 1909 (DDA NUI 1/10); NUI, Senate Minutes, vol. 1, 22 December 1909, 34.

101. NUI, Senate Minutes, vol. 1, 22 December 1909, 34.

102. NUI, Senate Minutes, vol. 1, 14 July 1911, 277.

103. IAWG, *Memorial from the Irish Association of Women Graduates*, July 1911 (DDA, NUI 2/28).

104. NUI, Senate Minutes, vol. 1, 14 July 1911, 277.

105. NUI, Senate Minutes, vol. 2, 30 October 1912, 522.

106. Coffey, *Number of Students 1910–11* (DDA NUI 2/23).

107. Susan Parkes, 'The First Decade, 1904–14: A Quiet Revolution,' in *A Danger to the Men*, ed. Susan Parkes (Dublin: Lilliput Press, 2004), 55–86.

108. Queen's University Senate, Minutes, 14 October 1910, *Statistics of Session 1909–10*.

109. NUI, Senate Minutes, vol. 3, 27 February 1913, 33; McCartney, *UCD*, 83.

110. NUI, Senate Minutes, vol. 1, 14 July 1911, 287.

111. McCartney, *UCD*, 83.

112. NUI, Senate Minutes, vol. 5, 27 October 1916, 197.

113. Parkes, 'The First Decade,' 84

114. Parkes, 'The "Steamboat Ladies: The First World War and After,"' in *A Danger to the Men*, ed. Parkes (Dublin: Lilliput Press, 2004), 107–8.

2

Universities in the Irish Free State

The foundation of the Irish Free State in 1922 saw a high level of continuity in university education. The university settlement established by the Irish Universities Act, 1908, commanded a high degree of consensus within nationalist Ireland. The new political and administrative elites generally did not intervene in the internal governance or workings of the universities.[1] Irish ministers promoted piecemeal initiatives to promote favoured policies, particularly revolving around cultural nationalism. But the vast majority of politicians and officials were content to leave regulation of disciplines to academics or professional bodies: in terms of Humboldt's concept of university autonomy as freedom for teaching and research, Irish universities enjoyed a high level of autonomy in their core activities.[2] The other side of the coin, however, was perennial financial neglect, allied to a traditionalist vision of higher education as professional training for a privileged elite. Higher education simply did not feature among the priorities of the new nationalist governing elite, not least because it was on the periphery of the dominant ideological narratives which shaped the early Irish state.

© The Author(s) 2018
J. Walsh, *Higher Education in Ireland, 1922–2016,*
https://doi.org/10.1057/978-1-137-44673-2_2

While there is a lack of comprehensive data on higher education enrolments outside universities and teacher training colleges up to the early 1960s, the dominance of the universities within a limited and fragmented tertiary space was apparent.[3] Over 85% of students attending higher education institutions up to the mid-1960s pursued their studies in the universities.[4] Admission to the universities occurred through different matriculation examinations in the NUI, Trinity and the Royal College of Surgeons (RCSI). While the Department of Education was critical in 1933 of the range of entrance tests of varying standards, which 'affects injuriously both the work of the school and the work of the universities', no serious attempt was made to link university entrance to the public examinations, such as the terminal Leaving Certificate, in the first generation after independence.[5] Entry was determined mainly by family or individual resources. As Coolahan notes, despite the enabling clause in the Irish Universities Act, the resources devoted to scholarships or other awards remained 'meagre'.[6] Financial support for access to university colleges was limited and haphazard, based on schemes of university scholarships administered by local authorities which varied in value and reached only a small minority of students—a total of 870 scholarships were held by about 14% of university students as late as 1967.[7]

De Valera expressed a widely held view when he told the Seanad in May 1940 that training for a professional career was the essential role of the university:

> …originally the universities were professional schools just as the modern universities have very largely to be professional schools, but the fact is that in our universities at present, excepting those particularly fortunate in having brains as well as means, the students have to think when they come to the universities of a career, and that they cannot live in them for a prolonged period.[8]

The Taoiseach's speech was notable for its embrace of the vocational concept of the university as a centre for professional training and his open acknowledgement that entry to university had more to do with means than merit. Very few politicians would have dissented from his conviction that Newman's ideal of university education belonged to a bygone age, although his commentary on Newman had more than a touch of caricature:

> ...the great majority of the students who go to the university are not like those whom Cardinal Newman had in mind who are able to go to Oxford and Cambridge, and who are leisurely and wealthy people in a position to approach their studies from mere love of the things in them, without any idea of using them, except in so far as they add to their own particular culture.[9]

De Valera's limited, pragmatic vision of the academy as a professional school for privileged individuals reflected deeply embedded perceptions within mid-twentieth century Irish society, which helped to dictate the limited government support for the universities.

The composition of the student body in the universities certainly underlined a strong popular attachment to professional careers. The colleges of the NUI saw a steady increase in the proportion of students pursuing professional qualifications, particularly in medicine, dentistry and engineering, between 1929–30 and 1947–48.[10] Arts humanities disciplines continued to attract a significant cohort of students, while science and commerce languished, attracting a relatively small and in some cases a declining segment of students. Coolahan suggests that the underdeveloped state of the Irish economy up to the 1950s helps to explain the neglect of science, commerce and agriculture.[11] Yet this hardly explains the limited appeal of agriculture, which was a vitally important sector of the state's economy during this period and was one of the few disciplines within the university to attract dedicated state funding. Certainly the lack of economic opportunity within Ireland encouraged a focus on stable, high-status occupations including the professions and the public service. Yet the strong demand among parents and students for entry to the humanities and the professions also reflected a profound social and cultural conservatism, which privileged professional status and academic subjects over scientific, 'practical' or technical disciplines.

The influence of social conservatism was reinforced by an essentially laissez-faire governing ideology and the persistence of a traditional institutional framework for higher education. University education was not included in the formal remit of the Department of Education, which was established in 1924 to assume responsibility for national, intermediate and technical education. The new department's remit embraced teacher training for national schools and later the nascent third-level provision under the Vocational Education Committees (VECs), but did not extend to universities or colleges until 1957. Responsibility for Universities and Colleges devolved to the Department of Finance, which was concerned primarily with fiscal rectitude. Yet the preoccupations of the Free State political and official elite were by no means exclusively economic and particularly embraced the cultural imperative of reviving the Irish language. The Minister for Finance, Ernest Blythe, showed a keen if one-sided interest in university education as another front in the struggle to restore the national language. The colleges of the NUI were also subject to local political influence in appointments through the participation of councillors on their governing bodies, but this tended to magnify the importance of localism and personal connections, rather than any facilitating any overarching attempt to shape institutional policy.

The Cumann na nGaedheal government headed by W. T. Cosgrave was preoccupied with establishing the institutions of the new state and reconstructing a stable, profoundly conservative social order following a decade of war and revolution.[12] The government's determination to establish the new state's reputation for fiscal rectitude, which manifested itself in a rigorous economy drive extending to most areas of the public service, ensured that university education was 'frugally financed' throughout the lifetime of the Free State.[13] Cosgrave aptly summed up the government's position in a letter to the Duke of Devonshire, the Colonial Secretary, in July 1923:

> ...The Government were...faced with the difficulty that the amount which they are in a position to devote out of public funds towards the assistance of University education in Ireland has necessarily to be kept within narrow limits, at least so long as the financial exigencies of the present time continue.[14]

While few could quarrel with prudent finance in the aftermath of civil war, the parsimonious financing of higher education extended well beyond the unstable period of the early 1920s and became an integral feature of budgetary policy which outlived the Free State. Eoin MacNéill, the first Free State Minister for Education, informed the Dáil in July 1924 that the grants for the NUI under the old regime amounted to no more than a 'beggarly provision', but frankly admitted that he was able to do very little about it: '…I was not able to recommend or to devise any proposal which would make the National University even approximately the organ of national progress that it ought to be.'[15]

MacNéill's statement was no more than a truism. The annual appropriations outlined in the reports of the Public Accounts Committee revealed a consistently low level of public investment in higher education up to the late 1940s. The net expenditure by the Exchequer on 'Universities and Colleges' in 1924–25 was £107,800, barely 0.44% of total net expenditure reported to the Public Accounts Committee for that year.[16] While expenditure on teacher training colleges was accounted for under a separate Vote, the meagre resourcing for higher education was unmistakable. Following a range of incremental government initiatives in the 1920s, almost all designed to ensure that the colleges of the NUI were more closely oriented towards national cultural and economic objectives, the net Exchequer spending for Universities and Colleges saw a modest increase to £155,500 by 1932–33 (0.64% of net expenditure).[17] But expenditure by the national government on higher education was effectively frozen between 1930 and 1947, with no long-term increases either in recurrent or capital expenditure. The only significant exceptions were special grants paid through supplementary estimates to clear the debts of UCC in 1934 and UCD a decade later, which were reluctantly conceded by the Department of Finance.[18] The net Exchequer spend under the corresponding Vote in 1945–46 was a mere £161,664, barely 0.34% of net spending by the national government, which was among the lowest totals recorded since the foundation of the state.[19]

State funding for universities and colleges stagnated over a fifteen year period, failing to keep pace with the growth in overall expenditure even in an era of financial retrenchment during the world economic depression and second world war. The underlying pattern of parsimonious financing of higher education, firmly established in the 1920s, was maintained until the late 1940s. This pattern was consistent enough that it could not be attributed simply to the poverty of the newly independent state: it had a great deal to do with the archconservative leadership of the Department of Finance, both under its first secretary, Joseph Brennan and his long serving successor, J. J. McElligott.[20] The minimalist provision for higher level institutions testified to a prevailing indifference and in some respects outright opposition to investment in higher education among influential elites in the new Irish state.

'Free State Fights for Supremacy...'

The colleges of the NUI enjoyed close connections with the political elite of the new state. The first two ministers for education were university lecturers: Eoin MacNéill (1922–25) and his successor John Marcus O'Sullivan (1926–32) were both professors of history in UCD. While both ministers operated in a financial straitjacket, their influential role almost certainly benefited the NUI, facilitating the creation of the Agriculture Faculty in UCD and the dairy science institute in UCC.[21] Later de Valera not infrequently proved willing to circumvent or at least mitigate the uncompromising hostility of the Department of Finance to public investment in the universities. Yet the prominence of NUI graduates, professors and members of the Senate in the political elite never translated into consistent financial support for its colleges. While political connections secured a sympathetic hearing for the college officers at moments of crisis, they did not prevent the stagnation in state funding for the NUI for most of this period.

The transfer of technical training in science and agricultural disciplines from the Royal College of Science to the NUI in the late 1920s freed up greater resources for UCD and UCC and went some way towards remedying the 'beggarly' grants to at least two of the universities. The University Education (Agricultural and Dairy Science) Act, 1926 allocated increased resources to both colleges for 'general purposes', usually related to the employment of new staff, as well as capital funding related to development projects in science and agriculture and earmarked annual grants from the Department of Agriculture for agriculture in UCD and dairy science in UCC. UCD was a major beneficiary of the legislation, securing a substantial increase in its annual grant from £52,000 in 1925 to £82,000 in 1927, as well as a once-off capital grant to clear debts incurred in building projects particularly due to wartime inflation.[22] The annual state grant to UCC doubled to £40,000, while the college's deficit due to cost of living and wage increases was also cleared by the Exchequer.

The legislation enabled the establishment of a new faculty of general agriculture in UCD, which operated mainly on the farms and buildings at Glasnevin.[23] The college secured badly needed additional space and facilities in Merrion St. and benefited from a significant infusion of academic and support staff in science, mathematics and agricultural disciplines.[24] The initiative was arguably even more significant in its long-term impact on UCC. The exchequer underwrote the cost of building and equipping a new institute of dairy science in Cork, through an initial allocation of £67,000.[25] The faculty of dairy science was established in 1926, headed by Connell Boyle, the recently appointed professor of agriculture; the newly founded institute consisted of a laboratory block for teaching and research, a lecture theatre and an experimental dairy. The faculty was hailed by government ministers as a milestone in elevating agricultural education to university level and a model for future collaboration between the university faculty and farmers.[26]

Cosgrave laid the foundation stone for the new dairy science building in July 1928, in a ceremony which underlined the firmly utilitarian rationale for investment in the new institute. The Free State president gave a nod to Cork localism by noting the county's 'long and honourable connection with dairying', as the port of Cork was a centre for the export of dairy produce and the faculty built upon the tradition of the Munster Institute, the first dairy college in the UK, established at the instigation of the former QCC president, William K. Sullivan.[27] More significantly, Cosgrave emphasised the practical benefits to be delivered by the faculty through 'the closest collaboration' with the farmers of the Free State, notably upgrading the technical education of dairy farmers and improving the production and marketing of milk, butter, poultry and meat: 'We believe that its professors and workers will regard it as their highest function to have the opportunity of dealing with, and solving, the problems which confront the farmers of this country...'[28] Despite his relative moderation on the National Question, it is unlikely that Cosgrave would have been pleased by the *Irish Times* headline on the following day—'First Dairy College in the British Isles'.[29] Yet the president's agenda was more aptly summarised by a less prominent headline—'Free State fights for Supremacy in the Butter Industry'.[30] Cosgrave's address underlined the economic motivation for investment in the dairy science faculty and official expectation that UCC would contribute to the government agenda for developing agriculture.

The government proved willing to increase the capital funding for the institute when the original allocation proved inadequate. The college officers had intended to locate the new building outside the college walls but this provoked threats of legal action from local householders. The resulting decision to build within the existing site escalated the cost of building materials, as an 'aesthetically correct' limestone building in keeping with the existing architecture was considerably more expensive than the original proposal.[31] The negotiations between the college and the government also identified a glaring shortfall in the original grant, which was diplomatically raised by the private secretary to the Minister for Agriculture in November 1929: '...it transpired that the matter of the provision of a suitable lecture theatre had been overlooked in the original estimate.'[32] Although the Department of Finance had approved a lecture theatre, no allocation for it had been included. The Department of Agriculture recommended an increase in the capital grant to £82,000, coupled with an extension of the grant for a further three years, to remedy this embarrassing omission.[33] As UCC was ready to go ahead with construction and no further expenditure could be made without amending legislation, a further university education bill was hastily drafted and rushed through the Dáil early in 1930.[34] The speed and relative generosity of the government's response was striking in the context of its general conservatism and parsimonious funding of higher education.

Yet the initiative did not mark a radical departure from the government's preoccupation with 'economy'. Ernest Blythe informed the Dáil in June 1926 that the increase in UCD's annual grant was still a saving to the state of £2000 set against the combined totals of the grants to UCD and the College of Science.[35] While the legislation involved a real increase in spending on UCC, Blythe stipulated that not all the college's debt would be covered, excluding a substantial outlay for the purchase of playing fields where the government believed 'the college itself should find a means of wiping out that debt'.[36] Both colleges also agreed not to make any further requests for increased funding for five years. Blythe emphasised that 'this increase is an increase which is not excessive. It is an increase which was due…' following capital development in the colleges, an increase in the student body since 1908 and the impact of wartime inflation.[37] Blythe was hardly exaggerating—the scale of the overall increase in funding for university education was modest and the increased subvention of UCD and UCC was mainly the result of the transfer of the two technical training institutions.

The Free State government's initiative to upgrade agricultural faculties in UCD and UCC was influenced by the strikingly high concentration of NUI academics within its ranks, but it was not simply a case of professors protecting their alma mater. The policy decisions of the mid 1920s marked a utilitarian *quid pro quo* between national objectives and academic self-interest. Minister for Agriculture Paddy Hogan, the leading advocate of the primacy of agriculture in Free State economic policy, supported the transfer of the College of Science, as part of a projected reorientation of university education to reflect the predominantly agricultural character of the Irish economy.[38] The colleges of the NUI in turn were expected to offer expanded facilities for training and research in agriculture and applied science to make a greater contribution to the agricultural sector. The increased financial support offered by the Free State government to the NUI in the first decade after independence supported institutional developments linked to national policy priorities, notably the development of agriculture as a central strand of its economic policy.

'...A Very Difficult Problem'

The revival of the Irish language was a fundamental political imperative which was integral to education policy under the Free State. While
this affected the NUI as a whole, government policy had the most
significant impact on the fortunes of UCG. The college, which had
secured modest additional payments from the Irish administration
between 1914 and 1922 to supplement the annual statutory grant of
£12,000, did not receive any additional support from the new government and did not benefit from the rationalisation of higher level
agricultural education in the mid-1920s. UCG also suffered from the
additional handicap that professorial salaries were linked with student
fees, which were not available for the general purposes of the college—a
traditional practice which had been discontinued in all the other university colleges by the early 1920s. The apparent neglect of the smallest college in the NUI provoked outrage among institutional leaders in UCG
and political and business elites in its Connacht hinterland. UCG's relations with the new government in the early to mid-1920s were characterised by mutual incomprehension and acrimony, with institutional
leaders fearing the downgrading of the college while politicians and senior officials were uncertain about its *raison d'etre*. The uncertainty within
government circles about the future of UCG was expressed, with more
honesty than tact, by MacNeill in a Dáil debate in July 1924:

> University College, Galway, is for me a very difficult problem... I leave
> Galway outside my proposals either one way or the other. I do not pro-
> pose to destroy. I do not propose to construct. I hold myself, and I put
> it to a representative body from the Galway College that I met not very
> long ago, that it was to my mind very questionable whether the efforts to
> carry on a university college in its present form and scope in Galway was
> the best way in which an institution of higher education could be carried
> on for Galway...[39]

He even floated the possibility that it could become an educational
centre for the fishing industry—an apparently bizarre proposal, but in
line with his general conviction that universities should serve national

priorities through greater specialisation and co-ordination of facilities, which was expressed more sensibly in the development of the dairy science faculty in UCC: 'Galway, I think, is an ideal situation from every point of view, from the point of view of sea fisheries, and from the point of view of inland fisheries, of being a centre for the purpose of education in and for that industry.'[40] This statement caused consternation in UCG. Three leading members of the governing body, Alexander Anderson, Rev. John 'Pa' Hynes and Dr. Thomas O'Doherty, the bishop of Galway, issued a letter to the national newspapers expressing 'grave anxiety' at the minister's statement. They deplored the idea that 'the Minister would like to see this College cease to be a University centre and become a fishing research station', while more diplomatically suggesting that he was merely proposing a fishing research station in conjunction with the college.[41] TDs for neighbouring constituencies also expressed dissatisfaction at the treatment of UCG, particularly the government decision to concentrate faculties for agriculture in Dublin and Cork.

The governing body of UCG, ably led by Anderson and Hynes, mounted an effective lobbying campaign to protect the college, which won support from politicians, business leaders and Catholic bishops in the west of Ireland. The college president circulated 'an appeal and a plea' to all Oireachtas members, county councils and national newspapers in October 1924; the appeal made a case for a sustainable government grant to UCG based on its achievements in medicine and engineering, the low salaries of its professors and the contribution which the college could make to the revival of Irish, particularly in teacher training.[42] MacNeill responded by proposing that the conduct of university teaching through the medium of Irish should become the distinguishing characteristic of the college and that a college-departmental conference should be held to consider how UCG could be transformed to undertake 'special work of national importance'.[43] The department's demand for UCG to become a central driving force behind the revival of the Irish language went well beyond the college's initial proposals. But the governing body accepted the proposal for a conference, in part due to genuine support for reviving the language among many of its members but mainly because they had no choice:

they had to engage with the minister on his own terms if they were to secure the long-term viability of the college.

The conference, consisting of seven members nominated by the minister and four representatives of UCG, produced a majority report in April 1926, which presented a gradualist model for Gaelicisation of teaching and learning. The report recommended the creation of four new lectureships to teach mathematics, history, commerce and education through the medium of Irish; reduction of student fees for courses through Irish and the establishment of a training college for primary teachers in conjunction with UCG. Vacancies in professorships would be filled 'as far as possible' by candidates able to lecture through Irish.[44] This evolutionary approach commanded the backing of the governing body: Anderson argued that the proposals would 'lead eventually under favourable circumstances to the Gaelicisation of the College'.[45]

But this gradualist model did not find favour with leading members of the government, who were sceptical of UCG's *bona fides* in the urgent national mission of language revival. Ministers pressed ahead with the legislation to develop agriculture and dairy science in UCD and UCC respectively, while postponing any move to assist Galway. UCG assembled a high powered deputation of leading political and ecclesiastical dignitaries to impress its case on Cosgrave and three of his ministers, including Blythe and O'Sullivan, on 27 May 1926. The delegation included O'Doherty, Thomas Gilmartin, the Catholic archbishop of Tuam, his Church of Ireland counterpart, Dr. Orr, and the Labour Party TD T. J. O'Connell. But while Cosgrave took a conciliatory line with the deputation, and one of its members indicated that he was 'fairly satisfied' with the outcome, the ministers gave no commitment to increase UCG's grant.[46] Moreover, Blythe advised the college authorities to close other faculties, such as Medicine, to concentrate on converting the institution into an Irish-speaking centre for university education.[47] Blythe, the foremost advocate for rapid Gaelicisation among Free State ministers, had no hesitation in ridiculing the sedate pace of change favoured by the college authorities. When several TDs questioned the lack of additional resources for Galway in the Dáil on 9 June 1926, the minister criticised the commission's report as 'a disappointing document' and called into question the college's commitment to Gaelicisation:

It did not, to my mind, indicate that the authorities of the college were really in earnest about the question. They are quite in earnest about the question of getting money, but I do not know that they are at all in earnest about the question of doing special work which would entitle them to money. If they would, perhaps, take that remark to heart we might get somewhere.[48]

Blythe, not content with illuminating the allegedly mercenary motives of the college authorities, bluntly warned that UCG's future status could not be guaranteed if it failed to accept its designated place in the movement for language revival:

If Galway is not going to do special work, then frankly as far as I am concerned I do not think it would be a wise course - it might be politically the only possible course to maintain it - to maintain it as a sort of toy college unless it does special work. On the other hand, if it does special work, and if the people concerned will give their minds to devising a scheme and the best method for doing this special work that the college can do, I do not think they will find the Government so difficult to deal with.[49]

It is unlikely that Blythe contemplated closing UCG, but his scathing attack was intended to pressure the college authorities into accepting a narrowly specialised function as an Irish-speaking institution taking a central part in the national project of Gaelicisation. Instead his harsh tone and contemptuous reference to a 'toy college' triggered the first significant conflict between university authorities and the Free State government.

Blythe's statement and the apparent threat of closure to UCG created a storm of protest against the government west of the Shannon. Anderson castigated Blythe in no uncertain terms in a letter to national newspapers on 11 June 1926, taking aim at the minister's demand for a sweeping Gaelicisation: 'If any one thinks that a sudden and radical change of this kind is practicable at the present, he must be the victim of educational hallucinations.'[50] The president also took issue with Blythe's wounding description of UCG as a 'toy college', asserting that considering the college's educational track record and the eminence of its graduates '…the nonsense of the description becomes manifest.'[51]

The governing body on 26 June adopted its own resolution protesting against 'the derisive and insulting language used by the Minister for Finance about Galway College.'[52]

Regional political, commercial and ecclesiastical elites combined to support the college, mobilising a public campaign against the apparently predatory designs of the government. A public meeting convened by the Chamber of Commerce in Galway Town Hall on 25 June 1926 saw an impressive show of strength in favour of UCG. The 'monster' meeting was attended by three bishops, representatives of all county councils throughout Connacht and local TDs, as well as trade unionists, employers and college representatives. Dr. O'Doherty proposed resolutions demanding that official threats to close UCG should cease and that the permanency of the college should be assured through adequate endowment.[53] Paddy Hogan, who had the thankless task of defending his ministerial colleagues, received a 'stormy reception', as he assured the meeting that the government had no intention of closing the college; meanwhile the *Irish Times* reported that virtually all the shops and business in the city closed at noon for two hours to protest against 'the aspersions of the Minister for Finance on University College Galway.'[54] The governing body's success in mobilising regional elites and popular support offered useful leverage in resolving the stand-off with government ministers.

The conflict proved sharp but short-lived. Blythe's wide-ranging criticism of UCG was not replicated by other government ministers, suggesting that he had overstepped the mark by threatening the closure of the college. Other Cumann na nGaedhael politicians sought to contain the popular backlash, as both Hogan in Galway and O'Sullivan in a Seanad debate on 30 June emphasised that the government's agenda envisaged only a reorganisation of UCG. The scale of elite and popular support mobilised by the governing body offered a compelling political incentive for an insecure, minority government to resolve the conflict with the college. The involvement in the negotiations of the Department of Education, which was more conciliatory than Blythe in its dealings with UCG, also facilitated a settlement. The representatives of the governing body concluded a 'memorandum of agreements' with the Ministers for Finance and Education on 15 October 1926, which affirmed that 'Galway College could render most useful service to the country by undertaking special work in connection with the Irish language...and that the Governing Body should henceforth endeavour to have an increasing proportion of the work of the College done through Irish.'[55] The governing body agreed to appoint three new lecturers (in history, mathematics and commerce) who would teach through Irish, with the nominees requiring approval by the Department of Education. They would also make 'every effort' to fill future academic vacancies with candidates 'able to impart instruction through the medium of Irish'.[56] The college would reduce its fees to approximately the pre-war level to encourage greater participation in UCG by students in Irish-speaking areas, 'which are generally speaking poorer districts' and establish a special scholarship scheme for native Irish speakers from traditionally Irish speaking districts in any part of the country. The government in turn agreed to increase the annual grant to the college from £20,800 to £28,000, with an immediate increase to be paid in 1926; allocate £1500 for repayment of the college's debt and allow fees previously paid to professors to be used for the general purposes of the college—a long-term objective of the college leadership. Equally important was a government commitment to increase the salaries of professors to a minimum level of either £650 or £700 annually, with an additional supplement depending on the continuation of County Council grants enjoyed by UCG.[57]

The involvement of the Department of Education in approving the three new lecturers (ostensibly to ensure their ability to teach through Irish) was a departure from the usual academic appointment procedures and the department took this clause seriously enough to require that two of the three posts be re-advertised to secure better qualified candidates. This potentially fractious situation was resolved when the department agreed to accept the appointment of any candidate on a list of nominees with the required qualifications and all three posts were filled by October 1928.[58] The settlement was a compromise which ensured the financial viability of the college and largely achieved the governing body's preference for a gradualist approach to Gaelicisation.

The agreement was implemented by the college authorities and government departments on a non-statutory basis for over two years, but legislation was required to confirm an increase in the annual grant. Blythe informed the Executive Council on 28 January 1929 that as the increased grants to UCD and UCC had been confirmed through legislation, 'it was felt impossible to refuse the request of the Governing Body of University College, Galway, that the same procedure should be followed in their case, especially as they had fulfilled all the conditions attaching to the increased grant.'[59] He also offered an incentive to the college authorities to accelerate the pace of Gaelicisation, as the Bill authorised the Minister for Finance to allocate additional funding of up to £2,000 to the college if they were 'in a position in the near future to increase the proportion of instruction given through the medium of Irish'. It was a short Bill of only four clauses, which gave legal force to the college's commitment to appoint academics capable of teaching through Irish: Section 3 required the NUI senate and governing body of UCG in filling vacancies to 'appoint to such office or situation a person who is competent to discharge the duties thereof through the medium of the Irish language: provided a person so competent and also suitable in all other respects is to be found...'[60] The Cabinet decision on 14 February to approve the draft Bill testified to a much closer understanding between ministers and the college authorities following the public confrontations of the mid-1920s. The strategic decision by the governing body and academic elite in UCG to adopt teaching through Irish as a key function of the college paid off in securing political and financial support from the Free State.

The University College, Galway, Bill, did not command universal support in the Dáil, as Fianna Fáil, now the main opposition party, argued that it did not go far enough towards Gaelicisation. The Galway TD, Frank Fahy, supported the increased grant but complained that no date was given for 'when we might expect complete Gaelicisation' and Section 3 allowed a 'loophole' in the legislation by introducing a proviso for competence and suitability.[61] Party leader Eamon de Valera also intervened in the debate on 24 October 1929 to urge that precedence be given to the Irish language over superior academic qualifications:

We are faced in this Bill...with a difficulty that we are faced with constantly, and that is the question as to whether we are going to make appointments on the highest qualification professionally, or whether we are going to give preference to the Irish language...I, for one, believe that there is far less danger that a person who knows Irish will be appointed who may be incompetent professionally than there is that we will have the claims of the Irish language neglected.[62]

Blythe did not dispute de Valera's thesis that the national importance of Irish outweighed concerns about the integrity of academic appointments. But he argued that coercion of the college by statute was unworkable and that the Dáil should rely on the good judgement of the governing body, which would be informed by both patriotic and practical considerations:

> ...there is a definitely new spirit in University College, Galway, and I believe that that condition will continue to improve there...even the people who do not care anything about the Irish language themselves will see - and this Bill is one of the ways for making that clear - that if this College is to increase in importance and to get additional endowments or favours from the Government it must sincerely and earnestly go ahead with the work of making itself an Irish College.[63]

Blythe, the fiercest critic of UCG three years earlier, was ironically the college's foremost advocate in the Dáil debate, defending the governing body's commitment to the Irish language policy. While it was hardly a resounding vindication of university autonomy, Blythe's statement highlighted a pragmatic conviction among ministers that it was more effective to co-opt academics in pursuit of national priorities than to adopt a coercive approach which undermined the autonomy of the universities. The Finance Minister's arguments proved convincing. Fahy's amendment to delete the proviso relating to competence and suitability from Section 3 was easily defeated, with a number of Labour TDs including T. J. O'Connell supporting the government.[64] This division marked the only real controversy over the Bill, which became law in December 1929.[65]

The settlement between government ministers and the college authorities exerted a long-term influence on the institutional mission and academic priorities of UCG. Fianna Fáil made no attempt to amend the UCG legislation when the party came to power less than three years later. The college's mission became more firmly associated with the national objective of Gaelicisation than any of its counterparts. The financial settlement underpinned a notable expansion of student enrolments in UCG, with the number of Galway students presenting for NUI examinations increasing from 236 in 1921 to 697 in 1932. Much of this increase was accounted for by Irish-speaking students, with 158 students attending lectures through Irish in various subjects by 1930–31.[66] The college authorities were able to manage the official requirements set out by the UCG Act without conceding their operational authority or provoking serious conflict with the Department of Education.

The most controversial element of the legislation was Section 3: decried by Fianna Fáil as too cautious in 1929, it later became the focus of criticism for upsetting the order of academic merit in appointments, although its defenders argued that only a minority of appointments were influenced by the Irish language requirement.[67] The clause survived intact for the remainder of the twentieth century, indicating that the government and college authorities had found a workable compromise which was broadly acceptable to politicians, officials, the governing body and professional academic elite in Galway. The government made no attempt to enforce a wider rationalisation of faculties or dictate academic decisions, once ministers were assured that UCG had adopted teaching through Irish as an integral part of its institutional mission.

UCG accommodated itself to the overarching policy and political imperatives, but was largely successful in securing financial stability while maintaining its character as an institution teaching 'universal' knowledge. The success of the college authorities in adapting to the new political dispensation owed much to effective leadership and valuable connections with regional elites, but was also facilitated by the essential conservatism of the Free State government. Ministers sought to secure the collaboration of universities for policy imperatives such as Gaelicisation, but stopped well short of any attempt at restructuring of university institutions. The Free State government had a remarkably strong representation of university professors in its ranks—ironically, this did little to increase the profile of universities in national political discourse, focused on state-building, constitutional conflict, development of agriculture and Gaelicisation. Yet the composition of the government was significant in discouraging structural innovation and reinforcing the established pattern of a university-dominated sector.

All four university colleges were largely left to their own devices by the Irish government after early policy decisions setting the level of support for particular institutions were taken in the 1920s. Academic elites within the universities were usually able to determine the institutional policies and educational practice of their institutions. The main limitation on their freedom of action consisted of stringent spending constraints maintained by the Department of Finance. The most consistent expectation of policy-makers, other than saving money, was that universities would contribute to national objectives, notably the restoration of the Irish language and the development of national resources, particularly agriculture. The drive to develop agriculture, particularly the livestock and dairy sector, by the first Free State governments was a consistent thread driving government initiatives in university education throughout the 1920s and 1930s, although it subsequently faded from view. Political and official pressure for Gaelicisation was much more pervasive, persisting as a significant factor in the relations between the new state and the universities for a generation after 1922.

'…There Need not Be Any Apprehension About It…'

Trinity College faced a financial crisis at the outset of the new dispensation, struggling with wartime inflation, loss of student fees due to military service and loss of rents during the military conflicts of 1919–23.[68] No financial provision was made for the college in the Treaty, although the Irish delegation led by Arthur Griffith and Michael Collins had no objection to the retention of the clause from the Government of Ireland Act.[69] When representatives of the southern unionists met the Prime Minister in London on 5 December 1921, immediately after the Treaty was signed, the provost expressed dissatisfaction about the omission of the clause guaranteeing a grant to TCD, but made no headway with Lloyd George: 'The Prime Minister acknowledged that it had escaped his memory but stated that he thought that there need not be any apprehension about it, as he felt sure that the majority in Southern Ireland would deal impartially with the minority.'[70] Lloyd George conveyed an unmistakable message that the college would have to come to terms with the new Irish government. Trinity College, once the rock on which initiatives for higher education had perished, no longer counted for much in the calculations of a government which had accepted the breaking of the union.

The provost's lobbying was not entirely unsuccessful, winning short-term financial backing from the coalition as departmental budgets were being cut by the Geddes Committee in Westminster.[71] Trinity received non-recurrent grants totalling £24,000 from the UK university grants committee in 1919–20 and a further instalment of £12,000 in 1921–22.[72] But these ad hoc payments allowed the college to maintain its annual budget without any scope for longer term investment and even with this support the college's deficit reached £13,700 in 1921–22.[73] A memorandum by Bernard in February 1922 argued that it would be 'extremely unfair and unjust if Trinity is placed in the position of a suppliant to the new Irish Parliament for the necessary financial support, which has already been guaranteed by an act of the Imperial Parliament.'[74] But appeals to imperial allegiance were largely a devalued currency in London.

The elevation of Bonar Law, a staunch unionist, to the premiership in November 1922, gave renewed hope to the Board. Yet while the Prime Minister expressed his 'deep sympathy with the situation in which Trinity College found itself', he ruled out any long-term aid from the British Treasury, conceding only that the college had an equitable claim for the brief period that the abortive Government of Ireland act was on the statute book.[75] British ministers, even traditionally sympathetic Conservatives, were never willing to accept a long-term commitment to Trinity once the union proved untenable. Bonar Law's ability to assist the college was limited by the terms of the Treaty and his own ill health, which forced his retirement as Prime Minister in May 1923. Nevertheless the lobbying of Law's short-lived government by the college representatives and English university MPs had some success. Stanley Baldwin, who succeeded Law as Prime Minister, announced the government offer to Bernard on 9 June 1923. While ruling out any future charge on the British exchequer, Baldwin confirmed a once-off grant of £20,000 to TCD through a supplementary estimate, to settle the college's claims from the Geikie Commission.[76] Baldwin noted that the decision was made as 'The Government was conscious of the difficulties, I trust temporary, which confront the College at the present time…'[77]

The Free State government had already guaranteed more generous representation to Trinity graduates than envisaged in the Anglo-Irish negotiations. The abortive parliament for southern Ireland provided for four representatives of TCD and NUI graduates, an arrangement maintained by the Dáil in 1921–22. Four TDs were returned unopposed to represent the TCD constituency in the Third Dáil in June 1922.[78] Collins and Griffith, the leaders of the Provisional Government, offered representation to southern unionists in the newly formed Senate. Irish ministers reached agreement with Winston Churchill, the Colonial Secretary, and a delegation of southern unionists including the provost, in London on 13 June 1922 that each university would have two representatives in the Senate under the constitution of the Irish Free State.[79] But university representation was transferred to the Dáil at the instigation of two of Trinity's parliamentary representatives, Gerald Fitzgibbon and William Thrift, during the debate on the constitution in September 1922. Kevin O'Higgins, Minister for Home Affairs, readily accepted Fitzgibbon's amendment to include university representation in the Dáil '…to assist in the legislation, instead of being put into the cooling chamber.'[80] The graduates of TCD and the NUI elected three representatives to the Dáil in every election between 1922 and 1933.

The financial negotiations between Trinity College and the Free State government proved more contentious. The Board submitted a memorandum to the Provisional Government in February 1922, setting out Trinity's claims for a state subsidy.[81] The college's nascent relationship with the new state was threatened by the death in August 1922 of Griffith and Collins, who had both offered to secure comparable support for TCD with the Government of Ireland Act: Griffith was sympathetic to Trinity's case and his death came as a bitter blow to Bernard, who later described his passing as a 'national misfortune'.[82] W. T. Cosgrave, who inherited the leadership of the newly established Irish

Free State in September 1922, was cautious in making any commitments to the universities. Tomás Irish suggests that Cosgrave's response
to Trinity's representations in 1922–23 was 'firm and unsympathetic'.[83]
Certainly Cosgrave was less accommodating than Griffith a year earlier,
not least because he was the leader of an embattled government in the
midst of a civil war which dragged on until the summer of 1923. Yet it
was the Department of Finance, rather than Cosgrave himself, which
offered the most stubborn resistance to Trinity's claims.

Cosgrave agreed to allocate a once-off grant of £6000 in November
1922, to compensate Trinity for the non-payment of rents during the civil war.[84] But this was a temporary expedient which did little to address the financial crisis. Following a meeting between Thrift
and Cosgrave in March 1923, the Board made a submission to the
Free State government seeking a state grant of not less than £10,000
per annum and the transfer to the college of the securities (amounting
to over £100,000) held by the Public Trustee on TCD's behalf, which
was intended to cover any loss of income that the college might suf-
fer due to compulsory land purchase under the 1903 Land Act.[85] The
prolonged negotiations which followed pitted the Board of Trinity
against the Department of Finance, which was hostile to the college's
claims and sought to assert greater official control in return for a limited
subsidy. The secretary of the department, Joseph Brennan, in a ques-
tionnaire issued to Thrift, sought detailed information on the college's
finances, management and support for students before any grant was
awarded. The Board, clearly regarding Brennan's missive as a delaying
tactic, appealed directly to Cosgrave on 9 June 1923, arguing that a settlement of their claim should not be delayed until 'the minute enquir-
ies indicated in Mr. Brennan's letter have been completed.' The Board's
submission argued that TCD was seeking only parity of esteem with the
NUI, which was receiving additional grants from the new state in addition to its statutory grant and directly challenged the Free State government to treat Trinity fairly:

> The University of Dublin is at this moment the only University in Great
> Britain or Ireland which does not receive an annual grant from the State
> supplementing its pre-war revenues and the Board of Trinity College are

unwilling to believe that the Irish Government intend to treat an institution of such national importance in an illiberal manner.[86]

Brennan's response on 23 June gave no ground to the Board's robust appeal. The department offered only a special grant of £5000 in 1923–24, which was linked to a series of onerous conditions regarding the management of the college and stipulated that 'no such grant will be paid to the university in any future year.'[87] The conditions included the introduction of minimum fixed salaries for the non-fellow professors and lecturers, stipulating specific improvements to be made by the Board immediately. This clause, later described by McDowell and Webb as 'humiliating', was in fact inspired by representations from the non-fellow professors, whose salaries compared unfavourably to their more privileged counterparts among the Fellows, to Michael Hayes, the then Minister for Education, in 1922.[88] Although the official offer proposed an amendment to the Land Act to allow the transfer of the securities held by the Public Trustee to the college, this too came with strings attached in the form of six conditions. The most sweeping of these recognised the government's right to undertake 'a comprehensive enquiry' into the college and required the Board's agreement to 'cooperate with the Government in rendering such inquiry as effective as possible and in putting into effect such recommendations resulting from the inquiry as the Government may approve.'[89] Adding insult to injury, Brennan noted that the Minister for Finance was not satisfied that the college authorities had yet done everything possible by 'internal re-arrangement for the purpose of securing the most economical and efficient application of its existing resources.'[90] The official conditions required a sweeping abdication of power by the Board and substantial curbing of the college's autonomy. The Department of Finance was hostile to TCD and sought much greater control over the university as the price for extremely limited financial support.

Yet differences emerged between senior officials and ministers, who had to consider the wider ramifications of a penny-pinching approach to the once privileged university. Free State ministers tended to view Trinity primarily through the political prism of its relations with Britain and concern to accommodate the interests of southern unionists within the state. Assiduous lobbying of government ministers by the university TDs, particularly Thrift who became a key intermediary between ministers and the Board, proved effective in achieving a settlement.[91] The college authorities issued an uncompromising response to Cosgrave. The Board's letter of 23 June briskly dismissed the official conditions and raised the prospect of open conflict between the government and Trinity College: 'It would be impossible for any academic authority to accede to the terms of the letter and they think it desirable that the matter should be further considered by the Government, before publicity is given to the correspondence.'[92] The authorities even warned ministers that their response should respect the academic calendar, requesting an urgent reply by 29 June as the college was about to enter the summer vacation and 'it will be necessary for them to come to a decision as to their future action at their last statutory meeting of the Term on 30 June.'[93] The Board's apparently high risk strategy, involving the threat of public confrontation with the new government, was less audacious than it appeared. Thrift had briefed Cosgrave on the university's parlous financial situation and its inability to meet costs without resorting to a bank overdraft 'for the first time in living memory'. Trinity's plight also attracted the attention of the British government, which had recently concluded its own settlement with the college. The Duke of Devonshire wrote to Cosgrave in May 1923 to express concern about the college's financial position.[94] The Free State president placed a high value on winning over the southern unionist minority to the new political dispensation. The sensitivity of Trinity's position within the complex nexus of relationships between the new state, the British government and the displaced unionist elite ensured that the college's claims were resolved at a political rather than official level.

The Board's calculated gamble paid off. The government's response, issued in a letter from Brennan only four days later but influenced by Cosgrave, was more conciliatory: it offered short-term financial support while tacitly abandoning the demands for tighter official control. The Cabinet agreed to allocate a special, non-recurrent grant of £5000 for 1923–24, on the basis that no further claim for a similar grant would be made for three years.[95] Ministers also offered a broadly favourable settlement of the complex arrangements for land purchase, agreeing to transfer to TCD the balance of the capital funds accumulated by the Public Trustee.[96] The college secured unrestricted use of the interest on the capital sum and was permitted to draw down up to £10,000 of the capital within the first three years subject to the approval of the Minister for Finance, while investment of the capital was placed under the joint control of the Minister and a college officer.[97] The college also received a small grant of £3000 'in the present and future years', on condition that it waived any further claims to an indemnity for operation of the land purchase legislation.[98] The government's conditions were relatively light, mainly amounting to financial safeguards to protect the state and the more onerous stipulations sought by the Department of Finance were dropped: the clause setting minimum salaries for non-fellow professors disappeared from the final version.[99] While the right of the government to initiate an enquiry into the resources of the college was acknowledged, the requirement for the Board to implement any recommendations arising from it was dropped, making this clause essentially meaningless. Having secured a relaxation of the official conditions and a modest improvement in the financial terms, the Board unanimously accepted the government's offer on 30 June, although its members allowed themselves a parting shot at the Department of Finance. The governing body's minutes noted that the special grant of £5000 was insufficient to meet all claims for increased salaries that might be made by staff members between 1923 and 1926: 'The Board will count themselves fortunate if the University and College can be kept out of debt by a rigid limitation of expenditure.'[100]

The settlement fell well short of the generous support proposed by the Geikie commission, but did much to alleviate the financial crisis facing the college. The agreement between the government and the Board allowed Trinity to weather the immediate financial crisis and ensured that the college's financial position was no worse than in the pre-war period, although it offered little scope for expansion. Thrift welcomed the agreement in the Dáil on 25 July 1923 as '...a fair attempt to meet the claims of the college'.[101] The agreement, whatever its financial limitations, maintained Trinity's traditional constitution and autonomous status, with the result that the predominance of the senior fellows was preserved well into the twentieth century. No enquiry into the college's financing or administration was undertaken under the Free State. While Cosgrave drove a hard bargain with the Board, Trinity was treated in a markedly more favourable way than proposed by the mandarins in the Department of Finance.

Yet the difficult negotiations and the failed attempt to impose a far-reaching enquiry did not augur well for future relations between Trinity and the new state. While the Board reserved their right in June 1923 to place the financial needs of the college before future governments once a three-year period had elapsed, in fact no submission to the government was made by the college authorities over the next 23 years. This marked a deliberate policy of avoiding interactions with the government which might draw unwelcome political or official intervention.[102] This low profile approach, characterised as a 'policy of inconspicuousness' by McDowell and Webb,[103] was adopted by the college administration in the 1920s and remained the defining feature of Trinity's engagement with the state for the following generation.

The strongly Catholic and nationalist orientation of the new polity shaped Trinity College's equivocal place within the independent state, encouraging the adoption of a calculated low profile and cautious interaction with state institutions. Despite their pragmatic acceptance of the Treaty, the governing elite of the college rose to prominence in a very different era when Trinity had espoused an unapologetic unionism; all but one of the senior fellows up to 1952 were elevated before 1920.[104] The cultural and religious ideologies which underpinned the independent Irish state also placed Trinity's traditional academic elite in a defensive, semi-detached position, reinforcing divisions between the older university and its 'national' counterpart.

This did not prevent practical collaboration with the new government or discreet lobbying of ministers, particularly by Trinity's parliamentary representatives. When a dispute over reciprocal recognition of medical qualifications between Ireland and Britain arose in the mid-1920s, Thrift played a significant role in brokering a compromise with Kevin O'Higgins that protected the university medical schools in Ireland.[105] The college administration achieved a cautious accommodation with the new government, symbolised by the award of an honorary degree to Cosgrave in 1926. As Irish points out, however, underlying differences remained: while Cosgrave and the Board were mutually respectful in their contributions to the ceremony, it was apparent that 'Cosgrave saw the event as a celebration of Irish freedom, while Trinity saw it as a celebration of continued imperial affinity.'[106] Trinity's enduring attachment to the imperial connection was underlined by its commitment to symbols of allegiance to the Crown. 'God Save the King' was the anthem played at most official events, including graduations, throughout the interwar period; a toast was given to the King (as well as Ireland) at official functions in the college as late as 1945.[107] Disputes over symbols of allegiance were all the more potent due to the contested definitions of nationality in the political disputes of the interwar period, both within Irish party politics and Anglo-Irish relations (which were largely inseparable in this period). The status of the oath of allegiance was the subject of bitter contention between Cosgrave and his opponents, until eventually removed by de Valera. The contested status of the state itself, at least until the mid-1930s, also added a sharp edge to debates around the disputed emblems of nationality or empire.

The symbols of nationhood caused sharp, albeit occasional, disputes in the college's relations with the new regime. When the Governor-General, James McNeill, was greeted with a rendition of 'God Save the King' at the college races in 1928, he attributed it privately to 'ignorance as well as prejudice'.[108] There was room for confusion about whether it was the anthem of the Commonwealth or purely of the UK; at any rate, the majority view in Trinity firmly favoured the traditional practice. At McNeill's request, the government confirmed in October 1928 that the Irish national anthem was 'The Soldier's Song' which should be played at all formal events attended by the Governor-General.[109] The anthem provoked a stand-off between the Governor-General and the college in June 1929, when McNeill was again invited to attend the college races. The Governor General requested the Trinity Week committee to ensure that the Irish national anthem was played or none at all, but the committee was determined to maintain the tradition of playing 'God Save the King.'[110] The Board, when appealed to by McNeill, defended the playing of the UK anthem as 'at once an expression of its traditional loyalty to the Throne, and an act of courtesy and respect to the King's Representative'. They ostensibly offered to meet

McNeill's conditions, but in a tone of pained regret that made clear they were acting under protest:

> ...the Board has every reason to believe that the omission of the usual observance will be acutely felt by the students who have invited his Excellency to their Sports, and by their guests: and the Provost and the Board apprehend that the College will incur much discredit in the eyes of its friends, both at home and beyond the boundaries of the Free State. Thus placed in a painful dilemma, the Board leave his Excellency to decide on what course he will take. If he desires to be present at the College Sports, they will feel bound to defer to his express wishes.[111]

This could only be interpreted as a broad hint that McNeill might be better off not attending at all if he persisted in his wrongheaded attitude to the Commonwealth anthem. Yet this was not a clash solely with McNeill, but with the Free State government. Having received the provost's letter, ministers quickly confirmed that the Governor General would not attend Trinity Week.[112] This was only partly about the expression of an ideological position. Free State ministers were concerned at the prospect of violent incidents triggered by the Union Jack or the UK anthem, which were far from unknown in the Ireland of the 1920s. The incident generated considerable controversy, attracting attention in British newspapers such as *The Times* and the *Sunday Chronicle* and provoking a number of complaints to Cosgrave from Anglo-Irish dignitaries such as Lord Granard and Lady Ardee.[113] J. W. Dulanty, the Irish representative in London, requested guidance from the Executive Council on an official 'line' to take in responding to complaints from British traders so as to minimise the impact on Irish goods in Britain.[114] While the dispute was publicly brushed off by ministers as a trivial spat, Cosgrave was angry at the Board's position, as he informed Lady Ardee: '...I do claim that in respect of matters where my discretion is exercised more confidence in my judgement should be shown, and in this case the persons in charge in Trinity have disappointed me'.[115] The clash of divergent identities within the college and in its relations with the state was not easily resolved, even if it only occasionally broke the surface to cause open conflict.

In this instance the row was eventually resolved by an early example of constructive ambiguity. The college administration decided three years later to play both anthems at the college races, with 'the Soldier's Song' being played at the opening to welcome the Governor General and 'God Save the King' at the end.[116] The dispute over anthems underlined the residual conflict between the strength of Trinity's traditional loyalties and its attempts to accommodate to new political realities. The ambivalence of the college's position was appropriately captured by its display of national emblems. Trinity continued to fly the Union Jack from the West Front, but also displayed the Tricolour and the college flag.[117] The college's official approach enshrined creative ambiguity in its ceremonial throughout the interwar period, reflecting an attempt to bridge or at least manage divergent cultural identities. While this appeared a reasonable compromise to the Board and most staff, it gave no shortage of ammunition to critics in the Dáil, the Irish language organisations and the Catholic Church, who portrayed Trinity as an outdated relic of a discredited imperial past.

The nationalist critique of Trinity as antiquated and hostile to national objectives, particularly Gaelicisation, retained a long-term resonance among political elites. Tom Derrig, Minister for Education in de Valera's government from 1932 until 1948, was among Trinity's most prominent critics, declaring in 1934 that 'its record, as far as Gaelicisation is concerned, has been such that it is no less than a scandal.'[118] Derrig also argued for good measure that Trinity was producing such a vast surplus of graduates 'in proportion to the special portion of the population for which it caters' (presumably Protestants) that three-quarters of them were obliged to emigrate. Derrig's attack on Trinity College drew an angry riposte from the *Irish Times*, which warned the government against sacrificing the welfare of the country to 'the claims of a blind and arrogant nationalism' and concluded that 'If Mr. De Valera's Government is able to parochialise the Free State's universities, it will have struck the deepest blow at the Irish people.'[119] In fact de Valera was conciliatory in his dealings with Trinity and in any case the government had limited leverage over an institution which received no state grant.

Trinity's isolation, which had real financial and demographic implications for the college, was far from complete. Trinity academics, including two future provosts (William Thrift and Ernest Alton) served in the Dáil up to 1936 and in the Senate subsequently. The college officers achieved a cautious rapprochement with Cosgrave and other Free State ministers in the 1920s. There were undoubtedly wide differences in outlook between Fianna Fáil and the conservative governing elite in Trinity during the 1930s but this did not prevent senior academics from opening lines of communications to the new regime. De Valera was invited by Thrift to open the college's new reading room in July 1937 and made a conciliatory address, stressing Trinity's historical contribution to the Irish nation and invoking the name of Thomas Davis and other prominent Trinity graduates who had embraced Irish republicanism.[120] If his message contained an implicit message that Trinity could do more to embrace the new state, it was also an example of careful bridge-building on both sides. De Valera maintained friendly relations with Thrift, whom he consulted over the creation of the Dublin Institute of Advanced Studies (DIAS) in 1938. The Taoiseach established a much closer friendship with Albert J. McConnell, professor of mathematics, based on their shared passion for mathematics, which became more significant in the 1950s during McConnell's reforming term as provost. Constructive individual connections did not change established allegiances, particularly among participants in the fierce political struggles of the early twentieth century, but helped to mitigate traditional antagonisms which were increasingly regarded as outdated by younger members of the college community. Yet Trinity remained in an ambivalent, semi-detached position in relation to the Irish state and even more within a predominantly nationalist and Catholic society well into the mid-twentieth century, due to the persistence of traditional divisions and conflicting national allegiances both in terms of the college's own cultural orientation and how it was perceived by powerful forces within nationalist Ireland.

Despite the tentative accommodation between the college authorities and the Irish government, diverging symbols of identity retained the potential to provoke conflict well into the 1940s. The second world war exposed divisions between Trinity staff and students, who strongly favoured the Allies and the official policy of the Irish state, which embraced neutrality throughout the conflict. A significant number of Trinity students enlisted in the British army and 113 perished in the conflict, at a time when the Irish state was neutral; four Fellows and a number of lecturers also took leave of absence to serve in the allied armed forces or undertake related 'war work'.[121] The college's leaders took steps to minimise conflict with the wartime policy of the state. Thrift ended the practice of playing 'God Save the King' in 1939 on the outbreak of war, while the college authorities also ceased to fly the Union Jack in the late 1930s. Although toasts to King George VI continued throughout the war, they were quietly discontinued from 1945.[122] These efforts were reasonably successful in preventing any conflict with the state, but could not contain tensions between Trinity and powerful currents of nationalist public opinion which remained staunchly anti-British. Such tensions led to clashes between Trinity students and their more nationalistic contemporaries in UCD, as well as hard-line nationalist groups in Dublin, around major commemorative anniversaries such as Armistice Day before and during the second world war.[123]

The end of the war in Europe on 7 May 1945 produced the most dramatic flashpoint between Trinity and the more hard-line strain of nationalism, pitting Trinity students against an eclectic combination of their UCD counterparts, republican sympathisers and a far right group, Ailtirí na hAiséirghe, which combined fascist sympathies with extreme nationalism. The incident was triggered by an unofficial celebration by a group of Trinity students, who ran up the Union Jack and other Allied flags (as well as the tricolour) on the main college flagpole, provoking a furious reaction from a crowd gathered in College Green. The *Irish Times* reported that 'A section of the crowd took exception to the position of the Eire flag and three attempts, frustrated by Guards were made to effect an entrance into the university…Guards had to make repeated baton charges in College Green to disperse the large crowds demonstrating in front of Trinity.'[124] A large-scale demonstration was eagerly fomented by Ailtirí na hAiséirghe, in which a Union Jack was burned in front of the college by protesters, including the then UCD student (and future Taoiseach) Charles J. Haughey; a group of Trinity students on the roof burned a tricolour, either in the midst of the clash or as a retaliatory gesture.[125] These incidents set off two days of rioting, in which the college was targeted by demonstrators and was 'virtually in a state of siege', bombarded by stones and threatened by a crowd of several thousand on the night of 9 May, who were held off by police.[126] The college officers, fearful that the provocative celebration and fierce backlash could wreck decades of cautious rapprochement with the Irish state, moved swiftly to limit the damage. The provost, Ernest Alton, personally apologised to de Valera for the treatment of the tricolour, emphasising 'the desire of the College to dissociate itself from the irresponsible acts of a few individuals.'[127] The Board took steps to prevent any recurrence, cancelling rag week (anyway regarded with suspicion as a source of riotous behaviour) and replacing the junior dean, who was responsible for student discipline. The riot underlined the devastating potential for conflict and even outright violence inherent in a conflict of identities exemplified by the display of divergent national symbols, a quarter of a century after Trinity had accepted the Anglo-Irish Treaty. Yet the incident had no long-term impact and effectively marked the end of an era in which the symbols of nationality divided the college from the Irish state. Alton's term saw a closer rapprochement with the Irish government, at least while de Valera was in office and the incident did not prevent the government granting Trinity's application for a state grant less than two years later. While the war brought traditional divisions into the open, it also encouraged Trinity to shed its more overt symbolic associations with the *ancien regime*.

'In Medicine and Surgery, There Is No North and South'

The new state continued the pre-independence practice of supporting higher education institutions or faculties offering specialised medical courses, such as the Royal College of Surgeons in Ireland (RCSI) and the School of Medicine in TCD. RCSI, which was among the oldest higher education institutions on the island of Ireland, was founded in 1784 to make discrete provision for surgical education.[128] When the Medical Act, 1886 required graduates to be educated in surgery, medicine and obstetrics, RCSI began to train doctors in its medical school and a con-joint board was established to oversee a joint diploma between RCSI and the Royal College of Physicians.[129]

Following the Treaty, self-government and the partition of the island caused a shock to the college, whose Fellows had opposed home rule legislation in 1893.[130] The Free State government recognised the estab-lished position of RCSI in medical education by appointing two mem-bers of its council to the first Senate, including president Sir William De Courcey Wheeler.[131] RCSI prided itself on being an all-Ireland insti-tution and this was reflected in the appointment of its annual officers. Andrew Fullerton, its president in 1927–28, was professor of surgery in Queen's University.[132] The first Governor General of the Irish Free State, T. M. Healy, who was a regular guest at the college's Charter day dinner, congratulated Fullerton on his appointment in February 1927 with the pious sentiment that 'In medicine and surgery, I believe, there is no North and South.'[133]

The presidents of RCSI also maintained close connections with both Trinity and UCD during the early decades of the Irish state. A contro-versial proposal by the Free State government in 1925 to introduce a separate general medical register, which would have excluded grad-uates of Irish medical schools from registering for practice in Britain, provoked strong protests from university medical schools and RCSI.[134] All three medical schools collaborated in lobbying the Free State gov-ernment to modify its plan. RCSI president, Charles Maunsell, warned ministers in 1926 that 'the uncertainty about the Register had shaken the great Irish schools of medicine and surgery to their very founda-tions…'[135] The legislation adopted in 1927 established a new med-ical registration council for doctors trained within the Free State, but sensibly provided for reciprocal recognition of medical qualifications. Controversy later arose over representation on the new Irish medical registration council, when RCSI and the College of Physicians were granted only a single joint nominee.[136]

RCSI received a small grant from the pre-independence Department of Agriculture and Technical Instruction (DATI) since 1910 for the teaching of science and this grant was continued by the Department of Education from 1924 under its vote for technical instruction.[137] The level of exchequer support was modest, ranging from £990 in 1922–23 to £1073 in 1931–32.[138] The college received £1500 annually by 1949, somewhat less than the School of Medicine in Trinity which secured support under the same heading.[139] The subvention was never designed to cover most recurrent costs and the college was mainly dependent on private funding and student fees for its resources.

The Era of De Valera

The election of Eamon de Valera as Taoiseach in 1932 did not signal any major policy shift in higher education, where differences between the two major parties were marginal. Several Fianna Fáil ministers were hostile to the universities, often on the basis of their shortcomings in promoting the revival of Irish. Tom Derrig, the Minister for Education, was the most outspoken in criticising the failure of the universities to embrace Gaelicisation, telling the Dáil on 9 March 1934 that 'If the universities do not solve the problem of progressively Gaelicising themselves, we shall have to seriously reconsider our whole attitude to them'.[140] Derrig acknowledged that UCG was beginning to play its part in the revival of Irish, while Cork and Dublin were not far behind, but claimed that the NUI still lagged far behind the secondary schools. More influential ministers, such as Séan MacEntee, a long serving Minister for Finance, expressed concerns about over-production of university graduates leading to emigration, a constant refrain promoted by senior officials of the Department of Finance.[141] On a less elevated plane many Fianna Fáil TDs were suspicious of the NUI because several prominent academics, particularly in UCD, were supportive of Fine Gael.

Yet de Valera's government was preoccupied during the 1930s with political and constitutional reform, along with the imposition of traditional Sinn Féin policies of economic self-sufficiency and development of indigenous industry behind high tariff barriers. Higher education was invisible in the rhetoric of protectionist economic development and Fianna Fáil ministers were no more inclined to intervene directly in the internal workings of the universities than their Cumann na nGaedhael predecessors, with the usual exception of intermittent efforts to promote Gaelicisation. Moreover, de Valera's position as Chancellor of the

NUI represented a significant stabilising factor in relations between Fianna Fáil and the National University. The Fianna Fáil leader served as Chancellor for over half a century, presiding over the NUI until his death in 1975. De Valera, unlike his predecessor, William Walsh, treated the position of Chancellor as a formal and ceremonial office: he was diligent in presiding over the activity of the National University, but rarely intervened to influence its decisions or to shape academic policies.[142]

De Valera was, however, alert to the implications for the NUI of the new constitutional settlement between the Irish state and the British Empire, which he engineered between 1932 and 1939. The King was recognised by the charter and statutes of the NUI as the Visitor of the National University, with the power to appoint a board to conduct a Visitation of the institution. This embarrassing legal anomaly emerged following a request for the appointment of a Board of Visitors to investigate the 'dairy science row' in UCC in 1934. This was a bitter dispute over control and administration in the new dairy science faculty, ranging the president, Patrick Merriman and Professor Connell Boyle against the lecturers of the faculty, backed by Alfred O'Rahilly, the influential registrar.[143] Fianna Fáil, which prized its republican credentials and was committed to removing the monarch from the constitution, could hardly allow the King to appoint a Board of Visitors. The Attorney General, Conor Maguire, proposed adapting the charter of the NUI to allow the Governor General to act as Visitor.[144] But the Executive Council, in a decision on 15 February 1935 which bore de Valera's personal imprint, rejected this halfway house and instead decided to make an order adapting the charter to replace the King with the Council itself as the body appointing the Board of Visitors.[145] After the order was laid before the Oireachtas, the government appointed two High Court judges, Murnaghan and O'Byrne, as the Board of Visitors for UCC in June 1935.[146] Ironically, the visitors were never obliged to adjudicate the dispute, as the governing body decided by a majority vote on 31 January 1936 to uphold the position of the lecturers.[147] But the dairy science row assumed a wider significance than it deserved in leading de Valera's government to clarify the obscure but legally significant position of the Visitor in the charter of the NUI.

The adoption of de Valera's constitution in 1937, which abolished all vestiges of royal authority except for the purpose of external association with the British Empire, led to a further intervention by the Taoiseach. Alex McCarthy, the newly appointed registrar of the NUI, sought clarification from de Valera in 1938 on the place of the King within the statutes of the university following the constitutional changes of the 1930s. The Taoiseach's response left no doubt about his determination to exclude the King from any lingering connection with the university. Maurice Moynihan, the secretary to the government, issued a detailed reply to the registrar's query on 28 July, which was approved by de Valera.[148] Moynihan asserted that the new constitution allowed the government to exercise all powers previously held by the King, unless other provisions were specifically made by the constitution: 'It is therefore regarded as being quite incompatible with Article 49 of the Constitution that any function of a Visitor should continue to be exercised by the King.'[149] The careful attention given to an apparently arcane statutory point testified to de Valera's concern to confirm the 'national' status of the NUI by removing the last symbolic legacies of imperial government. It marked a rare decisive intervention by de Valera in the affairs of the NUI, when university considerations became relevant to the wider constitutional agenda at the core of his government's ideology.

'...It Was Better to Leave the Text as It Stood...'

The only institutional reform affecting the relationship between universities and the Irish state adopted by Fianna Fáil did not involve higher education per se, but the abolition of university representation in the Dáil. This arrangement did not long survive Fianna Fáil's ascent to power in 1932. Fianna Fáil ministers objected to the special constituency for university graduates on impeccably democratic grounds: in introducing the constitutional amendment to delete article 27 of the 1922 constitution, Seán T. Ó Ceallaigh, vice-president of the Executive Council, argued for the abolition of graduate representation in the Dáil on the basis that it conflicted with the generally accepted principle of universal adult suffrage.[150] Yet while university representation could easily be portrayed as outdated and undemocratic, the party's motives were less altruistic. Fianna Fáil ministers had little sympathy with claims for special representation of Trinity graduates and indeed Ó Ceallaigh expressed the party's suspicion of the influence of graduates living abroad in terms which revealed a great deal about conventional attitudes to emigrants, graduates or otherwise: 'such persons should not be in a position to exercise an influence on our Parliamentary developments.'[151] Cumann na nGaedhael enjoyed the support of the independent TCD deputies and traditionally dominated representation in the NUI graduate constituency, which elected prominent UCD academics such as MacNeill, McGilligan and Michael Tierney as government supporters between 1922 and 1932. Ironically, Fianna Fáil secured two of the three seats in the NUI constituency for the first time in 1933 (with one being held by Attorney General Conor Maguire), but this was not enough to redeem university representation.[152] T. Desmond Williams, professor of history in UCD, gave a later reflection on the abolition of university representation which was more tactful than some of his counterparts at the time: 'College men felt, and possibly rightly so, that the previous record of the College (and the university) and the interpretation placed upon it by Fianna Fáil influenced to some extent at least that decision.'[153] Graduate representation in the Dáil was strongly defended by the TCD representatives and by W. T. Cosgrave, who warned that the abolition of the TCD constituency broke commitments made by the Free State in 1922 and would reduce the proportion of non-Catholic TDs.[154] But the outcome was a foregone conclusion considering Fianna Fáil's overall majority and the Dáil approved the constitutional amendment by a decisive majority of 51 to 29 on 5 July 1934.[155] The Senate fought a dedicated rearguard action, rejecting the amendment on 18 July. This followed a rancorous debate in which Oliver St John Gogarty, an independent senator best known for his occasional association with James Joyce, declared with more hyperbole than sense that it was '… the most tragic day in the history of all this disastrous republican government'.[156] The Senate's resistance succeeded in delaying the inevitable, until the abolition of article 27 was again approved by the Dáil in February 1936.[157]

But even this reform proved less radical than it appeared, as it was not the end of graduate representation. De Valera included a graduate constituency within a redesigned Senate in the new constitution adopted barely a year later. The 1937 constitution provided for three members to be elected by the NUI and Trinity graduate panels within a 60-member upper house. De Valera's initiative, unforeseen by either supporters or opponents during the frequently bitter debates over abolition, was almost certainly influenced by institutional pressure from the NUI. While the more vocal opposition to the abolition of graduate representation focused on the position of Trinity College, institutional leaders and many academic staff in the NUI were also disturbed by the disappearance of the graduate constituency. The NUI senate, acting in a more diplomatic fashion than parliamentary opponents of abolition, adopted a resolution on 12 April 1934 which was conveyed to de Valera: 'The Senate, learning of the proposed abolition of University Representation in the Dáil, wishes to place on record its opinion that, by this or other means, the University, as an important cultural corporation, should have representation.'[158] The NUI senate did not oppose abolition but quietly indicated to the Chancellor that some form of university representation was desirable. De Valera was also sensitive to charges that the representation of the Protestant minority in the Free State was being curtailed and concerned not to give ammunition to the unionist administration in Stormont, alert for any opportunity to depict 'Home Rule as Rome Rule'. He asked Michael MacDunphy after the draft constitution had been published to prepare a revised clause for graduate representation in the Senate which would be flexible enough in case of the unification of the island. The Cabinet secretary's draft was designed to cover the following contingencies:

1. The addition of Queen's College University, Belfast, in the event of the unity of Ireland being achieved.
2. The elevation of one or more of the constituent colleges of the NU to University Status.[159]

MacDunphy proposed a complex provision which involved the election of at least six but no more than ten senators by the university graduates, with the members divided equally among the universities and the precise numbers determined by statute. De Valera, however, decided to set out the level of representation for each university in the constitution. MacDunphy, tellingly, noted in a private memo that de Valera feared an adverse reaction from Trinity College:

> Though very much attracted by the scheme the President felt that to make the change after the original text had been published might be interpreted by Trinity College as an attempt to cut down representation of that body, and he thought that in the circumstances it was better to leave the text as it stood.[160]

The rejection of the alternative scheme illustrated de Valera's concern to reassure Trinity College and the Protestant minority that their interests would not be adversely affected in the new constitution, combined with a shrewd calculation that raising an outcry from Trinity graduates would hand a weapon to his domestic opponents and the Stormont administration. Ironically, the solution which he eventually adopted was very similar to the one agreed by his former opponents, Collins and Griffith, with the southern unionists in 1922.

'…The Whole Position…Is Destroyed in One Blow'

The bitter battle over university representation was exceptional because it was fundamentally not about higher education at all, but went to the heart of the partisan and ideological divisions of the early Irish state. Despite the considerable differences between Fianna Fáil and Cumann na nGaedhael over political and constitutional issues, de Valera's government was generally notable for its continuity with earlier Free State policies in university education, particularly in the new government's devotion to fiscal conservatism and Gaelicisation. De Valera's long-serving Minister for Finance, Séan MacEntee, gave no ground to Ernest Blythe in his commitment to 'economy' and implemented austerity policies more stringently due to the impact of the Economic War with

Britain and the world economic depression.[161] MacEntee included university colleges receiving statutory grants in legislation providing for a 10% reduction in the salary of civil and public servants, although the Department of Finance acknowledged that implementation of the public service cut presented unusual problems due to the autonomy of the universities and the difficulty in ascertaining the proportion of the statutory grants devoted to salaries. The Cabinet decided on 24 March to include a general clause based on similar legislation in New Zealand, empowering the government to reduce university grants on a temporary basis, while delegating to the universities themselves the unpalatable task of making the reductions: 'They would have to be invited to say how much, in total, the salaries of their officials would be reduced if the scale decided for Civil Servants of equivalent remuneration was applied to them.'[162] The Public Services (Temporary Economies) Bill allowed the college authorities to make deductions in salary and provided for 'consultation' between the Minister for Finance and colleges regarding the scale of cuts in grants and salaries. The government's relentless pursuit of economy provoked the sharpest clash between ministers and university authorities between 1922 and 1960, although in an era before twenty four hour media and spin-doctoring it took place almost entirely behind closed doors.

The authorities of the NUI adopted a common front in resisting the pay reductions, which caused particular outrage due to the authority given to the Minister for Finance to decide the cuts and the application of the legislation solely to the NUI. TCD was exempt from the pay cuts as the college did not receive a statutory grant. O'Rahilly and Tierney took the lead in rallying the opposition at a meeting of academic staff drawn from all three colleges on 21 April, with the elder statesman of university presidents, Alexander Anderson, in the chair. The academics agreed an uncompromising denunciation of the Bill in a memorandum to the government and appealed to de Valera to meet a deputation of NUI representatives. O'Rahilly and Tierney wrote to de Valera urging him to intervene, noting that they were 'most anxious to have a friendly discussion with you before the Bill reaches the Committee stage in the Dáil and hope to arrive at an agreed course of action.'[163] If their approach to the Chancellor was conciliatory, the academic statement which they drafted left no room for ambiguity, arguing that the Bill gave arbitrary power over the colleges to the Minister for Finance; undermined university education for Catholics and represented a fundamental threat to university autonomy:

> The most serious aspect of the Bill is the almost unconscious and innocent way in which it insinuates and initiates State control over our University Colleges. The principle has been strenuously opposed by the Catholic Church in every country. The absence (hitherto) of State control over the working of our Colleges was an indispensable precondition for their recognition by the Hierarchy as suitable for Irish Catholics. The withdrawal of this guarantee raises issues of far-reaching importance.[164]

Having held out the somewhat unlikely prospect that the emergency fiscal legislation could undermine the Catholic Church's support for the university settlement reached a generation earlier, the letter proceeded to raise the dreaded spectre of Communism:

> If the Bill is passed as it stands at present, the whole position, secured by generations of effort and struggle for Irish Catholic University Education, is destroyed in one blow. There is embodied in the Bill the principle of State control over University administration and personnel, with all its possible political, cultural and religious reactions. So far no country outside of Russia has adopted this principle.[165]

The extreme, dogmatic tone of the academic statement bore the hallmark of O'Rahilly, a dedicated exponent of integralist Catholicism and Tierney, a leading advocate of applying Catholic social teaching to the political realm.[166] Yet it was apparent that the academic leaders were willing to use any stick, however implausible, to beat the Department of Finance. Catholic social teaching was invoked to protect the professional interests of an academic elite: they appealed to the government not to include universities in the legislation and instead to reach agreement on economies through 'prior consultation' with the university authorities and if necessary, a special Bill dealing only with the universities.

The stinging academic critique of the Bill met with an equally intransigent response from MacEntee, who was not inclined to compromise with his critics. He warned de Valera on 24 April that if universities were exempted from the legislation other bodies would demand the same treatment; it was impossible to offer reliable estimates of the deductions for university staff as the colleges were refusing to provide the necessary information. While he conceded that the extent of the deductions for civil servants might not be appropriate for university teachers this did not excuse the academic opposition: '…the Colleges should be informative and otherwise helpful, instead of unhelpfully critical.'[167] The Department of Finance dismissed the academic argument that the Bill would extend state control over the university as 'to say the least, far-fetched' and rejected a special universities bill as impractical.[168]

The university representatives issued a more detailed indictment of the legislation in May 1933, submitting a thirteen page memorandum to the Executive Council. They reiterated their core objection that the legislation transformed the relationship between the state and the university by encroaching on their autonomy: 'This autonomy and this complete freedom, guaranteed to the Catholics and their staffs as well as to the Catholic community of Ireland by specific provisions set forth in their Charters, is now being swept away almost at random by one or two sections in an Economies Bill'.[169] The academic representatives characterised MacEntee's request that they identify appropriate deductions in the grant as 'a total injustice'; essentially under protest, they suggested modest deductions for each college which amounted to about 2% of the general purpose grants.[170] The academic critique did not sway the Finance Minister. MacEntee briskly rejected their case on 5 May, arguing that the unhelpful attitude of the university authorities made agreement without legislation impossible and 'it would probably be a fatal mistake to leave them out of the Bill.'[171] Their argument that the Bill threatened university autonomy, 'developed at great length and enveloped with the dust of verbiage' was absurd. MacEntee commented acidly that increases in the grant by legislation did not inspire claims of state control: 'A minor reduction in grant is no more an attack on autonomy than a large increase in grants was an attempt to corrupt University education at its source'.[172]

De Valera adopted a more measured line than MacEntee, seeking to scale down the conflict with the NUI representatives without undermining his government's stringent fiscal policy. De Valera received a deputation consisting of the three university presidents and other representatives of the NUI staff on 26 April, promising to have their representations examined by the Minister for Finance; not surprisingly, this did not bridge the gap between MacEntee and the NUI representatives.[173] The president also consulted privately with Denis Coffey, his closest associate among the NUI presidents, asking his view confidentially on the original O'Rahilly-Tierney memorandum and the departmental response. When de Valera sent the Department of Finance's unfavourable response to Coffey on 5 May, he did not commit himself to any particular course of action, noting only that he would inform Colley of the decision 'in some days'.[174]

De Valera moved to broker a compromise between the colleges and the Department of Finance. The government's decision later that month mitigated the impact of the cut on university salaries. MacEntee amended the original Bill on 26 May, excluding the universities from the general clause enabling the Minister for Finance to make unspecified deductions in the statutory grant and instead allowing the minister to reduce the grant to university colleges by a maximum of 5% in the current financial year.[175] This concession largely defused the row with the NUI authorities, without exempting the universities from the legislation. The final outcome was even less onerous, as the Department of Finance informed the NUI registrar in April 1934 that the minister had decided to make a deduction of 3% in the grant of £10,000 payable to the universities from the Irish Church Temporalities Fund.[176] The conflict, which had aroused strong feelings on both sides, ended with barely a whimper.

The compromise did not please everybody. Paddy McGilligan attacked the government in the Dáil debate for cutting the salaries of professors and sought unsuccessfully to reduce the cut to a nominal 1%. McGilligan mocked Fianna Fáil's claim that the university authorities freely accepted the new arrangement, commenting that it was 'easy to make an arrangement when you have a pistol at your head.'[177] McGilligan made an impassioned appeal on behalf of university professors threatened with 'The watercresses of starvation-land - that is the fare that we are going to mete out to a body of exceptionally qualified men...'[178] But there was little sympathy for university professors in the Dáil. Thomas Kelly, a Fianna Fáil TD, responded bluntly that '£800 a year is not bad now' and the government comfortably defeated McGilligan's amendment.[179] McGilligan, himself an academic and TD for the NUI, was the only deputy in the debate to question the impact of the legislation on the professorial staff, teaching and scholarship of the universities.

The legislation did not alter in any significant way the relationship between the Irish state and the universities. The outcome testified to the effective lobbying by the NUI representatives and the value of their political connections. De Valera's pivotal position as Chancellor mitigated the harsher elements of government economic policy. The initiative was inspired by a wider policy diktat to achieve 'economy' in the public service at a time of severe economic crisis, which affected higher education largely in the name of official consistency. While MacEntee was characteristically abrasive in his contacts with university authorities, his irritation at their resistance to his austerity budget did not signal a wider assault on the autonomy of the university: even the finance minister disclaimed any desire to influence the internal staffing structures of universities or review salaries of university staff on a regular basis. Yet if the Bill's academic critics overstated their case, they had no shortage of grounds for complaint in the parsimonious financing of university education by the Irish state since 1922 and the high-handed approach of ministers who were intolerant of any dissent. Perhaps the most striking feature of the dispute was that hardly any of the protagonists alluded to the potential contribution of the universities to the wider society or economy. Arguments on both sides were framed almost exclusively in terms of political, religious and financial imperatives, with much of the disagreement focusing on the relative weight given to university autonomy, denominational interests in higher education and the government's agenda of fiscal economy.

Despite the more militant rhetoric employed by some Fianna Fáil ministers around Gaelicisation, de Valera's government was generally cautious in its dealings with the universities. The conservative policy direction set by the first Free State government in higher education was maintained with few exceptions by de Valera. This was certainly true in the parsimonious financing of higher education, where the grants for all four universities and the statutory provision for the NUI remained static between 1930 and 1947, with the exception of a modest advance to support Gaelicisation in UCD and a more substantial once-off rescue package to relieve the college's debt in 1944. Both major parties in the first quarter of a century after 1922 adhered to an overarching framework of fiscal stringency in higher education, punctuated by piecemeal initiatives to support Gaelicisation or less frequently to underpin faculty developments linked to a predominantly agricultural economy.

'The Professor Was Very Nervous...'

If de Valera generally adhered to a conservative template in his dealings with the universities, he was responsible for a dramatic initiative in higher education, undertaken in very unfavourable circumstances. The foundation of the Dublin Institute for Advanced Studies (DIAS), which coincided with Europe's descent into the second world war, was de Valera's personal initiative, although he relied on detailed input from senior academics, especially Prof. E. T. Whittaker, former Astronomer Royal and professor at Edinburgh University, Arthur Conway and AJ McConnell.[180] The Taoiseach hoped to solve several problems at once through a new institute, notably the future of the neglected observatory at Dunsink, previously associated with the famous mathematician, William Rowan Hamilton; the development of advanced mathematical research in Dublin and the expansion of research on Irish language and literature. The Irish Studies committee of the Royal Irish Academy (RIA) had submitted a proposal to the Taoiseach for a separate institute of Celtic studies. De Valera was enthusiastic about the concept of a research centre for the study, collation and dissemination of manuscripts in Irish, but decided to locate Celtic studies alongside advanced scientific research within a specialised research institute.[181]

Following discussions with Whittaker and Thrift, now provost of TCD, in April 1938, de Valera decided on two separate projects, the

development of Dunsink in conjunction with the Meteorological service and establishment of 'an institute of higher studies such as that
of Princetown {sic}, where research work would be carried out under
the guidance of men of international reputation.'[182] De Valera's meeting with Whittaker on 8 April 1938 was the genesis of the Institute of
Advanced Studies, established two and a half years later. The inspiration for the idea was derived principally from the Princeton Institute
for Advanced Study, where the School of Mathematics was headed
by Albert Einstein, although officials also garnered information on a
diverse range of research centres for de Valera, including the Institute
of International Affairs in London (Chatham House), the College
de France and the Kaiser-Wilhelm Institute in Germany.[183] The proposed Institute bore de Valera's distinctive stamp, combining his particular interest in the Irish language and advanced mathematics: it
would be built initially around the disciplines of theoretical physics
and Celtic literature, offering a research centre for eminent academics
with an international reputation. The school of Theoretical Physics was
intended to have three senior professors, Conway, Whittaker and Erwin
Schrodinger, a Jewish physicist and Nobel laureate with a track record
of hostility to the Nazis.

The initiative proceeded throughout 1938–39 on two tracks—
one a conventional path involving departmental memoranda and
legislation for the creation of the Institute, and the other a distinctly
unconventional route involving high level official assistance in getting
Schrodinger and his family to Ireland. De Valera used informal channels to offer the Austrian-born physicist asylum. Whittaker succeeded
in conveying de Valera's offer to Schrodinger through a German exile,
Prof Max Born, another colleague based in Geneva, Prof Baer, and
Schrodinger's mother-in-law in Vienna. Stealth was necessary in con-
tacting the physicist, as Whittaker warned de Valera: 'He {Max Born}
said that S. was much disliked by the Nazis, who might not be content with dismissing him but might even kill him; and that it would be
unwise to write to him, as his letters would be opened and any plans
likely to lead to a good settlement for him would be frustrated.'[184]
The international academic network proved adept in evading the
Nazi censors, transmitting a message from Schrodinger that he would

be prepared to take up the Taoiseach's offer but any early preparations to leave Germany 'would involve him in serious trouble'.[185] But
his departure was not delayed for long, as Schrodinger was writing to
de Valera directly from Rome on 16 September 1938, confirming his
wish to proceed to Dublin and appealing for assistance with obtaining
the necessary visas for himself and his wife from the Irish legation in
Rome.[186] De Valera swiftly secured consular assistance for Schrodinger:
a week later the professor and his wife were on their way to England via
Switzerland and France, travelling on visas obtained by Irish embassy
staff. The Irish consul in Rome, showing a keen appreciation of his
minister's personal interest in the welfare of the travellers, reported
directly to de Valera that 'The Schrodingers left for Geneva last night.
I bought their railway ticket…The Professor was very nervous, as well
he might be.'[187] Schrodinger, having met de Valera in Geneva where the
Taoiseach was attending the League of Nations, was safely ensconced in
Magdalen College, Oxford by 2 October.

De Valera assembled an impressive cast of academics to welcome the
exiled Nobel laureate to Dublin and consider plans for the projected
school of Theoretical Physics. The Taoiseach convened a meeting in
Dublin on 21 November, involving Conway, Thrift, McConnell and
Schrodinger himself; de Valera's closest official collaborators, Maurice
Moynihan, the Cabinet secretary and Joseph Walshe, secretary of
the department of External Affairs also attended. De Valera outlined
his intention to establish 'an Institute of Advanced Studies', encompassing schools of Theoretical Physics, Celtic Studies and Medical
Research, with other sections possibly to be added subsequently.[188]
Both Conway and McConnell were supportive of the scheme for a
school of Theoretical Physics, while seeking to protect the interests of
their own institutions: Conway advised that the governing body for the
new school should include the senior professors in the appropriate subjects in UCD and TCD, while McConnell noted that if the Andrews
Professorship in Astronomy in Trinity was associated with the Institute,
the college wished to retain a connection with it. De Valera's determination to secure Schrodinger's participation was apparent from the outset: at the Taoiseach's instigation, Conway offered the exiled physicist
a temporary lectureship in UCD, to give him a regular income until

the institute was established.[189] Even more striking was de Valera's personal intervention to overcome any obstacles faced by Schrodinger within the Irish immigration system, which was extremely restrictive in accepting Jewish (or any political) refugees. This triggered a highly unusual exchange between the Taoiseach and the Department of Justice. Schrodinger requested that the department issue a visa for Hildegunde March, a native of Innsbruck, to come to Dublin on the basis that 'she was a friend of his wife'[190]: in fact, Frau March, the wife of his former assistant Arthur March, was Schrodinger's mistress and later the mother of his daughter. John Duff of the Department of Justice, taken aback at this request, sought direction from Moynihan on 24 November, noting pointedly that March did not qualify for inclusion in the limited quota of political refugees from Germany:

> ...Frau March is an 'Aryan'. She has a husband and child but there is no intention of seeking permission for the husband and child to follow her here. The Professor was very mysterious about the whole matter...I felt that it was extremely peculiar that a request should be made for facilities for this lady to abandon her family for the somewhat inadequate reason that she would be of assistance to Frau Schrodinger in establishing a home here.[191]

Moynihan responded on 13 December with a straightforward directive from the Taoiseach that Hildegunde March was to be allowed into the country: 'The Taoiseach is anxious that everything possible should be done in this matter to meet the wishes of Prof. Schrodinger as a Scientist of international repute whom it is desired to induce to pursue his scientific work in this country.'[192] De Valera noted that as March was not a political refugee, there was no need to consider her case in the light of the quota and implicitly no obstacle to her entry to Ireland. De Valera was not deterred either by Schrodinger's unconventional life-style or by the scientist's habit of seeking assistance directly from the Taoiseach on a wide variety of issues, ranging from serious—the renewal of his Irish visa when he was caught in Belgium at the outset of the war—to the mundane, how to transfer his furniture to Dublin.

Following Schrodinger's visit to Ireland, de Valera forged ahead
with the establishment of the new institute, which now moved from
semi-clandestine avenues into more formal bureaucratic channels.
Moynihan wrote to Joseph O'Neill, secretary of the Department of
Education, on 9 January 1939, asking for the department's advice in
producing a detailed scheme for the institute as the Taoiseach wished to
have proposals for the school of theoretical physics prepared 'as expedi-
tiously as possible.'[193] The priority given to theoretical physics reflected
de Valera's concern that the putative institute might lose Schrodinger's
services if he secured other employment in the meantime. Although the
Taoiseach involved the Department of Education in the planning for
the institute, he did not accept O'Neill's proposal that a small committee including representatives from the four university colleges should
draw up the scheme for the school of theoretical physics, which would
have delayed the process of founding the institute; instead de Valera
asked Conway to advise on drafting a scheme for the school. The initial scheme for the institute was drafted by Moynihan, who drew upon
extensive input from Conway and Whittaker. The purpose of the new
institution was 'to foster advanced work in various branches of study...
by providing an organisation and funds offering whole-time careers
to scholars of special distinction and international repute', as well as
opportunities for Irish and international students to work under the
guidance of such scholars.[194] The official memorandum envisaged that
each school would have its own governing body and exercise 'a considerable measure of autonomy', although Moynihan proposed that an
overall governing body might well be desirable. None of the schools
within the Institute would engage in teaching or confer degrees.[195] The
scheme proposed a maximum allocation of £7500 annually for the new
institution fixed by legislation, while the actual grant would be determined by the Minister for Finance within this envelope.[196] The creation of a specialised research institute, devoted essentially to advanced
theoretical study without any teaching or examination functions, was
innovative in an Irish context, but reflected developments in the USA,
Germany and Denmark during the early twentieth century.

All the major decisions in the creation of the new institution were taken by de Valera, who rejected Moynihan's preference for a single governing body. The Taoiseach decided in April 1939 that the institute would be overseen by a council with a limited co-ordinating function: each school would be controlled by its own governing body, which would include the permanent professors of the institute and nominees of the government, with a chairman appointed by the government. Decisions on appointment or removal of professors would be made by each governing body subject to the approval of the government and the first full-time professors would be named in the legislation.[197]

De Valera introduced the legislation for the establishment of the Dublin Institute for Advanced Studies to the Dáil on 6 July 1939. The Bill provided for the creation only of schools of Theoretical Physics and Celtic Studies, while enabling the government to add other departments later.[198] Despite its limited scope, the legislation was controversial, provoking opposition from senior Fine Gael politicians. General Richard Mulcahy opposed the Bill, arguing that a new institute would undermine the NUI as it could only mean 'the substitution, by some other body, of the faculties, say, in the National University of Ireland…'[199] De Valera's brief response illustrated the scale of his ambition for the institute, whatever its small beginnings: the new foundation would not supplant the NUI but undertake specialised research which went beyond the existing activity of the universities and the RIA. The contribution of the Institute would enable Ireland 'to be a world centre for Celtic studies' and re-establish an international reputation for the Irish state in mathematical research, building on the pioneering work of Hamilton in the mid-nineteenth century.[200] But the parliamentary criticisms of the Bill unnerved Schrodinger, who suspected, wrongly, that Nazi influence was behind the opposition and wrote an anguished letter to the Taoiseach, fearing that the school of theoretical physics might be dropped from the scheme:

> That I am alarmed by any trace of influence from that side, you will forgive me, Sir, knowing the experience I had with it…To sum up, I am seriously distressed by the present situation and know not what to do…I therefore beg you, Sir, restore my faith, if you deem it due to do so.[201]

De Valera quickly reassured Schrodinger on 31 July that the school of Theoretical Physics was an integral part of the Institute and would be approved by the Dáil, probably before the end of the year. He adopted a benign tone towards the opposition, dismissing Mulcahy's arguments as 'groundless' while acquitting his opponents of the charge of anti-Semitism: 'I am not, of course, in a position to say what precisely were the reasons actuating Deputy Mulcahy…but I think it most unlikely that he was influenced by any views such as those to which you allude as being held in another country.'[202]

The outbreak of the Second World War delayed the initiative until the spring of 1940. De Valera's preoccupation with the multiple foreign and security challenges of the Emergency ensured that the Bill was postponed for almost a year. The extent to which it was his personal initiative was highlighted by the lack of progress in the first year of the war, as no other minister had either the inclination or expertise to take up the project. De Valera's enthusiasm for a specialised research institute was not widely shared within the political elite. Mulcahy made a populist critique of the scheme, which he described in a Dáil debate on 10 April 1940 as 'a higher humbug production in the language of films…'; with more than a hint of anti-intellectualism, he accused de Valera of neglecting mathematics in poorly funded secondary schools to pursue an impractical scheme of no educational benefit to the mass of the public: 'The Taoiseach referred to the McCullaghs and the Hamiltons, but there are people called Pat Murphys. We are descending to the Pat Murphy argument now.'[203] McGilligan also presented a sharp indictment of the Bill on 1 May, albeit on very different grounds: the proposed institute created an unhealthy divergence between research and the universities and he would seek in a future government to associate the Institute with UCD so as to 'get this institute brought back to the academic group from which it should never have been separated'.[204] McGilligan forced a vote on the final stage of the Bill, much to de Valera's exasperation, although it was carried by a substantial majority. The Dáil debate was flavoured by wariness about the innovation of a research institute, laced with more general suspicion of de Valera's motives, on the part of Fine Gael deputies closely associated with the NUI.

The debate in the Seanad, where the legislation was approved without a vote, took a very different course. Most senators did not oppose the Bill but university members were critical of the extent of government control over the proposed Institute and the limited security for the professors. Among the contributors to a wide-ranging debate were two future university presidents, Michael Tierney and Ernest Henry Alton, whose contributions influenced the final shape of the Bill. The most searching criticism of the legislation was made by Tierney, who accepted the principle of an institute but questioned de Valera's determination to combine Celtic Studies and Theoretical Physics and argued that too much power was given to the government, particularly the Minister for Finance, over the financing and staffing of the Institute.[205] Tierney's concern about excessive official power was echoed by Alton (otherwise a strong supporter of the Bill) who warned that 'there is too much of the Minister for Finance about it. His dead hand, his deadening hand, is over it.'[206] De Valera was more receptive to these academic critics than his political opponents, accepting amendments to clarify that the governing body of each school was autonomous in its academic functions and that the power of the council of the institute was restricted to financial oversight and administration.[207] Other amendments guaranteed that the salary and conditions of senior professors would not be altered without their consent and offered protection against arbitrary removal from office. But the powers of the Minister for Finance to exercise financial oversight were retained and subsequent relations between the institute and the department largely vindicated the academic critics.

The more measured response of the senators to de Valera's initiative was not simply about the less partisan nature of the upper House. The more constructive reaction of the university representatives underlined that neither Trinity nor UCD were seriously disturbed by the new Institute, not least because senior university academics were consulted from the outset by de Valera. The reservations of professional academics related more to the prospect of state control of a new research institution rather than its distinctive, specialised character.

It was not the relatively weak domestic opposition or the more widespread indifference among the political elite which presented the greatest threat to the initiative. The world war threatened to derail the proposed institute, causing severe problems in assembling a distinguished cast of international scholars in a newly founded research institute, at a time when normal travel or educational exchange between Ireland and continental Europe was almost entirely disrupted. These problems led Whittaker, de Valera's closest academic collaborator, to advise in May 1940 that the project should be postponed for the duration of the war:

> In the circumstances the question must be faced, whether it is advisable to start the School of Theoretical Physics until the free flow of research students is restored by the ending of the war. Frankly, I am hesitant…I doubt whether, in the present state of the world, the most brilliant Professors could make a success of it as a school, though of course they could carry on their own personal researches.[208]

Whittaker's reservations, while sincerely held, were also influenced by his reluctance to abandon wartime Edinburgh: his sense of duty to the university, which was severely affected by the loss of staff to 'war work', would prevent him taking up his intended post in the institute. Moreover, another key supporter of the initiative was also unavailable, as Conway, whom de Valera had envisaged as director of the school of Theoretical Physics, was elected to succeed Coffey as president of UCD in 1940. But de Valera was determined to press ahead, even if the institute was to be only a 'modest beginning'. He told Whittaker on 20 May 1940 that 'it will be absolutely necessary to open the school in October, even though we have to do so without the full complement of Professors.'[209] He regretted Whittaker's inability to leave Edinburgh, 'which will be a sore loss to the School, but if you feel you cannot come I will, of course, understand.'[210] The logic of the professor's argument appeared undeniable, but de Valera worked on the more compelling political logic that if the foundation of the Institute was delayed it might never happen.

The Taoiseach moved to establish the institute in the autumn of 1940, even as the Battle of Britain raged over the neighbouring island. The Taoiseach's department informed the Department of Finance in October 1940 that steps were being taken to form the first council of the institute and establish the two constituent schools; the department was asked to approve a draft estimate of £7500 for the expenses of the institute in its first year.[211] The first council was appointed on 4 October 1940, signalling the creation of the new institution as a body corporate; Monsignor Pádraig de Brún, professor of Mathematics in Maynooth, Irish language scholar and a former student of de Valera, was its first chairman. The elevation of such an irreproachably respectable figure was calculated to disarm any criticism of the new venture. Schrodinger was installed as the sole senior professor and director of the School of Theoretical Physics on 29 October.[212] He remained the sole academic staff member, until his fellow German exile, Walter Heitler, described by Whittaker as 'a much younger but extremely brilliant man', became assistant professor in the school in June 1941. The newly founded School of Celtic Studies was more generously served with eminent researchers at the outset, with the appointment of Tomás O'Rahilly, Osborn Bergin, and R. I Best as senior professors. Daniel Binchy, an eminent Irish language scholar who had served as the Irish minister to Berlin during the dying days of the Weimar Republic, became the first chair of the governing body, beginning a long-standing association with Celtic studies within the institute.[213]

DIAS began on a deliberately modest scale, spending even less in its first year than allocated by the Department of Finance. It did not realise either de Valera's hopes that other research disciplines would gradually be grafted on to the institute, or the fears of his opponents that it was merely the first step towards the creation of a rival system of higher education to the universities. The only major addition to the new foundation was the School of Cosmic Physics, established in 1947 to specialise in the study of geophysics; the government acquired the observatory at Dunsink from TCD for the use of the new school.[214] Leo W. Pollak, another eminent Jewish scientist exiled under Nazi rule after a long association with the University of Vienna, was instrumental in the creation of a school specialising in geophysics and astronomy within the Institute. Pollak sent de Valera a proposal for the creation of the school of Cosmic Physics in 1943 and became its first director in 1947.[215]

The other two senior professors appointed from the outset, Hermann Bruck and Lajos Janossy, were also foreign scholars attracted to Ireland in the aftermath of the war.[216] The establishment of the School of Cosmic Physics was even more controversial than the institute, winning approval in the Dáil in February 1947 on a party line vote in which all the opposition parties rejected the initiative.[217] The new school drew a stinging attack from the *Irish Independent* which argued that the government was neglecting badly underfunded universities to endow 'institutions which are in their way rival universities'.[218] The predominance of continental European scientists in the School during its early years also drew critical attention, so that Pollak felt obliged to reject publicly claims that 'only foreigners had been employed in the School of Cosmic Physics…'[219] Irish candidates had been appointed at assistant professor and technical assistant level, although attracting leading international scholars was part of the *raison d'etre* of the Institute. Pollak told a lecture in UCD on 4 November 1950 that he had fulfilled a commitment to de Valera that Irish scientists would be employed where possible, but it was not easy 'to get Irishmen who are fully trained and qualified to fill certain technical positions.'[220] Pollak's argument (and its logical implication that Ireland lagged behind continental Europe in scientific and technical training) was controversial and arguably ahead of its time; it would be widely accepted by the political and official establishment a decade later, under de Valera's successor, Seán Lemass.

An equally significant obstacle to the progress of the new research centre was securing salaries commensurate with their expertise for junior academics. Pollak was writing to de Valera in December 1951 to note that his request for increased salaries for the two assistant professors in Cosmic Physics (Charles McCusker and T. Murphy) and the technical assistants had not been sanctioned. He feared that younger staff would accept employment abroad and 'their valuable services be lost to this country'.[221] Pollak's appeal to de Valera indicated frustration at the tight financial control maintained over the institute by the Department of Finance and the sometimes deliberate tardiness of the department in responding to funding requests. A lengthy struggle between the institute and the department over a pay increase for senior professors (from £1200 to £1800 per annum) extended over a four-year period, from January 1948 until May 1952, although it was eventually resolved in favour of the professors following pressure from the Department of the Taoiseach.[222]

The governing body of the institute waged a battle with the Department of Finance in the early postwar period on a series of issues, including salary increases, along with improved terms and conditions, for assistant professors and other junior academic employees; marriage and children's allowances for the permanent staff, both academic and non-academic and agreement for appointment of additional administrative staff.[223] The Department of Finance conceded a pay increase for academic staff (though not as much as DIAS had sought) but refused marriage and children's allowances outright. C. S. Almond, assistant secretary of the department, told Moynihan in May 1952 that while UCD gave such allowances, they 'are not such a feature of University remuneration generally that we should feel bound to give them to the Institute.' Almond argued that conceding this demand would establish an awkward precedent as it would 'embarrass us as regards State remuneration generally to concede marriage differentiation by way of allowances...'[224] As the state maintained an established policy of gender and marriage discrimination in the public service through a different pay scale for single men and women relative to married men, it was ironic that the department feared introducing further marriage differentiation that might spoil the pristine clarity of the pay scale. Significantly, Moynihan (and de Valera) accepted Finance's decision, perhaps taking the view that the institute had got at least half a loaf. The ageing Taoiseach did little during his penultimate term between 1951 and 1954 to challenge the restrictive financial policies pursued by Finance and its political head, Seán MacEntee. The institute, not unlike the universities, experienced severe financial constraints in the early postwar period. Even de Valera's patronage was no guarantee of generous funding in an era of semi-permanent austerity.

While it was never a large-scale research institution, DIAS enjoyed considerable success in attracting eminent international scholars to Dublin. Contrary to Whittaker's apparently well founded concerns in 1940, the international turmoil probably acted as a catalyst for the foundation of the institute, by creating a flow of highly educated exiles from Nazi Germany and its sphere of influence in Central Europe in the late 1930s. De Valera was the driving force behind the creation of the institute. He determined the unusual shape of the institute as an eclectic combination of Celtic studies, advanced physics and ultimately geophysics. De Valera offered an idealistic rationale for this particular combination of disciplines to sceptical members of the Seanad in 1940, arguing that a range of disciplines would ensure a greater international reputation for the new foundation than one focusing solely on Celtic studies: '…so that all the various rays of credit, the good name that we get, may be focussed into a single institute'.[225] Yet he made no effort to conceal the pragmatic reality that his approach was designed to reduce administrative functions and costs at the outset of the new project. The institute was established on a modest budget under the tight control of the Department of Finance. Yet the new venture (and particularly the school of Theoretical Physics) would not have happened at all, particularly in the bleak summer of 1940, without de Valera's determination to establish it, even in apparently unpropitious circumstances at the height of the Second World War.

'…A Certain Flow of Emigrants from This Country Is Inevitable…'

Although the Emergency did not derail the foundation of DIAS, it ensured that all higher education institutions operated within a regime of rigorous austerity during the first half of the 1940s. The universities saw an incremental but steady increase in student numbers during the first two decades of the Irish state: this was particularly marked in UCD, where the number of students doubled over a fifteen year period between 1926–27 and 1940–41.[226] Both UCC and UCD sought assistance from the Exchequer in the early 1940s to clear debts accumulated since the previous increase in the statutory grant and finance new building projects. The Department of Finance firmly opposed any proposals for greater state expenditure on the universities throughout the war, instead pressuring university leaders to increase student fees.

The governing body of UCC proposed to build a new student centre for the Cultural and Recreative Association of Students and Graduates as the college lacked any dedicated auditorium for student activities and to extend the Biological Building to relieve overcrowding in the natural sciences; the cost of £22,000 would be financed on a 50:50 basis between the college's existing budget and the Exchequer.[227] Joseph Downey, the college secretary, presented this proposal to de Valera personally in May 1940, hoping that the Taoiseach would intercede with the Department of Finance. But in this instance the NUI institutional back channel to the Chancellor, sometimes a valuable resource for college officials, failed to produce the desired result. The Department of Finance reminded the Taoiseach on 8 July 1940 that UCC was bound by the conditions attached to a previous grant to reduce its debts in 1934, when the governing body had agreed to assume full responsibility for all current and capital expenditure, except where 'the latter is of such exceptional amount and character as to justify a State contribution and is expenditure for which the Minister's prior approval has been obtained.'[228] Downey was told by the Taoiseach's office on 20 July that if the college authorities believed they could comply with this condition 'having regard to those times of emergency and extraordinary expenditure by the State', then UCC's application should be submitted in the normal way to the Department of Finance.[229] This polite rebuff was sufficient to sink the college's initiative for the duration of the war.

UCD fared better with an application to extinguish its debt, but only after a prolonged struggle which testified to the Department of Finance's jaundiced view of investment in higher education. Conway informed de Valera in January 1941 that the college was obliged to finance urgent repairs to 86 St. Stephen's Green, where 'the roofs of the Concert Hall and also of the Convocation Hall are very bad and as well the ceilings are so dangerous that no one is to be allowed in these Halls, a situation which will render our term examinations, now coming on, impossible.'[230] As the college already had an overdraft of £50,000 and faced additional expenditure for the repairs, Conway appealed for Exchequer support to cover UCD's burgeoning debt, which reached £82,000 in 1941. This appeal provoked a triangular struggle between the Department of Finance, UCD and the Department of Education lasting for almost three years. The secretary of the Department of Finance, the formidable J. J. McElligott, not only rebutted UCD's claim but demanded a reduction of Exchequer 'liabilities' in university education and a restriction of student numbers. McElligott enjoyed the support of his own minister, Tánaiste Seán T. Ó Ceallaigh, but was firmly opposed by Joseph O'Neill, secretary of the Department of Education, whose political superior, Derrig, showed little interest in the dispute. De Valera, the ultimate arbiter, was more sympathetic to UCD's position but did not impose a decision, allowing the protagonists to fight it out until an interim solution was agreed in 1943 which gave UCD most of what it sought. The first shot in what proved to be a prolonged struggle was fired by Ó Ceallaigh, who expressed his department's anger to de Valera at UCD's temerity in undertaking capital spending without prior approval:

> I must confess to receiving something of a shock when I read Prof. Conway's letter of the 10th instant addressed to you re: financial position of UCD. Apparently the College has run into debt to the extent of £50,000 without asking anybody's permission and it is now expecting us to foot the bill. Apparently, also, the renovating of 86 St. Stephen's Green is to cost £5,000 more than the £20,000 provided, which shows miscalculation somewhere.[231]

Ó Ceallaigh questioned the need for expanded university buildings at a time of national emergency: 'It seems a luxury to provide buildings of this kind, particularly in war time and more particularly when, according to Prof. Conway's letter, ordinary accommodation for students is very limited.' Moreover, he urged government action to reduce or at least limit the already modest allocations for university expenditure: 'We have always paid the piper so far without any control over the tune and it is time, I think, that we displayed a little more interest in College finances, with a view to limiting, if not reducing, our liabilities.'[232]

Ó Ceallaigh's letter, drafted by the senior officials, was not mere bureaucratic obstruction. Instead the Department of Finance went on the offensive, seeking to change the balance between public and private financing of the universities. Finance's preferred solution was to achieve a limitation of student numbers and transfer the burden of university financing to individual students (and their families) rather than the state. The subsequent exchange of correspondence between McElligott and Joseph O'Neill was unusually revealing about the dominant official paradigm which assigned minimal importance to higher education in national policy and regarded university studies as a private good conferring purely individual benefits. McElligott warned O'Neill on 8 February 1941, in seeking his counterpart's response to UCD's application, that the financial position regarding the universities was 'very unsatisfactory' and would get worse unless measures were taken to rectify it.[233] O'Neill, however, sharply disagreed with Finance's position on 21 February, warning that tinkering with university admission would not solve the wider 'social-economic problem'. He attributed increasing social demand for university education in Ireland, to economic underdevelopment:

> We are a poor country with comparatively few openings for our young people. If we keep the best brains of the poorer classes out of the University by raising fees, what are we to offer them as an alternative? There is not at the moment enough land to go around. All the commercial jobs are so crowded that the business firms can get people at a very low wage.[234]

O'Neill conceded that emigration among university graduates was high (although neither department was able to quantify the level of emigration among graduates) but warned that imposing financial restrictions on access to college would reduce the standard of university education and favour 'the better off classes.'[235] The Department of Education was willing to consider restrictions on the admission of students but only on the basis of more stringent matriculation requirements.

McElligott returned to the fray later in 1941, proposing to control the number of university students mainly through an upgrading of the standard of the entrance examinations 'so as to ensure that only the best brains get through.'[236] More stringent matriculation requirements should, however, be coupled with higher fees, which McElligott regarded as a positive incentive to attainment: 'The payment of fees helps people to take their work more seriously and a slight rise would offset any decline in numbers following from a raising of the admissions standard…'[237] McElligott's determination to reduce spending on the universities was grounded in a deeply conservative world view, which perceived universities at best as a luxury item but more usually as an albatross around the neck of the Exchequer. The NUI was criticised as wasteful, inefficient, engaged in over-production of graduates and facilitating emigration. He complained to O'Neill in the first of two letters on 9 September that the Exchequer was merely subsidising emigration:

> …a certain flow of emigrants from this country is inevitable. What I do not like is treating these emigrants to a University education largely at public expense and then seeing them go. At any stage their departure is a loss to us, but why should we serve them out to other countries, complete with degrees, etc., I cannot understand.[238]

McElligott was insistent on 30 December 1941 that the solution lay in restriction of student numbers. Significantly, this was rationalised not merely as financially necessary, but desirable to maintain the value of professional qualifications and preserve social stability:

> A limitation in the size of the student body is in my view justified by the crowded state of the professions, the number of graduates that are to be found competing against each other for jobs for which no university qualifications are required as well as by the steady emigration of trained people of this sort. Moreover, the existence of unlimited opportunities for higher education has a disturbing effect on young people who might otherwise settle into a trade or business of some sort instead of sending them off in the fruitless pursuit of "something better".[239]

The secretary's letter amounted to a staunch defence of an elitist order in university education, confined within narrow bounds so as not to upset established power structures or social mores. McElligott's chilling embrace of economic fatalism was flavoured with Victorian morality: restriction of student numbers was useful to control access to the professions and cap unwelcome aspirations among young people which might be subversive to the established order. The correspondence highlighted the rhetorical skill of the Department of Finance—universities could be indicted both for promoting emigration and for raising unrealistic expectations among graduates who remained at home.

The secretary's unequivocal hostility to public funding of higher education was not universally shared within the civil service but even opposition to it proceeded from assumptions which were not fundamentally dissimilar. O'Neill's response on 8 January 1942 did not address many of the more sweeping arguments made by his powerful counterpart, but focused on the damaging practical implications of McElligott's restrictive policy. O'Neill defended the standard of the entrance examination for the publicly funded National University, on the basis that it was pitched at a higher level than Trinity College or RCSI.[240] He also identified the political Achilles' heel of McElligott's proposal, namely the inter-institutional implications of any attempt to enforce more stringent entrance standards:

> …If it were to be applied in any drastic way to the National University only, one of its results would almost certainly be to drive students to Trinity College and the Surgeons, a result which would raise such a wave of indignation that the proposal could not be enforced…[241]

It would be equally unacceptable to force new entrance requirements on either TCD or the College of Surgeons. He concluded that the only effective way 'to reduce the number of our university students is to make alternative employment available for our young people.'[242] O'Neill did not attempt to present a wider social or economic rationale to justify expansion of university education, but challenged Finance on its own ground by raising daunting political and practical obstacles. He accepted the inevitability of emigration and hoped that increased entry to the university was a temporary phenomenon caused by limited economic opportunity, while making a plea for humane treatment of the poorer classes.

The internal official debate over support for UCD continued for another eighteen months, but the Department of Finance ultimately failed to impose a limitation of student numbers. De Valera was sympathetic to O'Neill's side of the argument: his private secretary, Kathleen O'Connell, told O'Neill in February 1941 that the Taoiseach was 'very pleased' at his response to McElligott.[243] While de Valera told Conway that he would not overrule the Minister for Finance, he manoeuvred behind the scenes to circumvent Finance's staunch opposition. When Conway submitted a *General Statement of Finances* at the Taoiseach's request in March 1942, making a robust case for an increased Exchequer grant for UCD, de Valera referred it jointly to the departments of Finance and Education. Soon afterwards, he asked Moynihan to seek Finance's view on a proposal that responsibility for the Vote for Universities and Colleges should be transferred to the Department of Education.[244] This offered the prospect of a more sympathetic hearing for UCD's application, even if it did not remove the need to secure approval ultimately from Finance. McElligott, however, objected to any change as 'a break with tradition' which would have no practical effect as almost all allocations in the Vote were fixed by statute. Moreover, he severely upbraided the Department of Education, which 'appears to over-emphasise the autonomy of the universities and colleges leaving the initiative all the time with them…', even suggesting that inaction by his counterparts in Education had contributed to irresponsible financial management in the universities: 'One result of this laisser-faire attitude has been that the Colleges tend to pile up debts, which after a time, they have little or no compunction in asking the State to discharge.'[245] Following this discouraging response, De Valera allowed the matter to drop and the transfer, which might well have had significant implications for higher education in the postwar period, was postponed until the late 1950s.

But the Taoiseach continued to prod the Department of Finance to address UCD's claim for emergency funding, with Moynihan issuing reminders to Finance throughout 1942. McElligott proposed in March 1942 that an interdepartmental committee be established to consider university expenditure, including such issues 'as whether an unduly large number of students were receiving university education and how this number might be controlled or restricted.'[246] But the Department of Education rejected the plan, arguing that any information necessary for consideration of UCD's application was easily available from the universities. Instead McElligott and O'Neill, along with senior officials of the two departments, met directly on 9 November 1942 to address UCD's application and Finance's concerns about university financing. The conference was tense and sometimes acrimonious. McElligott criticised the Department of Education for 'adopting an attitude of fatalistic acquiescence in the present situation', asserting that a cheap university education simply facilitated education for export. O'Neill invoked de Valera in response, noting that he had discussed the matter with the Taoiseach, 'who had expressed the opinion, with which he himself was in agreement, that if we must export people, it was better for us that they should be educated people who would enhance the national prestige abroad'.[247] The ensuing discussion underlined a sharp divergence between the two departments on reducing the number of graduates or the pitfalls of cheap university education, both consistent themes raised by McElligott. A minute of decisions was, however, produced agreeing that officials of both departments would meet with Conway and Prof. J. J. Nolan, registrar of UCD, to discuss terms for assistance in clearing their debt.[248] The minute, which papered over the conflict among the officials, did not specify upgrading matriculation standards and raising fees as a condition for further support, although both were raised with the UCD officers.

Despite McElligott's consistent pressure to reduce student numbers, the Department of Finance was obliged to settle for imposing stringent financial conditions on UCD in return for clearing most of its debts. The secretary told the Public Accounts Committee in May 1945 that when it became apparent that the college could not liquidate its overdraft of £82,000 through increased fees or other fund-raising, the minister 'accordingly decided to come to their assistance...'[249] McElligott, unsurprisingly, did not inform the committee of his own persistent but unsuccessful efforts to block such assistance or enforce a limitation of student numbers. McElligott wrote to Conway on 13 May 1943 setting out terms on which the minister was prepared to rescue UCD. The secretary sought 'categorical assurances' from the governing body that they would control future expenditure to avoid bank overdrafts and 'take entire responsibility in the future for all expenditure of a capital nature, save where this is of such exceptional amount and character as to justify a State contribution and is expenditure for which the

Minister's prior approval has been obtained.'[250] The onerous conditions reflected established official practice, particularly the exclusion of any state subvention towards capital expenditure other than in exceptional circumstances—the Department of Finance could be relied upon to interpret such a clause inflexibly. Yet it was notable that McElligott's letter made no reference to admission standards or raising of fees, even if he hoped that financial pressure would oblige the college to take such initiatives. The response of the governing body issued by Conway on 27 May was generally conciliatory, offering the assurances demanded by the Department of Finance while rejecting 'any inference...that the College finances have not been economically managed.'[251] Yet the governing body also issued a Parthian shot to the department, noting that:

In doing so, the Governing Body is bound to point out:

1. That the College is still growing.
2. That the public demands upon its services are still increasing.
3. That adequate provision of a capital nature has never been made for its proper housing and accommodation.
4. That it has before it a prospect of rising prices for every kind of material and service.

This warning proved prescient and could easily have applied across the university sector in the late 1940s. All four university colleges would be seeking greatly increased support from the state over the following decade, not least due to the long-term deficit in capital development.

UCD eventually secured funding to clear its debt without committing to reduced student numbers or more restrictive admission standards. The Dáil approved a supplementary estimate of £70,000 to UCD, proposed by Ó Ceallaigh in February 1944: the amount cleared most of the college's total debt, although the Exchequer contribution was also supplemented by savings achieved by the college and increased income from fees.[252] The college's financial situation improved somewhat due to a steady increase in the number of students throughout the second world war, ironically in view of McElligott's demands to reduce student enrolments. The rigorous conditions imposed by Finance would soon be eroded by a more dramatic upsurge in enrolments in the postwar era.

The opposition of the Department of Education and UCD's academic leadership mitigated Finance's relentlessly conservative agenda, while the Taoiseach made his influence felt through gradually wearing down opposition to a settlement of UCD's debts, in this case from one of the most powerful officials in the public administration. But the tortuous progress of the college's funding application and the sharp exchanges between the departments of Finance and Education underlined the absence of any coherent policy towards higher education other than consistent parsimony and the negligible importance of the university in political and official discourse. The de facto exclusion of capital expenditure by the Department of Finance imposed severe pressure on universities even at a time of modest expansion. The world view held by powerful figures within the public administration, characterised by Victorian morality, Gladstonian fiscal conservatism and protection of existing occupational and professional structures, revealed not so much indifference as hostility to the expansion of higher education.

Benign Neglect

The policy of successive governments towards university education in the quarter of a century between the early 1920s and the late 1940s amounted to little more than benign neglect. Higher education was peripheral to policy-makers preoccupied with state formation, assertion of national sovereignty and economic nationalism. This was not simply due to fiscal constraints or even a failure of imagination by political and administrative elites. The economic weakness of the new state certainly contributed to the stagnation in Exchequer support for 'universities and colleges', but it was not simply about poverty. The parsimonious funding regime reflected the peripheral status of university education in political and official discourse and the absence of a public debate on the place of universities in society. A traditional societal and cultural context militated strongly against investment in higher education, which was identified with academic education for the professions and high-status white collar occupations. It was no accident that higher education remained both underdeveloped and university dominated well into the middle of twentieth century. The Department of Finance was overtly hostile to public funding of university education and had no hesitation in pressuring institutions to increase fees and unsuccessfully, to reduce student numbers. The most influential department in the state regarded spending on higher education as a luxury benefiting only a small minority, many of whom were likely to be lost to Ireland through emigration and was unmoved by wider social or economic considerations. The dominant popular movements of the era perceived the universities as channels for the achievement of religious and cultural objectives. Otherwise higher education featured hardly at all in a dominant national discourse marked by integralist Catholicism, protectionism and social conservatism.

Notes

1. Coolahan, *Towards the Era of Lifelong Learning*, 87.
2. Von Humboldt, 'On the Spirit and the Organisational Framework of Intellectual Institutions in Berlin,' *Minerva* 8, no. 2 (1810): 242–50.
3. Patrick Clancy, 'The Evolution of Policy in Third-Level Education,' in *Irish Educational Policy: Process and Substance*, ed. D. G. Mulcahy and Denis O'Sullivan (Dublin: IPA, 1989), 100–1: information on student enrolments in the first three decades of the Irish state was not published by the Department of Education, as it was not responsible for the sector and information is not available on enrolments in professional and technological courses. This makes comparisons between universities and non-university institutions more difficult, but it is apparent that the vast majority of enrolments occurred in the universities up to the 1960s.
4. Department of Education, *Statistical Report 1965–66* (Dublin: Stationery Office, 1967), 5.
5. Department of Education, *Explanatory Memorandum Re University Entrance Tests,* 9 March 1933 (NAI TSCH S6403).
6. Coolahan, *Towards an Era of Lifelong Learning*, 101.
7. Department of Education, *Memorandum to the Government, Scheme of Grants for Higher Education*, 20 February 1968 (NAI TSCH 99/1/332 S.16890), 2.

8. Seanad Éireann, vol. 24, col. 1395, 15 May 1940.

9. Ibid., col. 1394.

10. John Coolahan, 'Higher Education in Ireland,' in *A New History of Ireland, 1921–84*, vol. 7, ed. J. R. Hill (Oxford: Oxford University Press, 2003), 767.

11. Ibid.

12. Joseph Lee, *Ireland 1912–85: Politics and Society* (Cambridge: Cambridge University Press, 1988), 105–6.

13. Ibid.,131.

14. Cosgrave to the Duke of Devonshire, 14 July 1923 (NAI TSCH/3/S1766).

15. Dáil Debates, vol. 8, no. 10, col. 1051, 11 July 1924.

16. Report of the Public Accounts Committee, *Appropriation Accounts 1924–25* (Dublin: Stationery Office, 1928), 299.

17. Report of the Public Accounts Committee, *Appropriation Accounts 1933–34* (Dublin: Stationery Office, 1936), 107.

18. J. J. McElligott to Arthur Conway, 13 May 1943 (NAI TSCH/3/S12544); S. O'Mahony to Joseph Downey, 20 July 1940 (NAI TSCH/3/S13258A).

19. Report of the Public Accounts Committee, *Appropriation Accounts 1946–47* (Dublin: Stationery Office, 1950), 112–17.

20. Lee, *Ireland 1912–1985*, 108–35.

21. See below (pp. 137–39) for the closure of the Royal College of Science.

22. University Education (Agriculture and Dairy Science) Bill, 1926 (NAI TSCH/3/S3780), 4–5.

23. T. D. Williams, 'The College and the Nation,' in *Struggle with Fortune: A Miscellany for the Centenary of the Catholic University of Ireland 1854–1954*, ed. Michael Tierney (Dublin: UCD, 1954), 166–92.

24. Donal McCartney, *UCD—A National Idea*, 113.

25. University Education (Agriculture and Dairy Science) Bill, 1926 (NAI TSCH/3/S3780), 4.

26. Murphy, *The College*, 222–3.

27. *Irish Times*, 'First Dairy College in the British Isles,' 21 July 1928.

28. Ibid.

29. Ibid.

30. Ibid.

31. Murphy, *The College*, 224.
32. Minister for Agriculture to the Executive Council, *Memorandum*, 18 November 1929 (NAI TSCH/3/S7375).
33. Private Secretary to the Minister for Agriculture to the Secretary, Executive Council, 18 November 1929 (NAI TSCH/3/S7375).
34. Michael MacDunphy to James McNeill, 4 March 1930 (NAI TSCH/3/S7375).
35. Dáil Debates, vol. 16, no. 7, col. 708–9, 9 June 1926.
36. Ibid., col. 710.
37. Ibid., col. 710.
38. Irish Times, 'A National Guarantee: Government Proposal,' 13 February 1924.
39. Dáil Debates, vol. 8, no. 10, col. 1053–4, 11 July 1924.
40. Ibid.
41. *Irish Times*, 'Letters to the Editor: University College Galway,' 14 July 1924.
42. Mac Mathúna, 'National University of Ireland Galway,' 71
43. Ibid.
44. Ibid.; Anderson letter to national newspapers, 15 June 1926 (NAI TSCH/3/S2409).
45. Anderson Statement, 11 June 1926 (NAI TSCH/3/S2409).
46. *Irish Times*, 'Education in the West: Finances of University College Galway,' 28 May 1926: The other members of the deputation were Anderson, Fr. Hynes, and J. B. Whelehan, Controller of the Stationery Office.
47. Anderson Statement, 11 June 1926 (NAI TSCH/3/S2409); Mac Mathúna, 'National University of Ireland Galway,' 74.
48. Dáil Debates, vol. 16 (7), col. 717–18, 9 June 1926.
49. Ibid., col. 718.
50. Anderson Statement, 11 June 1926 (NAI TSCH/3/S2409).
51. Ibid.
52. John Hynes to the Secretary of the Executive Council, 26 June 1926 (NAI TSCH/3/S2409).
53. *Irish Times*, 'University College Galway: Mr Hogan Gives Assurances; No Intention to Close It,' 3 July 1926.
54. *Irish Times*, 'The Galway College,' 26 June 1926.
55. Department of Education, *Memorandum of Agreements Reached at a Conference Between Representatives of the Governing Body University*

College Galway, and the Ministers for Finance and Education, 15 October 1926 (NAI TSCH/3/S2409).
56. Ibid., 1–2.
57. Ibid., 2.
58. Mac Mathúna, 'National University of Ireland, Galway,' 71.
59. Minister for Finance, *Explanatory Memorandum*, 28 January 1929 (NAI TSCH/3/S2368).
60. *University College Galway Bill 1929* (NAI TSCH/3/S2409), 3.
61. Dáil Debates, vol. 32, no. 2, col. 282, 24 October 1929.
62. Ibid., col. 293–4.
63. Ibid., col. 298.
64. Dáil Debates, vol. 32, no. 5, col. 696–8, 31 October 1929.
65. Dáil Debates, vol. 32, no. 8, col. 1108, 13 November 1929; Michael MacDunphy to James McNeill, 17 December 1929 (NAI TSCH/3/S2409).
66. Mac Mathúna, 'National University of Ireland, Galway,' 79.
67. Ibid., 77.
68. *Memorandum*, 11 April 1923 (MUN V/6/6/15), 3.
69. McDowell and Webb, *Trinity College Dublin*, 426–7
70. Minutes, Board Meeting, 10 December 1921 (MUN V 5/22).
71. Bernard to Hilton Young, 31 May 1921; Bernard to Greenwood, 18 June 1921; Bernard to Greenwood, 13 July 1921 (MUN V 6/5/116).
72. Bernard, *Memorandum Relating to Trinity College Dublin and the State Subsidy* (MUN V 6/5/119), 2.
73. Ibid.; McDowell and Webb, *Trinity College Dublin*, 427
74. Bernard, *Memorandum Relating to Trinity College Dublin and the State Subsidy* (MUN V 6/5/119), 2.
75. *Memorandum to the British Government*, 11 April 1923 (MUN V/6/6/15), 4–5.
76. Minutes, Board Meeting, 9 June 1923 (MUN V 5/22)
77. Ibid.
78. The four TDs elected to represent TCD were Thrift, Gerald Fitzgibbon, James Craig, and Ernest Henry Alton.
79. *Universities: Representation in Parliament*, 10 May 1924 (NAI TSCH/3/S2810), 2.
80. 'Enactment of the Constitution by Dáil Éireann,' Extract from Dáil debates, vol. 1, 1151–3, 4 September 1922 (NAI TSCH/3/S2810).
81. Minutes, Board Meeting, 15 February 1922 (MUN V 5/22).

82. Tomás Irish, *Trinity in War and Revolution 1912–23* (Dublin: RIA, 2015), 224–5.
83. Irish, *Trinity*, 224–5.
84. *Irish Times*, 'Grant to the Universities,' 17 November 1922.
85. Minutes, Board Meeting, 24 March 1923 (MUN V 5/22).
86. Minutes, Board Meeting, 9 June 1923 (MUN V 5/22).
87. Brennan to Louis Purser, 18 June 1923, Minutes, Board Meeting, 23 June 1923 (MUN V 5/23).
88. Irish, *Trinity*, 238.
89. Brennan to Lewis Purser, 18 June 1923, Minutes, Board Meeting, 23 June 1923 (MUN V 5/23).
90. Ibid.
91. Irish, *Trinity*, 238.
92. Purser to Cosgrave, 23 June 1923, Minutes, Board Meeting, 23 June 1923 (MUN V 5/23).
93. Ibid.
94. Cosgrave to the Duke of Devonshire, 14 July 1923 (NAI TSCH/3/S1766).
95. Minutes, Board Meeting, 30 June 1923 (MUN V 5/23).
96. Ibid.; *Irish Times*, 'Funds of TCD: Agreement with the Government,' 7 July 1923.
97. Minutes, Board Meeting, 30 June 1923 (MUN V 5/23).
98. Ibid.; Cosgrave to the Duke of Devonshire, 14 July 1923 (NAI TSCH/3/S1766).
99. Minutes, Board Meeting, 30 June 1923 (MUN V 5/23); Brennan to Purser, 18 June 1923, Minutes, Board Meeting, 23 June 1923 (MUN V 5/23).
100. Minutes, Board Meeting, 30 June 1923 (MUN V 5/23).
101. Dáil Debates, vol. 4, no. 17, col. 1413, 25 July 1923
102. McDowell and Webb, *Trinity College Dublin*, 429
103. Ibid.
104. Ibid., 429–33.
105. Irish, *Trinity*, 242; see below p. 159 for discussion of medical education.
106. Ibid., 244.
107. McDowell and Webb, *Trinity College Dublin*, 433–4.
108. James McNeill to W. T. Cosgrave, 17 September 1928 (NAI TSCH/3/S6535).
109. W. T. Cosgrave to James McNeill, 19 October 1928 (NAI TSCH/3/S6535).

110. McNeill to Cosgrave, 12 June 1929 (NAI TSCH/3/S6535).
111. Provost and Board of Trinity College to the Governor General, 25 May 1929 (NAI TSCH/3/S6535).
112. Extract from Cabinet Minutes, *National Anthem and Flag: Trinity College Sports, 1929*, 28 May 1929.
113. *Sunday Chronicle*, 'Free State Governor's Amazing Action,' 9 June 1929; *Irish Independent*, 'Anthem Crux: T.C.D. ban on the "Soldier's Song"', 'Governor General Obliged to Decline an Invitation,' 8 June 1929.
114. Dulanty to Diarmuid O'Hegarty, 24 June 1929 (NAI TSCH/3/S6535).
115. Cosgrave to Lady Ardee, 25 June 1929 (NAI TSCH/3/S6535).
116. *Irish Independent*, 'Trinity Race and Garden Party: A Dual Pleasure,' 9 June 1932.
117. Ibid.
118. *Irish Times*, 'Minister's Attack on the Universities,' 10 March 1934.
119. Ibid.
120. *Irish Times*, 'Trinity and Ireland,' 3 July 1937; Irish, *Trinity*, 263–4.
121. McDowell and Webb, *Trinity College Dublin*, 466; Irish, *Trinity*, 264.
122. 'Report made to the Board of Trinity College on 20 February 1947 by the Provost and Registrar' (Companion vol. 6, MUN V/6/7), 1; McDowell and Webb, *Trinity College Dublin*, 434; Irish, *Trinity*, 264.
123. *Irish Times*, 'Wild Armistice Scenes,' 12 November 1932.
124. *Irish Times*, 'Baton Charges in Dublin,' 8 May 1945
125. McDowell and Webb, *Trinity College Dublin*, 464–5; Irish, *Trinity*, 267.
126. *Irish Times*, 'T.C.D.,' 10 May 1945.
127. *Irish Times*, 'T.C.D.,' 10 May 1945; McDowell and Webb, *Trinity College Dublin*, 465.
128. *RCSI History Timeline*. Accessed 1 September 2017. http://www.rcsi.ie/history.
129. John Nolan, 'The Recognised Colleges,' in *The National University of Ireland 1908–2008 Centenary Essays*, ed. Dunne et al. (Dublin: UCD Press, 2008), 203.
130. *RCSI History Timeline*. Accessed 1 September 2017. http://www.rcsi.ie/history.
131. *RCSI History Timeline*. Accessed 1 September 2017. http://www.rcsi.ie/history.

132. *Irish Times*, 'Where Ireland is United: Science Knows No Border,' 21 February 1927.
133. Ibid.
134. *Irish Times*, 'The Medical Register,' 28 May 1926.
135. *Irish Times*, 'The Medical Register,' 28 May 1926.
136. *Irish Times*, 'Medical Register Agreement,' 3 May 1927.
137. Department of Education, Memorandum for the Executive Council, April 1933 (NAI TSCH/3/6442).
138. Department of Education, *Statement of Accounts* (NAI TSCH/3/6442), 3.
139. *Irish Times*, 'T.C.D. Grant Criticised by Bishop,' 31 May 1949.
140. *Irish Times*, 'The New Nationalism,' 17 March 1934.
141. MacEntee to Patrick Hillery, 26 August 1960 (NAI TSCH/S.16803A).
142. John Walsh, 'Eamon De Valera 1921–75,' in *The National University 1908–2008 Centenary Essays*, ed. Dunne, et al., 135–45: see this chapter for some exceptions to this pattern, including de Valera's willingness to vote (and occasionally use his casting vote) in academic appointments by the senate.
143. Murphy, *The College*, 225–7.
144. Private Secretary to Minister for Education to Secretary, Executive Council, 6 December 1934, *Copy of Minute of 14/11/34 from Attorney General to Minister for Education* (NAI TSCH/3/S6915).
145. National University of Ireland (Adaptation of Charters) Order 1935, 13 February 1935; Executive Council Minutes, 15 February 1935 (NAI TSCH/3/S6915).
146. MacDunphy to Secretaries of the Departments of Finance and Justice, 13 June 1935 (NAI TSCH/3/S7438A).
147. *Special Meeting of the Governing Body*, 31 January 1936 (NAI TSCH/3/S7438A); Murphy, *The College*, 227.
148. Maurice Moynihan to Alex McCarthy, 28 July 1938 (NUI, Box 419), 1.
149. Ibid.
150. Dáil Debates, vol. 52, no. 5, col. 479–80, 8 May 1934.
151. Ibid., col. 481.
152. NUI, Senate Minutes, vol. 13, 9 March 1933, 277.
153. Williams, 'The College and the Nation,' 166–92.
154. Dáil Debates, vol. 52, no. 5, col. 562, 8 May 1934.
155. Dáil Debates, vol. 53, no. 12, col. 1536–8, 5 June 1934.

156. Seanad Debates, vol. 18 (31), col. 1977–2006, 18 July 1934.
157. Government Minute, *Universities Representation in the Oireachtas*, 1 June 1936 (TSCH/3/S2810).
158. NUI, Senate Minutes, vol. 14, 12 April 1934, 138; F. H. Wiber to Michael MacDunphy, 16 April 1934 (NAI TSCH/3/S2810).
159. MacDunphy, *Minuted Note on the Universities Representation in the Oireachtas*, 10 May 1937 (NAI TSCH/3/S2810).
160. Ibid.
161. Murphy, *The College*, 301.
162. Secretary of the Department of Finance to the Executive Council, 16 March 1933 (NAI TSCH/3/S6341/8).
163. O'Rahilly and Tierney to De Valera, 21 April 1933 (NAI TSCH/3/S6341/8).
164. College Authorities of UCD, UCC and UCG, *Memorandum on the Public Service (TE) Bill*, 1933.
165. Ibid.
166. Murphy, *The College*, 299.
167. MacEntee to de Valera, n.d 1933 (NAI TSCH/3/S6341/8).
168. Department of Finance, *Public Services (Temporary Economies) Bill, 1933. Effect on Grants to Universities*, 25 April 1933 (NAI TSCH/3/S6341/8).
169. Representatives of the Colleges to the Minister for Finance, 13 May 1933.
170. Ibid.
171. MacEntee to de Valera, 5 May 1933 (NAI TSCH/3/S6341/8).
172. Ibid.
173. Coffey to De Valera, 22 April 1933; Private Secretary of President of Executive Council to Coffey, 24 April 1933 (NAI TSCH/3/S6341/8).
174. Private Secretary of President of Executive Council to Coffey, 5 May 1933.
175. Dáil Debates, vol. 47, no. 15, col. 1836–41, 26 May 1933.
176. NUI, Senate Minutes, vol. 14, col. 138, 12 April 1934; this was the fund originally set up following the disestablishment of the Church of Ireland in 1869.
177. Dáil Debates, vol. 47, no. 19, col. 2529–30, 2 June 1933.
178. Ibid., col. 2526.
179. Ibid., col. 2527–30.

180. Neasa McGarrigle, *The Establishment of the Dublin Institute of Advanced Studies, 1936–1948* (Ph.D. diss., TCD, 2017), gives a detailed exploration of the creation and development of DIAS in its formative years. This thesis is deposited in TCD Library on a four year stay and is unavailable for consultation until 2021.

181. Seanad Debates, vol. 24, no. 14, col. 1297–38, 15 May 1940.

182. Memorandum, *Institute for Advanced Studies* (NAI TSCH/3/S10602B).

183. J. P. Hackett to Maurice Moynihan, 26 February 1940 (NAI TSCH/3/S10602B); Joseph Walshe to Moynihan, 8 June 1940.

184. E. T. Whittaker to de Valera, n.d., April 1938 (NAI TSCH/3/S10602A).

185. Whittaker to de Valera, 25 May 1938.

186. Schrodinger to de Valera, 16 September 1938 (NAI TSCH/3/S10602A).

187. Ambassador to de Valera, 23 September 1938 (NAI TSCH/3/S10602A).

188. Moynihan, *Memo on Dunsink Observatory*, 23 November 1938 (NAI TSCH/3/S10602A).

189. Ibid.

190. John Duff to Moynihan, 24 November 1938 (NAI TSCH/3/S10602A).

191. Ibid.

192. Moynihan to Duff, 13 December 1938 (NAI TSCH/3/S10602A).

193. Moynihan to O'Neill, 9 January 1939 (NAI TSCH/3/S10602A).

194. Moynihan, *Memorandum: Proposed School of Theoretical Physics— Relation to Proposed Institute for Advanced Studies*, 1, 29 March 1939 (NAI TSCH/3/S10602A).

195. Ibid., 2.

196. Ibid., 11.

197. Moynihan, Note of decision by de Valera, 5 May 1939 (NAI TSCH/3/S10602A).

198. Dáil Debates, vol. 76, no. 16, col. 1966–7, 6 July 1939.

199. Ibid.

200. Ibid., col. 1969–70.

201. Schrodinger to de Valera, 29 July 1939 (NAI TSCH/3/S10602A).

202. De Valera to Schrodinger, 31 July 1939 (NAI TSCH/3/S10602A).

203. Dáil Debates, vol. 79, no. 10, col. 1087, 10 April 1940.
204. Dáil Debates, vol. 79, no. 17, col. 2204, 1 May 1940.
205. Seanad Debates, vol. 24, no.14, col. 1323–38, 15 May 1940.
206. Ibid., col. 1346.
207. Ibid., col. 1596–1606.
208. Whittaker to de Valera, 6 May 1940 (NAI TSCH/3/S10602B).
209. De Valera to Whittaker, 20 May 1940 (NAI TSCH/3/S10602B).
210. Ibid.
211. Ó Dubhthaigh to McElligott, 7 October 1940 (NAI TSCH/3/S10602B).
212. Memorandum, *Institute for Advanced Studies*, 2 (NAI TSCH/3/S10602B).
213. 'D. A. Binchy 1900–89,' http://www.ricorso.net/rx/az-data/authors/b/Binchy_DA/life.htm. Accessed 13 November 2015.
214. Memorandum, *Institute for Advanced Studies*, 3 (NAI TSCH/3/S10602B).
215. Ibid.
216. *Memorandum: Conditions of Service in Public Sector: Professors*, 22 January 1948 (NAI TSCH/3/15337).
217. *Irish Press*, 'New University Buildings,' 14 February 1947.
218. *Irish Independent*, 'The Irish Universities,' 3 February 1947.
219. *Irish Independent*, 'Denial That Only Foreigners are Employed,' 4 November 1950.
220. Ibid.
221. Pollak to de Valera, 10 December 1951 (NAI TSCH/3/S14202).
222. Tarlach Ó Raifeartaigh to N. S. Ó Nuallain, 13 May 1952 (NAI TSCH/3/S15337).
223. Registrar of DIAS to MacEntee, 5 February 1952.
224. Almond to Moynihan, 12 May 1952 (NAI TSCH/3/S15337).
225. Seanad Debates, vol. 24, no. 14, col. 1306, 15 May 1940.
226. Conway, *General Statement of Finances*, 3 February 1942 (NAI TSCH/3/S12544A).
227. *Memo re Buildings required by University College, Cork*, n.d., 1940 (NAI TSCH/3/S13258A).
228. Department of Finance to de Valera, 8 July 1940 (NAI TSCH/3/S13258A).
229. Seán O'Mahony to Joseph Downey, 20 July 1940 (NAI TSCH/3/S13258A).

230. Conway to de Valera, 10 January 1941 (NAI TSCH/3/S12544A).

231. Ó Ceallaigh to de Valera, 31 January 1941 (NAI TSCH/3/S12544A).

232. Ibid.

233. J. J. McElligott to Joseph O'Neill, 8 February 1941 (NAI TSCH/3/S12544A).

234. O'Neill to McElligott, 21 February 1941 (NAI TSCH/3/S12544A).

235. Ibid.

236. McElligott to O'Neill, 30 December 1941 (NAI TSCH/3/S12544A).

237. McElligott to O'Neill, 9 September 1941 (NAI TSCH/3/S12544A).

238. Ibid.

239. McElligott to O'Neill, 30 December 1941 (NAI TSCH/3/S12544A).

240. O'Neill to McElligott, 8 January 1942 (NAI TSCH/3/S12544A).

241. Ibid.

242. Ibid.

243. O'Connell to O'Neill, 24 February 1941.

244. Moynihan to Departments of Finance and Education, 16 March 1942 (NAI TSCH/3/S12544A).

245. Minister for Finance to Moynihan, 8 August 1942.

246. Department of Education to Moynihan, 26 September 1942 (NAI TSCH/3/S12544A).

247. *Financial Position of University College Dublin, Note of Conference on 9 November 1942* (NAI TSCH/3/S12544A), 1.

248. Ibid., 4.

249. Public Accounts Committee, *Appropriation Accounts 1943–44* (Dublin: Stationery Office, 1945), 9.

250. McElligott to Conway, 13 May 1943 (NAI TSCH/3/S12544A).

251. Conway to McElligott, 27 May 1943 (NAI TSCH/3/S12544A).

252. Public Accounts Committee, *Appropriation Accounts 1943–44* (Dublin: Stationery Office, 1945), 9.

3

Church, State and the University

Integralist Catholicism

The absence of a pro-active government policy on higher education did not mean that universities were isolated from society. The mission and values of higher education institutions reflected, sometimes in diverse ways, the political, religious and cultural milieu of early and mid-twentieth century Ireland. The predominant ideology of the institutional church and a variety of lay Catholic organisations in the early to mid-twentieth century was integralist Catholicism, which sought to make Ireland a more completely Catholic state than it had yet become and reached its peak in the early post war period.[1] Trinity College operated in an inhospitable cultural and political context, due to its traditional association with the displaced unionist elite and the firm opposition of the Catholic Church to 'neutral' educational institutions.[2] The NUI enjoyed a very different cultural inheritance from its more venerable counterpart, due to its origins as a non-denominational university which was designed to function within a denominational Catholic setting.

© The Author(s) 2018
J. Walsh, *Higher Education in Ireland, 1922–2016*,
https://doi.org/10.1057/978-1-137-44673-2_3

Despite the non-denominational statutory framework of the NUI, ecclesiastical power was an integral part of university life during the early to mid-twentieth century. McCartney suggests that the bishops 'acted in effect as patrons of all its colleges...a connection in part invited by the colleges themselves, especially at mid-century, when the church's influence was at its most pervasive.'[3] While the bishops exercised this function formally only on behalf of St. Patrick's College Maynooth, their prestige in an overwhelmingly Catholic society, the strength of clericalism in Irish political culture and the circumstances in which the National University was founded ensured that they commanded a great deal of influence. Formal episcopal participation in governing bodies or college administration was less significant than informal influence exercised through religious, clerical and lay Catholic networks in a cultural context shaped by the pervasive reach of integralist Catholicism.

All three colleges of the NUI saw significant religious influence in a variety of ways. Bishops of their local dioceses served on the governing bodies of UCG and UCC until the 1990s, while the government nominated a prominent ecclesiastical figure (usually a monsignor of the Dublin archdiocese) to the governing body of UCD between 1923 and 1976.[4] The presidency of UCG was held consecutively by two Catholic priests in the mid twentieth century. Rev. John 'Pa' Hynes, a native of Sligo, was a key figure in UCG's development in the early Irish state: Hynes was a long serving registrar of the college (1916–34), before ultimately succeeding Anderson as president in 1934. Hynes was succeeded in 1945 by another Catholic priest, Monsignor Pádraig de Brún, professor of mathematics in Maynooth College.[5]

Dr John Charles McQuaid, archbishop of Dublin (1940–72), a formidable exponent of integralist Catholicism, was deeply engaged in education at various levels, including the universities. As chairman of the episcopal committee on university education, McQuaid was effectively the hierarchy's specialist on higher education and maintained close connections with a network of college presidents within the NUI, especially Michael Tierney (1947–64) and his successor J. J. Hogan in UCD (1964–72), Alfred O'Rahilly in UCC (1943–54) and de Brún in Galway (1945–60).[6] McQuaid's power was felt particularly in

UCD, which he regarded as 'the lawful heir to the Catholic University founded by the Irish Bishops...'[7] The archbishop held both the symbolic title of rector of the dormant Catholic university and a great deal of practical influence due to his authority over the considerable number of Catholic priests working in the college and connections with a dense network of lay allies and collaborators. As theology lay outside the legal remit of the university, philosophy, education and later social sciences were the disciplines where the influence of the institutional church was most strongly felt.[8] The archbishop maintained a particular interest in the school of philosophy where the majority of students were seminarians in the mid-1900s and all three chairs in philosophy in UCD were held by priests between 1952 and 1971.[9] Teacher education too bore a strong religious imprint, as two of the three professors of education up to 1973 were Jesuits, TJ Corcoran SJ and Seán Ó Cathain SJ. Corcoran, the first professor of education in UCD (1909–42), enjoyed an influence which extended well beyond the college, as the most influential outside adviser to Free State governments on the revision of the primary education curriculum in the 1920s. McQuaid had a strong interest in the expanding disciplines of social science and sociology in the postwar period, asserting that 'It is perhaps in social philosophy, more than in technology, that the Catholic University student needs to be firmly instructed.'[10] Fr James Kavanagh, a protégé of McQuaid and head of the Dublin Institute of Catholic Sociology, was appointed in 1964 as the first professor of social science in UCD.[11]

Overt ecclesiastical participation in policy-making operated in concert with the enduring strength of clericalism and lay support for integralist Catholicism. The 'Catholicisation' of UCC reached its height under the presidency of Alfred O'Rahilly, a university leader, propagandist and educationalist who ended his life as a Holy Ghost Father.[12] O'Rahilly was a more aggressive advocate for integralist Catholicism than many bishops. As registrar of UCC he was the dominant figure in the college for much of the presidency of his low profile predecessor, Patrick Merriman (1919–43) and its de facto leader for a generation. O'Rahilly, memorably described by John A. Murphy as a 'Renaissance universal man who much preferred the Middle Ages...'[13] was an uncompromising advocate for traditional Catholicism and

Irish-Ireland nationalism. He enjoyed not only local predominance in UCC but considerable national notoriety as a prolific contributor to public debates on an impressive range of issues. The overtly Catholic nature of the appeal by the NUI representatives to de Valera over the economy Bill in 1933 was influenced by O'Rahilly's suspicion of state power and willingness to appeal to the church in defence of institutional interests. The fiercely denominational character of the letter also reflected the conviction by both O'Rahilly and Tierney that the NUI should develop as an overtly Catholic institution.[14]

Leading academics in the NUI were prominently involved in the political debates of the 1930s, often enunciating a corporatist ideology rooted in Catholic social teaching. Tierney and James Hogan, professor of history in UCC (1920–63), were the leading Irish advocates of a corporate society during the interwar period, urging a vocational re-organisation of society to create a new political structure.[15] The work of Hogan and Tierney referenced the social policy principles outlined by Pope Pius XI in *Quadragesimo Anno* (1931), rather than the brutal reality of Mussolini's regime in Italy and later Hitler's totalitarian dictatorship in Germany.[16] Yet corporatism entailed unsavoury political associations in the volatile politics of the 1930s and was hardly compatible with democratic government. Hogan's fervent anti-Communism, exemplified by his pamphlet *Could Ireland Become Communist*, caused him to embrace the Blueshirt movement led by General Eoin O'Duffy. The UCC historian offered intellectual respectability to the Blueshirts and was a member of the executive committee of the Fine Gael party on its foundation in 1933. But Hogan soon broke his links with the Blueshirts, denouncing O'Duffy's 'destructive and hysterical leadership' and contributing to the general's enforced departure from Fine Gael.[17]

Vocationalism enjoyed considerable popularity in the 1930s in academic and ecclesiastical circles. De Valera paid lip-service to the movement by establishing vocational panels for nominations to the Seanad in the 1937 Constitution, although the reconstituted Upper House outside the university panels was in practice dominated by party politicians. The embrace of corporatism by an influential section of the NUI elite had less to do with fascism than an overblown fear of Communism, as well as in some cases opposition to the dominance of

de Valera. It was an ill-fated attempt to construct an ideological alternative rooted in traditional Catholicism to both Communism and
extreme republicanism. While corporatism was comprehensively discredited by the defeat of the fascist dictatorships during the Second
World War, integralist Catholicism retained a formidable grip on public
and political attitudes in the early postwar period and remained a profound cultural influence on the NUI up to the 1960s.

Most private colleges in the early to mid-twentieth century were
established or controlled by religious institutions. These institutions
included St. Patrick's College Maynooth, which was legally a seminary
despite its dual status as a pontifical university and recognised college of
the NUI between 1908 and 1997, a number of smaller seminaries for
the education of Catholic clergy or religious and other institutions set
up to meet particular religious or social objectives by religious orders.[18]
This should not be seen as an Irish equivalent of Levy's notion of a religious 'wave' of expansion in private higher education, influenced by a
Catholic reaction to a secular, public monopoly in higher education.[19]
The development of religious higher education institutions in Ireland
was more a product of a distinctive socio-political context shaped by
the predominance of the Catholic Church and strength of integralist
Catholicism.

Perhaps the most innovative and resilient venture linked to religious initiative was launched by the Jesuit order, which established
the Catholic Workers College in 1951 at Sandford Lodge, Ranelagh.[20]
As Limond comments, the foundation of the CWC was part of 'a
much wider mobilisation on the part of the Catholic Church: the
Catholic social action 'project'…' designed to offer adult education to the Catholic working class and contain the perceived threat
of Communism.[21] Yet the Jesuits had a record of social action independent of the anti-Communist crusade and were influenced by the
progressive social ideas of Pope Leo XIII, expressed in the encyclical
Rerum Novarum.[22] The college began by offering a diploma combining
Catholic social ethics and practical industrial relations issues to trade
unionists, but soon offered parallel courses to managers as well, indicating the Jesuits' desire to advance Catholic social principles across

the industrial field.[23] The college established an influential niche in management education for industrial relations, organising the training programmes for the Institute of Personnel Management from the mid-1960s: its primary mission was underlined by redesignation in 1965 as the College of Industrial Relations.[24] The Jesuit leadership of the college undertook a series of reinventions over the following generation, adapting successfully to a free trade economy and in due course a liberalising society.

The Catholic bishops intensified their long-term opposition to the attendance of Catholic students at TCD in the 1940s, mainly because it was considered to be a repository of secular, irreligious and anti-Catholic influences.[25] McQuaid re-affirmed the ecclesiastical ban in particularly uncompromising terms through a Lenten pastoral in February 1944:

> No Catholic may enter the Protestant University of Trinity College without previous permission of the Ordinary of the diocese…Deliberately to disobey this law is a mortal sin, and those who persist in disobedience are unworthy to receive Sacraments.[26]

McQuaid stipulated that permission for Catholics to attend Trinity could only be given by the archbishop himself 'for grave and valid reasons…' conditional on measures to safeguard the faith and practice of Catholic students. Quoting his predecessor, Dr Edward Byrne, McQuaid later referred to Trinity College as a 'fortress of aggressiveness and ascendency'.[27] The bishops collectively reiterated the prohibition in equally stark terms at their plenary meeting in 1956:

We forbid under pain of mortal sin;

1. Catholic youths to frequent that College
2. Catholic parents or guardians to send to that College Catholic youths committed to their care;
3. Clerics or religious to recommend in any manner parents or guardians to send Catholic youths to that College…[28]

The ecclesiastical ban intensified Trinity's dependence on non-Irish students, which reached its height in the early postwar era. Much of Trinity's postwar expansion was accounted for by British and international entrants, as well as a continuing strong representation from Northern Ireland.[29] The college drew a majority of its students from outside the Irish state in the early postwar period and 46% of the student population of approximately 3000 in 1962–63 was admitted from outside the island of Ireland.[30] This distribution could not be attributed simply to the ban, as it was influenced by Trinity's international prestige and an influx of British students including veterans of the Second World War.[31] Yet the implementation of the ecclesiastical decrees against Trinity, pursued with renewed vigour and intensive administrative efficiency by McQuaid, had an undoubted impact, as Catholics accounted for only 17% of admissions in 1960.[32]

Trinity's isolation in a predominantly Catholic society up to the 1950s was underlined by the college's exclusion from the large majority of local authority scholarship schemes. Only 11 of the 28 councils in the Republic allowed scholarships to be held at Trinity without restriction in 1955. A further four permitted non-Catholic students to hold such scholarships and thirteen excluded Trinity in various ways, often due to qualifications linked to compulsory Irish for matriculation but sometimes due to overtly religious requirements.[33] A campaign instigated by A. J. McConnell in the 1950s, seeking to include the University of Dublin in local authority schemes, generated acrimonious debate at council meetings and probably ignited greater criticism of Trinity in the short-term. When Louth County Council was asked to include Trinity in 1953, the ensuing debate highlighted a notable hostility to the college. Alderman Peadar Martin opposed any change as 'he would not like to do anything that would tend to direct the youth of the country under Trinity's influence, because, politically and nationally, it had always been out of harmony with the aspirations of the vast majority of the Irish people.'[34] Alderman L. Walsh shared his sentiments, stating that 'the National University was for their own people. He would think very little of any Irish parents, brought up in the National tradition, who would not send their children there.' Both men were rebuked by the council chair, Senator McGee, who argued that virtually every Irish nationalist movement up to the beginning of the twentieth century 'had its origins inside Trinity.' But the council did not change its position in the short-term, deferring any decision pending legal advice.[35] The Board's lobbying also had some successes. Kerry County Council amended its scheme, which was restricted to UCC, in 1955 to include other university colleges including Trinity and Queen's.[36] Roscommon County Council also moved to widen its scheme in 1956, following advice by legal counsel that the existing scheme, which allowed only Protestant students to hold scholarships at Trinity, was illegal.[37]

The connections between the Catholic hierarchy and NUI college presidents deepened in the early 1950s, when a liaison committee was established to allow regular consultation between the bishops and the presidents. This committee, which included the three university presidents and on the ecclesiastical side McQuaid, Michael Browne, bishop of Galway, Cornelius Lucey, bishop of Cork and the three other archbishops, was active from 1951 until the late 1960s.[38] The liaison committee facilitated a considerable level of collaboration between college presidents and the bishops in relation to the position of Trinity College and government policies on higher education.

The alignment between the Catholic bishops and NUI presidents reached its peak in the mid to late 1950s, when it was notably effective in modifying government policies. James Dillon, Minister for Agriculture in the first two inter-party governments, proposed a restructuring of agricultural education through the creation of a higher level agricultural institute, which would be funded by the American Grant Counterpart fund drawn from Marshall Aid to Ireland. The proposal had been under consideration for almost five years when Dillon published draft legislation in the autumn of 1955.[39] The proposed institute was intended to embrace all higher education and research in agriculture and was highly contentious in UCD and UCC, which sought to protect their faculties of agriculture and dairy science respectively from absorption within a new state-sanctioned institute.[40] Dillon's plan was publicly opposed by Tierney and by Henry St John Atkins, O'Rahilly's successor in UCC, while the former president, not to be outdone, issued a statement denouncing the proposal as an attempt to 'expropriate and suppress existing institutions...'[41] Although the Taoiseach, John A Costello, insisted that the institute was about coordination of agricultural education rather than state control, the university critics enjoyed powerful ecclesiastical support. Browne and Lucey, who were members of the liaison committee, both objected to the institute in very similar terms in September 1955 as a state takeover of agricultural education which undermined the faculties of the NUI.[42] The weight of the opposition was sufficient to deter the coalition government from proceeding with the Bill.

Following de Valera's return to power in March 1957, the bishops made a definitive intervention to block the Bill in a letter issued by the secretaries to the hierarchy on 1 October 1957:

> The Cardinal, Archbishops and Bishops of Ireland felt it their duty to submit representations to the late Government in regard to the proposed Institute of Agriculture and to make clear that they would regard as most detrimental to Catholic interests the proposal to deprive the National University of the Faculties of Agriculture and Dairy Science...they would feel it their duty to oppose with determination any diminution of that University, which Catholics after a long struggle obtained as some measure of their just rights.[43]

The bishops also objected to the inclusion of Trinity College, which did not have an agriculture faculty, within the proposed institute or any move to place TCD 'on a par with the National University...'[44] It was a stark warning that any reduction of the NUI's role in agricultural education would embroil the government in conflict with the bishops. There was no ambiguity about a straightforward assertion of ecclesiastical power in an area where the bishops had no formal or statutory rights, but where they had identified a community of interest with the NUI presidents. Following this intervention, the original scheme was watered down to leave the university faculties untouched and establish An Foras Talúntais instead as a research institute in 1958.[45]

Shortly afterwards, Tierney secured influential support from McQuaid in opposing a joint board including UCD and Trinity nominees for the management of veterinary education and instead negotiated the continuation of separate veterinary faculties on favourable terms for the larger college.[46] Both O'Rahilly and Tierney proved adept at mobilising the support of the bishops to block government policies which they opposed. The collaboration between the bishops and Catholic university leaders reflected a shared ideological commitment to integralist Catholicism and a perception of common enemies, whether in Trinity College Dublin or the less tangible but real fear of statism and bureaucratic overreach at the height of the Cold War. Yet it was also a pragmatic attempt by Catholic university leaders to mobilise ecclesiastical power to benefit their own institutions in an era of minimal state support for university education.

Gaelicisation

The crusade for Gaelicisation achieved considerable resonance within the NUI, although its influence varied dramatically between different institutions. UCG adopted teaching through Irish as a central focus of its academic activity through its agreements with the Free State government.[47] More incremental initiatives were undertaken in the other colleges, due to the steady pressure maintained by the Gaelic League, successive governments and a significant section of the academic staff and graduates. UCD pledged to expand its department of modern Irish and established new oral Irish courses for the student body, as part of an agreement with de Valera's government in 1933–34.[48] UCC made lectures available through Irish in certain departments and launched a popular Gaeltacht scholarship scheme for students. The governing body determined in the 1930s that only Irish speakers should be appointed to the posts of president, registrar, secretary or librarian—in a move also influenced by the hope of greater exchequer funding.[49] This could be viewed either as a genuine commitment to Gaelicisation from the top down or a shrewd move to limit the impact of the cultural crusade on academic appointments.

Yet despite such apparent progress Gaelicisation was divisive within the NUI and in the university's relations with the cultural nationalist movement. An influential Irish-Ireland group on the governing body of UCC, clashed bitterly with Patrick Merriman in 1936 over the appointment of Frances Vaughan as professor of education, on the basis that she had no Irish.[50] There were also divisions among professors in UCD over the merits of teaching through Irish. Michael Tierney, a strong supporter of Irish scholarship and son-in-law of Eoin MacNeill, was a vociferous public critic of the government's policy of 'compulsory' Irish in schools, of which his fellow UCD professor Timothy Corcoran was the leading architect.

The NUI's commitment to the Irish language since the debate over 'essential Irish' did not shield the university from fierce criticism when university leaders sought to limit the impact of Gaelicisation. The Gaelic League and its supporters rapidly became disillusioned with the contribution of the NUI to the national project of language revival. The NUI general board of studies recommended in March 1924 that it was 'not possible at present that Lectures should be given in Irish in the various subjects of the Faculties.'[51] The senate also responded cautiously to the demands of the Gaelic League for an intensification of compulsory Irish within the university, agreeing only to seek the views of the academic councils in each university college on whether a first year examination in Irish should be introduced in every faculty.[52] The executive committee of the Gaelic League passed a resolution in April 1924, expressing anger at the senate's equivocal response:

> Since it is Irish money the University is spending, it is our strong opinion that the Senate should give better fair play to the language of the country; and we find fault with them on account of the injustice they are doing… it is not right for the National University to give a Degree to a student in any branch of learning unless he has a good knowledge of Irish.[53]

This uncompromising broadside had relatively little impact, as the senate decided later in the same year that the issue of a compulsory examination in Irish across all faculties 'should be decided by each College for itself.'[54] This was probably unavoidable as the academic councils of

UCD and UCG had expressed directly contradictory viewpoints on the proposal, with UCD opposing a compulsory Irish examination.[55] The demands of the language revival movement were regarded as counter-productive by some former supporters. Agnes O'Farrelly, a pioneer both in women's participation and the teaching of Irish in UCD, warned at a meeting of Convocation in 1924 against the adoption of 'extreme and ill considered resolutions and methods', declaring that 'The Irish language is suffering from its friends as well as from its enemies.'[56]

The most persistent thread in government policy towards the universities up to the 1940s was pressure to play their part in the Gaelicisation of society. But the actual impact of government support for Gaelicisation on institutional policy and practice was intermittent and piecemeal. The Cumann na nGaedheal government's agreement with UCG, which fell short of a full-scale Gaelicisation demanded by much of the political elite and drew sharp criticism from de Valera in 1929, was quietly accepted by Fianna Fáil governments. Official backing for cultural nationalism never translated into a systematic policy for Gaelicisation within the universities, which would have required an equivalent commitment of resources to match official rhetoric.

Significantly, the only additional statutory grant approved by de Valera's government for the universities in the grim economic circumstances of the 1930s involved a modest investment in Gaelicisation in UCD. Coffey, who was noted for his ability to maintain good relations with both sides of the Treaty split, managed to secure additional resources for the Irish department in UCD. Blythe agreed in November 1931 that the government would finance the re-organisation and expansion of the department of modern Irish up to a maximum grant of £3000: armed with this assurance, the UCD authorities proposed the creation of six new academic posts, as well as the conversion of an existing lectureship into a new Chair of Irish Poetry.[57] The change of government in March 1932 did not derail the negotiations. When Coffey met with de Valera and MacEntee on 2 April 1932, the incoming President was well disposed to the proposal, commenting only that increased government support would depend on convincing the public that 'the applicants were men of outstanding qualification.'[58] But the initiative was delayed by Derrig, an uncompromising advocate of the language revival crusade, who wrote to de Valera in May 1932 to oppose increasing the grant unless definitive guarantees were given to improve the teaching of Irish and give instruction in other subjects through Irish.[59] He noted that 'I do not think it right, considering the condition of Irish in this College presently, for the state to provide the new grant until the whole matter is examined carefully.'[60]

Derrig's intervention delayed a government decision for almost two years. Yet the Department of Finance regarded the initiative with equanimity because of its minimal cost: MacEntee confirmed the understanding reached by UCD with his predecessor as early as July 1932, allowing the college to go ahead in making two new appointments. The Cabinet agreed on 17 January 1934 to draft a special bill to give effect to the increased grant.[61] The University College Dublin Bill was approved by the Oireachtas in July 1934. Yet the agreement reached by UCD to secure the grant nullified some of the benefits, as the payment of the additional grant was dependent on the introduction of a staffing structure which the college was unable to implement fully and so the full grant was never allocated.[62] The compelling appeal of Gaelicisation could be deployed to challenge the normal constraints of inter-war austerity. Yet the ambiguous outcome was more reflective of the authentic spirit of the era, in which universities barely featured as a focus of political discourse or public policy.

Derrig's criticisms of UCD and UCC in 1933 for lagging behind the schools in their commitment to Irish were informed by representations to the government by discontented language revivalists. Shortly after taking office in May 1932, De Valera received a memorandum from Dr Seamus Ó Ceallaigh, who made a scathing attack on UCD, arguing that the standard of Irish studies in UCD was 'hopelessly low in view of the labour expended in the intermediate schools'.[63] Moreover, the shortcomings of the college authorities, in failing to promote Irish in the social and official life of UCD, were dissected with meticulous zeal:

> Quite anglicised. Public functions same as in Trinity. Irish never or hardly ever heard at lectures so frequently delivered to the public by savants from abroad. Social functions un-Irish. Toasts &c never in Irish. Irish gets no recognition as a matter of routine.[64]

Ó Ceallaigh was by no means a lone voice, as the Gaelic League frequently expressed dissatisfaction with the record of the NUI, especially UCD, over the following decade. Following Conway's appointment as president of UCD in 1940, the League circulated a resolution to county councils decrying 'the insult offered to Irish' when the senate refused to adopt a rule that the president of UCD should be an Irish-speaker and urging the local authorities not to offer further scholarships to UCD until the governing body 'was willing and ready to give justice to the language of the country.'[65] Although the corporations in both Dublin and Cork declined to adopt the resolution, it was a notable indication of the pressure that could routinely be brought to bear on university institutions to conform to the ambitious agenda of the cultural nationalist movement. Relations between UCD and the Gaelic League had reached a state of simmering hostility by the early 1940s.

The most dramatic confrontation of the crusade for Gaelicisation within the NUI erupted in 1943, over the appointment of W. J. Williams to the chair of Education in UCD. Williams, a long serving assistant lecturer in the school of education who did not speak Irish, was recommended for the chair by the academic council of UCD, in succession to Fr. Corcoran, the most famous champion of compulsory Irish.[66] Although Williams easily won the support of the governing body, the Gaelic League mounted a vociferous public campaign to block his appointment by the NUI senate, issuing an appeal for support to the Taoiseach, the Catholic bishops and TDs. A protest meeting was held at the Mansion House on 5 March 1943, where speakers denounced the governing body's action as 'shameful, treacherous and anti-Irish.'[67] The League's president, Diarmuid Mac Fhionnlaoich, disclaimed any intention to seek state control of the universities, but demanded the rejection of Williams' nomination by the senate in the interests of Irish-speaking students and Irish education in general. The Gaelic League's campaign provoked a stormy debate at a meeting of the NUI Convocation on 10 March, in which neither side gave any ground. An opponent of the League, Desmond Bell, claimed that 'outside bodies had taken it upon themselves to dictate to the staff and the graduates' and Convocation should back the governing body rather than 'support the views of a body who, when holding a street-corner meeting could not express themselves in Irish.'[68] A deeply divided

Convocation eventually passed the Gaelic League's motion that the professor of education be qualified to lecture in Irish by a margin of only 101 to 94. Student opinion in UCD was more favourable to Williams' appointment—the Literary and Historical Society passed a motion which probably reflected the views of many academics as well as its student membership: 'That this House,…having no limited interests, resents the attempt of the Gaelic League to interfere in University affairs.'[69]

The dispute culminated in violent clashes outside UCD on the eve of the senate decision. A protest march to Earlsfort Terrace was organised on 10 March by Glúin na Bua, a breakaway organisation from the Gaelic League led by Proinsias Mac Beatha. The protesters were opposed by a much larger group of UCD students, triggering a fight recorded by the *Irish Times* with barely concealed glee[70]:

> Protesters, against the appointment marched to the College after a meeting in O'Connell street, were met by about a thousand students who turned a hose on them from a top window of the College, then rushed them and captured their banners after a series of fights, in which the banners were used as weapons…The banners afterwards were burned on the steps of the College.[71]

The sound and fury generated by the League's campaign left the senate unmoved and may even have stiffened its resistance. The senate, meeting in private session on 11 March 1943, approved Williams' appointment by a decisive margin of 23 to 7.[72] De Valera, who presided at the meeting, favoured the appointment of the only other qualified candidate, Fergal McGrath SJ, but did not seek to challenge the decision of the senate. The verdict was a clear rebuke to the Irish language organisations, underlining the limits of their influence on the NUI. The debate on Gaelicisation within the NUI was far from over, but the senate was successful in resisting external pressures which were widely perceived as threatening the autonomy of its constituent colleges. Academic elites within the NUI dealt effectively and for the most part unsentimentally with the significant political and public pressure for Gaelicisation. College leaders and senior academics were pragmatic in accommodating official demands to secure greater resources but fiercely defended academic control over appointments and college management.

Women in Higher Education

Following the breakthroughs of the early 1900s, women's participation in university education in the new Irish state remained heavily restricted and prescribed by traditional gender roles for over a generation. Legal equality was a far cry from equal treatment in college life. The enrolment of female students levelled off and sometimes declined during the interwar period. The proportion of female students in UCD, which reached a peak of 36% in the mid-1930s, declined later in the decade and remained below 29% of enrolments for the following three decades. This decline was linked particularly to a fall in female enrolments in medicine, where the proportion of women students dropped from one sixth to one tenth of the total between 1919–20 and 1931–32.[73] UCC, which had admitted women since 1885–86, saw a significant increase in the proportion of female students following the creation of the NUI, not least due to the removal of the Catholic church's ban on the 'godless' colleges.[74] This advance in female participation continued in the 1920s, with an increase from 20% of the student population in 1917–18 to 32% in 1934–35.[75] But women's participation stagnated over the following two decades in line with wider trends throughout the NUI. Trinity showed a more distinctive demographic pattern, but the proportion of female students was very similar to the NUI by the 1950s. Women accounted for 23% of full-time students by 1939, compared to 15% in 1914—an even lower level than its NUI counterparts.[76] But female enrolment expanded rapidly in the late 1940s as part of a 'postwar rush', reaching 32% of the full-time student population in 1949. This expansion levelled off early in the following decade, but the proportion of women remained about one third in 1956 despite an overall decline in enrolments.[77] The demographic pattern of the student population in the three largest colleges in Ireland was similar in the mid-1950s, with women accounting for between one quarter and one third of full-time enrolments.

Discrimination against women remained firmly entrenched not only in the culture of the universities, but in a range of policies and regulations overtly designed to limit the impact of co-education. The universities legislation did not prevent institutional policies or practices which limited the influence of women graduates and staff or the freedom of female students. One of these was identified by a vigilant Mary Hayden, who wrote to Archbishop Walsh in June 1909, pointing out that the proposed statute for UCD restricted the franchise for election of the governing body to graduates of the colleges in Stephen's Green and Cecilia St, disenfranchising most of the women graduates of the Royal University.[78] Walsh responded sympathetically, inviting Hayden to draft a clause 'which would remedy the injustice to the Dublin women students…'[79]

Other forms of discrimination proved more enduring. Despite differences in their traditions and religious orientation, university colleges shared a traditionalist outlook in their rigorous attempts to regulate student life and control the activity of female students. UCC under O'Rahilly's presidency maintained an exhaustive list of regulations for both genders, but focused particularly on the potentially malign behaviour of women. Murphy commented that, 'If the rights of man were circumscribed, the rights of women were even more restricted.'[80] Female students were banned from smoking in the college, restricted in their dress code and subject to a higher level of supervision than men. Student lodgings were segregated by gender, while separate clubs were maintained for men and women.[81] The official policies of the college expressed a repressive, authoritarian spirit allied to a suspicion of women as potential harbingers of scandal.

Such restrictive university policies were the norm in mid-twentieth century Ireland. There were no great differences on gender between the ultra-Catholic O'Rahilly and the largely Protestant, ex-unionist leaders of Trinity College. The college administration in Trinity enforced a considerable level of segregation in social and recreational activity up to the 1950s. Female students faced significant practical restrictions, including a famous, long lasting rule requiring women students to leave campus by 6 p.m., strict dress requirements and exclusion from certain areas of the college.[82] Although an increasing number of societies were open to both genders in the interwar period, the prestigious debating societies excluded women until the 1960s. Trinity remained a male-dominated institution well into the second half of the twentieth century.

The apparently modest advance in academic appointments within the NUI in 1909–11 proved a notable landmark in women's participation which was not surpassed (or sometimes equalled) for most of the twentieth century. The position of women academics within the NUI deteriorated during the first generation of the independent Irish state. A total of four women professors in 1932 was a 'high water mark' for UCD, which declined in the mid-twentieth century.[83] Two women held senior academic posts by 1938 although there was a marginal increase in the proportion of women holding statutory lectureships; there was only a single female professor (Kathleen Cunningham in modern languages) between 1949 and 1957.[84] UCC showed a similar pattern, as a modest increase in the female academic staff was offset by a decline in the proportion of women in senior posts. A key factor in the lack of progression in UCC was the requirement for women holding non-statutory lecturing posts to retire on marriage.[85] This counterbalanced the college's willingness to employ a greater number of women in junior academic posts and reduced the available pool for promotion internally. Only four women held professorial posts in UCC in 1954–55, just 10% of the total senior academic cohort.[86]

Female academics also remained a small minority in Trinity, which due to its traditional constitution was in some respects even more restrictive than its NUI counterparts. Frances Moran was the sole female professor for most of the interwar period and only three women were serving as professors by 1939.[87] Eight women held full-time academic posts by the end of the 1930s, including four 'assistants to the professor', the most junior academic post.[88] Women were excluded from the main staff dining facilities and from membership of the Senior Common Room. More seriously, female academics were denied access to the distinction of Fellowship—and therefore membership of the body corporate of Provost, Fellows and Scholars—until 1967.[89] The college administration, however, increasingly relied on female employees in administrative and secretarial posts.[90] This reflected a gendered distribution of labour, in which secretarial/administrative roles were viewed as more suitable for women. As Parkes notes, "the position of women staff in TCD, therefore, was to continue to be 'second class citizens' until the 1960s…"[91]

Formal discrimination in national policies against women was the norm throughout the mid twentieth century, with the imposition of a marriage ban requiring female primary teachers to retire on marriage from 1933 to 1958, while the civil service marriage bar persisted until 1974. Such policies both restricted the employment of women and sometimes directly influenced university education, including UCC's policy on retirement of non-statutory lecturers. But formal regulations were only part of the story—the institutional culture of the universities was shaped by a conservative society, marked by strong cultural and religious pressures on women to conform to traditional gender roles linked to marriage and home-making.[92] The majority of higher education institutions, including the NUI, were shaped by integralist Catholicism, informed by conservative social teaching emphasising the place of the traditional family and the authority of an all-male ecclesiastical hierarchy. Trinity was equally conservative, influenced by the resilience of Victorian cultural mores and the predominance of elderly senior fellows in its governance until the early 1950s. Traditionalist—and straightforwardly misogynistic—attitudes towards women were not the monopoly of any one creed or institution. The universities were certainly slow to change, but their values and practices reflected conventional societal values and a wider cultural conservatism up to the mid-1900s.

The Academy and Society

Some historians have argued that the universities, particularly their leaders, adopted a low profile and did little to inform public opinion about the place of the university in society during the first generation of the independent state.[93] This traditional portrayal does not capture the complexity of the interaction between university leaders, academics, ministers, civil servants and church leaders in this period. Certainly institutional leaders rarely offered a public critique of the limited government support for their colleges before the 1950s. If anything senior academics perceived advantages in governmental conservatism, as the state rarely impinged on the autonomy of the academy or the activity of the academic elite. University leaders accepted without much public complaint, at least up to 1945, the other side of this coin—financial neglect of the universities by official and political elites. There was little public debate about the place of the academy in society and university leaders rarely linked the fortunes of their colleges to wider societal or economic advances.

Yet senior academics were both vocal and relatively successful in challenging or modifying political initiatives which they perceived as threatening the status of their institutions, such as Blythe's pressure for wholesale Gaelicisation of UCG or MacEntee's economy Bill. Prominent figures such as O'Rahilly and Tierney (though probably atypical in any profession) had no hesitation in promoting their views or entering public disputes with politicians, other universities and occasionally each other. More conventional was the quiet diplomacy practiced by senior NUI figures such as Coffey and Conway, which often proved effective in shaping government policies or securing exchequer support on an ad hoc basis. University leaders were usually (though not invariably) low profile in public discourse, particularly up to the late 1940s, but this did not equate with being ineffectual. Their relationship with government and other major institutions, such as the Catholic church, has to be understood in terms of the peripheral position of academic institutions in public discourse. The dominant ideologies of early to mid-twentieth century Ireland—integralist Catholicism and cultural nationalism—defined the cultural context in which the universities operated. University leaders and for that matter most academics accepted the underlying premises of a fundamentally conservative society.

Notes

1. J. H. Whyte, *Church and State in Modern Ireland 1923–1979* (Dublin: Gill and Macmillan, 1980), 158–61.
2. John Walsh, 'The Problem of Trinity College Dublin: A Historical Perspective on Rationalisation in Higher Education in Ireland,' *Irish Educational Studies* 33, no. 1 (2014): 4.
3. McCartney, *UCD*, 183–4.
4. Ibid., 160.
5. http://www.ainm.ie/Bio.aspx?ID=420, Biography of Padraig de Brún—Accessed 27 October 2015, http://www.ainm.ie/Bio.aspx?ID=420.

6. Nolan and Walsh, 'In What Orbit We Shall Find Ourselves, No One Could Predict,' *Irish Historical Studies* 41, no. 159 (2017): 77–96. https://doi.org/10.1017/ihs.2017.7.

7. John Charles McQuaid, *Higher Education for Catholics* (Dublin: Mc Gill & Son, 1961), 14.

8. McCartney, *UCD*, 216.

9. Ibid., 216.

10. McQuaid, *Higher Education for Catholics*, 11.

11. McCartney, *UCD*, 216.

12. Murphy, *The College*, 270–1.

13. Ibid.

14. Ibid., 299.

15. McCartney, *UCD*, 177; Lyons, *Ireland since the Famine,* 528.

16. Lyons, *Ireland Since the Famine*, 528.

17. Murphy, *The College*, 243; Lyons, *Ireland since the Famine*, 531.

18. Clancy, *Irish Higher Education*, 28; Séamus Smyth, 'National University of Ireland, Maynooth,' in *National University of Ireland 1908–2008 Centenary Essays*, ed. Dunne et al. (Dublin: UCD Press, 2008), 109.

19. Daniel C. Levy, *Higher Education and the State in Latin America: Private Challenges to Public Dominance* (Chicago: University of Chicago Press, 1986), 37.

20. Mark Duncan, Eoin Kinsella, and Paul Rouse, *National College of Ireland: Past, Present, Future* (Dublin: The Liffey Press, 2007), 9.

21. David Limond, 'Advanced Education for Working People: The Catholic Workers' College, a Case Study,' in *Essays in the History of Irish Education*, ed. Brendan Walsh (London: Palgrave, 2016), 252.

22. Ibid., 344–6; Duncan et al., *National College of Ireland*, 7.

23. Duncan et al., *National College of Ireland*, 9; Limond, 'Advanced Education for Working People,' 348.

24. Duncan et al., *National College of Ireland*, 22–3.

25. *Commission on Higher Education*, 26 May 1961, 141–61; James Lydon, 'The Silent Sister: Trinity College and Catholic Ireland,' in *Trinity College Dublin and the Idea of a University*, ed. C. H. Holland (Dublin, 1991), 39–43.

26. *Irish Times*, 'Archbishop Re-Affirms TCD Ban,' 21 February 1944.

27. McQuaid to the Convent of the Holy Child Killacoona, Killiney, 14 December 1967 (DDA, *McQuaid Papers*, XVIII/38A/10).

28. McQuaid, *Higher Education for Catholics*, 17.

29. Luce, *Trinity College Dublin*, 15.
30. Ibid., 183.
31. Nolan and Walsh, '"In What Orbit We Shall Find Ourselves, No One Could Predict": Institutional Reform, the University Merger and Ecclesiastical Influence on Irish Higher Education in the 1960s,' *Irish Historical Studies* 41, no. 159 (2017): 77–96. https://doi.org/10.1017/ihs.2017.7.
32. Luce, *Trinity College Dublin*, 196.
33. Ibid.
34. *Irish Times*, 'Trinity College Dublin,' 23 April 1953.
35. Ibid.
36. *Irish Times*, 'Kerry Scholarships for TCD and QUB,' 26 August 1955.
37. *Irish Times*, 'Scholarship Scheme "Illegal",' 14 July 1956.
38. McCartney, *UCD*, 184–5.
39. Costello to Dillon, 11 May 1950 (NAI TSCH/3/S14815A).
40. *Irish Times*, 'State Will Not Control Institute of Agriculture,' 15 August 1955; McCartney, *UCD*, 192; and Murphy, *The College*, 295.
41. *Irish Times*, 'Farm Plan a "New Dose of Statism,"' 5 October 1955.
42. *Irish Times*, 'Bishop Opposed to Plan for Agricultural Institute,' 17 September 1955; 'Bishop Criticises Plans for New Institute,' 17 September 1955.
43. William MacNeely, Bishop of Raphoe and James Fergus, Bishop of Achonry to de Valera, 1 October 1957 (NAI TSCH/3/S.12544).
44. Ibid.
45. McCartney, *UCD*, 193.
46. Ibid., 195.
47. See above, pp. 36–45.
48. Denis Coffey to Ernest Blythe, 4 March 1932; Seán MacEntee to Secretary, Executive Council, Memorandum, 9 January 1934 (NAI TSCH S6240).
49. Murphy, *The College*, 246.
50. Ibid., 247.
51. NUI Senate, Minutes, vol. 9, 14 March 1924, 224.
52. Ibid., 225.
53. NUI Senate, Minutes, vol. 9, 25 April 1924, 238.
54. NUI Senate, Minutes, vol. 9, 9 July 1924, 349.
55. Ibid., 347–8.

56. *Irish Times*, 'Teaching of Irish: Miss Agnes O'Farrelly's Criticism,' 10 December 1924.

57. Memorandum, Statute XVIII, UCD, *Additional Provision for Statutory Teaching Offices in the Department of Modern Irish Language and Literature* (NAI TSCH/3/S6240).

58. Minutes of Meeting Between the President and Coffey, 2 April 1932 (NAI TSCH/3/S6240).

59. Derrig to de Valera, 12 May 1932; Joseph O'Neill to Secretary, President of the Executive Council, 3 May 1932 (NAI TSCH/3/S6240).

60. Derrig to de Valera, 12 May 1932 (NAI TSCH/3/S6240).

61. Extract from Cabinet Minutes, 17 January 1934; Private Secretary, Minister for Finance, to Private Secretary, Executive Council (NAI TSCH/3/S6240).

62. Public Accounts Committee, *Appropriation Accounts 1952–53* (Dublin: Stationery Office, 1955), 8.

63. Ó Ceallaigh to de Valera, *Headings for Consideration of the Relations of University College, Dublin, to the Question of Gaelicisation* (NAI TSCH/3/S6240).

64. Ibid.

65. *Irish Times*, 'Irish in National University,' 24 July 1940.

66. NUI Senate, Minutes, 11 March 1943, 138; Biography of Paul Andrews SJ, Accessed 15 November 2015. http://www.jesuit.ie/news/jesuits-teaching-the-teachers/downloaded.

67. *Irish Times*, 'Meeting Denounces UCD,' 6 March 1943.

68. *Irish Times*, 'NU Convocation's Three Hour Debate in Three Languages,' 10 March 1943.

69. NUI Senate, Minutes, 11 March 1943, 141.

70. The sympathies of the *Irish Times* (then under the direction of the redoubtable R. M. Symllie) lay firmly with the governing body and students of UCD and the editorial on 10 March was strongly critical of the 'agitators' for their extravagant claims about the potential harm of the appointment and attacks on the governing body; the editor took pleasure in the discomfiture of the Gaelic League and possibly also at the open clash between UCD and the League.

71. *Irish Times*, 'Fight over the Chair of Education,' 11 March 1943.

72. NUI Senate, Minutes, 11 March 1943, 141.

73. McCartney, *UCD*, 83.

74. Murphy, *The College*, 130.

75. Ibid., 131.

76. Luce, *Trinity College Dublin*, 152.

77. Ibid.

78. Mary Hayden to Walsh, 8 June 1909 (DDA NUI 1/6).

79. Hayden to Walsh, 10 June 1909 (DDA NUI 1/9).

80. Murphy, *The College*, 286.

81. Ibid., 236.

82. Susan Parkes, 'The 1930s: Consolidation but Still Discrimination,' in *A Danger to the Men*, ed. Susan Parkes (Dublin: Lilliput Press, 2004), 113–41.

83. McCartney, *UCD*, 83.

84. Ibid.

85. Murphy, *The College*, 131.

86. Ibid., 346.

87. Parkes, 'The 1930s: Consolidation but Still Discrimination,' 135.

88. Ibid.

89. Elizabeth Mayes, 'The 1960s and '70s: Decades of Change,' in *A Danger to the Men*, ed. Susan Parkes (Dublin: Lilliput Press, 2004), 215–6.

90. Parkes, 'The 1930s: Consolidation but Still Discrimination,' 135.

91. Parkes, 'The First Decade,' 84.

92. McCartney, *UCD*, 83.

93. Coolahan, 'Higher Education in Ireland,' 763.

4

Higher Technical Education in Ireland

Origins of Higher Technical Education

Technical education in the early 1900s was a broad church, still ill-defined and embracing a variety of forms, including classes in science and art in intermediate schools; dedicated courses offered by technical schools under the auspices of local authorities and a small number of higher technological institutions. These included the Metropolitan School of Art, originally founded by the Royal Dublin Society and the Royal College of Science, established as a public institution in 1867.[1] Technical education received official recognition as a distinct educational strand, differentiated from preparation for the practice of a trade, for the first time in the late 1800s. The Technical Instruction Act, 1889, gave explicit recognition to technical education as the study of applied subjects in England, Wales and Ireland, excluding teaching the practice of any trade or employment from its legal definition. 'Technical instruction' was defined as 'instruction in the principles of science and art applicable to industries, and in the application of special branches of science and art to specific industries or employments.'[2] The act

© The Author(s) 2018
J. Walsh, *Higher Education in Ireland, 1922–2016*,
https://doi.org/10.1057/978-1-137-44673-2_4

empowered local authorities to organise schemes of technical instruction and offer financial assistance from the rates.[3]

The origins of technical education in Ireland owed more to private or philanthropic initiative and local authorities than any deliberate state policy up to the early twentieth century. A popular movement for the development of technical education gained momentum in the late 1800s, driven by an eclectic combination of educational reformers, philanthropists, business interests and labour leaders. Local authorities in the cities, prodded by educational reformers such as Arnold Graves in Dublin and W. H. Crawford in Cork, provided much of the organisation and finance for the early 'technical schools'. The first technical school in Dublin, was the product of a coalition between the Corporation, business interests in the city and the newly formed Dublin Trades Council, in which the land reformer Michael Davitt was a driving force.[4] The Kevin Street Municipal Technical School was founded in October 1887, supported by public subscriptions and a grant from the local authority. The school, offering evening courses in science, mathematical and art subjects, attracted 220 students in its first year.[5] A voluntary committee in Cork took the lead in establishing a School of Design as early as 1849, offering classes in arts and science subjects, which came under the direction of the Corporation from 1855. New schools of art and science were developed and presented to the city in 1884 at the instigation of W. H. Crawford and were subsequently designated as the Crawford Municipal Institute.[6] Cork Corporation adopted its own scheme from 1895, building on an early tradition of engagement with technical education. The Corporation in Limerick became deeply involved in the area for the first time in 1896, when the Athenaeum Society, a voluntary body which had set up a School of Art in the city a generation earlier, handed over its property in trust to the Corporation to administer its activities 'for the advancement of technical education.'[7]

The 1889 legislation, which proved ineffective outside the cities, was the forerunner of a more significant initiative a decade later. The catalyst for legislative change came from a broad based committee of political and civic leaders, convened at the invitation of Horace Plunkett, a liberal unionist MP and founder of the co-operative movement.

Plunkett was an influential advocate of technical or 'practical' education in rural areas, along with the creation of a separate department of agriculture for Ireland.[8] Plunkett presided over a cross-party committee including unionist and nationalist representatives, known as the Recess Committee as they met during the parliamentary recess in 1895. Despite political and sectarian divisions, the 'unofficial committee of Irishmen' produced a unanimous report informed by comparative research on the position of agriculture and industry in Ireland relative to other European countries.[9] The backwardness of Irish agriculture and the necessity for technical education as part of the solution were central themes of the conference. The main recommendations of the report were accepted by the government and embodied in the Agriculture and Technical Instruction (Ireland) Act, 1899. The most significant outcome was the creation of a new Department for Agriculture and Technical Instruction in Ireland (DATI).[10] The legislation embraced a similar conceptual framework to its predecessor in defining technical education, but excluded technical instruction in elementary schools. Technical education was envisaged as a post-compulsory endeavour involving applied studies relevant to trade and industry.[11] Pressure from civil society in Ireland proved influential in provoking action by the Irish administration, which fitted well with the mantra of constructive unionism. The report also fed into wider concerns by political elites to develop education for trade and industry at a time when Britain's traditional economic strength was being challenged by the rising power of Germany.[12]

The newly created department, headed during its formative phase by Plunkett himself, took over responsibility for administering grants for technical instruction from the Department of Science and Art in London, in addition to a wide range of responsibilities including agriculture and fisheries.[13] The department also assumed oversight of higher level agricultural and technical institutions, including the Royal College of Science, Albert College of agriculture in Glasnevin and the Metropolitan School of Art, most of which had previously come under the auspices of the Board of Education in London. DATI was led by Plunkett until he was replaced by the Liberal government in 1907; his close associate T. P. Gill, a former nationalist MP, enjoyed a more enduring influence as secretary of DATI until 1922. The legislation created an endowment fund of £55,000 for technical instruction, which was divided on a statutory basis into two allocations, one of £25,000 to be distributed between county boroughs in accordance with population and the remainder to be devoted to 'other purposes' and to schemes outside the major urban areas.[14] The resources for the latter allocation were disbursed on the recommendations of a Board of Technical Instruction, which acquired considerable influence as its agreement was necessary for the approval of all local schemes of technical instruction outside the boroughs.[15]

Perhaps equally significant in stimulating the development of technical education outside urban areas was the creation of democratically elected county councils, accomplished through the Irish Local Government Act in 1898. The reformed local authorities enjoyed the necessary rating base and popular support to establish viable schemes of technical instruction funded from the rates. Almost all the local authorities utilised the terms of the 1899 act to develop schemes of technical instruction which drew support from the endowment fund.[16] The ensuing surge in activity led to the establishment of 49 local technical education committees across the country.[17] There were marked differences in both the scope and form of technical education between urban and rural areas. Technical instruction in larger urban centres was offered in technical schools providing 'systematic courses of instruction', of the kind pioneered by early initiatives in Dublin and Cork, usually focusing on science, technology and arts in preparation for employment in trade and industry.[18] The pattern of technical education in rural counties was more varied and less tightly organised. While technical schools were formed in centres of population, much of the instruction was in woodwork, domestic science and agriculture, initially provided by itinerant teachers, many of whom were paid by DATI; home industries and commerce were also included in various county schemes.[19] The organisation and subject focus were often very different from urban areas, indicating both diverse local needs and differing levels of resources between rural and urban authorities. While the legislation on the brink of the new century had a significant influence in extending the practice of technical education across most of the country, the most extensive developments were still concentrated in the major urban areas during the early 1900s.

Dublin Corporation set up a technical education committee in 1900 to govern technical education in the city, which oversaw a significant expansion in the technical schools over the following decade.[20] The TEC established a new technical institute at Bolton St. in 1911, which was founded in the first building in Ireland designed specifically for technical education. The new institute took over courses in building construction and engineering, which were transferred from Kevin St. and soon offered courses in aeroplane construction as well.[21] The expansion of urban schemes of technical education was not restricted to the city of Dublin. A technical instruction committee established by the Rathmines urban district council instigated the foundation of the Municipal Technical Institute on Rathmines Road in 1901.[22] The new institute mainly provided business and language courses and emphasised its commitment to education in commerce for 'persons of either sex', enjoying strong participation from female students who made up a third of its initial enrolment.[23] The institute expanded rapidly, catering for 333 students in 1901 and 1620 by 1925.

The technical schools and institutes established by the urban local authorities were very different from traditional intermediate schools, both because of the form and content of their courses and their focus on adult education. The expansion of Kevin St. school led to a diversification of activity, as commercial classes were transferred from 1905 to a new centre at Rutland Square (later Parnell Square): this evolved into a new technical school specialising in commercial education and the teaching of domestic economy.[24] The technical institute in Bolton St. broke new ground by introducing the first day release apprenticeship courses in Ireland in 1914 for machine operators in printing and later developing a full time two year course from 1922 which counted for the first two years of a student's apprenticeship.[25] The TEC course in Bolton St. was the only day apprentice school in the Irish Free State during the 1920s, awarding apprentice scholarships to 'boys of not less than 14 years of age' and offering training mainly in engineering, printing, carpentry, cabinet-making and plumbing.[26] The TEC also provided a day dressmaking course for women aged 14–16 'to fit them for employment in the trade houses.'[27] Both apprenticeship courses operated on the basis of liaison with employers' associations to regulate numbers of apprentices admitted to the institute, but this was not always successful and 'difficulty has been experienced from time to time…in placing pupils in employment in their respective trades.'[28]

Higher level professional or technological studies emerged gradually within the urban technical schools in the early 1900s. Kevin St. technical school offered mainly second level courses for the 14–16 year old cohort, but also undertook higher level work to prepare students for teacher training and for external professional or university examinations.[29] Students presented for the degree examinations of the Royal University and external examinations of London University; the school's courses in physics and chemistry were recognised as satisfying the requirements for the first professional examinations of RCSI and the Royal College of Physicians.[30] While this was not the primary focus of the school's activity, it was a foretaste of how the technical schools would develop under the direction of the City of Dublin Vocational Education Committee (CDVEC) later in the twentieth century. The Rathmines technical institute offered higher level commercial subjects, including accountancy, economics and commercial law, from the early 1900s, as well as specialised courses for clerks in banking and insurance recognised by the professional institutes and for railway employees in conjunction with the Dublin railway companies.[31] The diversity of the courses offered by the TEC institutes reflected the extent to which they were a distinctive new phenomenon in Irish education and offered potential for development at higher level, even if this was not readily apparent in the early 1900s.

DATI aspired towards the achievement of distinct higher technological institutions, specialising in 'applied' disciplines such as science, engineering and architecture. When the Royal College of Science came under the aegis of DATI in 1900, a departmental committee recommended that the college should give 'advanced education in Applied Science of a character higher than that given in an ordinary technical or intermediate school without aiming at competition with existing University Colleges.'[32] The college was intended to perform a variety of functions in higher level education—train teachers for technical and intermediate schools where science was taught; offer instruction in elementary science mainly for teachers in primary schools and provide 'a complete course of instruction in Science as applied to Agriculture and the Industrial Arts for general students...'[33] The department expanded the scope of courses in the college, building new laboratories and extending its courses from three to four years, in line with colleges of applied science in continental Europe and the United States. A report commissioned in the first decade of the Irish Free State recorded with more than a hint of nostalgia that the College of Science 'reached its highest stage of development' in the early 1900s under DATI.[34]

The university settlement in the early 1900s opened up new opportunities for collaboration between higher technical institutions and the universities in Dublin and Belfast, but also exposed competing visions of higher education. The department fought tenaciously to prevent the absorption of technical institutions under its jurisdiction within the larger and more prestigious universities. Following an appeal by George C. Ashlin, an eminent architect, to Archbishop Walsh to use his influence to secure the establishment of a university school of architecture in the NUI, the Dublin commission established a part-time chair of architecture in UCD in 1909.[35] The existence of the new school was immediately challenged by Gill, who appealed to the commission in 1910 to defer the appointment of a new chair, as the department wished to concentrate architectural studies in the College of Science. But the commission rejected the department's plan, agreeing only to a brief delay while Gill was informed that 'the commissioners feel themselves bound to fill the vacancy' as courses in architecture had already been published.[36] It was an early indication of a long-term debate about how to develop technological and vocationally oriented disciplines in higher education, which would re-emerge in the second half of the twentieth century.

The department was more successful in negotiations with Queen's University, Belfast, where Gill blocked a proposal by the university senate and Belfast Corporation for the integration of the city's Municipal Technical Institute with proposed faculties of commerce and technology in Queen's, operating in association with the Corporation.[37] Instead a revised agreement was negotiated which led to the recognition of the Institute as a college of Queen's University and the abandonment in the short-term of the scheme for a university faculty of technology.[38] The department also reached agreement with all three universities on the island of Ireland, allowing university students on completing their first two years in agriculture and science disciplines to pursue a further two years of study at the College of Science in Glasnevin.[39]

DATI was open to collaboration with the universities through agreements which recognised complementary but distinct spheres of influence. This was partly a case of an assertive new department, led by formidable public figures such as Plunkett and Gill, marking out its territory. Yet Gill's negotiations with university authorities testified to a departmental preference for the concentration of higher level technical studies in science, agriculture and architecture within the fledgling technical institutes, while avoiding duplication of functions between the colleges and the expanding universities. DATI in the early 1900s implicitly embraced an emergent 'binary' structure for higher education rather than acceptance of a university-dominated sector. DATI evolved a creative approach involving formal collaboration with universities which maintained and enhanced an institutional space for the technical institutes. While this strategic orientation was not always explicitly articulated and certainly was never accepted by university authorities, the department's activism offered a more favourable climate for the development of nascent higher technical institutions than the laissez-faire political economy of the Victorian era or the conservative nationalism of the early Free State.

Higher Technical Education in the Free State

If the universities were peripheral to the nationalist world view of the new Irish Free State, higher technical education barely appeared on its radar. The innate conservatism of the Free State government and its close connections with the NUI ensured that government decisions reinforced the dominant position of the universities. The newly created Department of Education assumed responsibility for the technical education functions previously held by DATI in 1924. The only significant institutional recasting undertaken by the new government involved the closure of the Royal College of Science and incorporation of its scientific and agricultural disciplines within UCD and UCC; the Albert Agricultural College in Glasnevin, which worked closely with the College of Science, was also earmarked for transfer to UCD. The Free State government reversed the policy of DATI, which had sought to develop higher level studies in technical disciplines separately from the universities. Influential figures in the new government, notably Eoin MacNeill and Patrick McGilligan, definitively rejected this emergent diversified approach, in favour of integrating higher-level agricultural and scientific studies within the NUI.

'...Professors and Students Moved About like Chattels'

The fate of the College of Science was uncertain from the outset of new political dispensation. The government abruptly closed the college in October 1922 at the height of the civil war, following reports of a plot by anti-Treaty forces to blow up the college buildings.[40] The displaced students refused to transfer to UCD and held a protest meeting on 17 October calling for the restoration of the college, where the dean, Prof. F. E. Hackett, declared that 'in the Irish Free State they must claim academic freedom. Professors and students must not be moved about like chattels.'[41] A student speaker claimed that the bomb reported to have been found in the building was 'simply an aeroplane dynamo for demonstration purposes.'[42] Whatever the truth of the alleged bomb plot, the college's days as an independent entity were numbered. Although the work of the college continued temporarily in a number of different sites across Dublin, the buildings in Merrion St. were taken over as government offices. Paddy Hogan told the Dáil in October 1922 that it was an anomaly to have two separate establishments in UCD and the College of Science 'both teaching to a great extent the same subjects'.[43] McGilligan, the Minister for Industry and Commerce, took the same line in July 1924, arguing that the College of Science was 'a perfectly and completely redundant institution', which duplicated courses undertaken in UCD; he rejected DATI's approach of keeping technological studies separate from the university.[44] The government regarded a separate College of Science as an outmoded relic of the British administration, whose valued academic work in agricultural and science disciplines should be integrated within a university institution. Official parsimony, concerns about duplication of academic activity and political support for extending the agriculture faculties in the NUI combined to ensure the closure of the College of Science.

MacNeill recommended in a memorandum to the Executive Council on 8 May 1924 that the College of Science should be discontinued as a separate institution, with its staff and resources being transferred to UCD and UCC; this would allow 'special development' to create a faculty of agriculture in Cork, while UCD would 'absorb the other elements of the College of Science as far as is practicable'.[45] MacNeill made a policy statement to the Dáil on 11 July 1924, confirming that higher education programmes in agriculture and applied science would in future be based in new faculties of agriculture in UCD and UCC: 'The National University is more properly the university of the agricultural community, which is the main part of this nation, and the development of the agricultural community and the development of that rural civilisation, which I have spoken of before, ought to be one of its principal functions.'[46] When the government did not immediately act on his recommendations, the minister returned to the fray on 23 August, indicating that a government decision was 'urgently necessary' as MacNeill wished the transfer to take place for the new academic year: the college buildings and equipment were to be transferred to the control of UCD immediately, pending legislation to formalise the reallocation of resources to the two colleges. MacNeill's memorandum to the President of the Executive Council pointedly warned that the college's space and facilities should in general be returned to academic use, challenging official reluctance to agree to an early transfer because the buildings were being used as government offices: 'The Minister is strongly of the opinion that all the laboratories, lecture-halls and classrooms, formerly used for the purposes of the College should revert to their original use and be placed at the disposal of University College.'[47] This required the relocation of government offices currently based in the college buildings, retaining accommodation only for the state services for agricultural and chemical testing which could not easily be housed elsewhere. MacNeill's lobbying enjoyed strong support within the government, not least from McGilligan, who was also a lecturer in UCD. The Cabinet agreed on 26 August 1924 that the buildings and equipment of the College of Science would be handed over to the Department of Education, 'to be placed at the disposal of the Governor of University College, Dublin.'[48]

Yet the Department of Finance, which was responsible for the preparation of legislation, showed no great urgency in bringing forward a Bill to finalise the transfer of the college's functions to the NUI. Despite powerful voices within the Cabinet promoting the initiative, no bill materialised for almost two years after the Executive Council decision, An impatient McGilligan appealed to Cosgrave on 17 September 1925 to prod Finance into action; noting that the Bill had been 'promised again and again', he commented that 'seeing that Executive Council decision on this was announced eighteen months ago I do not feel that I am asking too much in pressing for the Bill required to carry out that decision.'[49] This official inertia may have been influenced by a political crisis which engulfed the government and particularly MacNeill, in 1925, but is more likely to have reflected the department's preoccupation with balancing the books, which required stringent examination of any new initiative, however modest. Michael MacDunphy, assistant secretary to the government, applied gentle pressure to his counterpart in Finance, in November 1925 seeking a report on the legislation.[50] Finance's response suggested that while the department was not opposed to the policy, it was determined to progress the initiative at its own pace. Leon McAuley told MacDunphy on 11 November that the 'whole question of the College of Science—a very complicated matter— has been under consideration for some time past in this Department…' and while his department was now in a position to take it up with the Department of Education, it was 'too soon, however, to say when a Bill can be introduced.'[51]

MacNeill was forced to resign as Minister for Education in November 1925, following his ill-fated participation in the Boundary Commission whose report was a devastating setback to the Free State government. This setback permanently derailed his political career but did not halt the momentum for the transfer of the College of Science. The initiative was supported by John Marcus O'Sullivan, MacNeill's successor and fellow UCD professor, McGilligan and Cosgrave himself. The president's office was influential in securing a draft bill from the Department of Finance. The University Education (Agricultural and Dairy Science) Bill was eventually approved by the Executive Council in June 1926.[52] The legislation provided for the transfer of the land and buildings of the College of Science and the Albert Agricultural College to UCD; the incorporation of most functions of the College of Science within UCD and the creation of a new faculty of dairy science for UCC.[53] Although several TDs, including the Labour deputy leader and Mayo deputy T. J. O'Connell, complained that UCG was being excluded, the legislation was rapidly approved by the Oireachtas in the summer of 1926.[54]

The closure of the College of Science removed one of the few significant institutions offering higher technical education in pre-independence Ireland. The initiative created unanticipated problems for the newly created technical instruction branch of the Department of Education, which could no longer rely upon the advice and assistance of the professional staff in a college under the direct control of the state, in developing science syllabuses at post-primary level or training science teachers.[55] Not all departmental officials agreed with the disappearance of the college and the technical instruction branch mourned the loss of a valuable public resource. Moreover, barely a year later, the report of the Commission on Technical Education made thinly veiled criticisms of the decision to close the College of Science, highlighting the deficits in the specialised expertise available to the department in scientific education and particularly in researching the interface between schools and the labour market: 'The Department can no longer command this valuable assistance,… and it has no facilities whatsoever for the scientific investigation of any industrial problem.'[56] But there was overwhelming political support for the transfer of the college's functions to the NUI. The initiative was consistent with national policies, particularly upgrading the status of agricultural studies within the university and was easily justified by appeals to Ireland's bucolic destiny as a 'rural civilisation'.

The predominant ideological paradigm of the early Irish state also dictated a limited role for the government in providing education, which was largely delegated at all levels to autonomous institutions aided by the state. The initiative reflected open hostility among the new political elite to institutions which were associated with the discredited imperial administration and most of all delineated a pervasive and highly influential bias in favour of academic education in a university setting over specialised vocational or technical training.

'…The Failure to Develop that Systematic Technical Training Which Is Recognised…as an Essential Factor of Industrial Success'

The preoccupations of the Free State government in education revolved around Gaelicisation and curriculum reform to establish the primacy of the Irish language. Yet innovative approaches to technical and vocational education were advanced with varying degrees of success by the Commission on Technical Education, established by the government in September 1926 to 'enquire into and advise upon the system of Technical Education in Saorstat Eireann in relation to the requirements in trade and industry.'[57] The commission came into being because the Department of Education informed the government that 'the information available to the Department as to the existing and probably future requirements of trade and industry in this country is wholly inadequate…to come to any satisfactory conclusion as to the needs of the country in the matter of Technical Education.'[58] Frustration within the new technical instruction branch, which did not share the traditionalist academic value system dominant among politicians and senior officials, at the lack of data on the relationship between demand for technical education and labour market requirements provided a decisive impetus for establishing the commission. Joseph O'Neill acknowledged in a frank letter to the Executive Council that neither his department nor Industry and Commerce had been able to discover how far trade and industry was held back through the lack of technical training:

'Technical Education' much more than any other form of Education must fit the prospective worker for a specialised occupation and without the governing information indicated above, it is impossible to know how far the existing system or any probably (sic) improvement in it can achieve this purpose.[59]

O'Neill recommended the establishment of a commission to conduct an in-depth investigation of the 'whole problem of technical education in Ireland' with a particular focus on the present or future needs of industry and commerce. The Free State Cabinet approved the establishment of a broadly based commission, containing departmental nominees from Education, Finance, Industry and Commerce and Agriculture and two TDs, John Good and Hugh Colahan, representing employers and trade unions respectively. The commission also included unusually strong external representation for an Irish official enquiry during this period, with the appointment of two academic experts, Dr. Arthur Rohn, president of the federal polytechnicum, Zurich and Nils Fredriksson of the Swedish Board of Education.[60] The two academics were chosen (almost certainly at the instigation of the technical instruction branch) because Sweden and Switzerland were smaller European countries which had pioneered the introduction of higher technical institutions of a comparable status and standard to universities. The senior inspector of the technical instruction branch, John Ingram, was also the chairman of the commission and the branch was deeply engaged in the formulation of the recommendations.

The commission was instrumental in the most significant structural innovation by the new state in education, the establishment of a new public system of vocational schools offering 'continuation' courses in practical skills for young people aged fourteen to sixteen.[61] Yet its report, presented with notable efficiency in October 1927, extended well beyond vocational schools and also included a highly critical analysis of higher technical education. Opening their critique by stating that the importance of higher technical education 'has not in our opinion been sufficiently realised in the Saorstát,' the commission left no doubt about the consequences of neglecting higher level technical and scientific courses, identifying a lack of appreciation among business and commercial occupations of the value of technical education and not coincidentally, 'the failure to develop that systematic technical training which is recognised, in other countries, as an essential factor of industrial success.'[62] The Irish state was compared unfavourably to Switzerland, where the Federal Institute of Technology offered third level education in a wide range of technical disciplines and 'may be regarded as a technical University…'[63] Similarly, Sweden had two technical institutes 'of university standard'—the Royal Technical School in Stockholm and the Chalmers Institute of Technology in Gothenburg.[64] Moreover, the commission highlighted the vital part played by graduates of higher technical institutions in achieving successful industrial development: 'Although others may contribute materially to this development, the motive force in the economic advance of a country will be supplied by those who possess the highest scientific and technological qualifications.'[65] This was a radical message in post-independence Ireland, especially coupled with the commission's implicit criticism of the closure of the Royal College of Science. It was not surprising that much of it fell on deaf ears within the political and official elite.

The commission offered only three recommendations on higher technical education, but each involved a fundamental re-appraisal of existing policies. Firstly, they advocated 'the continuance and wide development of the work which has hitherto been the function of the Royal College of Science…'—ensuring that courses of university standard were available in scientific disciplines 'to produce leaders in technical education, more especially on the scientific side.'[66] The commission envisaged both higher level courses in engineering and applied chemistry and more systematic professional training for teachers of science and technology. They argued that if science and engineering courses of this type were not delivered in future by the universities, 'the re-establishment of a separate institute for this purpose will have to be seriously considered.'[67] While couched in diplomatic language, this was one of the most far-reaching recommendations of the commission, challenging traditionalist understandings of the university and implicitly criticising the government's decision to give the universities a monopoly on higher level engineering and scientific courses.

Their other recommendations also had a transformative potential for the existing post-compulsory courses of technical education in Dublin, Cork and Limerick. The commission sought full-time day courses of 'secondary technical character', extending for three years after the Intermediate Certificate. These higher second level technical courses were intended to produce managers with scientific expertise and train teachers for the vocational schools. The commission proposed a similar expansion of commercial courses at upper second level in the technical institutes in Cork and Rathmines.[68] A noticeable feature of the report was its broad definition of higher technical education, which encompassed recognisably third level disciplines within the College of Science, professional teacher training and post-compulsory, senior cycle courses.

The commission's recommendations on higher technical education, while much less extensive than their detailed treatment of junior cycle vocational courses, were even more radical and proved to be far ahead of their time. Their recommendations diverged sharply from the narrower priorities of the Free State government, focused on the development of agriculture insofar as they acknowledged science at all. It would be another forty years before an Irish government accepted a report from another expert group for the creation of regional technical colleges, incorporating elements of the commission's recommendations, although on a dramatically increased scale. There was no meaningful support among politicians or senior civil servants (outside the technical instruction branch) in the first decade of the independent state for the revival of a separate third-level institution offering technological courses or for a significant upgrading of senior cycle technical education.

The major legacy of the commission was the Vocational Education Act, 1930, which provided for the creation of the vocational schools as a distinct second-level strand under the control of the Vocational Education Committees (VECs). Yet even at second level the scope and potential of the vocational sector was restricted by an agreement between the government and the Catholic bishops. O'Sullivan gave assurances to the Catholic hierarchy in October 1930 that the vocational schools would provide continuation and technical education of a strictly practical character: they would not provide general education, which would continue to be given in primary and secondary schools.[69]

Successive governments until the 1960s maintained the 'practical' character of the sector, which was guaranteed by the Vocational Education Act and the minister's assurances to the hierarchy.[70] Vocational school students were denied access to the Intermediate and Leaving Certificate examinations and restricted to a two-year continuation course leading to the Day Group Certificate until 1963. The restrictions imposed by the state helped to ensure that the status of the vocational system was vastly inferior to the prestige enjoyed by the private secondary schools.

Technical education at higher level, involving higher-level certificate or diploma courses or attainment of professionally recognised qualifications in technical subjects, remained much more underdeveloped than the vocational sector, which whatever its limitations, developed into a national system of schools: facilities for higher technical education simply did not exist in most areas of the country. The large majority of students pursuing higher level technical courses were concentrated in the colleges offered by the CDVEC up to the 1960s.[71] The opportunities for further education or technical training for most vocational school students outside the major urban centres were poor to non-existent. The only institutions offering courses in higher level technical education outside Dublin were the Crawford Municipal Technical Institute in Cork and a centre specialising in hotel management in Shannon: there were none at all serving rural areas. The development of higher technical studies was limited even in Dublin, which had the strongest tradition of technical education. The City of Dublin VEC, which took over responsibility for the technical institutes in Dublin from 1930, sought to expand the scope of higher technical courses in the city, with mixed results. The VEC, with Louis Ely O'Carroll, the former principal of Kevin St. technical institute as its chief executive, shared similar ambitions to the commission on technical education. A board of studies, led by O'Carroll and consisting of the principals of the five technical institutes within the city, was established in the early 1930s to advise the VEC, offering leadership and oversight for the colleges.[72]

A committee of the board developed an ambitious vision for the upgrading of technical education at both second and higher level in the city of Dublin. The board's report to the VEC in 1936 proposed the upgrading of the five technical institutes to incorporate a greater higher level component, involving the award of diplomas for approved programmes of study, alongside continuing second level courses.[73] The committee's blueprint proposed 'five central schools of specialisation' in the metropolitan area, located 'on principal thoroughfares, convenient of access from all the main residential districts in the Borough Area.'[74] Among other plans, the technical school in Kevin St. was to be relocated and redesignated as a College of Technology; the Rathmines technical institute would become a High School of Commerce, with its programmes in a city centre location and an upgraded School of Domestic Science would be established in a new building at Cathal Brugha St.[75] Two new regional technical schools based in the north west and south west of the city were also envisaged.[76] The centrally based colleges were intended to provide higher level courses accredited by the relevant professional bodies in various disciplines and professional courses for the training of teachers in science and technology.[77] Another key aspiration of the report was that the colleges were to develop an industrial research function for the first time.

The board's ambitious vision received cautious support from the Department of Education, which acknowledged 'a valuable report dealing with present and future accommodation requirements...'[78] But the plan faced formidable practical obstacles, not least the fiscal stringency imposed by the government during the economic depression and the second world war. Duff et al. in their official history of DIT, commented that 'circumstances changed and World War II intervened.'[79] Yet the challenge for the VEC was more that circumstances did not change at all. The parsimonious government funding of higher education was remarkably consistent throughout this period. The fiscal and social conservatism which shaped government priorities in education militated against significant investment in higher education generally and even more in technical education. The inferior place of vocational education in a society which placed a high value on professional status, academic learning and religious formation imposed sharp constraints on the ambitions of the VEC. The post-independence political and administrative elite with few exceptions regarded higher level courses as the preserve of the university and technical institutes as venues for vocational training.

The grand design of the board of studies made only limited progress over the following two decades and the more ambitious elements of its plan largely fell by the wayside. One of the few significant recommendations to be implemented was the establishment of St. Mary's College in Domestic Science in June 1941 as the first recognised third level college under CDVEC auspices.[80] Teacher training in home economics was a key function of the new college, although it also offered courses in hotel management and culinary training. The college in Cathal Brugha St. offered a three year diploma for domestic science teachers, taking over the functions performed previously by the Department of Education's training school in Kilmacud, which closed in 1941.[81] When the domestic science training courses were transferred to St. Angela's training college, Sligo, ten years later by agreement between CDVEC and the department, the college in Cathal Brugha St. became a centre of training for the hotel and catering industry.

Yet this rapid development of the board's blueprint proved exceptional. The VEC colleges were engaged mainly in a range of second level technical courses, part-time adult education leading to external professional or university examinations and apprenticeship training in this period, rather than embarking on new ventures in higher level diplomas where demand was uncertain and official support limited. The Apprenticeship Act, 1931 was based entirely on 'the principle of voluntary co-operation' by employers and trade unions and achieved extremely limited results.[82] The legislation was used to set up apprenticeship committees only in four craft trades which voluntarily put themselves within the scope of the legislation; committees for hairdressing and furniture making operated only in Dublin, while two other committees in painting and decorating and brush and broom manufacture had a national remit.[83] The impact of the committees on the education of apprentices was limited and the legislation itself was acknowledged as 'defective' by the Department of Industry and Commerce a generation later in 1958.[84]

CDVEC succeeded in developing relationships with craft trades despite the shortcomings of the legislation. Apprenticeship was an important focus of the Kevin St. institute, which offered training for electrical apprentices for the Electricity Supply Board (ESB) and established a new apprenticeship scheme for the bakery trade in the late 1930s.[85] The institute also offered a variety of courses leading to the external examinations of the City and Guilds of London Institute and the B.Sc. in the University of London, as well as a pre-university course in applied science which prepared students for the matriculation examinations of the NUI.[86] Kevin St. expanded its full-time programmes in science and engineering during the 1950s, offering post-compulsory education serving an eclectic range of occupations, including pharmacists, opticians and radio operators.[87] The development of the institute's full time courses and CDVEC's ambitions to expand its portfolio of higher level technician courses was reflected in its redesignation as a college of technology at the end of the 1950s.

The school in Parnell Square became a centre for apprenticeship training in the retail distribution trades, developing courses from 1949 attended by apprentices on day release leading to apprentice diploma and certificate awards.[88] The institute in Bolton St. also established a strong engagement with apprenticeship, especially through day release schemes in engineering and construction, while also maintaining a junior cycle technical school. Higher level studies began to develop more fully after the second world war, particularly due to the demand to prepare students for examinations of professional bodies in architecture, quantity surveying and engineering.[89] The Rathmines technical institute expanded its enrolment during the 1940s, but its focus remained mainly second level in this period, with a majority of its students pursuing full-time continuation education courses in general or business studies.[90] Yet like its counterparts the institute began to expand its higher level diploma provision during the late 1950s, beginning with evening part-time courses preparing candidates for the examinations of professional bodies in accountancy, banking and management.

Most of the VEC colleges by the late 1950s had developed a 'vertical' academic structure in which education in the principal disciplines was offered in distinct departments at all levels from craft training to professional diploma courses. The CDVEC valued this institutional structure on the basis that it offered an 'impetus to ambition provided by the continuous ladder...' for progression; a range of staff expertise within a single school and a 'fruitful interpenetration of craft and technology in the vital technician area…'[91] Yet this structure had developed more by accident than design, as the CDVEC accommodated the requirements for apprenticeship training particularly from craft trades and in the postwar period took advantage of the increasing demand for preparatory courses leading to certification by professional bodies.

The development of the CDVEC colleges fell well short of the ambitious vision sketched out by the board of studies in 1936. But the achievement of the colleges in this period should not be underestimated. They operated in a conservative society, which gave a privileged status to academic education for the professions, public service and white collar employment. This status differential was compounded by the reluctance of political and official elites to invest in higher education in any meaningful way. Yet the colleges were reasonably successful in developing a distinctive niche through collaboration with employers and industrial trades in training for the labour market. Most of the colleges by the 1950s offered an eclectic combination of apprenticeship training, second level technical courses and increasingly higher level certificate or diploma programmes. The aspirations set out in the 1936 report were never completely abandoned and several were realised in very different circumstances during the following generation.

The technical institutes occupied an ambivalent position in the early postwar period. Such institutions offered post-compulsory, higher level courses in an increasing variety of disciplines outside the traditional universities. Yet avenues for entry to higher technical colleges were limited and uneven, while systems for accreditation and recognition of their programmes remained inconsistent, fragmented and often linked to external bodies outside Ireland. The underdevelopment of higher technical education was no accident. It was the logical consequence of a traditionalist consensus in Irish education, shared by ministers, officials and prominent private stakeholders, for the first generation of the independent Irish state. A dominant ideological paradigm informed by religious and cultural nationalist imperatives placed a minimal value on vocational and technical studies, emphasising the primacy of religion, the humanities, classical studies and the Irish language. This ideology helped to shape a conservative consensus, characterised by a timid approach to policy formation on the part of the Department of Education and a general deference towards the powerful religious interests within the educational system, particularly the Catholic Church. Higher technical education did not feature at all in the traditionalist discourse of political and official elites and the underdevelopment of technical and vocational education, a defining feature of the Irish educational sector since the 1920s, was particularly marked at higher level.

Notes

1. Brian Kelham, 'The Royal College of Science for Ireland (1867–1926),' *Studies: An Irish Quarterly Review* 56, no. 223 (Autumn 1967): 297–309; Commission on Technical Education, Report (Dublin: Stationery Office, 1927), 1–2.
2. Commission on Technical Education, 33.
3. Ibid., 2.
4. Jim Cooke, *A History of the Irish Vocational Education Association 1902–2002* (Dublin: IVEA, 2009), 12–13.
5. Thomas Duff, Joe Hegarty, and Matthew Hussey, *The Story of the Dublin Institute of Technology* (Book Gallery: 2000), 4, http://arrow.dit.ie/ditpress/1. Accessed 2 May 2016.
6. Commission on Technical Education, 2.
7. Ibid.
8. Lyons, *Ireland Since the Famine*, 211.
9. Commission on Technical Education, 6; this was the description applied to them by the Commission thirty years later.
10. Ibid.
11. Ibid., 8.
12. Cooke, *A History*, 15.
13. Commission on Technical Education, 7; Lyons, *Ireland Since the Famine*, 213.
14. Commission on Technical Education, 9–10.
15. Ibid.
16. Ibid., 10.
17. Duff et al., *Dublin Institute of Technology*, 6.
18. Commission on Technical Education, 9–10.

19. Ibid.; Lyons, *Ireland Since the Famine*, 214; Duff et al., *Dublin Institute of Technology*, 6.
20. Duff et al., *Dublin Institute of Technology*, 6.
21. Ibid., 10.
22. Ibid., 8–9.
23. Ibid., 8–9.
24. Ibid., 9; the technical school was based first at 12 Rutland Square and then 18 Rutland Square from 1912 (Rutland Square was renamed Parnell Square from 1933).
25. Commission on Technical Education, 29; Duff et al., *Dublin Institute of Technology*, 10.
26. Commission on Technical Education, 29.
27. Ibid., 30.
28. Ibid., 30.
29. Duff et al., *Dublin Institute of Technology*, 7.
30. Ibid., 7.
31. Ibid., 9.
32. Commission on Technical Education, 33.
33. Ibid.
34. Ibid.
35. G. C. Ashlin to Walsh, 29 January 1909 (DDA NUI I/6).
36. Dublin Commission, Minutes, 29 December 1910 (DDA NUI 34), 3.
37. Minutes, Queen's University Senate, vol. 1.1, 26 February 1910, 5–6.
38. Minutes, Queen's University Senate, vol. 1.1, 14 October 1910, 1–2; Minutes, Queen's University Senate, vol. 1.1, 14 December 1910, Appendix 3, Jaffé to Senate, 5 December 1910, 5–6.
39. Commission on Technical Education, 33; Minutes, Queen's University Senate, 14 December 1910, Appendix 3, Jaffé to Senate, 5 December 1910, 5–6.
40. *Irish Times*, 'College of Science Closed: Building Taken over by the Government,' 21 October 1922.
41. *Irish Times*, 'Science Students' Difficulty,' 18 October 1922.
42. Ibid.
43. Dáil Debates, vol. 1, no. 23, col. 1654, 18 October 1922.
44. Dail Debates, vol. 8, no. 14, col. 1613, 17 July 1924.
45. Ó Dubain to Michael MacDunphy, 8 May 1924 (NAI TSCH/3/S3780).
46. Dáil Debates, vol. 8, no. 10, col. 1052, 11 July 1924.

47. Ó Dubain to MacDunphy, 23 August 1924 (NAI TSCH/3/S3780).
48. Assistant Secretary to the Government to MacNeill, 27 August 1924.
49. McGilligan to Cosgrave, 17 September 1925 (NAI TSCH/3/S3780).
50. MacDunphy to Leon McAuley, 9 November 1925.
51. McAuley to MacDunphy, 11 November 1925.
52. *Decision of the Executive Council:* 2/270—Item No. 4, 9 June 1926 (NAI TSCH/3/S3780).
53. University Education (Agriculture and Dairy Science) Bill, 1926 (NAI TSCH/3/S3780).
54. MacDunphy to T. M. Healy, 17 July 1926 (NAI TSCH/3/S3780).
55. Commission on Technical Education, 33.
56. Ibid.
57. Joseph O'Neill to Secretary, Executive Council, 18 September 1926 (NAI TSCH 3/S5001).
58. Joseph O'Neill to Secretary, Executive Council, 29 May 1926 (NAI TSCH 3/S5001).
59. Ibid.
60. Seán MacGiolla Fhaoláin to Secretary, Executive Council, 29 July 1926 (NAI TSCH 3/S5001).
61. Commission on Technical Education, 145.
62. Ibid., 106.
63. Ibid., 106–7.
64. Ibid., 107.
65. Ibid., 106.
66. Ibid., 108.
67. Ibid., 108.
68. Ibid., 108.
69. J. M. O'Sullivan to Dr. D. Keane, 31 October 1930, in *Irish Educational Documents*, vol. 2, ed. Aine Hyland and Kenneth Milne (Dublin: CICE, 1992), 219–22.
70. Seán O'Connor, *A Troubled Sky: Reflections on the Irish Educational Scene* (Dublin: Educational Research Centre, 1986), 28–29.
71. Government of Ireland, *Investment in Education. Report of the Survey Team Appointed by the Minister for Education in October 1962* (Dublin: Stationery Office, 1965), 4.
72. Duff et al., *Dublin Institute of Technology*, 13–14.
73. *Report of the Department of Education 1935–36* (Dublin: 1937), 69–70.
74. Ibid.

75. Ibid.
76. Ibid., 70.
77. Duff et al., *Dublin Institute of Technology*, 14.
78. *Report of the Department of Education 1935–36*, 69.
79. Duff et al., *Dublin Institute of Technology*, 14–15.
80. *Irish Times*, 'Dublin's New College of Domestic Science,' 17 June 1941.
81. Duff et al., *Dublin Institute of Technology*, 26–27; Coolahan, *Towards an Era of Lifelong Learning*, 82.
82. Minister for Industry and Commerce, *Memorandum for the Government, Proposals for Amendment of the Law Relating to Apprenticeship*, 7 June 1958 (NAI TSCH 3/S2402B), 4; *Dáil Debates*, vol. 177, col. 77, 21 October 1959; *Dáil Debates*, vol. 177, col. 377, 28 October 1959.
83. *Report of the Department of Education 1935–36*, 110; *Memorandum for the Government, Proposals for Amendment of the Law Relating to Apprenticeship*, 7 June 1958 (NAI TSCH 3/S2402B), 17–18.
84. Ibid., 4.
85. Duff et al., *Dublin Institute of Technology*, 17.
86. Ibid., 17–18.
87. Ibid., 18.
88. Ibid., 23–4.
89. Ibid., 25–6.
90. Ibid., 22.
91. HEA, *Report on the Ballymun Project,* Appendix II: City of Dublin Vocational Education Committee, 'Memo to the Higher Education Authority' (Dublin: HEA, 1972), 3.

5

Ministers, Bishops and Teachers

The emergence of state-aided but denominationally managed institutions for the training of national school teachers by 1900 testified to an equally significant but less visible accommodation between the Irish administration and the major churches in Ireland which preceded the university settlement. The commissioners for national education had established a public, non-denominational teacher training college in Marlborough St., which was linked to the model schools established by the national board as centres of teacher training from the mid nineteenth century. But non-denominational teacher education confronted insurmountable obstacles in nineteenth century Ireland, due to the opposition on very different grounds of both the Catholic bishops (who sought denominational teacher training institutions funded by the state) and the Church of Ireland authorities (who largely favoured separate denominational schooling).[1] The Irish administration gradually abandoned the embryonic public system for training teachers in the late 1800s, particularly after the Powis Commission in 1870 accepted the case by the Catholic bishops for state aid to denominational teacher training colleges.[2] The first Catholic college for male national teachers, St. Patrick's Teacher Training School in Drumcondra, was founded in

© The Author(s) 2018
J. Walsh, *Higher Education in Ireland, 1922–2016*,
https://doi.org/10.1057/978-1-137-44673-2_5

1875 under the direction of the Vincentian order. The first Catholic college for women candidates was founded by the Sisters of Mercy, first in
Baggot St. but later established at Carysfort College, Blackrock.[3]

The Irish administration agreed in 1883 to offer recognition to the
major non-vested training colleges, including St. Patrick's, Carysfort and
the Kildare Place College, overseen by the Church of Ireland.[4] The voluntary colleges received annual capitation grants from the board under
the Balfour scheme from 1890.[5] This decision completed a fundamental shift in policy towards state support for denominational, church-run
teacher training institutions. The acceptance of the scheme by both the
Catholic bishops and Church of Ireland General Synod was crucial to its
success.[6] The scheme led to the inauguration of the Church of Ireland
Training College in 1884 as a denominational training college financed
by the state, albeit including within its walls a 'non-government' college
for the training of teachers for the church which did not receive state
aid.[7] The public training college at Marlborough St., which was 'the
sole survivor of the National Board's grand plan for a nondenomina-
tional system of teacher education', continued to operate on this basis
but mainly served Presbyterian students up to 1922.[8] Teacher training
for elementary schools was provided from the late 1800s by state-aided,
denominational institutions under the auspices of the Catholic bishops
or the Church of Ireland, as the state's previous role in providing teacher
education was diluted and ultimately abandoned, in 'a major strategic
victory for the Catholic church'.[9]

Five Catholic colleges for the training of lay national teachers were
recognised by the commissioners, all single-sex institutions administered by religious orders. The De La Salle order established a college for
boys in Waterford from 1891, while St. Mary's College, Belfast served
Catholic women from 1900.[10] Mary Immaculate College, Limerick,
was founded in 1901 at the instigation of the local bishop, Edward
O'Dwyer, as 'a Training College for Female national School Teachers for
the Catholic religion', operated by the Sisters of Mercy.[11] Not all religious institutions entered the public system. The Christian Brothers
established St. Mary's college in Marino, as a 'senior novitiate' offering
teacher training to new members of the order, alongside their headquar-
ters in Ireland in November 1905.[12] St. Mary's was a private college

offering training at both primary and secondary levels for the first twenty years of its existence, as the Christian Brothers remained aloof from the national system until the 1920s.[13]

Candidates for the publicly funded colleges until 1910 included untrained assistant or principal teachers seeking official qualifications who followed a one year course and candidates for teaching who undertook a two year course. The younger age cohort included monitors (students at senior level in national schools who assisted with teaching younger pupils); pupil teachers recruited from the secondary schools and candidates for training selected through the King's Scholarship examinations overseen by the national board at Easter.[14] Successful completion of the two year course was required for all entrants to the colleges from 1910.[15] While the training colleges were privately administered and denominational, they were also subject to official oversight by the commissioners, who determined their admission procedures, level of enrolments, curriculum and financing.[16] This state-aided, church-run model established an enduring precedent for teacher education in the twentieth century.

The education of primary teachers emerged as a major focus of government action in the early Irish state, not least due to the emergence of Gaelicisation as a key policy imperative following independence. Following the transfer of power to the Irish Free State in 1922, the system of primary teacher training maintained a high level of continuity with the pre-independence period in terms of ownership and control. Any institutional changes following independence and partition reinforced the denominational, state-aided character of the system. The Marlborough St. college was closed in September 1922; St. Mary's college in Belfast passed under the control of the Stormont administration and Stranmillis college was opened as a non-denominational institution serving the new Northern Ireland state.[17] The Christian Brothers reached a rapprochement with the Free State government, paving the way for the Department of Education to recognise 'Coláiste Oiliúna Mhuire, Marino' in 1929 for the award of the two-year diploma for primary school teaching.[18] The most notable policy departures after 1922 were inspired by Gaelicisation, which impinged on primary teacher training more dramatically than any other strand of higher education.

The training of secondary and vocational teachers did not acquire a comparable importance, mainly because only 7% of children proceeded beyond primary education as late as 1932.[19] The Department for Education had no formal function in the training of most secondary teachers and minimum qualifications for the profession were set by the Registration Council established in 1918 under the Intermediate Education (Ireland) Act, 1914.[20] Among the requirements for registration were a university degree and 'a recognised diploma or qualification obtained after a satisfactory course of training in the theory and practice of education…'[21] Schools of education in all four university colleges offered the Higher Diploma in Education from the early twentieth century, usually as a one year course following a degree programme. While the H. Dip was 'nominally full-time', it was usually completed as a part-time course, had a poor reputation among many former students and was frequently criticised by school managers for excessive attention to theory over practice.[22] More significantly, registration was not required to secure employment in schools and almost 50% of secondary teachers were unregistered during the first three decades of the new state, testifying to the lack of public oversight of secondary teacher education.[23] The schools of education were poorly staffed and did not enjoy a high status within the universities: the Commission on Higher Education acknowledged their peripheral status as late as 1967 when it warned that "…education should not be regarded as the 'poor relation' of university studies".[24]

Training for vocational teachers varied widely not only in the content and duration of programmes but in entry requirements and qualifications received by students.[25] While the department was active in organising a range of training courses for different categories of vocational teachers, often through the VECs, no comprehensive plan was introduced and a significant minority of teachers, including university graduates, were not required to receive any formal training.[26] Teachers of general subjects were required to have a degree, while teachers of specialist subjects, usually identified as 'manual instructors', required a specific qualification in their subject.[27] The most consistent efforts by the department related to fluency in Irish. The Teastas Múinteoira Gaeilge, based on a one month summer course in oral Irish and teaching methods, was introduced for teachers of general subjects from 1932, while the Céard Teastas, a qualification indicating ability to teach through Irish, became compulsory for all vocational teachers.[28] The first course for woodwork instructors was held in the Metropolitan School of Art in 1925, while a more substantial programme later extending to eighteen months was offered in Bolton St. technical school from 1937.[29] The CDVEC also provided an eighteen month training course for instructors in metalwork at Ringsend Technical institute from 1937–38. A number of courses for manual instructors were later extended to two years and offered in Coláiste Charman in Gorey, Co. Wexford.[30] The Crawford Municipal Technical Institute in Cork provided training for rural and general science teachers from 1937, arranging for students to undertake a second year of their course in UCC.[31] This later developed into a three year rural science course organised by the department, in conjunction with the City of Cork VEC and UCC.[32]

Government activism in primary teacher training conformed to a wider pattern of development in Western European states, where state intervention was more significant, at least initially, in non-university institutions with a vocational or professional training mission.[33] The first decade of the new state saw major policy changes to serve the overarching national project of reviving the Irish language. A departmental memorandum at the end of the decade noted that the department undertook 'a complete reform of the Training College curriculum'.[34] Irish became a compulsory subject for entry to the training colleges and an essential qualification for national school teachers. A new programme for the training colleges in 1923 made Irish a compulsory subject, while the colleges were expected not only to adapt rapidly to teaching Irish but to produce a bilingual teaching profession.[35] The system for recruiting national school teachers was transformed. Entry to the colleges by monitors was terminated in 1925 and the King's scholarship examinations were first renamed as the Easter entrance examinations and then replaced from 1931.[36] An 'open competition' was introduced, based on a combination of preliminary tests at Easter in oral Irish, music and needlework (for girls) as a prerequisite for admission and assessment of Leaving Certificate results.[37] This remained a key element of the selection process until 1959. The 'open' process saw a high level of competition for entry, mainly drawing upon secondary school leavers who performed well in the examinations.[38] A revised teacher training programme was introduced by the department in 1932–33, which gave greater emphasis to professional components of the course, moving away from a dual focus on general academic studies and professional practice.[39] The revised programme also required colleges to give students experience of teaching practice in a number of national schools rather than the previous approach of using a single 'practising school' linked to a particular college.[40]

The most influential departure launched by the Free State in teacher training was the establishment of preparatory colleges which would 'reform the Training Colleges at the foundation by ensuring that the candidates for these Colleges shall have received a thoroughly sound secondary education.'[41] Departmental officials aimed to replace the discredited monitorial system with a new system of entry to the training colleges to establish secondary education as a baseline for entry and provide a reliable supply of Irish speaking candidates for training. The department proposed seven residential colleges conducted through Irish, providing free secondary education for students aged 13 and over for four years leading up to entry to the training colleges.[42] The departmental plan claimed to 'tap a source of supply hitherto largely neglected, viz. the children of the primary schools in the Gaeltacht, whose people have not sufficient means to enable them to pay for their children's education beyond the National School course.'[43] Yet the initiative was not motivated by egalitarianism and the benefits offered to poor families in the Gaeltacht were largely incidental. As the department's report for 1926–27 noted: '…it was decided to set up a number of Preparatory Colleges which would provide for clever boys and girls desirous of becoming teachers and other clever boys and girls with a good knowledge of Irish, a sound secondary education on Irish lines…, with the advantages of a collective school life lived in an atmosphere of Gaelic tradition.'[44] The official memo justified the new initiative on the basis that the colleges would not only remedy a shortage of male teachers but provide an ideal institutional setting to prepare candidates for training:

> These Colleges will provide a school…sufficiently large to permit the advantages of a collective life and the influence of the formative elements with youthful companionship in work, a school in which the young

candidates for the profession will be assembled in distinct homogeneous groups so that their teaching and training may be constantly inspired by the special purpose in view.[45]

The memo underlined official concern to exert a high level of control over candidates entering the teaching profession, allied to the positioning of teaching as an ideological vocation, not unlike the religious life. The prime motivation for the creation of the colleges was to provide a consistent supply of primary teachers competent to teach through Irish and underpin Gaelicisation of the training colleges.

The Free State government approved the departmental plan on 11 February 1926.[46] The department swiftly established six preparatory colleges for Catholic candidates between 1926 and 1929, including five in Gaeltacht areas. Three of the colleges catered for boys and three for girls; all six were delegated to the management of religious orders.[47] Although the government initially considered establishing a non-denominational college in Dublin, this proposal was opposed by the Church of Ireland authorities, led by John Gregg, archbishop of Dublin: instead the department offered a co-educational preparatory college under the control of the Church of Ireland.[48] Although Gregg was opposed to compulsory Irish, he collaborated with the department in establishing the new college to secure the prospects of Protestant teachers and safeguard the Church of Ireland training college, which struggled to attract candidates with a sufficient knowledge of Irish.[49] Coláiste Moibhi was founded in 1927 under the patronage of the Church of Ireland archbishop, initially on Moibhi Road, Glasnevin.[50] Coláiste Moibhi was effectively a gateway to CITC and as Relihan comments served for the following sixty years as 'a mainstay for CITC in the provision of candidates suitably qualified in the Irish language.'[51]

The Department of Education made substantial concessions to the new college to facilitate the co-option of the Church of Ireland in the crusade for Gaelicisation. The normally strict entry requirements in Irish were diluted for Coláiste Moibhi and it was the only college where entrance examination papers were presented in English.[52] When the preparatory college transferred from Glasnevin to new premises at the former Royal Hibernian Military School in the Phoenix Park seven years later, the acquisition of the property was facilitated by the department and its new building was financed by the state.[53] Both Gregg and de Valera were present at the formal opening on 8 May 1934, which showcased the pragmatic accommodation between the government and the Church of Ireland. Gregg paid tribute to the 'courtesy and goodwill' displayed by the government in establishing Coláiste Moibhi, noting that 'the Education Department had agreed to its foundation with the greatest readiness and goodwill…'[54] De Valera in turn declared that his presence at the opening was 'proof that the Government regarded the work of that College as of special importance.'[55] If this display of harmony carefully obscured the differences between the state and Church of Ireland over the Irish language policy, nevertheless the outcome served the interests of both parties. Coláiste Moibhi proved the most enduring of the preparatory colleges, surviving various policy changes until the 1990s and ironically outlasting the high tide of the Irish language crusade.

The reformed system of recruitment adopted from 1931 combined preferential access for preparatory college students to the training colleges with the open competition.[56] Preparatory college students were allowed entry without further competition, provided they fulfilled minimum Leaving Certificate requirements.[57] The department envisaged that half of the intake to the training colleges would be drawn from the preparatory colleges[58]: this proportion would be regularly exceeded over the following generation. The department also established a revised pupil-teacher scheme in 1926, designed to prepare candidates for entry to the colleges through a two year course undertaken in 'specially selected secondary schools where the instruction is given as far as possible through the medium of Irish.'[59] Pupil-teachers were selected from Intermediate Certificate candidates securing honours in Irish and admitted to the training colleges on passing the Leaving Certificate and a test in oral Irish conducted by the inspectorate.[60] Candidates from the pupil teacher scheme which operated until 1936 ranked next in preference to preparatory college students in terms of entry to teacher training.[61] The training colleges therefore had virtually no input in determining the entry or suitability of their students.

Gaelicisation presented far-reaching challenges to many of the colleges, demanding a realignment of examinations and curricula and an even more significant cultural readjustment. These challenges were particularly marked for CITC, where Irish had never been taught and the majority of its candidates and teachers had no knowledge of the language; the high standard of the revised entrance examination was a potentially insurmountable barrier for Church of Ireland candidates.[62] The Church of Ireland authorities were vociferously opposed to 'compulsory Irish', which did not improve CITC's ability to adapt to the new policy. Yet if its long serving principal, Henry Kingsmill Moore, was tentative in responding to the new dispensation, his successor E. C. Hodges was committed to implementing the language policy on pragmatic grounds, as 'it was incumbent on the college to adjust to the Irish language requirements if it was to survive as an educational establishment.'[63] The college authorities succeeded in negotiating favourable arrangements with the Department of Education, which allowed CITC to devise its own entrance examination in Irish and permitted the college to accept students who were not proficient in Irish.[64] Moreover, the department accepted that Irish would not be used as a medium of instruction in the college, settling for 'marked improvements from year to year' in the students' fluency in the language.[65] Joseph O'Neill, the first secretary of the department and successive ministers were willing to compromise on the stringency of language requirements to reconcile CITC to the new dispensation. CITC was the sole training college open to both genders operating in the Irish state until the 1960s, although its intake was overwhelmingly female for much of this period.

The department in its report for 1927–28 expressed gratification at the advance of Gaelicisation in the colleges, hailing '...the remarkable extension of the use of Irish as a medium of instruction.'[66] Yet the new policy did not command universal acceptance initially, even in the Catholic training colleges. The stringent entrance examination and rapid introduction of Irish as a compulsory subject caused difficulties for students and staff in St. Patrick's College, underlined by high failure rates in final examinations in Irish during the early 1920s.[67] The department attributed such issues to the weak command of Irish among entrants from the Easter scholarship examinations, in which only 7% of papers were taken through Irish in 1927—this was a factor in phasing out these examinations.[68] The introduction of higher and lower courses for Irish in 1925 eased the problem, but did not reconcile all of the professors to the level of compulsion or the department's efforts to enforce Gaelicisation. Some prominent lecturing staff in the college were sceptical of the language revival crusade, notably Revd. E. J. Cullen, its president from 1920 until 1937, who resisted official efforts to make Irish the normal language of instruction.[69] This reluctance contrasted with the greater strength of cultural nationalism in most of the other Catholic colleges. Mary Immaculate rapidly embraced the new policy, as Irish became the established language of the college and all courses were taught through Irish from the early 1930s.[70] The Irish language movement was embraced from the outset by St. Mary's, Marino, where it conformed closely to the ideological orientation of the Christian Brothers; among the order's objections to the national system was the extent of Anglicisation under the commissioners.[71] Irish became the medium of instruction for teaching practice lectures and lecturing staff from the 1920s were expected 'to be sympathetic towards, if not fluent in, the Irish language.'[72] Carysfort also adapted readily to the new dispensation. Although Irish was introduced as a compulsory subject only from 1923, 92% of examination papers were taken entirely in Irish in the summer examinations by 1932 and Irish was used as a medium of instruction from the mid-1930s.[73]

The radical ambitions of the language revival movement provoked a backlash among national teachers, leading to the convening of the second national programme conference in 1925, in which both Catholic and Protestant educators from the training colleges participated. The conference report, which was accepted by the department, recommended a more gradual transition to 'compulsory Irish' and a more measured assessment taking account of aptitudes; among other modifications, the colleges were allowed to introduce higher and lower courses in Irish and English, in the Easter entrance tests and college examinations.[74] The college authorities also pushed back on more extreme plans floated by the department, including a proposal in 1929 that all professors in the training colleges should teach through the medium of Irish or retire from their posts: college representatives led by Cullen successfully resisted this proposal, partly on the grounds that it would be detrimental to the progress of Irish.[75]

The practical impact of Gaelicisation, underpinned by a panoply of state policies which had a far-reaching influence on the training colleges, was sometimes more variable than its advocates hoped. While the preparatory colleges provided a steady stream of Irish-speaking students, policy and practice towards the national language varied even within the Catholic training colleges. The department was satisfied that in the Catholic training colleges 'practically all the work is done through the medium of Irish' by the early 1930s, based on an analysis of examination papers which were almost all taken through Irish.[76] This was a valid if somewhat narrow metric, but the report may have overstated the extent to which Irish became 'the everyday language' of the colleges.[77] Ferriter points out that English was still used as a language of record in St. Patrick's College, including much of the college's correspondence and the teaching practice reports.[78] Carysfort's authorities employed Irish as the medium of instruction for its programme, but English continued to feature in its administration and student life; the college's centenary booklet noted only that Irish 'was being used with increased effect in the social life of the College'.[79] O'Connor notes in her official history of MIC that Irish had become the 'everyday language' of the institution, while the revised programme adopted in 1933 encompassed Irish literature and history as well as study of the language.[80]

The preparatory colleges became the single most important avenue of recruitment to primary teaching for the first generation of the independent state. Entrants from the preparatory colleges and the pupil-teacher schemes comprised 64% of all entrants to the colleges in 1932, compared to 28.3% from the open competition.[81] St. Patrick's College, Drumcondra was dominated from the early 1930s by students from the western seaboard, with a significant intake from the Gaeltacht.[82] Two-thirds of the students as late as the early 1960s were drawn from the counties of the western seaboard, of which Kerry, West Cork, Clare, Galway, Mayo and Donegal were especially strongly represented, with only a handful each year coming from Dublin. This later became a bone of contention for McQuaid who was dissatisfied at the minimal intake of students from his archdiocese.[83] The system was controversial almost from the outset, drawing criticism from the Labour Party, the INTO and even some Catholic bishops.

The authorities of the Catholic training colleges were divided in their views on the preparatory colleges. Fr Killian Kehoe, president of St. Patrick's College (1948–57), informed McQuaid in 1957 that a minority of students were 'here more or less against their will', due to their background in the preparatory colleges. Kehoe underlined a key criticism of the system, which involved a legal contract with the state to enter the teaching profession. The students were '…caught in a financial web spun by the Department of Finance…They are really victims of the system that sent them to us.'[84] His successor, Dr. Donal Cregan (1957–76), shared a similar perspective, arguing that a system which forced students from frequently remote areas on the western seaboard to work in urban schools with large classes created 'a cultural shock' for both teachers and pupils.[85] But the Sisters of Mercy in Carysfort were supportive of the system which they helped to operate—the college's centenary publication noted that 'the Preparatory Colleges Scheme… continued to provide excellent candidates for Our Lady of Mercy College until these colleges were closed…'[86] Similarly, the Christian Brothers operated Coláiste Caoimhin, a Catholic preparatory college for boys in Dublin, until its closure in 1939.[87] Moreover, the Department of Education, particularly led by Derrig, staunchly defended the preparatory colleges and criticisms by union leaders or educational authorities made little impact during the high tide of Gaelicisation. The cultural crusades of the early Irish state had a more dramatic and long-term impact on teacher training than any other strand of higher education.

Yet once the significant curricular and pedagogical changes linked to Gaelicisation were implemented, the Free State government did not seek any fundamental reform of existing institutional relationships and academic structures, which conformed to the pre-independence pattern. A departmental committee which examined the workings of the training colleges in 1929 was narrowly focused on internal administration and financing of the colleges.[88] The main outcomes of this report were a reduction in the annual fixed grants per student from the exchequer, on the grounds of the severe financial situation facing the new state and introduction of revised financing mechanisms in which exchequer grants were calculated based on the approved number of students and the total in residence on each campus.[89] The department showed no interest in taking up proposals made periodically by the INTO or senior professors for an extension of the training course to three years. This proposal was floated by John J. Piggott, professor of education in St. Patrick's Training College, in 1942 and supported by the president, Fr Jerome Twomey, but received no support from senior civil servants.[90] The first wide-ranging official report on teacher education in Ireland did not occur until 1970, when it noted baldly that 'No fundamental changes have taken place in such training generally since the State was founded.'[91]

The INTO began to agitate for university qualifications for teachers during the 1920s. The union's annual congress adopted a resolution in June 1922 seeking a four year training course for primary teachers in conjunction with the universities.[92] The first university-college alliance was the result of an alignment between TCD and CITC at a time when both faced an uncertain future following the world war and the collapse of the traditional political order. The Board of TCD agreed to create a formal institutional relationship with CITC in 1919, allowing its students to attend arts lectures in Trinity while receiving their professional training in Rathmines.[93] Although progress was delayed by objections from the Treasury and the political crisis in Ireland, the scheme was introduced from September 1921. Candidate teachers in CITC were recognised as Trinity students and secured a university diploma in elementary education at the conclusion of the two year training course, when they could proceed to a degree by passing the Senior Freshman TCD examinations which gave access to the final two years of the BA course.[94] This proved a long-term arrangement which survived until 1975 and in a modified form into the twenty-first century.

The Department of Education did not share the INTO's zeal for teachers to secure university degrees, but allowed the NUI senate and Catholic training colleges to develop modest collaborative arrangements. The NUI senate agreed in April 1924 to introduce assessment by college professors in conjunction with the final year training college examinations, allowing students who succeeded in this common examination an exemption from the first year arts courses and examinations in the NUI.[95] The senate considered this arrangement 'most satisfactory' as it did not require any change in the university statutes and was also acceptable to the department.[96] The outcome for students, however, was much less favourable, as only 17% of the second year students who applied for the first year exemption in 1924 reached the standard set by the NUI examiners; no doubt as a consequence, very few students (51 of 291) applied in 1925 and only 36 reached first year university standard.[97] This solution fell far short of the INTO's demand for a university degree for teachers, which remained a distant aspiration in the early decades of the new state. The department showed no inclination to instigate more intensive linkages between teacher training and the universities, leaving institutions to work out their own ad hoc arrangements.[98]

The institutional regime established in the 1920s, which persisted for over a generation, was based on a close alliance between the state and the church authorities. The management and provision of teacher training was delegated to private, denominational institutions under ecclesiastical management. The day-to-day administration and student discipline of the Catholic training colleges was in the hands of religious orders or clerical managers. But the Department of Education established admission procedures, determined student numbers and approved curricula and examinations. The Departments of Finance and Education approved annually the number of students which each college was 'licensed' to admit.[99] Departmental inspectors conducted the Easter tests; prescribed the college courses, served on the committees which devised training college examinations and inspected the work of the lecturers.[100] They also monitored the efforts of the colleges to expand teaching through the medium of Irish.[101] The colleges never enjoyed autonomy on the Humboldtian model, not least because they served essential functions for both the new state and the church authorities. As O'Donoghue et al. point out, the colleges were 'largely isolated' from other higher education institutions and as residential institutions largely under religious or clerical management maintained a distinctive culture and discipline which prized conformity and respectability.[102] The colleges were positioned as important agents of state policy in terms of Gaelicisation and the wider post-independence project of nation-building. Perhaps even more fundamental to the twentieth century system of teacher training was its function in reproducing the denominational system of national schools which commanded consensus between all the major churches and the state.

The Department of Education responded to a decline in the primary school population which began in 1933–34 by enforcing tight control over the supply of teachers.[103] A regulation requiring women national teachers to retire on marriage was imposed from October 1934, signalling the restrictive direction of government policy. Rule 72 (1) was justified on the basis of a surplus of teachers and fiscal retrenchment in the midst of the world economic depression. Yet traditionalist cultural values about the primary place of women in the home were also influential, which were subsequently reflected in legislation and in the 1937 Constitution.[104] A series of initiatives were taken to restrict the recruitment of teachers during the mid to late 1930s with the explicit rationale of alleviating unemployment among trained teachers, particularly younger men. These included the abolition of the pupil-teacher scheme from 1936 and the withdrawal of privileges previously allowed to teachers trained outside Ireland to qualify for recognition in national schools.[105] The open competition examination and the entry of university graduates to the colleges were suspended from 1938; admission was restricted to students in the preparatory colleges, members of religious communities and untrained temporary teachers who were either teaching religious or native Irish speakers.[106] The number of lay male candidates in the colleges in 1937–38 was only half of the total six years earlier, while the total of lay women in training was reduced by a third from 'the normal number in residence' in 1938–39.[107] The preparatory colleges system was effectively the sole route of entry to teaching for lay candidates between the late 1930s and early 1940s: 62% of entrants to teacher training in 1938 were drawn from the preparatory colleges, with 31% consisting of untrained assistants, mainly members of religious orders.[108] Even more strikingly, only 30 students were admitted to Mary Immaculate in 1940, with 28 drawn from the preparatory colleges.[109] The department's report for 1937–38 noted bluntly that 'the avenues of recruitment for National Teachers have, for all practical purposes, closed.'[110]

The restrictive policies continued throughout the second world war, when the department resorted to even more drastic measures to control teacher supply. The licensed number of students in a training college for men was capped at 135 in 1942–43 and kept at this level in 1943–44, while the comparable level for a training college for women was reduced from 100 in 1942–43 to 80 in 1943–44.[111] Class size did not feature at all in policy decisions in this period. Severe restrictions were imposed on the level of teachers entering training despite very high class sizes in urban areas.[112] The department did not hesitate to curtail the activity of teacher training institutions or even close them temporarily. De La Salle, Waterford, ceased to operate as a general training college for male teachers following a ministerial decision in September 1939, instead becoming a secondary school, although it continued on a modest scale as a training centre for teachers from the De La Salle, Presentation and Marist orders.[113] Coláiste Caoimhin, the preparatory college for boys in Dublin, was closed in 1939, ostensibly on the grounds that it was too distant from the Gaeltacht, but in reality as a further control measure.[114] More significantly, the department decided in 1943 that St. Patrick's College should be closed for the following academic year.[115] The college premises in Drumcondra was occupied for a year by St. Enda's preparatory college, whose normal site in Salthill was taken over for military use by the Department of Defence.[116] Although the college re-opened in September 1945, it did so in a tentative fashion with only 33 students undertaking the first year examination in 1946.[117] Other colleges were also severely restricted. The number of entrants to Carysfort reached its lowest level in 1943 and the college authorities noted that the wartime period was 'a time of much enforced austerity in the College.'[118] It was only at the end of the war that the college was allowed to accept the number of students for which it had accommodation. The temporary closure of St. Patrick's College was the most striking exercise of the department's power in teacher education, but it was only the most drastic in a series of restrictive measures, which underlined the limited influence of the religious managers and still more the teaching staff in the colleges over decisions involving admissions, composition of the student body and even their survival.

The early postwar period saw a transformation in the previously dismal prospects for teacher education. Following an increase in the birth rate from 1942, primary school enrolments in the late 1940s saw the first significant expansion since the early 1930s: enrolments increased by 10,131 between June 1947 and June 1950.[119] This foreshadowed a long-term surge in student numbers which was mitigated but not halted by a high level of emigration in the 1950s, as average enrolment increased from 472,536 in 1953–54 to 490,700 in 1957–58.[120] The department's report for 1947–48 noted that 'The unemployment of some years ago has now disappeared and indeed it has now become a question as to whether existing training facilities for Catholic lay students will be adequate for future requirements…'[121] St. Patrick's College was already 'full to capacity' only three years after its re-opening and accommodation for an additional 40 places was made available in Carysfort. Departmental officials recognised the altered demographic context but struggled to respond effectively. Any doubt had disappeared in the departmental report for 1948–49, which pointed to a shortfall in the level of trained teachers to fill vacancies, noting that 'If present trends persist, this inadequacy is likely to continue'.[122] But the officials did not propose any initiatives to expand teacher supply or augment accommodation in the colleges. Minister Richard Mulcahy had announced the formation of the Council of Education to review the primary school curriculum and so 'any proposal to augment the number of training colleges must be approached cautiously…' as the Council's enquiry would have implications for primary teacher training.[123] The department deferred decisions on teacher training pending the deliberations of the Council, which was established in April 1950 and produced its first report on primary education in 1954.[124] This led to stasis in policy on teacher education for much of the 1950s, even as the department acknowledged that the accommodation in the Catholic training colleges 'had been utilised to the fullest extent in recent years…' and school managers were unable to find trained teachers.[125]

The inadequate supply of trained teachers was a constant refrain of annual departmental reports throughout the 1950s, as officials identified a particularly acute shortage of women teachers.[126] The department responded with incremental increases in the level of student teachers in the mid-1950s, increasing the number of first year places in the major Catholic training colleges from 294 in 1953 to 402 in 1957, with the large majority of the additional places for women.[127] But despite an increase of 64% in the output of trained teachers between 1954 and 1959, the shortfall in teacher supply persisted and untrained teachers, particularly the recognised category of Junior Assistant

Mistress, comprised 22% of all national schoolteachers in 1957–58.[128] The shortfall in trained teachers was driven not only by demographic expansion and a tardy official response to the baby boom but systemic problems caused by government policies, such as the increased retirement of trained women teachers, not least due to the marriage ban.[129] Policies adopted a generation earlier had created an impasse which could no longer be resolved by incremental tinkering with student numbers. The palpable failure of established policies, often adopted due to wider political or societal pressures which had little to do with education, provoked a fundamental re-appraisal of teacher training beginning in the late 1950s.

Teacher training at primary level occupied a distinctive place in the first generation of the Irish state, offering practice-based pre-service training at post-compulsory level but operating largely outside the formal accreditation and assessment systems of the university. The colleges offered higher level courses without the prestige of a degree qualification at a time when the concept of a differentiated third level higher education system still lay well in the future. Yet the training colleges served a central function for a new state whose founding ideology was closely intertwined with the establishment of political and cultural independence and attracted a high level of intervention from the political and administrative centre. Paradoxically the colleges were denominational, privately administered institutions which attracted a much more intrusive form of state control than any other strand of higher education. Teacher training was effectively a public-private partnership between the Catholic and Protestant churches and the Irish state, with a governance model of state-aided education closer to the primary managerial system than the autonomy of the traditional university. Financial and political power rested with the department, while administrative control by the bishops and religious orders was the daily reality in almost all colleges. The triangular relationship between church, state and academics which influenced the development of the universities was starkly apparent in the training colleges and characterised by a very different balance of power.

Notes

1. Susan Parkes, *Kildare Place: The History of Church of Ireland Training College and College of Education 1811–2010* (Dublin: CICE, 2011), 53.
2. Susan Parkes, '"An Essential Service": The National Board and Teacher Education,' in *Essays in the History of Irish Education*, ed. Brendan Walsh (London: Palgrave, 2016), 71–2.
3. Carla King, 'The Early Years of the College, 1875–1921,' in *St. Patrick's College Drumcondra: A History*, ed. James Kelly (Dublin: Four Courts, 2006), 96–7.
4. Department of Education, *Report of the Department of Education for the School Year 1924–25 and the Financial and Administrative Years 1924–25–26* (Dublin: Stationery Office, 1926), 33.
5. Ibid.; Parkes, 'An Essential Service,' 74.
6. Parkes, *Kildare Place*, 78.
7. Ibid., 62–3.
8. Parkes, 'An Essential Service,' 74.
9. Tom Walsh, 'The National System of Education,' in *Essays in the History of Irish Education*, ed. Brendan Walsh (London: Palgrave, 2016), 19.
10. *Report of the Department of Education for the School Year 1924 and the Financial and Administrative Years 1924–25–26*, 38.
11. Ibid.; Sr. Loreto O'Connor, *Passing on the Torch a History of Mary Immaculate College, 1898–1998* (Dublin: Mary Immaculate College, 1998), 6–9.
12. Donal Blake, *St Mary's Marino Generalate and Teacher College Century of Educational Leadership, 1904–2004* (Dublin: Marino Institute of Education, 2005), 5.
13. Ibid., 79.
14. *Report of the Department of Education for the School Year 1924 and the Financial and Administrative Years 1924–25–26*, 36–7.
15. Ibid., 34.
16. King, 'The Early Years,' 100–1; Parkes, *Kildare Place*, 55.
17. *Report of the Department of Education for the School Year 1924 and the Financial and Administrative Years 1924–25–26*, 34; Parkes, 'An Essential Service,' 74.
18. Parkes, 'An Essential Service,' 83.

19. Lee, *Ireland 1912–85*, 133–6.
20. Government of Ireland, *Report of the Commission on Higher Education 1960–67* (Dublin: Stationery Office, 1967), 216.
21. Ibid.
22. Ibid.; Tom O'Donoghue, Judith Harford and Teresa O'Doherty, *Teacher Preparation in Ireland: History, Policy and Future Directions* (Emerald: 2017), 98.
23. O'Donoghue et al., *Teacher Preparation in Ireland*, 98.
24. Government of Ireland, *Commission on Higher Education*, 220.
25. Government of Ireland, *Commission on Higher Education*, 224–5.
26. Coolahan, *Era of Lifelong Learning*, 82.
27. O'Donoghue et al., *Teacher Preparation in Ireland*, 107.
28. Department of Education, *Statistical Report 1937–38* (Dublin: Stationery Office, 1939), 72–3.
29. O'Donoghue et al., *Teacher Preparation in Ireland*, 107.
30. Ibid.; Department of Education, *Statistical Report 1937–38*, 86–7.
31. Department of Education, *Statistical Report 1937–38*, 85.
32. *Government of Ireland, Commission on Higher Education*, 226.
33. Guy Neave, 'The Changing Boundary Between the State and Higher Education,' *European Journal of Education* 17, no. 2 (1982): 231–41.
34. Department of Education, 'Unification and Co-ordination,' n.d. (NAI DFA/GR/623-8), 4.
35. Diarmuid Ferriter, '"For God's Sake Send Me a Few Packets of Fags": The College, 1922–45," in *St. Patrick's College Drumcondra: A History*, ed. James Kelly (Dublin: Four Courts, 2006), 133; Parkes, *Kildare Place*, 146.
36. O'Connor, *Passing on the Torch*, 52–3.
37. *Report of the Department of Education 1931–32* (Dublin: Stationery Office, 1933), 12.
38. O'Donoghue et al., *Teacher Preparation in Ireland*, 58.
39. *Report of the Department of Education 1931–32*, 13–14.
40. Ibid., 14–15.
41. Department of Education, 'Unification and Co-ordination,' n.d. (NAI DFA/GR/623-8), 4.
42. Department of Education, 'Scheme for Preparatory Colleges,' 22 February 1926 (NAI TSCH/3/S.4828), 1.
43. Ibid.

44. *Report of the Department of Education for the School Years 1924–25–26 and the Financial and Administrative Year 1926–27*, 21.

45. Department of Education, 'Scheme for Preparatory Colleges,' 22 February 1926 (NAI TSCH/3/S.4828), 1.

46. Minutes of Executive Council, C. 2/243, 'Preparatory Training Colleges,' 11 February 1926 (NAI TSCH/3/S.4828).

47. John Walsh, *The Politics of Expansion: The Transformation of Educational Policy in the Republic of Ireland, 1957–72* (Manchester: Manchester University Press, 2009), 43; the colleges for girls were Coláiste Íde, Dingle; Coláiste Muire, Tourmakeady and Coláiste Bríde in Falcarragh; those for boys included Coláiste na Mumhan, Mallow, Coláiste Éinne, Galway and Coláiste Caoimhin, Glasnevin.

48. Parkes, *Kildare Place*, 62.

49. Martina Relihan, 'The Church of Ireland, the State and Education in Irish Language and Irish History, 1920–1950s,' in *Educating Ireland, Schooling and Social Change, 1700–2000*, ed. Deirdre Raftery and Karin Fischer (Kildare: Irish Academic Press, 2014), 156–7.

50. Valerie Jones, 'Coláiste Moibhi: The Last Preparatory College,' *Irish Educational Studies,* 15, no. 1 (1996): 101–11.

51. Relihan, 'The Church of Ireland,' 156.

52. Ibid., 156.

53. 'St. Moibhi's Preparatory College,' 8 May 1934 (NAI TSCH/3/97/9/1138, RA 53/51), 1–3.

54. Ibid., 1.

55. Ibid., 3.

56. Eileen Randles, *Post-primary Education in Ireland 1957–70* (Dublin: Veritas, 1975), 29.

57. Seán O'Connor, *A Troubled Sky*, 29.

58. O'Donoghue et al., *Teacher Preparation in Ireland*, 53.

59. *Report of the Department of Education for the School Years 1924–25–26 and the Financial and Administrative Year 1926–27*, 22.

60. Ibid., 23; O'Connor, *Passing on the Torch*, 53.

61. O'Connor, *Passing on the Torch*, 53.

62. Parkes, *Kildare Place*, 146.

63. Relihan, 'The Church of Ireland,' 158.

64. Ibid., 147.

65. *Report of the Department of Education 1931–32*, 15.

66. *Report of the Department of Education 1927–28* (Dublin: Stationery Office, 1929), 15.
67. Ferriter, 'The College, 1922–45,' 135.
68. *Report of the Department of Education 1927–28*, 13.
69. Ferriter, 'The College, 1922–45,' 141.
70. O'Connor, *Passing on the Torch*, 37.
71. Blake, *St Mary's Marino*, 36.
72. Ibid., 185.
73. Our Lady of Mercy College, Carysfort Park, *Centenary 1877/1977, Our Lady of Mercy College Carysfort Park, Blackrock, Co. Dublin* (Dublin: Carysfort College, 1977), 26–8.
74. Parkes, *Kildare Place*, 148–9.
75. O'Connor, *Passing on the Torch*, 36.
76. *Report of the Department of Education 1931–32*, 15.
77. Ibid.
78. Ferriter, 'The College, 1922–45,' 141.
79. Carysfort College, *Centenary 1877/1977*, 27.
80. O'Connor, *Passing on the Torch*, 37.
81. *Report of the Department of Education 1931–32*, 6.
82. John Walsh, 'An Era of Expansion, 1945–75,' in *St. Patrick's College Drumcondra: A History*, ed. James Kelly (Dublin: Four Courts, 2006), 133.
83. Memorandum by Dr. Donal Cregan, October 1972 (SPCA, A/19/IV), 1.
84. *Annual Report to the Archbishop of Dublin and Manager of St. Patrick's Training College 1956–57* (DDA, *McQuaid Papers*, AB8/B/XVIII/18), 2.
85. Memorandum by Cregan, October 1972 (SPCA, A/19/IV), 3.
86. Carysfort College, *Centenary 1877/1977*, 27.
87. Blake, *St Mary's Marino*, 98.
88. O'Connor, *Passing on the Torch*, 35–6.
89. Ibid.; Public Accounts Committee, *Appropriation Accounts 1943–44* (Dublin: Stationery Office, 1945), 57.
90. Ferriter, 'The College, 1922–45,' 135–6.
91. HEA, *Report to the Minister for Education on Teacher Education* (Dublin: HEA, 1970), 2.
92. *Irish Times*, 'Commission on Education: Suggestion by the Teachers,' 21 April 1922.

93. Parkes, *Kildare Place*, 129.
94. Ibid., 132–3: McDowell and Webb, *Trinity College Dublin*, 450; *Irish Times*, 'Trinity College and Teachers,' 30 June 1921.
95. NUI Senate, Minutes, vol. 9, 25 April 1924, 232–3; Nolan, 'The Recognised Colleges,' 200.
96. NUI Senate, Minutes, vol. 9, 25 April 1924, 232.
97. *Report of the Department of Education for the School Year 1924–25*, 39: only 44 students out of 255 who applied for first year university status reached the required standard in 1924.
98. Department of Education, 'Unification and Co-ordination,' n.d. (DFA/GR/623-8), 4.
99. Public Accounts Committee, *Appropriation Accounts 1943–44* (Dublin: Stationery Office, 1945), 57.
100. Department of Education, 'Unification and Co-ordination,' n.d. (DFA/GR/623-8), 4; O'Donoghue et al., *Teacher Preparation in Ireland*, 59.
101. Department of Education, 'Unification and Co-ordination,' n.d. (DFA/GR/623-8), 4.
102. O'Donoghue et al., *Teacher Preparation in Ireland*, 59–62.
103. *Report of the Department of Education 1936–37* (Dublin; Stationery Office, 1938), 8–9.
104. Walsh, *Politics of Expansion*, 15.
105. *Report of the Department of Education 1936–37*, 8–9.
106. Ibid., 8.
107. Ibid., 8.
108. *Report of the Department of Education 1937–38* (Dublin: Stationery Office, 1939), 10.
109. O'Connor, *Passing on the Torch*, 39.
110. *Report of the Department of Education 1937–38*, 8.
111. Public Accounts Committee, *Appropriation Accounts 1943–44*, 9.
112. Blake, *St Mary's Marino*, 96.
113. *Report of the Department of Education 1939–40* (Dublin: Stationery Office, 1941), 11; *Irish Times*, 'Training College Decision,' 1 September 1939.
114. Blake, *St Mary's Marino*, 97–8; *Report of the Department of Education 1938–39* (Dublin: Stationery Office, 1940), 10.
115. Public Accounts Committee, *Appropriation Accounts 1942–43* (Dublin: Stationery Office, 1945), 46; Ferriter, 'The College, 1922–45,' 155.

116. Public Accounts Committee, *Appropriation Accounts 1944–45* (Dublin: Stationery Office, 1947), 33.

117. Walsh, 'An Era of Expansion,' 158.

118. Carysfort College, *Centenary 1877/1977*, 26.

119. *Report of the Department of Education 1947–48* (Dublin: Stationery Office, 1949), 4; *Report of the Department of Education 1949–50* (Dublin: Stationery Office, 1951), 4.

120. *Report of the Department of Education 1957–58* (Dublin: Stationery Office, 1959), 57.

121. *Report of the Department of Education 1947–48*, 6.

122. *Report of the Department of Education 1948–49* (Dublin: Stationery Office, 1950), 3.

123. Ibid.

124. *Report of the Department of Education 1949–50*, 3.

125. Ibid., 6.

126. *Report of the Department of Education 1950–51* (Dublin: Stationery Office, 1952), 6; *Report of the Department of Education 1951–52* (Dublin: Stationery Office, 1953), 5.

127. *Report of the Department of Education 1952–53* (Dublin: Stationery Office, 1954), 7; *Report of the Department of Education 1955–56* (Dublin: Stationery Office, 1957), 5; *Report of the Department of Education 1956–57* (Dublin: Stationery Office, 1958), 5.

128. *Report of the Department of Education 1950–51*, 6; *Report of the Department of Education 1951–52*, 5; *Report of the Department of Education 1958–59* (Dublin: Stationery Office, 1960), 6.

129. *Report of the Department of Education 1952–53*, 7.

Fig. 1   Dublin University OTC guard being inspected by Sir Robert Tate at Dublin Castle, 17 March 1920. Tate was a senior fellow of TCD. Image Courtesy of the National Library of Ireland

Fig. 2   Postcard of Kildare St. Training College 1880–1900. Lawrence Collection, Image Courtesy of the National Library of Ireland

Fig. 3 Students at De La Salle College, Newtown, Co. Waterford, 31 May 1924, Poole Collection, Image Courtesy of the National Library of Ireland

Fig. 4 Student at the National University of Ireland, Earlsfort Terrace, 1940–60. Cardall Photographic Collection, Image Courtesy of the National Library of Ireland

Fig. 5 President Seán T. Ó Ceallaigh, meeting delegates attending the Federation of University Women in Dublin, 13 August 1957. Independent Newspapers Ireland, Image Courtesy of the National Library of Ireland

Fig. 6 Students in Front Square, Trinity College, Dublin, 1964. Wiltshire Collection, Image Courtesy of the National Library of Ireland

Fig. 7   UCD, Earlsfort Terrace, 1969. Wiltshire Collection, Image Courtesy of the National Library of Ireland

Fig. 8 Patrick Kavanagh giving a poetry lecture, lecture hall in UCD, 1958. Wiltshire Collection, Image Courtesy of the National Library of Ireland

Please write your name and address on the reverse of this card and include it with any future communications.

This card will then be returned to you as acknowledgement of receipt of the communication.

Dear Applicant,

This is to acknowledge receipt of your communication received on

Fig. 9 Central Applications Office, Postcard receipt from CAO to applicant, undated. Image Courtesy of the National Library of Ireland

6

The End of the Old Order

The Irish Universities are short of money. They are short of staff and short of space. Their lecture-rooms are overcrowded and their professors underpaid. They are so cramped for space that in some institutions the students have no place to put their bicycles or hang their coats.[1]

The *Irish Independent* offered a lament for university education in the quarter of a century since independence on 3 February 1947. Few academics or students would have dissented from the *Independent* editorial, which took the opportunity to attack the government for financing the Dublin Institute of Advanced Studies, while 'universities are starved of resources.'[2] The place of higher education in society emerged as a significant issue in the public sphere during the early postwar period and received a more favourable response from political and administrative elites. Yet traditionalist understandings of the university as a training ground for the professional classes and an elite institution offering individual rather than collective benefit persisted: so too did the even more enduring association of higher education exclusively with the university. Finance Minister Frank Aiken told the Dáil on 26 February 1947 that 'they could not afford to make every boy a

© The Author(s) 2018
J. Walsh, *Higher Education in Ireland, 1922–2016*,
https://doi.org/10.1057/978-1-137-44673-2_6

graduate and he thought it was only fair that those who got the advantage in life of a University degree should contribute a fair share of the cost of their education.'[3] Aiken's restrictive view of university education as a training ground for a privileged male minority, caused no dissent from TDs; it accurately reflected most politicians' attitudes towards the universities, still firmly associated with the traditional academy and the upper middle class.

An international upsurge in higher level participation began during the early postwar period in most West European states, including Belgium, West Germany, France, the Netherlands and the UK.[4] This trend accelerated to produce 'an explosion of enrolments' from the second half of the 1950s.[5] While only about 5% of the relevant school leaving age group in economically advanced countries enrolled in higher education programmes in the early 1950s, this rate of enrolment exceeded 40% based on OECD data by 2000 and was even higher depending on varying definitions of 'tertiary education.'[6] The upsurge in participation during the early postwar era was linked to the establishment or extension of welfare states in the UK and Western Europe and the postwar economic revival informed by Keynesian economics; both interrelated developments were underpinned by a 'welfare liberal' consensus based on an activist role for the state in economic management and provision of social services.[7]

The upsurge in popular participation in Ireland began considerably later than the more developed European states, especially West Germany, the Netherlands and the UK: Ireland was closer to Mediterranean countries such as Portugal and Greece in a distinctive pattern of expansion which took off from the 1960s.[8] The Irish economy stagnated during the 1950s, as industrial employment declined by 14% and emigration reached a record level, with over 400,000 people leaving the country between 1951 and 1961.[9] Yet enrolments in higher education in Ireland still increased by 56% between 1950 and 1960, indicating an increasing social demand for higher education even at a time of economic stagnation and perceived national crisis.[10] The universities saw a gradual expansion in enrolments during and immediately after the second world war. The number of full-time students in the four universities doubled from 6796 in 1948–49 to 13,006 in

1964–65, with a more consistent rate of expansion in the colleges of the NUI.[11] This represented a limited increase in participation by the school-leaving population, in which widening of participation beyond traditional middle class entrants was virtually non-existent. But the universities struggled to accommodate increasing enrolments following a quarter of a century in which there was no significant capital investment by the state.[12]

The composition of enrolments differed between the NUI and Trinity, with the latter more influenced by postwar European trends. The student body in UCD increased from 2396 to 3037 between 1940–41 and 1944–45 and the college had over 3400 students by the mid-1950s.[13] UCC saw more than a doubling of its student population in a twenty year period, from 441 in 1926–27 to 1067 in 1944–45.[14] This trend of consistent but moderate expansion over time contrasted with a more volatile pattern in Trinity College, which saw a marginal decline in student numbers during the war, but experienced a 'postwar rush', as the full-time student body increased from a prewar total of 1543 in 1939 to 2351 in 1950, due in part to an influx of wartime veterans.[15] The composition of the student population in Trinity was very different from almost all other higher education institutions in Ireland, with over 40% of its students drawn from outside the state, mainly from Britain or Northern Ireland, in 1945–46.[16] The proportion of students from the Irish state in the colleges of the NUI remained around 90% from 1948–49 to the mid-1960s.[17]

'…No Further Educational Reorganisation Is Intended…'

The government took tentative steps in the mid-1940s towards postwar planning of education. De Valera urged Derrig in December 1944 to undertake a wide-ranging examination of education from primary to university level, with a view to considering improvements in educational facilities, particularly in the light of wartime policy initiatives in Britain and Northern Ireland, including the Butler Education Act in

1944.[18] The Taoiseach's main concern was that educational developments in the Irish state should not lag dramatically behind Northern
Ireland, particularly as the Stormont government under Sir Basil Brooke
was eagerly highlighting disparities in social services and living standards between North and South.[19] An internal departmental committee
was established by Derrig in March 1945 to examine the existing educational system, including university education and make recommendations 'as to what changes and reforms, if any, are necessary in order to
raise the standard of education generally and to provide greater educational facilities for our people.'[20]

But the government's flirtation with educational planning was
short-lived and in any event hardly extended to higher education at
all. Derrig was unenthusiastic, warning in August 1945 against the
early publication of a White Paper on his department's current plans,
as these extended only to the improvement of national school buildings and extension of continuation education and issuing a White
Paper 'would suggest that no further educational re-organisation is
intended.'[21] Even when the report of the departmental committee was
available its recommendations would require consultation with the
Catholic bishops and his department 'may not be in a position to deal
with its recommendations for a considerable time.'[22] The committee's
report in June 1947 focused on raising the statutory school leaving
from 14 to 16, but proposed to do so through the gradual abolition of
the vocational system.[23] This conservative solution to the second class
status of vocational schools would have provoked conflict with local
politicians and vocational teachers. Against this unpromising background no White Paper on education materialised and the committee's recommendations were quietly shelved. None of the committee's
recommendations dealt with university education, which had been
postponed for consideration 'at a later stage', while higher technical
training did not even make it on to its agenda.[24] Higher education
did not feature among the department's priorities, in part because the
universities remained formally outside its remit but mainly due to
institutional conservatism and inertia.

'...Absolutely a Disgrace...'

While a general re-appraisal of educational policies did not materialise in the early postwar period, ministers were more open to incremental initiatives in higher education, while the position of universities attracted greater political and media attention. The government sought statements of financial needs in 1946 from the colleges of the NUI, with the intention of increasing their grants—a potentially significant departure from the austerity of the previous two decades. No comparable official invitation was given to Trinity College, which government departments regarded as a private institution.[25] De Valera gave an unusually lengthy statement on university education in the Dáil on 14 February 1947, rejecting claims by opposition TDs Patrick McGilligan and James Dillon, that the universities had been starved of resources. Yet he also acknowledged that the NUI required additional public investment both for salaries and capital development amounting to 'several millions for buildings alone'.[26] He announced that a proposal by the UCD officers to provide for the college's accommodation needs in a city centre site around the Iveagh Gardens, was receiving 'sympathetic examination' within the government.[27] It was a rare public admission by the long serving Taoiseach that universities were underfunded in relation to increasing student numbers and comparable institutions in Britain. De Valera even made the striking admission that professorial salaries were 'at the present time absolutely a disgrace', an implicit indictment of government policy since independence.[28] The postwar era briefly appeared to herald a new beginning in higher education, as an Irish government held out the prospect of significant investment for the first time since 1922.

Government decisions in the late 1940s initiated a gradual upward trend in Exchequer support for the universities. The net expenditure from the Exchequer for Universities and Colleges in 1948–49 (£323,916) represented a modest 0.45% of net Exchequer spending approved by the Oireachtas.[29] State spending under the main Vote for higher education doubled in absolute terms over the following decade. Spending on Universities and Colleges was broadly consistent with the trend in overall expenditure in the 1950s: the comparable level of state

spending on higher education in 1958–59 (£692,180) increased marginally to 0.62% of net audited expenditure.[30] Yet this did not signal any
radical realignment of official priorities. The increased resources were
oriented almost entirely towards current spending in the universities
or associated institutions such as St. Patrick's College, Maynooth. The
expansion in public spending occurred from a very low base following a
period of stagnation in the public resources devoted to higher education
and had more to do with crisis management than coherent planning.

The leaders of all three colleges in the NUI submitted ambitious proposals for postwar development in 1945–46. These appeals for assistance highlighted the low level of academic salaries which had been
fixed at the same level since the late 1920s, the crippling requirement
to meet capital needs from regular income and a gradual increase in
student numbers. All three universities drew on comparisons to salaries
and capital development in British universities, which had benefited
from a postwar surge in Exchequer support from the Attlee government.

The most ambitious proposals were submitted by UCD, informed
by the report of a committee appointed by Conway to investigate the
college's financial position. UCD sought a trebling of its annual grant
and capital funding of over £2.1 million.[31] O'Rahilly had already submitted in April 1945 a wide-ranging memorandum, seeking 'guidance
as much as finance…some indication of policy as regards post-war
development.'[32] This was a remarkably blunt and outspoken document,
amounting to a critical survey not only of UCC's position but the lack
of coherent policies or institutional structures in higher education.
O'Rahilly, bemoaning the absence in Ireland of any such body as the
University Grants Committee in Britain to serve as a 'buffer body'
between universities and government, commented that he had no alternative but to appeal directly to the Taoiseach. He was 'therefore, under
the unpleasant necessity of appearing in the guise of an importunate
mendicant.'[33] De Valera had encouraged O'Rahilly to undertake this
unpleasant duty, as the president noted: '…in Limerick, at the conse-
cration of Dr. O'Neill, you whispered to me that UCD had submitted a document more detailed than mine. Hence I had better submit
some further observations.'[34] He submitted another detailed memo
to the Taoiseach on 23 April 1946, focusing mainly on salaries and

development of new buildings. O'Rahilly argued that 'staff find it hard to live' on existing salaries, proposing that full-time professors receive a comparable salary to principal officers.[35] He sought an increase in the annual grant of 37.5% to increase salaries, coupled with capital funding of £160,000 for new buildings, particularly enlargement of the library. O'Rahilly characterised this proposal as 'by comparison with the other document to which you referred…a very moderate claim'.[36]

UCG submitted a more ambitious application, seeking roughly a doubling of its annual grant combined with extensive capital funding. Pádraig de Brún also raised particular concerns about the low salaries of professors and lecturers, not least because professors in Galway were paid less than their counterparts in Dublin and Cork; the salaries of full-time assistants was 'a disgrace to us, and a matter of conscientious scruple'.[37] While acknowledging that it was unrealistic to augment the grant at the same level as England, the UCG president argued that Irish universities could not compete effectively with Belfast, 'where the Grant to Queen's University from public sources has trebled'.[38]

The Board of TCD also decided to make its first submission for assistance in twenty-three years in December 1946. The Board was hesitant about drawing the Irish state into its affairs: the senior fellows had not forgotten the fraught negotiations with the Free State and feared the imposition of onerous conditions as a prerequisite for a state grant, notably the introduction of compulsory Irish for matriculation.[39] But the Board eventually responded to pressure from younger academic staff and the lack of available alternatives to achieve financial stability.[40] Provost Alton hinted at the internal debate in his letter to de Valera on 18 December 1946: 'It is only after long consideration that we resolved to forward this appeal. We have tried our best to solve the problem ourselves but are convinced that the help of the Government are necessary.'[41] Trinity sought a regular state grant of £35,000 and non-recurrent capital funding of £75,000; the latter amounted to about three-quarters of the college's projected building requirements, with the remainder to be raised by private benefactions.[42] The decision to seek a state grant was an early indication of a generational and ideological shift in the balance of power within the college, which came to fruition under the leadership of A. J. McConnell.

The government established an ad hoc interdepartmental committee in 1946 to consider the submissions by the colleges of the NUI, including McElligott, O. J. Redmond of the Department of Finance and Micheál Breathnach. The committee identified salaries for academic and non-academic staff as 'the principal difficulty confronting the Colleges at present', conceding the case for significant increases in pay which had generally been fixed at the same level since 1929.[43] The officials were, however, unconvinced by comparisons between the NUI and British universities. The committee acknowledged 'an able and interesting report' by the UCD officers, but concluded:

> The Report tends unduly to measure the financial requirements of the College by the standards of highly endowed provincial universities in Great Britain and without sufficient regard to the capacity of the Irish taxpayer to assist University education in a country which is already suffering from over-production of university graduates.[44]

The officials argued that the UCD submission did not acknowledge the poverty of the Irish state compared to its wealthier neighbour—a constant refrain within the civil service up to the 1950s—and also validated McElligott's long held conviction about the 'over-production' of graduates. The committee recommended a 40% increase in the grants to each college, coupled with a 50% hike in fees, which they considered sufficient 'to improve suitably the remuneration of their staffs', meet the higher costs of maintenance due to the low value of the pound and offer additional scholarships.[45] This proposal partly met the demands of the universities for an increased annual income, but at the price of a substantial up-front fee increase, in line with a tried and tested official strategy. Significantly, the committee declined to make any recommendations regarding capital expenditure, on the basis that the colleges' proposals were 'so extensive that it seemed that consideration of them must be deferred, or alternatively, that they be examined by some body which would have the time and opportunity to consider the proposals in detail...'[46] While the committee was given only a limited timeframe to prepare its report, this elegant evasion of responsibility meant that decisions on university capital development were postponed indefinitely.

The university leaders were more successful in securing an upgrading of academic salaries. All three NUI presidents resisted the proposed official split between state grants and student fees, instead proposing the opposite ratio of a 50% rise in the grant and a smaller fee increase. The governing body of UCG protested in January 1947 that a 40% increase in the annual grant was 'totally inadequate' as the college had never been adequately endowed and an increase in fees, though acceptable if absolutely necessary, could reduce student numbers. For good measure, de Brún added that the amount of 'our College scholarships (£25 and £30) are in present circumstances, a shame on us.'[47] The university presidents feared not only the uncertain impact of fee increases but that additional income would be absorbed by increased salaries, leaving little or nothing for other requirements. The committee's report to the government in January 1947 made some concessions to university lobbying, proposing a 50% increase in both grants and fees but did not change the official strategy; the officials also offered a modest front-loading of the increased grants, which would come into effect from 1 September 1946, two months before the upgrade in salaries.[48] The committee also, 'without presuming to interfere with the traditional autonomy of the Colleges', sought 'a general understanding' that salaries should not rise more than 20–40% over pre-war levels.[49] While the government could not unilaterally impose an increase in fees, any leverage held by the presidents was limited by their acute need for financial support.

The settlement reached with the NUI early in 1947 largely conformed to the official blueprint. The government accepted the strategy offered by the committee, although ministers showed greater flexibility on financial details. De Valera, Derrig and Aiken agreed the terms at a conference with the three NUI presidents on 19 February 1947, allowing the first significant infusion of public resources in university education since the 1920s. While the government indicated its 'general approval' for the 50% increase in the grants, the NUI leaders agreed to raise fees 'within a few years' to half again their level in 1939–40: the main departure by de Valera from the committee's favoured model was that the colleges could raise fees by instalments if they wished.[50] UCG also received an additional £8000 annually to provide more lectureships through Irish: an appeal to Gaelicisation was rarely wasted on de Valera. Although the governing body of UCD thanked the Taoiseach on 2 April 1947 for promising 'sympathetic consideration' for future capital expenditure on buildings, student hostels and equipment,[51] the thorny problem of capital development was left unresolved. The proposed expansion of UCD's accommodation near Iveagh House was also abandoned, largely due to opposition from the Office of Public Works (OPW), dealing a final blow to UCD's efforts to find a solution to its accommodation crisis in the city centre.[52]

An attempt was also made to clarify the ambiguous (and sometimes acrimonious) relationship between the Departments of Finance and Education: the minute of the meeting noted that 'The Minister for Education undertook to use his good offices to act as intermediary whenever a College required financial or other help from the Government. (This does not imply that the Universities are under the Department of Education).'[53] This curious arrangement suggested that the Minister for Education was perceived, not least by the institutions themselves, as a mediator between universities and the Department of Finance. The clause was much too ambivalent to clarify the awkward triangular relationship between Finance, Education and the universities, which re-emerged as a bone of contention during the 1950s. But its appearance at all indicated dissatisfaction, by university representatives and probably de Valera, with the Department of Finance's miserly stewardship of the universities and colleges.

The agreement was a mixed bag for the NUI. It facilitated a significant (and badly needed) salary increase for its employees: for example, salaries in UCG increased across the board, ranging from a rise of £400 for full-time professors to £240 annually for library clerks.[54] But the deferral of decisions on capital development meant that any upgrading of building or equipment was limited and drawn from regular annual income. All three colleges increased their fees substantially, with UCD opting for an immediate 50% hike from September 1947, while UCG adopted a comparable increase for most undergraduate faculties.[55] O'Rahilly approved a more gradual increase for undergraduate courses in UCC, which still brought fees to a level 50% higher in 1947 than when the state grant was last fixed twenty years earlier.[56]

'Extraordinary Discrimination…'

Trinity's first application for a state grant in 23 years never came under the remit of the interdepartmental committee and was instead decided directly by de Valera. The committee offered to examine Trinity's proposals but also ventured to ask 'whether…the time is not ripe for an inquiry into the whole organisation of University education in the country, with a view to such reforms as would ensure greater efficiency, educational or otherwise.'[57] The government did not act on this recommendation and instead de Valera took personal charge of negotiations with Trinity College, reflecting the sensitivity of TCD's position relative to the Irish state.

The college's case for funding, drafted mainly by the registrar, Kenneth C. Bailey, shared much common ground with its NUI counterparts, emphasising the challenge of competing for academic staff following 'the sharp rise in salaries' in British universities as a result of 'the greatly increased grants…given by the State and by local authorities' and legitimate demands for wage increases among its staff following the end of wartime restrictions on wages.[58] The submission also referenced the college's inability to finance essential improvements in buildings, laboratory space and student accommodation.[59] Yet the Trinity memorandum was distinctive in calling upon wider historical and political arguments, which were very different from the appeals to Gaelicisation strategically advanced by the NUI. Trinity's glorious past and international reputation were invoked to support its case: 'In the course of its long history of three and a half centuries, Trinity College has become known all over the world…It seems to us important that, in spite of the difficulties of the times, her traditions of scholarship and public service should be preserved and amplified'.[60] Yet the college representatives also made a bolder claim that Trinity could contribute to national reconciliation as an all-Ireland institution, drawing a significant proportion of its students from Northern Ireland:

> Within our own country the College has a peculiar service to render, for through all the changes of the last twenty-five years she has continued to be able to attract large number of students from Northern Ireland, and thus to make a very important contribution towards that increased understanding between North and South which is the surest foundation for the Ireland of the future.[61]

This argument that Trinity transcended the border did not commend universal assent within a political culture imbued with traditional, irredentist nationalism and would soon be fiercely disputed by Catholic bishops. But the appeal had an undoubted attraction to de Valera, a leading architect of the culturally homogeneous, twenty-six county Irish state, who nevertheless retained a deeply felt ideological aspiration to Irish unity.

Alton and Bailey met the Taoiseach on 7 December 1946 with the intention of 'laying before you some of the needs of the college in this difficult era'.[62] The subsequent application would not have been made at all if de Valera was unsympathetic to their case. The government's swift and favourable response bore the Taoiseach's personal imprimatur. De Valera and Aiken met the provost and registrar on 20 and 21 February 1947, accepting the college's case for an annual grant and confirming at the second meeting that the government would give the full amount of £35,000 requested by the Board.[63] They also gave an assurance that 'when the time comes for provision of money for capital expenditure by the National University, consideration will be given to the needs of Trinity College also in this respect.'[64] This commitment did not amount to much, as Trinity was simply included in the general deferral of decisions on capital investment. No specific conditions regarding college governance or curriculum were attached to the grant, which was allocated for the general purposes of the college. The grant was offered, however, on the basis of understandings reached between de Valera and the college officers. The most significant undertakings given by the Board were financial, as Alton confirmed that the highest salaries, mainly those of the pre-1919 senior fellows, would not be increased and that the overall advance in salaries would not generally exceed the comparable increases in the NUI—both stipulations made by the Taoiseach to avoid 'unfavourable comment' on the government decision.[65] De Valera also warned Alton and Bailey that 'nothing should be done which would give critics of the college just cause for regarding the College as an institution out of sympathy with Ireland. The flying of the Union Jack was particularly mentioned.'[66] The flag burning incident on VE Day was undoubtedly fresh in de Valera's mind, along with previous official displays of the British flag by the college. Alton quickly confirmed that 'the Union Jack had not been flown officially since 1939'.[67]

The Taoiseach's concerns were mainly about managing the politics of the decision and minimising any opportunity for criticism of his government by Trinity's numerous opponents. The only substantive change in academic policy sought by de Valera related, predictably, to Gaelicisation. The Taoiseach urged the college officers 'to do more to promote the study of Irish and particularly the knowledge of the living language.'[68] This meant in practice the appointment of lecturers to teach courses through Irish. Yet when the college representatives raised practical concerns about identifying lecturers with the necessary fluency in Irish along with the required subject expertise, de Valera indicated that the government had no intention of applying compulsion and would be satisfied with 'comparatively slow progress if goodwill and a desire to help were present.'[69] The Board made a gesture in this direction, agreeing on 1 March 1947 to 'endeavour, as soon as possible, in the latest 12 months, to secure the services of two or three scholars capable of teaching appropriate University subjects to full University standard through the medium of Irish.'[70] Fee remission was also to be offered to students attending lectures in courses available through the national language, along with prizes for excellence in examinations through Irish. This gesture did not have much practical impact. The college experimented with a small number of courses through Irish, in mathematics and Irish archaeology, which later did not survive.[71] It was a far cry from the fears of traditionalists that compulsory Irish would be imposed as the price for financial survival.

The first formal exchange on university finance between an Irish government and Trinity College in almost a quarter of a century was very different from the chilly encounter between Free State ministers and ex-unionist dignitaries in the early 1920s. Alton thanked de Valera on 1 March 1947 for the 'promise of speedy and generous assistance'.[72] T. C. Kingsmill-Moore, one of the Trinity Senators, also expressed appreciation to the government 'for a grant which is as generous as it is wise', noting that it was the first grant-in-aid for general purposes awarded to the college since the pre-Union Irish Parliament.[73] De Valera's decision marked a significant turning point in the state's relations with Trinity College, traditionally distant and conducted at arm's length on both sides. Yet it also exposed Trinity's finances to greater scrutiny, as the state grants were subject to review by the Comptroller and Auditor General and the Public Accounts Committee. There was some hostility among backbench TDs to the grant for Trinity College. A Clann na Poblachta TD, Michael Fitzpatrick, questioned the basis for the grant at a PAC meeting in November 1949: 'I, not being a Fellow of Trinity College, should like to know something about this matter...I want to know the reason for the amount.'[74] While Fitzpatrick's contribution was ruled out of order, the committee's examination of public funding for Trinity sometimes allowed backbench TDs to ventilate their hostility to the college.

The new departure did not end Trinity's isolation within an over-whelmingly Catholic society. Hostility to Trinity persisted within elements of the political and official establishment, while criticism of the college by the Catholic bishops intensified in the late 1940s. The most trenchant critic of de Valera's decision was Michael Browne, bishop of Galway. Browne, a deeply conservative prelate, demanded an explanation in an address at St. Mary's College, Galway on 30 May 1949, for the 'extraordinary discrimination' displayed by the government grant to Trinity College, when no public support was given to St. Patrick's College, Maynooth.[75] Browne reminded his audience that Trinity was the product of the Reformation and the Penal Laws:

> No explanation has been given why an institution which still enjoys the proceeds of vast confiscated estates, and for centuries did everything to prevent Catholics having university education should now receive £35,000 from this State, while nothing at all is given to Maynooth.[76]

The bishop also ridiculed the political rationale for assisting Trinity: 'Some people thought that it would induce the North to come in. The North had shown itself remarkably indifferent to all their parading of their tolerance, and has gone its own way.'[77] Most bishops were more circumspect in their public remarks, but his attack captured the collective sentiments of the Catholic hierarchy. Browne's fusillade left no doubt that whatever the government might do the bishops had not relented in their hostility to TCD.

Palace Revolutions

The *Irish Independent* combined its jeremiad at the financing of the universities in February 1947 with criticism of the 'strange aloofness' of university leaders, who failed to take citizens into their confidence about the plight of their institutions.[78] Yet a generational change in the leadership of two of the largest universities, Trinity and UCD, brought more sharply defined objectives and a more assertive style to the previously genteel lobbying of the government. Michael Tierney was elected as president of UCD in October 1947, in a ballot within the NUI senate which effectively overturned the preferences of the governing body.[79] Tierney's victory was regarded by contemporaries as a significant break with the past. Tierney, a classicist, was the first humanities academic to hold the presidency of UCD and his dynamism and ambition, allied to a world view rooted in integralist Catholicism, shaped the fortunes of the college over the following generation.[80] His elevation marked a crucial change of direction in the college's postwar development. Tierney championed the transfer of the entire college to a new suburban site at Belfield along the Stillorgan Road, a cause which defined his presidency.[81] Tierney became a controversial figure both within UCD and in the political realm: both allies and detractors testified to his predominant position in UCD throughout his 17-year presidency.

An equally radical transition occurred in Trinity College early in the 1950s. Alton's term as provost (1942–52) saw increasing conflict between the influential senior fellows, an elderly elite who had almost all attained their eminence by 1919 and younger academic staff, seeking a more representative governing body and more professional college administration. The *Irish Times*, despite its consistent sympathy for Trinity, noted in 1952 that 'One criticism which might be levelled against it with some justice of recent years is that it has stuck too slavishly to the tradition that a university ought to be administered by elderly men.'[82] The conflict came to a head following Alton's death in February 1952. A. J. McConnell, a 48 year old mathematician and outgoing registrar, was selected in a ballot of the fellows and professors on 11 March 1952.[83] McConnell, a native of Ballymena, Co. Antrim, was the first Presbyterian to be appointed provost. But more significantly

McConnell's elevation transformed the leadership and governance of Trinity College. The new provost curtailed the power of the senior fellows, by appointing his own nominees as annual officers and later expanding the membership of the Board to widen the representation of more junior academic staff in 1958.[84]

McConnell departed from the 'policy of inconspicuousness' pursued by the college authorities for a generation. He criticised 'violent attacks' made on Trinity College in contributing to a debate on partition at the Blackrock Literary and Debating Society on 22 October 1955, arguing that Trinity promoted 'full co-operation and mutual confidence… between Protestant and Catholic, Northern and Southern'.[85] He rebutted attacks on the college by its numerous critics, such as Cornelius Lucey, whose characterisation of Trinity as '…free-thinking or indifferent to religion' he dismissed as untrue.[86] McConnell's administration also brought pressure to bear on county councils which did not allow students to hold their grants at TCD.[87] Despite occasional rebuffs and a fair amount of angry debate at local authority meetings, this campaign had a gradual impact, as 25 councils had included Trinity in their schemes by 1967.[88]

The other two university colleges did not have a comparable 'palace revolution' in the 1950s, but experienced a similar turning point in the following decade. De Brún, towards the end of his term, clashed with the governing body in UCG, which regarded his style as autocratic and sought unsuccessfully to restrict the powers of the presidency after his retirement in 1960.[89] Prof. Martin Newell, who was elected by the NUI senate in July 1960, although an overwhelming majority of the governing body favoured Liam Ó Buachalla, was the first lay president of UCG in twenty-six years.[90] Newell's presidency (1960–75) marked a key period of transition for UCG, in which student enrolments trebled. Newell's administration oversaw rapid expansion of the college, including a new site development plan and a large-scale expansion in the range of academic departments.[91]

UCC, which was led for over a decade after O'Rahilly's retirement by conservative, low profile presidents,[92] experienced a more dramatic turning point in the late 1960s. Following the retirement of J. J. McHenry, effectively a 'caretaker' president, a substantial majority of the governing body supported Tadhg Ó Ciardha, the outgoing registrar, for the succession.[93] But the NUI senate selected M. D. McCarthy, a native of Cork but director of the Economic Research Institute, by a single vote in July 1967.[94] Although McCarthy enjoyed influential support among academic staff, it was still a striking exercise of discretion by the senate, which was often more receptive to academic lobbying than governing bodies with strong local authority representation.[95] McCarthy proved a successful reforming president, not only overseeing expansion of the college through a twenty-year site development plan adopted in 1972, but modernising its administration and appointments system.[96] It was notable that in key appointments in all three constituent colleges across several decades the NUI senate exerted decisive influence on the appointment of a new president, in each case rejecting the favoured choice of the governing body.

Muddling Through

The report of the interdepartmental committee in 1947 set the pattern for government-university relations for the next decade—sometimes significant, but piecemeal, support through recurrent grants; intermittent pressure for fee increases and virtually no public investment in capital development. Overall a coherent political or official vision for higher education was conspicuously absent. The Department of Finance, under McElligott until 1952 and his successor O. J. Redmond (1952–56), remained suspicious of any extension of state commitments in higher education, even if its officials tacitly acknowledged that a restriction in enrolments was no longer possible. The sharp increase in governmental instability in the early postwar period, which saw four changes of government between 1948 and 1957, was not conducive to long-term planning. But probably more significant than political instability was its opposite—an underlying continuity in political and official attitudes towards higher education, which assumed that third-level participation was a privilege for an elite minority. The brief postwar optimism evoked by tentative gestures toward educational planning by de Valera's government in the mid-1940s soon evaporated in the face of official and political indifference, if not outright hostility towards investment in higher education.

The election of the inter-party government led by John A. Costello in 1948, in which McGilligan became Minister for Finance and the veteran soldier-politician General Richard Mulcahy took charge of the Department of Education, did not lead to any new departure in higher education. The financial settlement in 1947 proved inadequate to support the postwar expansion of the universities or even maintain their solvency. UCD applied for 'immediate financial assistance' of over £115,000 in November 1949, to cover increased salaries, a deficit in the pension fund and a substantial overdraft on capital spending. Tierney also began to lobby for government support on a much more ambitious scale, for a development plan on the Stillorgan Road involving a building programme of £2.5 million.[97] Almost all the university leaders were seeking to improve upon the terms of the settlement in 1947, without necessarily scaling the same heights as Tierney. O'Rahilly submitted a substantial funding application for UCC in September 1950, to meet increased running costs partly due to inflation.[98] Trinity also sought an 80% increase in its state grant, while renewing its original application for capital funding.[99]

The proposal by the interdepartmental committee for a commission of inquiry on the future of university education did not find favour with Costello any more than it had with de Valera. Instead the new coalition moved tentatively towards devising its own longer-term policy. The Cabinet agreed on 28 April 1950 to set up a ministerial committee on university education, composed of the Taoiseach, Tánaiste William Norton and the Ministers for Finance, Education, Defence and Health.[100] This was an eclectic combination, lacking an obvious rationale for its composition other than a wide representation of three of the parties in government—Fine Gael, Labour and Clann na Poblachta. The brief for the Cabinet committee was to consider:

1. The coordination of existing institutions providing University education and providing training for the medical profession.
2. The basis on which financial assistance by the State to such institutions should in the future be provided.
3. The question of financial assistance by the State towards the solution of the problem of accommodation in UCD.

The Cabinet committee's terms of reference reflected traditionalist understandings of higher education, conceptualised essentially as the universities and medical institutions (such as RCSI) operating at an equivalent level, among ministers and the public administration. Yet the establishment of the committee illustrated the government's search for a coherent policy involving greater coordination between the major institutions of higher education, which were all seeking increased public support. This was the first indication of one of the most consistent preoccupations of successive governments in the second half of the twentieth century, namely how to resource an expanding higher education sector and ultimately influence its development. The 'problem of accommodation' in UCD also emerged as a major issue—it would become a recurring theme of government and parliamentary debates for the next two decades.

The inter-party government fell before the Cabinet committee could devise any serious policy recommendations. But its deliberations contributed to the government's decision to approve a supplementary estimate providing incremental support to most universities and Maynooth College in December 1950. The government approved a total supplementary estimate of £162,000 for the NUI, with the most substantial allocation of £104,000 being devoted to UCD.[101] The increased grant and the appearance of UCD's development programme on the government agenda testified to effective lobbying by Tierney, as well as McGilligan's close connections with the college. UCC and UCG also secured an increase in their grant, although neither O'Rahilly nor de Brún regarded it as adequate and both were soon making renewed representations to the next government. Yet if most university leaders were far from satisfied with their lot, the Board of Trinity College was outraged at receiving an increase of only £10,000, which the then registrar, McConnell, described as 'altogether inadequate'.[102]

Pressure from the Catholic bishops was instrumental in securing the first state subsidy to St. Patrick's College, Maynooth, since disestablishment of the Church of Ireland in 1869.[103] Pádraig de Brún had made an initial approach to de Valera for a grant to Maynooth in 1947. Financing the college raised awkward questions about constitutionality under Article 44.2.2, which ruled out endowment of any religion by the state. The Attorney General, Cearbhall Ó Dálaigh, advised that a straightforward subvention to St. Patrick's College would be unconstitutional due to 'the preponderating character of the institution as a whole'.[104] Ó Dálaigh did not rule out assistance to 'secular' courses of study within the college, but a government decision was still pending when de Valera was replaced by Costello.

The Catholic bishops, as trustees of St. Patrick's College, undertook a two-pronged offensive on behalf of Maynooth, combining a public appeal with private lobbying of the inter-party government. The bishops launched a national collection in every parish across the island of Ireland in October 1948, seeking to raise £300,000 for Maynooth college: the appeal was necessary because the college was heavily in debt and unable to undertake any major refurbishment of buildings which were mainly over 150 years old.[105] The college's case received overwhelming support in most national newspapers. The *Irish Independent*, representing the conventional religious fervour ignited by the appeal, commented with no shortage of hyperbole that the college was 'the nerve centre of Irish religious life, the living fire from which the torch of the Faith has been carried to the ends of the Earth.'[106] While the national collection in 1949 did much to solve the immediate financial problems of the college, the bishops maintained pressure on the government for a regular grant. Michael Browne was the most outspoken ecclesiastical advocate of state aid to Maynooth and his public criticisms of the state grant to Trinity College were buttressed by an indictment of the state for its failure to offer comparable support for St. Patrick's College.[107] Both the college authorities and their ecclesiastical allies saw the recent state grant to Trinity College (with its Divinity School) as a useful lever to make the case for Maynooth.

Monsignor Kissane, president of Maynooth College, appointed an internal committee in 1949, which prepared a memorandum making a more subtle case than Browne's public statement for an annual state grant to Maynooth. The Maynooth submission referenced the House of Commons parliamentary debate over the original endowment granted by Sir Robert Peel's government in 1845, to underline an essential distinction between endowing an educational institution and endowing the Catholic religion. The grant to TCD was highlighted, among other official policies such as support for chaplains in secondary schools, as validating the legality of support for Maynooth.[108] The memorandum also made a pragmatic case for support to Maynooth College as a contribution to societal stability, arguing that 'Even from the point of view of civil society Maynooth is probably the greatest single stabilizing influence in the country'.[109] This essentially conservative argument strikingly echoed the rationale enunciated by Peel a century earlier, when he had urged the House of Commons to approve the grant to Maynooth to make the college a stabilising influence in Ireland and '… break up…that formidable confederacy which exists in that country against the British Government… by acting in a spirit of kindness, forbearance and generosity.' [110]

The claim for parity with TCD was well calculated to appeal to Costello, whose conventional Catholic piety was both sincere and deployed for effect in parliamentary debates. Costello took the lead in negotiations with the bishops, meeting with a deputation including Kissane and the bishops of Limerick and Raphoe, on 6 February 1950. Kissane handed the memorandum to the Taoiseach, who explicitly endorsed Maynooth's claims for support. An official note of the meeting recorded Costello's agreement with the deputation, albeit expressed as a personal position because no government decision had yet been taken:

> The Taoiseach's personal views are that no difficulty should arise on constitutional grounds in regard to the making of a State grant in respect of secular studies in the College, as a recognised college of the National University and that, in view of the grants already payable to other University Institutions in the State, there are no good grounds on which such assistance could be refused.[111]

The Taoiseach asked Kissane to submit a second memorandum, setting out the extent of the assistance required to improve facilities and staff salaries in Maynooth. This submission, received by Costello on 29 April 1950, explicitly stated that Maynooth College consisted of 'two divisions'—the faculties of arts, science and philosophy leading to BA and B.Sc. degrees and the faculties of theology and canon law recognised by the papacy.[112] The memo noted that 'The former division is of the same general character as the Faculty of Arts and Science in other Universities…This Department forms the Recognised College of the National University of Ireland…' and its academic courses were overseen by the NUI senate.[113] This distinction between the theological faculty of the pontifical university and the college of the National University succeeded in removing any legal objection to a state grant, although Maynooth remained a seminary and both arts and theological courses were being pursued solely by clerical students in this period. The Taoiseach secured a favourable opinion from the Attorney General's office, which advised on 9 May that 'Information now furnished shows that the Faculties of Arts, Science and Philosophy comprise a separate and distinct establishment in Maynooth…the provision of financial assistance for that part of St. Patrick's College does not in any way contravene the 44th article of the Constitution.'[114] This legal imprimatur allowed McGilligan to include a grant of £15,000 to Maynooth in the supplementary estimate announced in November 1950. The Taoiseach's involvement in the negotiations expedited a favourable government decision on Maynooth and ensured that any legal or political obstacles were quickly overcome. The explicit distinction between the recognised college and the pontifical university in the second memorandum emerged from the deputation meeting and the formulation may well have been influenced by Costello, a distinguished lawyer. While Costello was instrumental in approving the first state grant to Maynooth, the decision owed a great deal to the traditionalist cultural context in which ministers operated at the peak of the power of integralist Catholicism in Irish society.

The inter-party government saw a severe, albeit temporary, deterioration in the state's relations with Trinity College. The Board of TCD made three applications for increased state assistance between December 1948 and January 1950, none of which were successful. Alton addressed his appeals to Costello, suspecting correctly that the Taoiseach was more sympathetic to Trinity's case than McGilligan.[115] The provost sought a supplementary grant in April 1949 to provide for a salary increase, designed to keep pace with a significant salary readjustment in Britain. Following the Spens report on remuneration in the newly established

National Health Service, which led to the upgrading of the salaries of post holders in clinical schools such as medicine and dentistry, the Chancellor of the Exchequer, Sir Stafford Cripps, approved a general upgrading of salary scales for academic staff in the universities from October 1949.[116] McGilligan, however, refused on 23 May 1949 to authorise any supplementary allocation for Trinity in 1949–50, on the basis that the proposal to give 'further State aid to Trinity College cannot properly be considered apart from the financial needs of the Constituent Colleges of the National University…'—an ostensibly reasonable position shared by the Department of Education.[117] The college authorities appealed for a doubling of the annual grant to £79,000 and capital funding for a new building in December 1949, arguing that the college's position was 'much more critical' than a year earlier.[118] Yet the overall review of university financial requirements by the Department of Finance in 1950 proved equally unfavourable to Trinity. The miserly allocation of £10,000 to TCD in the supplementary estimate for 1950–51 triggered the most severe clash between the college leaders and an Irish government since 1922.

The college authorities appealed to Costello in January 1951 to receive a deputation about the treatment of Trinity, presenting a memorandum setting out comparisons in salaries of staff and financial support between the college and UCD.[119] Costello and McGilligan received the Trinity deputation, consisting of Alton, McConnell and the bursar, Harry Thrift, on 19 March 1951. Patrick Lynch, Costello's influential adviser, also attended, although as it transpired neither he nor the Taoiseach had much influence on the meeting, which was dominated by McGilligan. The normally moderate Alton made a pointed criticism of McGilligan: 'It would seem… that the Minister for Finance was inclined to treat Trinity harshly. If so, his recent treatment would leave a permanent stamp of inferiority on Trinity College.'[120] But it was McConnell who presented a detailed critique of the government's policy, arguing that average endowment per student between Trinity and UCD, almost identical in 1947, was almost two to one in favour of the larger college four years later. This discrepancy would make it 'quite impossible for Trinity College to maintain a comparable standard with University College.'[121] McGilligan flatly rejected Trinity's case on the

basis that comparable standards could not prevail between such dissimilar institutions: "If the Trinity authorities were aiming at such an objective, 'that was the rock on which they would founder'".[122] When the
registrar asked whether the minister favoured 'discrimination' against
Trinity College, McGilligan responded bluntly that Trinity was a college
for Protestants and still worse accommodated a strong British element
in its student body:

> The fact was that University College was part of a public institution the
> National University which catered for 93% of the population. Trinity
> College, on the other hand, was not a public institution and it catered for
> only 7% of the population...there were many students in Trinity College
> who might be described as immigrants from Britain.[123]

McGilligan's argument had an obvious historical resonance and
reflected long-term concerns among senior civil servants about the high
proportion of British students in Trinity. But it ignored the impact of
the ecclesiastical 'ban' and showed an apparent desire to turn back the
clock to the pre-1947 period when the college had received no regular
state grant.

The meeting developed into a sulphurous confrontation between
McGilligan and McConnell, with occasional interventions by the provost or Taoiseach, usually attempting to moderate the main protagonists.
A particularly sharp exchange gave a flavour of the acrimony between
the two men:

> ...The Minister said that he did not think any reasonable person could
> maintain the proposition that Trinity College, situated as it is in its par-
> ticular circumstances, should be equated to University College by the use
> of State funds. It was not possible to put the two Colleges on the same
> footing because the natures of both were different. The same average state
> endowment per student would produce...gross inequality for a public
> institution such as University College Dublin.
> 37. The Registrar asked whether the Government intended to strangle
> Trinity College.[124]

For good measure McGilligan argued that 'Many students...went to Trinity because it had low entrance standards and Irish was not compulsory,' reviving the traditional nationalist indictment of the college.[125] McConnell for his part did not hold back, vigorously disputing McGilligan's arguments and demanding whether 'the Minister wanted to drive the Trinity College staff out of the country.'[126]

Costello took a more conciliatory line, denying any intention to discriminate against Trinity and seeking, unsuccessfully, to moderate the confrontation. The Taoiseach also floated the idea of a single university in Dublin, commenting that '...it was a pity that it has not been possible to have only one university in Dublin which, if necessary, might include a number of Constituent Colleges'.[127] This fascinating observation, offered almost as an aside in the midst of the row, was largely brushed aside by most of the other participants, including Costello's Cabinet colleague. Merger was not an objective of the inter-party government, which had not yet developed any settled policy for higher education. But Costello's observation was significant as an augury of future policy in the very different circumstances of the 1960s, indicating that merger was being discussed within the political and official establishment as early as 1951.

Although McGilligan's trenchant opinions were not shared by the Taoiseach, the minister's hostility to Trinity was an insuperable obstacle to any agreement. Perhaps his most striking intervention came when Costello sought to end the meeting on a conciliatory note by promising to bring the representations of the deputation before the government: 'The Minister for Finance said he would oppose the proposals of the deputation to the point that he would not remain Minister for Finance if the proposals were accepted.'[128] McGilligan's extraordinary threat of resignation underlined that Trinity could expect no assistance from the inter-party government.

Following this disastrous encounter, relations between the government and Trinity were at such a low ebb that Costello avoided sending the provost an official minute of the meeting, presumably because the divergence was so stark that any attempt at compromise was pointless. The Board circulated its own report of the confrontation to the TCD Senators criticising 'the discrimination shown against the College in the distribution of University grants by the Minister for Finance...[129] McDowell and Webb, writing from a Trinity perspective but not minimising McConnell's part in the row, offered the pithy verdict that it was 'an argument before two impotent spectators between a Ballymena Presbyterian and a Derry Catholic – a confrontation that was unlikely to end in détente'.[130] Long-term cultural divisions certainly formed the backdrop to the dispute, but it would be a mistake to attribute it simply to religion. McGilligan's hostility to Trinity College was consistent with his earlier opposition to the foundation of DIAS on the basis that it would drain resources from UCD; his tenacious support for the NUI (and particularly UCD) throughout his public career left no room for compromise. McGilligan took no prisoners in defending his own college and the cherished national project of the NUI. The minister's hostility to UCD's metropolitan rival was certainly expressed with a vehemence unusual among government ministers (though not backbench TDs) in the postwar era. But his contention that Trinity was a privately controlled, Protestant enclave within the Irish state was conventional wisdom in the public service until the late 1940s and retained considerable currency during the 1950s, reflecting a deeply held suspicion of Trinity among nationalist political and official elites.

The wider political context may also have contributed to the confrontation. Costello and McGilligan received Trinity's deputation just as a conflict within the government over the Mother and Child Scheme was about to come to a head. The attempt by Dr. Noel Browne, Minister for Health, to introduce a scheme providing for free ante and post-natal care for mothers and free medical care for children under sixteen, was rejected by the Irish Medical Association and more significantly the Catholic bishops. When the Cabinet disowned the scheme, Browne was forced to resign in April 1951 and the controversy erupted into the public domain, fatally destabilising the government.[131] Browne's status as a Trinity graduate soon came under attack from opponents across the political spectrum, as well as Catholic prelates. The government leaders, seeking to avoid conflict with the Catholic Church on health, were hardly likely to open another front with the bishops in higher education by acceding to Trinity's ambitious funding application. Yet the Mother and Child scheme did not explain the failure of Trinity's earlier applications for aid in 1948–50 and is unlikely to have been crucial in the rejection of its case in 1951, although it may well have exacerbated the confrontation. It is more likely that McGilligan's pivotal position within the government was decisive in determining the disparity in resourcing between the universities.

The inter-party government struggled to manage increasing demands from a moderately expanding university sector in the early postwar period. Although its members sought a more definitive policy toward higher education and increased resources at least in terms of recurrent grants, the government's approach remained notably fragmented and was dictated more by the influence of individual power brokers than any coherent policy. A Cabinet committee was appointed over two years into its term, but even then few policy decisions were taken and the attempt to chart a more long-term roadmap even for university education petered out. A notable illustration of the coalition's inability to develop a coherent position on university financing came in the confrontation between McGilligan and the TCD representatives, which Costello was unable to mediate. This political failure was far from unique. Successive governments throughout the 1950s were seeking to move beyond the austerity of the interwar and wartime period, but proved unable to clarify policy priorities or evolve a longer term plan for higher education.

Paradoxically a government led by Fine Gael, previously the Commonwealth party which had defended TCD's representation in the Dáil, proved markedly more hostile to Trinity's financial demands than de Valera. Following Fianna Fáil's return to office in June 1951, the college officers resumed negotiations with de Valera and a partial settlement was reached in February 1952. The government approved an increase of £40,000 in the annual grant and a more modest grant of £10,000 in 1952–53 'for the repair of the College buildings.'[132] While the latter estimate represented only a fraction of the capital funding sought by the college and was officially non-recurrent, it was renewed annually over a number of years, offering a valuable resource for the maintenance of historic buildings.[133] De Valera's more generous

response to Trinity's lobbying may be attributed to a variety of considerations, many of which had little to do with education. Certainly de
Valera was friendly with a number of prominent Trinity professors or
graduates, including Thrift and particularly McConnell and the value
of personal connections should never be underestimated in Irish political culture. McCartney asserted that at a time when his opponents
retained strong connections with UCD, 'it was in de Valera's political
interest to show the smiling face of Irish nationalism to an institution
which…found itself in danger of suffering the consequences of its former unionism'.[134] Yet while political calculation was undeniably present
in his reversal of McGilligan's decision, de Valera's record in university
education suggests more complex motivations. Probably more significant was de Valera's concern not to offer any propaganda gifts to the
Ulster unionist administration in Stormont through mean-spirited
treatment of Trinity College, following a similar logic as his decision
in framing the 1937 constitution to guarantee TCD graduates representation in the Senate. Yet de Valera's decision was not an isolated
incident but perhaps the most notable example of his willingness to
intervene in favour of university authorities on particular issues, sometimes going against the grain of dominant political and official attitudes, whether expressed by the Department of Finance or political
opponents.

If political and official elites struggled to define policy priorities in
higher education, they were more effective in reacting to crises, especially where shortfalls in university facilities threatened to undermine
professional faculties or the state's international reputation. Such a crisis
emerged during the mid-1950s in medical education, when a combination of long-term underfunding and critical external reports threatened the viability of university medical schools in the Republic. The
unfavourable reviews by examiners from the General Medical Council
and the Medical Registration Council of Ireland in 1955 exposed
deficiencies in facilities and staffing in the three medical schools of
the NUI, raising the prospect that the reciprocal recognition of Irish
medical qualifications in Britain might be withdrawn.[135] Similar
shortcomings in a professional discipline came to a head at the same
time, when the board of the Dublin Dental Hospital, the main centre

for the training of dentists in Ireland which served both Trinity and UCD, sought support for a full reconstruction of the Dental School on a new site. Meanwhile the facilities for the smaller Dental School in Cork, linked to UCC, were so inadequate that it was described privately by Mulcahy in February 1956 as 'a sitting bird for non-recognition.'[136] The plight of the two professional disciplines provoked a spate of increasingly frenetic contacts between university leaders and ministers during the second inter-party government (1954–57).

All three university presidents within the NUI appealed to the Department of Education for substantially increased grants, in which the upgrading of the medical faculties featured prominently. The senate adopted a resolution in October 1955, proposed by De Brún and Tierney, which impressed upon the government 'the urgent need of considerable and immediate financial help…to bring the medical schools of our Constituent Colleges to such a standard as will preserve the international recognition which they have hitherto enjoyed'.[137] Tierney put the case more bluntly in a letter to Costello in January 1956, warning that 'We are now dangerously close to a situation in which, if adequate provision is not made as soon as possible for bringing our whole system of medical and dental teaching up to date, the recognition hitherto accorded to our graduates in Great Britain may be summarily refused.'[138] The university lobbying was amplified by an even more influential figure. De Valera wrote to Costello as Chancellor of the NUI on 7 November 1955, urging him to intervene personally to ensure that 'any short-comings here as regards medical teaching cannot be attributed to State indifference or neglect.'[139] He too raised the risk of damage to the international reputation of Irish medical education: 'A bad name given to us now by such bodies as the American Medical Association and the General Medical Council would be hard to outlive: it would not only have a disastrous effect on our reputation abroad but would tend to lower our proper self-esteem and our domestic standards.'[140] It was an exceptional intervention by de Valera, who was both the titular head of the NUI and leader of the opposition; he emphasised that only the 'extreme urgency' of the situation led him to lobby the Taoiseach but his intervention certainly raised the stakes by highlighting the political costs of inaction by the government.

The combination of academic and political lobbying for the Irish medical schools proved effective. Costello promptly circulated the appeals from the NUI and de Valera to Mulcahy and a number of other ministers; shortly afterwards the Department of Education recommended in November 1955 a substantial increase in the grants for all three colleges of the NUI in the estimates for 1956–57, including the full amounts requested for medicine and dentistry.[141] The Department of Finance was less generous, but approved a 10% increase in the general purposes grant for each college, coupled with allocations for medicine and dentistry which conceded between 81% and 100% of the original applications.[142] Trinity, which had first highlighted the need for increased public investment in medical education during the late 1940s, also received a 10% increase and a comparable allocation for its medical faculty. A delay in announcing the estimates led to another rocket from Tierney, who told the Taoiseach on 1 March 1956 that the problems facing UCD Medical school had developed to such a point that '…it is now a question whether the most immediate and large-scale assistance may not be already too late'.[143] Costello spoke personally to Tierney to reassure him that he would be informed of the budget for UCD within a week and the Department of Education informed all four university presidents of the revised estimates early in March.[144] The inter-party government responded decisively to the apparent crisis facing the Irish medical faculties. Indeed the speed of the official reaction was exceptional at a time when the process of considering new initiatives of any significant cost, in higher education or elsewhere, was rarely less than tortuous. The swift governmental response testified to the consensus within the political establishment that international recognition of Irish medical qualifications had to be preserved whatever the costs. This position was sensible, but also reflected the persistence of a traditionalist world view about the value and purpose of university education. The political elite was united in protecting the international reputation of Irish medical courses in Britain and the USA and preserving the prestige of the medical and dental professions. This did not translate, however, into a wider concern with the underdevelopment of higher education or even reputational damage to universities facing competition for staff with better endowed British institutions in the early postwar period.

The political establishment was ineffectual in resolving more complex, longer-term challenges, such as the increasingly chronic accommodation problems in all the university colleges due to the prolonged absence of capital investment and more fundamentally the emerging social demand for higher levels of education. Successive governments from the late 1940s grappled with the bitterly contested development plans for UCD without reaching any definitive conclusions. Tierney's development plan, which was unanimously approved by the governing body of UCD in November 1951, ultimately involved the transfer of the entire college to newly purchased sites at Belfield and Merville along the Stillorgan Road.[145] The governing body's plans were opposed by a section of the college's academic staff and their differences were periodically fought out in national newspapers during the mid to late 1950s. Dr. Roger McHugh criticised the governing body for underestimating the cost of the development at Belfield and neglecting the potential for expansion at Earlsfort Terrace. McHugh commented acidly in 1957, in response to claims by his opponents that no binding decisions had been taken, that 'six years of taking no decisions seem to have involved us in considerable expense (in the way of fees for advice etc.)…'[146] Another critic of the plan, John J. O'Meara, professor of classical languages, floated a close association between UCD and Trinity College as an alternative to the Belfield project in 1958, arguing that 'Dublin would have one of the greatest universities in the English-speaking world, if to the old and great tradition of Trinity College were joined the traditions of Newman's Catholic University'.[147] O'Meara favoured a pooling of resources and collaboration in securing public and private funding rather than a full merger, but either option was equally unwelcome to the UCD administration. Such contributions fed into a prolonged and contentious public debate over the principle and financing of the Belfield project, which was not finally resolved until 1960.

The minority governments led by both de Valera and Costello between 1948 and 1957 proved willing to offer piecemeal, often substantial, support to UCD's plans, but shied away from a definitive decision in favour of the controversial and costly transfer of the college. McGilligan, an early advocate of the plan, gave a green light to UCD to extend its holdings on the Belfield site in 1949 and for the purchase of Merville, the largest acquisition to date, in 1951. Four ministers, including Costello and McGilligan, met Tierney and other UCD officers in July 1949, agreeing that the government would raise no objection to the purchase of further property by the college in Stillorgan.[148] Although senior ministers were well aware of UCD's plans, no formal proposal was approved by the Department of Finance or the government and McGilligan 'verbally sanctioned' the college's purchases of land.[149] But McGilligan's successor as Minister for Finance, Seán MacEntee, was firmly opposed to the transfer of UCD. An internal departmental memo noted that MacEntee had 'serious misgivings over the whole matter…' which if anything understated the vehemence of the minister's views.[150] An influential section of Fianna Fáil TDs and activists remained opposed to the plan up to 1960, even when de Valera eventually bestowed his own, somewhat elliptical, blessing upon it.

The UCD administration sought to circumvent the Finance Minister by appealing directly to de Valera. Tierney sought the services in 1952 of Raymond McGrath, the chief architect of the OPW, as a member of an advisory board to oversee the technical details of the building project. This was blocked by MacEntee on the basis of McGrath's official position. Instead de Valera advised Tierney that arrangements should be made for ongoing consultation between the college officers and official representatives, including McGrath and civil servants in Education and Finance, from the time that preliminary plans were prepared: these officials would report back to their departments but 'would not be empowered, on their own responsibility, to commit the government to approval of any particular proposals.'[151]

Tierney appealed to the Taoiseach on 9 February 1953 for a capital endowment of £200,000 to cover the costs of the land purchased since 1949 and allow further expansion in Stillorgan.[152] De Valera consulted with MacEntee and Seán Moylan, the Minister for Education (1951–54), before inviting Tierney to make a formal request for the additional grant to the Department of Education, with the crucial assurance that ministers would attempt 'to convey a decision on the question of the capital endowment by the end of this week'.[153] A reluctant MacEntee urged in vain a wide-ranging investigation of higher education (a proposal eventually adopted by Lemass' first government in 1960). Meanwhile, Tierney was lightly rapped on the knuckles by de Valera for making informal agreements with McGilligan on 'a matter involving a sum of such a magnitude.'[154] The Department of Education on 11 March 1953 couched the official decision in favour of UCD in diplomatic language, confirming that the Finance Minister would 'consider providing in his next Budget for the endowment concerned but on the condition that it be clearly understood that such provision must not be regarded as committing the Government in any way to…approval of the College proposals for new buildings or any action in respect thereof.'[155] This apparently crucial qualification, inserted by MacEntee, attempted to clarify that no government imprimatur had yet been given to the Belfield project. Yet despite MacEntee's reservations, the government had been drawn into supporting UCD's plans, although de Valera was cautious in the face of scepticism by influential officials and outright hostility from the Finance Minister. While MacEntee's reservation was technically correct, the decision marked the first, albeit heavily qualified, commitment by the Irish government to the transfer of the college. De Valera informed a deputation from UCD in August 1953 that he and Moylan were in favour of 'the proposal for new College buildings on the Stillorgan site, adding, however, a remark to the effect that Government approval would be necessary.'[156] This carefully qualified statement glossed over the divisions within the government, not least MacEntee's staunch opposition to the plan. It was almost certainly intended to postpone any decision in the context of unfavourable economic circumstances and the government's precarious position in the Dáil. Certainly no Cabinet decision followed before de Valera's government lost power in 1954.

The second inter-party government, confronted by a sharp deterioration in the balance of payments and a renewed economic contraction following the Suez crisis, sought to curtail spending on education and was equally cautious in making any decisions on the transfer to Belfield. Costello's administration was less divided than Fianna Fáil on the principle of UCD's plans. The party's traditional connections with UCD ensured that Fine Gael was even more receptive than Fianna Fáil to lobbying by the college authorities and most Fine Gael ministers, including Mulcahy in his second term as minister, were sympathetic to the transfer.[157] But the Department of Finance remained sceptical of such a costly development programme without any wider investigation of the universities' fiscal demands on the Exchequer.

The second inter-party government, like its predecessors, was essentially reactive in its approach to higher education. Costello, who had quietly floated the idea of merger between Trinity and UCD during his first term, publicly signalled his support for the expansionist direction set by Tierney in an address during the celebrations of the centenary of Newman's Catholic university in November 1954.[158] But the government made no attempt to address the vexed question of the transfer of the college until 1956, when Tierney's lobbying acted as a catalyst for action. When the UCD president warned Costello on 1 March 1956 that 'the College's position in regard to buildings and equipment is growing steadily more desperate…', the Taoiseach agreed to receive a deputation of college officers to consider the Belfield plans.[159] Following this meeting on 11 April (which was not minuted at Costello's request), Costello and Mulcahy agreed that the Minister for Education would make a submission to the government on the college's proposals for the Belfield site. Mulcahy advised the government in May 1956 that UCD could no longer function effectively on its existing site and he saw 'no reasonable alternative to the proposed transfer.'[160] Mulcahy sought government approval in principle of the transfer on the basis that it would be financed by the Exchequer over a twenty year period. Although his submission was co-ordinated with the Taoiseach, the proposal was opposed by the Department of Finance, which held out for its traditional solution of a commission of enquiry as well as urging the college to reassess the prospect for expansion at Earlsfort Terrace.[161]

The issue was controversial enough that the Cabinet ultimately settled on a compromise. The Cabinet decided on 28 June 1956 to approve in principle the proposed transfer, but this was hedged with so many conditions as to make the decision almost meaningless. Crucially the Cabinet determined that no expenditure should be incurred by the college except on planning until the government clarified 'the availability of resources to finance the State capital programme as a whole in the coming years.' Moreover, the start date and timeframe for the project would 'be decided by the Government having regard to the availability of financial resources from time to time, due regard being had to the prior requirements of directly-productive capital works and of urgent capital works of a social character, including housing…'[162] The note of an earlier Cabinet meeting on 15 June expressed the true position more bluntly—while approval in principle might be given 'UCD would have to take its place in the queue' in relation to other demands on limited resources available for capital expenditure.[163] The tortuously formulated Cabinet decision had no immediate impact and was not even publicised by the government, perhaps because it was so convoluted that it defied explanation. Tierney was informed privately of the government decision, but the copy he received was marked 'to be kept secret until further notice'—not surprisingly, he concluded that it was not possible to take any effective action based on this decision.[164] It was an almost comical commentary on the hesitancy which marked government policy not only towards the Belfield transfer but with regard to longer term policy decisions on higher education throughout the 1950s.

The interim decisions by both inter-party and Fianna Fáil ministers up to the late 1950s left a high degree of uncertainty about UCD's ultimate fate, while also reducing the freedom of action of later politicians and officials. The incremental support offered by successive governments allowed Tierney and his collaborators to create facts on the ground by their extensive purchase of land and initial allocation of accommodation on Stillorgan Road to college departments.[165] The president himself began to use a recently acquired house in Whiteoaks as his official residence, which was presented as 'an act of faith in the future.'[166] Yet this was not a unilateral initiative by Tierney but a complex negotiation in which ministers were involved at almost every stage. The college authorities received sufficient encouragement, sometimes unofficially by leading members of the government, to suggest that their initiative would ultimately receive official support, as a confidential memo by officials of the Department of the Taoiseach acknowledged in July 1955: 'Generally the authorities of University College, Dublin, have fairly substantial grounds for anticipating that Government approval will eventually be given to their proposals for the erection of new buildings on the Stillorgan site and for the transfer of the College to that site…'[167] This would prove a prescient analysis in a more favourable political and economic climate from the late 1950s.

An Elite System

Whatever the differences in their cultural or religious traditions, the university colleges shared similar characteristics in the early postwar era. All four colleges attracted only a small minority of the population, were severely under-resourced and were oriented towards training for the professions. A seminal report on long-term needs for educational resources, *Investment in Education*, which was produced by an Irish survey team under the auspices of the OECD between 1962 and 1965, graphically highlighted the restrictive, elitist nature of university institutions up to the early 1960s.[168] Only 2% of the population aged 15–19 and 3.4% of the population aged 20–24 at the time of the 1961 census were enrolled in third-level education, excluding theological training for the priesthood.[169] Moreover, universities were predominantly the preserve of the upper middle class, as the report noted that 'the strong association between university entrance and social group is unmistakable'.[170] 65% of university entrants drawn from the Leaving Certificate cohort in 1963 (the overwhelming majority of entrants) were the children of professionals, employers and higher white-collar employees: only 2% of university entrants were drawn from the unskilled and semi-skilled manual working class, while 4% were the children of the unemployed or widows.[171] Entry to universities was almost exclusively determined by social and family background and university education remained the preserve of a small privileged elite well into the mid-twentieth century.

De Valera's tenure as Chancellor of the NUI, described as 'grotesquely long' by Fanning, has often been perceived as a recipe for stagnation and a barrier to change in the relationship between government and the universities.[172] Yet this is an over-simplified portrayal during his various terms as Taoiseach. His presence at the head of the NUI certainly precluded any adventurous initiatives by his ministers, but no minister of any political persuasion up to the late 1950s showed inclination towards policy activism other than as a prop for Gaelicisation. De Valera proved receptive to appeals for assistance from college authorities and tended to mitigate the influence of the Department of Finance. He showed political courage, laced with calculation, in authorising the first exchequer grant to Trinity College by an Irish government. The Fianna

Fáil leader accepted the conventional view of universities as professional training schools for a privileged minority, but was more sympathetic to the concerns of professional academics than most politicians. Yet de Valera almost invariably acted in response to appeals for assistance from university authorities: he was ready to champion the upgrading of academic salaries and protection of professional qualifications, but notably wary of authorising finance for the more long-term, costly and complex task of capital development. De Valera's sympathy for universities did not translate into a coherent policy for higher education.

Governments in the early postwar period were more open than their predecessors to taking incremental initiatives, but were reactive and hesitant in developing coherent policies and focused almost entirely on university institutions. Political and official elites still subscribed to a traditionalist world view about the value and purpose of higher education. This world view associated higher education almost exclusively with the universities and explicitly accepted a limited vision of the university as a narrowly defined elite institution. Government initiatives usually responded to a particular crisis in finances, staffing or professional recognition of courses within the universities. The real increase in state funding for universities and colleges in this period could not keep pace with increasing social demand for higher education, which was significant in a period of economic instability. Yet the peripheral status of higher education was no longer universally accepted: the universities at least secured greater attention in the national media and institutional appeals for assistance no longer met with blanket hostility or efforts to curtail enrolments. A growing sense of crisis in the university sector could be detected in this period, exemplified by the threatened non-recognition of medical schools and the intermittent but significant cash infusions made several times since 1945. The traditionalist consensus on higher education, defined by a laissez faire government philosophy and parsimonious financing of the sector, proved increasingly unsustainable in the face of demographic demands and a more vocal public sphere, including a more assertive university leadership. The growing societal demand for higher education, combined with the impact of political and administrative neglect over the previous generation, forced a re-appraisal of traditionalist policies, although this was both piecemeal and incomplete during the 1950s.

Notes

1. *Irish Independent* editorial, 'The Irish Universities,' 3 February 1947.
2. Ibid.
3. *Irish Press*, 'Bigger Grants for Universities,' 27 February 1947.
4. Patrick Clancy, 'Evolution of Policy in Third-Level Education,' 100–1.
5. Ibid., 99.
6. Ulrich Teichler, 'Changing Structures of the Higher Education Systems: The Increasing Complexity of the Underlying Forces,' in *Diversification of Higher Education and the Changing Role of Knowledge and Research* UNESCO Forum Occasional Paper Series No. 6 (Paris, 2004), 4.
7. Mark Olssen and Michael Peters, 'Neoliberalism, Higher Education and the Knowledge Economy: From the Free Market to Knowledge Capitalism,' *Journal of Education Policy* 20, no. 3 (2005): 314.
8. HEA, *Interim Report of the Steering Committee's Technical Working Group* (Dublin: HEA, 1995), 26.
9. Diarmaid Ferriter, *The Transformation of Ireland 1900–2000* (London: Profile 2004), 465–6.
10. HEA, *Interim Report of Technical Working Group*, 26.
11. Government of Ireland, *Report of the Commission on Higher Education 1960–67*, 21.
12. Ibid., 126.
13. Report of the Interdepartmental Committee to the Minister for Finance, 31 January 1947, 3 (NAI TSCH/3/S14018A); Ó Raifeartaigh to GPS Hogan, 16 January 1958 (NAI TSCH/3/S12544).
14. O'Rahilly Memorandum, 'The Post-war Development of University College Cork,' 27 April 1945 (NAI TSCH S13258); Murphy, *The College*, 305.
15. Luce, *Trinity College Dublin*, 144; Memorandum on the Needs of Trinity College Dublin, December 1946 (NAI TSCH/3/S13962A).
16. Memorandum on the Needs of Trinity College Dublin, 6 December 1946 (NAI TSCH/3/S13962A).
17. *Report of the Commission on Higher Education*, 86.
18. De Valera to Derrig, 16 December 1946 (NAI TSCH/3/S12891B).
19. Ferriter, *Transformation of Ireland*, 450–1.

20. Liam Ó Laidhin to Private Secretary to the Taoiseach, 1 November 1947 (NAI TSCH/3/S12891B).
21. D. MacConchrada to Maurice Moynihan, 29 August 1945 (TSCH/3/S12891B).
22. Ibid.
23. *Recommendations for the Reorganisation of the Educational System to Meet a Raising of the School Leaving Age*, 27 June 1947 (NAI TSCH/3/S12891B), 19–20.
24. Ibid., L. Ó Muirithe to Derrig, 27 June 1947.
25. Luce, *Trinity College Dublin*, 146.
26. *Irish Independent*, 'New University Buildings,' 14 February 1947.
27. *Irish Press*, 'New University Buildings,' 14 February 1947.
28. *Irish Press*, 'New University Buildings,' 14 February 1947.
29. Public Accounts Committee, *Appropriation Accounts 1948–49* (Dublin: Stationery Office, 1950), 102.
30. Public Accounts Committee, *Appropriation Accounts 1958–59* (Dublin: Stationery Office, 1959), 88.
31. Report of the Interdepartmental Committee to the Minister for Finance, 31 January 1947 (NAI TSCH/3/S14018A).
32. O'Rahilly Memorandum, 'The Post-war Development of University College Cork,' 27 April 1945 (NAI TSCH S13258).
33. Ibid., 4
34. Memorandum from the President of UCC, 23 April 1946, TSCH/3/S14018A.
35. Ibid., 2.
36. Ibid., 3.
37. Memorandum from Pádraig de Brún to J. J. McElligott, 27 January 1947 (NAI TSCH/3/S14018A).
38. Ibid.
39. McDowell and Webb, *Trinity College Dublin*, 474.
40. Luce, *Trinity College Dublin*, 146.
41. E. H. Alton to de Valera, 18 December 1946 (NAI TSCH/3/S13962A).
42. Memorandum on the Needs of Trinity College Dublin, 10 December 1946 (NAI TSCH/3/S13962A).
43. Report of the Interdepartmental Committee to the Minister for Finance, 31 January 1947 (NAI TSCH/3/S14018A), 2.
44. Ibid., 3.

45. Ibid., 5.
46. Ibid., 3.
47. De Brún to J. J. McElligott, 27 January 1947 (NAI TSCH/3/S14018A).
48. Report of the Interdepartmental Committee to the Minister for Finance, 31 January 1947, 7 (NAI TSCH/3/S14018A).
49. Ibid., 5–9.
50. O'Rahilly, *Confidential Report: Meeting on 19 February 1947 Between an Taoiseach, the Minister for Finance, the Minister for Education and the Three President of the Constituent Colleges*, 22 February 1947, 1 (NAI TSCH/3/S14018A).
51. A. J. O'Connell to de Valera, 2 April 1947 (NAI TSCH/3/S14018A).
52. McCartney, *UCD*, 120–1: see McCartney for a detailed discussion of UCD's efforts, particularly under Conway's presidency, to expand the Earlsfort Terrace site.
53. O'Rahilly, *Confidential Report*, 1 (NAI TSCH/3/S14018A).
54. *Increases in Salary for Members of Teaching Staff* (NAI TSCH/3/S14018A).
55. *Irish Independent*, 'Increase in University Fees,' 13 September 1947.
56. Memo from the President of University College, Cork, 17 July 1947 (NAI TSCH/3/S14018A); Coláiste na hOllscoile, Gaillimh, Statement showing increase in students' class fees (NAI TSCH/3/S14018A).
57. Report of the Interdepartmental Committee to the Minister for Finance, 31 January 1947 (NAI TSCH/3/S14018A), 11.
58. Memorandum on the Needs of Trinity College Dublin, December 1946 (NAI TSCH/3/S13962A), 2.
59. Ibid., 4–7.
60. Ibid., 10.
61. Ibid., 10.
62. Alton to de Valera, 8 November 1946, Government Note, 7 December 1946 (NAI TSCH/3/S13962A).
63. 'Report Made to the Board of Trinity College on 20 February 1947 by the Provost and Registrar,' (MUN V/6/7, Companion vol. 6), 1; Board Minutes, 12 March 1947 (MUN V/5/26), 244–45.
64. Alton to De Valera, 1 March 1947 (NAI TSCH/3/S13962A).
65. Ibid.
66. 'Report Made to the Board of Trinity College on 20 February 1947 by the Provost and Registrar,' 1 (MUN V/6/7, Companion vol. 6).

67. Ibid.
68. Ibid.
69. Ibid.
70. Ibid.
71. McDowell and Webb, *Trinity College Dublin*, 475.
72. Alton to De Valera, 1 March 1947 (NAI TSCH/3/S13962A).
73. Seanad Debates, vol. 33, no. 15, col. 1322, 20 March 1947.
74. Public Accounts Committee, *Appropriation Accounts 1947–48* (Dublin: Stationery Office, 1950), 14
75. *Irish Independent*, 'State Grant to TCD: Explanation Required, Bishop Says,' 31 May 1949.
76. Ibid.; *Irish Times*, 'TCD Grant Criticised by Bishop,' 31 May 1949.
77. *Irish Independent*, 'State Grant to TCD: Explanation Required, Bishop Says,' 31 May 1949.
78. *Irish Independent* editorial, 'The Irish Universities,' 3 February 1947.
79. McCartney, *UCD*, 132–3.
80. Ibid.
81. Ibid., 134.
82. *Irish Times*, 'Trinity College,' 17 March 1952.
83. *Irish Times*, 'New Provost of Trinity College,' 15 March 1952; Luce, *Trinity College Dublin*, 148; for more detailed analysis of McConnell's election and its implications, see McDowell and Webb, *Trinity College Dublin*, 493–7.
84. Luce, *Trinity College Dublin*, 148–9.
85. *Irish Times*, 'Provost Replies to "Violent Attacks" on Trinity College,' 24 October 1955.
86. Ibid.
87. Luce, *Trinity College Dublin*, 155.
88. Ibid., 156; See above pp. 111–12 for this campaign.
89. Mac Mathúna, 'National University of Ireland Galway,' 81.
90. NUI, Senate Minutes, vol. 23, 7 July 1960, 144–5. Newell was also the first native of Galway to become president of UCG.
91. Seán Tobin, 'Dr. Martin J. Newell 1910–85,' *IMS Bulletin* 19 (1987): 13–21. Accessed 1 December 2017. https://www.maths.tcd.ie/pub/ims/bull19/bull19_13-21.pdf.
92. Murphy, *The College*, 318–9.
93. Ibid., 319–20.
94. NUI, Senate Minutes, vol. 40, 15 July 1967, 69–70.

95. Murphy, *The College*, 318–20.
96. Ibid., 325–28.
97. *Memorandum on the Financial Position of University College, Dublin*, 8 (NAI TSCH/3/S12544).
98. Murphy, *The College*, 306.
99. Government Note, 8 December 1948 (NAI TSCH/3/S13962B).
100. *Extract from Cabinet Minutes*, G.C.5/171 (NAI TSCH/3/S13962A): The Committee included Costello, McGilligan, Mulcahy, Norton, Noel Browne (Health) and T. F. O'Higgins (Defence).
101. Public Accounts Committee, *Appropriation Accounts 1950–51*, 11.
102. Deputation from Trinity College Dublin to Taoiseach and Minister for Finance, April 1951 (NAI TSCH/3/S13962B).
103. Public Accounts Committee, *Appropriation Accounts 1950–51*, 11.
104. Note by Attorney General, 21 October 1947 (NAI TSCH/3/S14086).
105. *Irish Times*, 'Maynooth College Needs £300,000,' 13 October 1948.
106. *Irish Independent*, 'Maynooth's Appeal to Ireland,' 13 October 1948.
107. *Evening Herald*, 'Taxpayers £35,000 Subsidy for TCD: Most Rev. Dr. Browne's Disclosure,' 30 May 1949.
108. Memorandum on State Assistance to Maynooth College, 1950 (NAI TSCH/3/S14086), 1–3.
109. Ibid., 3.
110. Hansard, House of Commons vol. 79, col. 1040, 18 April 1845.
111. Note of Meeting, 10 February 1950 (NAI TSCH/3/S14086).
112. Memorandum: St. Patrick's College, Maynooth, 29 April 1950 (NAI TSCH/3/S14086), 1.
113. Ibid.
114. O'Donoghue to the Attorney General, 9 May 1950 (NAI TSCH/3/S14086).
115. Government Note, 8 December 1948; Alton to Costello, 2 March 1949; Alton to Costello, 1 April 1949; A. J. McConnell to Costello, 31 January 1951 (NAI TSCH/3/S13962B).
116. Alton to Costello, 1 April 1949; Department of Education, Trinity College Dublin: Application Dated 1 April 1949 for Increased State Assistance (NAI TSCH/3/S13962B).
117. McElligott to Moynihan, 23 May 1949.
118. *Memorandum on the Needs of Trinity College*, 2 December 1949 (MUN/6/8, Companion vol. 7).

119. McConnell to Costello, 31 January 1951 (NAI TSCH/3/S13962B).
120. Deputation from Trinity College Dublin to Taoiseach and Minister for Finance, 1 March 1951 (NAI TSCH/3/S13962B).
121. Ibid., 3–4.
122. Ibid., 6.
123. Ibid.
124. Ibid., 9.
125. Ibid., 11.
126. Ibid., 9.
127. Ibid., 9.
128. Ibid., 17.
129. Minutes, Board Meeting, 25 April 1951, 121–2 (MUN V/5/27).
130. McDowell and Webb, *Trinity College Dublin*, 479.
131. Lee, *Ireland 1912–85*, 299.
132. Minutes, Board Meeting, 5 March 1952, 121–2 (MUN V/5/27).
133. McDowell and Webb, *Trinity College Dublin*, 479.
134. Donal McCartney, *The NUI and De Valera* (Dublin: UPI, 1983), 39–40.
135. De Valera to Costello, n.d. 1955 (NAI TSCH/3/S14018C).
136. Richard Mulcahy to John A. Costello, 8 February 1956 (NAI TSCH/3/S12544).
137. Seamus Wilmot to Costello, 27 October 1955 (NAI TSCH/3/S14018C).
138. Tierney to Costello, 16 January 1956 (NAI TSCH/3/S12544).
139. De Valera to Costello, 7 November 1955 (NAI TSCH/3/S14018C).
140. Ibid.
141. National University of Ireland, *Grants for Medical Schools in Constituent Colleges*, August 1956 (NAI TSCH/3/S12544), 1–3.
142. Ibid; Moynihan to Private Secretary to Eamon de Valera, 10 September 1956: UCD secured 100% of the funding sought for Medicine and Dentistry; UCC 85% and UCG 81.5%—although the latter college increased its demand from £7500 to £10,000 while the application was already under consideration.
143. Tierney to Costello, 1 March 1956 (NAI TSCH/3/S12544).
144. Moynihan to Private Secretary to Eamon de Valera, 10 September 1956 (NAI TSCH/3/S12544).
145. Memorandum, 27 October 1952 (NAI TSCH/3/S14018C); McCartney, *UCD*, 234–6; Whiteoaks and Montrose were acquired in 1949 and Merville in 1951.

146. *Irish Times*, 'Letters to the Editor—UCD,' 6 April 1957.
147. J. J. O'Meara, *Reform in Education* (Dublin: Mount Salus Press, 1958), 18–19; *Irish Times*, '"Some Union" Between TCD and UCD Urged: Welding of Tradition,' 28 March 1958.
148. Department of Education Memorandum, *University College Dublin: Proposed Transfer to Stillorgan Site*, 21 July 1955 (NAI TSCH/3/S13809B).
149. Government Note, 23 February 1953 (NAI TSCH/3/S12544); McCartney, *UCD*, 235.
150. Department of Education Memorandum, *University College Dublin: Proposed Transfer to Stillorgan Site*, 21 July 1955, TSCH/3/S13809B (NAI TSCH/3/S13809B).
151. Department of the Taoiseach Memorandum, 27 October 1952 (NAI TSCH/3/S14018C).
152. Tierney to de Valera, 9 February 1953 (NAI TSCH/3/S12544).
153. Government Note, 23 February 1953 (NAI TSCH/3/S12544).
154. Ibid.
155. Secretary of the Department of Education to Tierney, 11 March 1953 (NAI TSCH/3/S12544).
156. Department of Education, *University College Dublin: Proposed Transfer to Stillorgan Site*, 21 July 1955 (NAI TSCH/3/S13809B).
157. Costello and Mulcahy were UCD graduates, while McGilligan (Minister for Finance in the first and Attorney General in the second inter-party government), was both a graduate and a college professor.
158. *Irish Times*, 'UCD's Independence Would Be "Disaster,"' 16 November 1954.
159. Tierney to Costello, 1 March 1956 (NAI TSCH/3/S12544).
160. Memorandum for the Government, *Proposed Transfer of University College, Dublin, to Belfield Site, Stillorgan Road* (NAI TSCH/3/S13809C), 1.
161. Ibid., 8.
162. Maurice Moynihan to James Dukes, 28 June 1956 (NAI TSCH/3/S13809C).
163. Government Meeting, Note, 15 June 1956 (NAI TSCH/3/S13809C).
164. Note of meeting between the Taoiseach and Minister for Education and Dr. Tierney and Prof. Hogan, 25 May 1957 (NAI TSCH/3/S12544), 1–4.
165. McCartney, *UCD*, 240.

166. Ibid., 233.
167. Department of Education, *University College Dublin: Proposed Transfer to Stillorgan Site*, 21 July 1955 (NAI TSCH/3/S13809B).
168. Government of Ireland, *Investment in Education*, 172.
169. Ibid., 120.
170. Ibid., 172.
171. Ibid., 172.
172. Ronan Fanning, 'T. K. Whitaker 1976–96,' in *The National University of Ireland 1908–2008 Centenary Essays*, ed. Dunne et al. (Dublin: UCD Press, 2008),149.

7

The Transformation of Higher Education

A radical transformation of higher education occurred in the thirty-year period from the 1950s to the 1980s, encompassing major policy, institutional and structural changes.[1] Far-reaching policy changes were driven mainly by an interventionist state in a context of societal and cultural modernisation. The radical transition in HE policy reflected the breakdown of the traditionalist consensus on the role of higher education and its relationship with the state: this testified to attitudinal and generational change among domestic political elites, linked to a wider re-appraisal of traditional ideological frameworks and the impact of human capital ideas mediated through the OECD. Governmental intervention on an unprecedented scale was designed to deliver a more highly skilled work force and accommodate increasing social demand for third-level education.[2] The outcome was the emergence of a recognisable higher education system for the first time, which was diversified, sectorally differentiated and radically different in scale, organisation and ambition than the fragmented collection of institutions in the post-compulsory education space of the previous era.

Martin Trow's theoretical model for the development of higher education indicates a progression from 'elite' to 'mass' systems of higher

© The Author(s) 2018
J. Walsh, *Higher Education in Ireland, 1922–2016*,
https://doi.org/10.1057/978-1-137-44673-2_7

education and ultimately to 'universal' access.[3] Trow argued that the entry of over 15% of the relevant school leaving age cohort to higher education marked the transition from traditional 'elite' institutions to 'mass' education, with 50% identified as a similar threshold for 'universal' education.[4] Perhaps the most valuable insight of Trow's model was not its concept of linear progression which was subsequently questioned, not least by its author, but its focus on the transformative nature of expansion which exerted a far-reaching influence at all levels of institutional life, work and culture: 'Mass higher education systems differs from elite higher education not only quantitatively but qualitatively… the differences between these phases are quite fundamental and go through every aspect of higher education'.[5] Yet Trow's reinterpretation of his original ideal typology presented a more nuanced and complex portrayal in which 'mass' higher education developed alongside 'elite' HE, providing a greater range of opportunities for prospective students, but co-existing with rather than replacing the earlier pattern both across and within institutions. Instead elite HEIs were able to persist within a mass HE system, while both elite and mass characteristics could be maintained in a HE system moving towards universal access.[6]

O'Sullivan posits a gradual socio-cultural transition in which religious ideals associated with a dominant 'theocentric' paradigm, which provided the ideological backdrop for educational policy in the first generation of the Irish state, were displaced from the 1950s by a 'mercantile' paradigm with economic considerations at its core.[7] Human capital theory, which held that investment in people produced a greater return of investment than investment in physical capital, emerged as a major strand of international economic thinking in the early 1960s.[8] The Irish political and administrative system enthusiastically embraced 'human capital' theory as a key institutional rationale for investment in education.[9] While O'Sullivan's theoretical framing of the debate is valuable, it risks understating non-economic variables in a period of policy, institutional and cultural ferment, notably increased social demand for post-compulsory education and the influence of egalitarian ideas among politicians, expert advisers, academics and students. The imperative of national economic development in the mid-twentieth century was a key driver of educational policy change, but the wider context of political and societal modernisation was also crucial. Generational and attitudinal change within the political and official elite, demographic expansion from the mid-1960s for the first time in a century and the greater appeal of egalitarian policies all combined to break down the traditionalist consensus and make education a key focus for political action. The reforms launched by the Second Vatican Council (1962–65) had a profound influence on Irish Catholicism, contributing to a decline of traditional attitudes of deference among lay Catholics and to some extent clergy to the bishops.[10] A broadly based ideological reorientation underpinned major policy, institutional and cultural changes in Irish higher education. While economic imperatives undoubtedly played a crucial part in the rapid expansion of the system, labour market considerations co-existed with increasing political and social pressures linked to societal demand for third-level places and the influence of egalitarian ideas in the public sphere. Political elites sought to legitimise policy changes through an appeal to political and egalitarian objectives, seeking to demonstrate that their agenda was defined neither by narrowly economic priorities nor by the traditional pieties of an earlier era.

Séan Lemass, who succeeded de Valera as Taoiseach in June 1959 on the older man's elevation to the Presidency, initiated a far-reaching transformation of economic and educational policies, which within a short time exerted a profound influence on higher education. Lemass, working in conjunction with T. K. Whitaker and other reform-minded officials in the Department of Finance, completed a radical reorientation of economic policies, marked by a gradual transition from a protectionist regime to free trade and from self-sufficiency to sustained promotion of foreign investment.[11] The Department of Education, led by a number of younger, dynamic ministers appointed by Lemass, was given responsibility for the universities from 1957–58, in a long awaited change approved by Whitaker.[12] Patrick Hillery, who authorised the landmark *Investment in Education* study in 1962 under the auspices of the OECD and the Department of Education, recognised the value of an externally validated study in legitimating major reform: the initiative '…meant opening cupboards and all the dark holes and highlighting everything that was lacking.'[13] The reforms adopted by the government, notably the introduction of free second-level education and raising of the statutory school leaving age to fifteen by 1972, contributed to an extraordinary upsurge of enrolments, which intensified societal demand for access to higher education.[14]

Changing attitudes among domestic political elites dovetailed with an emerging international consensus that investment in education at all levels was essential to economic development. The Cold War added a crucial impetus to educational expansion, as global rivalry between the superpowers offered a compelling imperative for scientific and technological development in the West. The Organisation for European Economic Co-operation (OEEC) warned explicitly in 1961 that the success of the competing systems in achieving social and economic progress would 'affect their respective influence in the world at large' and that educational investment was significant in 'the world competition' between the democracies and the Communist world.[15] The OECD promoted investment in 'human capital' among the developed countries of the West from the early 1960s, identifying the development of education and scientific research as vital to achievement of economic growth. Human capital ideas mediated primarily through the OECD contributed significantly to a radical change of direction by the political and administrative elite.[16] The limitations of educational provision were underlined by a series of expert group reports, of which *Investment in Education* was the most significant. Many (though not all) of these re-appraisals were linked with the OECD, including an influential review of technical training.

'...Break-Down Point Has Almost Been Reached...'

The first critical re-appraisal of the position of the universities since 1922 was offered by a commission on accommodation needs, which despite its limited remit served as a catalyst in transforming government policy. The commission was established by de Valera's final government in August 1957 with the remit to 'inquire into the accommodation needs of the Constituent Colleges of the National University and to advise as to how in the present circumstances these needs could best be met.'[17] The commission fulfilled several purposes—offering an authoritative investigation by an 'expert' group of the contentious Belfield proposal; assessing the equally pressing accommodation concerns of UCC and UCG and meeting a longstanding demand of the Department of Finance for a longer term review of the universities' financial requirements. Jack Lynch, the newly appointed Minister for Education, hoped that the commission would relate the universities' accommodation problems to 'the national need', while de Valera sought a definitive recommendation on the Belfield problem, recognising that it could not be dealt with in isolation from the other colleges in the NUI.[18] Justice Cearbhall Ó Dálaigh chaired a small commission composed mainly of members drawn from the business community and government departments, including the stockbroker J. J. Davy and Aodhogán O'Rahilly, a director of Bord na Móna.[19] Trinity College was not included in its terms of reference. When O'Rahilly sought to have the option of amalgamation considered by the commission, the Cabinet explicitly ruled out this out in March 1958.[20] O'Rahilly threatened to resign from the commission, but was persuaded to remain a member by the Taoiseach.[21] De Valera was instrumental in determining the restrictive terms of reference, not least because he had already indicated his support for the Belfield project. The Taoiseach wished to avoid raising the politically explosive question of merger, which would provoke conflict with the Catholic bishops. Cardinal John D'Alton, archbishop of Armagh, warned publicly on 23 June 1958 against 'any ill-considered experiment in the education field', singling out a merger between Trinity College and UCD as 'a union of incompatibles'.[22] The idea of merger was outside the realm of practical politics in the late 1950s, not least due to the ecclesiastical ban on the attendance of Catholics at TCD and the reluctance of influential political leaders, including de Valera, to contemplate a radical reconstruction of university education.[23]

De Valera assured Tierney, who was sceptical of the commission, in August 1957 that it was not a device to delay a decision on Belfield further and would be required 'to report this side of Christmas'.[24] While this proved optimistic, the commission completed its work swiftly, issuing an interim report on UCD in June 1958 and the final report by May 1959. The expert group exposed the accommodation crisis in the universities, highlighting the absence of state funded capital development for a quarter of a century: 'The result has been that the Colleges have become more and more over-crowded, and arrears of building have been accumulating...'.[25] The commission issued a blunt warning about the legacy of benign neglect:

> The problem, however, cannot, in our opinion, await a protracted solution. Already break-down point {sic} has almost been reached in the colleges...Under such conditions the quality and standards of both the teaching and the work of the university cannot for long go unaffected.[26]

The report recommended an ambitious building programme financed by the state, costing £8 million over a ten-year period. Among the recommendations were general principles for university development, including maintaining the physical unity of each institution, accommodation of the sciences in new buildings and providing accommodation open to adaptation, which had relevance for all future developments not only in the NUI but throughout the emerging third-level sector.[27] The commission also sounded the alarm about the economic implications of a failure to invest: 'a crisis in these training centres would have the gravest consequences for the national life and economy...The solution of the problem, therefore, is urgent and its place in national planning should be high'.[28]

The commission's first interim report on UCD proved influential. The commission recommended the transfer of the entire college to Belfield to deliver 'a final and satisfactory solution to the College's accommodation problems'.[29] The majority of the commission gave a definitive imprimatur to the transfer of UCD despite a vigorous dissent by O'Rahilly, who argued for the amalgamation of UCD and Trinity College. The commission's report was a key factor in breaking the deadlock within successive governments since 1951 over the Belfield development. The Department of Education under successive ministers had championed the Belfield project and the secretary, Tarlach Ó Raifeartaigh, was a firm advocate for the transfer of UCD to Belfield. MacEntee, now the Minister for Health and Social Welfare, mounted a dedicated rearguard action, objecting to the proposed transfer which would be accomplished only 'at an enormous capital cost'.[30]

But the Department of Finance proved willing to authorise large-scale investment in university education based on the recommendations of the commission. Moreover, the report enjoyed the crucial support of the Taoiseach. De Valera advised the Cabinet to approve the transfer of UCD to Belfield with the proviso that any decision in principle would require the approval of the Dáil.[31] The government adopted de Valera's favoured approach, approving the transfer of UCD subject to the agreement of the Dáil, on 26 May 1959.[32]

Lynch's successor, Dr. Patrick Hillery, presented a token Vote to the Dáil in March 1960 to secure parliamentary approval for the proposal. Hillery rejected amalgamation in his Dáil statement as a threat to the parental and religious freedoms guaranteed in Article 42 of the constitution, which required the state to respect the lawful preference of parents not to send their children to any educational institution in violation of their conscience.[33] Hillery's statement was drafted by Ó Raifeartaigh, a devout Catholic layman who consulted closely with McQuaid on university education. McQuaid, as chairman of the episcopal commission on university education, wrote to both Hillery and Ó Raifeartaigh on 24 March 1960 to offer his congratulations on the minister's statement: 'I regard it as a document of unusual historic value. For the first time a Government has stated in effect that the Catholics have a right to their own University education.'[34] Ó Raifeartaigh's prompt response underlined the extent of the collaboration between McQuaid and senior departmental officials. He paid tribute to McQuaid for his staunch advocacy of higher education for Catholics which both men saw as being vindicated by Hillery's statement: '[Catholic higher education] has now been publicly and officially accepted, after its loss for more than four hundred years.'[35] McQuaid's collaborative relationship with Ó Raifeartaigh testified less to overt ecclesiastical pressure than a shared world view defined by integralist Catholicism.[36] The bishops did not determine the state's policy in favour of the transfer to Belfield, which was driven by Tierney's persistent lobbying, strong elite backing for the project and ultimately de Valera's intervention. But the opposition of the bishops to Trinity College effectively defined the acceptable parameters for policy: the development of Belfield was a pragmatic solution for a government and political elite which had no desire for conflict with the ecclesiastical authorities.[37] The official decision was a striking illustration of the extent to which the complex interpenetration of ecclesiastical and state power shaped policy-making in practice despite the formally non-denominational status of the unversities.

The commission served as a catalyst in ending the long term drought in capital investment. The report underlined that the existing accommodation for UCC and UCG was inadequate, recommending that necessary building projects for the two colleges should be funded mainly by the exchequer.[38] A university development committee was proposed as a liaison mechanism between colleges and the government. This recommendation influenced the establishment of the Commission on Higher Education in the following year.[39] Subsequently, the establishment of the Higher Education Authority (HEA) in 1968 created an institution fulfilling many of the functions proposed by the report.

The report had a wider significance which has not always been recognised, making an eloquent appeal for public investment in third-level education as a national priority, which both reflected and contributed to changing attitudes among political and official elites. The commission ensured that the expansion of university education appeared on the government's radar for the first time since independence. The importance of the commission as an inflection point in terms of policy change was underlined by the appropriation accounts for 1959–60. The net expenditure for 'Universities and Colleges' for 1959–60 amounted to £948,560, a very modest allocation by subsequent standards, which nonetheless represented an increase of 37% from the previous year.[40] This allocation amounted to 0.8% of net exchequer spending, representing a more substantial advance for higher education in a single year than the cumulative increase over the previous five-year period. Lynch publicly committed the government in April 1959 to financing the commission's recommendations on the urgent accommodation requirements of the universities.[41] This marked an explicit break with the practice of successive governments since 1922, which had given capital grants grudgingly and on strict conditions, if at all. Moreover the commission's argument that 'The well-being of university education and of the country are closely linked' had a long-term resonance which would be felt for the rest of the twentieth century and beyond.[42]

The commission operated in a political and institutional context which was favourable to its message that universities were at crisis point. The Department of Finance under Whitaker's direction adopted a strategic approach to expenditure on higher education, encompassing a wider reconceptualisation of spending on education as a necessary investment for societal and economic benefit. This shift in the department's traditional orientation was crucial in paving the way for expansionist policies in higher education for most of the following generation. The internal debate between the Departments of Finance and Education between the 1950s and the early 1980s focused more on how to finance new initiatives, beginning with the transfer to Belfield, rather than the ideological objections to public support for higher education expressed by McElligott's generation. Ironically the investigation of university financing sought by McElligott since the mid 1940s to restrict spending on university education, proved a catalyst for long-term expansion underpinned by public capital investment.

A wider investigation into third-level education was announced by Hillery in March 1960, with the establishment of a new Commission on Higher Education.[43] The commission, again headed by Ó Dálaigh, was charged with a re-appraisal of the entire third-level sector encompassing all third-level institutions.[44] The commission was the first committee of enquiry appointed by an independent Irish government in higher education: the sole restriction on its freedom of action was that the die was cast on the transfer of UCD to Belfield.[45] But its impact was diluted because the government set out to ensure that no influential interest group would be offended by exclusion from it. Its membership included university academics, Catholic and Protestant bishops and representatives of business and the public service.[46] But at twenty-eight members the new group was three times the membership of its highly effective predecessor. The new commission struggled to reach consensus on key issues or to report in a timely fashion. The commission's report was not submitted until 1967 and its lengthy deliberations limited its influence in an era when educational policy was in ferment.

More significant than the deliberations of the commission was an emergent consensus among political and official elites in favour of investment in higher education. The upward trend in spending in the late 1950s was the prelude to a dramatic expansion of public investment. The net exchequer spending on higher education increased from £948,560 in 1959–60 to £11.2 million in 1971–72, amounting to 2% of net state spending.[47] The HE sector maintained a broadly comparable share of overall exchequer spending over the following decade, despite a marked deterioration in economic conditions. The state was spending £84.4 million on higher education by 1980–81, just under 2% of net state spending reviewed by the PAC.[48] Government expenditure on HE as a percentage of total state spending on education reached 18% by 1980.[49]

The rationale for state investment in the universities was influenced by 'human capital' considerations, linked to the perceived contribution of higher education to national economic development. The Department of Education noted in 1962: 'The university project of transcending importance in relation to economic development in the 1963–68 period will be the provision of the new Science Block in University College Dublin'.[50] The development of the new campus proceeded apace throughout the 1960s, underpinned by substantial public funding, with the opening of the science building in September 1964 and the completion of new arts and administration buildings between 1968 and 1973.[51]

The prominence of higher education in official discourse was intertwined with an increasingly influential strand of government policy, namely the development of science and technical education at higher level. The accommodation commission drew attention to 'marked development' internationally in the sciences, which were not adequately supported in the NUI.[52] Capital funding allocated to the colleges of the NUI sought to correct the historical neglect of science, with the construction of science buildings and libraries usually receiving a high priority, beginning with the science block at Belfield in 1960–64. The government approved in February 1964 the development of a new science building in UCC, accommodating chemistry, physics and mathematical sciences, as well as a new science library for the college; the new science block was completed between 1967 and 1970 at a cost of £2.1 million.[53] Similarly, the Exchequer financed a new science and library complex in UCG between 1968 and 1973.[54]

Yet the upsurge in public investment was not exclusively targeted towards science. The department embarked upon a large-scale programme of capital investment at higher level, underpinning a far-reaching expansion of the university infrastructure. The exchequer provided half of the necessary funding for the building of the new Berkeley library in TCD (first proposed by the Board in 1950) up to a total cost of £736,000.[55] This programme of capital investment was extended throughout the 1970s, with the allocation by the government to the HEA in 1970 of £15 million for capital projects in the universities over a six-year period.[56] The ambitious programme of public investment reflected the newly dominant consensus at elite level that higher education would contribute to the needs of an expanding economy.

University education was also influenced by cultural and institutional changes within the Catholic church. The trustees of Maynooth initiated in 1966 the most far-reaching institutional reform since the foundation of the seminary, opening the college to lay students on a co-educational basis.[57] The decision led to a long-term phase of development, in which the design and building of a new campus was initiated, including a new arts building funded by the state as part of the programme of third level capital development.[58] The motivation behind this initiative was less radical than it appeared in the heady days immediately after the Second Vatican Council and it did not lead to any reform of the college statutes. As Smyth notes, the decision was prompted by hard-headed financial calculation and was 'a conservative defence and retention of a collegiate mission and identity that had flourished on campus for more than 150 years.'[59] Ecclesiastical power remained a reality in an institution which was both a seminary and a recognised college of the NUI. Two professors in the college were dismissed by the trustees in 1977 following their decision to secure laicisation from the priesthood.[60] The Irish Federation of University Teachers (IFUT) took up their cause, but ultimately lost in the Supreme Court; a judgement in the High Court affirmed that Maynooth in 'its fundamental status and character' was still legally a seminary, regardless of its recognised college status and acceptance of state grants.[61] Despite its physical and demographic transformation, the college's traditional constitution and dual status remained intact for another generation.

When the commission on higher education finally submitted its report in February 1967, it had largely been overtaken by events. Yet the commission produced an immensely detailed report, which offered a comprehensive assessment of higher education. A central theme of the report was the protection of academic standards by limiting the expansion of university education, coupled with the absorption of increasing social demand by new non-university institutions. The commission drew a fundamental distinction between training, presented primarily as a vocational function that should occur outside the university and basic research, which should remain the primary mission of the university. Their vision was informed by Newman's ideal of the university as 'a place of teaching universal knowledge', although they accorded a higher place to research than the founder of the Catholic university.[62] This ideological position, while sincerely held, buttressed the commission's preoccupations with safeguarding academic standards and limiting professional training within the university. The commission also owed a debt to Von Humboldt's ideal of freedom for research and teaching as the defining principle of the university.[63]

The commission identified real problems of inadequate staffing and accommodation in higher education and warned against further expansion in the universities in the short-term. The necessity to protect academic standards at a time of increasing demand for higher education and traditionally low levels of state support informed their report:

> If the universities should falter, they must inevitably be swamped by the flood of undergraduates; and the consequent lowering of standards will be transmitted throughout the entire educational system, with grave consequences in every department of the nation's activities.[64]

The commission proposed the creation of a new type of third-level institution, the New College, to meet much of the expanding demand for higher education. These new institutions, in Dublin and Limerick, would award a pass degree for three-year courses and diplomas for shorter courses. The teacher training colleges would be linked to the New Colleges, while the training of secondary school teachers would remain concentrated in schools of education in the universities.[65]

The commissioners were wary of major changes at institutional level, opposing amalgamation between Trinity College and UCD: their most significant recommendation for institutional reform was the dissolution of the NUI and the reconstitution of its constituent colleges as separate universities. A strong affirmation of institutional autonomy was a notable feature of the report, although the commissioners acknowledged that such autonomy was subject to limitations imposed by dependence on state funding. They favoured more formal collaboration between the universities, overseen by a Council of Irish Universities established by the Oireachtas.[66] The council, composed of members from each college, would provide for collaboration between universities without impinging upon their autonomy. The commissioners also proposed improvements in college governance and procedures, recommending that academic appointments in all universities should be made by the governing authority on the basis of nominations by expert committees.[67] They also proposed the establishment of a statutory Commission for Higher Education reporting directly to the Taoiseach, to act as an intermediary agency responsible for planning, budgeting and distribution of funding.[68]

The distinction between university education and professional training was a central preoccupation of the report. The commissioners argued that 'the university is not a professional academy…existing merely to provide training for several professions…The university is a place for the study and communication of basic knowledge'.[69] This conviction that the function of the university consisted of education in fundamental principles echoed Newman's *Discourses* a century earlier and led the commissioners to propose the exclusion of vocational training and most 'applied' research from the university. They argued, however, that new research developments should usually be accommodated in the universities or existing research institutes.[70] Technological studies should be conducted outside the universities under the auspices of a Technological Authority, which would 'promote and assist technological training and research'. Yet this distinction between vocational training and university education sat uneasily with the well established function of the university in offering education for the professions, which the commission sought to retain. The report favoured the retention of high-status professional disciplines such as law and medicine within the university, while newer disciplines such as business and social studies were to be 'firmly based on fundamental sciences', with vocational training in such disciplines being provided outside the universities.[71] The liberal ideal of university education advanced by the commission had never commanded universal assent, but was now increasingly at odds with the 'human capital' assumptions at the heart of state policy.

'They May Have the Subtlety, But I Have the Money'—The University Merger

The commission's report was quickly sidelined by Donogh O'Malley, the third up and coming Fianna Fáil politician appointed by Lemass as Minister for Education. O'Malley, a flamboyant figure best known for the introduction of free second-level education, was equally pro-active, although ultimately less successful, in promoting a radical restructuring of higher education. The minister was convinced that it was essential 'to rationalise the university position in Dublin' by combining the two colleges in a single University of Dublin.[72] O'Malley's preference for a major structural reform was well timed, due to the delay in the commission's report, the increasingly rapid expansion of student enrolments and the priority assigned by Lemass to educational reforms.[73] Trinity College experienced an upsurge in student numbers during the 1960s, in line with an international trend for increasing enrolments in higher education: the student body increased by 75% within a decade from 2443 in 1960 to 4032 in 1970.[74] Trinity's autonomous status provoked tensions with the Department of Education. The department was furious at the Board's decision in 1965 to expand the student body up to 4000 students by 1970 'without consultation with the Minister for Education'.[75] Ó Raifeartaigh informed McQuaid privately that 'though Mr. Winkelman had been explicitly warned orally not to go beyond the figure of 3000 students and had been told to await a written confirmation, he had not paid the slightest attention but increased the numbers. This was an action that could not be passed over.'[76] O'Malley was determined to end Trinity's semi-detached position within Irish society, which he attributed both to its own unaccountable elite and the policy of the Catholic bishops.[77]

O'Malley first raised the prospect of a merger between Trinity College and UCD with the Cabinet on 15 December 1966. O'Malley's submission to the government, bluntly entitled '*The Problem of Trinity College Dublin*', was revealing about the actual motivations for a merger. He warned the government that '…the problem is now brought to a head by Trinity's present student numbers, policy and capital claim. Its present policy, if accepted, would evidently not stop there and would indeed draw in its train implicit further commitment on the part of the State'.[78] The expansion of the college involved a large-scale building programme, including a new arts building, which led to a request for capital funding from the state of just under £2.4 million. It was Trinity's request for major capital investment, at the same time as UCD forged ahead with the move to Belfield, which raised duplication of academic resources as a key issue and provided an important catalyst for the university merger. O'Malley argued that 'the State should not have to shoulder the enormous expense of duplication that will be involved' in financing the expansion of two rival universities in Dublin, especially as the additional funding for TCD represented a commitment to the education of non-Irish students.[79] The minister commented that the majority of non-Irish and Northern Ireland students in Trinity 'consti- tute a present to Britain and other countries of technical assistance of the highest quality'.[80]

O'Malley's concerns were not simply about money or nation- alist angst at subsidising the children of the ancient imperial oppressor—although neither were entirely absent from his reflec- tions on the university question. The minister perceived TCD as a non-Catholic institution, dominated by a narrow elite of (mainly Protestant) senior academics, dependent on British students for its sur- vival and isolated from contemporary Irish society.[81] O'Malley argued that Trinity's independent position was intolerable: '…we cannot allow a position to continue in which one University in Dublin would be allowed to remain apart from the main stream of the nation and con- tinue to recruit its student body to a large extent from foreigners.'[82] TCD's autonomy was problematic because it underpinned the college's ability to remain apparently impervious to the priorities of the Irish government. The department's memorandum was explicit in its criticism of the power enjoyed by its traditional academic elite:

> The answer is not in anything that the Trinity authorities may be expected to do, for a body with absolute power has never been known willingly to abdicate it... If Trinity is really to fit into Irish life – and it can scarcely be done without, for it has the means of providing for up to 3,000 Irish students who will undoubtedly be seeking for university places which will not otherwise be available, - then it would appear to be necessary for its constitution and government organisation to be democratised in the same way as are those of the other University Colleges.[83]

The dissatisfaction of the minister and senior officials at the de facto independence of the Board was a key rationale for the merger and formed common ground with Catholic bishops, such as McQuaid.[84] O'Malley and the officials were seeking to resolve several problems at once—Trinity's semi-detached position within Irish society, the restrictions imposed by the ecclesiastical ban and duplication of academic activity due to unplanned expansion of enrolments.

O'Malley acted decisively to sideline the commission's report immediately after its submission to the government in February 1967, seeking the approval of the Cabinet for a merger on 9 March 1967. O'Malley argued that the state had to address the anomalous position of TCD, claiming that 'the Commission has to all intents and purposes shied away from the problem'.[85] The Cabinet agreed on 31 March that O'Malley should approach the university authorities to propose a single University of Dublin, with Trinity College and University College as its two constituent colleges 'and with each complementary to the other'.[86] The sidelining of an expert commission was unusual at a time when other expert groups—notably the *Investment in Education* team—played an important role in shaping and legitimating policy change in education. Merger was a reversal of government policy from Hillery's statement only seven years earlier and testified to O'Malley's personal imprint on policy formation. The policy change marked the adoption by the government of a pro-active, authoritative approach to policy-making in higher education, which became the focus of significant government intervention for the first time since 1922.

Yet the initiative was also based on a secret understanding between O'Malley and McQuaid.[87] The minister consulted McQuaid well before any government decision and the archbishop recorded in January 1967 his impressions of the initiative:

> Mr. Donogh O'Malley, the new Minister for Education, spoke to me of his determination to alter T.C.D. constitution and charter. I learned that he had the permission of the government to negotiate. At once I added: 'Permit me to say that you ought to be very clear about the points of negotiation. You are dealing with very subtle people.' 'They may have the subtlety, he answered, but I have the money'.[88]

O'Malley's willingness to curb the autonomy of TCD helped to cement an informal, but influential alliance between the minister and archbishop in favour of the merger, which remained unknown until very recently.[89] McQuaid recorded approvingly that 'The Scheme would break up the T.C.D. system of a private University, self governing and self perpetuating, according to the Letters Patent of 1911.'[90] The announcement of the new policy was preceded by secret negotiations between the archbishop and minister, with Ó Raifeartaigh as a crucial intermediary: McQuaid met the secretary on seven occasions between January and April 1967, in the run-up to the policy announcement by O'Malley.[91] The archbishop advised Ó Raifeartaigh on the content and timing of the minister's statement and O'Malley incorporated several changes suggested by McQuaid to underline the merger's compatibility with Catholic social teaching.[92] McQuaid enjoyed extraordinary access to senior departmental officials and was treated as an indispensable ally and partner in policy-making, in sharp contrast to the provost of Trinity and UCD president who were simply informed of the policy change.[93]

The minister's policy statement on 18 April 1967 identified the merger of Trinity College and UCD as the cornerstone of the government's policy for restructuring higher education.[94] A. J. McConnell and J. J. Hogan were informed by the minister of the sweeping nature of his statement only on the morning of the press conference.[95] O'Malley commented that the commission had 'served the nation truly and well', at the same press conference where he sidelined their report.[96] The announcement was in line with O'Malley's favoured tactic of pre-empting opposition by publicly announcing new policy initiatives. He proposed the creation of a single university authority, established on a statutory basis, with a subsidiary authority for each constituent college: the powers and composition of each governing body were not yet decided and no detailed plan for the rationalisation of faculties was outlined. *The Irish Times* commented that the Minister had assumed 'a cheerful, confident, shoot-first-and-ask-questions-afterwards mood'.[97]

The minister's statement was informed by a pragmatic economic and political rationale for merger. He warned that the state could not be expected to subsidise 'avoidable duplication' of university services due to the competing claims of two universities in a single metropolitan area, emphasising that 'the whole thing cries out for some kind of complementary allocation'.[98] O'Malley mixed idealistic appeals to history and national tradition with his pragmatic analysis of economic realities, asserting that merger would end 'a most insidious form of partition on our doorstep' and allow Trinity College 'to take the final step across the threshold of that mansion to which it properly belongs, the Irish nation...'[99] The reconstituted University of Dublin would be multi-denominational rather than 'neutral', in a formulation agreed by O'Malley with McQuaid.[100]

The minister was keen to convince academic opinion that the initiative was not driven solely by economic necessity, arguing that 'what makes economic sense makes educational sense too'.[101] Yet educational considerations were the least important among the policy imperatives driving the merger. Educational benefits figured only briefly in the two memoranda on merger submitted by the department to the government. O'Malley failed to set out any plausible educational rationale for the merger: his commentary on the educational benefits of the initiative was brief and defensive, acknowledging that he had 'treated mostly of the economic side of things and of training for the professions' and including a highly ambivalent reference to Newman—'we are all to some extent followers of Newman in the belief that a university has something more to give its students than mere training'.[102]

O'Malley's dramatic initiative committed the government to the most radical restructuring of the institutional architecture of higher education since the foundation of the state. O'Malley and McQuaid found common ground in their shared distaste for the status quo in Trinity College and the alliance between the most powerful representatives of the state and the Catholic Church in education gave a vital impetus to the merger. The bishops issued a statement on 20 June 1967 which did not explicitly support the merger but welcomed O'Malley's efforts to achieve 'a satisfactory solution' of this problem, while entering a proviso that any sound system of university education had to respect 'the fundamental religious and moral principles of our people'.[103] McQuaid privately held out the prospect of removing the ecclesiastical ban provided that Trinity was itself transformed by breaking down the traditional independence of its academic elite and bringing it under a strong central university authority, in which Catholics would have a majority and UCD would be the stronger partner.[104]

Yet both O'Malley and McQuaid underestimated the resilience of academic elites determined to maintain their autonomy.[105] The governing body of UCD immediately came out in favour of 'a complete unification of the two institutions', which was the favoured solution of Hogan and the college officers.[106] But TCD had no intention of accepting a merger based on the unitary model favoured by the UCD administration and McQuaid, which was a thinly veiled attempt to absorb Trinity College into a larger, merged institution.[107] T. W. Moody, professor of Irish history and a former member of the commission on higher education, spoke for many Trinity staff when he wrote in *Studies* that a unitary university would mean 'the extinction of TCD' and would never be accepted: 'There being no death-wish in TCD, it will resist a unitary university to the utmost'.[108] The unitary path to merger did not command universal support in UCD, where the Academic Staff Association (ASA) and a number of prominent academics favoured a two-college structure. A minority of the governing body itself, including Dr. Garret FitzGerald, a university senator, dissented from the position of the administration, arguing for a more flexible approach which did not make unified departments the cornerstone of a merger: this group caused considerable irritation to the officers of UCD, although they were outvoted at meetings of the governing body.[109] Yet the divergence over a unitary/federal model marked a fundamental division between the most influential forces in each college, which could not be readily overcome. The negotiations between the two institutions between November 1967 and February 1968, facilitated by Ó Raifeartaigh, not surprisingly proved inconclusive, breaking down over the allocation of faculties between the two colleges. Prof. James Meenan, a member of UCD's negotiating team, commented that the negotiations were increasingly 'an attempt to square a circle'.[110]

Coolahan points to the failure of the government to consult adequately among stakeholders or offer a convincing conception of what constituted university education as key weaknesses in the merger initiative.[111] Yet O'Malley's pre-emptive strike was deliberate and had worked in presenting traditional stakeholders with a fait accompli in announcing free post-primary education.[112] The profound institutional differences regarding a unitary or two-college model, allied to professional academic resistance to unwelcome encroachment by the state, were more significant in undermining the initiative. The lack of detailed preparation for the merger was also a serious failure. Seán O'Connor, an influential assistant secretary who supported the minister's plans, admitted subsequently that the department lacked detailed information about the staffing and accommodation needs of various faculties in the event of merger.[113] This omission explained the absence of any coherent plan for re-organisation at the outset and limited O'Malley's ability to develop a plausible educational rationale for the merger, which was a fundamental weakness of the initiative. Donogh O'Malley died suddenly in March 1968, depriving merger of its most determined advocate. Ferriter even suggests that the idea 'lost steam' after O'Malley's death.[114] But departmental officials privately regarded the outlook for merger as problematic from an early stage: O'Connor commented subsequently that even during O'Malley's term, 'many of us feared that the battle could not be won'.[115]

The detailed plan for the reorganisation of the universities announced by O'Malley's successor, Brian Lenihan, on 6 July 1968 was arguably a turning point in the debate, exposing publicly the formidable obstacles to merger. The minister's plan allocated the professional disciplines of law, medicine, dentistry and veterinary science to Trinity; engineering, social sciences and commerce would be based in UCD, with each college retaining a range of disciplines in Arts and Science.[116] While Lenihan's statement provided much of the detail missing from O'Malley's earlier announcements, a convincing educational rationale which engaged with the aims and mission of the university was still conspicuously absent. Although the Board of TCD was willing to consider the plan, the Fellows, still a powerful force within the institution, voted overwhelmingly to reject merger.[117] Moreover, the proposed redistribution of faculties was particularly unacceptable to UCD. The loss of medicine (the original core of the Catholic university) and law provoked strong opposition and Lenihan's plans were decisively rejected by various faculties, as Meenan highlighted in September 1968: 'It could be said with great truth that University College has never been so united about any issue throughout its existence as it is about this.'[118] The governing body of UCD condemned Lenihan's plan in April 1969 as a recipe for 'the partial destruction and total discouragement' of UCD as a university institution.[119]

Merger was also undermined by a rapidly changing societal and cultural context, as traditional religious influences gradually declined and previous denominational divisions in university education began to lose their previous salience. Official assumptions that Trinity College was unattractive to Irish students proved outdated, as the ban had a steadily declining impact during the late 1960s. The dramatic impact of O'Malley's announcement may have contributed to the increased popularity of the college: Martin O'Donoghue, an economics lecturer and adviser to the College officers on the merger, believed that following the ministerial announcement 'there was a flood of applications from Catholics almost immediately'.[120] Yet the increasing attraction of TCD to middle-class Catholics was also the product of wider cultural change, associated with the Second Vatican Council and the transformation of economic and educational policies during the 1960s. McQuaid warned the bishops in 1968 that the ban was increasingly being flouted: 'Already Catholics have in large numbers been treating our Statute as non-existent …'[121] The college's records indicated that Catholics comprised 48% of the first year undergraduate cohort in 1969–70, while departmental estimates suggested that Catholics already formed a small majority of the new intake as early as 1968.[122] Ó Raifeartaigh advised the Taoiseach, Jack Lynch, in February 1969 that TCD would have a large majority of Catholic students within a decade—a prediction that proved accurate.[123] Trinity College had crossed a Rubicon in its ability to attract Catholic students within the state by the end of the decade. The increased flow of entrants from the Republic allowed TCD to reduce its previous dependence on British students.[124] Traditional denominational divisions ceased to be a significant dividing line in higher education, as Trinity broadened its appeal to encompass a larger, more diverse and increasingly more liberal Catholic middle class.[125]

The university authorities ultimately found common ground in their mutual scepticism about the merger. The authorities of the NUI and Trinity conducted successful negotiations in the spring of 1970, which were facilitated by M. D. McCarthy, president of UCC, producing 'a unanimously agreed alternative to the Government's proposals for the future provision of higher education...'[126] The NUI senate and Board of TCD agreed to propose this alternative solution to the HEA in April 1970.[127] The NUI/TCD agreement envisaged two independent universities in Dublin, which would collaborate closely together and rationalise their academic activity in a number of faculties, including science, engineering and health sciences.[128] The successful negotiations between the NUI and TCD forestalled the government's plans by offering the prospect of effective collaboration between the two universities, which stopped well short of merger. The agreement was a defensive innovation designed to prevent a restructuring imposed by the state. While official aspirations for a radical university re-organisation were not fulfilled, the outcomes of the NUI/TCD agreement in terms of institutional coordination also proved limited. The NUI/TCD initiative was a strategic defence of institutional power by previously antagonistic elements of a professional elite, who ultimately united to forestall a further assertion of power by the political centre.

This pragmatic accord between institutional leaders was closely followed by the removal of the ecclesiastical ban. The Catholic bishops agreed in June 1970 to withdraw their regulation restricting the entry of Catholics to TCD, citing 'positive developments' in the relations between the two universities.[129] Yet the bishops were also responding to the reality that the ban was increasingly being ignored, as McQuaid had foreseen two years earlier.[130] The removal of the ban confirmed the decline of traditional religious and cultural divisions in university education.

The effective resistance of a professional university elite to the grand design promoted by both O'Malley and McQuaid played a key role in the failure of the merger.[131] The outcome underlined that even an alliance between the Catholic bishops and an interventionist minister could not guarantee radical institutional reform in the face of academic elites which staunchly defended their autonomy and traditional institutional structures.[132] Yet while O'Malley's initiative for merger proved abortive, this did not signal any retraction of state intervention within HE. Indeed the initiative foreshadowed a long-term expansion of the power of the state in HE, which was exemplified by the unceremonious rejection of the commission's report and later the foundation of the HEA as a statutory intermediary agency between the department and the universities.

'The Issue Is Fundamentally a National One...'

The Department of Education played a crucial role in shaping the newly authoritative approach towards policy-making in higher education from the mid 1960s. An internal committee, headed by Ó Raifeartaigh and including the most senior officials of the department, was appointed by O'Malley in 1967 to produce a detailed response to the commission.[133] The officials, whose deliberations remained confidential, were sceptical and frequently scathing in their commentary on the report, which addressed almost all recommendations other than the merger, where government policy had apparently been predetermined. Seán O'Connor, a member of the committee, reflected its views in commenting that 'the Commission was determined to protect the universities at all costs and to make them even more elite than they already were.'[134] The recommendation for New Colleges was categorically rejected, on the basis that a non-university institution awarding pass degrees would undermine the status of all Irish degrees; the officials believed that 'the idea is psychologically unsound', as colleges with inferior degrees would merely promote an inferiority complex among their students and staff.[135] The recommendation for a Technological Authority was also rejected due to a government decision to proceed with the new Regional Technical Colleges.[136] The committee dismissed unequivocally a central plank of the commission's report, namely that the universities were responsible for matching student numbers with the available resources: 'The issue is fundamentally a national one...it would be a grave abuse of the universities' autonomy...' if they attempted to restrict the level of student access to their institutions without prior consultation with the state.[137] This blunt assertion of the power of the political and administrative elite, albeit in a confidential report, signalled the end of an era in which the state adopted a laissez faire approach to the universities. Ironically it also marked a complete reversal of earlier official policies, pursued particularly by the Department of Finance, focusing on restriction of third level enrolments. Arguably the major shortcoming of the commission from an official perspective was not so much any specific recommendation, but its concern to protect the institutional autonomy of university institutions. While the universities retained control over their internal operations and academic activity, the emergence of an interventionist state redefined the context in which they operated, particularly at a 'macro' level where decisions were made on capital development, inter-institutional relations, expansion and admissions.

James Dukes, an assistant principal officer in the department's universities section, reflected the jaundiced official view of the commission, commenting that 'they had no impact that I can recall'.[138] Coolahan offers a more nuanced perspective, arguing that it would be unfair to conclude that the commission's report had no effect, as several key recommendations were ultimately adopted; White points to up to 13 areas where the commission's recommendation could be 'shown, or at least argued, to have had an influence.'[139] Yet the evidence supports Dukes' more critical view. The painstaking deliberations of the commission left remarkably little influence on government policies over the following two decades, not least because most of its recommendations did not survive the critical scrutiny of the departmental committee. The controversial proposal for 'New Colleges' disappeared, with the department instead giving priority to the expansion of higher technical education. Similarly, the commission's recommendations for a diversified system of teacher training were rejected in favour of introducing a university degree for primary teachers. Where ministers did adopt recommendations of the commission, mainly in the creation of a new system of governance for HE, they usually did so only where the committee had given its imprimatur.

The establishment of the Higher Education Authority in 1968, initially on an ad hoc basis, as a permanent executive body to advise the minister and allocate state funding to institutions of higher education, was the most significant legacy of the departmental agenda for institutional reform.[140] The creation of a new authority to oversee the development of third-level education was a rare point of agreement between the commission and their critics in the department, although the committee's view that it should report to the Minister for Education rather than the Taoiseach prevailed.[141] The government delegated wide-ranging functions to the new authority, which was established on a statutory basis in 1971. The HEA was required to maintain 'a continual review of the country's needs in higher education' and advise the minister on issues related to higher education. But the authority was also given significant powers for oversight and financing of the universities, including examination of budgets prepared by the institutions of higher education and recommending the allocation of state funding for each institution.[142] The HEA enjoyed executive functions for 'designated' institutions, mainly the universities at the outset, but was restricted to an advisory role for most non-university institutions, especially the expanded higher technical sector which emerged from the radical policy changes of the 1960s.

Diversification and the Transformation of Higher Technical Education

The most radical change of direction during the 1960s involved non-university education. The government created a regional network of higher technical colleges within a reconfigured and greatly expanded technical sector, leading to a far-reaching diversification of higher education at system, institutional and subject levels.[143] These reforms were less dramatic than O'Malley's ill-fated initiative for merger, but left a more enduring legacy and defined the configuration of an expanded higher education system for the following two generations. International pressures, mediated particularly through the OECD, proved an important catalyst in stimulating the policy changes in technical education, but the OECD's input was deliberately sought and quickly embraced by Irish politicians and civil servants.[144]

The first indications of a reassessment of traditional, laissez-faire approaches at the interface of further education and the labour market affected apprenticeship, traditionally a largely unregulated area which did not require formal engagement with educational institutions, although CDVEC was extensively involved in apprenticeship training schemes since the 1930s. The Apprenticeship Act, 1958 created a new national framework for the regulation of apprenticeship, replacing the ineffective 1931 legislation.[145] The new legislation drew on recommendations of the Commission on Youth Unemployment in 1951 for effective statutory regulation of the selection and training of apprentices and provided for the establishment of a national apprenticeship board.[146] Lemass, then still the line minister, commented that 'faulty apprenticeship can have a profound effect on the national economy.'[147] An Chéard Chomhairle, which was established on 11 April 1960 under the terms of the Apprenticeship Act 1958, was empowered to 'regulate the recruitment, training, progress, general well-being and final certification of apprentices.'[148] Among the powers delegated to the board was the right to set up apprenticeship committees in different trades which would maintain a compulsory register of apprentices and determine conditions for selection from the register; the new board would also approve minimum educational qualifications necessary for entry to apprenticeship.[149] An Chéard Chomhairle was intended to enlist the collaboration of employers and trade unions, who were strongly represented on the board and also included nominees from the VECs, following representations to Lemass by members of CDVEC.[150]

An Chéard Chomhairle established a minimum age for entry into apprenticeship of fifteen years and required minimum post-primary qualifications (usually linked to pass level in specific subjects in the Intermediate Certificate or Day Group Certificate for vocational schools) for all potential apprentices after 1 September 1963.[151] The upgrading of educational standards formed part of a deliberate strategy by the Department of Industry and Commerce to eliminate restrictive practices around the entry and training of apprentices so as to overcome 'these abuses in the manner best calculated not to antagonise employers and workers on whose goodwill the success of the measure will… depend.'[152] The upgrading of apprenticeship had immediate implications for second-level technical education, as apprenticeship committees were empowered to require the attendance of apprentices at technical courses and compel employers to release apprentices to attend such courses without loss of earnings.[153] While the implications for third-level education were less immediate, the heightened importance attached to apprenticeship was an early indication of the explicit linkage between upskilling and a successful economy and accommodating improved training for apprentices was a factor in third-level policy initiatives such as the RTCs.

A more far-reaching re-appraisal of government policy towards higher technical education came in the early 1960s, when the Department of Education invited two OECD examiners, Alan Peacock and Werner Rasmussen, to undertake a review of technical education and training.[154] The international experts criticised the absence of an adequate preparatory course at second level for potential entrants to the colleges of technology and the lack of any educational ladder from the vocational school to university.[155] The critical analysis by the OECD examiners shaped key policy changes announced by Hillery. The minister's policy announcement on 20 May 1963 included the first official proposal for 'Regional Technological Colleges', which would provide technical education at an advanced level. The proposed colleges were originally intended mainly as a bridge to third-level education or skilled technical employment for post-primary students with technical aptitudes and were linked to a proposal for a Technical Schools Leaving Certificate, which never materialised.[156] Hillery's statement was the first government initiative which aimed to diversify a higher education sector dominated by 'elite' universities and meet social demand increasingly through non-university institutions.

O'Malley appointed a Steering Committee on Technical Education headed by Noel Mulcahy in September 1966, including trade union and employer nominees, to formulate an educational plan for the colleges. The Steering Committee's report in April 1967 exerted a profound influence on the expansion of higher technical education during the following decade. The report reflected the growing importance of vocational imperatives linked to economic development in higher education policy. The Regional Technical Colleges (RTCs) were designed to provide a greater supply of skilled technical employees, which was perceived as an essential requirement if the economy was to adapt successfully to free trade with Britain and the accession of the state to the European Economic Community (EEC).[157] The main long-term function of the new institutions was to provide education for employment in trade and industry over a wide range of occupations.[158] Planning for the colleges explicitly took account of the economic and social needs of developing regions, where investment in education was considered a necessary element of industrial development. The committee envisaged a wide variety of courses for different age cohorts, including Leaving Certificate courses in science and technical subjects, apprenticeship training and adult education.[159] Yet from the outset the RTCs had a significant remit in third-level education, offering technician qualifications at various levels and higher-level professional courses in technical subjects.[160] The committee believed that the new institutions should not only meet a short-term demand for skilled technical workers, but also expand the traditionally neglected area of higher technical education. Among the Steering Committee's most influential recommendations was the establishment of a national council for educational awards, which would validate courses and award qualifications for the higher technical sector.[161] The National Council for Educational Awards (NCEA) was first established on an ad hoc basis in April 1972, providing an institutional framework for the recognition of technical courses and qualifications.[162] The report reflected an emerging consensus among politicians, civil servants and business leaders that investment in higher technical education was indispensable to economic progress.

O'Malley shared this conviction, warning the government in June 1967 that 'The availability and demand for technical education are of the essence in relation to our future industrial progress'.[163] The Cabinet quickly agreed that the state would finance the building costs of the RTCs on a phased basis, with larger colleges in Cork and Galway being built over a marginally longer timeframe.[164] The only major disagreement among ministers concerned O'Malley's determination to establish an additional college in Letterkenny, which was staunchly opposed by the Department of Finance. But the minister ultimately won government approval for an RTC in Donegal, assisted by lobbying from Anthony MacFeely, the Catholic bishop of Raphoe and Neil Blaney, the powerful Minister for Local Government.[165] The policy decisions taken by the government in 1967–68, informed by the report of the Steering Committee, guaranteed the establishment of a network of new technical colleges extending to most regions of the country.

The first five RTCs in Athlone, Carlow, Dundalk, Sligo and Waterford were founded in 1970, while a further three colleges in Galway, Letterkenny and Cork were in operation by 1974 and a ninth college in Tralee by 1977.[166] Six of the first seven colleges offered senior cycle Leaving Certificate courses with a scientific, technological or business orientation.[167] But as a HEA report acknowledged, while RTCs were originally intended to 'reinforce the technical dimension of the second-level system', the new institutions soon found themselves called upon 'to cater increasingly for third-level demand.'[168] When the new RTC in Cork opened its doors in 1974, the third level courses of the Crawford Municipal Technical Institute were incorporated from the outset.[169] As demand for more specialised higher level courses increased, the colleges phased out their Leaving Certificate subjects and focused primarily on third-level programmes across a wide range of disciplines, including applied science, business studies, engineering and construction studies, as well as to a lesser extent apprenticeship training and adult education.[170] The creation of An Chomhairle Oiliúna (AnCo) in 1967 as an industrial training authority created a separate framework for the training of apprentices and the proportion of apprentices within the newly established colleges was smaller than anticipated.[171] AnCo reduced the role of the education system in training apprentices and helped to ensure that the RTCs were primarily focused on third-level education.[172] The colleges displayed from the outset a strong vocational orientation, designed to prepare students for employment in trade and industry.

The development of the National Institutes for Higher Education (NIHE) was another significant landmark in the diversification of higher education. The Limerick University Project Committee mounted a sustained public campaign for a new university in the city since 1959: their case was supported privately by the internal departmental committee on higher education and publicly by successive ministers including O'Malley and Lenihan.[173] But ministers were wary of conflict with the existing university authorities who were opposed to a new university and Lenihan referred the issue to the newly formed HEA to 'avoid any danger of a clash with the Higher Education Authority.'[174] The HEA in its first report in March 1969 saw 'no national need' for another university but instead offered an innovative proposal for a new type of third-level institution which would go beyond the more restricted remit of the RTCs or colleges of technology.[175] The authority identified the development of higher technological education as an urgent national requirement, echoing the steering committee in its comment that technological studies in Ireland 'has not yet found its proper level'.[176] The HEA recommended the establishment of a national institute of higher education, combining extensive specialisation in technical courses at diploma and certificate level with the prestige of degree courses in arts humanities and science.[177] The HEA was influenced by the report of the Robbins Committee in Britain in 1963, which led to the development of the Polytechnics as an important sector in English higher education.[178] This recommendation was quickly accepted by Lenihan as a compromise between the competing pressures of the Limerick University lobby group and university leaders. The National Institute for Higher Education in Limerick opened its doors to students in September 1972.[179] The NIHE, led by Dr. Edward Walsh, quickly made its mark as a distinctive higher education institution with a strong technological and commercial focus; it was the first institution in Ireland to introduce modularisation as the core principle of programme design.[180] The NIHE incorporated degree courses in arts and science, traditionally associated with university education, as well as innovative elements, including industrial placement within all full-time programmes.

The expansion of higher technological education on a national scale stimulated a gradual repositioning of the VEC colleges. The colleges faced increasing demand for apprenticeship training particularly in the engineering trades, due to the stimulus provided by An Chéard Comhairle.[181] More significantly, CDVEC identified higher level training in 'technician education' as a key area of expansion: in a submission to the HEA in 1969, the VEC noted that 'the technician sector is lacking in organisation and yet the need for technicians is proportionately considerably greater than for apprentices.'[182] The VEC colleges increased the number and scope of their higher level certificate and diploma courses during the 1960s, while their second level activity was gradually transferred to other institutions within the VEC system.[183] The Bolton St. college launched the first full-time technician courses in architecture and construction in the Irish state during the mid-1960s.[184] Similarly the institute in Kevin St. developed a number of post Leaving certificate courses at technician level during the 1960s and relaunched its professional electrical engineering course as an honours diploma in 1966, which rapidly secured recognition as the equivalent of a university degree course. The increasingly rapid move up the value chain by the techological colleges was also reflected by new initiatives in management and business education. The Rathmines institute launched the first full-time four year course in business outside the universities in the early 1960s.[185] The redesignation of the Bolton St. and Kevin institutes as colleges of technology at the end of the 1950s and the Rathmines institute as a College of Commerce in 1956 expressed CDVEC's ambitions for expansion of their higher level programmes. Over 60% of the activity of these three colleges consisted of third-level programmes by the end of the 1960s.[186] Overall the VEC colleges deepened their engagement with higher level education at technician and professional levels during the 1960s, gradually sidelining their previously substantial involvement in second level.

CDVEC positioned itself as a key institution in fulfilling the labour market requirements of an expanding economy. Martin Gleeson, CEO of the VEC, appealed to Lemass in December 1959 to facilitate plans for a new building to accommodate the Kevin St. college which had been under discussion since 1953, receiving a sympathetic response from the Taoiseach.[187] Following an enquiry by Lemass, the Department of Education approved the plans for the new building, part funded by the exchequer, in January 1960.[188] CDVEC was successful in securing high level political support for the development of its colleges for the first time. The completion of the new building in 1968 gave about 14,000msq of new accommodation to the Kevin St. college, including specialised laboratory space for engineering and science.[189] This redevelopment enabled the rapid expansion of higher level diploma courses in engineering and applied science, but did not relieve overcrowding among its cohort of apprentice electricians, as the VEC acknowledged in 1969: 'The College of Technology…already cannot hold the large electrical apprenticeship population to which it is committed.'[190]

The apprentices were accommodated off site in temporary accommodation in Whitefriar St. until 1968, but the apparent downgrading of apprenticeship in the VEC's scale of priorities caused tension with some of its traditional stakeholders. J. McConway, general secretary of the Electrical Trades Union, complained to Brian Lenihan in June 1968 that the Kevin St. college was 'slowly divorcing itself' from the training of apprentices in electrical trades: he threatened that the union would object to the recruitment of additional apprentices unless adequate educational facilities were provided.[191] The VEC took this shot across their bows seriously enough to find additional temporary accommodation for apprentices and secured a new site for apprenticeship training adjacent to the college in Bolton St.[192] The committee did not intend to abandon its long term engagement with apprenticeship, but was struggling to manage expansion in multiple fields with finite resources. Yet the exchange underlined a gradual shift within the VEC colleges towards a greater concentration on higher level certificate and diploma courses which sat uneasily with its traditional stakeholders.

The combination of overcrowding in its existing colleges and the CDVEC's ambition to expand its foothold in higher level technical education led to a far-reaching plan for the repositioning of its higher level programmes. A VEC planning committee produced an ambitious proposal for a new higher education institution at Ballymun, incorporating higher level courses in technological, higher technician, management and commercial education.[193] The VEC saw the opportunity to utilise the site of Albert College which was being vacated by UCD and was available to Dublin Corporation. It was a radical break with previous practice for CDVEC, which accepted that its traditional combination of disciplines at different levels within a 'vertical structure' could no longer be maintained, proposing instead a 'horizontal' integration of related schools operating at similar qualification levels.[194] The new college would be a purely third level institution 'concerned only with the technician and technological levels…'[195] Commercial and management education at higher level would be concentrated in the Ballymun college, which would also incorporate all the engineering schools offering certificate and diploma courses previously based in Kevin St. The new college was intended to operate in conjunction with Kevin St. which would specialise in higher scientific education and food technology. Meanwhile the Bolton St. college would serve as a hub combining apprenticeship education for both the industrial trades and the electrical trades previously offered in Kevin St.[196] This ambitious proposal did not command universal enthusiasm within the VEC, as it involved both a move from a city centre location for much of its third level activity and a break from the principle of offering 'ladders of opportunity to students more or less under the same roof'.[197] The initiative proved very influential for the future direction of higher education in Dublin, but not precisely in the way that CDVEC had hoped.

The government response to the VEC plan was favourable to the principle of a new third level institution, but ambivalent about the VEC's role in providing it. The Department of Education in 1970 made a successful application to the World Bank for a loan to support new initiatives in second and third level education, including the RTCs and an NIHE in Dublin: the World Bank loan ultimately included up to £400,000 for a new third level institution in Ballymun.[198] The VEC proposal was referred by Lenihan to the HEA and a working party appointed by the authority endorsed most of the VEC recommendations for a higher technological college in Ballymun in December 1970.[199] But the HEA also stipulated that the new college and Kevin St. should form a joint college with a single governing body, which would be a designated institution under the HEA.[200] The governance recommendation dismayed the VEC and ensured that the new institution would develop autonomously from the VEC system with its own governing body.[201]

While the government did not immediately act on the HEA report, the VEC misjudged the level of political support for its vision of the Ballymun project.[202] The Fine Gael-Labour coalition appointed an interim governing body in March 1975 for the proposed NIHE in Dublin, which was independent of the VEC and tasked with reporting directly to the minister on 'the form and structure of the Institute.'[203] Then in December 1976 the NIHED was designated by the minister as an institution under the remit of the HEA. The writing was on the wall for the original VEC project and CDVEC had little to gain by remaining involved in an enterprise over which it had no control but which might well absorb many of its higher level programmes. Although a working party on technological education in Dublin was set up to consider the relationship between NIHED and a redesigned VEC institution, the discussions failed to make any headway: CDVEC finally withdrew from involvement in the project in 1977, instead embarking on the restructuring of its colleges to create the Dublin Institute of Technology (DIT).[204] The NIHE was established in September 1980 on the Albert College site as a new institution developing its own distinctive portfolio of courses. The new institute operated entirely at degree level, offering a range of business, technology and computer applications programmes.[205] The establishment of the NIHEs in Dublin and Limerick reflected the rapid transformation of higher technical education, which had emerged as a defining feature of the state's educational policy during the 1960s.[206]

The diversification of the higher education sector reshaped the institutional balance between universities and higher technical institutions. The RTC/DIT sector experienced a particularly dramatic expansion: this sector accounted for only 5% of student enrolments in 1965, but expanded rapidly to 26% in 1980 and 38% by 1992.[207] The proportion of first time entrants to HE in this sector was even more striking, accounting for 40% by 1980–81 and a small majority of all first time entrants by 1991.[208] The striking expansion of the higher technical colleges was underpinned by the European Social Fund (ESF), in an early example of successful Irish negotiation to secure EEC support for higher level vocational training. Following a decision by the Council of Social Affairs as part of its social action programme in 1975 to support the employment and geographical mobility of young people under 25 through the ESF, an application by the Department of Education was successful in securing funding for students pursuing courses in middle level 'technician skills' in the new RTCs.[209] Irish ministers and civil servants were cautious in promoting these ESF funded courses, not least because EEC funding was in principle available for training rather than education: as White notes, Irish negotiators were 'pioneers in extending the boundaries of the European Social Fund.'[210] A substantial proportion of certificate and diploma programmes were funded by the EEC from 1975 and following a significant infusion from the Social Fund in 1984, almost 90% of new entrants to full-time courses in the RTCs were receiving ESF grants by the mid 1980s.[211] The proportion of new entrants starting full-time diploma and certificate courses in Ireland was higher than OECD and EC averages by 1990–91. This entry pattern reflected the impact of a coherent national strategy designed to direct much of the demand for higher education towards non-university institutions and technical courses.

The shift to a diversified system also drove changes to the traditional pattern of participation by field of study. The most significant changes within the universities included a rapid expansion in business courses, from 8% of total enrolments in 1965–66 to 13% in 1980–81, coupled with a similar decline in medicine and dentistry from 17% to 13% of the total in the same period.[212] Arts, law and social science disciplines experienced a marginal decrease, but consistently attracted over 40% of new entrants. The changes by discipline at university level were incremental, but marked the beginning of a gradual decline in the previous dominance by professional courses. The distribution of student enrolments in non-university institutions showed a sharp divergence from the universities, reflecting the predominance of vocationally oriented disciplines in the higher technical colleges. The most marked feature was the high participation in business courses, which accounted for 35% of total enrolments by 1985–86; engineering and architecture and to a lesser extent science were the other major subject areas in the non-university sector.[213]

The rapidly expanding higher technological sector was positioned as the main avenue for vocationally oriented courses linked to the labour market up to the 1980s. Yet the universities were also drawn into new initiatives at the interface of educational and industrial policy, largely at the instigation of the Industrial Development Authority (IDA). The Manpower consultative committee, established by the Department of Labour in December 1978, operated as 'an initial forum for dialogue between the IDA and the education system'.[214] The IDA, which reflected the concerns both of Irish employers and the multinational corporations that it was seeking to attract to Ireland, became increasingly engaged with higher education policy, particularly lobbying the HEA about skill shortages.[215] The Manpower committee identified a substantial shortage of graduates to meet labour market demand in engineering and computing. The HEA took the lead in persuading universities to expand student intake in these areas, with a commitment of resources from the Manpower committee.[216] This targeted investment mainly in programmes in Trinity, UCD and UCC produced dramatic results, with an increase in the engineering graduate cohort of 40% and a tenfold expansion in graduate numbers in the newly developing area of computer science.[217] The Manpower programme was a precursor to more intensive demands on the universities to engage more fully with the market during the closing decades of the twentieth century.

The policy changes adopted by the government in the mid to late 1960s led to the emergence of a significant higher technological sector for the first time. Higher technical education emerged as a distinctive strand within the third-level sector, offering an alternative route to higher or professional qualifications alongside the more traditional disciplines pursued by the universities. The foundation of the RTCs and NIHEs also transformed the educational opportunities available to vocational pupils, who had previously been denied any real avenue to higher education, especially in rural areas.[218] Official commitment to the expansion and upgrading of the higher technical sector reflected a strong vocational emphasis in higher education policy, as the new institutions were explicitly designed to meet the labour force needs of an expanding industrial economy.[219]

The diversification of higher education, achieved mainly through the expansion and reimagining of higher technical education on a national scale, was one of the most radical educational reforms of the twentieth century. The extent of the transformation should not be underestimated. Irish ministers and officials promoted the expansion of technical education, which had been neglected and restricted by the state and the Catholic bishops until the 1950s, as an indispensable element in the economic development of the nation.[220] The upgrading of higher technical education marked a decisive break with the conservative approach of political and clerical elites up to the 1950s, which had severely limited the potential of the vocational sector. The influence of the OECD dovetailed with changing domestic priorities and effective political leadership to chart a new direction for higher education, which marked a dramatic reversal from the past.[221]

Teacher Education

The prospect for teacher training was transformed by demographic change but still more by the ideological reorientation which underpinned interventionist policies from the late 1950s. Teacher training for national schools emerged as a key field for policy innovation, reform and expansion, not least due to the importance of primary and second-level education to the state's expansionist policies. A combination of expansionist policies and demographic growth created a surge in the demand for teachers of a kind not seen since the foundation of the state. The department's decision in 1958 to end the recruitment of Junior Assistant Mistresses and start phasing out the high proportion of untrained teachers in national schools reinforced the importance of the training colleges.[222] The colleges enjoyed substantial capital investment for the first time in a generation to accommodate unprecedented student enrolments. Teacher training also experienced a more fundamental transformation, driven by policy changes such as the abolition of the preparatory colleges and a pragmatic institutional response to wider cultural changes, which transformed many of the traditional features of the colleges. The training of primary teachers was reconceptualised as 'teacher education' and linked explicitly to the university system.

The wider re-appraisal among policy-makers of the contribution of education to economic and societal progress had an early influence on teacher training. Among the first indications of attitudinal change was the reversal of the marriage ban. Jack Lynch, the first of several reform-minded ministers, announced the withdrawal of the marriage ban as 'educationally indefensible' in May 1958, accepting a departmental recommendation to prioritise the supply of trained teachers.[223] A partial reform of recruitment procedures was also introduced in 1958, when an order of merit was introduced for all candidates based on the Leaving Certificate results: the highest placed candidates undertook an oral test in Irish and English and an interview, conducted by a board drawn equally from departmental inspectors and training college representatives.[224] The reform of selection procedues allowed the college authorities to undertake an initial evaluation of candidates and ended the privileged position of the preparatory colleges in relation to entry to teacher training.[225] The re-appraisals announced by Lynch signalled that senior figures within the department were no longer content with the status quo.

This was followed by a radical reconfiguration of the traditional system of admission. Lynch's successor, Patrick Hillery, proposed in November 1959 the closure of the five Catholic preparatory colleges, indicating in a memorandum to the Cabinet there were 'fundamental objections' to the system, notably the undesirable segregation of future teachers from other sections of the population and the pressure placed on pupils as young as 13 to determine their future careers.[226] This proposal marked a dramatic reversal by senior officials in the Department of Education, who quietly dropped a central plank of Gaelicisation and explicitly rejected the arguments advanced by their predecessors thirty years earlier. The system was a liability by the late 1950s: the state secondary schools were expensive, attracted numerous critics and their academic reputation was difficult to defend, not least because the standard of the Preparatory College students at the Leaving Certificate was lower than the standard reached by successful candidates in the open competition.[227] The government quickly approved the abolition of the preparatory college system, which was replaced by an expanded scheme of secondary school and university scholarships for Gaeltacht students.[228] The only exception was Coláiste Moibhi, which was allowed to continue in operation, as the department believed that the Protestant secondary schools were still unable to provide candidates for the teaching profession with adequate Irish.[229] All five Catholic colleges were closed from 31 July 1961, with four being transferred to religious orders or diocesan clergy to offer 'A' secondary schools conducted entirely through Irish.[230]

The abolition of the preparatory college system, which attracted little opposition or even public debate, transformed the process of recruitment and selection for the primary teaching profession. Apart from the embrace of the meritocratic principle through the Leaving Certificate results, the decision reversed a crucial building block of the state's traditional policy for the revival of Irish and was part of a wider dilution of the primacy of Irish in the educational system inaugurated by Hillery.[231] The policy reversal was crucial for the evolution of the Catholic training colleges over the following two decades, giving the authorities greater control over recruitment of candidates, allowing a more diverse intake of students and facilitating other innovations, such as admission of day students and acceptance of co-education. The initiative contributed to a rapid transformation in the composition of the student body in St. Patrick's College, Drumcondra, facilitating its transition from a purely residential training institution. The college admitted male day students from Dublin for the first time in 1968–69, in a change of direction approved by McQuaid, who informed the department that 'a larger intake in St. Patrick's of Dublin youths' was desirable.[232] About half of the students were non-resident within the college by 1972–73, while entrants from the Dublin region accounted for a plurality among the student body, in stark contrast to the dominance of preparatory college students only a decade earlier.[233]

A more striking policy change was the embrace of co-education, previously frowned upon by the Catholic bishops. Sr. Loreto O'Connor, president of Mary Immaculate College, indicated that 'The move with the times in the 1960s called for a change in the enrolment of only women...' and MIC became the first Catholic training college to adopt co-education when male students were admitted in September 1969.[234] Cregan also indicated his willingness to accept female day students in St. Patrick's College but was initially denied permission by the Department of Education.[235] The department, however, allowed the college to accept women students from 1971–72, initially on a non-residential basis. Female participation helped to drive an unprecedented increase in enrolments to over 600 by 1972–73, which Cregan acknowledged was 'in the nature of a minor explosion' for the college.[236] The acceptance of co-education by the Catholic training colleges was an important break with the past and marked a profound change in the traditional character of almost all the teacher training institutions. A decline in religious vocations also prompted a reappraisal of traditional conventions. De La Salle college was closed in 1970 and Marino became the sole centre for teacher training for male religious orders. This soon proved insufficient to maintain a steady intake and St. Mary's college opened its doors to lay students of both genders for the first time in 1972.[237] Women soon accounted for a majority of students even in the colleges previously reserved for men.

The expansion of the colleges was underpinned by public investment, including exchequer support for capital development. The first major project authorised by the department was the reconstruction of St. Patrick's College, allowing the college to accept approximately 100 additional students annually.[238] The minister financed the full cost of the redevelopment subject to conditions set by the Department of Finance, which spread the costs over thirty-five years. The exchequer provided half of the necessary funding directly through block grants and the remainder was secured through a bank loan of £750,000, repaid by the state which covered the annual interest charges incurred by the college.[239] McQuaid was uneasy about such reliance on the state to guarantee the loan, complaining to Seán MacGearailt, assistant secretary of the Department of Education, about interference from the Department of Finance which he regarded as sorely lacking in knowledge about education. But it was a very favourable arrangement which allowed for the completion of an ambitious redevelopment programme in the mid 1960s.[240] The surge in public investment in teacher education continued up to the early 1980s. MIC benefited from a similar development programme to accommodate over 800 students by 1980, which led to the opening of a new extension incorporating a new library, lecture threatre and TV and communications studio.[241] Carysfort also secured a new extension allowing capacity for 800 students, which was completed in 1983—ironically, only three years before the announcement of its closure in the midst of a renewed economic crisis.

The fortunes of CITC were also transformed in this period, benefiting from effective institutional leadership and the expansionist orientation of the department. The governing body decided in 1961 to move the college from the city centre to Rathmines, due to long-term concerns over the condition of its building in Kildare Place, which was already over 150 years old.[242] The Department of Education supported their case, noting '…the unsatisfactory and unsuitable accommodation in their College in Kildare Place…Because of its age and the cramped, outmoded facilities available, a scheme of reconstruction to bring the college up to modern standards is not feasible.'[243] The governing body acquired an alternative site at Rathmines Castle in 1963, selling the Kildare Place building to Laing development company. The Church of Ireland authorities experienced similar problems as McQuaid in securing an adequate bank loan to finance the redevelopment and instead the Department of Finance negotiated a loan of £535,000 on favourable terms for the college.[244] The loan was advanced by the Representative Church Body and a consortium of insurance companies under the auspices of Irish Life Assurance Company.[245] The government approved a state guarantee of the loan for CITC in July 1966, which was a precondition for the involvement of the insurance companes in the arrangement and Finance authorised annual grants to the college to allow repayment over a thirty year period.[246] This guarantee facilitated the swift redevelopment of the Rathmines site. The transfer of CITC to a more spacious site, complete with new lecture halls, residential accommodation and a chapel was completed in 1968–69.[247] The transfer of the college saw a consolidation at Rathmines of the Church of Ireland teacher education institutions, which became known as the Church of Ireland College of Education (CICE). Coláiste Moibhí was accommodated on the same site as a 'juniorate' for the training college, offering a two year senior cycle course through Irish until the mid 1990s.[248]

The rapid expansion of the training colleges during the 1960s gave renewed impetus to demands for the introduction of a university degree for primary teachers. The Commission on Higher Education recommended the extension of the two year course to three years, but envisaged association of primary teacher training colleges with the abortive New Colleges.[249] But the internal departmental committee favoured a more significant re-positioning of teacher training, proposing validation of an extended three year training programme for national teachers through the universities.[250] Successive ministers favoured this option, but were cautious about arousing opposition within the universities. The government was therefore slow to evolve a coherent position on teacher education in the late 1960s. Brian Lenihan first promised the INTO in 1968 that he would establish a linkage between the colleges and universities, but then in January 1969 referred the future of teacher education to a working party within the HEA.[251]

The authority's report on teacher education in May 1970 marked the first comprehensive re-appraisal of teacher training at primary and second level since the foundation of the Irish state. The HEA working party recommended a large-scale expansion of teacher training programmes at primary and second-level, on the basis that the educational sector would require an output of approximately 9500 primary and 9275 post-primary teachers by 1980.[252] They criticised the fragmented, underfunded and poorly co-ordinated structures for teacher training, recommending the establishment of an independent teacher training authority, An Foras Oideachais.[253] Their most influential recommendation was that the primary teacher training programme should be restructured as a three-year course combining academic and pedagogical content and leading to the award of an undergraduate degree.[254] The HEA identified multiple advantages in a degree course which had as much to do with wider policy objectives as the educational development of the individual teacher: 'It would enhance the status of the primary teacher and the teaching profession in general,…bring the aim of a unified teaching profession a step closer, and it would help to counterbalance any possible drift of students from the Training Colleges to the Universities.'[255] Introduction of a degree qualification for all teachers was consistent with the government's policy of developing a more integrated profession with a common salary scale for primary, secondary and vocational teachers. Yet while the working party favoured closer links between the colleges and the universities, they also recommended that the newly introduced degree programme should be awarded by the NCEA—a conclusion which drew sharp criticism.[256]

The working party favoured upgrading the status of the larger training colleges rather than incorporating primary teacher education programmes within the universities and did not hesitate to propose a rationalisation of the existing institutions. They envisaged the reconstitution of St. Patrick's College, Mary Immaculate and Carysfort as Colleges of Education with broad based, autonomous governing bodies, but advised that due to the small number of their students the colleges in Marino and Waterford '…should cease to operate as centres of teacher training.'[257] The working party was more cautious about CITC due to its minority status, noting that '…for reasons of conscience its authorities may wish to retain its separate existence.'[258] A measure of rationalisation was achieved through the closure of De La Salle college, but this had more to do with the decline in vocations and proportion of religious entering teacher training than the report itself.[259] Perhaps not surprisingly, several of the more controversial recommendations were sidelined by the government, notably a teacher training authority independent of the department and the closure of Marino. Yet the report was a decisive step towards reconceptualising teacher education, offering a plausible rationale for public investment, encouraging policy and attitudinal changes in a previously traditional sector and presenting a blueprint for programmatic and curriculum reforms.

If the report was a manifesto for radical reform of teacher education, it was also an apparent setback for advocates of a university qualification for primary teachers. The proposed linkage with the NCEA was rejected by the INTO, the Association of Training College Professors and student representative bodies in the training colleges.[260] This dismay was shared by the college authorities. Cregan complained to the bishops that the Department of Education aimed to retain 'almost complete control of primary teacher education' and was unwilling to devolve greater responsibility for primary education to the universities: he also speculated that the HEA was seeking to confer greater academic status on the awards given by the NCEA by including primary teachers within its remit.[261] The latter conclusion was more accurate, as senior departmental officials favoured a university degree for national teachers, but the HEA which was more influenced by its university members, took the opposite view.

Following the election of a Fine Gael-Labour coalition in March 1973, the incoming Minister for Education, Dick Burke, resolved the debate in favour of a university degree for primary teacher training. Cregan informed the bishops early in 1973 that Burke was sympathetic to demands by the INTO and college authorities that primary teachers should be able to take a university degree.[262] Seán O'Connor, now secretary of the department, asked the presidents of UCD and UCC in June 1973 to open negotiations with the larger Catholic training colleges in Dublin and Limerick on a three year course leading to a university degree.[263] Burke, meanwhile, announced a restructuring of the higher education system on a 'comprehensive' basis, which ultimately failed to materialise. But his more modest proposal for teacher education proceeded despite the failure of the government's wider initiative. The negotiations with the governing bodies of UCD and UCC were already well advanced, when the leaders of Mary Immaculate College, Carysfort and St. Patrick's College applied for recognition as recognised colleges of the university on 11 July 1974.[264] The NUI general board of studies recommended the approval of all three applications based on agreements reached by UCC with Mary Immaculate and UCD with St Patrick's College and Carysfort.[265] The conditions included introduction of assessment boards incorporating representatives of the relevant university college for appointment of teachers in the colleges of education; protocols for each examinations board approved by the university and appointment of additional academic staff.[266] The NUI senate approved the recommendations in April 1975, according recognised college status to the three institutions and allowing them to offer the new three year B.Ed. degree programme from the 1974–75 academic year.[267] St. Angela's college, Sligo, which specialised in training teachers of home economics, was subsequently given recognised college status in 1978, following agreement with the governing body of UCG.[268] The NUI's decision in 1975 was a seminal moment in the transformation of teacher education and the culmination of a process of policy change and institutional reform which began in the late 1950s.

Yet as Nolan comments, if the decision was an 'important milestone' in launching a university degree for primary teachers, many details remained unresolved.[269] These included the status of the new B.Ed. as a pass or honours award and progression for teachers to postgraduate degrees, as well as variations which emerged between the UCD and UCC course structures.[270] If the senate's decision on the principle of the new degree was uncontentious, this was emphatically not true of its discussions on the complex issues arising from the new dispensation. The issue of an honours award at undergraduate level caused particular contention. When the senate sought guidance from its constituent colleges on a number of issues including the honours award, it received diverse and often contradictory responses. The academic council in UCD agreed that honours should be available to students at the degree examinations from 1977, but their counterparts in UCC argued that honours should not be awarded 'on the existing three-year course', although they were open to a four year honours course.[271] The UCG council also rejected the principle of an honours award on the three year course. The contradictory responses from the colleges produced a lengthy and contentious debate at a senate meeting on 9 December 1976. This was resolved only when the Chancellor, T. K. Whitaker, put the question to a vote and the senate agreed by 14 votes to 11 that 'Honours should be available at the B.Ed. Degree Examination on completion of a three year course of study.'[272] The senate allowed wide variation on other contentious issues, facilitating variable course structures and different arrangements for exemption from university arts examinations between the two Dublin colleges linked to UCD and Mary Immaculate in relation to UCC.[273] This may have avoided further conflict within the NUI but effectively sanctioned less favourable arrangements for exemption and academic progression among students in the Dublin colleges.[274]

The transition to a three year degree in primary teacher education led to an intensification of the traditional relationship between Trinity College and CICE, coupled with a more unexpected alliance with three smaller Catholic colleges. CICE opened negotiations with Trinity in 1974 to offer the new degree programme.[275] The academic council

recommended the introduction of the new B.Ed. degree in association with CICE in June 1975: the college Board approved the initiative with the caveat that additional financial aid should be sought from
the Minister for Education and in the absence of such assistance 'the
course for primary teachers would have no greater claim on the general
resources of the College than others already in existence.'[276] CICE's relationship with Trinity was long established but sometimes volatile, featuring tension with the college authorities and its school of education.

The negotiations subsequently encompassed Marino and two
Catholic training colleges managed by the Dominican order, Froebel
College and St. Catherine's in Sion Hill. The Christian Brothers found
an unexpected ally in Trinity after their initial approaches to UCD
and UCG for an association with Marino proved unsuccessful.[277] The
apparently incongruous alliance was facilitated by the withdrawal of the
ecclesiastical 'ban' and a convergence of interests between Trinity and
the smaller Catholic colleges, which required a university to accredit
their degree programmes, while the authorities in TCD were able to
secure greater student numbers and demonstrate their ecumenical credentials by forging an alliance with Catholic religious providers.[278]
Perhaps more significantly, uncertainty over the merger made alliance
with smaller, Dublin-based colleges more attractive to academic leaders
in Trinity, especially to forestall the more radical realignment favoured
by successive governments. The Board agreed in February 1976 to
recognise Marino and Froebel as associated colleges offering the three
year B.Ed. from 1976–77, while similar arrangements were extended
to St. Catherine's college to offer a B.Ed. in home economics.[279] The
new institutional configuration was managed by a B.Ed. co-ordinating
committee, including representation from the four colleges and Trinity's
school of education.

The three year B.Ed. was a concurrent programme with education as
the central area of study, incorporating the academic/foundation disciplines of education; specific curricular content related to particular subjects and teaching methods, as well as teaching practice in schools.[280]
While assessment was conducted by academic staff in the colleges of
education and the programmes were overseen by the accrediting university, the Department of Education continued to determine entry

requirements and level of enrolments on each programme.[281] The TCD approved programme differed from the NUI model, as it was an integrated education programme with no co-operating arts subject.[282] The agreement between TCD and its associated colleges established a four year requirement for an Honours degree in line with Trinity's existing programmes, although an ordinary B.Ed. degree could be attained after three years. Students from the colleges attended lectures in academic subjects offered by the school of education for one day a week in Trinity as an integral part of the degree. This was a mixed outcome for B.Ed. students: as Susan Parkes, the first registrar for the new B.Ed. in 1976, noted subsequently, the integrated programme was a coherent offering designed for trainee teachers, but the student experience of the university was limited and fragmented.[283] The relationship between the colleges and TCD over the following generation was sometimes difficult, reflecting cultural divergences and the inherent complexity of managing a major programme offered across a number of diverse institutions.

The repositioning of teacher education also had a significant impact on the formation of second-level teachers. Pre-service secondary training remained the preserve of university schools of education. The surge in second-level enrolments from the early 1960s and demand for training of more second-level teachers gave enhanced importance to schools of education and helped to stimulate reform of the existing training programmes. The H.Dip in Education was transformed into a one year, full-time course in Trinity, UCD and UCC during the 1970s.[284] The schools of education benefited from greater investment in staffing and facilities and each university filled chairs of education which had sometimes previously been left vacant, facilitating the emergence of a new group of leaders in the field.[285] The schools also launched new initiatives at postgraduate level during the 1970s, introducing Master of Education (M.Ed.) taught postgraduate courses which offered opportunities for further study and engagement with research in education, while MA and doctoral research was also expanded.[286]

The training of vocational teachers was largely delegated by the department to the VECs in the early decades of the state. There was no specialised course in Ireland offering degree level courses in physical education, although training was offered to girls in three women's colleges operated by religious orders. Demand for higher level courses was met in the early 1970s through St. Mary's College, Twickenham, where Irish students undertook courses funded by Irish government scholarships; four of these students received the first degrees awarded by the NCEA in 1975.[287] The Fianna Fáil government decided in 1970 to establish a National College of Physical Education in Limerick, offering a four year degree to men and women.[288] The college opened in 1973 on the same site as the NIHE with an initial enrolment of 200 students. Almost immediately Burke announced in October 1973 that its remit would be expanded to include training for a wider variety of vocational teachers, including woodwork and metalwork.[289] The training functions for physical education and 'specialist subjects', initially envisaged as separate institutes on the same site, were combined under a single governing body and designated as Thomond College of Education in 1975.[290] Thomond was immediately embroiled in the maelstrom around the coalition's wider plan for a 'comprehensive' system and in line with this plan secured approval from the NUI senate as a recognised college in December 1976.[291] This association proved short-lived and acrimonious. The students' union in Thomond fiercely attacked the new alignment in March 1977, ostensibly on the basis of a downgrading of continuous assessment in their programme, but mainly because they objected to the linkage with UCC: '...the whole general character and ethos of the Thomond College of Education is being endangered by an over-hasty and badly thought-out university link, brought about in the first place for doubtful reasons.'[292] The student teachers refused to accept a B.Ed. degree from the NUI for 1976 and withdrew from college courses temporarily early in 1977 to 'highlight the grievances which have arisen from the negotiations with University College Cork re assessment of our degree course.'[293] Thomond's turbulent association with the NUI lasted almost exactly a year, as it was brought back under the NCEA following the return of Fianna Fáil to power in June 1977.[294] While the government's plans for second-level teacher education had an ad hoc flavour due to the wider debate over system structure, the development of Thomond College was an important incremental step in offering higher level education to a significant subset of second level teachers in PE and a range of vocational subjects.

The impact of reforming policies on primary teacher training was more fundamental. The inauguration of the B.Ed. programme offered by the newly redesignated colleges of education was one of the most significant reforms of the second half of the twentieth century. The training colleges, which had been largely insulated from other higher education institutions and shared many features with residential secondary schools, were drawn into a diversified higher education system. Whatever its limitations, this model of primary teacher education proved enduring and persisted into the early twenty-first century. The initiative testified to the ability of the political and adminstrative elite to negotiate long-term policy change in higher education when pursuing clearly articulated goals with a strong educational rationale and institutional support. Significantly, public officials were careful not to challenge the denominational basis of the teacher training colleges, which in turn proved willing to accept and frequently to initiate radical institutional changes. The repositioning of primary teacher education was achieved with relative ease, reflecting the traditional responsiveness of teacher training institutions to government policy but also the willingness of religious providers to adapt to wider cultural changes and the absence of any fundamental challenge to the continuing denominational imprint within the system.

The Binary System

Perhaps the most striking outcome of the government's policies for diversification was the emergence of a binary system governing third-level education, characterised by differentiation in mission and governance between universities and the new technical institutions and much tighter official control over the management of most non-university institutions. While the government delegated important executive functions to the HEA regarding the universities (and later the NIHEs), a varied non-university sector including the RTCs, CDVEC colleges and colleges of education remained outside the remit of the authority. An unpublished report by the Department of Education in 1974 explicitly referenced the 'separation between the autonomous sector (the universities) and the integrated sector (Colleges of Technology, Regional Technical Colleges etc.)' as the hallmark of the binary system, noting for good measure that the model 'envisages that the universities would tend to be under public control to a lesser extent than other institutions of higher education.'[295] The RTCs were placed under the authority of the VECs, which appointed their boards of management, but were also subject to control by the Department of Education, which funded the new institutions directly by a dedicated grant channelled through the VECs.[296] The department was unwilling to surrender its power over higher technical education or teacher education, still less to concede to the new institutions the autonomy traditionally enjoyed by the universities. This decision had lasting implications for the development of the newly expanded higher technical sector, which lacked the support of an influential 'buffer' agency and remained subject to direct control by the Department of Education.

The composition of the first authority provided some reassurance to the universities that the HEA was not intended to infringe upon their autonomy. The authority consisted of fourteen members, including at least seven drawn from the universities and other institutions of higher education, with a similar number of non-academic members. Ó Raifeartaigh was appointed as the first chairman of the HEA, with James F. Dukes as the first secretary. Ó Raifeartaigh commented in a letter to Seán MacGearailt, his successor as secretary of the department, on 7 March 1970 that the achievement of rationalisation and co-ordination in higher education was the 'raison d'être' of the HEA.[297] Yet the HEA was never simply an extension of the Department of Education. Dukes, an independent minded civil servant who was a strong advocate of increased resources for higher education, argued that 'Many of them were university figures; it wasn't about state control. What we wanted was to develop the universities'.[298] The HEA operated in the context of the state's educational policies but did not hesitate to challenge or modify government policies with which it disagreed, especially in the first two decades of its existence.

The HEA enjoyed considerable influence on government policy in the 1970s, when it frequently acted to modify initiatives which attracted hostility from the universities and sometimes came into conflict with the minister. The authority's report on university re-organisation, which was presented to the minister on 9 December 1971, sounded the death-knell for the university merger. The authority accepted that there should be two universities in Dublin, in accordance with the NUI-TCD agreement, although they also recommended the establishment of a Conjoint Board linking the two universities to oversee a joint approach to collaboration.[299] The HEA's recommendation for a change in the government's policy enhanced its reputation with the universities, which generally opposed the merger.[300]

Apart from its role in giving merger a decent burial, the authority produced influential reports on new structures and institutions in a rapidly changing higher education system, contributing particularly to policy formation on the NIHEs and teacher education. The authority also collaborated with the universities in creating the Central Applications Office (CAO), which was established as a limited company controlled by the institutions in January 1976.[301] The CAO provided a centralised process from 1977 for administering an increasing volume of applications to the universities. Points were first used as a mechanism to allocate university places by the School of Medicine in UCD from the late 1960s. The CAO oversaw the introduction of a competitive points system which converted the top six grades in the Leaving Certificate into points offering entry to college programmes.[302] The NIHEs and Thomond College were soon included in the CAO, as were degree courses in DIT from 1982.[303] Most non-designated institutions were initially outside the CAO, but the RTCs participated in a similar central applications system in the 1980s and the CAO incorporated both the RTCs and colleges of education from the early 1990s.[304] The CAO became the standard entry route to the vast majority of third-level courses by the 1990s and its emergence reinforced the importance of the Leaving Certificate as the key gateway to higher education. Trinity suspended its matriculation examinations for most subjects in 1979, while the NUI 'matric' survived as an alternative entry route until 1992.[305] The centralised applications process and associated points system were among the most enduring legacies of the far-reaching policy changes of the 1960s and 1970s.

The HEA soon established a constructive relationship with the institutions within its remit, which usually recognised the value of a 'buffer agency' between universities and the state. Séamus Ó Cathail was well qualified to comment on the interface between the state and academia, serving as secretary to the Commission on Higher Education before becoming academic secretary of UCG. Ó Cathail, commenting on institutional perceptions of the HEA in 1982, suggested that '... the model would generally be regarded as suitable and indeed that, the procedures for the operation of this model are in themselves, tolerable, even if occasionally irksome'.[306] Ó Cathail acknowledged that the universities had various complaints about the HEA, including the increasingly familiar refrain that 'its attitudes were over-influenced by the State agencies in the background, for which it becomes the public face'.[307] Yet such complaints were driven by concern that the HEA was not sufficiently robust in negotiating with the Department of Education, not by any institutional desire to question the intermediary role of the agency.

The binary structure did not, however, go unchallenged in the contentious political debates of the 1970s. The election of a Fine Gael-Labour coalition in 1973, which ended a sixteen-year period of Fianna Fáil rule, led to a dramatic, though short-lived, policy change on system structure. Minister Burke set up a Cabinet sub-committee to prepare a White Paper on the reorganisation of higher education in January 1974.[308] The new committee included several members with an academic background, including Dr. Garret FitzGerald, the Foreign Minister, Justin Keating, Minister for Industry and Commerce and Dr. Conor Cruise O'Brien, Minister for Posts and Telegraphs (previously a civil servant and an academic in the USA).[309] The creation of such a high powered cabinet committee indicated the increased political importance and sensitivity of the higher education brief since the 1950s and reduced Burke's freedom of action. The minister commissioned a report on system structure and organisation from an internal departmental committee in 1974, which recommended maintaining the binary system in the short-term, while keeping open the option of "a possible future transition to a 'comprehensive' system on a gradual basis."[310] The committee dissented from the HEA recommendations on the merger, arguing for closer integration between Trinity and UCD than the NUI-TCD agreement. The minister's proposals to the Cabinet for restructuring the system on 11 September 1974 generally reflected the perspective of his officials. Burke sought to resurrect the merger, proposing a reconstituted University of Dublin with joint faculties of medicine and science between Trinity and UCD.[311] His plan also envisaged a reduced NUI containing UCC, UCG and St. Patrick's College Maynooth and a more radical proposal for an 'Institute for Technological and Technical Education', serving as a national institution with supervisory functions over the entire technological sector including the new NIHEs. The proposed institute was potentially a state-wide technological university, although the department considered that 'the time has not yet come…to establish the third institution as a technological University in its own right'.[312] Burke's plan displayed a logic in building on the existing binary framework, although it also sought to resurrect the ill-fated merger.

Yet Burke's original plan never saw the light of the day, mainly because of the opposition of other ministers. A note of the Cabinet meeting on 18 September 1974 recorded that 'After full discussion, M/E said he would reexamine his proposals in the light of the points made by his colleagues'.[313] Burke's proposals were opposed by most ministers on the Cabinet sub-committee, including the Finance Minister Richie Ryan and Conor Cruise O'Brien, while objections were also raised on more specific grounds by the Departments of Health and the Gaeltacht.[314] Influential ministers such as Cruise O'Brien and FitzGerald were sceptical of merger, while the Department of Finance offered a critique from the opposite direction, suggesting that Education was not going far enough in achieving rationalisation of faculties between Trinity and UCD.[315] The decisions reached by the Cabinet in early October 1974 differed sharply from Burke's original plan. The government agreed an alternative model involving three separate universities: the University of Dublin 'comprising T.C.D.—progressively an N.C.T structure involving Ballymun, Bolton St. etc….'; UCD which would be reconstituted as an independent university, including Maynooth as a constituent college and a reduced NUI consisting of UCC and UCG.[316] NIHE, Limerick, would become a recognised college of the NUI, while NIHE Dublin (and potentially the colleges of technology as well) established a similar relationship with Trinity College; the National College of Art and Design

(NCAD) would be incorporated as a faculty within UCD. The NCEA would be replaced by a new co-ordinating committee on technological education to validate courses and award qualifications at diploma and certificate levels, while degree awarding powers would be reserved for the universities.[317] Finally all third level education institutions would be brought under the authority of the HEA.

Burke and his senior officials were sceptical of the government decisions and repeatedly sought to reverse or at least modify them. Burke warned his colleagues on 25 October 1974 that their decisions could jeopardise the prospect of EEC funding for the RTCs through the Social Fund, which was dependent on their 'vocational' character and would also require a referendum to change the university panels in Seanad Éireann to allow representation for graduates of three universities.[318] Burke's salvo confirmed his opposition in no uncertain terms, alluding to 'the Minister's conviction that the decisions are detrimental to Higher Education generally, but particularly to Technological Education.'[319] The minister's case was inspired by the strenuous objections of the Department of Education, which pulled no punches in characterising the restriction of degree awarding powers to the universities as 'reactionary in concept and out of line with the trends of a technological age'.[320] The minister appealed to the Cabinet to back his original proposals or adopt the previous HEA blueprint based on the NUI/TCD agreement.[321]

But the government initially refused to deviate from its original decision involving a 'comprehensive' system structure. The Cabinet decided on 13 December 1974 to re-state its commitment to three universities in the state, '(i) a University to be constituted from the present University College, Dublin (ii) the University of Dublin (Trinity College) and (iii) the National University of Ireland, comprising University College, Cork and University College, Galway.'[322] A conjoint board would be established to co-ordinate the two universities in Dublin and oversee a redistribution of faculties between them 'with a view to ensuring rational use of resources'.[323] While each university would retain its autonomy, the proposed redistribution of faculties was more favourable to UCD: the burgeoning disciplines of business studies and social science were allocated solely to UCD, along with agriculture and veterinary medicine, while dentistry and pharmacy were conceded to Trinity.[324] The government made only minor concessions to Burke's appeal, agreeing that NIHED could in due course be linked with either Trinity or UCD and that Maynooth, bizarrely, would have the option of becoming a constituent college of any one of the three universities. Ministers also confirmed that the NCEA would be replaced by a Council for Technological Education to 'validate and award non-degree third-level qualifications' in the NIHEs and RTCs.[325] The government plan amounted to a fundamental reversal of previous policy on diversification, seeking to develop new higher education institutions within a unitary model and placing the prestigious degree courses under the auspices of the universities.

Burke announced the government plan in a press statement on 16 December 1974, putting a brave face on an initiative imposed on him by more influential members of the Cabinet. He commented that 'a valid binary system could not be maintained without a degree of duplication of scarce resources, both of money and of talent, which would be unacceptable in a country of this size'.[326] The minister's statement suggested that the initiative was driven by utilitarian considerations, rejecting a binary division as wasteful and inefficient. Yet this portrayal understated the more overtly political motivations for the decision. Most ministers had no desire to revive the university merger and sought an alternative which would be more acceptable to the universities. The Department of Finance sought to curtail the costs of expansionist policies by imposing tighter co-ordination (and in Dublin rationalisation of faculties) on HEIs. The government's plan was framed based on these diverse and potentially contradictory impulses and emerged from a muddled policy-making process which sidelined the HEA and rejected the input of the Department of Education. The coalition in retreating from the merger had produced a blueprint for restructuring the system, which was equally controversial and so convoluted that it was almost impossible to justify.

Burke portrayed himself as a construction manager clearing up after a visionary if somewhat impractical architect: 'Mr O'Malley hit the system like a thunderbolt when he announced his proposal for a merger. Perhaps it has been my lot to pick up the pieces and produce a coherent plan for the last quarter of this century'.[327] This proved to be wishful thinking. White comments that following the failure of the merger, the coalition government 'was opting for even more elaborate trench warfare on different terrain, and with a much larger and angrier group of adversaries.'[328] More significantly, the latest plan was being advanced by a minister and department which did not really agree with it. The initiative suffered from the additional handicap that it undermined a newly established and workable model without offering an alternative which was either credible or attractive to most institutions.

Burke's initiative attracted a chorus of condemnation from a wide variety of institutions, student organisations and even official agencies, securing support only from Ed Walsh and the governing body of UCD. Few institutional stakeholders matched the vehemence of the Union of Students in Ireland (USI), which denounced Burke's attempt to bring non-university institutions under the auspices of the existing universities as 'a charter for disaster…infantile and simplistic'.[329] But the authorities of UCC and UCG were sharply critical of the initiative which left them as sole residents of a rump NUI. The provost of Trinity, Leland Lyons, opposed a conjoint board 'as a very real threat to the autonomy of the universities' and criticised the proposed redistribution of science and professional faculties between Trinity and UCD.[330] The government initiative was produced without any consultation with HEIs and was quietly opposed by the HEA: Ó Raifeartaigh commented publicly that the HEA had 'no part whatever' in formulating the minister's initiative.[331] The HEA chairman wrote to the minister on 15 April 1975, commenting diplomatically that 'a number of problems have presented themselves' with regard to the government's plan.[332] Ó Raifeartaigh enumerated the authority's reservations about the government initiative. Firstly, 'equality of status' betweeen universities and the non-university sector could not be achieved by setting up technical institutions as recognised colleges; instead 'the possibility of constituting a Technical University in the existing non-university sector' should be explored.[333] Ironically, the views of the minister and departmental officials on this point were much closer to the HEA's perspective than the government decision. The HEA also favoured independent university status for UCC and UCG rather than participation in a rump NUI and sought 'a better balance' in the disciplines allocated between Trinity and UCD.[334] While the authority's objections were expressed in a diplomatic vein, the state's 'buffer agency' made no secret of its opposition to the government's plan.

The ambitious restructuring of higher education envisaged by the government initiative was never implemented. Degree-awarding powers were removed from the NCEA, which acquired instead ill defined powers of planning and coordination over non-degree programmes, although this move was vocally opposed by Fianna Fáil.[335] Burke secured Cosgrave's support to modify the original government plan in the face of almost universal institutional opposition. Cosgrave agreed that Burke should bring the policy before the government again and also advised him to meet the members of the HEA authority, 'so that we will have a clearer picture of their views on the points they raise.'[336] The HEA's intervention contributed to a course correction by the government, probably because it gave Burke the necessary leverage to persuade his colleagues to change direction. The minister announced a partial change of direction in August 1976, proposing a restructured system based around five separate universities and appointing a joint working party, including representatives of the department, HEA and university colleges.[337] This working party produced the heads of a detailed Higher Education Bill for circulation to ministers. The outline Bill offered independent university status to UCD, UCC, UCG and Maynooth: Trinity would remain a separate institution but an amendment to the TCD Letters Patent would allow five government nominees on the Board.[338] A joint universities council was proposed to secure greater co-ordination between the five universities on entry requirements, recognition of courses and mobility of staff and students.[339] The proposals for the two NIHEs and colleges of education reflected the government's policy, envisaging that they would conclude institutional agreements with a neighbouring university to accredit their degrees: the NCEA was to be retained, albeit solely for the award of qualifications at diploma/certificate level.[340] Yet Burke's appointment as Ireland's second EEC commissioner in November 1976 reduced the momentum for legislation, while the political timetable conspired against such a far-reaching reform so late in the lifetime of the administration.[341] Burke's successor, Peter Barry, sent the draft to Cosgrave on 16

December 1976, noting that 'it was for the confidential information of the Taoiseach.'[342] But no legislation was introduced before the national coalition was defeated in a general election in June 1977.

The only tangible outcomes of the coalition's ambitious plans for the restructuring of higher education were the association of teacher education with the universities (a significant institutional change which stood the test of time) and a modest re-allocation of health sciences disciplines between Trinity and UCD. Veterinary medicine had traditionally been offered in both universities, with a much greater concentration of students in UCD. Successive government plans and the NUI/TCD agreement envisaged a single faculty of veterinary medicine located in Trinity, but this was reversed by the coalition's plan in December 1974, which allocated veterinary medicine to UCD while dentistry and pharmacy were reserved for Trinity.[343] This was almost the sole element of the government's initiative which was realised in practice, largely at the instigation of Mark Clinton, Minister for Agriculture. Lyons fought hard to retain the veterinary faculty, but in this instance the political elite moved decisively to enforce a rationalisation of two small faculties. Clinton wrote to Lyons and Tom Murphy, the president of UCD, on 11 August 1975, 'to confirm that the government's decision on Veterinary Medicine is absolutely final and irrevocable.'[344] Lyons strongly protested at the minister's decision, warning Clinton that 'the Board and the College would take a grave view of what, in the circumstances, would undoubtedly be regarded in Trinity as an arbitrary and unjustifiable proceeding'.[345] While the provost fought a dedicated rearguard action in defence of the veterinary faculty, seeking advice from Darley and Co. solicitors on the legality of the government action, even J. V. Luce (a college officer from 1977–85), recognised that the college's case was 'weakest at this point', considering the high cost of maintaining two faculties and the disparity of numbers between Trinity and UCD.[346] Clinton, who was implementing a Cabinet decision, insisted on the centralisation of veterinary medicine in UCD, which was accomplished in 1977. The change of direction at political level was also influenced by UCD's stronger connections with the coalition (particularly its major Fine Gael component) than the previous administration. The concentration of veterinary medicine in UCD was a rare example during this period of the imposition of a government decision by *force majeure* within the university sector, which still retained a high level of autonomy. The coalition's wider initiative, however, shared the same fate as the merger and any attempt to undertake a radical restructuring of higher education was postponed indefinitely.

Yet even the prospect of a major restructuring had significant implications for higher education in Dublin, stimulating a new alliance between Trinity and the CDVEC. The TCD engineering school and its counterparts in Kevin St. and Bolton St. were already sharing laboratory space and resources so there was a precedent for closer collaboration. But the nascent alliance was stimulated by a shared distrust of the coalition government's attempt to overturn the binary model.[347] The Board of TCD was disturbed by several aspects of the government's plan, including the creation of a joint science faculty between Trinity and UCD and denial of capital investment to the faculty of engineering science in TCD; the status of the VEC's higher professional courses was threatened by the prospect of an independent NIHE in Dublin and apparent eclipse of the NCEA.[348] Negotiations between two institutions traditionally at different poles of the higher education spectrum quickly revealed a convergence of interests. The uncertainty generated by the latest government plan, Trinity's suspicions that the coalition was biased towards UCD and pressure from British professional bodies in engineering for degree qualifications as a prerequisite for membership gave impetus to the negotiations, which were instigated by Patrick Donegan, the chairman of CDVEC.[349] An initial proposal was quickly agreed, allowing VEC students who successfully completed the final diploma examinations in engineering to be awarded a new B.Sc. (Engineering) degree by the university from 1975: this plan for 'a closer relationship with the Colleges of Technology in Dublin…' was quickly ratified by the university council and Board in May 1975.[350] This proved the first step in a more long-term alliance, leading to the establishment of a joint working group to create an operational framework for future relations between Trinity and CDVEC.[351] A partnership agreement was concluded between CDVEC and the University of Dublin in April 1976, committing both parties to work together to 'generate greater educational possibilities and enhance the capabilities of both our educational institutions...on a basis of absolute parity.'[352] The partnership agreement confirmed that each institution would maintain their independent identity, respecting 'the distinctive character and ethos of the other.'[353] The agreement provided for the validation of awards to VEC students for degree purposes through the University of Dublin and co-operation in the development of courses, sharing of resources and mobility of students.[354] A liaison council was established, consisting of six representatives of each partner, to oversee and promote 'this co-operative association'.[355] The agreement established an institutional framework for recognition of professional diploma courses at degree level, beginning with diploma courses in architecture and engineering. Yet the institutional alliance also recognised 'a community of interest in educational, academic and professional matters greater than the specific connections...between us', leaving scope for joint action in response to future developments in higher education.[356] The alliance soon extended well beyond the initial collaboration, ultimately encompassing a wide range of courses across six colleges of techology, including applied sciences, business studies, human nutrition and dietetics (from 1982) and music education (from 1985).[357] The TCD-CDVEC alliance was a pragmatic response to the upheaval within the emerging higher education system, which offered valuable gains to each partner.[358] The VEC colleges secured recognition of their higher level professional courses through the university, while Trinity secured an institutional alliance which, unlike the government plan, did not compromise its autonomy or existing range of disciplines.

The newly minted alliance with TCD and the unsatisfactory outcome of the Ballymun project from a VEC perspective led to the reconfiguration of the CDVEC colleges with the intention of creating a unified third-level institution. The VEC made an order on 25 May 1978 to 'commence a process of unification' of the six colleges, establishing a single governing body for the newly formed Dublin Institute of Technology from 1 September 1978.[359] The new governing body, operating as a sub-committee of the VEC, was given authority to develop 'a fully integrated third level institute' and a similar apprentice institute across the colleges; an academic council was also established to integrate the academic activity of the different colleges in terms of examinations and assessment.[360] The governing body had a broadly based membership, including VEC members and nominees representing staff, students, Dublin Council of Trade Unions and industry.[361] The new institute did not, however, lead to the rapid formation of a unitary structure, as the colleges retained considerable autonomy and continued to operate as distinct academic units under the control of their principals.[362] But the alliance with Trinity endured for almost a quarter of a century, as many of the DIT's degree courses continued to be validated by the University of Dublin until 2001.

The return of Fianna Fáil to power in 1977 brought a reversal of the coalition's policy on higher education.[363] The incoming Minister for Education, John Wilson (1977–81), restored the binary system and introduced a statutory framework for the NIHEs. The Fianna Fáil government restored a key role to the NCEA in the validation of higher technological courses and qualifications, deciding in November 1977 to reinstate its degree awarding powers for non-university institutions including the NIHEs, RTCs and Thomond College.[364] The newly formed DIT was not included in the NCEA's remit, although its individual colleges were, testifying to the CDVEC's reluctance to embrace the NCEA as the main accreditation agency for its awards.[365] The government also moved to establish the NIHEs on a statutory basis with their own governing bodies, which were independent of the local VECs. Wilson showed a preference for incremental legislation, albeit following consistent objectives, rather than the more sweeping restructuring plans advanced by his predecessors since 1967.

The government's deliberations on NIHE Limerick revealed ambivalence on the extent to which the new institutions should be engaged in research or postgraduate education, traditionally the preserve of the universities. The decision on 9 February 1979 to approve the general scheme of a Bill for the NIHE was subject 'to the consideration of the question of including a provision enabling post-graduate work with suitable controls', indicating uncertainty among ministers as to how far graduate courses in the new institute should go.[366] The Department of Education included a section providing for postgraduate degrees and research in the draft Bill which was brought to the Cabinet almost a year later, noting that '…the term "degree level courses" comprehends post-graduate degrees and…the word "research" comprehends research at post-graduate level.'[367] The memorandum (and subsequently the Bill) stipulated that 'control' over such programmes and research would be exercised by the academic council and governing body, underlining a residual ambivalence over a research mission for the NIHEs, coupled with genuine uncertainty over the eventual remit of the new institutes. The legislation approved by the Cabinet in January 1980, retained significant powers of oversight and supervision for the minister, despite the NIHE's status as a designated institution under the HEA. The majority of the governing body was appointed by the government on the recommendation of the Minister for Education. Moreover, the governing body was obliged to submit an annual report to the minister and to supply him 'with such information regarding the performance of its functions as he may from time to time require.'[368] The NIHE's finances and staffing policies were also subject to closer regulation than the universities: the institute's power to appoint staff was dependent on the approval of the minister 'given with the concurrence of the Minister for Finance', while its officers could not be removed or suspended from office without ministerial consent.[369] The student fees set by the governing body also required ministerial approval.

The scope for political control over the institute and the danger of localist influence over academic appointments featured heavily in the debate on the Bill in the Senate. Wilson defended the legislation against criticisms by T. K. Whitaker and John A. Murphy, both independent senators on the NUI panel, that it gave excessive control to the minister over the number of staff appointments and even the admission fees, the latter vividly described by Murphy as 'ministerial interference gone mad'.[370] Whitaker and Trevor West, a Trinity senator, also sought to enforce a statutory process for academic appointments. The two senators proposed an amendment requiring public advertisement for academic posts 'in media of wide circulation in Ireland and at least two other member countries of the European Economic Community,' as well as nomination by a board of assessors including a majority of members external to the institute 'of whom…not less than two shall be nationals of member states of the European Economic Community other than Ireland…'[371] As an additional safeguard the governing body would be able to overturn a recommendation from such a board only by a two-thirds majority. Despite a warning by Whitaker in the debate on 3 July 1980 against 'a tendency towards inbreeding' in third level institutions, Wilson rejected the amendment as unduly restrictive.[372] The legislation was approved by the Oireachtas without a vote in July 1980.

The new NIHE in Dublin conformed to the same template in terms of its constitution, functions and relationship with the state. The government accepted the HEA recommendation that the new college at Ballymun would develop autonomously from CDVEC with its own governing body.[373] Yet as with its Limerick counterpart, separate governance did not mean autonomy from the government. The coalition appointed both the interim governing body in March 1975 and the first director of the institute, Daniel O'Hare, in 1977.[374] The legislation to establish the new institute on a statutory basis, approved by the Oireachas in November 1980, was modelled on the NIHE Limerick Act, reserving the same powers to the minister.[375] Legislation was also adopted in 1979 giving statutory recognition to Thomond College, with a separate constitution and academic authority, but also maintained a comparable level of control for the minister.[376]

The policy decisions of the late 1970s confirmed the independent trajectory of the two universities in Dublin. Wilson clarified unresolved issues left over from the debris of the initiatives for university restructuring since the late 1960s, especially regarding the distribution of university faculties between Trinity and UCD. The most contentious issue concerned the allocation of the rapidly expanding faculties of business and social studies, which were designated solely for UCD in the coalition's plan. Lyons made the case to Wilson for the retention of the two disciplines in both colleges, alluding with some asperity to the recent transfer of veterinary medicine:

> …The Provost stressed that the continued existence of Business Studies in the College must be regarded as of crucial importance to the relations of Trinity with the world of business and that 'having been cut off from any contact with agriculture, it is more than ever essential for us to be able to go on contributing to industry in the way we have conspicuously done for so many years'.[377]

The college officers also argued that social studies should be retained in Trinity, not only due to the advantages of its integrated course structure, facilitating students to secure both a professional qualification and a university degree, but also because of 'the significance of a difference of emphasis in the discipline in the context of a pluralist society.'[378] While this argument was not teased out by the department, it was notable as one of the first references in a departmental memo on education to the concept of a 'pluralist society', which was by no means uncontroversial but was becoming a popular reference point in public debate as the influence of integralist Catholicism declined and for the related implication that diverse perspectives in university courses deserved protection by the state. Wilson accepted the college's case and the government agreed in April 1978 to rescind the coalition's decision, allowing the retention of business and social studies in both colleges.[379] It was a sensible decision considering the increase in student enrolments in those disciplines in both universities, although it had as much to do with the reluctance of the government to become embroiled again in a futile struggle over the redistribution of academic units. Significantly, the department no longer referenced (positively or otherwise) traditional political or religious arguments around Trinity's representation of a minority or its links with Northern Ireland, reflecting the decline of traditional denominational divisions in higher education and the reduced salience of religious and cultural objectives among policy-makers.

Wilson issued the first white paper on education published by an Irish government in 1980, a long awaited development which proved largely anti-climactic. The *White Paper on Educational Development* re-affirmed the binary system in higher education, underlining official commitment to 'flexibility and diversification of educational institutions' which would 'play complementary and supportive roles…'.[380] The government's policy statement confirmed the enduring nature of the binary structure, which would remain a defining characteristic of higher education in Ireland for the following generation. The policy statement also endorsed the dissolution of the NUI and reconstitution of UCD, UCC and UCG as separate universities.[381] The White Paper was otherwise notable mainly for a firmly utilitarian vision of higher education informed by national economic requirements, emphasising the importance of technological courses at higher level and the contribution of higher education to the labour market in which the role of 'higher education institutions in recent years towards meeting the highly qualified manpower required by an expanding economy is readily recognised'.[382] The White Paper noted that the government had set out 'priority objectives for third-level education' and would examine the funding arrangements for the sector to ensure priority in the allocation of resources for 'such identified areas of national development.'[383] The minister publicly expressed dissatisfaction with the HEA's responsiveness to government policies regarding the allocation of funding to institutions, highlighting tension between the authority and the department and pressure among senior departmental officials for greater control over the agency and its spending decisions.[384]

The White Paper offered a high level of continuity with existing policy frameworks based on expansion, diversification and upskilling. The transformation of policy and system structure since the late 1950s was now an established orthodoxy. The NIHEs in Dublin and Limerick were inaugurated by ministerial order with the NCEA as their awarding body in 1981, in accordance with the recommendations of the White Paper.[385] Yet the proposed dissolution of the NUI was quietly shelved by successive governments and comprehensive universities legislation would not re-emerge as a serious project until the 1990s. While a referendum was held in 1979 to permit the extension of the franchise within the university panels for the Seanad to graduates drawn from outside the traditional universities, lack of interest in any reform of the Seanad at political level ensured that the existing panels remained unchanged. The White Paper was more significant in confirming the expansionist, pragmatic and utilitarian direction of government policy in HE than for breaking new ground in any dramatic way.

Increasing Participation

The most notable features of the Irish higher education system from the 1950s to the mid 1980s were a rapid expansion of student enrolments allied to far-reaching institutional and system diversification. The level of first time entrants to third level courses increased from 10% of the relevant school leaving age cohort in 1965 to 22% in 1980–81 and 28% by 1985. There were 20,698 full-time students attending publicly funded higher education institutions in 1965: over 85% were registered with the four university colleges and the recognised college at Maynooth.[386] Enrolments had almost trebled only twenty years later, as 55,087 full-time students were enrolled in a diverse range of HEIs including the RTC/DIT sector.[387] While data on part-time participation is limited up to the 1990s, the expansion of the universities was oriented mainly towards full-time students. Part-time participation was more significant in the RTC/DIT sector, where part-time students accounted for a majority of enrolments in the late 1970s.[388]

The evolution of the Irish system was broadly consistent with international trends for the OECD, particularly in Western European states. Yet Irish higher education followed a distinctive chronology of expansion, linked to later postwar economic development and a more abrupt transformation in national policies. The peak in enrolments began later than in other Western European countries, especially more economically advanced states such as West Germany and was sustained at a higher level throughout the 1980s compared to a majority of European states.[389] The steady expansion of student enrolments, particularly at undergraduate level, involved a striking quantitative growth of the sector, linked to the diversification and restructuring of non-university institutions which was the most notable legacy of policy and institutional reform.

The societal demand for higher education, linked to increasing expectations among parents and students, was intensified by reforming policies in second level education, particularly the introduction of free second-level education. The first scheme of higher education grants emerged from the wider initiative for free post-primary schooling in 1967. The Cabinet initially resisted O'Malley's proposal to divert the funding from the limited schemes of post-primary and university scholarships to a new scheme of financial assistance at university level. Charles Haughey, the Minister for Finance, criticised the plan as 'open ended…and altogether too costly to adopt in present circumstances.'[390] But O'Malley and Haughey reached agreement on a scheme of higher education grants in February 1968, which was means tested and linked to attainment: families with incomes below £1200 annually were eligible for the full grant, amounting to £175 for each student whose family residence was 'in or adjacent to a University town' or £300 for those living away from home.[391] The academic cut-off point for a grant was deliberately pitched above the minimum matriculation standard for the universities, requiring four Honours in university matriculation subjects at the Leaving Certificate, with a 70% requirement in at least one subject.[392] The scheme required co-funding by local authorities, who were mandated to supply annually the equivalent of their existing allocation for scholarships and the exchequer, which would provide the remainder.[393] Despite vociferous opposition from Neil Blaney, the Minister for Local Government, who criticised the statutory burden imposed on local authorities as a 'retrograde' step, the government agreed the principle of the scheme on 27 February 1968.[394] The Local Authorities (Higher Education Grants) Bill was approved by the Cabinet on 2 April 1968 shortly after O'Malley's death and became law in time for the 1968–69 academic year.[395] The legislation was the first real attempt by the state to reduce traditional barriers restricting access to university for low-income families, particularly from rural areas and was a genuine improvement on the fragmented scholarships' scheme. Yet it was a relatively limited scheme which applied only to the universities initially and was still intended to reach only about 14% of students receiving higher education.[396]

The new grants scheme had the advantage of offering a flexible template for improvement, as the Ministers for Education and Finance had discretion to alter eligibility limits and grant rates without resorting to legislation. A combination of increasing student enrolments and rising inflation throughout the 1970s generated continual pressure from the Union of Students in Ireland and intermittently from university leaders for a more generous scheme. The scheme was restructured in September 1972, dividing the grant into a fee element (initially to a maximum of €156 annually) and a maintenance element, consisting of a non-adjacent rate of £250 and adjacent of £100 per annum; this concession met a long-standing USI demand, although the national students' union was quick to point out that it failed to keep up with the cost of living.[397]

The means test for new grants was also revised upwards from £1200 to £1600.[398] The coalition increased the maximum levels for maintenance grants by 20% in 1974–75, while the maximum fee element was raised by 38% to £215 over a three year period by 1975–76.[399] Burke also sought agreement in February 1976 to raise the means test and improve the maintenance element by a further 25%, but was rebuffed by the Department of Finance.[400]

Successive governments were willing to recognise higher technical colleges for grant purposes on an ad hoc basis, but were slower to place eligibility for such students on a statutory basis. The coalition approved a draft Bill in February 1977, but failed to act on it before the government lost power.[401] John Wilson decided in January 1978 to proceed with the coalition's Bill, which gave statutory recognition for grant purposes to attendance at 'approved courses of not less than two years duration' at diploma level in the RTCs and colleges of technology.[402] The legislation, which became law in December 1978, confirmed the extension of the grants scheme to most full-time students in the non-university sector.[403] The gradual improvement of the third level grants scheme testified to the influence of egalitarian impulses on public policy during this period, as ministers such as O'Malley both adopted equality of opportunity as a key reference point in legitimating policy innovations and responded to expectations within a public sphere which was both more egalitarian and more vociferous than it had been in the previous generation.

Yet despite incremental advances in the student support schemes in this period, the transition to third-level education was still marked by sharp socio-economic inequalities. Massification and diversification did not translate into greater equality in participation at least up to the 1980s. The scale of class-based inequality in higher education was illustrated firstly by *Investment in Education* and then in a number of major studies led by Patrick Clancy between 1979 and 2001.[404] *Investment* underlined that participation in the small 'elite' sector in 1963 was sharply skewed by socio-economic status: entrants from middle class families in the professional, managerial or intermediate non-manual socio-economic groups (SEGs) outnumbered entrants from the semi skilled/unskilled manual group by approximately thirty three to one at university level.[405] The estimated entry rate for the former SEG was far in excess of any other group at 12.8%, while entry for the latter SEG was negligible at 0.3%. The subsequent studies of university entrants revealed only a marginal improvement even in absolute terms by 1980, with corresponding figures of 19% and 1.8% for the professional/managerial and semiskilled/unskilled SEGs respectively.[406] There was also a close association between social class and participation in a newly massified higher education sector as a whole. Five of the eleven SEGs as identified in the CSO data were under-represented in higher education in 1980 as compared to their numbers within the population as a whole, while the six 'higher' SEGs were over-represented, sometimes by a dramatic margin.[407] The combined rate of entry for the six higher SEGs was 35%, compared to only 8% for the lower SEGs.[408] Although improvements in absolute levels of participation for almost all SEGs were achieved during the 1980s, relative disparities between social groups remained striking even when the diversification of the system was well advanced. A HEA report using data from 1992 pointed to a participation rate of 89% for the upper middle class higher professional SEG and 13% for the unskilled/semiskilled manual SEG.[409]

The persistence of significant class inequalities supported Raftery and Hout's thesis of 'maximally maintained inequality' in their 1993 study of expanding educational enrolments in Ireland. This thesis posited that although expansion would allow a greater absolute number of people to make the transition to the next stage of education, relative inequality between classes would be maintained until the point when demand for a given level of education was 'saturated for the upper classes'.[410] Certainly class inequalities remained deeply embedded within a massified, diversified system. While these inequalities were largely the result of long-term structural and cultural factors derived from a traditional society, the type of reforms prioritised by policy-makers in this period also played their part in perpetuating socio-economic disparities in participation. Government policies up to the 1980s were focused on increasing participation by school leavers, providing a wider range of vocationally oriented courses and directing social demand into a newly diversified system rather than on reducing socio-economic inequalities or opening up higher education to 'nontraditional' students. Yet the achievement of greatly increased participation in a newly expanded system amounted to a gradual but far-reaching democratisation of higher education, which unleashed consequences not planned by policy-makers and presented profound challenges to traditional policies and practice in elite institutions.

Student Dissent

Students did not figure in policy-making or governance of higher education institutions up to the 1960s, except as passive recipients of institutional decisions. Irish university leaders up to the 1960s were rarely tolerant of dissent and were frequently willing to suppress or at least restrict student societies which might challenge their authority. The decline of deference to traditional authorities during this period was particularly notable among students and came as a rude shock to a generation of university administrators who had come to maturity in early post-independence Ireland.

Large-scale student protests emerged in Irish universities during the late 1960s, reflecting global trends of dissent among young people against established policies and institutions. Such protests were often inspired by the famous student rebellion in France in May 1968, which led to a more general popular mobilisation that rocked President de Gaulle's regime and by an international wave of protests against US participation in the Vietnam War.[411] Yet student dissent also had more local causes, from the lack of any student influence in college government to the flawed implementation of specific policies, such as the transfer of UCD to Belfield.[412] The most large-scale and well publicised protests occurred in UCD and Trinity, not least because of the extensive attention which they attracted from the metropolitan media. But major campus based protests also occurred in UCC and UCG in the late 1960s, featuring opposition to the war, but also more national concerns such as the absence of student representation on the HEA. Student activists in each college sought to coordinate pickets and lecture boycotts in November 1969 in protest at 'the mediocrity and limitations of the HEA...'[413]

Protests targeted at specific grievances were mounted by student teachers in Thomond College and the students' union representing participants in hotel management courses in Galway RTC in 1976–77, opposing the removal of degree awarding powers from the NCEA and its impact on their qualifications.[414] Other student-led protests were linked to popular progressive causes, such as the opposition to apartheid. A demonstration directed at the Irish Rugby Football Union over their invitation to the Springbok team to tour Ireland was organised in December 1969 by clerical students from Maynooth and drew about 100 participants, including priests and professors as well as seminarians.[415] Organised student movements emerged as a serious factor in third level colleges across the country and contributed to the development of students' unions as a normal feature of college life.

It was a truism among the many critics of student movements that student activists made up only a small minority of the student body and were often pursuing a wider political agenda. While it was certainly true that groups such as the Maoist Internationalists in Trinity or the more broadly based Students for Democratic Action in UCD were highly politicised minorities and often had links with left-wing movements, the protests in universities and other HEIs from the late 1960s were not simply the product of left-wing militancy but reflected a wider frustration with university and state institutions. Often action by a dedicated minority served as the catalyst for a wider mobilisation, especially if the militant group was fortunate enough to attract an over-reaction from the authorities. A small protest by the Internationalists in Trinity against a visit by King Baudouin of the Belgians on 15 May 1968 led to some heavy handed policing and a sensationalised commentary on the student protest by the *Evening Herald*.[416] The apparent combination of 'police brutality and on top of that, misrepresentation in the press' immediately provoked a series of mass meetings and demonstrations in Trinity, including a march by 1000 students to Independent Newspapers offices in Middle Abbey St., as well as Pearse St. Garda station.[417] The demonstration was led by the Students' Representative Council (SRC), which opted strategically to take the lead on the mass protest, not least to sideline the Internationalists—the *Irish Times* noted approvingly that 'It was organised, significantly by the S.R.C…It was entirely peaceful, sober and responsible and brought no clash with the authorities.'[418] If this seemed a far cry from the tumultuous challenge to state authority in France around the same time, it was also a new departure in student activism, foreshadowing a more militant student organisation over the following two decades. As J. V. Luce, who dealt with subsequent student protests as the college's senior dean, comments it was "the first manifestation of 'student power' on the Trinity campus" and the prelude to 'more than a decade of organised demonstrations, occupations, boycotts and harassment of visiting Ministers of State.'[419] The reform-minded administration of A. J. McConnell approved representation by students on school committees in May 1968 and allowed student representatives to participate as 'observers' with speaking rights at the Board from 1969, making TCD one of the first Irish universities to include students on its governing body, although they did not secure full membership until 2000.[420] This relative openness did not, however, prevent periodic outbreaks of militancy by various student groups over the following two decades or a particularly acrimonious clash between the college administration and the students' union led by Joe Duffy in 1980–81.

The most dramatic manifestation of student protest occurred in UCD in 1968–69. The 'Gentle Revolution' drew most of its impetus from persistent grievances with the college administration regarding overcrowding at Earlsfort Terrace, lack of meaningful student representation and inept management of the transfer to Belfield, although its leading figures were influenced by the international context of student revolt.[421] Students for Democratic Action (SDA), a broad left group including Kevin Myers, John Feeney and Ruairi Quinn, took the lead in organising 'direct action'—mainly mass meetings and occupations of college buildings—from the autumn of 1968.[422] As in Trinity, there was tension between the SDA and the more mainstream SRC, which sought to retain the initiative by mobilising students through mass 'teach-ins'.[423] But the most dramatic confrontation was triggered in February 1969 by a two-day SDA occupation of the administration block in Earlsfort Terrace, ostensibly to protest at the way in which students and departments were being transferred to Belfield before its facilities, especially the library building, were fully completed. A mass meeting of students on 27 February called for a radical restructuring of the governing body to provide for 'effective delegation of power to a joint staff and student body' and establishment of a staff-student committee to control the move to Belfield.[424] This was a direct challenge to the established order in UCD, which was quickly rejected by the governing body.[425] A second mass meeting on 5 March, by some accounts including 'over half the total student body...' but certainly a large proportion of students, resolved to boycott lectures until further notice; instead they would engage in a rolling series of seminars on the governance of UCD and in a more ambitious vein on the function of the university itself.[426] This approach was openly supported by a number of junior staff and tacitly by some members of the governing body, as an alternative to more militant action. The conflict was defused over the following weeks, in part due to divisions among the student activists and negotiations in which the ASA was involved. Most of the student demands were not met, although departmental staff-student committees which had already been under consideration were established and a student representative was nominated by the government to the governing body.[427]

The Union of Students in Ireland (USI), founded in 1959 as an all-Ireland national representative body, secured momentum and visibility as a result of the wave of student protests. USI gained prominence as a campaigning and lobbying organisation during the 1970s, operating also as a training ground for student leaders who later became active in national politics and journalism, such as Pat Rabbitte, Eamon Gilmore and Paul Tansey. Pressure from USI contributed to a gradual restructuring of the nascent higher education grants system. USI highlighted its campaign for a 'comprehensive grants system' extending to all full-time higher education courses through multiple student demonstrations, but also mobilised pressure on politicians by securing the backing of university leaders for its demands.[428] The Board of TCD supported USI's objectives in a letter to Nicholas Nolan, secretary to the government, in November 1971.[429] The governing body of UCC made a submission on student finance to the Minister for Education in May 1978, seeking the extension of the grants scheme to all third-level courses attended by full-time students and more generous criteria linked to acceptance by a recognised college in the scheme: the UCC submission was quickly referenced by student leaders, not least in appealing to Taoiseach Jack

Lynch, who represented Cork city in the Dáil.[430] Successive governments improved the scheme during the 1970s, widening its scope and delivering incremental improvements in student support payments.[431]

The practical impact of the 'student revolution' in 1968–69 appeared limited, not least to its most radical activists. McCartney even argued that 'Like the merger, it was a case of the mountain groaning in labour and a ridiculous little mouse being born.'[432] The more idealistic objectives of student leaders for societal transformation or fundamental institutional change were not fulfilled and even more modest demands for student representation within institutional governing structures were not fully conceded.[433] Yet the longer term influence of the protest movement should not be underestimated. Students' unions represented by full-time sabbatical officers were established in UCD and Trinity by 1975 and became a normal element of college life in most higher education institutions by the 1980s.[434] While this emphatically did not preclude resort to militant action, the existence of a stronger student institution offered a representative interlocutor for the college authorities and a more stable framework for resolving disputes. The development of student representation within institutional structures was a more long-term process, which had already started but accelerated in the aftermath of the protests.

The student protest movements also marked a sharp break with a culture of authoritarianism and deference which had prevailed to a greater or lesser degree in all Irish higher education institutions.[435] The numerous policy changes from the mid 1950s and the erosion of religious and cultural influences which were central to traditionalist understandings of higher education opened up new lines of critique against established authorities and institutions. Even reform-minded university leaders sometimes found that their understanding of reform was much too timid for student activists seeking radical transformation not only of the university but of society as a whole. Major development projects in more conservative institutions, such as UCD, also served as a catalyst for protest when development was not combined with reforms of governance allowing wider participation by the college community. Student activism had become a force to be reckoned with on college campuses and if student politics sometimes disappointed its practitioners and constituents, new forms of activism and organisation were there to stay.

'...The Unprecedented Expansion of Post-compulsory Education...'

An influential HEA steering committee concluded in 1995 that 'considerations of economic growth and technological development have been the main forces behind the unprecedented expansion of post-compulsory education...', while social justice considerations had been important in 'legitimating' such expansion.[436] The influence of vocational imperatives on government policies since the mid-1960s was unmistakable. The diversification of higher education and emergence of a higher education system on a binary model were shaped by economic objectives, notably the development of a wider range of technologically oriented institutions and courses to meet the demands of an expanding economy. Yet government policies in an era of reform and expansion were not grounded solely in crude economic calculations: meeting a vastly increased societal demand for post-compulsory higher education was a genuine political preoccupation during this period and contributed significantly to policy decisions on diversification. Egalitarian ideas and appeals were influential in a more vociferous public sphere consisting of a wider cast of institutional leaders, academics, trade unions and for the first time student representatives. Policy-makers were both more responsive to egalitarian appeals and concerned to emphasise an egalitarian rationale for their actions than they had been in an earlier period. It was a confluence of economic and social demands within a transformed political and cultural context that created a potent consensus in favour of expansionist policies. The emergence of the modern Irish higher education system occurred in a wider context shaped by the breakdown of the protectionist economic consensus, the decline of traditional religious divisions and the erosion of deference towards various forms of authority.

Notes

1. John Walsh, 'Creating a Modern Educational System: International Influence, Domestic Elites and the Transformation of the Irish Educational Sector, 1950–75,' in *Essays in the History of Irish Education*, ed. Brendan Walsh (London: Palgrave Macmillan, 2016), 235.
2. Ibid.
3. Martin Trow, *Problems in the Transition from Elite to Mass Higher Education* (California: Carnegie Commission, 1973), 7.
4. Ibid.
5. Ibid., 6.
6. Martin Trow, *Reflections on the Transforming from Elite to Mass to Universal Access: Forms and Phases of Higher Education in Modern Societies Since WWII*, Working Papers (Berkeley: University of California, 2005), 65. Accessed 1 December 2017. https://escholarship.org/uc/item/96p3s213.
7. O'Sullivan, *Cultural Politics*, 104.
8. O'Sullivan, *Cultural Politics*, 143; Walsh, *Politics of Expansion*, 64–9.
9. Coolahan, 'The National University of Ireland and the Changing Structure of Irish Higher Education,' in *The National University of Ireland 1908–2008 Centenary Essays*, ed. Dunne et al. (Dublin: UCD Press, 2008), 261–79; O'Sullivan, *Cultural Politics*, 143; Walsh, *Politics of Expansion*, 324–5.
10. Louise Fuller, *Irish Catholicism Since 1950 the Undoing of a Culture* (Dublin: Gill and Macmillan, 2002), 201–4.
11. Gary Murphy, *In Pursuit of the Promised Land, the Politics of Post-War Ireland, 1945–61* (Dublin: Mercier Press, 2009), 302–9.
12. Public Accounts Committee, Appropriation Accounts 1956–57, 5.
13. Hillery Note, n.d. (UCDA Hillery Papers, P205, Folder 4).
14. Walsh, *Politics of Expansion*, 311–27.
15. Ibid., 63; Governing Committee for Scientific and Technical Personnel, *STP/GC (61) 1, Outline Programme for Scientific and Technical Personnel 1961–62*, 30 January 1961 (NAI D/FIN 2001/3/546, D500/2/62), 4.
16. John Walsh, 'International Influence, Domestic Elites and the Transformation of Higher Technical Education in Ireland,' *Irish Educational Studies* 30, no. 3 (September 2011): 365–81.
17. CAB 2/18, G.C. 8/38, Cabinet Minutes, 20 August 1957, 2–3.

18. Decision Slip, Government Meeting, 6 August 1957 (NAI TSCH/3/S.13809C).
19. *Irish Press*, 'Commission on NUI Named,' 28 September 1957.
20. Decision slip, *Cruinniú Rialtais, Commission on Accommodation Needs of University Colleges: Terms of Reference*, 14 March 1958.
21. O'Rahilly to de Valera, 13 March 1958 (NAI TSCH/3/S.16289).
22. *Irish Press*, 'Cardinal's Warning on Education: Should Not Merge Universities,' 24 June 1958.
23. Nolan and Walsh, '"In What Orbit We Shall Find Ourselves, No One Could Predict": Institutional Reform, the University Merger and Ecclesiastical Influence on Irish Higher Education in the 1960s,' *Irish Historical Studies* 41, no. 159 (2017): 77–96. https://doi.org/10.1017/ihs.2017.7.
24. 'University College Dublin—Notes of Discussion on 12 August 1957 (in the Department of An Taoiseach) Betweeen an Taoiseach, the Ministers for Finance and Education, and the President and Registrar, University College Dublin' (NAI TSCH/3/S.13809C).
25. *Report of the Commission on Accommodation Needs of the Constituent Colleges of the National University of Ireland* (Dublin: Stationery Office, 1959), 128.
26. Ibid.
27. Ibid., 127–8.
28. Ibid.
29. Ibid., 44.
30. Memorandum for the Government, 20 May 1959 (NAI TSCH/3/S.16289), 12.
31. Walsh, *Politics of Expansion*, 141–2; Moynihan to Ó Raifeartaigh, 29 April 1959 (NAI TSCH/3/S.16289).
32. Government Information Bureau, 2 June 1959 (NAI TSCH/3/S.16289).
33. Dáil Debates, vol. 180, 940–1, 23 March 1960.
34. McQuaid to Hillery, 24 March 1960 (DDA, *McQuaid Papers*, XVIII/38/200/3).
35. Ó Raifeartaigh to McQuaid, 24 March 1960 (DDA, *McQuaid Papers*, XVIII/38/200/2).
36. Nolan and Walsh, '"In What Orbit We Shall Find Ourselves, No One Could Predict,"' *Irish Historical Studies* 41, no. 159 (2017): 77–96. https://doi.org/10.1017/ihs.2017.7.
37. Walsh, *Politics of Expansion*, 54–5.

38. *Commission on Accommodation Needs*, 125.
39. Coolahan, 'Higher Education in Ireland, 1908–84,' 774.
40. *Public Accounts Committee, Appropriation Accounts 1959–60* (Dublin: Stationery Office, 1962), 100.
41. Dáil Debates, vol. 174, col. 72–3, 8 April 1959.
42. *Commission on Accommodation Needs*, 128.
43. Dáil Debates, vol. 180, col. 952–3, 23 March 1960.
44. Cabinet Minutes, 16 August 1960 (CAB 2/20, G.C. 9/90).
45. Walsh, *Politics of Expansion*, 56.
46. Cabinet Minutes, 13 September 1960, 3–4 (CAB 2/20, G.C 9/94).
47. Public Accounts Committee, *Appropriation Accounts 1971–72* (Dublin: Stationery Office, 1975), 196.
48. Public Accounts Committee, *Appropriation Accounts 1980–81* (Dublin: Stationery Office, 1982), lvi.
49. HEA, *Interim Report of the Steering Committee's Technical Working Group* (Dublin: HEA, 1995), 44.
50. Department of Education, *Forecast of Developments*, 6 January 1962, 7 (NAI TSCHS.12891D/1/62).
51. HEA, *Progress Report 1974* (Dublin: HEA, 1974), 39.
52. *Commission on Accommodation Needs*, 125.
53. Cabinet Minutes, 22 May 1962; HEA, *Progress Report 1974*, 39.
54. HEA, *Progress Report 1974*, 39.
55. Government of Ireland, *Second Programme for Economic Expansion (Part 2), Laid by the Government Before Each House of the Oireachtas, August 1963* (Dublin: Stationery Office, 1964), 206.
56. HEA, *Progress Report 1974*, 37.
57. Smyth, 'National University of Ireland, Maynooth,' 108–9.
58. Ibid.
59. Ibid., 109
60. Marie Coleman, *IFUT—A History 1963–1999* (Dublin: IFUT, 2000), 23
61. Ibid., 26–8: IFUT was founded in 1963 as a representative association of university teachers.
62. Newman, *Discourses*, ix.
63. Von Humboldt, 'On the Spirit and the Organisational Framework of Intellectual Institutions in Berlin,' *Minerva: A Review of Science, Learning and Policy* 8, no. 2 (April 1970): 242–250.
64. Government of Ireland, *Report of the Commission on Higher Education 1960–67* (Dublin: Stationery Office, 1967), 97–8.

65. See Section on Teacher Education 269–81 below.
66. Government of Ireland, *Commission on Higher Education*, 53.
67. Ibid., 64
68. Ibid., 54.
69. Ibid., 119–20.
70. Ibid., 95–96; John Coolahan, 'Higher Education in Ireland, 1908–84,' in *A New History of Ireland, 1921–84*, vol. 7, ed. J. R. Hill (Oxford: Oxford University Press, 2003), 781.
71. Government of Ireland, *Commission on Higher Education*, 95–6.
72. Minister for Education, 'The problem of Trinity College Dublin,' 15 December 1966 (NAI TSCH 98/6/195).
73. Nolan and Walsh, '"In What Orbit We Shall Find Ourselves, No One Could Predict,"' *Irish Historical Studies* 41, no. 159 (2017): 77–96.
74. HEA, *Progress Report 1974*, 46.
75. Minister for Education, 'The Problem of Trinity College Dublin,' 15 December 1966 (NAI TSCH 98/6/195), 1.
76. McQuaid, 'T.C.D. and the Ministry—At Occasional Functions in the Autumn of 1966' (DDA, *McQuaid Papers*, ABXVIII/38/212A/1). Franz Winkelman was the Treasurer of Trinity College from 1962.
77. Nolan and Walsh, 'In What Orbit We Shall Find Ourselves, No One Could Predict,' *Irish Historical Studies* 41, no. 159 (2017): 77–96.
78. Minister for Education, 'The Problem of Trinity College Dublin,' 15 December 1966 (NAI TSCH 98/6/195), 21–2.
79. Ibid., 2.
80. Ibid., 9.
81. John Walsh, '"The Problem of Trinity College Dublin" a Historical Perspective on Rationalisation in Higher Education in Ireland,' *Irish Educational Studies* 33, no. 1 (2014): 6. https://doi.org/10.1080/0332 3315.2013.867095.
82. Department of Education Memorandum, 9 March 1967 (NAI TSCH 98/6/195), 1.
83. Minister for Education, '"The Problem of Trinity College Dublin,"' 15 December 1966 (NAI TSCH 98/6/195), 11–12.
84. Ibid., 23; Nolan and Walsh, '"In What Orbit We Shall Find Ourselves, No One Could Predict,"' *Irish Historical Studies* 41, no. 159 (2017): 77–96. https://doi.org/10.1017/ihs.2017.7.
85. Department of Education Memorandum, 9 March 1967 (NAI TSCH 98/6/195), 1.

86. Department of Education Memorandum, 9 March 1967 (NAI TSCH 98/6/195), 1; Cabinet Minutes, 31 March 1967, 3–4 (NAI 99/5/1, G.C. 12/22).
87. Nolan and Walsh, "'In What Orbit We Shall Find Ourselves, No One Could Predict,'" *Irish Historical Studies* 41, no. 159 (2017): 77–96. https://doi.org/10.1017/ihs.2017.7.
88. McQuaid, '*T.C.D. and the Ministry*,' (DDA, *McQuaid Papers*, ABXVIII/38/212A/1), 1.
89. I am grateful to Dr. Ann Nolan for the research on this point.
90. McQuaid, '*T.C.D. and the Ministry*,' (DDA, *McQuaid Papers*, ABXVIII/38/212A/1), 1–3.
91. Ibid., 2.
92. Ibid., 4.
93. Nolan and Walsh, "'In What Orbit We Shall Find Ourselves, No One Could Predict,'" *Irish Historical Studies* 41, no. 159 (2017): 77–96. https://doi.org/10.1017/ihs.2017.7.
94. *Irish Times*, 'TCD and UCD to Be United: O'Malley Announces Wedding Plans,' 19 April 1967; *Irish Press*, 'UCD and TCD to Merge: Opening of New Era in Our Higher Education,' 19 April 1967; *Irish Independent*, 'UCD and TCD to Merge: Minister Outlines University Plan,' 19 April 1967.
95. Ibid.
96. *Irish Times*, 'TCD and UCD to Be United: O'Malley Announces Wedding Plans,' 19 April 1967.
97. Ibid.
98. Donogh O'Malley, 'University Education in Dublin: Statement of Minister for Education—18 April 1967,' *Studies* 56, no. 2 (1967): 113–21.
99. Ibid., 118.
100. Ibid., 121–2.
101. Ibid., 120.
102. Ibid., 121.
103. Tarlach Ó Raifeartaigh, 'Towards a Satisfactory Outcome of the Forthcoming Negotiations on the U.C.D.-T.C.D. Merger,' 10 April 1968 (DDA, *McQuaid Papers*, XVIII/38A/18/2).
104. McQuaid to Ó Raifeartaigh, 11 June 1967 (DDA, *McQuaid Papers*, XVIII/38/212a/11).

105. 'Amalgamation of Trinity College Dublin and University College Dublin' (DDA, *McQuaid Papers*, XVIII/38A/1–25).
106. J. P. MacHale, 'The university Merger,' *Studies* 56, no. 2 (1967): 122–9.
107. Walsh, *Politics of Expansion*, 241.
108. T. W. Moody, 'The University Merger,' *Studies* 56, no. 2 (1967): 173–5.
109. Paddy O'Flynn, *A Question of Identity: The Great Trinity and UCD Merger Plan of the 1960s* (Dublin: Farmar, 2012), 110–11.
110. James Meenan, 'The University in Dublin,' *Studies* 57, no. 3 (1968): 314–20.
111. Coolahan, 'The NUI,' 267.
112. Walsh, 'The Problem of Trinity College Dublin,' *Irish Educational Studies* 33, no. 1 (2014): 10. https://doi.org/10.1080/03323315.201 3.867095.
113. Seán O'Connor, *A Troubled Sky*, 203.
114. Diarmuid Ferriter, *Ambiguous Republic: Ireland in the 1970s* (London: Profile, 2012), 635.
115. O'Connor, *A Troubled Sky*, 204.
116. Minister for Education, *Higher Education: Statement Issued by the Minister for Education on Behalf of the Government*, 6 July 1968 (NAI TSCH 2000/6/655), 4–6.
117. Luce, *Trinity College Dublin*, 189; Interview with Prof. Martin O'Donoghue, February 2005.
118. James Meenan, 'The University in Dublin,' *Studies* 57, no. 3 (1968): 314–5.
119. J. J. Hogan, *The Case for University College Dublin*, April 1969 (NAI TSCH 2000/6/655), 14.
120. Interview with Prof. Martin O'Donoghue, February 2005.
121. McQuaid Notes, 18–19 September 1968 (DDA, *McQuaid Papers*, AB8/B/XXXIV).
122. Luce, *Trinity College Dublin*, 197; Ó Raifeartaigh to Lynch, 6 February 1969 (NAI TSCH 2000/6/655), 1–3.
123. Ibid., 2–3.
124. Lyons, *Ireland Since the Famine*, 655.
125. Walsh, 'The Problem of Trinity College Dublin,' *Irish Educational Studies* 33, no. 1 (2014): 12. https://doi.org/10.1080/03323315.201 3.867095.

126. NUI, Senate Minutes, vol. 42, 23 April 1970, 44.
127. Ibid.
128. HEA, *Report to the Minister for Education on University Reorganisation* (Dublin: HEA, 1972), 83–7.
129. Minutes, General Meeting of the Hierarchy, 22–24 June 1970 (DDA AB8/B/XV/b/07), 5.
130. Nolan and Walsh, "'In What Orbit We Shall Find Ourselves, No One Could Predict,'" *Irish Historical Studies* 41, no. 159 (2017): 77–96; Fuller, *Irish Catholicism Since 1950*, 188.
131. Walsh, 'The Problem of Trinity College Dublin,' *Irish Educational Studies* 33, no. 1 (2014): 11. https://doi.org/10.1080/03323315.2013.867095.
132. Nolan and Walsh, "'In What Orbit We Shall Find Ourselves, No One Could Predict,'" *Irish Historical Studies* 41, no. 159 (2017): 77–96.
133. The committee included the Deputy Secretary, Seán MacGearailt, the assistant secretaries and chief inspectors.
134. O'Connor, *A Troubled Sky*, 173.
135. Department of Education, 'Departmental Committee's Observations on the Recommendations of the Commission on Higher Education,' n.d. 1967 (NAI TSCH 99/1/438, S.17744), 11.
136. See below pp. 257–62 for development of the RTCs.
137. Ibid., 10.
138. Interview with James F. Dukes, 2003.
139. Tony White, *Investing in People: Higher Education in Ireland from 1960 to 2000* (Dublin: IPA, 2001), 48; Coolahan, 'Higher Education in Ireland, 1908–84,' 781.
140. Hyland and Milne, *Irish Educational Documents* 2, 424–5.
141. Department of Education, 'Departmental Committee's Observations,' 1967, 30 (NAI TSCH 99/1/438, S.17744).
142. 'Statement Issued by the Minister for Education on Behalf of the Government,' 16 August 1968 (DDA AB8/B/XVIII/18), 1–3.
143. John Walsh, 'The Transformation of Higher Education in Ireland,' in *Higher Education in Ireland: Practices, Policies and Possibilities*, ed. Andrew Loxley, Aidan Seery, and John Walsh (Basingstoke: Palgrave Macmillan, 2014), 5–32.
144. John Walsh, 'A Quiet Revolution—International Influence, Domestic Elites and the Transformation of Higher Technical Education in Ireland, 1957–72,' *Irish Educational Studies* 30, no. 3 (2011): 365–81.

145. Office of the Minister for Industry and Commerce, *Proposals for Amendment of the Law Relating to Apprenticeship*, 7 June 1958 (NAI TSCH 3/S2402B), 4.
146. Ibid., 4–5.
147. Ibid., 6.
148. Ibid., 7.
149. Ibid., 13; *The Apprenticeship Act 1958, as Passed by Both Houses of the Oireachtas*, 9 December 1959 (NAI TSCH 3/S.16808), 12–13.
150. Office of the Minister for Industry and Commerce, *Proposals for Amendment of the Law Relating to Apprenticeship*, 7 June 1958 (NAI TSCH 3/S2402B), 7.
151. Circular 12/61, Department of Education, March 1961.
152. Office of the Minister for Industry and Commerce, *Proposals for Amendment of the Law Relating to Apprenticeship*, 7 June 1958 (NAI TSCH 3/S2402B), 7.
153. Walsh, *Politics of Expansion*, 47.
154. OECD, *Reviews of National Policies for Science and Education, Training of Technicians in Ireland* (Paris: OECD, 1964), 81.
155. Ibid., 88–9.
156. Hillery Statement, 20 May 1963 (NAI TSCH 17405 C/63), 13; White, *Investing in Education*, 57.
157. Government of Ireland, *Steering Committee on Technical Education, Report to the Minister for Education on Regional Technical Colleges* (Dublin: Stationery Office, 1969), 7.
158. Ibid., 11.
159. Ibid., 12.
160. Ibid., 11–12.
161. Ibid., 8.
162. NCEA, *First Annual Report 1972–73* (Dublin: Stationery Office, 1973), 7.
163. Office of the Minister for Education, 'Memorandum to the Government, Regional Technical Colleges,' 15 June 1967 (NAI TSCH 98/6/831, S.18047A), 6.
164. Cabinet Minutes, 11 July 1967 (NAI 99/5/1, G.C. 12/46), 4–5.
165. Anthony MacFeely to Lemass, 23 August 1966 (NAI TSCH 97/6/510); Cabinet Minutes, 17 October 1967 (NAI 99/5/1, G.C. 12/65), 3.

166. HEA, *Progress Report 1974*, 57; Talk by Tomás Ó Floinn, *Recent Developments in Education in Ireland* (NAI DFA 2003/17/383), 14.
167. HEA, *Progress Report 1974*, 58.
168. Ibid., 57.
169. White, *Investing in Education*, 86.
170. HEA, *Progress Report 1974*, 57–58; Government of Ireland, *White Paper on Educational Development* (Dublin: Stationery Office, 1980), 74.
171. Marie Clarke, 'The Development of Vocational and Technical Education in Ireland, 1930–2015,' in *Essays in the History of Irish Education*, ed. Brendan Walsh (London: Palgrave Macmillan, 2016), 313.
172. White, *Investing in Education*, 59.
173. Press Release, *Speech by Brian Lenihan TD, Minister for Education, Opening This Year's Festival of Shannonside, Limerick*, 18 May 1968, 1–2, *Statement by Limerick University Project Committee*, 7 September 1968 (NAI TSCH 99/1/311, S.16735B).
174. Memorandum from the Minister for Education, *University Education in Limerick, Additional information*, 19 November 1968 (NAI TSCH 99/1/311, S.16735B).
175. Walsh, *Politics of Expansion*, 358–9.
176. HEA, 'Memorandum B, Recommendation of the Higher Education Authority on the Provision of Third-Level Educational Facilities at Limerick,' (NAI TSCH 99/1/311, S.16735B), 3.
177. Ibid., 6–8.
178. Clancy, 'Policy in Third-Level Education,' 120.
179. Address by Jack Lynch, 27 September 1972 (NAI TSCH 2004/21/95.)
180. White, *Investing in People*, 74.
181. HEA, *Report on the Ballymun Project: Appendix II:* CDVEC, 'Memo to the Higher Education Authority' (Dublin: HEA, 1972), 69–70.
182. Ibid., 69.
183. Duff et al., *Dublin Institute of Technology*, 18–26.
184. Ibid., 26.
185. Ibid., 23.
186. White, *Investing in People*, 90.
187. Ronan Foley to Lemass, 12 December 1959 (NAI TSCH 97/6/510).
188. Foley Note, 6 January 1960 (NAI TSCH 97/6/510).

189. Duff et al., *Dublin Institute of Technology*, 18–19.
190. HEA, *Report on the Ballymun Project, Appendix II*, 69.
191. McConway to Lenihan, 4 June 1968 (NAI TSCH 99/1/124).
192. H. J. O'Dowd to McConway, 30 September 1968 (NAI TSCH 99/1/124).
193. HEA, *Report on the Ballymun Project, Appendix II*, 68–79.
194. Ibid., 70.
195. Ibid., 71.
196. Ibid., 73.
197. Duff et al., *Dublin Institute of Technology*, 30–31.
198. Memorandum to the Government, 'National Institute for Higher Education, Dublin,' Appendix A, 28 February 1980 (NAI TSCH 2010/53/413), 1.
199. HEA, *Report on the Ballymun Project*, 61–65.
200. Ibid., 64; White, *Investing in People*, 91.
201. HEA, *Report on the Ballymun Project*, 56.
202. Duff et al., *Dublin Institute of Technology*, 31–32.
203. Memorandum to the Government, 'National Institute for Higher Education, Dublin,' Appendix A, 28 February 1980 (NAI TSCH 2010/53/413), 2.
204. Duff et al., *Dublin Institute of Technology*, 32–33.
205. HEA, *General Report 1974–84* (Dublin: HEA, 1985), 52.
206. Walsh, *Politics of Expansion*, 362.
207. HEA, *Interim Report of the Technical Working Group*, 18.
208. Ibid., 25.
209. Frank Barry, 'Outward Economic Development and the Irish Education System,' *Irish Educational Studies* 33, no. 2 (2014), 213–23: The ESF was mobilised to support the objectives of the Social Action Programme devised by the *cabinet* of Commissioner Patrick Hillery, which helps to explain both Ireland's success in securing advantages from the expanded programme and the caution of Irish ministers in addressing this publicly.
210. White, *Investing in People*, 164.
211. Ibid., 180; HEA, *Interim Report of the Technical Working Group*, 25.
212. HEA, *Interim Report of the Technical Working Group*, 29.
213. Ibid., 30
214. White, *Investing in People*, 186–7.
215. Ibid., 257–8.

216. Antonia McManus, 'The Transformation of Irish Education: The Ministerial Legacy, 1919–1999,' in *Essays in the History of Irish Education*, ed. Brendan Walsh (London: Palgrave Macmillan, 2016), 279.
217. Ibid., 280; HEA, *General Report 1974–84*, 51; White, *Investing in People*, 186–7.
218. Ó Buachalla, *Education Policy*, 281.
219. Clancy, 'Policy in Third-Level Education,' 123.
220. Walsh, 'A Quiet Revolution,' *Irish Educational Studies* 30, no. 3 (2011), 365–81.
221. Ibid.
222. Walsh, *Politics of Expansion*, 15.
223. *Dáil Debates*, vol. 161, col. 696–707, 1 May 1957; *Dáil Debates*, vol. 168, col. 638–40, 22 May 1958.
224. *Dáil Debates*, vol. 168, col. 640–41, 22 May 1958.
225. O'Connor, *A Troubled Sky*, 29; O'Donoghue et al., *Teacher Preparation in Ireland*, 56–7.
226. Department of Education, Memorandum to the Government, 9 November 1959 (W26/2, M2001/5, D/Education); Walsh, Politics of Expansion, 43–4.
227. O'Connor, *A Troubled Sky*, 52–4.
228. Cabinet Minutes, 15 December 1959 (NAI CAB 2/20, G.C. 9/36), 3–4.
229. Valerie Jones, 'Coláiste Moibhí: The Last Preparatory College,' *Irish Educational Studies* 15, no. 1 (1996): 109.
230. Public Accounts Committee, *Appropriation Accounts* 1961–62 (Dublin: Stationery Office, 1963), 55
231. Walsh, *Politics of Expansion*, 45–6.
232. McQuaid to Tomás Ó Floinn, 27 March 1969 (DDA, *McQuaid Papers*, AB8/B/XVIII/18).
233. 'Memorandum by Dr. Donal Cregan,' October 1972 (SPCA, A/19/IV), 1.
234. O'Connor, *Passing on the Torch*, 60–1.
235. 'Memorandum by Dr. Donal,Cregan' October 1972 (SPCA, A/19/IV), 1.
236. Ibid.
237. Blake, *St. Mary's Marino*, 136–7.

238. Department of Education, *Forecast of Developments*, 6 January 1962 (NAI TSCH S.12891D/1/62), 1; *Second Programme for Economic Expansion (Part 2)*, 195.

239. Public Accounts Committee, *Appropriation Accounts 1962–63* (Dublin: Stationery Office, 1964), 101; Public Accounts Committee, *Appropriation Accounts 1965–66* (Dublin: Stationery Office, 1967), 117; McQuaid to Seán MacGearailt, 14 June 1960 (SPCA, D/10/II).

240. McQuaid to MacGearailt, 14 June 1960 (SPCA, D/10/II).

241. O'Connor, *Passing on the Torch*, 69.

242. Parkes, *Kildare Place*, 182–3.

243. Office of Minister for Finance, 'Memorandum to the Government, State-Guaranteed Loan for the Church of Ireland Training College for the Building of a New Training College,' 6 July 1966.

244. Ibid., 2.

245. The RCB advanced £200,000 to the governing body, with the remainder being drawn from the consortium.

246. Office of Minister for Finance, 'Memorandum to the Government, State–Guaranteed Loan for the Church of Ireland Training College for the Building of a New Training College,' 6 July 1966, 3–4.

247. Parkes, *Kildare Place*, 186–7.

248. Ibid., 189; Relihan, 'The Church of Ireland, the State and Education,' 158.

249. *Report of the Commission on Higher Education 1960–67, Summary* (Dublin: Stationery Office, 1967), 95.

250. Department of Education, 'Departmental Committee's Observations,' 1967 (NAI TSCH 99/1/438, S.17744), 30.

251. Annual Report of the CEC 1968–69 (Dublin: INTO, 1969), 40.

252. HEA, *Report to the Minister for Education on Teacher Education* (Dublin: HEA, 1970), 4–5.

253. Ibid., 9–10.

254. Ibid., 13–14.

255. Ibid., 14–15.

256. Ibid., 15.

257. Ibid., 18.

258. Ibid., 18.

259. Blake, *St. Mary's Marino*, 132.

260. Donal Cregan, *Memorandum on Colleges of Education*, 1973 (SPCA, A/19/IV), 1.

261. Ibid.
262. Ibid.
263. John Nolan, 'The Recognised Colleges,' in *The National University of Ireland 1908–2008 Centenary Essays*, ed. Tom Dunne et al. (Dublin: UCD Press, 2008), 202–3; O'Connor, *Passing on the Torch*, 67–8; Tadhg Kelly, 'St. Patrick's College,' 42
264. NUI Senate, Minutes 74–12, 11 July 1974, 103.
265. NUI Senate, Minutes 75–9, 17 April 1975, 19; O'Connor, *Passing on the Torch*, 67–8.
266. Nolan, 'The Recognised Colleges,' 203.
267. NUI Senate, Minutes 75–9, 17 April 1975, 19–20.
268. Nolan, 'The Recognised Colleges,' 212.
269. Ibid., 203.
270. Ibid., 204.
271. NUI Senate, Minutes, 9 December 1976, 203–4.
272. Ibid., 205.
273. Ibid., 202–5.
274. Nolan, 'The Recognised Colleges,' 204
275. Parkes, *Kildare Place*, 190.
276. Board Minutes 154/2, 11 June 1975 (MUN V/5/42), 4.
277. Blake, *St. Mary's Marino*, 136–7.
278. Ibid.
279. Board Minutes 91/1, 18 February 1976 (MUN V/5/43), 9.
280. O'Donoghue et al., *Teacher Preparation in Ireland*, 130; the foundation disciplines were philosophy of education, sociology of education, psychology of education, history of education and comparative education.
281. Ibid.
282. Parkes, *Kildare Place*, 191.
283. Ibid.; Board Minutes, 14 July 1976 (MUN V/5/43), 4.
284. Coolahan, *Era of Lifelong Learning*, 146.
285. O'Donoghue et al., *Teacher Preparation in Ireland*, 133.
286. Ibid.; Coolahan, *Era of Lifelong Learning*, 146—this discussion draws particularly on Coolahan's work in teacher education.
287. White, *Investing in People*, 120.
288. Dáil Debates, vol. 248, no. 12, 23 July 1970, col. 1926–7.
289. Dáil Debates, vol. 268, no. 3, 23 October 1973, col. 401–2
290. Dáil Debates, vol. 286, no. 6, 4 December 1975, col. 925–926.

291. Dáil Debates, vol. 294, no. 2, 17 November 1976, col. 173; Nolan, 'The Recognised Colleges,' 208.
292. James L. Kelly to Minister for Education and the Taoiseach, *Thomond College of Education Link-Up with UCC—Its Implications for Course Assessment*, 14 March 1977 (NAI TSCH 2007/116/274).
293. Ibid.; White, *Investing in People*, 160
294. Nolan, 'The Recognised Colleges,' 209.
295. 'Report of the Departmental Committee on the Organisation of Higher Education with Special Reference to the Dublin Area,' 1974 (NAI TSCH 2005/7/352), 2.
296. White, *Investing in People*, 83–4; Coolahan, 'The NUI,' 269
297. Ó Raifeartaigh to MacGearailt, 4 March 1970 (NAI TSCH2001/6/405).
298. Interview with James F. Dukes, 2003.
299. HEA, *Report on University Reorganisation, Appendix III: Proposals (the NUI/TCD Agreement) Put Forward by the National University of Ireland and Trinity College Dublin* (Dublin: HEA, 1972), 83–87.
300. Clancy, 'Policy in Third-Level Education,' 106–7
301. HEA, *General Report 1974–84*, 53.
302. Damian Murchan, 'Changing Curriculum and Assessment Mindsets in Higher Education,' in *Higher Education in Ireland: Practices, Policies and Possibilities*, ed. Loxley et al. (Basingstoke: Palgrave Macmillan, 2014), 187–8.
303. HEA, *General Report 1974–84*, 20.
304. Ibid., 20; Clancy, *Irish Higher Education*, 88.
305. Fanning, 'T. K. Whitaker, 1976–96,' 153–5
306. Séamus Ó Cathail, 'Ireland: The University and the State,' *Cre-Information* 58, no. 2 (1982): 44–55.
307. Ibid.
308. Note, 'Cruinniú Rialtais,' 10 January 1974 (NAI TSCH 2005/7/352).
309. Ibid.: the other members were Tánaiste Brendan Corish, Richie Ryan (Finance) and Mark Clinton (Agriculture and Fisheries). FitzGerald was a former member of the governing body of UCD, while both Keating and Cruise O'Brien were former university lecturers and Clinton had worked in medical and university administration.
310. 'Report of the Departmental Committee on the Organisation of Higher Education with Special Reference to the Dublin Area,' 1974 (NAI TSCH 2005/7/352), 2.

311. Memorandum for the Government, *Reorganisation of Higher Education*, 11 September 1974 (NAI TSCH 2005/7/352), 1–3.
312. Ibid., 10–11.
313. Note, 'Cruinniú Rialtais, Higher Education: Reorganisation,' 18 September 1974 (NAI TSCH 2005/7/352).
314. Memorandum for the Government, *Reorganisation of Higher Education*, 11 September 1974 (NAI TSCH 2005/7/352), 15–18.
315. Ibid.
316. Note, 'Cruinniú Rialtais, Higher Education: Reorganisation,' 1 October 1974: the reference to 'N.C.T.' indicates that the University of Dublin was being positioned as the awarding body for the VEC colleges of technology.
317. Note, 'Cruinniú Rialtais, Higher Education: Reorganisation,' 4 October 1974; Daniel O'Sullivan to Private Secretary, Minister for Education, 4 October 1974 (NAI TSCH 2005/7/352).
318. Minister for Education, Memorandum for the Government, *Reorganisation of Higher Education*, 25 October 1974 (NAI TSCH 2005/7/352), 1.
319. Ibid.
320. Ibid., 5.
321. Ibid., 5.
322. O'Sullivan to Private Secretary, Minister for Education, 13 December 1974 (NAI TSCH 2005/7/352).
323. Ibid., 2.
324. Ibid., 3.
325. Ibid., 1.
326. 'Statement by the Minister for Education, Mr Richard Burke TD, When Announcing on Monday, 16 December 1974, the Government Proposals in Relation to Higher Education' (NAI TSCH 2005/7/352).
327. *Irish Times*, 'Higher Education Plans Final, Says Burke,' 17 December 1974; *Irish Times*, 'Education Bill to Be Prepared, Says Burke,' 19 December 1974.
328. White, *Investing in Education*, 119.
329. *Irish Times*, 'UCD Welcomes Education Plan; UCC and UCG Critical, Proposals a "Charter for Disaster", Says USI,' 18 December 1974.

330. 'Press Release by the Provost of TCD', 16 December 1974 (MUN V/5/42), 1–2.
331. *Irish Times*, 'UCD Welcomes Education Plan; UCC and UCG Critical, Proposals a "Charter for Disaster", Says USI,' 18 December 1974.
332. Ó Raifeartaigh to Burke, 15 April 1975 (NAI TSCH 2005/151/297).
333. Ibid.
334. Ibid.
335. White, *Investing in Education*, 125.
336. Cosgrave to Burke, 29 April 1975 (NAI TSCH 2005/151/297)
337. White, *Investing in Education*, 126.
338. 'The Higher Education Act,' December 1976 (NAI TSCH 2006/133/217), 34–5.
339. Ibid., 38.
340. Ibid., 48–9.
341. White, *Investing in Education*, 129.
342. Private Secretary to Minister for Education to M. F. Murray, 16 December 1976 (NAI TSCH 2006/133/217).
343. Minister for Education, Memorandum for the Government, Appendix (NAI TSCH 2008/148/224), 3–4.
344. Clinton to Lyons, 11 August 1975 (NAI TSCH 2005/151/297).
345. Lyons to Clinton, 14 August 1975 (NAI TSCH 2005/151/297).
346. Luce, *Trinity College Dublin*, 193; Board Minutes, 12 November 1975 (MUN V/5/43), 3.
347. O'Flynn, *A Question of Identity*, 161; Martin O'Donoghue Interview, February 2005.
348. 'Press Release by the Provost of TCD', 16 December 1974 (MUN V/5/42), 1–2; White, *Investing in Education*, 122; Duff et al., *Dublin Institute of Technology*, 72
349. Board Minutes, 28 May 1975 (MUN V/5/42), 6; White, *Investing in Education*, 122.
350. Board Minutes, 28 May 1975 (MUN V/5/42), 6.
351. Minutes of Joint Meeting of Board and Council, 29 April 1976 (MUN V/5/42), 134–5.
352. 'Agreement Between the City of Dublin Vocational Education Committee and the University of Dublin: Appendix to Minutes to Special Board and Council Meeting of 29 April 1976,' (MUN V/5/43), 2.

353. Ibid.
354. Ibid.
355. Ibid., 3.
356. Ibid., 2.
357. Duff et al., *Dublin Institute of Technology*, 73–6.
358. Martin O'Donoghue Interview, February 2005.
359. Dáil Debates, vol. 310, no. 6, 7 December 1978, col. 1151–2.
360. White, *Investing in Education*, 141; Duff et al., *Dublin Institute of Technology*, 37.
361. Duff et al., *Dublin Institute of Technology*, 37.
362. Ibid., 39–41.
363. Coolahan, 'The NUI,' 267–8.
364. Government Information Service, Press Statement by the Minister for Education, 18 November 1977, 1–4; Note, 'Cruinniú Rialtais,' 15 November 1977 (NAI TSCH 2007/116/274).
365. White, *Investing in Education*, 143.
366. Minister for Education, C.O.3 H11/01/09, Memorandum for the Government, 'National Institute for Higher Education Bill, 1980,' 24 January 1980 (NAI TSCH 2010/53/462).
367. Ibid., 1.
368. 'National Institute for Higher Education, Limerick, Bill,' 1980, No. 25 of 1980, 9.
369. Ibid., 7.
370. Seanad Éireann Debates, vol. 94, no. 14, 3 July 1980, col. 1776.
371. Seanad Éireann NIHE Limerick Bill 1980, Committee stage, 'Amendments,' 1–2.
372. Seanad Éireann Debates, vol. 94, no. 14, 3 July 1980, col. 1760–1.
373. HEA, *Report on the Ballymun Project*, 56.
374. Minister for Education, Memorandum for the Government, 'Heads of a Bill for the Establishment of the National Institute for Higher Education,' 28 February 1980 (NAI TSCH 2010/53/413).
375. Bertie O'Dowd to M. Ó hOdhráin, 28 November 1980 (NAI TSCH 2010/53/413).
376. White, *Investing in Education*, 160.
377. Minister for Education, Memorandum for the Government, 'Business and Social Studies in the University Institutions in Dublin,' January 1978 (NAI 2008/148/224), 1–2.

378. Ibid., 2.
379. D. O'Sullivan to Private Secretary, Minister for Education, 18 April 1978 (NAI 2008/148/224).
380. Government of Ireland, *White Paper on Educational Development* (Dublin: Stationery Office, 1980), 74.
381. Ibid., 70.
382. Ibid., 70.
383. Ibid., 70.
384. Clancy, 'Policy in Third-Level Education,' 109.
385. Government of Ireland, *White Paper on Educational Development*, 70–72.
386. Department of Education, *Statistical Report 1965–66* (Dublin: Stationery Office, 1967), 5.
387. HEA, *Interim Report of the Technical Working Group*, 25–7; OECD, *Review of National Policies for Education: Review of Higher Education in Ireland* (Paris: OECD, 2004), 7.
388. White, *Investing in People*, 194.
389. HEA, *Interim Report of the Technical Working Group*, 26.
390. Department of Education, Memorandum to the Government, 'University Scholarship Schemes,' 21 June 1967 (NAI TSCH 98/6/951), 1–7.
391. Ibid., 21.
392. Department of Education, Memorandum to the Government, 'Scheme of Grants for Higher Education,' 20 February 1968 (NAI TSCH 99/1/332 S.16890), 2.
393. Ibid., 1.
394. N. S. Ó Nualláin to Tony Ó Dálaigh, 27 February 1968 (NAI TSCH 99/1/332 S.16890).
395. Walsh, *Politics of Expansion*, 199; Ó Nualláin to Ó Dálaigh, 2 April 1968 (NAI TSCH 99/1/332 S.16890); Ó Nualláin to M. Ó Flatharthaigh, 10 July 1968.
396. Walsh, *Politics of Expansion*, 199; Department of Education, 'Memorandum, Scheme of Grants for Higher Education,' 20 February 1968 (NAI TSCH 99/1/332 S.16890), 3.
397. *Memorandum from the Union of Students in Ireland*, 20 July 1976 (NAI TSCH 2006/133/151, S.16890), 1; see section below for the impact of USI.

398. Department of Education, 'Higher Education Grants Scheme, Memorandum, Appendix A: Higher Education Grants,' 31 August 1976 (NAI TSCH 2006/133/151, S.16890), 3.
399. Ibid.
400. Ibid., 4.
401. 'Note by Department of the Taoiseach of conversation with Liam Ó Laidhin, Department of Education' (NAI DFA 2009/135/283).
402. John Wilson to Lynch, 18 January 1979 (NAI DFA 2009/135/283).
403. Ibid.
404. *Interim Report of the Technical Working Group*, 121.
405. Government of Ireland, *Investment in Education*, 172.
406. Clancy, *Irish Higher Education*, 68.
407. Ibid.; Séamus Ó Buachalla, 'Policy and Structural Developments in Irish Higher Education,' *European Journal of Education* 19, no. 2 (1984): 165–71.
408. Clancy, *Irish Higher Education*, 68.
409. HEA, *Interim Report of the Technical Working Group*, 121; the SEGs were disaggregated more fully in this analysis, so it is not a precise basis of comparison with the figures above.
410. Adrian Raftery and Michael Hout, 'Maximally Maintained Inequality: Expansion, Reform and Opportunity in Irish Education, 1921–75,' *Sociology of Education* 66, no. 1 (1993): 56–7.
411. *Irish Times*, 'France Debates a Return to Work,' 3 June 1968; *Irish Times*, 'The Student Revolution,' 16 November 1968.
412. *Irish Times*, 'Student Action—The Case For,' 4 March 1969.
413. *Irish Times*, 'Vietnam War Protest March in Cork,' 20 January 1968; *Irish Times*, 'Students to Picket UCC, 'Wave of Protest Continues,' 29 November 1969.
414. James L. Kelly to Minister for Education and the Taoiseach, *Thomond College of Education Link-Up with UCC—Its Implications for Course Assessment*, 14 March 1977 (NAI TSCH 2007/116/274); John Raftery to Cosgrave, 15 December 1976 (NAI TSCH 2006/133/217).
415. *Irish Times*, 'Protest Against Apartheid,' 1 December 1969.
416. Luce, *Trinity College Dublin*, 200.
417. *Irish Times*, 'Student Protest Misrepresented—S.R.C Versus Communists,' 20 May 1968.
418. Ibid.

419. Luce, *Trinity College Dublin*, 201.
420. Ibid., 199–201.
421. *University Observer*, Accessed 30 October 2017. http://www.universityobserver.ie/features/a-campus-in-crisis-ucds-gentle-revolution/. The author of the piece was Amy Gargan; McCartney, *UCD*, 348–52.
422. McCartney, *UCD*, 348–52.
423. Ibid.
424. *Irish Times*, 'Threat to Radical Students,' 1 March 1969.
425. Ibid.
426. *Irish Times*, 'UCD Students Not to Attend Lectures—To Study Terms for Reform,' 6 March 1969; *University Observer*, http://www.universityobserver.ie/features/a-campus-in-crisis-ucds-gentle-revolution/. Accessed 30 October 2017: the *Irish Times* article claimed that over half the student body was in attendance.
427. McCartney, *UCD*, 386.
428. *Memorandum from the Union of Students in Ireland to All TDs and Senators on the Issue of Student Grants*, 20 July 1976 (NAI TSCH 2006/133/151, S.16890), 1.
429. G. H. H. Giltrap to Nicholas Nolan, 4 November 1971 (NAI TSCH 2006/133/151, S.16890).
430. Breda Sheehan to Jack Lynch, 13 November 1978 (NAI TSCH 2009/135/283).
431. *Memorandum from the Union of Students in Ireland*, 20 July 1976 (NAI TSCH 2006/133/151, S.16890), 1; See pp. 298–300 above.
432. Ibid.
433. McCartney, *UCD*, 386–7.
434. Ibid.; Luce, *Trinity College Dublin*, 199–201.
435. McCartney, *UCD*, 386–7.
436. HEA, *Interim Report of the Technical Working Group*, 120.

8

Reform and Resistance

The massification of higher education imposed new demands on HEIs, while greatly enhancing the visibility of higher education in the public sphere. The fiscal contraction in the early 1980s imposed severe financial constraints on higher education institutions, particularly in terms of recurrent spending. Yet while the scale of public resources devoted to higher education was curtailed, successive governments maintained a significant capital investment programme and official policies both responded to and sought to underpin a contining upsurge in participation. Following the dramatic upsurge in Ireland's economic fortunes during the 1990s, higher education became the focus of a wide-ranging institutional and legislative reform agenda. Pressure on HEIs to achieve commercialisation through closer linkages with industry also emerged more strongly during this period, although it was by no means the central motif of government policy. The expansion of enrolments, coupled with dramatically increased levels of public investment, stimulated greater central oversight focusing on accountability, quality assurance and value for money—all of which were increasingly contentious at the interface between academic institutions, the HEA and government departments. The drive for greater authority over the university sector

© The Author(s) 2018
J. Walsh, *Higher Education in Ireland, 1922–2016*,
https://doi.org/10.1057/978-1-137-44673-2_8

from an increasingly interventionist state provoked effective resistance from academics and institutional leaders.

Higher education throughout the developed world was influenced by the erosion of the postwar political consensus following stagflation and the shock of the oil crises in the 1970s. Keynesian economics was displaced as the dominant discourse of the OECD states by neo-liberalism, adopted enthusiastically in the 1980s by the Thatcher government in the UK and the Reagan administration in the USA, which promoted a resurgence of free market economics enforced by a powerful state.[1] Neo-liberalism was aptly described by Vaira as 'not only a political rhetoric, or ideology, but a wide project to change the institutional structure of societies at a global level.'[2] As an institutional project, neo-liberalism was informed by a very different and markedly more sceptical vision of the public sector, including higher education, than the 'welfare liberal' mode which it displaced: as Olssen and Peters commented, under a neoliberal mode of regulation 'markets have become a new technology by which control can be effected and performance enhanced, in the public sector.'[3] Thatcher's government was equally suspicious of academics and students' unions—both often portrayed as selfish producers engaged in protecting their own positions. Neo-liberalism and its associated organisational discourse of 'new public management' (NPM) emerged as the dominant paradigm in reforms of higher education in the UK, Australia and New Zealand.[4] NPM at least in the English-speaking world was characterised by strong performance management and monitoring systems to enforce formalised accountability rather than professional self-regulation; assertive, empowered management, rather than collegial approaches to decision-making and employment of market mechanisms within areas traditionally associated with the 'public realm'.[5] Yet the influence of UK policies inspired by a neoliberal script was extremely limited in Irish higher education during the 1980s. Irish ministers occasionally paid rhetorical homage to the new doctrines in their policy statements, but had no intention of embracing them wholesale and favoured a consensual, evolutionary style of policy-making which was the antithesis of Thatcherism, seeking to build on the policy changes of the 1960s and 1970s, rather than imposing a sharp break with a statist past.

Crisis and Retrenchment

Educational policy in the 1980s struggled to reconcile the demographic reality of a rapidly increasing student population with the political imperative of financial retrenchment. A high birth rate by international standards until 1980, combined with the long-term impact of the introduction of free post-primary education, fuelled a steadily increasing demand for higher education.[6] The subsequent decline in the birth rate from 1980 was expected to reduce the numbers taking the Leaving Certificate in the 1990s, but the short-term demographic pressures were reinforced by the increased social demand for higher education, particularly among more advantaged socio-economic groups. This surge in enrolments coincided with a crisis in public debt and a prolonged economic recession in the early to mid 1980s. The *Programme for Action in Education*, launched in 1984 by Gemma Hussey, Minister for Education in the Fine Gael-Labour administration, aptly highlighted the official dilemma: 'The greatest growth in demand…will be at third level which is also the most costly. This rising social demand for education…poses exceptional problems in the face of the deterioration in recent years in the state of the public finances'.[7] Hussey proved an effective negotiator in resisting demands from the Department of Finance to suspend capital investment in third-level education, although she also became a lightning rod for criticism of the government's austerity policies among teacher unions and some religious orders.

The Department of Finance imposed a temporary freeze on new third level building projects in January 1983, pending a comprehensive review of capital expenditure in education. The Taoiseach, Garret FitzGerald, was informed that this review was 'insisted upon by officials of the Department of Finance…after they had taken a stand on the practice of the Department of Education to submit capital expenditure estimates from year to year without having obtained sanction for the individual components of such expenditure.'[8] Finance objected to being asked to approve capital expenditure in education on a piecemeal basis without an overarching plan outlining priorities for the remainder of the decade.[9] This decision mainly impinged on higher education projects, including a new engineering building at Belfield and a clinical sciences complex at St James' hospital for Trinity, where the planning process was suspended pending the review. The suspension of the high profile engineering project to facilitate the transfer of the college's engineering faculty to Belfield, provoked outrage in UCD. Prof John Kelly, dean of engineering, appealed to FitzGerald that the decision was 'not in the best interests of the country at this time'.[10] Kelly warned Fine Gael TDs that the government was pursuing 'a false economy' by delaying the new engineering building which 'is much more than a UCD matter. It is one of national importance with immediate and serious effects on the industrial development plans of the country.'[11] The Department of Education was almost as trenchant in its private criticisms, warning in a submission to the government in September 1983 that 'the interruption of planning on a major project of this size is wasteful and uneconomic...'[12]

The dispute was a microcosm of a wider struggle which pitted the Department of Education and the HEA, seeking to maintain a third-level capital programme, against the Department of Finance, straining to reduce public expenditure and looking with a jaundiced eye on the steady expansion of public investment in higher education. Hussey's department outlined an extensive investment programme for the 1980s in their submission to the government in September 1983.[13] The minister sought 'a declaration that it is Government policy to cater for the increased numbers of students projected at third-level and that it is not Government policy to impose a numerical limitation per se on the number of students which may be so catered for...'[14] The minister also asked the Cabinet to authorise a number of third-level projects, which had been suspended at the instigation of the Department of Finance.[15] The department's most urgent priorities included immediate resumption of planning for UCD's engineering building, the clinical science complex in St. James hospital and the second phase of NIHED. Other priorities included the development of two new RTCs in Dublin by 1988 and four more (two in Dublin and two in Castlebar and Thurles) by 1990.[16] The memo noted that the necessary expertise for planning third-level developments within the overall capital allocation 'must be considered to reside in the institutions, the HEA and the Department of Education.'[17] This was a rebuke to the Department of Finance, supporting Hussey's argument that her department should only have to consult Finance before seeking tenders on building projects of over £5 million.[18]

Hussey appealed directly to the Taoiseach for assistance in maintaining third level capital investment. FitzGerald, who was often sceptical of the economic analysis of the Department of Finance, was willing to intervene periodically to protect the capital budget for HE.[19] Nevertheless Hussey noted privately that the government's discussion of the capital investment programme in June 1984 was 'a great big worry because of the huge amount required for third level.'[20] Hussey was successful in maintaining a third level capital programme despite pressure from the Department of Finance. The Cabinet did not impose any limit on student enrolments and allowed a number of projects at the planning stage to go ahead, accepting Education's argument that major capital projects would have to be funded if enrolments were not capped. Yet the ambitious development programme outlined by the department was severely scaled back. No new colleges were established in the 1980s, despite the recommendations of the White Paper for four new RTCs and NIHE Dublin was the last new HEI to be established until 1992.

The *Programme for Action in Education* unveiled by Hussey in January 1984 was a compromise between the attempt of the Department of Education and HEA to accommodate rapidly increasing student enrolments and Finance's determination to cut public spending. The programme pledged that the government would continue 'to provide third-level education for as many young people as possible', while seeking to secure a more cost-effective and productive HE system.[21] The minister proposed various initiatives to absorb increasing student numbers at a reduced cost, including rationalising similar courses between institutions; redesigning third-level courses based on a four-term academic year to deliver a greater throughput of students and the reduction of four-year degree courses to three years.[22] The *Programme for Action* also proposed a new model of resource allocation based on identifying unit costs at faculty and departmental level to achieve a more economic use of resources. Very few of the recommendations for rationalising programme or institutional structures were implemented, not least due to opposition from universities. No institution was inclined to embark on large-scale rationalisation and Trinity was determined to retain its four year degree structure. The main innovation foreshadowed by the *Programme* was the development of a unit cost mechanism for financing higher education, which was adopted by the HEA from 1995.[23]

The *Programme for Action* underlined, however, that the government would maintain a substantial level of investment in higher education despite severe fiscal retrenchment. The policy statement noted that even allowing for more efficient use of existing facilities, 'there will be need to provide new accommodation', referencing projects at the planning stage such as the second phase of NIHE Dublin and a new building at Bishop St. for the DIT College of Marketing and Design.[24] The *Programme* was more cautious in referring to projects where planning had been suspended by the Department of Finance, noting that such decisions would be made by the government in determining the public capital programme.[25] The engineering building for UCD was one of the capital projects included in the government's national plan, *Building on Reality*, launched in 1984.[26] A number of capital projects, such as the second phase of NIHE Limerick and an extension to the UCD library, were also completed in this period despite the financial constraints. While many of the cost-saving initiatives fell by the wayside, the commitment to sustaining capital investment in higher education was fulfilled, albeit at a reduced level.

The government's position on capital investment contrasted with previous periods of economic decline and neglect of higher education during the interwar period and again in the 1950s. Crucially not only was higher education the object of greatly increased societal demand a generation later, it was also perceived as a key factor in achieving economic recovery. Human capital considerations underpinned the programme, in which vocational training of graduates for a competitive economy took pride of place. Priority in financial support would be given to 'academic developments, either by way of new courses or extensions to existing courses, which are geared to developments in modern society and thus ensure that our graduates are kept abreast of rapidly changing technology and can compete with graduates of other countries'.[27] Such targeted support for academic courses perceived to have direct relevance to the labour market had already manifested itself in the Manpower programme. In the short-term pragmatic economic considerations functioned as a powerful rationale to maintain investment in higher education at a sufficient level to satisfy social demand. Although expenditure on education declined as a proportion of GDP during the 1980s, government expenditure on higher education increased as a percentage of state spending on education, from 18.1% in 1980 to 24% in 1993.[28] This increase was linked to a rapid expansion of student numbers throughout the decade—while full-time student enrolments quadrupled between 1965 and 1992, almost half of the increase occurred after 1980.[29]

This did not mean that higher education was insulated from the unfavourable economic environment. The recurrent state grants for universities declined as a proportion of total operating costs from 86% in 1980 to 62% in 1993. The continuing expansion in student enrolments was not matched by a proportional increase in academic staff: staff-student ratios increased between 1980 and 1993 from 16:1 to 22:1 in the universities and 9:1 to 14:1 for the non-university sector.[30] The fiscal contraction led to a sharp increase in student fees, which accounted for about a third of total institutional budgets by 1993.[31] The state grant expenditure per student within the RTCs declined even more dramatically by 57% during the same period. This decline was mitigated largely by the availability of EC funding through the ESF, which was augmented in 1984 following negotiations between Hussey and the European Commission.[32] The funding of diploma and certificate courses through ESF grants ensured that the vast majority of students in the RTCs and DIT did not pay tuition fees. Equally significant in the longer term was the emergence in 1984 of another EC initiative, the Framework Programme for Research and Technological Development, providing the first dedicated funding stream for research in higher education, which traditionally received no national funding.[33]

The availability of ESF funding also underpinned a major expansion of post-compulsory, pre-employment courses to promote 'transition' from school to work. The PECs were funded by the ESF and originally offered in vocational and community schools from 1978.[34] Following the amalgamation of several different types of 'transition' courses in the mid 1980s, such vocational training courses were increasingly offered both post junior and senior cycle and became identified as post leaving certificate courses (PLCs).[35] Enrolment in the one year PLCs doubled from 10,000 to 20,000 during the 1980s, with much of the growth occurring in Dublin, not least due to the low level of diploma and certificate places in the Dublin region, where DIT remained the sole provider until 1992.[36] The PLCs evolved into a nascent further education sector, although they remained strongly linked to post-primary education in organisation and staffing structures and lacked any national certification body. The National Council for Vocational Awards (NCVA) was established as a non statutory body in 1993 to validate further education courses and particularly to offer certification to the PLCs.[37] The lack of coordination of the emergent further education area with higher education helped to provoke major policy change in the late 1990s.

The impact of economic retrenchment on teacher education was particularly severe, leading to reductions in enrolment and more dramatically the closure of Carysfort College, one of the oldest third level colleges in Ireland. The vulnerability of the colleges of education was reinforced by the first significant decline in primary school enrolments since the 1940s. The fall in the birth rate of over 10,000 between 1980 and 1984 led to a reassessment of official projections for teacher numbers at primary level and halted abruptly the surge of investment in teacher education.[38] Moreover, austerity policies in the early 1980s meant that the long-term objective of reducing class sizes was downgraded. The intake for the six colleges of education was curtailed by 40%, from 1000 enrolments in 1980 to 600 five years later; all the colleges were operating well below their site capacity by the mid 1980s.[39] The graduate diploma in primary education was suspended from 1981 to 1991, while enrolments on the B.Ed. in all the colleges were sharply reduced.[40] The government identified the need for further rationalisation in teacher education, but discussions between the Department of Education and college authorities in Carysfort about alternatives uses for the space, such as in-service education, proved inconclusive. FitzGerald believed that the government had to address 'considerable overcapacity in the system', as the remaining colleges would have four times the level of places needed by the end of the 1980s.[41]

This was the context for one of the most controversial decisions in education by an Irish government.

Hussey announced on 4 February 1986 that Carysfort College would be closed, indicating that the decision was primarily about the need to contain public expenditure and achieve 'a better reallocation of resources' in view of the decline in pupil numbers.[42] While Hussey became the public face of the closure, she had initially opposed it and later sought a more gradual process of consultation which was pre-empted by a leak of the government decision.[43] The decision triggered a firestorm of controversy, as it was immediately denounced by the INTO, IFUT and USI, as well as opposition politicians and staff in the college. The Catholic archbishop of Dublin, Kevin McNamara, expressed dismay at the end of 'the proud educational tradition' represented by the Sisters of Mercy for 109 years, while the college president, Sr. Regina Durcan, denounced the government for ensuring 'a totally pointless waste of a superb third-level facility.'[44] Hussey confided to her diary the '...ongoing hassle and chaos over Carysfort, which has escalated to being a political disaster of amazing proportions...'[45] The government's case was damaged by the abrupt announcement of the decision and by the absence of any plan for the implementation of the closure and the position of the staff. Fianna Fáil's criticism of the government in the Dáil on 7 February that the decision was 'clumsy and crude' enjoyed considerable resonance, although Hussey's rejoinder that her opponents were guilty of opportunism was not unfounded.[46] The controversy certainly damaged Hussey, who was moved from Education to Social Welfare in a Cabinet reshuffle the following week.[47] Her successor Patrick Cooney, a veteran Fine Gael politician, promised a review of the decision, although ultimately the only concession made by the government was over the timing of the closure, as Carysfort was allowed to remain in operation until the end of the 1987–88 academic year.[48] While Fianna Fáil politicians including the party leader, Charles Haughey, fiercely criticised the decision to close Carysfort, the closure was implemented under Haughey's government which took office in March 1987.

Ultimately at a time of austerity and retrenchment in teacher education, Carysfort was particularly vulnerable, due to political, geographical and cultural factors pinpointed by Christina Murphy, the formidable education correspondent of the *Irish Times*:

> Why was Carysfort the one chosen? It would have been impossible to close Limerick, the only college outside Dublin; the only Church of Ireland College couldn't go either, neither could Marino, the only college training teachers entirely through the Irish language. St Pat's is on the Northside of Dublin – badly served by third-level colleges already – it is bigger than Carysfort and has an educational research centre attached to it...So the axe fell on the oldest and possibly most renowned of the colleges.[49]

Whatever the shortcomings of the government's tactics, the unsentimental decision to close Carysfort underlined the decline of ecclesiastical power in education: neither the dismay of the archbishop nor the strenuous protests of the religious managers had any impact on the government. Indeed the influence of traditional religious stakeholders in teacher education had declined to the point where their protests about Carysfort barely featured on the radar of ministers struggling to contain political, trade union and media opposition.

The trade union response to the closure was more effective, at least in protecting the position of its staff. IFUT failed to prevent the closure of Carysfort, but was successful in securing recognition from the new government that its staff could not be made redundant on a compulsory basis.[50] Following a threat of legal action by IFUT, the government conceded in 1988 the principle of 'reasonable redeployment' or voluntary redundancy for the staff.[51] Although the dispute was eventually resolved only in 1991, the large majority of staff were redeployed to universities, other colleges of education and in some cases the department itself, with a smaller number accepting voluntary redundancy. The significance of the IFUT-departmental negotiations extended well beyond the Carysfort dispute, as the government recognised the principle of tenure—while this was not yet the subject of a legally binding determination, it was understood by IFUT to mean an indefinite contract up to the age of 65.[52] This interpretation of tenure was implicitly accepted by ministers in sanctioning the redeployment of staff from Carysfort.

The abrupt shift from economic expansionism to austerity in the early 1980s impinged on teacher education with exceptional severity. The decline in the birth rate, combined with the severe budgetary climate, placed the colleges of education in a particularly vulnerable position, relative to other HEIs where enrolments were still expanding. The first year intake to the B.Ed. in St. Patrick's College, Drumcondra, was reduced by 63% between 1981 and 1991.[53] The Department of Education floated a proposal to close three of the five schools of education in the late 1980s and while this did not happen it highlighted the exceptional pressures on teacher education. The restrictions on enrolment continued until the early 1990s, even as the economy showed signs of recovery. St. Patrick's College and Mary Immaculate responded to the unfavourable economic climate by introducing new or extended in-service courses for teachers and by planning a general BA degree alongside their existing programmes.[54] The proposed BA, a notable departure for institutions whose remit was traditionally located in specialised teacher preparation, was attractive in offering a new source of income and widening of their academic mission which had the potential to safeguard the apparently beleaguered colleges following the closure of Carysfort. Any move in this direction was blocked by the Department of Education on financial and demographic grounds during the 1980s, but revived in more favourable economic circumstances during the early 1990s, when it was unexpectedly linked to the newly redesignated NIHEs following their transition to university status.

'…The Creation of Universities Did Not Loom Large on My Horizon…'

Ministers lacked the scope and inclination to promote new policy initiatives involving institutional or structural innovation for most of the 1980s. The major institutional reform of the decade was driven by the ambition of the NIHEs to secure university status. Ed Walsh, a leading advocate of business-oriented higher education and equally articulate critic of the traditional universities, proved particularly adept in winning political support for his case.[55] In response to sustained pressure from the two institutions and their regional lobby groups, Hussey established an international review group headed by Dr. Tom Hardiman in 1986 to consider the establishment of a technological university with the two NIHEs as constituent colleges.[56] The review group's recommendation for the establishment of the NIHEs as independent universities was presented to Mary O'Rourke, who took over the Department of Education in 1987. O'Rourke later conceded that on taking up office 'the creation of universities did not loom large on my horizon, because there were all these huge, horrendous cuts to be made everywhere…'.[57]

But the beginning of a modest economic recovery in 1989 offered an opportunity to take up the recommendations of the review group, which had the advantage of pacifying a highly effective regional lobby for a university in Limerick, as well as a more recent one in north Dublin. Walsh and his Dublin NIHE counterpart, Danny O'Hare, were credited by O'Rourke for lobbying 'mercilessly' in favour of university status for their institutions.[58] O'Rourke introduced minimalist amending legislation to the NIHE acts which upgraded the institutes to university status, allowed them to award degree, diploma and certificate qualifications independently and gave their directors the status of university president.[59] The legislation was passed with all-party support on 25 May 1989, the same day that the Dáil was dissolved following an unexpected defeat of the minority Fianna Fáil government.[60] While the debate was truncated due to the imminent general election, significant contributions were made by Garret FitzGerald, whose government had commissioned the Hardiman review and Labour Party TD, Michael D. Higgins, both academics.[61] Both TDs expressed concern that the legislation did not establish sufficiently the autonomy of the new universities or their power to establish and make appointments to academic posts, not least because the minister retained the power to appoint the governing authorities.[62] Yet despite such reservations the legislation to establish the University of Limerick and Dublin City University was approved by the Dáil within a single day in an unusual display of cross-party consensus. The success of the legislation was due to its minimalist nature, as it avoided more fundamental long-term issues around the reconstitution of the NUI or the wider legislative framework for the universities, and was not harmed by the imminence of a general election. Yet the act was the first legislative change to the existing university framework inherited by the Irish state, leading to the recognition of the first new universities since 1908.

The government responded more cautiously to discontent within the RTCs with their traditional governance structure. A high level of political and administrative control was built into the RTC sector from its inception. Legislation was brought forward in 1991–92 by successive ministers to establish the RTCs on a statutory basis and introduce self-governing management structures.[63] The Bill removed the colleges from the authority of the VECs, which was regarded as unduly restrictive by many institutional leaders and staff.[64] But the legislation was strongly criticised by a cross party lobby of TDs who reflected deep hostility within the VECs to the move: deputies including Jim Higgins (Fine Gael), Brian O'Shea (Labour) and Tomás MacGiolla (Workers Party), variously portrayed the Bill as 'an outright attack on local democracy…' and a centralisation of power to ensure that 'the Minister rules OK.'[65] Following strenuous lobbying by TDs and the Irish Vocational Education Association (IVEA), several amendments were accepted which maintained a residual role for the VECs in the governance of the colleges.[66] The Regional Technical Colleges Act passed by the Oireachtas in 1992 allowed the VECs to nominate six representatives to each governing body (as well as identifying five other organisations which could nominate members for appointment by the minister) and to ratify college programmes and budgets before forwarding these to the minister for approval.[67] The VECs remained stakeholders in the colleges, but no longer oversaw their administration and their traditional role in providing higher technical education had effectively been sidelined. Yet the legislation did not alter the subordinate relationship of the RTCs to the Department of Education, reserving substantial powers for the Minister for Education, including selection of the chairperson of the governing body, control over levels of staffing and approval of programmes and budgets.[68] Separate legislation approved by the Dáil in July 1992 established the Dublin Institute of Technology as a self-governing institute, while giving CDVEC a veto on the incorporation of any additional college to the institute.[69] The DIT Act, 1992, allowed the institute to confer diploma, certificate and other qualifications and permitted degree-awarding powers to be assigned by the minister, although this was delayed for six years.[70] Both acts re-affirmed in almost identical language the core economic and vocational function of the institutions to provide 'vocational and technical education and training for the economic, technological, scientific, commercial, industrial, social and cultural development of the State…'[71]

The transition of the NIHEs to university status facilitated a repositioning of the major teacher education institutions in the state, which enabled them to fulfil their ambition of offering a BA degree, although not in the way they had originally envisaged. Both St. Patrick's and MIC initiated discussions with the NUI about the introduction of a BA programme at the end of the 1980s, but their association with the National University was unexpectedly terminated following an intervention by the Department of Education. Although the NUI senate got as far as approving a recommendation for the BA in both colleges,[72] the department blocked the proposal and instead succeeded in enforcing a new association between the two colleges and the newly redesignated universities based on geographical proximity. The secretary of the department, Noel Lindsay, was instrumental in brokering a memorandum of understanding between MIC and the newly minted University of Limerick in October 1991.[73] This agreement facilitated the development and launch of a new BA degree from September 1992, when MIC became the first college of education to offer a liberal arts degree accredited at university level; the new four year programme was distinctive in offering an off campus placement year, taken in Ireland or more usually abroad.[74] Thomond College, which had maintained a distinct institutional life on the same campus since the early 1970s, was integrated into UL, following a reconfiguration of internal university structures to recognise a new 'college' of education, between 1989 and 1991.[75] Similarly, despite the apparent conclusion of successful negotiations between St. Patrick's College and UCD, the department instructed the college authorities instead to embark on a new association with DCU.[76] The resulting negotiations, in which departmental officials were heavily involved, led to a linkage agreement with DCU in August 1993, facilitating the introduction of a new BA in St. Patrick's College accredited by the university. The new programme started only two months later despite concerns among academic staff at its abrupt introduction.[77] The department's intervention was decisive in forging the new alignment, as the college authorities and staff in each instance acceded to the political and official pressure for a regionally based alliance rather than the traditional association with the NUI.

A combination of pressure from institutional leaders and a powerful regional lobby in Limerick, allied to a strategic response by policy-makers, led to far-reaching institutional restructuring in the non-university sector. White suggests that the successful campaign for university status by the NIHEs 'provided a fascinating insight into how a complex and elusive policy, such as the binary approach, could be deflected in the Irish political system by a well crafted lobby built around a single manageable issue...'[78] Yet the NIHEs had always occupied an ambiguous place within the diversified system as non-university institutions designated under the HEA and the regional campaign for a university in Limerick spanned a generation. Moreover, the decision reinforced the determination of policy-makers in the department and HEA to consolidate the binary divide, which was emphasised in a series of policy statements in the early 1990s, including the Green Paper in 1992 and White Paper in 1995.[79] Concerns about 'academic drift' involving the emulation of established universities by non-university institutions eager to move up the value chain and a corresponding decline of diversity within the system gained currency in Western European states from the 1970s.[80] Fears of 'dedifferentiation' and loss of the distinctive mission of the non-university technical colleges emerged as a key issue among departmental and HEA officials by the late 1980s.[81] Preserving the binary system, albeit with some concessions to regional pressures, was a notable preoccupation of successive ministers in the 1990s. The state's commitment to the binary system was underlined by the retention of the RTCs under the remit of the Department of Education and political caution over the status of DIT.[82] Departmental officials also exerted effective pressure on the colleges of education to forge linkages with neighbouring institutions which had only recently achieved university status rather than deepening their association with more established universities. This was an early example of regional collaboration which would become a key element of government policy in the 2000s, but can also be seen as an attempt to minimise disruption to the binary model.

Higher Education and the Celtic Tiger

The OECD in 2004 referenced economic analyses suggesting that upskilling of the labour force since the 1960s was a major contributor to the Celtic Tiger economy in the mid to late 1990s, accounting for 'almost 1% per annum of additional national output over the last decade or so', which was the most striking phase of economic advance since the foundation of the Irish state.[83] Ó Buachalla argues that a transformation in HE policy occurred from the late 1980s, moving from expansion driven primarily by social demand to a long-term policy based on vocational imperatives and the demands of the market: this transition led to greater intrusion by the state in higher education, involving external pressures on institutions to develop a 'competitive' ethos and abandon the traditional ideal of academic freedom associated with Humboldt.[84] This presents an over-simplified portrayal of the character and ideological underpinnings of policy change in the 1990s. Societal demand was one of a number of factors behind government policies in opening up higher education to popular participation between the mid 1960s and early 1980s, but had always co-existed with a strong emphasis on supplying the needs of the labour market. HE policy since the 1960s overtly positioned higher education as an important contributor to economic development. While Ó Buachalla highlights a significant 'policy intensification' at higher level since the late 1980s,[85] this did not mark an ideological turning point but more of a reinforcement of existing policies.

The extent of ideological change in terms of policy and discourse during the 1990s should not be overstated, as the combination of economic and social justice imperatives at the heart of policy formation since the 1960s remained influential in the late twentieth century. The imposition of radical reforms linked to NPM on higher education in England by Conservative governments in the 1980s had a minimal influence in Ireland.[86] This may have reflected the calculated embrace of European integration by successive Irish governments, in contrast to Britain's volatile interaction with the European project. The EC was a more significant reference point for Irish politicians and civil servants in this period, especially with Ireland's participation first in the Single European Act which led to the single market and later in economic and monetary union following the Maastricht Treaty in 1991. The contribution of higher education in adapting to the single market featured in the Green Paper in 1992. But university education was not a key focus of the Community's activity, which focused mainly on vocational training up to the 1990s. Irish policy-makers were also pragmatic and selective in how they engaged with the Community institutions, valuing the EC mainly for the resources of the ESF to support non-university courses and on a more limited scale the targeted support for research through structural funds. Many initiatives adopted in the late 1900s evolved over a lengthy period and reflected long-term priorities by national political and bureaucratic elites, modified by pressure from institutional leaders, academics and students. Egalitarian priorities in meeting social demand and widening participation in higher education co-existed with an increased emphasis on international competitiveness and engagement with business.

Higher education was an increasingly central element of the ongoing project of national economic development in this period. The emergence of the Celtic Tiger economy in the mid-1990s was often ascribed, at least in part, to high levels of education within the Irish workforce and an increased output of highly qualified graduates. Yet Ireland had historically low levels of average educational attainment by international standards across the population as a whole for most of the twentieth century.[87] Policy-makers were concerned to close the gap with developed states, both trading partners and competitors in the international marketplace, as well as adapting to the demands of the single European market. Official re-appraisals of the HE system in the early to mid 1990s underlined that Ireland had not yet overcome a traditional deficit in third-level participation by the school leaving age cohort compared to other developed countries.[88]

A notable policy shift in the late twentieth century was a gradual 'intensification' of state intervention in university education.[89]
Government departments and agencies sought to influence not only
the system structure and institutional relationships, but also the type
of programmes offered, seeking mainly to reposition university offer-
ings to meet labour market demands more effectively. While the RTC/
DIT sector had always been assigned a key labour market role, government policy increasingly prioritised the economic mission of universities as well. This suited HEIs, the state and employers in the late 1980s:
an agreement between the government and universities in 1990 led to
expansion in targeted disciplinary areas, providing 3600 new places over
three years in electronic engineering, information technology and business studies.[90] The government intervened to support priority areas in
business, engineering and later ICT, following the logic of the earlier
Manpower programme and the *Programme for Action*.[91] The increased
demand for engagement with the market by universities at this stage
was pragmatic and selective.

This focus on the economic contribution of HEIs across the sector
was apparent in official preparations for wide-ranging educational legislation. The department commissioned a discussion paper to prepare the
way for legislation at the instigation of Mary O'Rourke. The amended
Green Paper *Education for a Changing World* was published in 1992 by
her successor Séamus Brennan. The Green Paper was a significant inflection point in terms of policy change, providing a political imprimatur
to intensification of state intervention in higher education, allied to the
promotion of a more business-oriented approach by HEIs both in terms
of management and engagement with industry. The policy statement
sought greater accountability from HEIs in the form of annual reports
and recommended a unit cost system to facilitate the targeting of state
funding 'towards nationally important activities'.[92] Programmes of professional development for academic staff and procedures for quality
assurance of teaching and learning were identified as key requirements
for all institutions, reinforced by a new monitoring role for the HEA.
The Green Paper also proposed reform of the membership and functions of third-level governing bodies and a stronger executive role for
college presidents, as part of a more tightly defined managerial model.[93]

The Green Paper extolled the benefits of 'college-industry interaction', urging institutions to develop explicit policies for engagement with industry to promote research and development and support technical training. A key government objective, informed by the advent of the EC single market at the end of 1992, was to increase the transfer of graduates in science and technology to Irish industry, which was 'necessary if Ireland is to close the technology gap that exists between small industry in Ireland and its competitors in Europe'.[94] The Green Paper assigned a key function to the higher education system in supplying graduates 'with the technical expertise and management capacity' to allow Irish industry to compete successfully in a European market. It was notable for offering early official backing to the concept of a knowledge based economy, not yet explicitly defined in those terms:

> The development of knowledge-intensive industry based on 'brains rather than fixed assets' will largely depend on the ability of higher education institutions to produce sufficient numbers of leaders, innovators and those capable of managing and exploiting the opportunities of the new technology and its applications, both as employees and as entrepreneurs.[95]

The Green Paper explicitly promoted the reorientation of universities towards national economic objectives, through more corporate style management and engagement with industry. Brennan, a centre-right minister who favoured a movement towards entrepreneurial universities, undoubtedly left a distinctive imprint on the Green Paper. The emphasis on accountability and reform referenced developments in higher education in the UK under the Thatcher government, but it was a muted echo which fell far short of an embrace of neoliberalism.

The Green Paper was part of a gradual evolution of higher education policy rather than a radical shift and not all of its priorities were given the same weight in the ensuing White Paper. Niamh Bhreathnach, the first Labour Party Minister for Education (1993–97), adopted the accountability measures promoted by her predecessor while incorporating a stronger emphasis on equality of opportunity. The new minister established a steering committee in December 1993, headed by Noel Lindsay, chairperson of the HEA, to advise on the future development of higher education. The steering committee was supported by a technical working group, led by Prof. Jerry Sexton of the ESRI, which undertook detailed analysis of the projected future expansion of the sector under alternative scenarios.[96] The interim report of the technical working group in January 1995 produced detailed findings and recommendations, informed by analysis both of the quantitative expansion of higher education and the disparities in participation linked to socio-economic group and age.[97] The interim report was central to the conclusions of the Steering Committee and the higher education section in the White Paper *Charting our Education Future*.

The technical working group expressed concern that the rate of entry within the relevant age cohort to full-time higher education in Ireland at 35% in 1991 remained below average on a comparative basis among OECD states.[98] The group recommended a participation target of 50% of the Leaving Certificate age cohort by 2006. The report favoured both 'increasing' and 'widening' participation, combining renewed expansion of the age participation rate with more targeted intervention to overcome deeply entrenched inequalities within the system. The technical working group recommended 'significant intervention' at primary and second level to counter under-achievement and school leaving, along with measures to address both economic and cultural barriers to access at higher level for under-represented SEGs.[99] These proposals included an enhanced maintenance grant for 'students from disadvantaged backgrounds' and introduction of a quota of reserved places in HEIs for such students, coupled with access courses to facilitate 'take-up of places and successful completion of higher education programmes'.[100] The group also proposed a range of initiatives to widen participation by mature students, including consistent admission procedures at institutional level, increased grants for mature students from low income backgrounds and improved support services for non-traditional learners within HEIs.[101]

The working group also commented on the 'disposition of growth between the University and RTC/DIT sub-sectors and by qualification level'[102]: the report favoured maintaining the 'current relativity' in size—about 50-50 in the early 1990s—between the university sector and the non-university technical institutions and retaining the existing balance in entry and graduate output between sub-degree and degree courses.[103] Yet this did not preclude further expansion of the RTC sector, particularly at levels 6 and 7. The technical working group highlighted very low entry rates to certificate/diploma courses in Dublin relative to the rest of the country, which were linked to high levels of socio-economic disadvantage in many areas of the city. They recommended enhanced third-level facilities in the South-East and West of the country, but noted that 'in view of the scale of the disparities, priority should be given to the provision of additional facilities at certificate/ diploma level in Dublin.'[104] This gave momentum to the establishment of new technical colleges in Dublin, envisaged by the White Paper in 1980 but sidelined during the recession.

The interim report informed the minister's White Paper *Charting our Education Future*, which was published in 1995. The White Paper was the product of an extensive process of re-appraisal, incorporating the HEA study and a wider process of consultation culminating in the National Education Convention, a consultative conference including representatives from a wide range of educational partners at Dublin Castle in 1993.[105] A core principle of the White Paper was its commitment to 'balance institutional autonomy with the needs of public policy and accountability, having due regard to the respective rights and responsibilities of the institutions and the State'.[106] This tension between institutional autonomy and accountability to the state was central to public debates on higher education throughout the 1990s. The White Paper included many of the proposals advanced by the Green Paper, including the unit cost funding system which was introduced by the HEA in the mid 1990s; the establishment of institutional quality assurance procedures monitored by the authority and long awaited legislation on the position of the universities.[107] The minister sought to maintain mission differentiation between the two sectors, emphasising that the RTCs should offer only 'limited levels of degree provision', while all their programmes were expected to have an applied orientation.[108] The White Paper envisaged an extended role for the HEA, involving an expansion of its remit to include all publicly funded colleges and charging the agency with overall co-ordination of the higher education system.

The White Paper, reflecting the influence of the technical working group and Bhreathnach's social democratic outlook, prioritised egalitarian social objectives, focusing on gender equality and widening participation for traditionally under-represented groups.[109] The minister adopted many of the recommendations of the interim report, backing proposals for access programmes and improvements in student support schemes: the HEA was also asked to advise on how to achieve a target for an increase of 500 students annually from lower socio-economic groups in third-level education.[110] Greater flexibility in course structures to facilitate participation by mature and part-time students in full-time employment was also recommended.[111]

The latest policy statement emphasised the themes of innovation and knowledge transfer from HE to the economy which had emerged in the Green Paper: 'higher education institutions have an important leadership role in providing and continually renewing the skills and knowledge base which are vital to our future progress'.[112] More systematic engagement by HEIs with the economy was required to promote upskilling for professional, managerial and technical workers and 'the diffusion of scientific knowledge and technological and managerial innovations'.[113] The White Paper also foreshadowed the development of a coherent research policy for higher education, indicating that the underdeveloped area of HE research would receive significant state support for the first time.

The technical working group's recommendations for new diploma/certificate courses in Dublin were quickly implemented. A new RTC at Tallaght had already been established in 1992, belatedly implementing departmental plans first mooted in 1980. The steering committee recommendation paved the way for the rapid establishment of two new technical colleges in Dublin. The new RTC at Blanchardstown, which opened in 1999, had a strong focus on providing for 'non-traditional' students entering third-level education through alternative routes than the Leaving Certificate, including students from low-income families, mature applicants, and students with disabilities.[114] An existing college of art and design in Dún Laoghaire was reconstituted as the Institute of Art, Design and Technology (IADT) in April 1997, conforming to the steering committee's recommendation for a new technical institute which would 'develop new specialisations in association with local industry'.[115] This proposal had powerful allies, not least the minister, who represented Dún Laoghaire in the Dáil.

The White Paper set out an ambitious reform agenda, which foreshadowed significant institutional and policy changes in higher education. A key objective prioritised by Bhreathnach was the abolition of third-level tuition fees, undertaken in conjunction with the removal of regressive tax relief on covenants.[116] While the impact of the policy proved highly controversial, the rationale for the abolition of third-level tuition fees was explicitly to widen participation, particularly to traditionally under-represented SEGs. Bhreathnach carried through the free fees initiative in the face of considerable public opposition from university leaders, educational commentators and even some students' unions.[117] University presidents were critical of a measure which made their institutions dependent on the state once again for 80–90% of their funding. Critics of the initiative, including opposition politicians, academics and student unions in Trinity and UCD, also argued that it would do little to enhance participation by under-represented socio-economic groups, particularly in the absence of any meaningful increase in maintenance grants.[118] But the minister overcame opposition within the government, including the scepticism of the Department of Finance, and the initiative was implemented on a phased basis by September 1996. The Irish decision to abolish tuition fees came barely two years before the British government began a phased reintroduction of third-level fees following the publication of the Dearing report in 1997.[119] The initiative subsequently attracted criticism from the ESRI on the basis that significant advantages accrued to graduates in terms of career earnings and that those who could afford to contribute should do so.[120] The minister secured little political credit for her initiative, which damaged her relations with university presidents without provoking a significant popular groundswell for 'free fees'.[121] More significantly, the public debate on 'free fees' rumbled on and the initiative never secured the iconic status accorded to Donogh O'Malley's démarche on free second-level education. While few politicians openly sought the return of tuition fees, the decision did not have a similar lasting legacy, as it proved vulnerable to domestic and international criticism and deteriorating economic circumstances in the early 2000s.

The scope and pace of major reforms in this period was facilitated by the unprecedented boom in economic growth and employment at the height of the Celtic Tiger. Yet the extensive process of policy innovation was underpinned by a high level of political support for investment in higher education and a broad consensus in government, civil society and academia that HE should be a key focus of government policy to pursue both economic and social justice objectives. Expenditure per student surged by 54% in a five year period during the second half of the 1990s, underlining a dramatic upsurge in both recurrent and capital funding of the HE sector. Although expenditure per student in Ireland increased by over four times the average for all OECD countries between 1995 and 2010, most of this increase occurred in the second half of the 1990s.[122] If this level of spending was not wholly exceptional in a period of economic buoyancy, it was certainly associated with a strong political and official commitment to extending mass participation, expanding a diversified system and achieving a higher level of education across the population. This policy framework had a strong economic orientation linked to knowledge transfer and upskilling to sustain a competitive economy, which coexisted with explicitly egalitarian objectives in terms of widening participation by traditionally under-represented groups.

Widening Participation

Increasing participation by successive generations of school leavers was a defining feature of the Irish higher education system in the second half of the twentieth century. The HEA technical working group recognised the likelihood of further expansion, offering a range of projections assuming that a decline in the birth rate between 1980 and 1995 would be partly counterbalanced by increasing participation rates and a moderate increase in the number of mature students; the group estimated total full-time enrolments of 118,300 to 125,400 in 2010 depending on the scenario adopted by government.[123] But the HEA study dramatically underestimated the scale of the next wave of expansion. The increasing completion rate at senior cycle helped to sustain third-level participation, as the number of Leaving Certificate candidates continued to increase until the late 1990s despite a declining birth rate.[124]

Third-level enrolments more than doubled once again over the following generation, as student numbers in publicly funded HEIs increased from 107,950 to 222,618 between 1992–93 and 2015–16.[125] There was a corresponding increase in full-time enrolments from 84,073 to 179,354.[126] The age participation rate saw a striking advance from 20% to 1980 to 44% in 1998 and 58% in 2015.[127] The proportion of new entrants to undergraduate higher education had almost trebled within a generation, with 43,460 new entrants entering full-time undergraduate courses in 2015, compared to 15,000 in 1980.[128] Higher education remained strongly oriented towards full-time participation, especially at undergraduate level: the 'free fees' initiative was restricted to full-time programmes and part-time students accounted for under 7% of undergraduate entrants in HEA designated institutions in 2006–07.[129] The level of full time to part time enrolment across the HE system in 2014–15 was 85:15, showing a more marked bias towards full-time participation than the OECD or EU 21 average of 77:23.[130]

The extraordinary upsurge in enrolments testified to the strength of societal demand for third-level education, despite a temporary easing of demographic pressures from the early 1980s to the mid 1990s, and the enduring impact of policy initiatives over the previous generation. Increased participation was reflected in the relatively high levels of attainment among the younger age groups entering the labour market since the 1980s. Ireland was fifth highest in the OECD rankings by 2007 in terms of higher education qualifications secured by the 25–34 year old age group.[131] The expansion in enrolments consisted mainly of school leavers up to the late 1990s: 90% of entrants to tertiary education through the CAO in 2002 were drawn from the 17 to 19 age group.[132] The proportion of mature students in higher education remained very low at the end of the twentieth century—the level of new entrants to full-time higher education aged 23 or over in 1998 was only 4.5%.[133]

Expansion was largely concentrated among the full-time undergraduate population up to the 1990s, although postgraduate entrants as a proportion of overall student enrolments increased moderately over a twenty year period from 8% in 1975 to 14% in 1994.[134] The Steering Committee found an 84%:16% balance between undergraduate and postgraduate enrolments in the universities in 1992–93 and their projections assumed a continuation of this trend pending a more long-term review of the appropriate balance between undergraduate and postgraduate participation.[135] While this estimate referred only to the universities, the balance between the different levels was broadly similar across higher education almost 20 years later, suggesting that expansion in postgraduate numbers more than kept pace with the increase at undergraduate level. There were 34,740 postgraduates in all HEA funded higher education institutions, amounting to 18% of total enrolments in 2010–11 and recent data in 2015–16 showed an almost identical proportion of postgraduate students.[136]

Widening participation to traditionally under-represented groups, as distinct from driving mass enrolment, emerged as a significant factor in public policy from the early 1990s. The Steering Committee was influential in making widening participation a key objective of government policy. The technical working party drew on a burgeoning research literature on access to higher education, which had highlighted marked disparities in participation linked to class since the 1970s and more recently imbalances relating to age, disability and ethnic origin.[137] Access to higher education emerged as a distinct field for policy action from the mid 1990s, exemplified by a series of expert group reports, ministerial initiatives and schemes at both national and institutional level. The most recent analysis by Fleming et al. considers access as a 'continuum ranging from relatively simple mechanisms and routes into HE, such as alternative matriculation criteria amd foundation programmes, to the other end, which encompasses comprehensive and integrated systemic change both inside and outside of HE.'[138] Access in terms of policy formation was conceptualised broadly in this period as encompassing entry, persistence and successful completion of higher education courses.[139]

All seven universities and most other colleges developed access programmes, involving linkages with designated second-level schools; allocation of a limited number of third-level places to students from 'disadvantaged' areas or schools through non-standard entry routes and preparatory 'foundation' programmes for undergraduate studies.[140] The social partnership process, which incorporated trade unions, employers and the voluntary/community sector as contributors to policy-making, also helped to bring equity of access to the fore. An action group on access to third level education was established in September 2000, implementing a recommendation by the latest national agreement between the 'social partners', the *Programme for Prosperity and Fairness*. The report of the action group in 2001 was a key factor in devising a coherent policy on access to higher education, prioritising widening participation among traditionally under-represented target groups.[141]

The action group acknowledged 'a vast amount of good work' already carried out by HEIs, schools, voluntary organisations and state agencies to widen participation, but noted the haphazard development of such initiatives in the 1990s: 'This work is uncoordinated. It lacks cataloguing, and there is no structure to take responsibility for identification and dissemination of best practice.'[142] The solution was not a doubling down on a plethora of piecemeal interventions, but a coordinated national framework to increase participation by traditionally disadvantaged groups: '...a proliferation of additional interventions is unlikely to bring about any radical change...unless they are deployed in a suitable structural environment that can coordinate and intensify their effect.'[143] The action group identified seven critical stages where intervention was necessary to improve equity in access, drawing on the work of Clancy and Wall to highlight the importance of intervention at primary and secondary levels in addressing socio-economic differentials in educational transitions.[144] But significant initiatives at Leaving Certificate and third level were also envisaged and it was in this sphere that the action group had the most impact. The group recommended the establishment of a co-ordinating body within the HEA to develop policy proposals and oversee the implementation of the proposed national framework. The primary objective of the new National Office for Equity of Access to Higher Education would be 'to put in place and oversee an integrated national programme to bring about significant improvement in equity in access to higher education among the target groups'.[145]

The report focused on socio-economically disadvantaged families and communities, mature students and students with disabilities, recommending the setting of numerical targets for each group. Participation was viewed as a holistic process, incorporating access programmes leading to third level and support for students after entry to higher education.[146] The action group also urged the allocation of increased resources, including a doubling of the existing level of excheq-uer financial assistance on access initiatives.[147] Other recommendations at institutional level encouraged HEIs to 'mainstream' their existing access programmes to ensure that key access posts became permanent and place equity in access policies 'in the mainstream of policy-making and internal academic and resource decisions...'[148] The Department of Education in turn was urged to reform student support schemes to target resources towards a special maintenance grant supporting the most disadvantaged students, pitched at a reckonable income limit of 75% of average industrial earnings.[149]

The ambitious report of the action group reflected strong egalitarian impulses. The action group enjoyed considerable influence on government policy and institutional strategies in the early 2000s. The new national office (soon retitled the National Access Office), arguably the central recommendation of the group, was established within the HEA in 2003 and generated three action plans on equity of access in HE between 2004 and 2015. The plans were informed by an increasing richness and sophistication in terms of the data relating to access.[150] The student support schemes were reformed over the following decade, partly implementing the recommendations of the action group. A special rate of maintenance grant for 'disadvantaged students' was introduced in September 2000 as an initial step pending the report.[151] This was a top-up grant for undergraduate students with very low incomes already in receipt of the maintenance grant.[152] Successive ministers prioritised enhancing the special rate over the standard maintenance grant—the top-up grant was increased by 19% in 2004, compared to 2% for the standard rate.[153] The rate of the special grant continued to increase for the rest of the decade, so that the additional non-adjacent rate was €2980 by 2013 and the income limit reached 54% of average industrial earnings.[154] This fell short of the action group's recommendation for the grant to cover actual student living costs at a reckonable limit of 75%, but represented almost a doubling of income support for non-adjacent recipients. The action group had also urged a more radical reform of student support, to include a capital test in addition to the income limit: this was intended to address successful manipulation of the grants scheme by wealthy individuals, identified by the earlier de Buitléir report in 1993.[155] But this recommendation was quietly sidelined by successive governments, not least because it would have adversely affected the interests of more privileged socio-economic groups such as the self-employed and large farmers.

Breaking the Circle?

The democratising influence of mass education transformed the gender composition of the student body from the 1960s. Female participation in the universities, which amounted to barely a third of university enrolments in 1965–66, increased to 43% by 1980–81 and 52% by 1992–93.[156] Women formed the majority of full-time students in Trinity, UCC and UCD in the early 1990s.[157] Women also took up 65% of places on arts and social science courses in 1992–93 (45% in 1965–66) and 56% in medicine/dentistry (26%)—solidifying a long-term trend in the case of arts but dramatically reversing female under-representation in professional medical disciplines.[158] Traditional variations by discipline persisted, although some were gradually eroded over time—previously male dominated disciplines such as science and agriculture were close to parity in terms of female participation in the 1990s. Female students continued to be under-represented in engineering, where the proportion of female students doubled but still remained below 20% by 1992.[159]

The combination of massification and diversification at institutional level also opened up new opportunities for women. While the emergent higher technological sector as a whole drew greater male participation by a margin of about two to one in 1980, this disparity was significantly reduced by the early 1990s, when women accounted for 43% of enrolments in the RTC/DIT sector.[160] The emergence of new art & design and business courses proved particularly attractive to female students. Women accounted for 59% of business students and a massive 79% of entrants to art, design and humanities courses in 1992–93.[161] The strong female participation in business programmes was more significant due to its status as the fastest growing discipline in the technological sector. While men still outnumbered women in the RTC/DIT sector, female participation expanded between 1980 and 1992 in almost all disciplines, with only engineering/architecture showing an insignificant rate of increase. The traditional demographic profile of higher education was transformed over a thirty year period, as increasing participation and massification eroded traditional gender differentials.[162]

Fleming et al. argue that gender equality had 'improved enormously' by the beginning of the twenty-first century, with most colleges having either a majority or at least parity in terms of female students.[163] While this was true of student participation, the situation among academic staff was very different. The number of female academics increased incrementally both in absolute and relative terms in the late 1900s, but the increased participation of women in academia was combined with marked inequalities. *Breaking the Circle*, a study conducted by Ailbhe Smyth, an academic in UCD, in 1984 found that women comprised less than 19% of academic staff in third-level institutions and were generally concentrated in the lowest promotional grades.[164] The study concluded that 'women are not formally excluded from the academic profession but... are most surely confined to a small and powerless space within it'.[165] A committee on the position of women academics in Ireland was established by the HEA in 1985 following the report at the instigation of Gemma Hussey, the first woman to serve as Minister for Education.[166]

The committee produced extensive data on the gender breakdown of academic staff in universities and other designated institutions (then the two NIHEs, NCAD and Thomond College) in 1984–85, while conducting a survey of career profiles which reached 651 male and female academics across the entire third-level sector.[167] The report found 'striking imbalances…between men and women academics in third-level', in terms of grades and fields of study.[168] There was a modest increase in the proportion of female academics since the early 1970s, from 10.5% to 14.5% in the universities and 15.5% to 18% in the other designated institutions, although this lagged well behind the expansion in the level of female students and women securing postgraduate degrees.[169] But women were heavily under-represented in the senior lecturing grades across all HEIs. Only 2% of professors and 5% of associate professors at university level were female, compared to 34% of assistant lecturers. The designated institutions showed an almost identical distribution despite their recent origins—women accounted for only 6% of senior lecturers compared to 29.5% of assistant lecturers and none at all at professorial level.[170] The study showed similar findings for the RTC/DIT sector, where women comprised 12% of academic staff in 1985, although a more detailed breakdown of numbers by grade was not available.[171] The colleges of education were an outlier, as 44% of their staff were female: this reflected not societal modernisation but the strong tradition of female religious orders in providing teacher education and the feminised nature of the teaching profession.

The survey of career profiles confirmed the striking under-representation of women across the third-level system: women accounted for 17.5% of junior lecturers, but only 3.5% of professors among the respondents.[172] The increased representation of women in the academic profession was concentrated almost entirely in the lower grades and there was no meaningful change since the early 1970s in the gender distribution of academic posts. The survey also underlined gender differentiation by field of study. Over half of female academics were concentrated in arts and social science disciplines, compared to 27% of their male counterparts.[173] Decisions on promotion remained almost entirely a male preserve—almost all respondents reported being interviewed 'by a board which was all or predominantly male.'[174] While the report did not allege overt discrimination, its findings highlighted pervasive inequalities in terms of gender and the resilience of traditional power structures which relegated women to a peripheral role.

The position in the country's oldest universities offered a case study in the persistence of gender disparities. The *Report of the Committee on the Promotion of Women* in TCD, compiled by a committee led by Prof Frances Ruane in 1989, offered similar findings to the national study, namely a notable gender imbalance which intensified as one moved up the academic ladder. The committee identified not only a low overall level of female academics in 1988–89, despite a modest improvement since 1970, but also particularly poor representation of women at senior levels, with most 'clustered in the lower ranks.'[175] The report found that while women accounted for almost 17% of all academic staff, they made up 29% of lecturers but only 5% of professors and 9% of senior lecturers.[176] Although Fellowship had been open to women since 1968, there were only five women out of 133 Fellows.[177]

The colleges of the NUI showed comparable gender disparities. Although UCD appointed an increasing number of women to junior academic posts by the early 1980s, there were no female professors or associate professors at all in 1980–81. McCartney notes that 'As far as senior academic positions were concerned, women had reached their lowest point.'[178] This was in stark contrast with the level of female participation at senior level achieved by the Dublin commission seventy years earlier and testified to the structural advantages enjoyed by men in UCD. The position in UCC was only slightly better—while the proportion of women among the ranks of senior academics marginally increased over a forty year period between 1954 and 1994 (from four to six), this was a significant relative decline among a cohort of professors which had more than doubled. John A. Murphy, a sympathetic but insightful historian of the college, commented in 1995 that 'It's still a man's world at the top in UCC.'[179] The same comment could accurately have been applied to almost all Irish HEIs outside teacher education. It was striking too that the traditional pattern of female under-representation at senior levels persisted even with the gradual modernisation of Irish society and the decline of religious influence in higher education.

Gender equality in higher education did not feature on the agenda of national policy-makers or institutional leaders until the mid 1980s. The

HEA study in 1987 focused attention on the gender imbalance among academic staff. The report urged HEIs to adopt policy statements on equal opportunity and review their procedures for recruitment, promotion and governance to secure more balanced representation of men and women.[180] But the report was couched in cautious language and its short-term impact was limited. The main impact of the study was to heighten awareness of gender inequality and generate debate about policy and practice within HEIs—not an insignificant result in the grim economic circumstances of the 1980s. The Higher Education Equality Unit (HEEU) was established in UCC and served as a forum for research and debate in the area. A publication by HEEU in 1995, consisting of contributions to conference proceedings incorporating a range of female voices, reiterated the peripheral status of women in higher education. A follow-up pilot study to *Breaking the Circle* by Smyth indicated that while the numerical representation of women academics in universities had improved to about a fifth of the full-time staff, they continued to be poorly represented in senior grades and 'the gendered division of labour in the Academy is still very marked.'[181] The institutions were more inclined to avoid all male interview or promotion boards, but their efforts often resulted in a sole female member on committees, raising suspicions of tokenism. Moreover, gender inequality was even more striking among non-academic staff within the college administration: women made up 79% of the administrative grades but held less than a quarter of senior administrative posts.[182]

Other contributions to the HEEU conference drew attention to various aspects of gender disparity. O'Sullivan pointed to the low rate of progression by women to senior administrative posts in UCD and UCC, despite the predominance of female employment in lower grades.[183] Mary Rose Burke highlighted 'a dearth of women' in senior posts within the under-researched RTC sector and a virtual monopoly by men of key leadership roles.[184] Muldowney and Leahy commented from a trade union perspective on the precarious status of the largely female catering and cleaning staff in TCD and the extent to which career advancement was linked to gender.[185] The consensus of the women contributors was that while gender equality was no longer contested in principle, actual progress at a practical level over the previous decade was minimal.

Yet the major reforms of the 1990s gave statutory underpinning to the achievement of gender equality for the first time. The White Paper in 1995 recommended that all HEIs should develop policies for gender equality, including gender balance on staff selection boards and greater participation by female students in traditionally male-dominated disciplines, such as engineering.[186] Niamh Bhreathnach gave a high priority to reducing gender disparities, promoting more women to the governing bodies of HEIs. The Universities Act, 1997, required institutions to promote 'gender balance and equality of opportunity among students and employees of the University'.[187] The development of policies to achieve 'equality, including gender equality, in all activities of the university' became a statutory obligation for the first time.[188] The adoption of equality policies and committees by the universities offered a forum to address concerns relating to gender equality, even if it did little to guarantee equity in practice, particularly in senior management. It was notable that the first real initiatives to address gender disparities in higher education were launched by women ministers. Gemma Hussey instigated the report on the position of women academics in 1985, in response to *Breaking the Circle*. Niamh Bhreathnach established equality policies as a statutory requirement in primary legislation. The de facto exclusion of women from positions of power in higher education offered ample evidence that such initiatives were necessary, even if they offered no guarantee of early change on the ground.

'A regulatory regime built on mistrust...'

Universities legislation had been contemplated since the mid 1960s, but finally became a reality in the 1990s. The expansion of the HE system produced greater fiscal, demographic and political pressures, intensifying official demands for tighter regulation and more rigorous accountability measures. A position paper issued by the minister in November 1995 sketched out a new legislative and regulatory framework for university education. This policy statement envisaged a reconstitution of university governing bodies to incorporate substantial external representation and a significant increase in the powers of the HEA with regard to oversight of university budgets, finances and staffing structures.[189] The paper also included the reconstitution of the three university colleges and the recognised college at Maynooth as constituent universities within the NUI.

The minister had floated the idea in July 1995 that the NUI might be dissolved following the reconstitution of its colleges, contrary to proposals made by the NUI senate for the retention of the charter and the federal link in a modifed form.[190] This proposal triggered a vigorous response from Whitaker, as the NUI standing committee noted: 'These proposals…provoked a quick and vehement response from the Chancellor. The Presidents, collectively and individually, had also responded to the Department's new proposals, as a result of which the Department now intends that the original White Paper commitment will be implemented.'[191] The department quickly clarified that the NUI would not be dissolved and this commitment was incorporated in the final position paper.[192] Following negotiations between the NUI officers led by Whitaker and departmental officials early in 1996, the senate's proposals for four constituent universities within a federal NUI were included in the Bill and a senate meeting in April 1996 noted that the NUI's representations had been 'substantially accepted'.[193]

The departmental plans for increased regulation of the universities in terms of governance, staffing and finance proved much more contentious. The first shot in what proved to be a prolonged struggle was fired by Dr. Seán Barrett, an economics lecturer and Fellow of TCD, who argued in the *Sunday Independent* that leaks of the proposed legislation were designed 'to soften up public opinion for changing Trinity College Dublin from an autonomous university into a Labour Party quango'.[194] Perhaps more significantly, most university presidents were firmly opposed to the extension of state control envisaged by the position paper, with the exception of the presidents of UL and DCU where the legislation gave greater autonomy to the new universities.[195] Both the content and tone of the position paper aroused anger among academics: a number of contributions at a special meeting of the NUI senate in December 1995 revealed irritation at the apparent lack of sympathy with university education:

> It is regrettable that the Position Paper, which should be projecting towards the new millennium in a language of hope, is presented in such a negative form….

> Many of the provisions in the Position Paper…depict a regulatory regime built on mistrust, which becomes the underlying theme.[196]

The publication of the universities Bill in July 1996 did not allay the fears of university leaders or other academic critics represented by IFUT regarding state control over management, pay and staffing. The legislation provided for the appointment of up to four ministerial nominees to university governing bodies, including external nominees to the Board of TCD for the first time and additional external nominees to the other governing authorities. But the most contentious feature of the Bill was a dramatic expansion in the regulatory authority of the HEA, including new requirements on universities to submit strategic development plans and annual reports to the authority; issuing of guidelines on the detail of university budgets by the HEA; greater control by the authority over staffing and restrictions on borrowing by universities without ministerial consent.[197] The department was hardly surprised when the Fellows of TCD rejected the Bill as an 'unnecessary intrusion' which undermined the autonomy of all Irish universities.[198] But opposition to the Bill extended far beyond Trinity, with representatives of the NUI and all three of its university colleges criticising aspects of the legislation. Whitaker told the NUI senate in October 1996 that the 'main criticism of the Bill was its invasion of the legitimate management freedom of the university…', citing particularly 'the ultimate control by the HEA' over the number and grades of staff and distribution of institutional budgets between different activities.[199] The NUI issued a public response seeking 18 substantive changes to the Bill, reflecting a high level of consensus among senior academics across its colleges on the shortcomings of the legislation. The governing body of UCG issued an even more trenchant statement, attacking the Bill as 'a heavy handed and bureaucratically stifling' piece of legislation which gave the HEA a 'presiding presence' in every aspect of university operations.[200]

Opposition to the Bill quickly moved beyond the groves of academe. Garret FitzGerald, the leader of the previous Fine Gael-Labour coalition, pulled no punches in attacking the Bill in September 1996. Describing the legislation as 'an extraordinarily authoritarian, indeed Thatcherite Bill', the former Taoiseach criticised the additional powers envisaged for the HEA as an unacceptable restriction of university autonomy.[201] This level of public and institutional opposition was ominous for a three-party coalition government which lacked a majority in Seanad Éireann. The government's precarious position in the Seanad gave exceptional leverage to the six university senators, as the Bill faced the prospect of defeat if all the university senators combined with the opposition parties, Fianna Fáil and the Progressive Democrats.[202] The exceptional political context paved the way for an influential academic, graduate and political lobby to transform the legislation.

Yet there were differences among university leaders and particularly within academic institutions over the optimal response to the Bill. Most university leaders sought to amend the Bill, albeit drastically, while a section of academic opinion sought to block it completely as a fundamental threat to university autonomy: among the most outspoken opponents of the Bill were Barrett and TCD Senator Shane Ross (ironically the only senator to hold a party whip as a member of Fine Gael). Trinity also had a distinctive agenda, seeking a private member's bill to amend the 1911 Charter and Letters Patent in line with wider universities legislation, to limit the impact of legislation on the college's statutes.

Bhreathnach signalled her willingness to compromise, assuring the Dáil on 30 October that she wished to 'dispel any impression that this Bill indicates that the Minister intends to take control of the universities…'.[203] The minister's conciliatory statement was only the starting point for a wholesale transformation of the original Bill through an exceptionally effective process of lobbying by university leaders in the Conference of the Heads of Irish Universities (CHIU), senators and a wider academic lobby championed by IFUT. The transformation of the Bill was facilitated by an extraordinary intervention from the HEA, which placed an advertisement in national newspapers on 30 October

1996 defending its own role and emphasising its support for the existing relationship between the authority and the universities: 'The HEA
believes that this process has worked well, with a satisfactory outcome
for both the universities and the State. It has not sought and would
not wish that any change in this process would be reflected in the legislation'.[204] John Walshe, the education editor of the *Irish Independent*,
commented that the Bill had set out to confer powers on the HEA
'that it clearly did not want'.[205] The striking intervention by the HEA
helped to produce a more acceptable Bill. The minister presented 106
amendments to the original bill in December 1996, which significantly
reduced the powers assigned to the HEA: proposed 'guidelines' on
budgets and staffing would not be mandatory and the block on borrowing without ministerial consent was removed. The maximum size of
a governing authority was increased from 31 to 38 to allow for greater
representation by academic staff and students.[206] The revised legislation
met many of the objectives of university leaders, although it did not
go far enough to satisfy more ideological opponents of state intervention. The HEA's initiative reflected its willingness to act as a 'buffer'
agency at a moment of conflict between the government and the universities, as it had done a quarter of a century earlier on the merger and
NIHE Limerick.[207]

The university senators enjoyed a pivotal position in the Seanad
debate on the Bill. The second reading in March 1997 was approved by
four votes (27–23), with only three university senators supporting the
Bill at that stage.[208] The outcome highlighted the government's precarious position and maintained the pressure for further concessions. The
critics of the legislation fell into two main camps—those who opposed
the Bill as an unacceptable encroachment on university autonomy and
those who objected to its original interventionist impulses but now
saw an opportunity to secure an acceptable version of the legislation.
Ross, who resigned from Fine Gael to oppose the legislation, was firmly
in the first camp: he attacked the Bill as 'a fundamentally retrograde
step' based on the principle of state control of third-level education.
For good measure he expressed stupefaction at the prospect of county
councillors on the board of TCD 'as the most absurd suggestion I ever
came across': this intervention drew an angry rejoinder from fellow

Senator Maurice Manning (an academic in UCD), who accused his colleague of 'ignorant, baseless snobbery'.[209] Most university senators, however, sought to amend the bill to meet the objections of CHIU, IFUT and university governing bodies. Among the substantial amendments secured during the tortuous process of parliamentary ratification were restricting the proposed financial oversight of the institutions by the HEA; placing responsibility for quality assurance primarily with the governing body and the addition of a section offering explicit protection to academic freedom for individual staff and institutional autonomy.[210] A late change was also made in the clause providing for academic councils to protect Trinity's council structure, following a last minute intervention by the provost, Tom Mitchell and Senator David Norris.[211] 37 amendments were made during the Seanad debates and over 200 were accepted throughout the parliamentary process: the Bill was 'one of the most amended pieces of legislation in the history of the State'.[212]

The concessions were sufficient to win the support of the governing bodies of UCC, UCD and Maynooth, as well as de facto acceptance by the Board of TCD. The process of transformation was so complete that by April 1997 the main concern of the NUI standing committee was that 'the revised Bill risks not being enacted because of the possible early dissolution of Dáil Éireann'.[213] The standing committee was alarmed enough at this prospect, which would have prevented the long awaited reconstitution of the NUI, that it not only called for the legislation to be passed but offered to meet university senators to promote the Bill.[214] The final legislation passed the Seanad on 24 April 1997 without a vote, having secured the support of five of the six university senators.[215] The final Bill was quickly approved by the Dáil, with the sole dissenting voice coming from the former PD leader, Des O'Malley.[216] The approval of the universities Bill without a vote in the Oireachtas, which would have seemed inconceivable a few months earlier, reflected the extent to which the legislation had been transformed out of all recognition.

The Universities Act, brought into effect by Bhreathnach on 13 June 1997 in one of her final acts as minister, was the first comprehensive legislation on the position of universities in Ireland in the independent Irish state. The minister received little credit for the tortuous process of conflict and conciliation which produced the final legislation. Yet the

Universities Act was one of the most significant initiatives by the Irish state in higher education since 1922. The legislation created a common statutory framework for all universities in Ireland for the first time and redefined the relationship between universities and the state. The 1997 act reconstituted the NUI, establishing UCD, UCC, UCG and the recognised college at Maynooth as constituent universities, while maintaining the federal institution in a diluted form.[217] The legislation also signalled the end of Maynooth's long-term dual status, prompting an institutional division between the seminary and recognised college which had been considered over a long period. The arts and science faculties of the recognised college secured constituent university status within the NUI, while St. Patrick's College continued as a seminary and pontifical university.[218] The legislation allowed a separate Private Members' Bill for Trinity College, amending the royal Charter and Letters Patent of TCD in a form consistent with the universities act, provided that such an act was passed within three years.[219] The private members' act, approved by the Oireachtas in 2000, implemented the universities legislation while confirming the remainder of the Charter and Letters Patent.[220]

The Universities Act recognised the right of the university to 'preserve and promote the traditional principles of academic freedom in the conduct of its internal and external affairs' and affirmed the freedom of academic staff in their teaching, research and other activities.[221] The autonomy of the institution was qualified, by specific requirements to promote equality of access and maintain 'obligations as to public accountability', although the act also confirmed that in subsequent interpretation of the legislation, an interpretation favouring the principles of academic freedom would be preferred.[222] Institutional autonomy was recognised within a framework of enhanced accountability and implicitly, responsiveness to national priorities. New statutory obligations were imposed on universities, notably the adoption of regular strategic plans and establishment of QA procedures.[223] The universities were also required to develop and implement equality policies promoting access to university education for under-represented groups and gender equality in all university activities. The governing authority was obliged to submit annually a draft statement of income and expenditure to the HEA, which continued to allocate state funding for the university budget: the chief officer of the university was required to inform the HEA of any 'material departure' from the budget.[224] The authority was empowered to issue guidelines to universities on staffing and the detailed breakdown of the budget, but such guidelines were not binding on the institutions.

Academic and political opponents of the legislation, including Ross and Barrett, insisted that the act represented unacceptable intrusion by the state on the academy. College presidents were equally convinced that they had protected the autonomy of the universities. CHIU even released a press statement in May 1997 thanking the minister and department for their 'open and constructive approach' to consultation with the universities.[225] Much of the subsequent commentary on the legislation has been favourable to the new university settlement. Walshe suggested that despite flaws in the initial process of consultation Bhreathnach eventually succeeded in achieving a 'balanced bill'.[226] Coolahan considered that the legislation 'represented a modernisation of the university system in line with contemporary thinking...' and achieved 'a reasonable balance' between safeguarding institutional autonomy and the legitimate demands of public policy and accountability, a conclusion shared by most university senators.[227] Clancy offered a more qualified conclusion that the universities, in neutralising the most threatening features of the universities legislation, achieved "something of a success in resisting the 'evaluative state'", although this may have been a 'pyrrhic victory', as it did not prevent a subsequent rebalancing of state-university relations in the early 2000s.[228]

The Universities Act was a response to the transformation of the higher education system over the previous generation. The legislation originally envisaged a significant redefinition of the boundary between the Irish state and the universities. This interventionist agenda, driven more by senior officials of the Departments of Education and Finance than by politicians or the HEA, met strong, vocally articulated resistance from a variety of actors within the university system, including institutional leaders, trade unions and senators. Hedley argued that the final shape of the legislation was a product of its time, as its promoters were 'powerful enough to force the legislation through, but not powerful enough to resist changes designed explicitly to subvert it.'[229] Certainly a well organised university lobby enjoyed considerable success, not least due to the exceptional political context and the intervention of the HEA, in transforming the original legislation in a manner which largely frustrated the official agenda for a more radical assertion of power by the regulatory state. It was the most successful example of resistance to an interventionist state by the university sector since the failure of the original plan for merger in the early 1970s.

Yet as Clancy indicated the outcome was by no means an unqualified success for the universities. While the far-reaching powers originally envisaged for the HEA were dramatically scaled back, the legislation enhanced the regulatory role of the authority, which would review three-year institutional strategies and oversee quality assurance procedures, while maintaining its pivotal role in the allocation of resources and oversight of university budgets. Although the Universities Act affirmed the right of each institution to regulate its own affairs in accordance with its own ethos and 'the traditional principles of academic freedom...', there was an implicit tension between this clause and the increased monitoring role of the HEA. While the HEA's role was primarily to advise and oversee universities, rather than direct their activity, it was never made clear to what extent institutions had to observe the wishes of the authority or its political masters.[230] This balance between university and government would be determined by negotiation and ultimately by financial pressure. Moreover, the explicit provision for quality assurance procedures in legislation was another innovation with long-term consequences, even if universities retained direct ownership of the quality assurance system.[231] The outcome was ultimately a compromise between the 'reform' agenda of influential actors within the political and official realm who sought intensification of official regulation and the still robust claims of institutional autonomy.

The debate over the universities legislation also had reverberations throughout the higher education system, as the government sought to contain demands for university status by the larger technical colleges. The HEA and departmental officials opposed the creation of any new universities but were willing to contemplate upgrading the status of

DIT and the larger RTCs. The Steering Committee in 1995 recommended a redesignation of the RTCs as regional institutes of technology, 'without changing the current thrust of their activities or the distinctive role of the colleges.'[232] A determined campaign by DIT to secure university status failed to convince two governments between 1995 and 1998.[233] The DIT president, Brendan Goldsmith, lobbied vigorously for university status during the debates over the Universities Act, but despite qualified support from an international review panel for university status within five years, the college's application was rejected by the HEA.[234] The institute was given full degree awarding powers up to doctoral level from 1998 and the long-term association between Trinity and DIT was phased out by 2001.[235]

Yet attempts to offer incremental advances to the non-university colleges inevitably created precedents, not to mention being fraught with political danger. A long-term campaign for university status by Waterford RTC brought the issue of redesignation to the fore in the run-up to a general election in 1997.[236] Following a recommendation by the Steering Committee for an expanded institute in Waterford with greater degree level courses, Bhreathnach announced in January 1997 that Waterford RTC would be upgraded to Institute of Technology status, with the power to award its own qualifications within a new national framework.[237] This initiative provoked an angry response among the other RTCs; outrage among staff and students in the Cork college was particularly marked and even provoked an independent campaign for the Dáil by the students' union in June 1997.[238] A review group established by the minister quickly reported in favour of the redesignation of all 11 RTCs to institute of technology status. Following the election of a new Fianna Fáil-led government, Bhreathnach's successor, Micheál Martin (not coincidentally a TD representing Cork city), first upgraded Cork to IoT status and in January 1998 signed an order to redesignate all the remaining RTCs as Institutes of Technology.[239] The department emphasised that the change was 'one of name not of status', indicating that it was mainly about improving the image of the colleges at home and abroad.[240] Certainly the tangible result of the change was relatively limited, as it did not include automatic delegation of independent degree awarding powers, which was linked instead to the development of a new national qualifications system. Yet the redesignation occurred in response to sustained pressure for increased autonomy from the RTC sector, allied to demands for university status from DIT and Waterford. The response of the government, while certainly influenced by regional and constituency concerns, was to offer incremental advances in status and prestige while holding the line on any new universities.

The Universities Act formed part of the most extensive body of legislation in education adopted since 1922, which had longer-term implications for the different strands of higher education.[241] The Teaching Council Act, 2001, provided the legal underpinning for the creation of the Teaching Council as the statutory agency responsible for the regulation of the teaching profession and the education, training and professional development of teachers: while the Council was established only in 2006, it soon forged an influential role in approving third level programmes in initial teacher education.[242] The raft of legislation encompassed a modernisation of the framework for higher technical education. Bhreathnach established TEASTAS as an interim national certification authority on an ad hoc basis in September 1995, with the remit of combining a number of disparate accreditation systems for the RTC/DIT sector, further education and second-level vocational courses.[243] The activity of TEASTAS attracted its fair share of controversy, not least because it engaged with a wide range of diverse groups which had no previous history of collaboration and was unable to identify any consensus among them: O'Sullivan suggests that the only thing that they agreed on was 'that everybody is opposed to TEASTAS'.[244] The interim authority upset a number of stakeholders in the area by proposing the replacement of the NCEA and a number of other awarding bodies in further education and training with two new awarding bodies for higher education and training and further education outside the third level sector respectively.[245] Yet TEASTAS proved influential in shaping the new legislative framework for qualifications and quality assurance, providing much of the road map for legislation, although the group itself was wound down in 1998.[246]

The Qualifications (Education and Training) Act, 1999 established a national system for the validation of higher education qualifications and a new framework for quality assurance for non-university institutions.[247] The legislation completed a sometimes messy process of policy clarification, innovation and reform which had been ongoing for the most of the 1990s.[248] Martin announced that the Bill was designed to establish for the first time 'a national framework of qualifications and routes for access, transfer and progression…'.[249] He also emphasised the need in developing the national framework to protect 'the balance of provision' in HEIs, such as DIT, operating at multiple qualification levels, so as '…not to undermine provision for sub-degree level programmes in particular, which have such a crucial role in meeting the skills needs of the future.'[250] While the legislation offered a process for future development by the IoTs, this was intended to be 'both detailed and exacting'.[251] Whatever else might have changed, limiting 'mission drift' and preserving the non-degree functions of the technological sector remained a priority for policymakers.[252]

The cornerstone of the legislation was the National Qualifications Authority of Ireland (NQAI), which was established in 2001, to devise the national framework of qualifications; assure the standards of awards in non-university higher and further education and facilitate access, transfer and progression between institutions.[253] The legislation also provided for the creation of the Higher Education and Training Awards Council (HETAC), which replaced the NCEA for the IoT/higher technical sector.[254] The Further Education and Training Awards Council (FETAC) was assigned a similar function for further education programmes and awards.[255] HETAC was empowered to delegate the power to recognised institutions to make their own awards. Waterford and Cork IoTs were the first to be allowed to make non-degree awards, in line with the recommendations of a review group led by Prof Dervilla Donnelly; this was extended to degree awarding powers for both IoTs in 2003 and to research degrees for WIT.[256] This did nothing to reduce agitation for degree awarding powers and increasingly university status by a majority of IoTs, all of whom were engaged in studies to degree, masters and sometimes doctoral level by the early 2000s, although the scope of such programmes varied dramatically.

A series of policy and legislative reforms which germinated over the previous two decades came to fruition in the mid to late 1990s, which was a period of exceptional creativity in educational policy analysis and legislation.[257] Yet while the volume of legislation was exceptional by historical standards, the level of re-appraisal and policy innovation was comparable to the mid to late 1960s when the modern HE system was forged and the intensive policy activity sought to manage and regulate the massified, diversified system largely created by the earlier reforms. The range and ambition of government initiatives contributed to a high level of contestation over the relationship between the state and academic institutions, which reached a comparable intensity to the debates over merger a generation earlier. The reforms sought by an interventionist state inspired resistance from university leaders and academics, who were often successful in blocking or substantially modifying major government initiatives, and from the VECs, whose role in non-university higher education was curtailed. The transformation of the universities legislation, achievement of university status by the NIHEs and the upgrading of the RTCs to IoT status all testified to the efficacy of well organised lobby groups rooted in academic institutions, which proved capable of mobilising regional and political alliances to influence policy and legislative outcomes. Yet many aspects of policy and institutional reform in the 1990s created the potential for a stronger, more authoritative political and administrative centre. The abolition of tuition fees; emergence of a new institutional settlement for the university sector and development of a national framework for programme validation and quality assurance for non-university institutions, increased the power of the government, HEA and other state agencies in higher education at the beginning of the twenty-first century. The long-term consequences of this shift in the balance of power were not entirely appreciated in an era of unprecedented economic success and only became fully apparent after the crash of 2008

Notes

1. Mark Olssen and Michael Peters, 'Neoliberalism, Higher Education and the Knowledge Economy: From the Free Market to Knowledge Capitalism,' *Journal of Education Policy* 20, no. 3 (2005): 313–4.

2. Massimiliano Vaira, 'Globalisation and Higher Education: A Framework for Analysis,' *Higher Education* 48 (2004): 487.
3. Olssen and Peters, 'Neoliberalism, Higher Education and the Knowledge Economy,' *Journal of Education Policy* 20, no. 3 (2005): 316.
4. Ibid., 313.
5. Ewan Ferlie, Christine Musselin and Gianluca Andresani, 'The Steering of Higher Education Systems: A Public Management Perspective,' *Higher Education* 56, no 3 (2009): 325–48.
6. Tony Fahey and John FitzGerald, 'The Educational Revolution and Demographic Change,' in *Medium Term Review: 1997–2003*, ed. David Duffy et al. (Dublin: ESRI, 1997), 9–13.
7. Department of Education, *Programme for Action in Education* (Dublin: Stationery Office, 1984), 3.
8. C. O'Grady to Private Secretary to the Taoiseach, 15 July 1983 (NAI TSCH 2013/100/208).
9. Ibid.
10. John Kelly to Garret FitzGerald, 8 March 1983 (NAI TSCH 2013/100/207).
11. Kelly to Nuala Fennell TD, July 1983 (NAI TSCH 2013/100/208).
12. Memorandum to the Government, 'Investment Programme for Third-Level Education,' September 1983 (NAI TSCH 2013/100/208).
13. Ibid.
14. Ibid., 2.
15. Ibid., 1.
16. Appendix A to Memorandum to the Government, 'Investment Programme for Third Level,' September 1983 (NAI TSCH 2013/100/207), 1–2.
17. Memorandum to the Government, 'Investment Programme for Third-Level Education,' September 1983 (NAI TSCH 2013/100/207), 4.
18. Ibid.
19. Gemma Hussey, *At the Cutting Edge, Cabinet Diaries 1982–87* (Dublin: Gill and Macmillan, 1990), 78.
20. Ibid., 102.
21. Department of Education, *Programme for Action*, 28–9.
22. Ibid., 29–30.

23. Clancy, *Irish Higher Education*, 236.
24. Ibid., 31.
25. Ibid., 31.
26. HEA, *General Report 1974–84*, 43–4.
27. Ibid., 29.
28. HEA, *Interim Report of the Technical Working Group*, 44.
29. Ibid., 18.
30. Ibid., 40; HEA, *Report of the Steering Committee on the Future Development of Higher Education (Based on a Study of Needs to the Year 2015)* (Dublin: HEA, 1995), 26; White, *Investing in Education*, 200.
31. HEA, *Interim Report of the Technical Working Group*, 39–40.
32. Hussey, *At the Cutting Edge*, 194–5: Hussey believed that she was the first minister to negotiate with the EC on ESF funding for the RTCs—while this was incorrect, it underlined the caution and even secrecy which attended the ESF negotiations and official pronouncements on the level of support for diploma and certificate programmes.
33. Ellen Hazelkorn, Andrew Gibson, and Siobhán Harkin, 'From Massification to Globalisation: Reflections on the Transformation of Irish Higher Education,' in *The State in Transition: Essays in Honour of John Horgan*, ed. Kevin Rafter and Mark O'Brien (Dublin: New Island, 2015), 256.
34. Rory O'Sullivan, "From the 'Cinderella' to 'the Fourth Pillar' of the Irish Education System—A Critical Analysis of the Evolution of Further Education and Training in Ireland" (Ph.D. diss., TCD, 2018), 162.
35. Ibid., 164.
36. Ibid., 164–5; White, *Investing in People*, 198.
37. Dáil Debates, vol. 504, no. 7, 18 May 1999, col. 1287.
38. *Irish Times*, 'Carysfort a Victim of Falling Rolls,' 6 February 1986.
39. Ibid.
40. Ciarán Sugrue, 'Three Decades of College Life, 1973–1999: The Old Order Changeth?' in *St. Patrick's College, Drumcondra 1875–2000: A History*, ed. James Kelly (Dublin: Four Courts, 2006), 244.
41. Garret FitzGerald, *All in a Life* (Dublin: Gill and Macmillan 1991), 621–2.
42. *Irish Times*, 'Government Decides to Close Carysfort College,' 5 February 1986.
43. Hussey, *At the Cutting Edge*, 101.

44. *Irish Times*, 'Carysfort a Victim of Falling Rolls,' 5 February 1986.
45. Hussey, *At the Cutting Edge*, 196.
46. *Irish Times*, 'Carysfort Decision "Clumsy,"' 7 February 1986.
47. Hussey, *At the Cutting Edge*, 196–7.
48. Coleman, *IFUT*, 31.
49. *Irish Times*, 'Carysfort a Victim of Falling Rolls,' 6 February 1986.
50. Coleman, *IFUT*, 31–2.
51. Ibid.
52. Ibid., 32.
53. Sugrue, 'Three Decades of College Life, 1973–1999: The Old Order Changeth?' 252.
54. Ibid.; O'Connor, *Passing on the Torch*, 71–2.
55. O'Flynn, *A Question of Identity*, 157; White, *Investing in Education*, 211–15.
56. Coolahan, 'The National University of Ireland,' 270.
57. Mary O'Rourke, *Just Mary: A Memoir* (Dublin: Gill and Macmillan, 2012), 62–3.
58. Ibid.
59. White, *Investing in Education*, 214.
60. Dáil debates, vol. 309, 25 May 1989, col. 1410.
61. A former Foreign Minister, FitzGerald served two terms as Taoiseach (1981–82; 1982–87) and was later chancellor of the NUI (1997–2007). Michael D. Higgins is a long serving Labour Party TD and Cabinet Minister who was elected as President of Ireland in 2011.
62. Dáil Debates, vol. 309, 25 May 1989, col. 1388–1409.
63. Oireachtas Éireann, No. 16 of 1992.
64. Clarke, 'The Development of Vocational Education,' 313.
65. Dáil Debates, vol. 420, no. 7, 4 June 1992, col. 1477–1536.
66. Ibid.; Dáil Debates, vol. 421, no. 2, 1 July 1992, col. 2006–54; Cooke, *Irish Vocational Education Association*, 586–7.
67. Dáil Debates, vol. 421, no. 2, 1 July 1992, col. 2006–54; Cooke, *Irish Vocational Education Association*, 586–7.
68. Oireachtas Éireann, No. 16 of 1992.
69. Dáil Debates, vol. 421, no. 2, 1 July 1992, col. 2247–86: this assurance was regarded as crucial by the IVEA and was also included in the RTC legislation.
70. Oireachtas Éireann, No. 15 of 1992.
71. Ibid.; Oireachtas Éireann, No. 16 of 1992.

72. Nolan, 'The Recognised Colleges,' 206; O'Connor, *Passing on the Torch*, 72–3.
73. O'Connor, *Passing on the Torch*, 75.
74. Ibid., 76.
75. White, *Investing in Education*, 189; O'Donoghue et al., *Teacher Preparation in Ireland*, 140–1.
76. Sugrue, 'Three Decades of College Life, 1973–1999: The Old Order Changeth?' 252.
77. Ibid., 252–3.
78. White, *Investing in Education*, 215.
79. Department of Education, *Education for a Changing World: Green Paper on Education* (Dublin: Stationery Office, 1992), 184; Department of Education, *Charting Our Education Future: White Paper on Education* (Dublin, Stationery Office, 1995), 92–3.
80. Guy Neave, 'Academic Drift: Some Views from Europe,' *Studies in Higher Education* 4, no. 2 (1979): 143–59. https://doi.org/10.10 80/03075077912331376927; Ludovic Highman, 'A Case Study on Differentiation in the Mission and Role of Higher Education Institutions in Ireland' (Ph.D. diss., TCD, 2015), 43–5.
81. Coolahan, *Era of Lifelong Learning*, 234.
82. See below pp. 370–1 for the failure of DIT's campaign for university status in the 1990s.
83. OECD, *Review of Higher Education in Ireland*, 7.
84. Ó Buachalla, 'Self-Regulation and the Emergence of the Evaluative State: Trends in Irish Educational Policy, 1987–92,' *European Journal of Education* 27, no. 1/2 (1992): 69–78.
85. Ibid., 72–4.
86. Hazelkorn et al., 'From Massification to Globalisation: Reflections on the Transformation of Irish Higher Education,' 256.
87. Malcolm Skilbeck, *Towards an Integrated System of Tertiary Education: A Discussion Paper* (Dublin: DIT, 2003), 15. Accessed 1 September 2013. https://dit.ie/media/newsdocuments/2003/Skilbeckdiscussionpaper_march2003.pdf.
88. HEA, *Interim Report of the Technical Working Group*, 27.
89. Ó Buachalla, 'Self-Regulation and the Emergence of the Evaluative State: Trends in Irish Educational Policy, 1987–92,' *European Journal of Education* 27, no. 1/2 (1992): 74.
90. Ibid., 70.

91. Coolahan, *Era of Lifelong Learning*, 234.
92. Department of Education, *Education for a Changing World*, 21.
93. Ibid., 196.
94. Ibid., 201.
95. Ibid., 201–2.
96. HEA, *Interim Report of the Technical Working Group*, 1.
97. Ibid., 2.
98. Ibid., 27: the rate identified first time entrants at typical age of entry. This made comparisons somewhat problematic as not all countries could identify first-time entrants to tertiary education programmes.
99. Ibid., 11.
100. Ibid., 12.
101. Ibid., 13–5.
102. Ibid., 2.
103. Ibid., 5.
104. Ibid., 10.
105. Coolahan, 'The NUI,' 274.
106. Department of Education, *Charting Our Education Future*, 88.
107. Ibid., 103–5.
108. Ibid., 95.
109. See below p. 362 for the White Paper's recommendations on gender equality.
110. Department of Education, *Charting Our Education Future*, 100.
111. Ibid., 96.
112. Ibid., 96.
113. Ibid., 97.
114. HEA, *Interim Report of the Technical Working Group*, 18; *Irish Times*, 'West Dublin to Get First College Aiming Courses at Disadvantaged,' 30 January 1998; *Irish Times*, 'Martin Launches New Institute of Technology,' 1 October 1998.
115. HEA, Steering Committee, 18–19.
116. Department of Education, *Charting Our Education Future*, 101.
117. *Irish Times*, 'Abolition of Fees May Be Liked or Loathed But It Is Historic,' 29 December 1995.
118. *Irish Times*, 'A Farewell to Fees,' 7 February 1995; the free fees issue triggered a sharp division between student unions, attracting the strong support of USI but being opposed by students' unions in UCD and Trinity.

119. *Irish Times*, 'Ripples from Report on Student Fees Will Cause Waves Across Sea,' 2 August 1997.
120. John FitzGerald et al., *National Investment Priorities for the Period 2000 to 2006* (Dublin: ESRI, 1999), 201.
121. John Walshe, *A New Partnership in Education: From Consultation to Legislation in the Nineties* (Dublin: IPA, 1999), 124–5.
122. Clancy, *Irish Higher Education*, 243.
123. HEA, *Interim Report of the Technical Working Group*, 51–5.
124. Department of Education, *Statistical Report 1997–98*, 83.
125. HEA, *Interim Report of the Technical Working Group*, 154; HEA, *Higher Education 2015–16—Key Facts and Figures* (Dublin: HEA: 2016), 6.
126. HEA, *Interim Report of the Technical Working Group*, 24; HEA, *Higher Education 2015–16*, 6.
127. HEA, *National Plan for Equity of Access to Higher Education 2015–19* (Dublin: HEA, 2015), 14; Report of the Expert Group on Future Funding for Higher Education, *Investing in National Ambition—A Strategy for Funding Higher Education* (Dublin: Department of Education and Skills, 2016), 14: the baseline age cohort is not the same for different years, which explains some variations in the age participation rate in figures presented by the HEA in the early 2000s and more recently.
128. HEA, *Higher Education 2015–16*, 2.
129. HEA, *National Plan*, 33.
130. HEA, *Higher Education System Performance 2014–16—Second Report of the HEA to the Minister for Education and Skills* (Dublin: HEA, 2016), 29.
131. Department of Education and Skills, *National Strategy for Higher Education to 2030—Report of the Strategy Group* (Dublin: DES, 2011), 31.
132. OECD, *Review of National Policies for Education: Higher Education in Ireland—Examiners' Report* (Paris: OECD, 2004), 11.
133. Ibid., 27.
134. White, *Investing in Education*, 194: if the Higher Diploma in Education where numbers fluctuated significantly over time was included in this total, the proportion of postgraduate enrolments remained broadly the same over this period.

135. HEA, *Steering Committee*, 36–7: the report did not include precise figures for postgraduate numbers in the non-university sector.

136. HEA, *Higher Education System Performance 2014–16*, 2.

137. Patrick Clancy and Ciaran Benson, *Higher Education in Dublin* a *Study of Some Emerging Trends* (Dublin: HEA, 1979); Patrick Clancy, *Who Goes to College? A Second National Survey of Participation in Higher Education* (Dublin: HEA, 1988).

138. Loxley et al., 'Access and Widening Participation: Stories from the Policy Domain,' in *Access and Participation in Irish Higher Education*, ed. Ted Fleming et al. (London: Palgrave, 2017), 49.

139. Ibid., 49–50.

140. Department of Education and Science, *Report of the Action Group on Access to Third Level Education* (Dublin: DES, 2001), 150–1; Loxley et al., 'Routes In: Access Categories, Mechanisms and Processes,' in *Access and Participation in Irish Higher Education*, ed. Fleming et al. (London: Palgrave, 2017), 88–91.

141. DES, *Report of the Action Group*, 119.

142. Ibid.

143. Ibid.

144. Ibid., 35.

145. Ibid., 124.

146. Ibid., 125.

147. Ibid., 44.

148. Ibid., 133.

149. Ibid., 53–5.

150. Loxley et al., 'Access and Widening Participation: Stories from the Policy Domain,' in *Access and Participation in Irish Higher Education*, ed. Ted Fleming et al. (London: Palgrave, 2017), 57–8.

151. DES, *Report of the Action Group*, 53.

152. Clancy, *Irish Higher Education*, 228.

153. *Irish Times*, 'Higher Education Grant to Increase by 2%,' 29 June 2004.

154. Clancy, *Irish Higher Education*, 228.

155. DES, *Report of the Action Group*, 59.

156. HEA, *Interim Report of the Technical Working Group*, 19.

157. Luce, *Trinity College Dublin*, 153; McCartney, *UCD*, 83; Murphy, *The College*, 131.

158. HEA, *Interim Report of the Technical Working Group*, 29.

159. Ibid.
160. Ibid., 30.
161. Ibid., 30.
162. See Chapter 9 for continuing under-representation of women among senior academic staff.
163. Fleming et al., *Access and Participation in Higher Education*, 28.
164. HEA, *Women Academics in Ireland: Report of the Committee on the Position of Women Academics in Third Level Education in Ireland* (Dublin: HEA, 1987), 6.
165. Ailbhe Smyth, 'Reviewing Breaking the Circle: A Pilot Project,' in *Proceedings of Conference Held in UCG*, 22–23 September 1995. Accessed 1 September 2017. https://www.ucc.ie/publications/heeu/womenstf/1_smyth.htm#top.
166. HEA, *Women Academics in Ireland*, 6.
167. The RTCs and colleges of education were non-designated HEIs in the 1980s, limiting the data available to the HEA and the report also drew attention to deficits in data about applications, interviews and appointments of staff in terms of gender.
168. HEA, *Women Academics in Ireland*, 5.
169. Ibid., 15.
170. Ibid., 16.
171. Ibid., 22.
172. Ibid., 22.
173. Ibid., 22–8.
174. Ibid., 25.
175. Maryann Valiulis, 'The Establishment of the Centre for Gender and Women's Studies,' in *A Danger to the Men*, ed. Susan Parkes (Dublin: Lilliput Press, 2004), 224.
176. Ibid.
177. Ibid., 223.
178. McCartney, *UCD*, 84.
179. Murphy, *The College*, 346.
180. HEA, *Women Academics in Ireland*, 30.
181. Ailbhe Smyth, 'Reviewing Breaking the Circle: A Pilot Project,' in *Proceedings of HEEU Conference Held in UCG*, 22–23 September 1995. Accessed 1 September 2017. https://www.ucc.ie/publications/heeu/womenstf/1_smyth.htm#top.
182. Ibid.

183. Irene O'Sullivan, 'Administrative Staff in a University Environment,' in *HEEU Conference Proceedings*, 22–23 September 1995. Accessed 1 September 2017. https://www.ucc.ie/publications/heeu/womenstf/6_sullivan.htm#top.

184. Mary Rose Burke, 'Women Staff in the RTC Sector,' in *HEEU Conference Proceedings*. Accessed 1 September 2017. https://www.ucc.ie/publications/heeu/womenstf/2_burke.htm#top.

185. Mary Leahy and Mary Muldowney, 'Catering and Cleaning Workers in a University Environment,' in *HEEU Conference Proceedings*, 22–23 September 1995. Accessed 1 September 2017. https://www.ucc.ie/publications/heeu/womenstf/5_leahy.htm#top.

186. Department of Education, *Charting Our Education Future: White Paper on Education* (Dublin: Stationery Office, 1995), 102.

187. Oireachtas Éireann, Universities Act, No. 24 of 1997, S. 1.12.

188. Ibid., 36.1.

189. Department of Education, *Position Paper* (Dublin: DES, 1995), 13.

190. Ronan Fanning, 'T.K Whitaker, 1976–96,' 160.

191. NUI, Senate Minutes, *Report of the Meeting of the Standing Committee Held on 24 October 1995*, 9 November 1995.

192. NUI, Minutes, Special Meeting of the Senate, 13 December 1995.

193. NUI, Senate Minutes, 25 April 1996.

194. *Sunday Independent*, 'Why Trinity Should Defend Its Reputation,' 15 October 1995.

195. Walshe, *New Partnership*, 137–41.

196. NUI, Special Meeting of the Senate, 13 December 1995.

197. Department of Education, *Position Paper*, 21–2.

198. *Irish Times*, 'TCD Fellows Reject Bill "In Present Form,"' 31 October 1996.

199. NUI, Minutes, Special Meeting of the Senate, 3 October 1996.

200. *Irish Times*, 'UCG Adds to Criticism of "Stifling" Bill,' 5 November 1996.

201. *Irish Times*, 'Thatcherite Bill Threatens College System,' 24 September 1996.

202. White, *Investing in People*, 226.

203. Dáil Debates, vol. 470, no. 7, 30 October 1996, col. 1396.

204. HEA Statement, 'Proposed University Legislation, Statement on Behalf of An tÚdarás Um Ard-Oideachas' (Higher Education Authority), 30 October 1996.

205. Walshe, *New Partnership*, 154.
206. *Irish Times*, 'Role of HEA Much Reduced in Amended Bill,' 19 December 1996.
207. White, *Investing in Education*, 229.
208. Seanad Debates, vol. 150, no. 14, 26 March 1997, col. 268.
209. Seanad Debates, vol. 150, no. 14, 26 March 1997, col. 240.
210. Clancy, *Irish Higher Education*, 259–60.
211. *Irish Times*, 'Trinity College Intervention Leads to Last-Minute Change in Bill,' 25 April 1997.
212. *Irish Times*, 'Universities Bill Finally Ready to Be Signed into Law,' 8 May 1997.
213. NUI, Senate Minutes, *Report of the Standing Committee 15 April 1997*, 24 April 1997.
214. Ibid.
215. Seanad Debates, vol. 151, no. 4, col. 318–58, 24 April 1997.
216. *Irish Times*, 'Universities Bill Finally Ready to Be Signed into Law,' 8 May 1997.
217. Coolahan, 'The NUI,' 279.
218. Smyth, 'National University of Ireland, Maynooth,' 114.
219. Oireachtas Éireann, No. 24 of 1997.
220. Oireachtas Éireann, No. 1 of 2000.
221. Oireachtas Éireann, No. 24 of 1997.
222. Ibid.
223. Ibid.
224. Oireachtas Éireann, No. 24 of 1997.
225. *Irish Times*, 'Universities Bill Finally Ready to Be Signed into Law,' 8 May 1997.
226. Walshe, *New Partnership*, 155.
227. Coolahan, *Era of Lifelong Learning*, 238.
228. Clancy, *Irish Higher Education*, 259.
229. Steve Hedley, 'Managerialism in Irish Universities,' *Irish Journal of Legal Studies* 1, no. 1 (2010): 117–41.
230. Ibid., 117–41.
231. Clancy, *Irish Higher Education*, 259.
232. HEA, *Report of the Steering Committee*, 33.
233. Coolahan, *Era of Lifelong Learning*, 236.

234. Dáil Debates, vol. 507, no. 4, 18 May 1999, col. 1285; *Irish Times*, 'DIT's Next Five-Year Plan,' 3 March 1998; White, *Investing in Education*, 233–4.
235. Coolahan, *Era of Lifelong Learning*, 236.
236. White, *Investing in Education*, 130–1.
237. Ibid.; HEA, *Steering Committee*, 33.
238. Walshe, *New Partnership*, 159–63.
239. *Irish Times*, 'Minister Signs Order Changing Titles of 10 ITs,' 29 January 1998.
240. Ibid.
241. This surge in policy and legislative activity included the Education Act, 1998 which gave a modern legislative base to primary and second-level education in Ireland: while this is outside the scope of the present work, the importance of the Education Act is addressed in Coolahan, *Era of Lifelong Learning*, 207 and O'Donoghue et al., *Teacher Preparation in Ireland*, 167.
242. Teaching Council Act, 2001, No. 8 of 2001, 8–9, Accessed 1 March 2018. http://www.irishstatutebook.ie/eli/2001/act/8/enacted/en/pdf; O'Donoghue et al., *Teacher Preparation in Ireland*, 186–7.
243. Walshe, *New Partnership*, 161–2.
244. O'Sullivan, "From 'Cinderella' to the 'Fourth Pillar' of the Irish Education System," 256–7.
245. Dáil Debates, vol. 507, no. 4, 18 May 1999, col. 1278–80; Walshe, *New Partnership*, 161–2.
246. Dáil Debates, vol. 507, no. 4, 18 May 1999, col. 1278–80; O'Sullivan, 'From "Cinderella" to the "Fourth Pillar" of the Irish Education System,' 256–7.
247. Oireachtas Éireann, No. 26 of 1999.
248. Dáil Debates, vol. 507, no. 4, 18 May 1999, col. 1278–80.
249. Ibid., col. 1281.
250. Ibid., col. 1286.
251. Ibid., col. 1284–5.
252. Ibid., 1286; White, *Investing in Education*, 237.
253. Oireachtas Éireann, No. 26 of 1999.
254. Dáil Debates, vol. 507, no. 4, 18 May 1999, col. 1287.
255. Ibid., col. 1282.
256. OECD, *Higher Education in Ireland*, 19.
257. Coolahan, *Era of Lifelong Learning*, 234.

9

Globalisation and the Primacy of Economics

It is recognised, perhaps more strongly than anywhere else in Europe, that tertiary education is a key driver for the economy—OECD review (2004).[1]

The repositioning of higher education as a key driver of knowledge based economic development intensified in the early twenty-first century, influenced by globalisation, international competition and ultimately economic crisis. A new phase in the transformation of the Irish higher education system emerged from the late 1990s, characterised by sustained national and international pressures on HEIs to prioritise economic objectives; more fine-grained intervention by state agencies at institutional and programme levels; more intensive commercialisation and a decline in public resourcing of HE. Enhancing human capital emerged as a key priority not only to achieve upskilling of the work force but to promote research and development (R&D) underpinning high-value industrial enterprises.[2] University leaders embraced managerialist agendas to transform the internal governance of institutions, triggering conflict within academic communities and facilitating greater centralisation of power at institutional level. Following the economic

© The Author(s) 2018
J. Walsh, *Higher Education in Ireland, 1922–2016*,
https://doi.org/10.1057/978-1-137-44673-2_9

crash in 2007–08, the primacy of knowledge based economic imperatives sidelined all other considerations in an era of renewed austerity which continued well into the following decade.

The concept of globalisation remains contentious—Vaira argues that there is 'no univocal and neat definition of its fundamental features, contents and above all, outcomes.'[3] But the global reach of finance capitalism, the communications revolution exemplified by the internet and the technological revolution in travel are all characteristics of a globalised world. Marginson and Rhoades' characterisation of globalisation as 'becoming global' to denote 'the development of increasingly integrated systems and relationships beyond the nation…' is useful in considering the impact of global forces and processes on higher education systems.[4] Globalisation is often linked to neoliberalism, particularly in its dissemination of free trade and open markets, but globalisation is a much broader phenomenon linked to changes in forms of technology which have transformed communications, travel and media.[5] Widely differing interpretations have been advanced to explain the progress of globalisation, exemplified by the competing poles of the convergence and divergence theses. The convergence thesis emphasises a progressive trend towards homogenisation, while the alternative interpretation highlights the diversity of the effects of globalisation and the ability of local and national institutions to interpret, adapt and sometimes resist top-down international pressures.[6] Attempts have been made to reinterpret the two competing perspectives to account for the varied influence of global, national and local elements: notably, the glonacal agency heuristic theorised by Marginson and Rhoades highlighted the 'reciprocity' of activity and influence between global, national and local dimensions and sought to move beyond a dominant focus on national states, systems and markets.[7]

Despite its contested status conceptually and particularly in its outcomes, it is widely accepted that globalisation has had a profound impact on higher education. This is not in itself a new phenomenon, as dominant global forces, movements and ideologies have shaped national higher education institutions since the Middle Ages. Yet the intensification of global relations underpinned by 'the shrinkage of distance'[8] has enhanced the power and immediacy of global forces and reinforced the incentives for national and local actors to respond strategically to such pressures. Moreover, while neoliberalism and globalisation are not identical, the dominant discourses associated with globalisation in its late twentieth century form have had a pronounced free market-oriented tinge. The most notable global trends in HE since the late 1900s have been the emergence of an entrepreneurial model as a key organising principle for higher education systems and institutions and the adoption of a dominant discourse of the 'knowledge economy' or 'knowledge society', which positions higher education as "the fulcrum of innovative knowledge production, whose task is to contribute actively to the 'national good' of economic competitiveness and development…"[9]

Higher education in developed nation states has been the site of a multitude of reform initiatives since the 1980s, often explicitly framed as responses to a globalised world. Ferlie et al. have linked reform agendas in HE with three broad narratives of public service reform, new public management (NPM), network governance and neo-Weberianism, offering a useful theoretical insight into the evolving state-HE relationship.[10] NPM attracts the most scholarly attention in Ireland, not least due to its close association with neoliberalism and its influence in the UK, but should not be seen as the only relevant narrative in terms of understanding policy and organisational changes in HE. The network governance narrative describes a more consensual type of policy formation and implementation, where power is shared between social actors and the state plays more of an influencing than a directive role, steering interactions through 'alliance building, partnership and persuasion rather than hierarchy'.[11] The neo-Weberian narrative is a more explicitly statist re-working of the original bureaucratic ideal associated with continental European states such as Germany and France, involving a re-assertion of the role of the state in 'steering' the HE sector, combined with a re-orientation of traditional modes of operation informed by bureaucratic rules towards 'outwards facing' service planning to meet the needs of citizens.[12] These ideal types are rarely implemented in an absolutist form and specific national cultural contexts are crucial in mediating the application of such reform narratives.[13]

Internationalisation

Irish higher education has been influenced by global forces and ideologies since the early modern period and more intensively by international expert groups and supranational bodies since the 1960s. The power of integralist Catholicism until the late twentieth century was closely linked to the dominance of ideologies such as ultramontane Catholicism and later the embrace of corporatist ideas in the international church. Yet the emergence of internationalisation as a key national and supranational agenda in the early 2000s, encompassing global competition for students, staff and resources, altered the calculations of policy-makers, while also having a transformative impact on the orientation, strategies and composition of higher education institutions. The launch of student exchange programmes by the EC, beginning with the Erasmus programme in 1987, led to a dramatic increase in student mobility across member states and had a profound long-term impact on higher education systems across Europe; previously 'national' issues such as academic credits, quality of provision and even structural features of the system acquired an international resonance, as higher education systems had to adapt to a greater influx of non-native students.[14]

The EC and later the EU played a significant and sometimes understated role in stimulating internationalisation within the Irish HE system and shaping the context in which policy-makers operated, even while responsibility for HE remained primarily with member states. At a macro policy level the explicit positioning of higher education within a wider official narrative focusing on knowledge based economic development was reinforced by EU initiatives in the early 2000s. The EU was a partner to the Bologna process and supported the adoption of a three cycle 'qualifications architecture' and the introduction of ECTS to underpin course transfer and student mobility.[15] The Lisbon strategy adopted by the EU heads of state and government in 2000 set the objective of making Europe 'the world's most competitive and dynamic knowledge-based economy and society' by 2010, confirming an embrace of knowledge based economic development which dovetailed neatly with the preoccupations of Irish policy-makers.[16] Among the key objectives of the EU agenda was the creation of a European area for research and innovation, involving stimulation of joint research programmes across member states, the removal of all obstacles to the mobility of researchers and actions 'to attract and retain high-quality research talent in Europe.'[17] The lofty ambitions of the Lisbon agenda, which encompassed economic, social and later environmental pillars, fell short of attainment and a revised strategy was accepted by the European Council in 2005, incorporating a narrower focus on growth and jobs.[18]

The EU Commission issued a number of policy documents promoting a 'modernisation agenda' for higher education in the early 2000s.[19] The Commission in a communication on 'The role of European universities in the Europe of Knowledge' in 2003 supported a movement in continental Europe and the UK towards greater differentiation between research-intensive and teaching-focused universities.[20] The EC paper argued for a more intensive concentration of research funding in a smaller number of institutions, allied to greater specialisation among the universities. The Commission referenced the 'precariousness of resources' and the pressure of global competition, particularly from better funded US universities, as key factors requiring 'a European critical mass which can remain competitive in the international league.'[21] This involved a dilution of the Humboldtian ideal of the university pursuing both teaching and research: 'While the link between research and teaching naturally continues to define the ethos of the university as an institution and while training through research must remain an essential aspect of its activity, this link is nevertheless not the same in all institutions, for all programmes or for all levels.'[22] Irish national policy-makers interviewed by Highman in 2014 acknowledged the influence of the EU through its research funding and exchange programmes, while minimising the policy influence of the Commission. Yet the Commission's arguments for a more differentiated HE system involving greater specialisation and diversity of mission by HEIs were echoed by the Irish national strategy for higher education in 2011, indicating the emergence of 'a common discourse' between Irish and EU policy-makers, despite the reluctance of national policy-makers to acknowledge explicitly any influence by their European counterparts.[23]

A key impulse behind the demand for greater concentration and spe-cialisation was achieving more effective competition by European HEIs in a globalised world.

The drive for internationalisation was sharpened by reduced pub-lic resources in the early 2000s. Recruitment of international students had not featured on the agenda of national policy-makers or most Irish HEIs up to the 1990s, with the exception of RCSI and university med-ical faculties which traditionally attracted students from developing countries. Debate around international students in an earlier era tended to focus on the cultural benefits of diversity or the possible denial of places for Irish students.[24] But research-intensive institutions sought to position themselves to attract international students paying lucrative non-EU fees, as public funding for HE became more conditional and constrained in the early 2000s. The increasing influence of university ranking systems, employed as a reference point particularly by 'elite' and research intensive institutions, was closely linked to the drive for inter-nationalisation. The ranking systems drew intense controversy about the reliability of their methodologies and limitations in capturing the full range of educational activity, especially in more teaching intensive insti-tutions, but there was no mistaking their influence as a key comparative benchmark for the prestige and credibility of leading universities in the early 2000s.[25]

The economic crisis in 2007–08 gave a further impetus to interna-tionalisation in higher education, as governments pressurised HEIs to find alternative sources of revenue to the public purse. The elevation of internationalisation as a key policy aim for Irish HE was crystallised in the Hunt report, which echoed earlier EU documents in pointing to the opportunities and threats of global competition: 'Internationalisation provides important new opportunities for Irish higher education, but equally, and as other countries also compete for talent and resources, Ireland cannot afford to be left behind.'[26] This invoked an almost Hobbesian struggle for survival in a pitiless global marketplace, which would be decided by the ability of Irish HEIs to hold their own in attracting international students, prestigious research staff and new sources of funding.

Teaching and Learning

Massification, globalisation and the entry of more diverse cohorts of students to higher education, particularly in non-university institutions, had a gradual but substantial impact on teaching and learning, assessment and course development. Reform of course structures and programme development was informed by the Bologna Declaration, agreed by 29 European ministers for education in 1999, which aimed to establish a common European Higher Education Area (EHEA).[27] Successive government policy statements beginning with the Green Paper in 1992 emphasised quality in teaching and learning and the redesign of course frameworks on a modular basis to achieve greater flexibility.[28] HEIs were frequently pro-active in promoting more structured, systematic approaches towards teaching and learning and course development, both to adapt to the extraordinary expansion of enrolments and at least in the case of Irish universities to forestall unwelcome government intervention.

The Bologna process which ultimately embraced 47 countries promoted a series of initiatives by member states to ensure the comparability and transferability of qualifications and the mobility of students and employees throughout the common higher education area.[29] Among the key priorities of Bologna from the outset were the introduction of a comparable three cycle 'qualifications architecture' at bachelor, master and doctoral levels across the EHEA and the adoption of the European Credit Transfer System (ECTS) as a transparent mechanism for comparability of education awards.[30] Irish HEIs adapted to the Bologna process quickly and with remarkably little internal or public debate. The recommended three cycle degree structure of undergraduate, masters and doctoral qualifications was already in place in Ireland well before the 1990s and ECTS was also adopted by most Irish HEIs, ensuring that the extension of ECTS across all programmes was relatively straightforward.[31] A more significant innovation was the rapid shift to outcomes based education in terms of formal programme and module development. The NQAI launched the Irish national framework of qualifications in 2003, setting out a comprehensive structure of awards in ten levels from primary to PhD defined by learning outcomes. Ireland was the first country to establish the compatibility of its NFQ with the Bologna framework for qualifications in the EHEA.[32]

Despite the relative compatibility of Irish higher education structures with the Bologna process, the implications of the NFQ were significant, including new award titles, redefining awards in terms of learning outcomes and provision for access routes to and progression from each qualification level.[33] NQAI gave considerable attention to the adoption of new award titles, which involved amendment of titles by the IoTs, although the recommendations essentially mirrored existing practice in the universities.[34] Gleeson identified the introduction of outcomes based education, based on measurable standards of knowledge, understanding, skills and competence, which owed a strong debt to behaviourist theories associated with Bloom's taxonomy, as 'a paradigm shift' in Irish higher education.[35] The development of generic learning outcomes and programme descriptors occurred firstly for awards at programme level, but the learning outcomes model soon encompassed the more granular module level, where the new curriculum model impinged directly on student learning.[36] Outcomes based education was embraced in a largely uncritical fashion by Irish policy-makers and institutional leaders, despite potentially far-reaching academic and pedagogical implications. This process was sometimes viewed sceptically by academic staff. Gleeson considers that the process of implementing learning outcomes involved 'technical adjustments to programmes and modules', divorced from the implications for teaching and learning or the logical implication of a revised form of pedagogy.[37] The construction of learning outcomes was often experienced by academics as a technicist process driven by managers in HEIs, who issued templates to their staff for the reconstruction of modules in terms of learning outcomes.[38] O'Farrell challenges this perception of the implementation of Bologna purely as 'an exercise in bureaucracy', suggesting that 'the successful implementation of learning outcomes…points to the possibility of embedding a culture of professional development where policy drives the necessity to do so.'[39] Yet a number of key issues remained unresolved, notably the extent to which outcomes based education had actually been internalised within academic practice, or whether it had simply been layered onto existing programme content and pedagogical approaches as the path of least resistance. Also the impact of the shift to outcomes based education, if any, in terms of the quality of teaching and learning has not yet been sufficiently explored: as Murchan points out, there is a need for ongoing analysis on 'the extent to which the supposed transparency, comparability and mobility associated with the use of learning outcomes to underpin courses enhances teaching and learning or whether the approach may unnecessarily constrain pedagogy in higher education.'[40]

Academic professional development in Irish HEIs is a relatively recent phenomenon, influenced by increased demands and expectations due to mass higher education, external pressures from the HEA and the example of initiatives in the USA and UK. The growing importance of pedagogical skills and professional development in teaching and learning was a notable departure from a more traditional academic conceptualisation of teaching, particularly in the university, as purely discipline centred dissemination of knowledge.[41] The first teaching and learning centre in the Republic of Ireland was established in DIT in 2000 and all the universities set up academic development units in the early 2000s. The vast majority of IoTs have also established a professional development function, either operating in distinct centres or aligned with particular schools.[42] A number of these units (although not all) were associated with the development of specific courses leading to teaching and learning qualifications for academic staff. The new staff development programmes were frequently underpinned by public investment, starting with the Training of Trainers programme initiated in 1994 and later the Strategic Innovation Fund (SIF) in 2007.[43] The emergence of the scholarship of teaching and learning as a distinct strand within educational theory and practice from the 1990s, not least through the reconceptualisation of the 'scholarship of teaching' by Ernest Boyer, offered a philosophical reference point for the new cohort of academic developers.[44] Several new professional networks also emerged as fora for the exploration and improvement of teaching and learning in higher education— among these are the All-Ireland Society for Higher Education (AISHE), a membership based professional society 'dedicated to the promotion of good practice in learning and teaching' on an all Ireland basis and the Education Developers in Ireland Network (EDIN), a forum for educational developers from Irish HEIs, including universities, IoTs and private colleges.[45] Yet the role and status of academic developers within HEIs remains uncertain and HEIs have often struggled to define their expectations of academic development units. As O'Farrell pointed out in 2013, academic development units perform diverse functions in different HEIs and there is 'little consensus' internationally about the role and positioning of academic development within academia.[46]

A National Forum for the enhancement of teaching and learning was established in November 2012 with a broad mission 'to enhance the teaching and learning for all students in higher education.'[47] The Forum was intended to centralise public funding for innovation in teaching and learning at higher level and overcome duplication in terms of teaching and learning initiatives.[48] The Forum launched a number of initiatives, including the development of a national learning impact awards scheme to showcase high quality teaching and a digital platform offering online resources and publications in the scholarship of teaching and learning. Potentially the most significant departure was the development of a national framework to underpin and inform professional development activities within HEIs.[49] It is early to evaluate the longer term influence of the Forum and overall the impact of the varied academic development programmes and activities in HEIs is a work in progress. The wide variety of institutional and national initiatives have created greater awareness of the scholarship of teaching and learning and encouraged the use of a wider range of teaching methodologies and assessment approaches, incorporating formative assessment and online or blended learning. Yet quality enhancement—which is inherently problematic and difficult to measure in terms of teaching and learning—has attracted less sustained attention from policy-makers than the more mechanistic and apparently straightforward task of quality assurance (QA).

The traditional academic approach to oversight of teaching and learning and programme development in the universities was summed up by a senior humanities academic as a kind of 'Tory anarchy'[50]: in effect the responsibility rested loosely with departments and individual academics had a great deal of autonomy in conducting their own teaching or delegating it to selected postgraduate assistants. Procedures to safeguard the standard of programme content and assessment at university level rested entirely with individual institutions. A system of external examiners was used in the universities to monitor the standard of achievement by students and the quality of programmes.[51] The RTC/IoT sector secured external validation of courses and qualifications through the NCEA and later HETAC from 1999. A key policy departure from the 1990s was the development of formal, cross-institutional systems of QA with a sectoral remit, influenced by national and European pressures for accountability and comparability of qualifications. The development of formal QA systems was also a key expectation of the Bologna process.

The Irish system of QA emerged from a process of internal reform and extensive negotiation by university leaders with the HEA and government officials. The Green Paper in 1992 proposed an academic audit unit within the HEA to oversee QA in designated institutions.[52] But institutional leaders instead took the lead in shaping QA processes before these were imposed centrally. University governing bodies devised a common framework for institutional QA procedures through an Inter-University Quality Steering Committee in 1995–96. This pilot initiative established the key features of QA in Irish universities which have largely persisted to the present day. The key elements were a self-assessment report by the school or department under review, which included student participation; evaluation by a peer review team including external members which presented a report to the institution and subsequently an implementation plan to put recommendations by the reviewers into practice.[53] Through this innovation, the universities retained control of the emerging QA system under the Universities Act, subject to the supervisory role of the HEA and successfully forestalled a centralised audit unit. QA became a core feature of university policies and practice from the late 1990s, although controversy continued over the extent to which such processes contributed to improving student learning.[54] Centralised institutional oversight of quality assurance and course development was established in the first decade of the twenty-first century.[55]

Following the qualifications legislation in 1999, HETAC was charged with ensuring that the institutions within its remit developed 'fair and consistent' procedures for assessment of learners and credible processes for assuring quality.[56] HETAC's remit included the IoTs, most other non-university publicly funded colleges and private colleges offering higher education courses of three months or more.[57] DIT was required to work directly with the NQAI in developing procedures for QA for its programmes.[58] The legislation had limited implications for the universities, who were required only to advise and give information to the NQAI in performing its functions.

This system was formalised in 2003, when all seven university governing authorities delegated to an Irish Universities Quality Board (IUQB) the mission of arranging institutional reviews of the efficacy of QA procedures in each university.[59] Clancy suggests that Irish systems for QA developed through 'a paralell process of national reform,' occurring concurrently with the Bologna process: while national initiatives preceded the declaration, Irish QA systems mirrored initiatives at a European level.[60] The IUQB was established in the same year as the Berlin conference of 40 European ministers for education, which brought QA to the fore as a key objective of the EHEA.[61] Both HETAC and the IUQB were successfully reviewed in terms of European standards and included in the European Quality Assurance Register for Higher Education established in 2008.[62]

A radical shake up of the sectoral QA agencies occurred between 2009 and 2012 as a result of the economic crisis. A new national agency, Quality and Qualifications Ireland (QQI) was established through legislation in 2012, leading to the amalgamation of NQAI, HETAC and FETAC.[63] This amalgamation followed the announcement by the Minister for Finance of the merger or abolition of 44 'quangos' in the 2010 budget. The new agency also superseded the IUQB and the Universities Act was amended to require existing universities to 'consult' with the agency before establishing QA procedures.[64] Universities were not obliged to secure approval from the agency for their QA policies, in contrast to all the other providers regulated under the legislation where QQI had the power to approve their procedures, make recommendations or reject them outright.[65] Yet the creation of a single national agency to oversee the national qualifications framework and QA procedures across the higher and further education system was a significant innovation with the potential to expand the regulatory authority of the state. QQI's strategy statement for 2016–18 indicated its broad remit which extended to 'learners in diverse areas – schooling, vocational training, higher education, adult education, community education and English language training.'[66] QQI also set out an ambitious agenda at higher level, including implementation of an international education mark for providers of programmes to international students and introduction of a comprehensive system of QA guidelines.[67] It is early to assess the influence of QQI, but the agency is the latest and certainly most powerful actor to date in the evolving QA regime in Irish higher education.

'Making Knowledge Work for Us'?

Another new departure embraced by the Irish political establishment at the end of the twentieth century was a belated but highly effective attempt to upgrade the previously fragmented research space in higher education. Investment in research was a late development in Ireland: expenditure on R&D and the number of researchers in Ireland lagged behind international indicators for most of the 1900s. As Hazelkorn et al. noted, during the twentieth century 'Ireland had no national research policy, investment strategy or noteworthy international reputation in scientific research.'[68] Enhancing research capability emerged as a key policy objective for the Irish state for the first time in the late 1990s.[69] Although support for scientific research was acknowledged to be inadequate by the Ó Dálaigh commission as early as 1959, the significant upsurge in capital investment that followed up to the early 1980s focused mainly on providing or upgrading infrastructure for teaching, college buildings and libraries—all badly needed considering the capital deficit of the previous generation. Higher education research received support, if at all, through relatively small-scale initiatives, usually supported by the EC, such as the Programmes for Advanced Technology established in 1987 (funded in part through EC structural funds) to promote industry-higher education research links supporting indigenous enterprise.[70] Research was not conceptualised as a distinct area in its own right requiring coherent policy formation and dedicated investment until the late 1990s.

Two reports in the 1990s signalled a new policy direction in higher education research. The Science Technology and Innovation Advisory Council (STIAC) led by Dan Tierney issued a key report in 1995, with the evocative title of 'Making Knowledge Work for Us', which set out a road map for the upgrading of science, technology and innovation (STI) research. Loxley suggests that the report 'gushed forth optimism like a fortune cookie', in its zeal to show how an enhanced STI environment underpinned by public and business investment could sustain the Irish economy.[71] The Tierney report proposed an ambitious partnership between state, industry and HEIs, on a scale which had not previously been seen in Irish HE, involving doubling the level of R&D undertaken by the business sector by 1999 and increasing funding for basic HE research from £1.5 million to £6 million.[72] The report sought the creation of a coherent higher education research system linked to systematic engagement by HEIs with private enterprise. Tierney advanced a series of recommendations which amounted to a manifesto for transformation in higher education research:

- The adoption by HEIs of a research charter to underline their 'proactive attitude towards research activities and in particular towards interaction with commercial users of research expertise';
- The introduction of a research equipment fund of £5 million annually to 'address the equipment shortfall problem' in the third level sector;
- A fund of £200,000 to encourage 'global participation' by Irish scientists through international collaboration;
- An improved three-year funding cycle for doctoral students, who were to receive at least £3000 annually and a system of postdoctoral fellowships.[73]

Higher education research was positioned as a key cog in the wheel of a nascent Irish 'system of innovation', with Tierney emphasising the importance of enhanced links between 'the third level and other elements of the National System of Innovation'. Equally significant was STIAC's concern to raise the status and profile of scientific research as a key contributor to economic innovation. This would be achieved through the creation of a Cabinet committee on science and technology chaired by the Taoiseach or his nominee; establishment of a permanent STI Council as an independent advisory body and a national office for STI within the Department of Enterprise.[74] A number of the STIAC recommendations were quickly implemented, including the appointment of the new Cabinet committee, led by Minister of State Pat Rabbitte, to pursue the recommendations and the upgrading of the national office for STI. Others fed into subsequent policy-making exercises such as the Foresight report. The STIAC vision of an integrated national system of innovation, incorporating HEIs as key actors serving national economic objectives in conjunction with enterprise, became central to government policy over the following decade. The Tierney report began a reorientation of HE research in which knowledge generation was positioned as a key contributor to economic innovation and HEIs were drawn into regular rather than occasional collaboration with industry.

If STIAC offered an alluring vision of a future with unlimited possibility, a comparative study on university research in Ireland and Europe commissioned by the HEA adopted a more prosaic style. The report by the CIRCA management consultancy group gave a harsh assessment of research in Irish universities: '…it is apparent from our analysis that there is something seriously amiss with public policy towards the support of higher education research in Ireland….the equipment position appears to be particularly bad…the overall position is bleak'.[75] Irish universities lagged behind their European counterparts in planning, coordination and assessment, in part due to inadequate core funding for research, which also severely limited opportunities to secure external funding on a collaborative basis.[76] The report sought a more strategic approach by both government and institutions, incorporating explicit institutional planning and greater inter-institutional collaboration, underpinned by an increase in core research funding.[77] Both reports highlighted the low status and funding of HE research in Ireland. The two reports helped to trigger a fundamental re-appraisal of government policy, which paved the way for large-scale public investment in research and the emergence of a distinctive research tier within HEIs in the early twenty-first century.

The announcement of the Programme for Research in Third Level Institutions (PRTLI) in 1998 was the first practical example of the newly minted commitment to 'fourth level' research. The PRTLI drew on the rationale for action supplied by Tierney and CIRCA.[78] The PRTLI, particularly in its early incarnations, was not explicitly linked to short-term economic returns, but was designed to build 'basic research capability' and create the conditions which would allow 'the right type of activities and projects to subsequently proceed'.[79] The programme set out to lay the foundations for a national system of innovation by creating facilities for basic research and supporting centres for the training of researchers.[80]

The PRTLI was rolled out over five cycles between 1999 and 2010, distributing about €1.2 billion in funding to 48 projects through a competitive awards process.[81] About a third of the total funding was raised from non-exchequer sources, including the European Union (EU), private industry and philanthropic donors. Atlantic Philanthropies led by Chuck Feeney was the most significant philanthropic contributor over the first three cycles, providing €178 million or 30% of the programme investment between 1999 and 2002.[82] The funding was allocated on the basis of competitive institutional proposals to establish or build on specialised research initiatives; this usually involved support for dedicated research centres, although a small number of other significant projects also received funding, including the new Ussher Library in TCD and the Boole Library in UCC. The core elements of the programme included resources to support staff and capital investment, such as the cost of laboratories, facilities for researchers in humanities/social sciences and library developments. The PRTLI was envisaged from the outset as a collaborative venture on a 'triple helix' model, encompassing the state, institutions and private enterprise.[83] The HEIs were required to provide significant funding towards capital costs, maintenance of equipment and postgraduate scholarships, as well as allocating academic staff as principal investigators to the newly funded centres. Despite the official aspiration to develop basic research capability across a range of disciplines and institutions, over half of the PRTLI funding (53%) in the first three cycles was allocated under the bioscience and biomedical theme, with only 15% going to social sciences and humanities.[84] Moreover, the programme investment was heavily concentrated in the universities, which received 83% of the funding in the first three cycles, compared to 13% for two non-university institutions with strong research capacity, RCSI and the Dublin Institute of Advanced Studies, and only 4% for IoTs.[85]

The government also established two new research councils in 2000–01 to support individual researchers at PhD or early stage post-doctoral level in line with the STIAC recommendations.[86] The Irish Council for Science, Technology and Engineering (IRCSET) and its counterpart in Humanities and Social Sciences (IRCHSS) developed a significant role in the funding and organisation of HE research, particularly at postgraduate and early career researcher levels in the first decade of the twenty first century. The centrality of research to economic development was underlined by the scale of the upsurge in public investment, with the allocation of €2.5 billion to research, technology, innovation and development in the National Development Plan 2000–2006, a five-fold increase in exchequer spending on research.[87]

A key milestone in developing a coherent policy on HE research was the Technology Foresight initiative undertaken by the Irish Council for Science Technology and Innovation (ICSTI)—the successor of STIAC—at the request of the government.[88] The Technology Foresight process, completed in 1998, took the form of a series of reports on eight different research areas, conducted by panels drawn from industry, academia and government departments. This initiative incorporated many of the STIAC insights, but on a much grander scale, reflecting the ambitions of the Irish political and official elites at the height of the Celtic Tiger. The initiative was underpinned by two key assumptions—that 'technology is a key driver for knowledge societies' which would shape the future structures of society and that 'Strategic investments in research, science and technology must be used effectively to underpin Ireland's development as a knowledge society…'.[89] The Foresight process favoured a repositioning of the Irish economy so it was internationally recognised as a 'knowledge based economy', identifying the key gap within the Irish system as the absence of 'a world class research capability of sufficient scale in a number of strategic areas within our universities and colleges, research institutes and industry.'[90]

This could only be achieved through an all-embracing partnership, conceptualised as a knowledge 'pyramid', consisting of private industry, government, the higher education sector and society 'with its four interlinked faces forming a partnership at all levels.'[91] This quadruple helix was a more elaborate version of Tierney's call for state, private and institutional collaboration to create an integrated national system of innovation.

The Foresight process produced not only a range of specific recommendations by particular panels but ambitious policy prescriptions, notably a substantial increase in national research capability to make Ireland 'a centre of excellence' in ICT and biotechnology; introduction of a Technology Foresight Fund to support the development of 'world class research capability' and incorporation of the Foresight findings into all future government planning exercises.[92] The intended outcomes of the Foresight initiative amounted to a transformation of the underdeveloped higher education research landscape through dramatically enhanced exchequer support and engagement with industry. Among the innovative features of the initiative were its espousal of strategic partnership with a key role for the state in promoting a culture of innovation[93]; the expectation of intensive engagement by HEIs with corporate partners and incentives to develop higher education research in domains of strategic economic importance. Not all of its recommendations were welcomed by the universities, which pushed back successfully against a recommendation by the ICT panel for the creation of independent research institutes outside the universities. But overall CHIU adopted a positive strategy, designed to take full advantage of the proposed investment.[94] The Foresight initiative commanded wide support among policy-makers, corporate executives and institutional leaders. The strategy marked the culmination of a lengthy process of re-appraisal since the early 1990s. The reconceptualisation of higher education as an integral part of a national system of innovation, in which competitive bidding for state funding and partnership with private enterprise in niche areas played a crucial role, signalled that engagement with industry was a key policy expectation, allied to the emergence of market mechanisms as a major factor in allocating resources.

Clancy argues that the new research initiatives, with their competitive funding models and rigorous evaluation of institutional research strategies, 'heralded the introduction of unbridled market principles into the steering of HE and represented the government's most serious attempt to exert control over the internal workings of the university'.[95] Yet not all research initiatives were created equal: the earliest research programmes, including PRTLI, can be distinguished from later developments influenced first by the Foresight process and subsequently the economic crisis. While the imperative for engagement with industry remained consistent, the first research initiatives between 1998 and 2000 were not prescriptive in terms of economic outcomes and were potentially open to a wide range of research areas proposed by academics. The PRTLI in its first three cycles up to 2002 did not require short-term commercial returns and supported initiatives across five thematic areas incorporating a wide range of disciplines, with the declared intention to 'embed a research culture across the higher education sector.'[96] Despite the allocation of the largest share of resources to science and technology, the programme funded a wide variety of centres and initiatives, including 16 in the social science/humanities and environment/marine thematic areas which did not generate commercial impacts.[97] The PRTLI initially pursued a 'generalist' approach to intervention which sought to address 'a research deficit' by focusing on the development of basic research capabilities at institutional level.[98] The programme introduced competitive funding mechanisms, but did not seek to dictate research priorities or academic practice.

Yet the Foresight report revealed a more sharply focused commercialisation agenda and readiness to leverage funding to influence institutional policy and practice. The establishment of Science Foundation Ireland (SFI) in 2000, to administer the new technology foresight fund of £646 million, channelled public funding towards research activity in strategic areas, such as ICT, biotechnology and renewable energy. SFI from the outset was focused on developing economically strategic areas for research and drawing prestigious international scientists into the Irish research system.[99] Ó Riain argues that SFI effectively introduced 'the logic of FDI attraction' to science and technology in higher education. SFI was the most significant source of research funding in the early

2000s and soon acquired a key role in formulating research policy.[100] The influence of SFI was enhanced when the role of chief scientific adviser was transferred to the director of the SFI in 2012. Moreover, the Research Prioritisation Exercise launched by the Department of Jobs, Enterprise and Innovation in 2011 established a top down approach 'to accelerate delivery of specific economic outcomes from our investment in research…', identifying 14 priority areas which were closely linked to the Irish enterprise base.[101] The RPE explicitly set expectations that investment in each of these areas should achieve 'real and demonstrable economic impacts…within a five year period.'[102] The scale of the public resources allocated to scientific research, introduction of rigorous competitive mechanisms in securing funding and narrower targeting of public resources after the crash increased the responsiveness of universities to government priorities and placed considerable power in the hands of new executive agencies, particularly SFI.

The outcomes of the dramatic policy shift in the late 1990s were substantial but not always in line with the intentions of policymakers. Total expenditure on research and development in higher education (HERD) more than doubled between 2002 and 2008, when it peaked at almost €750 million.[103] This was among the highest rates of increase in expenditure among the OECD states and brought Ireland from a low base to a mid table position in terms of investment in HERD as a percentage of GNP, where Ireland was 15th in the OECD by 2010.[104] Yet the desired engagement of business in higher education research did not fully materialise. Business expenditure on R&D outside higher education increased substantially between 1992 and 2010, but the proportion of HERD funded by industry remained well below the OECD average and even declined marginally in the early 2000s.[105] The surge in spending by the state easily exceeded any other contribution to HERD: although funding from private sources also increased, this also included a temporary infusion from Atlantic Philanthropies.[106] Public investment was crucial in underpinning the repositioning of higher education research and the much vaunted 'triple helix' envisaged by Tierney and the Foresight report was by no means fully achieved even in the specialised research arena.

Among the intended outcomes of this surge in investment was 'human capital development' by expanding the supply of postgraduates, particularly doctoral students. The *Strategy for Science Technology and Innovation* (SSTI) launched in 2006 set out to double the number of PhD graduates by 2013 and this was certainly achieved.[107] 780 PhDs were awarded across Irish HEIs in 2005, compared to 1100 in 2008 and 1447 by 2011.[108] An average of 29% of PhD graduates between 2005 and 2008 were drawn from PRTLI supported centres or initiatives.[109] Both PRTLI and the Foresight funding contributed significantly to the wider expansion in postgraduate enrolments in the early 2000s.

The upsurge in research funding, apparently an unequivocal benefit to HEIs, proved a mixed blessing over the longer term. An abrupt 'pause' in PRTLI funding in 2002 triggered protests from HEIs which were obliged to defer or curtail infrastructural projects, with the dean of research in UCC complaining that 'The infrastructure of this country and indeed this economy is not just the road network.'[110] The pause, which lasted for almost four years, created uncertainty about the government's support for research and impinged on the ability of HEIs to plan future research projects. The suspension of PRTLI contributed to a sharp reduction in capital funding for higher education in 2002–03 and was coupled with a freezing of recurrent budgets for HEIs[111]; for many institutions this meant a de facto reduction in non-pay budgets, which persisted well beyond the immediate financial crunch.

Ó Riain argues that the 'pause' in PRTLI operated as "a process of 'softening up' of the universities", before the re-introduction of streams of funding from 2005 linked more explicitly to a corporate vision of the university.[112] It is doubtful whether policy-makers were adopting a deliberate strategy rather than reacting to short-term economic and educational challenges. But the policy decisions in 2002–03 certainly signalled the end of a buoyant period in terms of state investment in higher education and the beginning of a more parsimonious and targeted approach to resource allocation, coupled with efforts to influence institutional policy and academic practice at a fine-grained level. The Minister for Education, Mary Hanafin, announced in 2005 the introduction of a strategic innovation fund (SIF), which would be awarded on a competitive basis to universities and IoTs to support innovation in higher education and research.[113] Over €510 million was allocated under the SIF between 2006 and 2013 to a range of projects, often promoting collaboration between HEIs and sometimes cross-sectoral collaboration between universities and IoTs. The projects supported by the SIF sought to underpin improvements in teaching and learning; promote access and retention; support 'managerial reforms' and develop postgraduate or 'fourth-level education'.[114] While many (though not all) of these objectives were uncontroversial, the fund gave leverage to policy-makers to change traditional approaches within HEIs, where these were perceived as outmoded, inefficient or unresponsive to societal (and primarily economic) concerns. The SIF was designed to promote or reward changes in policy and practice within HEIs, in line with government policy priorities. The fund was also employed to stimulate or support 'managerial reform' initiatives, designed to transform the traditional patterns of academic governance and administration on a corporate model.

Managerialism

Contemporary public and academic debates on the rise of managerialism (or NPM) are highly contested both in Ireland and internationally, sometimes shedding more heat than light on what is actually happening within or beyond HEIs. As Hedley notes, there is no universally agreed definition of what constitutes managerialism, but a widespread conviction exists among academics across the English-speaking world that 'they have been deposed by a new breed of bureaucrats, both within and without the university.'[115] More specifically, Hedley suggests that managerialism in higher education may be seen as a counterpoint to the traditional academic understanding of the university and involves 'rigorous control of a university's activities from both within and without.'[116] This resonates with a wider scholarly understanding of NPM, as embodying more hierarchical, authoritative management of employees; a greater role for markets in traditional public service domains and 'steering' at a distance by the state.[117]

The legal framework for the Irish universities was set by the Universities Act, which was a compromise between traditional academic and managerial understandings of the university. Arguably the advent of managerial influence within HEIs was a much earlier phenomenon, with the emergence of a professional corps of administrators in almost all Irish higher education institutions at least from the 1970s, due to the pressures of massification and increased state intervention in higher education. The newer universities, which began life as the NIHEs, had less autonomy from government and were characterised by a more assertive management from the outset, accentuated in both cases by the lengthy tenure of a powerful president—Ed Walsh in UL and Danny O'Hare in DCU. The RTCs had very limited autonomy even on an operational level for the first two decades of their existence, as they were subject both to local political oversight through the VECs and overarching policy control by the Department of Education. While the IoTs established statutory status and greater freedom to award degree qualifications in the late 1990s, they remained constrained by the power of the Department of Education.

The universities legislation was a hybrid which both facilitated the exercise of managerial power by institutional leaders and contained it. The legislation gave a high status to the chief officer of each university, who was legally responsible for its financial and operational management. But safeguards were built into the legislation, not least due to lobbying by IFUT, to confer explicit guarantees of academic freedom; provide for tenure for full-time permanent academics and establish formal procedures for appointment, dismissal and dispute resolution.[118] Subsequent litigation drawing on the Universities Act confirmed the existence of tenure for all those appointed to permanent academic positions, although the extent of the protection offered by tenure was not defined by the courts.[119]

Yet managerialism has gained ground since the adoption of the Universities Act, even if as Hedley notes, many developments in Irish universities cannot be neatly categorised as "either 'advances for managerialism' or 'victories for traditionalists'".[120] The rise of managerialism in the early 2000s is inseparable from the changing balance of power between the HEIs, the state and private industry. Both Clancy and

Ó Riain suggest that university management embarked on 'unprecedented restructuring' in the early years of the millennium, attributing this activism to a competitive funding environment and a more unfavourable political climate.[121] The restructuring initiatives, which shaped most universities in the early 2000s, were certainly influenced by more intensive competition for finite research funding and pressure from government to reconfigure traditionally collegial and decentralised university structures. Yet a key catalyst for internal restructuring in the pre-1989 universities was the emergence of a new cadre of university leaders, who were more focused on competition for both public and non-exchequer funding and frequently more impatient of internal dissent. The major restructuring initiatives mostly preceded the creation of the SIF and in the case of UCC, even the freeze in PRTLI, although all can be seen as responding to a harsher political and economic climate. The role of university leaders in the three largest universities in the state was crucial to varying degrees in triggering a multi-layered process of restructuring and facilitating a notable advance towards managerialism.

UCC was the first of the pre-1989 universities to experience far-reaching internal restructuring. Prof Gerry Wrixon, president from 1998, introduced plans for reshaping existing academic structures to create a more powerful managerial tier and a streamlined administrative structure, which later served as a model for other 'reform' plans. Wrixon was successful in driving through the main elements of his restructuring programme, reducing the college's seven faculties to four and asserting control over the appointment of faculty and department heads.[122] This was accomplished, however, at the cost of fierce internal division. Wrixon became a hugely controversial figure, described by an education journalist as a leader who 'dominates the college like a colossus...who draws admiration and criticism in equal measure'.[123] Opposition to his agenda from a significant segment of academics was played out not only in the board rooms of UCC but in national newspapers and the courts.[124] Dissent crystallised around Wrixon's attempt to secure a full ten year term allowing him to serve as president beyond the age of 65, which was opposed by the academic council and a minority of UCC's governors, but sanctioned by government ministers in

2005. Wrixon, however, announced his resignation in May 2006 and his final year of office was marked by intense conflict in which 'UCC was convulsed by supporters and opponents of Wrixon'.[125]

The winds of change were also felt in UCD following the appointment of Dr. Hugh Brady as president in 2003. Brady, the first president to be appointed through a search and interview process rather than elected by the governing body and NUI senate, acted decisively to transform the institutional governance and management of UCD. Brady appointed a management team on a corporate model, with four new vice presidents and established a one year term for all heads of department, subject to re-appointment by the president.[126] This was the overture to a more radical overhaul of traditional academic structures, underpinned by a consultancy report from the Washington Advisory Group, in which the president secured the amalgamation of 11 faculties into five colleges and over 90 academic departments into 34 schools. The colleges were headed by principals appointed by the president with managerial authority to set targets and monitor research outputs.[127] Brady's strategy, characterized by an European Universities Association review in 2010 as a 'big bang' approach to reform leading to a 'tumultuous' period for UCD, provoked a backlash from the UCD branch of IFUT, the students' union and some discontented senior academics.[128] Yet Brady's presidency marked a decisive change of direction in establishing a more hierarchical, powerful management with greater control over the policy, practice and administration of the university. Significantly, Brady, like his counterpart in UCC, was a scientist who prioritised research and commercialisation and sought to reposition UCD as a leading research intensive university, benchmarked by university rankings systems embraced by most Irish universities.

Trinity College was to some extent an outlier in the embrace of managerialism by university leaders: by the early 2000s it was the only remaining university in the Irish state in which academic staff elected its provost. Yet TCD, led by provost John Hegarty, embarked on its own process of internal restructuring in 2004, albeit in a more consensual fashion than its NUI counterparts. Hegarty, a scientist and former dean of research, prioritised a reformed college administration and a streamlined department structure involving the creation of larger, inter-disciplinary schools. This reform agenda proposed abolition of the traditional six faculty structure; merger of 81 academic departments to form no more than 18 interdisciplinary schools and enhancing the capacity of the central administration.[129] This agenda shared common features with managerial reform in the NUI in terms of an empowered central administration and a concentration of stronger academic units. Yet the outcome in Trinity was somewhat different from its NUI counterparts, where the presidents largely overcame academic opposition. The provost's plans triggered significant opposition from the local branch of IFUT which threatened industrial action, the students' union and from professional schools such as Law and Education, which refused to merge into larger units.[130] The college administration ultimately compromised in allowing a three faculty structure with elected deans and the persistence of a number of single discipline schools. While internal criticism of managerialism by prominent academics, including economist and Senate candidate Seán Barrett, did not prevent the creation of two powerful new executive posts overseeing academic affairs and corporate operations, the reconfigured senior management team also included three elected faculty deans. If Trinity was a more centralised institution with fewer academic units by 2010, it was also true that checks on the power of the administration, represented by the Fellows within the body corporate and a collegial tradition of governance, remained in place. TCD was on the more traditional end of a continuum in governance and leadership within a university spectrum which had shifted dramatically toward managerialism in the early 2000s.

The embrace of managerialism by most university leaders attracted a fierce critique among many academics, particularly those from humanities and social science who feared that their disciplines, traditionally central to the university, were being left behind by the new orthodoxy. Tom Garvin, professor of politics in UCD, took aim at the predominance of commercialisation and corporate management: 'in the newly governmentalised academy, an obsession with money and peculiarly half-witted form of benchmarking, usually referred to pejoratively as 'box-ticking' replaced any real concern with scholarship or blue-sky research.'[131] Other critics drew attention to the valorisation of research over teaching and the narrowing of institutional priorities. Seán Barrett, in a lengthy analysis of restructuring in 2006, concluded that managerial reform had 'done more harm than good', arguing that the economics of university reform were severely flawed, as it was financed initially by borrowings and internal transfers within the institutions, before being underpinned in some cases by state support through SIF.[132] Barrett criticised a downgrading of arts humanities and social science in favour of STEM disciplines which were more attractive for research funding and a decline in the status of undergraduate teaching in pursuit of 'improved research performance in international league tables.'[133] While these arguments were controversial, such critics were not isolated voices but reflected a high level of internal conflict and resistance to the managerial reform agenda. Much of this debate was inconclusive, ventilating simmering internal conflicts in the national media.

The undeniable shift towards managerialism in the governance and management of universities in the early 2000s was dictated by economics: 'managerial reform' was intended to enable more effective competition for resources both nationally and internationally, facilitate greater commercialisation and collaboration with industry, enhance research performance and leverage targeted government support. Clancy argues that 'the decisive move' was the state's successful mobilisation of market mechanisms to achieve government objectives: the introduction of competitive funding mechanisms marked a turning point, as it triggered the subsequent centralisation of authority within institutions.[134] Certainly the creation of competitive research funding instruments pitting institutions against each other and the more explicit valorisation of research, as opposed to teaching, transformed the context in which HEIs had operated in the twentieth century. Yet this was not the whole story: 'managerial reform' was not simply instigated by policy change in terms of research funding, but was complementary to it and sometimes even preceded official initiatives to influence the internal workings of institutions. Moreover, Irish political elites made only selective use of market mechanisms, retaining a strong attachment to bureaucratic authority associated with a traditional departmental culture or the more recent regulatory function of the HEA.

The embrace of managerialist agendas reflected a strategic choice by leading university figures and was not simply imposed by an interventionist state, although ministers and officials encouraged and to some extent financed it. University leaders in the 1990s had, not infrequently, clashed with ministers and the Department of Education over fundamental policy issues such as institutional autonomy and academic freedom. Their successors in the early 2000s were more focused on the search for competitive advantage, internal restructuring and securing state support for institutional 'reform' projects. They could reasonably argue that they were adapting both to globalisation and a less favourable fiscal and political climate. But the restructuring initiatives also reflected the prominence of leaders drawn from STEM disciplines and a largely uncritical acceptance of the value of centralisation in management and commercialisation in terms of engagement with society. Increasingly, university leaders adopted a similar discourse to politicians and civil servants regarding the positioning of higher education in relation to the economy, which prioritised commercialisation, knowledge generation and corporate style management, no matter how much they disagreed over resources and policy details.

Access and Inequality

The outcome of government and institutional initiatives on widening participation since the 1990s was mixed, revealing a combination of incremental progress by under-represented groups and persistent relative differences. The second action plan issued by the HEA in 2008 featured both an extension in the range of objectives (to include targets for part-time and flexible learning, non-standard entry routes and lifelong learning) and more ambitious participation targets for each target group.[135] The action plan envisaged an entry rate of at least 54% for all socio-economic groups by 2020 in the context of an overall age participation rate of 72%; the target for mature students was equally ambitious at 27% of all entrants by 2013.[136] The HEA took a more fine-grained approach in terms of access for students with a disability, proposing to double the number of entrants with sensory, physical or multiple disabilities by 2013.[137] The plan's aggressive target setting was influenced by a labour market agenda, citing the headline entry rate of 72% in the school leaving age cohort set by the National Skills Strategy in 2007. The strategy issued by Forfás regarded widening participation as a useful tool in meeting skills shortages in the labour market: 'This strategy estimates that a higher-education entry rate of 72% will be required by 2020 to meet the rising demands for higher-education qualifications.'[138] Other targets, particularly the entry rate for under-represented SEGs, were devised in the context of the demand for a higher headline participation rate. The ostensibly egalitarian agenda set by the action plan, while genuine in terms of its aspirations for widening participation, owed a great deal to the demand for highly qualified graduates in an apparently buoyant economy.

Such targets would have been optimistic in any scenario but proved unrealisable following the economic crash in 2008. Participation within the 18–20 year old cohort in all the target SEGs as a proportion of new entrants increased moderately from 20% in 2011–12 to 26% in 2014–15, albeit well below the original HEA target.[139] But this picture of incremental progress was punctuated by enduring class inequalities at a more granular level. Third-level participation differed dramatically across postal districts in Dublin city and county in 2011–12, reflecting results of earlier studies on urban differentials, particularly by Clancy and Benson, going back a generation to 1978.[140] Half of all postal districts showed rates of participation below the regional average of 47% and the estimated participation rate in the affluent Dublin 6 area was 99% compared to only 16% in Dublin 17.[141] A large-scale research study conducted by an ESRI team focused attention on class in a more nuanced way, exploring the way in which schools shaped young people's post-school pathways. A mixed methods longitudinal study, *Leaving School in Ireland*, followed a cohort of young people from their entry to second-level education to their outcomes three to four years after completing school, highlighting the way in which the social composition of the school influenced young people's access to higher education, over and above the impact of individual family background.[142] The study also pointed to the emergence of social class divergences in aspirations to higher education 'as early as junior cycle'.[143]

More recently, Byrne and McCoy found evidence of 'effectively maintained inequality' (EMI) in transitions from second to third level, suggesting that qualitative distinctions at the same level of education tended to 'maintain socio-economic differences in students' probability of progressing through an educational system'.[144] This analysis of EMI, informed by the regular School Leavers' survey between 1980 and 2006, indicated that a qualitative distinction could be found in the type of HEI (university or non-university) attended by students of similar academic achievements from different backgrounds, concluding that such qualitative differences represented 'a key barrier to greater equality in the Irish context'.[145] A 'diverging trajectories' pattern was particularly marked in the cohorts progressing from upper second level between 1984 and 1995, when students from higher SEGs were more likely to be enrolled in university while those from less advantaged SEGs were likely to be attending an IoT or college.[146] Institutional differentiation in the late twentieth century had a clear socio-economic dimension, linked not only to the type of courses offered, but to institutional status, socio-economic background and parental expectations. Yet Byrne and McCoy also found differences in the educational trajectories of distinct age cohorts pursuing a similar academic second level track, as there was a declining level of EMI in terms of accessing university education for cohorts leaving school between 1996 and 2005.[147] This was an intriguing finding which cut against conventional wisdom on the failure of the 'free fees' initiative, suggesting that the abolition of tuition fees had some impact on the post-school destinations of students from more disadvantaged SEGs who had pursued an academic route at second level.

The most popular alternative route to HE remained entry by mature students. Significant improvements were achieved in the level of mature entry between 1998 and 2006, with mature students accounting for 12.8% of full-time entrants in 2006, although the proportion of the adult population in higher education or training remained below the EU average.[148] Yet the participation of mature students declined during the economic crisis; having peaked at 15% of new entrants in 2010–11, the proportion of full-time mature students fell back to 12% in 2014–15.[149] While the number of part-time mature entrants fluctuated more dramatically, overall mature entry declined slightly over a four year period.[150] The HEA noted in 2016 that Ireland remained below 'average international performance' in terms of lifelong learning benchmarked against EU comparators and 'far below leaders such as Sweden where the share of the working-age population in education or training is over 70 per cent.'[151]

Several HEIs participated in other admissions routes for target groups, such as the Higher Education Access route (HEAR), which allocated reserved places at reduced points to young people from socio-economically disadvantaged backgrounds and the Disability Access Route to Education (DARE), which offered a similar entry route for students with disabilities.[152] These routes were taken by 2.5 and 0.9% respectively of applicants accepting a place in higher education in 2010.[153] Progression from FE courses at NFQ levels 5 and 6 was another supplementary pathway referenced in HEA action plans. But the FET route to HE which developed in the early 2000s was complex and restrictive: access for FET students was restricted to certain programmes, usually linked to quotas and conditional on minimum course requirements.[154] The number of students availing of the FET route reached only 6.6% of all new entrants in 2011.[155] The proportion of students entering HEIs through non-standard entry routes either outside or additional to the highly competitive CAO reached 24% of net acceptances by 2010—the large majority of this group were mature students.[156]

Progress in widening participation fell well short of the ambitious targets in the second action plan in terms of under-represented SEGs, mature students and lifelong learning.[157] The target of doubling the number of students with disabilities was achieved, while the HEA objective for enrolment on non-standard access routes was also close to attainment. The third action plan issued in 2015 scaled back the more unrealistic targets with regard to socio-economic inequality and mature entry, while maintaining the overall approach of focusing on 'equity groups' and developing more coherent pathways to higher education.[158] Loxley et al. argue that the plan was 'less bombastic in tone' than its predecessor and its continuing strong focus on economic concerns was tempered by 'a more democratic and inclusive sensibility' closer to the original action group report.[159] Certainly the plan paid homage to the conventional script of the knowledge based economy, noting that 'our educated workforce is Ireland's greatest economic asset and we need more people to take up higher education to drive economic progress.'[160]

Yet the eight principles set out by the plan revealed a strong emphasis on relationships between families, schools and HEIs and collaborative partnerships between stakeholders designed to build 'social capital' in communities with low levels of participation.[161] Only one of the principles, on improving pathways from further to higher education, featured labour market concerns in terms of meeting national skills needs.[162] The plan was less mechanistic than the 2008 document with its focus on high level action and targets, prioritising a wider cultural transformation to overcome more intangible barriers in terms of attitudes, aspiration and educational engagement. The 2015 document also posited a more fundamental change in the practice of HEIs, arguing that equity policies should be 'mainstreamed into the everyday life of higher education institutions', not least to enhance the progression rate among the target groups.[163] This echoed the thrust of the original action group report 14 years earlier but also implicitly underlined the limitations to change at institutional level: the integration of access policies and approaches to support students from target groups into everyday practice remained incomplete. The latest plan was more subtle and nuanced than its predecessor, seeking to strike a more sustainable balance between labour market requirements and the complexities inherent in the process of widening participation.

Consideration of the scale of inequality within the contemporary HE system is beyond the scope of this work, but it is possible to reflect on the impact of policy and institutional change over the last two generations. Genuine advances in participation by under-represented groups have been achieved, with the growth in mature entry a particularly notable change in the early 2000s, although it appears to have levelled off in the recent economic crisis. The position of students with disabilities has improved both in terms of entry rates and of the greater efforts at institutional level to facilitate their full participation and progression. The evidence regarding traditionally under-represented SEGs is more ambiguous or at least open to conflicting interpretations. The Irish HE system has seen an impressive range and quality of studies regarding access and participation since the 1970s. Sustained attention by policy-makers to widening participation at higher level was much slower to materialise, with the mid 1990s marking a significant transition point towards a more focused policy approach. Clancy suggests that the Irish HE system has made considerable progress, pointing to a reduction in class inequalities at entry since the 1990s and a comparative analysis of European research studies, which would place Ireland in the top third of European countries with regard to social inequalities in access to higher education.[164] Yet social class has remained a key influence on participation in HE both in terms of headline entry rates and perhaps to an even greater extent qualitative indicators relating to participation in differing types of institutions (particularly university and IoT) and fields of study.[165] Finally, while it is early to evaluate the impact of the recession on participation by under-represented groups, it is apparent that widening participation did not figure highly in the state's priorities during the economic crash. Influential political elites relegated egalitarian concerns to a secondary position in an era of crisis, while reinforcing pressure on HEIs to meet labour market demands. The most recent HEA plan suggested the re-emergence of a more egalitarian agenda as relative prosperity returned, although this remains vulnerable to further external shocks and to a frequently cautious and selective embrace of equity in the Irish context.

Gender

Gender did not feature in the first two action plans on access produced by the HEA between 2004 and 2013, except in terms of concerns over the under-representation of men among new entrants to HE. As Loxley et al. note, this was arguably a missed opportunity to explore nuanced relationships between gender, social class and labour force participation after graduation.[166] Moreover, gender imbalances among higher education employees traditionally did not command the same level of attention from policy-makers as the various disparities in participation by students.

Gender disparities in promotions provoked serious conflict within HEIs for the first time in the late 1990s. A group of women academics challenged the outcome of UCD's promotions round in 1997–98, noting that 20 promotions to associate professor included only one woman: they accused the college of discrimination and of breaching new employment equality legislation. The governing body overwhelmingly approved the promotions in June 1998, but the national Employment Equality Agency pointedly criticised 'the pattern of promotions in UCD.'[167] The dispute in UCD was one of a number of flashpoints which testified both to the resilience of entrenched structural inequalities in most HEIs and to increasing resistance to the perpetuation of traditional power structures. Trinity College faced criticism on a different front in 2000, when former president Mary Robinson wrote to the provost, Thomas Mitchell, to protest at the low proportion of women among recent recipients of honorary degrees. Robinson's concerns were well founded, as only 25 of 150 honorary degrees had been awarded to women over the previous decade and none at all in the most recent list. Mitchell conceded the point, urging the honorary degrees committee to ensure 'that the situation will not occur again'.[168] Tokenism and lack of representation of women on college decision-making bodies were still prevalent: Áine Hyland, professor of education in UCC, noted in 1998 that she was often the sole woman sitting on committees or promotions boards.[169]

The most dramatic conflict over gender disparities came in NUI Galway, which had the lowest representation of female academics at senior level of any university. The college's promotions round in 2008–09, which led to the elevation of 16 male candidates and one woman, was challenged before the Equality Tribunal by one of the unsuccessful candidates, Dr. Micheline Sheehy Skeffington, a lecturer in botany (and granddaughter of the famous suffragist, Hanna Sheehy Skeffington). Sheehy Skeffington won the case in November 2014, when the Tribunal found that NUIG had discriminated against her based on gender and instructed that she be promoted to senior lecturer and awarded compensation.[170] It was a landmark gender discrimination case whose implications extended far beyond the flawed competition in NUIG. The college administration accepted the decision and appointed a task force on gender equality, although it was boycotted by the academic section of SIPTU due to a perceived lack of independence. But the decision triggered a wider discrimination case lodged in the High Court in 2015 by four other women lecturers overlooked in the 2009 promotions round.[171] The task force recommended far-reaching changes in policy and institutional structure, including mandatory gender quotas for senior academic posts and the appointment of a new vice-president for equality and diversity—the first such post in an Irish HEI. While NUIG faced criticisms for slowness in implementing gender quotas, the implications of the Sheehy Skeffington case are likely to be far-reaching and will hardly be restricted to NUIG.

The combination of top down pressure through equality legislation and bottom-up demands for change from female academics, often linked to the feminist movement, produced incremental changes in the policy and staffing of higher education institutions. Women entered senior leadership posts in significant numbers by the early 2000s. Caroline Hussey was elected as registrar of UCD in 1994 and ironically was involved in defending the controversial promotions round four years later; Frances Ruane, bursar of TCD in the early 1990s, was the first woman candidate for provost in 2001.[172] Jane Grimson became the first female vice provost of Trinity in 2001, while Linda Hogan took up the influential role of chief academic officer at VP level in 2011. Áine Hyland headed the Points Commission in 1999 and later became vice-president of UCC. Women took up top leadership roles in the IoTs to a greater extent than the universities in the early 2000s. Marion Coy became president of Galway-Mayo IoT in 2002, later serving as chairperson of IOTI and as a member of the Hunt strategy group.[173] Maria Hinfelaar served as president of Limerick IoT between 2004 and 2016, before being recruited to head Glyndwr university in north Wales in a move which drew academic and media attention in the UK.[174] The IoT sector saw a gradual improvement in the participation of women in decision-making bodies—over two thirds of IoT governing bodies and 43% of academic councils met the HEA's recommendation for 40% representation of women in 2016.[175] If the glass ceiling had not been shattered, it was certainly displaying a number of cracks.

But there were also sharp limitations to the upward mobility of women at senior level. No Irish university has yet appointed a female president and the 40% recommendation for gender balance in senior management teams was not met by any university in 2016.[176] The IoT sector performed somewhat better—three IoTs out of 14 had female presidents by 2016, but similarly only three met the 40% guideline for gender balance at senior management level.[177] The three HEA funded colleges stood out in terms of gender balance, although admittedly within a small sample—one of the three college presidents was female and two of the three had at least 40% female representation within their senior management team and governing body.[178] An international, EU-sponsored study of six countries in 2006 found that women held only 15% of positions at senior management level in Irish universities, while Ireland also had the lowest proportion of female professors in the study.[179] A qualitative study of senior management at university level by Prof Pat O'Connor, which was published in 2010, highlighted a 'gendered organisational culture reflected in gendered processes and procedures.'[180] The study involved a series of interviews which encompassed roughly half of those in senior executive positions in Irish universities and concluded that 'the gender disparities at senior management level are striking.'[181] O'Connor noted that professorial status was perceived by most participants as a necessary prerequisite for such roles, although not all men in senior management were at this level and there was little awareness that such an expectation had gendered implications.[182]

The most recent HEA data on gender profiles in 2016 also underlined the persistence of gender disparities among both academic and non-academic staff in different institutional types. Women now formed a majority of all higher education staff in universities (54%) and colleges (66%), as well as half of all staff in IoTs; 44% of core-funded academic staff in universities and IoTs were female—a striking change from the traditional pattern two decades before.[183] But despite genuine incremental improvement, notable gender imbalances were still apparent at higher grades. Men comprised 79% of university professors, 71% of associate professors and 64% of senior lecturers, although women accounted for roughly half of the lecturer grade.[184] The IoTs showed a less steep imbalance, but a comparable gender distribution—women comprised only 32% of senior lecturers but 50% of assistant lecturers, the lowest system grade.[185] Only in the HEA funded colleges did women come close to parity at senior lecturer level, but in these institutions they made up 70% of junior academics.[186] The traditional 'clustering' of women at lower grades identified a generation earlier was still evident in the vast majority of HEIs.

This trend was even more marked among non-academic grades. Women made up only 19% of the most senior administrative/professional grade in the IoTs and 28% in the universities, despite accounting for almost two thirds of all non-academic staff.[187] Female participation was also much more precarious—a majority of contract employees were women in both academic and non-academic grades; part-time employment was also predominantly female, particularly among non-academic staff where an overwhelming 92% of part-time, permanent employees at university level were women.[188] The figures were sufficiently stark to attract warnings from government ministers that higher education institutions would face funding sanctions if they failed to address gender inequality more effectively.

The inequalities in the culture and practice of HEIs proved persistent and largely unaffected by massification and even demographic transformation of the student body. The interest of policy-makers in gender equity at this level was intermittent and up to 2000 at least, pressure for reform was driven largely by feminist advocates in the public sphere and the commitment of individual, usually female ministers. A combination of top down and grassroots pressures certainly led to incremental advances, particularly in the proportion of women academics, who are no longer the marginal minority described by Smyth and Valiulis in the 1980s. The Sheehy Skeffington case offers a precedent for further action and may yet be seen as a tipping point in the debate over gender equality. Yet progress in overcoming gender disparities has been uneven, as structural inequalities remain influential and traditionally privileged groups in positions of power are usually slow to relinquish it.

The OECD Review

It was not surprising that an Irish government turned to the OECD to instigate a formal review of higher education, at a time when policy was once more being reoriented to reflect a different balance between the interests of HEIs, the state and the market. The government could expect reinforcement from the Paris-based think tank for many of its priorities, notably the development of 'fourth level' postgraduate education and research, linked to competitive funding mechanisms; 'managerial reform' of governance and strategic planning of the HE sector as a whole. The OECD could be expected to express an authoritative view on the future financing of higher education, where the 'free fees' regime remained an issue of perennial controversy. Noel Dempsey, Minister for Education (2002–04), made no secret of his view that tuition fees should be reintroduced, with the resources freed up being allocated to widen access through improving maintenance grants for low-income students. Dempsey's position was opposed by the government's minority partner, the Progressive Democrats and several Fianna Fáil ministers.[189] Referring the vexed issue of college financing to the OECD offered a means of containing the government's divisions.

Government aspirations for the future were encapsulated in the terms of reference for the OECD review team, which envisaged that 'the higher education sector would be open and flexible in meeting an increasing diversity of needs and demands associated with the knowledge society, lifelong learning, globalisation, meeting the needs of national and regional economies and local communities, together with contributing to social cohesion and equity.'[190] Most striking was the range of functions assigned to higher education and their close linkage to wide-ranging societal and economic objectives. The HE sector required strategic planning and management in line with 'an integrated and cohesive approach to the development of the roles of different higher education institutions...'[191] Achieving QA in teaching and learning; developing research and innovation coupled with effective application of its outcomes to social, cultural and economic progress; and solutions to the financing dilemma, all featured in the terms of reference. Internationalisation was also a key preoccupation of the review. The OECD was asked to consider how 'a critical mass of consistently high quality and standards' could be developed to guarantee international competitiveness in the context of increasing internationalisation and mobility of staff and students.[192]

The team of OECD examiners, composed of academics, former politicians and officials drawn from continental Europe, Australia and the USA, considered a background report prepared by Prof John Coolahan and undertook a country visit to Ireland from 15–27 February 2004.[193] Their report offered wide-ranging recommendations on system structure, institutional reform, research, widening participation and third-level financing. The broad thrust of the report dovetailed with the priorities of Irish ministers and officials who had initiated it, but the examiners offered criticisms of existing policies couched in diplomatic language and advanced alternative approaches in some areas. While the review was presented in pragmatic, non-ideological terms, its underlying perspective was firmly rooted in theories of human capital formation. The report noted approvingly that 'Ireland was one of the first European countries to grasp the economic importance of education'.[194] The examiners both lauded and sought to reinforce an existing political consensus on the economic value of higher education: 'It is recognised, perhaps more strongly than in any other country in Europe, that tertiary education is a key driver for the economy.'[195] Investment in higher education was positioned as a key imperative to develop a highly innovative economy and the report was blunt in its identification of the system's outcomes in economic terms: '…the effectiveness of the tertiary education system, and the relevance of its products, is so critical to the long-term nature of Ireland's economy…'[196] The identification of programmes and qualifications as 'products' was striking and indicated a narrow interpretation of human capital in which higher education was positioned largely as an 'arm of economic policy.'[197]

This positioning of higher education as an integral part of a knowledge based economy influenced the team's view of postgraduate research: 'At the postgraduate level numbers do not match national aspirations and in particular PhD numbers are far too low'.[198] They recommended an intensification of government policies to promote postgraduate research, advising a doubling of the number of PhD students.[199] This recommendation was central to the new *Strategy for Science, Technology and Innovation 2007–2013* (SSTI), which embraced its vision of doctoral education.[200] The government also implemented other recommendations by the team for improved co-ordination of research policy, including the creation of a cabinet committee on research and the appointment of a chief scientific adviser.

The OECD team emphasised preserving the binary model, recommending 'differentiation in mission' between universities and IoTs, not least to maintain the traditional role of the IoTs in offering sub-degree qualifications and supporting regional economic development.[201] The examiners urged the government to resist pressures from IoTs for university status, arguing that 'for the foreseeable future there should be no further institutional transfers into the university sector'.[202] Yet they also recommended a unified governing framework for the tertiary sector, bringing IoTs and universities together under a new tertiary education authority, as 'policy towards tertiary education is fragmented...'; this was to be achieved within a structure maintaining differentiation of institutional functions and preventing 'mission drift'.[203] The existing managerial controls on the institutes were to be reviewed with the intention of 'drastically lightening the load of external regulation'[204]— an implicit criticism of the tight control maintained by the department over the IoTs since their inception, supporting the case made by IoT directors for operational freedom.

The OECD team was critical of the absence of a national strategy for higher education and identified a general fragmentation of responsibilities between different government departments which included education and research within their remit. The report favoured a new co-ordinating tier consisting of a permanent 'National Council for Tertiary Education, Research and Innovation', bringing together all government departments operating in higher education to 'lay down strategic guidelines to steer the system's operational machinery'.[205] The report also backed 'reform' in the governance of HEIs, reflecting the views of government ministers and some university leaders. Among their recommendations were that the post of university president or institute director should be publicly advertised and open to external candidates; the size of university governing bodies would be reduced to a maximum of 20 with 'a substantial majority' of lay members and universities should introduce more rigorous conditions for tenure.[206]

The OECD review supported the expansionist strategy pursued by the Irish state in higher education since the 1960s, suggesting that 'the great strength of the Irish tertiary education system is the way it has expanded student numbers while preserving quality…'.[207] But the reviewers struck a discordant note in their critique of existing policies on widening participation, noting that expansion had been achieved mainly by increasing participation among the 18–21 year old cohort and drawing heavily on the managerial and professional classes. The team was critical of the HEA projection for an age participation rate of over 60% by 2010, which 'perpetuates the sense that manpower needs will only be satisfied by increasing the numbers of full-time students…'[208] Further expansion in the age participation rate should not be achieved 'by simply drawing more on the dominant socio-economic groups currently entering tertiary education, as has happened, for example, in the expansion of numbers in the UK'.[209] The report recommended the removal of the distinction between part-time and full-time students with regard to payment of fees and eligibility for maintenance grants. Asserting that the abolition of tuition fees had not delivered the impact hoped for in widening participation, the team recommended the re-introduction of undergraduate fees, combined with reform of the means-tested support schemes and introduction of targeted grants for low-income students and students with special educational needs.[210] The resources raised by the tuition fees should represent a real increase in HEIs' income, rather than being simply offset against reduction in exchequer funding. The OECD team believed that the re-introduction of tuition fees was 'a necessary strategic step which will invigorate the tertiary education system and make it more competitive worldwide…', without compromising initiatives for widening participation.[211]

While not all of its recommendations were adopted, the OECD review exerted substantial influence on government policies. The most significant institutional change brought the IoTs and DIT under the remit of the HEA, through the Institutes of Technology Act, 2006, in line with the recommendations from the OECD team.[212] The HEA assumed responsibility for allocation and oversight of funding to the IoT/DIT sector for the first time. The authority's role in overseeing the colleges was similar in some respects to its interface with the universities, involving similar powers to review strategic plans and equality policies. The new legislation explicitly established for the first time the right of the colleges to promote the principles of academic freedom and affirmed the freedom enjoyed by academic staff in identical terms to the universities act. Yet despite the hopes expressed by the OECD team, autonomy at institutional level remained limited by legal and political constraints. The minister retained much greater powers over most non-university colleges than the universities. The governing authorities were required to comply with 'policy directions as may be issued by the minister from time to time', including those regarding the level and range of their academic programmes.[213] The governing bodies were also required to ensure that the colleges contributed to 'the promotion of the economic, cultural and social development of the State', as well as having regard to a range of other official objectives, including equality of access and promotion of the Irish language.[214] These clauses, which mirrored the language employed by the RTC legislation in 1992, confirmed political and business expectations of the technical colleges since their inception. Significantly, the government did not act on the OECD's proposal for a new national council to take a lead role in overseeing a coherent national system of innovation, which would have curtailed the role both of the HEA and the departments of Education and Enterprise. The report's perspective on college governance was not acted on immediately, but later received a definitive official imprimatur in the national strategy for higher education, which endorsed smaller university governing bodies and greater accountability by academic staff.[215]

The report's most critical commentary of the status quo in HE regarding widening participation and tuition fees also had the least influence. While debates in the early 2000s had suggested support within the Fianna Fáil-led government for replacing 'free fees' with a more generous higher education grants scheme benefiting low-income social groups, a major reform of higher education finance never materialised. Successive governments rejected the reintroduction of tuition fees due to strong political opposition linked to concern about the impact on middle-class families, particularly voiced by the minority parties in the government, the Progressive Democrats in 2003 and later the Greens in 2009–10. Instead student fees were increased incrementally by the back door through hiking the registration fee, initially set at £150 in 1995, to €670 by 2002–03, even before the Celtic Tiger began to sputter.[216] Similarly, the report did not inspire any action to remove the financial disincentives facing part-time students, despite much rhetoric about the importance of lifelong learning. The financing of higher education did not change significantly as a result of the OECD review and remained strongly oriented towards increasing full-time participation. In this respect, whatever the merits of its proposed solutions, the OECD review was certainly a missed opportunity to address the flawed higher education financing system at a time of relative affluence.

Sustainability

Funding for Irish higher education on a per capita basis was modest by international standards in the early 2000s and continued to be heavily dependent on public resources. While Ireland was close to the OECD average in terms of the level of public investment in higher education (about 1% of GDP) in 2006, private investment in HE at a mere 0.2% lagged well behind the international average for developed countries.[217] The upsurge in expenditure per student during the 1990s tailed off in the following decade well before the end of the economic boom: the rate of increase in spending per student was only 9% between 2000 and 2010, approximately a fifth of the level it had reached in the previous five year period.[218] Overall funding for higher education became more parsimonious even as the sector was positioned by national policy-makers as a key contributor to knowledge based economic development through research and innovation.

The very impressive growth rates of the early Celtic Tiger period began to subside from 2001, to be replaced by a rapidly inflating but unsustainable property bubble. The 'stop-go' approach decried by institutions was provoked by a post-election financial retrenchment by the

Fianna Fáil-led government in 2002; this was, however, also linked to a longer term shift in policy on HE influenced by demographic factors. The number of Leaving Certificate candidates peaked in the late 1990s and declined by about 12,000 between 1998 and 2006, raising the prospect of a falling student population.[219] Don Thornhill, secretary of the HEA, referenced a recent decline in applications under the CAO in 2002, warning that the sector was moving into 'a more complex and competitive era in which colleges may have to learn to live with less money and specialise more...'.[220] In fact, the number of Leaving Certificate candidates began to increase again from 2008 and the HEA's fear of falling enrolments proved dramatically wide of the mark before the end of the decade.[221] Yet such predictions left their mark on government policy, creating a more unfavourable political environment to justify investment than in the 1990s. Moreover, policy-makers within the HEA and DES increasingly sought to reshape the internal functioning of institutions as the price for continuing exchequer support for research and infrastructural investment.

A revised system of allocating resources for publicly funded HEIs was introduced gradually in the early 2000s, building on the formula based unit cost model implemented from 1995.[222] The revised allocation model was introduced for the universities from 2006 and later phased in for the IoTs from 2009.[223] The dominant element was a block grant paid as a single allocation with the internal budgeting determined by the HEIs themselves, subject to review by the HEA. The introduction of the modern block grant completed a long-term transition from an earlier 'line-item' model in which government departments provided funding for distinct budgetary lines, usually grouped together within a particular Vote.[224] The block grant includes a core recurrent grant (originally known as the Recurrent Grant Allocation Model) allocated through a funding formula determined by weightings for the relative costs of education in different disciplines, complemented by additional weightings for research and access and limited performance based elements linked to research outcomes and skills provision.[225] Other components within the block grant include the 'free fees' grant paid to HEIs since 1995–96 'in lieu of tuition fees'; core grant support for research linked mainly to research student numbers and core funding for 'access performance' assigning an additional weighting of one third to the normal student weighting to promote recruitment and retention of students from traditionally under-represented groups.[226] Available funding has been split into two 'pots' for universities/colleges and IoTs, according to historically based proportions of 60 and 40% respectively. The ringfencing of funding for each sector was a deliberate decision by the HEA, in response to the OECD recommendation to maintain the differentiated roles of the two main sectors and to concerns from both sectors to prevent 'leakage' of funding from one to the other.[227]

The other key elements of the funding model are 'directed' funding earmarked for specific purposes and 'performance' funding linked to the quality of an institution's performance in meeting targets relating to government objectives.[228] Earmarked funding to meet identifiable skills gaps has been a feature of the system since the late 1970s, when funding from the Manpower programme was used to develop engineering and computing. More recently, earmarked funding has been ringfenced and 'topsliced' from the block grant to support specific projects of strategic importance such as the National Forum for the Enhancement of Teaching and Learning and discipline based restructuring following thematic reviews in medical and nursing education.[229] Directed funding has increasingly been awarded competitively to serve strategic objectives, notably through the SIF between 2006 and 2013.[230] Performance based funding is a much more recent development in Ireland—although it was proposed by the HEA as early as 2005, it remained aspirational until the launch of the Hunt report in 2011.[231] The performance funding element established since 2013 envisaged the withholding of up to 10% of the block grant allocated for a particular year 'on the basis of verified performance against agreed targets in the preceding year.'[232] This performance based component was linked to a series of mission based compacts agreed between HEIs and the HEA from 2014.[233] This was a potentially radical recasting of the funding allocation model and held out the prospect of punitive sanctions against institutions if they failed to show sufficent progress in meeting government objectives.

The collapse of the Celtic Tiger economy in 2007–08 and the resulting adoption of austerity policies, later underpinned by the joint European Union-International Monetary Fund bailout programme from November 2010, had a dramatic and sustained impact on higher education. State investment in higher education declined by 38% between 2009 and 2016, even as student numbers increased by 34,000.[234] Public expenditure accounted for only 51% of overall funding of higher education in 2014–2015 (including capital funding but excluding contract research income).[235] This was less than the share of public expenditure in 1993 following the previous recession, at a time when both enrolments and projected participation figures were considerably lower. Even more striking was the severe decline in the per capita funding base of higher education—total income per student (incorporating core public funding, student contribution and other student fees) declined by 22% over a seven year period.[236] The decline in public funding was particularly severe in the first three years of the recession, when the HEA estimated that a 15% reduction in per capita funding had occurred. Clancy suggests that the Irish system experienced a steeper decline in the per capita funding base between 2007 and 2010 than any European country other than Lithuania, Greece and Hungary.[237] Moreover, this decline coincided with an upsurge in student enrolments, which accelerated throughout the recession: overall numbers in HEA-funded institutions grew from 196,000 in 2011–12 to 210,000 in 2014–15.[238] As Clancy noted, higher education faced 'something of a perfect storm', as declining public funding combined with a continued increase in student enrolments and reduced staffing levels since the start of the recession.[239] The notable decline of public funding during the crisis marked the most significant withdrawal of resources from higher education since the emergence of mass education in the third quarter of the twentieth century.

This erosion in the per capita resource base for higher education occurred in tandem with a dramatic increase in student fees. The registration payment was increased by successive governments from €900 to €3000 per annum between 2008 and 2015 and recategorised as a 'student contribution' from 2011–12, dropping the threadbare rationale that it was intended purely to fund specific student services.[240]

The trebling of the student contribution effectively reversed the 'free fees' policy introduced in the mid 1990s, while maintaining the formal scheme of remission for the tuition fee. The return of significant student fees had little to do with equity but was driven by the financial demands of austerity and the contested status of the 'free fees' policy itself, which had never won universal public or elite acceptance. This increase brought Ireland in line with funding systems in a plurality of European countries, in which a majority of students pay fees and a minority receive grants, while restoring the 'private' contribution to about one-third of the total cost, similar to the average level before the mid-1990s.[241] Austerity policies also led to the termination of maintenance payments to postgraduate students and some restrictions in grants at undergraduate level in the 2012 budget. The rapid re-imposition of fees was offset to some extent for lower and middle income entrants by a significant increase in the proportion of undergraduate students receiving third level grants in publicly funded colleges, which reached 48% of full-time students in 2014–15 compared to one third only six years before.[242] Yet this was more accidental than a matter of deliberate policy, resulting from increased student numbers and a substantial rise in the number of students qualifying for a grant, not least due to declining incomes during the recession.[243] Moreover, while overall public investment in the student support schemes grew by over 30% since 2008, over half of this funding was required to cover the cost of the student contribution and the maintenance element of the grant was reduced; the Cassells report in 2016 acknowledged that maintenance payments 'fell well below actual living costs'.[244]

The 'free fees' policy, which never commanded wholehearted support within government departments, was a notable casualty of the crisis and the de facto undermining of this policy was not accompanied by any corresponding moves to widen participation. Significantly, the increase in the student contribution was accomplished without much difficulty compared to other austerity measures which attracted large-scale public protest. This reflected the contested status of the policy and the fragmented nature of lobbying within the higher education sector where university and student leaders disagreed over the restoration of fees. Yet the re-emergence of a de facto third level fee, albeit capped due to a continuing state subsidy, in the absence of any corresponding initiative to target widening participation, also reflected the sidelining of egalitarian priorities in national policy during the economic crisis.

The erosion in the per capita funding base for higher education was damaging to HEIs in various ways, not all immediately visible. The reduction in core recurrent grants from the HEA, allied to tight employment control frameworks which restricted the recruitment and replacement of exchequer funded posts from 2009, led to a deterioration in the staff: student ratio from 16:1 to 20:1 by 2015.[245] The decline in capital expenditure, always vulnerable in an era of crisis, was nevertheless striking—exchequer capital funding on higher education was slashed by over half, from €202 million in 2009 to €87 million six years later.[246] The effect of this reduction was felt in an effective suspension of state investment in new buildings and minimal updating of equipment or ICT facilities.[247] The crisis also led to an agreement in 2009 between the government and the pre-1989 universities in which the state took over responsibility for university pension schemes. This agreement appeared a symbiotic arrangement, offering a state guarantee of the pension fund while the assets appeared on the state balance sheet; but the 'rescue' of the schemes by the state also gave increased leverage to government agencies over the staffing and management of the universities.[248]

The post-crisis budget in October 2016 offered an increase of only €37 million for higher education, which was derided by Mike Jennings, general secretary of IFUT, as 'a sponge held to the lips of a man dying of thirst.'[249] As the end of the recession brought only a very limited recovery in terms of recurrent or capital investment, at least some national policy-makers sounded the alarm. A HEA report on system performance in December 2016 chronicled the scale of the devastation in terms of institutional finances, identifying 'major sustainability problems facing the sector.'[250] 11 of the 26 HEA-funded institutions were in deficit in 2014–15, while the university sector as a whole was running at a loss of €1.5 million. The plight of the IoT sector was more acute and led to a dedicated financial review of the sector which confirmed that half of the 14 IoTs were in 'unplanned deficit' and five of these were 'vulnerable' in terms of short-term financial solvency.[251]

The de facto freeze on capital development even as enrolments steadily increased also had an enduring legacy. Space utilisation was at a premium as Irish HEIs provided 25% less physical space per student than international norms: 'Major repair or replacement is required on 41% of the total space in the sector.'[252] The financial reviews underlined an increasing risk not only to the quality of teaching and learning or the much vaunted student experience, but to the stability of HEIs, many of which lacked the reserves or the ability to leverage sufficient private funding to operate effectively or even guarantee their sustainability.

The IMF-EU bailout certainly constrained the options of government between 2010 and 2014, but official rhetoric around the importance of higher education to economic recovery was at odds with the absence of any practical attempt to limit the impact of the crisis on HE. The government response to the Great Recession was twofold—to seek an increase in the student contribution, which trebled in a seven year period and to urge cost-saving rationalisation on HEIs, deliberately lowering expectations of any medium-term assistance from the public purse. Moreover, even in a reviving economy conflicting demands for public service spending commanded greater support than the claims of higher education, not least because other lobby groups were more powerful and effective than the fragmented voices of the higher education sector. Ironically, this decline in public funding and political leverage occurred as policy-makers sought to achieve a strategic re-positioning of higher education, reinforcing its importance to the overriding goal of economic salvation.

Private Higher Education

Private higher education institutions have traditionally formed only a small element of higher education in Ireland. Yet for-profit colleges, which were a marginal element for most of the twentieth century, have recently taken a more prominent role in areas traditionally dominated by public HEIs and have established an increased profile at a time of reduced funding of the state-aided sector. A historical analysis of privately funded colleges which receive no state subsidy presents challenges which are not present to the same extent in the state-aided sector. Firstly, as Clancy notes, the privately funded sector is the most poorly documented strand of higher education, as a majority of private colleges make no return of enrolments to the HEA.[253] Distinctions arise between not for profit colleges and corporate for profit institutions, which have tended to gain ground in the last two decades. Complex issues of definition also arise in a historical context, as the boundaries between public and private were not always clear-cut. Trinity College Dublin, a leading 'public' research intensive university, was regarded by the Department of Education as a private institution up to the late 1940s and ambiguity about TCD's status in terms of the state persisted into the late twentieth century.[254]

International scholarship on private higher education (PHE) is of variable relevance in the Irish context. Levy's analysis of higher education and the state in Latin America, posits 'three waves of private growth', namely (i) Catholic, (ii) elite, and (iii) demand absorbing, which followed earlier waves of expansion in the public system.[255] But Levy's characterisation of the latest wave of expansion in PHE as 'demand absorbing',[256] responding to the failure of the public sector to meet the increasing demand for college places has limited resonance in the Irish context, where massification was achieved almost entirely through publicly funded HEIs and underpinned by an interventionist state agenda. The evolution of PHE in Ireland during the twentieth century was more in line with the 'peripheral private sectors' identified by Geiger, which developed in European countries such as France, Sweden and the UK, rather than the 'mass private sectors' in Japan and the Philippines.[257] Yet much of the international literature predates the more recent expansion of for profit PHE since the 1990s.[258]

The boundary between 'public' and 'private' may be subject to change over time. The Catholic Workers College was transformed over two generations from a Catholic trade union institute into a major state aided, business-oriented institution. The final and most radical transition for the college occurred in the 1990s, when the Jesuits relinquished their control of the institution, transferring it to lay control. The college also acquired significant exchequer funding for the first time, when the DES provided core grant funding of £600,000, while its full-time students became eligible for the higher education grants scheme.[259] The embrace of state aid was linked to an expansion of student enrolments and a repositioning of the college as a key provider of business, humanities and ICT courses, leading to its rebranding as the National College of Ireland (NCI). The most ambitious phase of this latest repositioning occurred between 1999 and 2002, when the NCI leadership drew on capital investment of €8.8 million from the exchequer, allied to substantial private funding, to finance the transfer of the college to a new site at the Irish Financial Services Centre in Dublin's Docklands.[260] The transfer of NCI to the new campus testified to the success of its leadership in mobilising alliances with both government and business. NCI was the largest of a number of colleges, state aided but operating on a non-profit basis, which occupied an intermediate position between the publicly funded HEIs and private for profit institutions by the early 2000s.

It is important to acknowledge the limited data on the enrolments, organisation and sometimes even existence of for profit colleges for most of the twentieth century.[261] For-profit higher education expanded in the final quarter of the twentieth century. Several of these colleges were established initially to prepare students for the examinations of professional bodies, particularly in business and accountancy and therefore prioritised business and social science courses.[262] The more notable providers of this type included Dublin Business School (DBS) and Griffith College Dublin (GCD). DBS, established in 1975, initially offered evening courses for students preparing for professional examinations in accountancy.[263] The college was unsuccessful in securing recognition from the NCEA in the mid 1980s and some private sector leaders regarded the NCEA board, influenced by the Teachers Union of Ireland (TUI), as hostile to recognition for private colleges; DBS instead secured accreditation for its undergraduate courses from Liverpool's John Moores University from 1989.[264] DBS took over a number of other private providers in the early 2000s, including Portobello College in 2007.[265] Griffith, established in 1974 as a business/accountancy college, followed a similar trajectory, securing recognition from the University of Ulster.[266] Griffith absorbed a number of smaller regional providers in the 2000s, expanding its activity to Cork and Limerick and also established an international presence, with satellite campuses in

Russia and Pakistan.[267] Griffith and DBS both vied for the mantle of Ireland's leading 'independent' institution and their historical development and vocational orientation was very similar.[268]

A potentially more significant expansion of for profit HE occurred in the early 2000s, as existing for profit providers expanded their footprint and the first for-profit online education college was established in the Republic. Hibernia College, set up in 2001 by Seán Rowland, developed a range of undergraduate, postgraduate and professional development courses through online platforms, which were validated by HETAC.[269] Hibernia was best known for its postgraduate teacher education programme, which attracted a steady influx of student teachers but provoked controversy with the established colleges of education. St Patrick's College and Mary Immaculate, as well as the INTO, protested when the Department of Education approved Hibernia's online programme for primary teachers in 2003, objecting to lack of consultation and more fundamentally to the absence of any tradition of teacher education or engagement with a university by the new provider.[270] The college's management claimed in November 2003 that Hibernia was being targeted by 'vested interests within the traditional teacher training sector'.[271] While the controversy rumbled on at an Oireachtas committee in 2004, Hibernia emerged as a major player in teacher education over the following decade. The decision to permit a for profit provider to enter the field of teacher education underlined the growing prominence of private higher education in the early 2000s and the closer engagement of for profit colleges with the state.

The larger for-profit colleges, including Griffith and DBS, established validation relationships for their degree programmes principally with UK universities up to the 1990s.[272] But more recently for profit providers established formal linkages with Irish executive agencies and came within the public regulatory system.[273] The White Paper in 1995 promised 'new control regulations' for private colleges offering state validated programmes.[274] The collapse of three small for-profit colleges in Dublin during 1996–97 shone a spotlight on the need for consumer protection, as the absence of financial bonding left students vulnerable to losing their investment.[275] The White Paper proposed regulation to address the vacuum in QA, prescribe 'institutional norms' in terms of academic standards and protect the financial investment of students.[276] A number of private colleges became designated providers under the NCEA, which validated 65 programmes in private colleges in 1998.[277] The Qualifications legislation in 1999 gave a statutory basis to regulation of private colleges for the first time, requiring compulsory bonding arrangements to recoup student fees on any programmes sanctioned by state awarding bodies.[278] The voluntary incorporation of many private providers within the new regulatory regime underlined the 'complementary needs' of private colleges and the state.[279] Diarmuid Hegarty, president of Griffith, welcomed the 1999 legislation 'in the interests of both the consumer and the colleges'.[280] DBS became a designated institution under HETAC in the 1990s and more recently decided to seek accreditation of all of its awards by QQI.[281] National policy-makers aimed to achieve a minimum level of regulation while larger private providers sought the seal of approval from the state to validate an expanding range of programmes.

The expansion of the larger private colleges and development of institutional relationships with the state contributed to the foundation of the Higher Education Colleges Association (HECA) in 1991 by four private colleges whose programmes were designated under the NCEA.[282] HECA spanned the diversity of private higher education by 2016, incorporating larger for profit colleges including DBS, Griffith and Hibernia, major non-profits including NCI and smaller institutions with a specialised remit such as St. Nicholas' Montessori College.[283] HECA was supportive of the qualifications legislation and the engagement of private colleges with the state awarding bodies, not least because its members had a vested interest in protecting their reputation and limiting the excesses of unregulated operators.

Despite the expansion of various forms of private provision in the early 2000s, private colleges remained a relatively small strand of higher education. The sector accounted for about 7% of the overall student cohort from levels 6–9, based on data supplied to the Cassells report in 2016, which noted a 'small but prominent private higher education sector.'[284] About 15,000 students are enrolled in private colleges, with three large institutions, Griffith, DBS and Hibernia, accounting for 80% of the total.[285] Diversity in scale and function is a notable feature of the private sector, which makes meaningful analysis more problematic: a research intensive institution with an international reach such as RCSI has little in common with small specialised Montessori colleges. The development of PHE was broadly consistent with Geiger's conceptualisation of a 'peripheral' private sector certainly up to the 1990s.[286] The most recent data indicates that the established pattern has not changed significantly, despite the recent expansion of for profit colleges and indications of government support for greater private provision in areas traditionally served by publicly funded HEIs.

The Hunt Report

The repositioning of higher education as an economic asset, linked to a narrow conceptualisation of human capital, became pervasive in national policies following the economic crash. The national strategy for higher education to 2030, issued by a strategy group led by Dr. Colin Hunt in January 2011, positioned higher education as 'a sustaining force for social and economic regeneration'.[287] This was not a new phenomenon, as policy-makers had allotted a central function to education in economic development for two generations. Yet the extent to which the report was shaped by its economic context is striking: the Hunt report was published three and a half years into the most severe economic crisis affecting the Irish state since the 1950s and barely two months after the Irish government was obliged to accept the joint EU-IMF bailout programme in November 2010. The leadership role assigned to Colin Hunt, the Dublin division director of the Australian bank Macquarie Capital Advisers, as chairman of the strategy group underlined the priorities of the Fianna Fáil-led government. Hunt, an economist whose career had been spent mainly in the higher echelons of the corporate and banking sector, had served as a special adviser to government ministers, including Taoiseach Brian Cowen.[288] As one insider close to the group noted, '...he knew absolutely nothing about higher education – had no experience of academia at all.'[289] The composition of the strategy group, particularly the predominance of members drawn from outside higher education, attracted criticism from university leaders. Only four of its 15 members were academics, while public officials from the departments of the Taoiseach, Finance, Education and Enterprise were strongly represented on the group, which also included members from Microsoft Ireland and EMC Manufacturing and representatives of agencies such as Forfás which tended to reflect an industry viewpoint.[290] Ferdinand von Prondzynski, outgoing president of DCU, commented in 2010 that most members of 'the undead higher education strategic review…' lacked knowledge of higher education and was sceptical that they would produce recommendations which were 'evidence-based rather than anecdote-inspired'.[291] The recommendations did little to disprove Von Prondzynski's analysis.

The Hunt report made the sweeping assertion that higher education 'is the key to economic recovery in the short-term and to longer-term prosperity'.[292] A litany of almost exclusively economic challenges was set for HE. The Irish economy faced a transition from application of knowledge developed elsewhere to knowledge generation—'we will increasingly have to be knowledge creators ourselves'; the educational level of the Irish population had to be raised to facilitate greater knowledge creation and the HE system repositioned to face these challenges.[293] The role and purpose of higher education was conditioned by the economic demands of Irish society in the twenty-first century, particularly the imperative of overcoming the economic crisis triggered by the Great Recession and by an international discourse around managerial reform and structural rationalisation mediated particularly through the OECD.

An important theme of the strategy, namely increasing the level of participation in higher education, was informed by a notably utilitarian rationale. The report was explicit in acknowledging the human capital paradigm as the rationale for widening participation: 'it is essential to create and enhance human capital by expanding participation in higher education'.[294] The report declared that:

More higher education graduates are needed to:
Provide a workforce capable of dealing with the increasingly complex demands of the global economy...
Attract high value-added investment and create high-skilled jobs, which will bring significant benefits to the wider economy;
Develop the research base which will provide opportunities for the development of new ideas, products and services;....[295]

The report acknowledged in a cursory fashion the 'less tangible social and civic benefits' flowing from participation in higher education, while leaving no doubt that the key rationale for increasing participation was greater economic productivity in an era of intense global competition. The more nuanced analysis of the value and complexities of widening participation in successive national action plans on access had no counterpart in the Hunt report. A single column was devoted to an analysis of differing entry rates to HE by socio-economic status, compared to a detailed three page discussion of 'Future skills: graduates for the 21st century'.[296] The report's vision for expanding participation had little to do with equity, but was about raising the educational level of the Irish population as the key to successful competitive performance in the globalised marketplace.[297]

Achieving greater efficiency and concentration of resources in HE was a key theme of the report, following the trail blazed by the OECD review. The strategy group set out a programme of reform encompassing institutional governance and system structure. This programme was explicitly linked to a demand for improving performance levels on the part of Irish HE relative to other high-performing (and better resourced) states within the OECD.[298] The report proposed significant reform in the governance of HEIs, involving both a reduction in the size of governing authorities and the appointment of a majority of external members. Governance structures were to be reformed at system level as well, with a similar reduction in the board of the HEA.[299] The proposals on governance were drawn directly from the recommendations of the OECD examiners seven years earlier.

The strategy envisaged a more 'coherent' higher education landscape characterised by a smaller number of larger institutions. Consolidation was a consistent mantra of the report, which argued that smaller stand-alone institutions lacked the scale required 'to deliver the necessary advances in quality and efficiency'.[300] Hunt envisaged that a number of IoTs could be merged to create technological universities, distinguished from existing universities through their commitment to 'career-focused higher education', particularly delivering programmes at levels 6–8 in STEM disciplines.[301] The technological universities were assigned a key role in achieving upskilling of the labour force by delivering significant increases in the level of part-time students, taking up somewhat belatedly another issue raised by the OECD.[302] The emergence of up to three new technological universities was explicitly linked to meeting performance challenges driven by vocational requirements and collaboration with industry.[303]

Rationalisation was justified not simply because it saved money, but particularly on wider economic grounds linked to national competitiveness, based on the debatable assumption that 'the next phase of economic development will require an even greater concentration of resources and expertise'.[304] The development of 'critical mass' in research, particularly on the part of universities, was a necessary prerequisite to allow Irish HEIs to compete effectively at a global level. This impulse for rationalisation, consistent with 'managerial reform' approaches over the previous decade, was potentially in conflict with the Irish tradition of regional economic and social development, exemplified at higher level particularly by the role of the IoTs.[305] This conflict was not teased out in the report, but complicated efforts by national policy-makers to implement a strategy of 'consolidation', which impinged on established regional interests and networks.

The report was definitive about the need for rationalisation at programme and institutional level, seeking new service level agreements as part of a 'strategic dialogue' between the HEA and third-level institutions. This was no mere consultative exercise, but an ongoing process of engagement in which the HEA would ensure the compatibility of institutional strategies with national policies.[306] A key element of the 'strategic dialogue' was the introduction of an explicit performance based funding element to 'incentivise good performance and penalise institutions which fail to deliver'.[307] The 'strategic dialogue' was intended to achieve rationalisation within and between HEIs. The strategy group aimed to reduce duplication in academic programmes and services, 'by rationalising programmes and offering them in fewer institutions'.[308] A favoured model of rationalisation presented by Hunt was a regional cluster approach, which stopped short of merging HEIs, at least in the case of the universities. Instead it was envisaged that HEIs of various types would engage in close collaboration, involving rationalisation of programmes and sharing of services.[309] The report drew its inspiration and many of its specific recommendations from the OECD review.

Clancy suggests that the national strategy, in failing to offer a detailed contextual analysis of the Irish HE system or to undertake primary research, essentially 'relied on reproducing the policy consensus emanating primarily from the OECD.'[310] The Hunt report was compared unfavourably to previous government-led reviews of higher education, including the report of the Steering Committee in 1995, which presented a contextualised analysis of the system, backed up by the extensive research of the technical working group.[311] The Hunt report certainly adopted an essentially bureaucratic, top-down approach to policy formulation, which contrasted even more sharply with the evidence-based education policy reviews of the 1960s, notably the *Investment in Education* study, which was informed by a comprehensive survey of educational provision in school districts throughout the country and production of detailed educational and labour market projections.[312] The strategy group's dependence on the OECD both for data and policy inspiration reflected a common discourse between national policy-makers and the OECD on higher education. The key recommendations were the product of a narrow conceptualisation of the role and mission of higher education, framed almost entirely in terms of its contribution to human capital.

Yet if the ideological inspiration for the national strategy's recommendations was clear-cut, a more complex and nuanced picture emerges in considering the process of its formulation. The content of the report reflected divisions within the strategy group, which never developed a unified perspective on the future of the higher education system. Persistent tensions emerged within the group, particularly between academic members and senior departmental representatives, as well as nominees from state agencies working closely with enterprise. A minority of members were strongly opposed to the drive for technological universities favoured by most public officials and considered resigning from the strategy group in protest at an advanced draft of the report, although they reluctantly accepted the final version.[313] An insider with a detailed knowledge of the process commented that 'there were a number of business people and civil servants on it who despised the universities…'[314] Another insider commented that Hunt, while hindered by his lack of knowledge of HE, also 'faced the task of chairing a group where views were often diametrically opposed.'[315] Early drafts of the report were more critical of HEIs for failing to adapt to economic and societal imperatives and sought to reposition higher education around an overarching concept of 'innovation'.[316] Yet such an emphasis on the shortcomings of the system was flatly contradicted by an ECOFIN report in 2009, pointing out that Ireland ranked first in the EU in terms of the esteem in which graduates were held by employers.[317] Progress on the report stalled in 2009, partly due to the economic crisis and lack of internal leadership, but mainly due to disagreements within the group. The final recommendations were drafted by senior public officials independently from the backroom team working on the main body of the text.[318] The report which eventually emerged was a compromise between the different civil service, business and academic interests on the group. The tortuous process of producing the report, allied to difficulties in reaching consensus within the group, did much to explain the sometimes uneasy coexistence of differing objectives and ambivalent language within the report.

The strategy group's recommendations in some key areas, notably governance and structure, reflected the imprint of NPM. The recommendation for the restructuring of university governing bodies to create a majority of 'lay' members was justified not only by their expertise in governance, but their status as external nominees distanced from traditional academic stakeholders.[319] This recommendation was consistent with an NPM philosophy, which sought to reduce the influence of 'insiders', notably academics and trade unions, while increasing the power of managers and the responsiveness of institutions to government policy and private industry.[320]

The powerful role given to the HEA in driving forward the process of rationalisation was consistent with the NPM practice of delegating significant authority to devolved executive agencies, which were empowered to deliver a 'managerial reform' agenda.[321] Significantly, at the heart of the proposed funding system were performance related mechanisms to promote efficiency, value for money and implementation of official priorities. These initiatives included a performance incentive mechanism where HEIs delivering an agreed level of service at a lower cost would retain the resulting savings for reinvestment, as well as the introduction of dedicated performance funding linked to national policy priorities.[322] This initiative was similar to public management and funding systems in the UK, New Zealand and Australia based on strong performance management and auditing of public service institutions.[323] The strategy group drew upon the rhetoric and to some extent the reality of NPM ideas.

Yet the national strategy in practice was far from being a charter for radical market reform or even managerial transformation. Irish higher education policy was closer in some respects to the network governance approach identified by Ferlie et al., characterised by the development of strategic alliances and networks between HEIs, combined with alliance building, negotiation and co-option of such networks by the state.[324] The network governance narrative is consistent with the Irish social partnership model stemming from the late 1980s, which was essentially a tripartite compact between the state, employers and trade unions, with more recent participation by voluntary and community organisations.[325] Although the partnership model was eclipsed by the advent of economic crisis, a deeply rooted commitment to achieving 'consensus' with major social groups was diluted rather than abandoned and found expression in the Croke Park I and Haddington Road agreements in 2010 and 2013 respectively: such agreements were focused mainly on maintaining a workable truce between government and organised labour to prevent large-scale industrial conflict.[326] National policy-makers also sought to work through existing or newly developed collaborative networks to achieve policy objectives, rather than imposing structural or institutional change through legislation or executive diktat. A number of inter-institutional alliances had developed in the early 2000s, largely in response to the competitive funding programmes offered by the PRTLI and more specific incentive funding through the SIF.[327] These included the Dublin Region Higher Education Alliance (DRHEA) financed by SIF; the TCD-UCD Innovation Alliance and a regional network of HEIs in Munster known as the Shannon Consortium.[328] The report sought to mobilise and build on such collaborative networks through the formation of regional clusters.[329]

Despite its advocacy of greater centralised control of higher education, the Hunt report did not amount to an unequivocal embrace of NPM approaches on the model of England or Australia.[330] The report affirmed that the preservation of 'a diverse range of strong, autonomous HE institutions is essential if the overall system is to respond effectively to evolving and unpredictable societal needs'.[331] Unsurprisingly, this support for autonomy was informed by a utilitarian rationale, as the extent of autonomy in major research intensive universities such as the US Ivy League was strongly associated with capacity for innovation.[332] Although national policy-makers adopted much of the rhetoric of NPM around the need for strong performance management linked to national and regional priorities, they were more cautious in translating this into practice.

While the 'strategic dialogue' was by no means an open-ended process of consultation between the state and HEIs, nor did it amount simply to a veneer for a predetermined process of rationalisation. The formation of regional clusters was predicated on securing input from and ultimately the support of influential constituencies within HEIs.[333] This arguably reflected a residual attachment to partnership norms within the Irish HE system and certainly underlined official preferences to achieve significant rationalisation through negotiated, collaborative processes. The 'strategic dialogue' aimed to align institutional strategies with national priorities, but this in itself was not novel: if anything, it replicated the strong if intermittent efforts by the Irish state to reshape higher education since the 1960s, with the original evolution of a binary system in HE an early example of effective state intervention linked to economic and social priorities.

The prospect of 'consolidation' applied mainly to the non-university sector and involved a carrot and stick approach to the IoTs: smaller publicly funded institutions would have to merge into larger HEIs through 'a process of evolution and consolidation', or survive based solely on private funding.[334] Yet the strategy also held out the alluring prospect (at least for institute presidents and managers), that newly amalgamated IoTs could achieve re-designation as technological universities. The essentially utilitarian rationale for technological universities was strikingly similar, taking account of the prominence of the research agenda, to the official preoccupations with labour market requirements, higher technological education and regional economic development that informed the RTCs and NIHEs forty years earlier.[335]

The Hunt report was not a manifesto for marketisation. Another notable departure from the key axioms of NPM was the limited role of market mechanisms as a tool for rationalisation of programmes and institutions in Ireland. In contrast to the UK, where a more laissez faire approach was adopted through increased tuition fees and valorisation of student choice to generate a different distribution of programmes, Irish policy-makers assigned the task of rationalisation to the HEA.[336] The report was ambivalent in its treatment of academic freedom, supporting the preservation of the 'intellectual autonomy' of academics in HEIs, albeit on the pragmatic basis that such autonomy was indispensable to engagement with society. Hunt made considerable efforts to show that traditional university values of institutional autonomy and academic freedom were consistent with greater accountability and responsiveness to state policies. This approach suggested not so much a philosophical confusion at the heart of the report, as a convoluted balancing act between very different values and views of the HE system.[337] The strategy group ultimately offered a qualified endorsement of NPM approaches, balanced by a residual attachment to the language and practice of partnership.

The reorientation of the activity of HEIs to serve narrowly economic objectives, largely focused around the salvation of an economy in crisis, was a defining feature of the Hunt report. The report was firmly located within a human capital paradigm and set out a vision for structural reform and institutional rationalisation through more centralised control of the higher education system in a context defined by reduced public funding. The dominant discourses linked to internationalisation and global competition, mediated through both the OECD and the EU institutions, profoundly influenced the content and recommendations of the strategy. Yet the report was also an uneasy halfway house of potentially inconsistent ideas, including clearly recognisable NPM instruments; elements of a partnership approach consistent with a network governance narrative and traditional bureaucratic priorities.[338] Pragmatic utilitarianism was the hallmark of the strategy, emphasising the necessity for rationalisation and managerial reform to enhance human capital formation, but avoiding consistent imposition of NPM approaches and advancing an eclectic range of measures to co-opt HEIs in accordance with government policies.

Contemporary Initiatives

Whatever the shortcomings of the Hunt report, its key recommendations became the template for policy formation in an era of crisis. The Fine Gael-Labour government elected in March 2011, constrained by unwelcome dependence on an international-European bailout programme, accepted the Hunt report as a base camp for the reform of higher education. The newly elected Minister for Education, Ruairi Quinn TD, in his first major address on higher education in May 2011 backed the report as a 'sufficient blueprint' for HE policy.[339] Quinn later acknowledged, however, that at the outset of his term as a reforming minister, 'it would be wrong to say that higher education was a priority.'[340] While the new government was supportive of a reform agenda in HE, managing (and ultimately emerging from) the economic crisis was their governing imperative and this reality imposed strict limitations on both the resources and political capital to be expended in higher education.

The independence of the HEA had been questioned by the McCarthy review of the public service in 2009, which recommended its merger back into DES, but this recommendation was rejected by the Hunt report in favour of allocating 'a strong central oversight role' to the agency.[341] The HEA was the main engine of policy activism following the report, launching a series of initiatives between 2011 and 2014. The authority initiated the 'strategic dialogue', issuing a consultation document in late 2011 which called for the establishment of regional clusters and produced initial guidelines for institutional consolidation.[342] Regional clusters were pitched as strategic, mutually beneficial agreements between groups of autonomous institutions in particular regions.[343] A limited number of 'thematic clusters' were also envisaged, notably in initial teacher education (ITE) and the creative arts in the Dublin region.[344] In a revealing indication of the HEA's priorities, the authority stated that 'Ultimately, mergers may or may not take place but regional clusters must develop.'[345] The HEA was more tentative about the prospect for mergers, noting correctly based on international data that 'institutional mergers can be very complex and potentially difficult ventures.'[346] Mergers across the binary divide between universities and IoTs were not contemplated and the HEA foresaw incorporations into larger institutions almost entirely involving smaller stand-alone institutions such as the colleges of education.[347]

A more far-reaching agenda for structural reconfiguration emerged in February 2012, with the HEA paper 'Towards a Future Higher Education Landscape'.[348] The paper identified 'a crowded and unstructured landscape', in which 44 institutions offered undergraduate programmes through the CAO.[349] Ireland had 39 HEIs receiving public funding, serving over 200,000 students at a cost of €1.5 billion annually.[350] The HEA endorsed a transition from 'a simplistic binary notion' of two separate sectors towards a coherent HE system involving a range of institutional types with 'clearly differentiated missions and clear strategic orientations.'[351] Echoing the Hunt report, the HEA sought the adoption of a system-level approach incorporating universities, newly created technological universities and IoTs, maintaining differentiated missions informed by the original binary concept but developing inter-institutional collaboration to meet national objectives. The landscape document offered a vision of 'directed diversity', involving diversity of mission at sectoral level, inter-institutional collaboration and rationalisation of programmes and structures, in which each institution '…by playing to its strengths…can make the biggest impact both for itself and for Irish society'.[352] Each institution was invited to provide its own strategic plan within six months, indicating how it proposed to position itself within the overarching framework set by the HEA.[353] The authority aimed to achieve a coherent HE system comprised of 'a smaller number of larger autonomous institutions with diverse but complementary missions.'[354]

The latest reformulation of government policy was completed when the HEA submitted a comprehensive report to the minister in April 2013, outlining the key principles for system reconfiguration.'[355] Among the authority's priorities were attaining a revised balance between institutional autonomy and accountability to the state; a coherent system based on complementary strategies across different institutions and 'critical mass' through consolidation and development of regional clusters.[356] The main instrument for achieving official objectives was the process of strategic dialogue between the HEA and HEIs and the main 'success factor' was defined as the evolution of regional clusters. The report envisaged mission based compacts, which would be formal agreements for three year periods developed through the 'strategic dialogue', with funding allocated based on performance and progress toward agreed outcomes.[357] The HEA's primary focus was on system reconfiguration in which universities and IoTs would retain a distinctive role, albeit within a more centralised framework, but a more directive approach to rationalisation would be taken with smaller institutions, including the colleges of education, which were expected to merge or incorporate with neighbouring universities.[358] Two more specialised reviews were commissioned by the DES in 2012, an international review of ITE led by the Finnish academic Pasi Sahlberg and a regionally focused review of creative and performing arts and media in Dublin, indicating a level of policy activity characterised by Clancy as unprecedented in the HE context.[359]

The surge of policy activism in 2011–14 testified to the influence of the Hunt report and even more to the impact of the economic crisis, which rendered acceptable policy agendas prioritising rationalisation and system reconfiguration that would have been avoided in a less tumultuous period. Policy-makers, from Ruairi Quinn to Tom Boland, the CEO of the HEA and senior officials of the DES, observed the admonition of US politician Rahm Emanuel 'not to waste a good crisis.'[360] Yet in a historical perspective such policy activism in higher education was not at all unprecedented: it had strong paralells to the late 1960s, when the crucial decisions on the creation of the RTC sector, the NIHEs and the merger were all brought forward within a five year period, and the mid to late 1990s, when major reforms were implemented with regard to universities legislation, redesignation of the higher technical colleges, a national qualifications framework and the repositioning of HERD.

The immediate impact of the Hunt report was to increase the power of the HEA. The national strategy assigned the key role to the HEA in directing and implementing policy in HE, indicating that the DES should remove itself from operational issues and focus more on policy and strategy in line with the OECD review.[361] The HEA became the de facto 'regulator' of the system, driving a policy agenda defined by structural reform and institutional rationalisation.[362] The agency played the central part in launching the process of 'strategic dialogue' and was instrumental in negotiating mission based compacts with each HEI. The HEA also took responsibility for implementation of a new Higher Education system performance framework announced by the DES in 2013, which sought to chart short to medium term objectives for the HE system as a whole informed by statistical data.[363] The production of comprehensive data on the system for the first time was one of the more valuable outcomes of the contemporary surge in policy activism. The HEA introduced a series of reports on system performance from 2013, providing detailed profiles of all HEA-funded institutions across a wide range of indicators, including enrolments; staff numbers and profiles; participation and progression; internationalisation;

research and knowledge transfer and financial data.[364] The HEA emerged as the lead agency in promoting interventionist government policies and regulating the institutional plans and strategies of HEIs in a pro-active (and arguably intrusive) fashion.[365]

Yet national policy-makers retained an attachment to ostensibly consensual forms of decision-making, allied to a pragmatic desire to co-opt institutional leaders, which militated against imposing drastic structural reform. The HEA referenced pragmatism as a key principle in its approach, noting the importance of 'the opportunity…that is offered by a number of alliances and clusters being developed through the initiative of higher education institutions.'[366] This underlined the authority's preference to achieve reconfiguration through collaborative initiatives agreed by HEIs themselves rather than bureaucratic diktat. The HEA was, however, demanding major system and institutional restructuring in a fiscal context where HEIs had limited options other than collaboration. The embrace of pragmatism did not conceal the increase of bureaucratic power over HEIs, exerted primarily through the HEA. It was a striking transformation from the role of the authority in its first two decades as a 'buffer agency' which often challenged government plans and priorities, to a more powerful, but less independent, regulatory body charged with implementation of a far-reaching agenda of structural reconfiguration.

The drive for consolidation impinged most dramatically on ITE, which experienced 'an unprecedented level and rate of change' between 2012 and 2017.[367] Pressure for reform of teacher education was reinforced by the wider international context, including the global education reform movement emphasising standardisation, concentration on literacy and numeracy and higher stakes accountability: a process of international benchmarking through the Programme for International Student Assessment (PISA) proved influential, causing a sensation in 2009 when the results for Irish 15 year olds in literacy and numeracy deteriorated sharply.[368] The minister announced in 2011 a series of policy changes within the framework of a new strategy to improve literacy and numeracy, including an extension in the duration of ITE programmes for

primary and post-primary teachers.[369] The undergraduate B.Ed. programme was extended from three to four years, with the equivalent of
at least one year as 'a school based professional development experience',
while postgraduate programmes in ITE for primary and second-level
teachers would run for two years with enhanced emphasis on school
based placement.[370] The Teaching Council was given a central role in
overseeing implementation of the strategy for teacher education.[371] The
influential part played by the Teaching Council in prescribing the content of the revised programmes and establishing a new model for school
placement of student teachers between 2011 and 2014 raised concerns
among academic staff in university schools of education that their traditional autonomy was being curbed.[372]

The international review of ITE in 2012 intensified the momentum for change, proposing a radical reconfiguration of publicly funded
ITE programmes and institutions. The Sahlberg report envisaged that
'teacher education should be facilitated in a university setting', which
would be achieved through the restructuring of existing programmes
and institutions into six centres, each built around one or more universities.[373] Sahlberg reflected admirably the official policy of consolidation, expressed by the landscape document which noted that '…public
funding of these small institutions will not be continued except in circumstances where there are significant reasons of a strategic kind for
continuing funding as separate institutions.'[374] The report was explicit
that teacher education in small-scale publicly funded providers, such as
St. Patrick's College, Thurles and Galway-Mayo Institute of Technology,
should be discontinued, while all the remaining providers were to be
integrated within the six proposed clusters.[375] All of the centres were
intended to offer research-based teacher education and professional
development on 'a continuum ranging from early childhood to in-
service training of teachers and leaders.'[376]

Progress in implementing the Salhberg report varied widely across
the six proposed centres. The report was influential in acting as a catalyst for rationalisation where institutional leaders were already open to
closer alliances or incorporation. The report endorsed the incorporation
of Froebel College of Education with NUI Maynooth, which was already
well in progress before the review and was completed in September

2013.[377] More significantly, Sahlberg recommended a new institute of teacher education embracing DCU, St. Patrick's College, Drumcondra and Mater Dei, which was favoured by institutional leaders on each campus.[378] The development of this institute, involving the incorporation of SPD and Mater Dei into DCU and the creation of a new faculty of education based in Drumcondra, was the major institutional legacy of the Sahlberg report. The position of CICE added an additional layer of complexity to this rationalisation. The college's traditional association with Trinity ended acrimoniously in 2013, following the breakdown of negotiations over incorporation.[379] The Church of Ireland authorities initially opened discussions with NUIM, before ultimately reaching agreement to enter the 'new' DCU faculty.[380] The negotiations with DCU were encouraged by the DES, where Ruairi Quinn and his advisers were apprehensive about the incorporation of CICE within NUI Maynooth on broader political grounds, as John Walshe, the minister's chief adviser, acknowledged: '…try explaining to Northern unionists the difference between the lay-run National University of Ireland Maynooth and the co-located seminary called St. Patrick's College Maynooth. All they would see was Rome Rule.'[381] The agreement with DCU did not command universal support within the Church of Ireland or staff in CICE, but was strongly backed by Michael Jackson, the archbishop of Dublin.[382]

The incorporation required a complex balancing act by DCU, a secular university, which was incorporating three well established colleges offering teacher education on a denominational basis. The structure of the new faculty maintained a denominationally neutral ethos in the core curriculum for teacher education, while recognising specialist programmes offered by distinct centres for Catholic and Church of Ireland education within the institute.[383] The formal incorporation to establish the new institute was completed in October 2016, although contentious issues around the transfer of staff from CICE to the new faculty were not fully resolved.[384] The new faculty of education, which began to operate on a refurbished St. Patrick's college campus in 2016, became the largest provider of teacher education in the Irish state.[385]

While the incorporation of smaller colleges within the universities to achieve critical mass in teacher education was the logical implication of

Sahlberg's analysis, the report also produced a more convoluted scheme for merger involving Trinity and UCD. The schools of education in Trinity and UCD, along with Marino Institute of Education (MIE) and the National College of Art and Design (NCAD), were included in a single cluster, envisaged as a possible 'flagship' institute of teacher education.[386] This proposal envisaged an unwieldy construct which departed from the report's own rationale for distinct university based centres, combining two colleges with very different missions and university schools of education offering second level teacher education programmes in two of the largest universities in Ireland. The HEA soon accepted that the proposed institute involving Trinity and UCD would be a 'virtual centre', involving collaboration but not merger on a single campus and the prospects for further integration across this cluster proved remote.[387]

The report's recommendation for UL and Mary Immaculate College to form a single integrated centre for excellence in teacher education was more logical in geographical terms, but cut across MIC's institutional strategy and determination to maintain its autonomy.[388] MIC under the presidency of Fr. Michael Hayes (2012–2017) pursued a distinctive strategy of asserting the college's Catholic identity and seeking alliance with Catholic institutions in Ireland and the USA, which caused tensions with Minister Quinn.[389] The college's programme of religious education also drew criticism from the HEA and Teaching Council, although the authorities strongly defended their commitment to educating 'students from all faiths and none.'[390] While MIC agreed to develop a joint BA with UL, the college authorities avoided incorporation: they also achieved the absorption of St. Patrick's College, Thurles within MIC in September 2015 to create 'the largest Catholic third-level college in the country.'[391] Marino pursued a more diplomatic approach and deepened its institutional alignment with Trinity in 2011, concluding a joint trusteeship in which TCD became a trustee with the Christian Brothers of Coláiste Mhuire, Marino.[392] Both Mary Immaculate and MIE were successful in avoiding outright incorporation into their nearest university, although each developed closer alliances with UL and Trinity respectively.

The impact of the Sahlberg report was uneven and linked to its acceptability to institutional managers, church leaders and to some extent academics. Yet a notable outcome identified by O'Donoghue et al. was a reduction in the influence of the Catholic church: while all state funded ITE programmes for primary teachers were located in denominational colleges in 2011, the majority of ITE programmes were brought within the fold of secular universities five years later, while only Mary Immaculate and Marino (in association with TCD), retained a denominational patron.[393] The review served as the catalyst for a fundamental restructuring of teacher education and eroded traditional alignments shaped by denominationalism which had persisted throughout the twentieth century.

Yet outside the field of teacher education the outcome of the structural reform agenda embraced by the HEA and government ministers since 2011 remained inconclusive and considerably more limited than sought by its promoters. The fate of an international review commissioned by the HEA underlined the limits of reform even in an era of upheaval. The international panel led by a Dutch HE specialist, Frans Van Vught, was asked to review the configuration of the system in an international context. The panel produced a controversial report in August 2012, recommending a radical reconstruction to achieve 'a small number of large, fit for purpose autonomous institutions with the critical mass necessary to determine achievable and flexible missions'.[394] The report favoured outright merger over voluntary institutional alliances and comprehensive, regional universities over maintaining the binary model.[395] Among its more far-reaching recommendations were a merger of Trinity and UCD; a similar integration of DCU and NUIM and the creation of a single national university of technology, incorporating both university and non-university colleges.[396] While it was the venerable idea of the TCD-UCD merger which attracted headlines when the report was leaked to the *Irish Times* in September 2012, perhaps more significant was the panel's strategy of reshaping the system on the basis of regional universities, which would have incorporated local IoTs and colleges of education.[397] The Van Vught report proposed discarding the binary model and its replacement by a 'comprehensive', university based structure with a stronger regional orientation, not unlike the ill-fated restructuring initiative proposed by the coalition in the mid-1970s.

The review proved much too radical not only for institutional leaders, who reacted with varying degrees of horror, but for the Department of Education. Quinn quickly rejected the leaked report, commenting on 26 September that the TCD-UCD merger 'was neither feasible nor desirable', while other key recommendations were not acceptable to the government.[398] The HEA Board had no prior warning of the report's contents and most of its members were aghast both at its proposals and the failure to give them advance notice of its appearance; the report also triggered tensions between the HEA and departmental officials.[399] The international report was 'dead on arrival' and the instant rejection of its recommendations led to some adverse commentary on the HEA for commissioning a report, which proved unacceptable to the minister and senior departmental officials.[400] The process of producing the report did much to explain the outcome. The absence of advance consultation made the report tone deaf to Irish institutional realities and sensitivities, as well as ensuring that its recommendations had no influential advocates when it was leaked, probably deliberately to ensure its rapid demise. The fate of the report illustrated the extent to which support for maintaining binary type differentiation, even within a reconfigured system, proved remarkably enduring.

The HEA, perhaps absorbing the lessons of the abortive expert review, prioritised the development of regional clusters of distinct HEIs, intended to promote a coherent system and more fine-grained institutional rationalisation on an incremental basis. Among the objectives of regional clusters were 'co-ordinated regional engagement' with business, particularly SMEs; an increased range of student pathways for access, transfer and progression in HEIs within the cluster; 'critical mass' in academic disciplines and a model of shared services to reduce duplication.[401] A key objective identified by the HEA was achievement of coordinated academic planning within the cluster, including development of joint programmes, coordination in research and 'removal of unnecessary duplication of provision.'[402] Coordination of academic programmes and development of shared student pathways were the first two priority objectives for the regional clusters, with elimination of duplication in programmes taking pride of place. It was an ambitious agenda, which placed a great deal of weight on the ability of the HEA to corral or persuade HEIs with distinct interests and very different cultures to sign up to significant rationalisation. Clancy noted 'formidable obstacles' to progressing the HEA's structural reform agenda, including financial constraints severely limiting the potential for incentive funding on the SIF model and the failure to develop regional administrative structures which might have offered direction to rationalisation.[403]

The HEA sought to mobilise a mixture of bureaucratic and collaborative mechanisms to bring HEIs in line with its rationalisation agenda. The authority applied financial pressure through the development of mission based compacts and sought to build upon existing regional networks such as the DRHEA, Shannon Consortium and the UCD-TCD Innovation Alliance. The HEA was dissatisfied at the initial response of HEIs to the landscape document and took the lead in identifying regional clusters bringing together universities, IoTs and colleges of education; the final shape of the clusters, however, was broadly in line with the proposals of the Irish Universities Association (IUA).[404] The HEA's reconfiguration strategy ultimately identified five regional clusters, categorised as South, Mid-West, West, Dublin/Leinster Pillar I and Dublin/Leinster Pillar II.[405] The Dublin/Leinster cluster was divided into two distinct pillars as the authority recognised that the greater Dublin region posed 'a greater challenge than other regions in terms of coordination and coherence' due to the number of institutions involved.[406] Pillar I included TCD, UCD, MIE, NCAD and Dún Laoghaire IADT; Pillar II involved an even more varied cast, including DIT, Tallaght and Blanchardstown IoTs, DCU and its linked colleges within the new education faculty, NUI Maynooth, Dundalk and Athlone IoTs, RCSI and NCI.[407] The clusters incorporated the major private and nonprofit institutions in Dublin, RCSI and NCI, although privately funded HEIs remained outside the remit of the HEA.

Yet despite intensive activity by the HEA, notably in securing agreement on the first round of mission based compacts with 26 HEIs, the tangible results of the drive for clustering were limited. The agency's report on system performance for 2014–15 noted diplomatically that some clusters achieved more progress than others. Although the Dublin II cluster reported 'a particularly strong performance…other clusters, such as Dublin I (UCD, TCD, IADT and NCAD), and Munster could not report similar levels of performance.'[408] The report indicated that the HEA was continuing to emphasise 'the importance of cluster development' but recognised that its level of success was variable at best.[409] A member of the HEA board subsequently commented that there was 'no enthusiasm' for clusters among the institutions and that clustering looked very much like 'a failed policy.'[410]

The HEA Board itself was divided about the implementation of technological universities (TUs), but accepted a political imperative to facilitate TUs. Quinn commented that the rationale for technological universities was 'substantially political', driven by pressure for the upgrading of Waterford IoT (WIT) from influential ministers representing constituencies in the south-east, as well as DIT's long-term campaign for university status.[411] The evolution of detailed metrics for recognition of TUs proved divisive within the HEA Board, as several members insisted on well defined criteria, including minimum numbers of academic staff holding PhDs in participating institutions; representatives of participating IoTs later claimed that some members of the HEA had an 'ideological aversion' to TUs.[412] The criteria unveiled in 2012 represented a compromise among HEA board members, designed to fulfil the political commitment to give a new type of university to DIT and Waterford, while attempting to ensure that recognition of a TU did not allow a general race up the educational value chain. The criteria involved a four stage process, incorporating benchmarks for proposed TUs in terms of research, staff and student profiles and the evaluation of applications by an international panel.[413] The process required consolidation of the participating institutions through a legally binding merger agreement at stage two, in advance of evaluation by the international panel at stage three and finally decision by the minister on possible designation as a technological university.[414] Quinn noted that one of his priorities, shared with the HEA, was to re-assert the original vocational mission of the IoTs and 'stop the mission drift of institutes of technology into becoming Maggie Thatcher type universities…'[415] The majority of national policy-makers were supportive of TUs, but had no desire to repeat the English experiment of adopting a 'unified' HE system in 1992, when the polytechnics were elevated to university status, but the system remained stratified in practice based on prestige, tradition and income among the universities. This amounted to a potentially significant contradiction at the heart of the new policy, which probably slowed the implementation of TUs.

Three expressions of interest for TU status were made in response to the landscape document. DIT, Blanchardstown and Tallaght IoTs set out to form TU4Dublin; Cork and Tralee IoTs proposed the formation of the Munster Technological University (MTU), while WIT and Carlow IoT reluctantly combined in an application for a TU for the south-east. Subsequently, the Connacht Ulster Alliance (Galway-Mayo, Sligo and Letterkenny IoTs) expressed interest in forming a technological university early in 2015.[416] The HEA recommended in 2013 that the first three consortia should proceed to the second stage of the process, while the Connacht Ulster Alliance received approval to go to the same stage in October 2015.[417] The path towards TU status was protracted and uncertain, with mixed outcomes for the participating institutions. The TU4 Dublin and Munster consortia were the most successful, receiving the minister's imprimatur following review by an expert panel in 2014 to proceed to the final stage before designation.[418] At least one of the consortia experienced severe internal disagreement, as WIT withdrew from negotiations with Carlow in 2014 and had to be coaxed back to the table with the assistance of an external mediator, former HEA chairperson Michael Kelly.[419] Legislation for the proposed TUs was repeatedly postponed. Progress was delayed due to controversy over the original criteria, disagreements within participating consortia, and especially trade union objections to the position of academic staff within the proposed TUs. A Technological Universities Bill was not published until December 2015 and was opposed by the TUI, which criticised the precondition for merger, contractual implications for academic staff and attempted rationalisation at a time of financial crisis: the government withdrew the bill from the Dáil in January 2016, just before the Dáil was dissolved for a general election.[420] The TUI reached agreement with the DES on a revised scheme in June 2017, in which merger was to occur simultaneously with designation as a TU.[421] The revised legislation was approved by the Oireachtas in March 2018, but the agreement diluted the original drive for consolidation as a precondition for TU status.

A notable weakness of the proposed mergers was that no detailed academic rationale for the TUs was properly articulated: indeed as Clancy noted, the rationales for merger embraced by policy-makers (rationalisation and critical mass) and institutional leaders (enhancing the position and status of their institutions) were different, if not potentially divergent.[422] The rationale for technological universities largely remains political as much as educational—satisfying a regional demand shared by institutional leaders and local politicians for enhanced institutional status, while protecting the differentiated character of the system and drawing a line in the sand against further movement into the university sector.

While it is too early to evaluate the long-term impact of clusters or TUs, the available evidence indicates the limitations of a rationalisation agenda based largely on co-opting existing institutions in the absence of strong financial investment or a wider political vision for the HE system. It was apparent by 2016 that the universities had escaped large-scale rationalisation in terms of institutional mergers or major programme restructuring. Seán Flynn, then education editor of the *Irish Times*, as early as September 2012 decried the Hunt report as too conservative and regretted that 'a radical shake up' of the universities was not envisaged.[423] Teacher education within the universities was an exception as schools of education were included in the far-reaching Sahlberg review, but other thematic reviews envisaged by the HEA either did not materialise or did not have a major impact. The determination of national policy-makers to maintain a binary imprint within an evolving system structure was a significant limitation on structural reform, while the unceremonious rejection of Van Vught indicated that structural changes would be incremental rather than radical. This incremental approach made sense for policy-makers in the government and DES for whom higher education was, ultimately, not a major strategic priority. The HEA was more invested in the structural reform agenda, but despite the impetus given by the Hunt report its power was constrained by the preferences of political leaders, differences within its board particularly over the fate of TUs and the ability of HEIs to limit radical change within collaborative networks.

The 'consolidation' agenda advanced by the HEA, DES and government ministers shared many of the flaws of earlier initiatives for restructuring in the twentieth century. The drive for rationalisation was most successful where a definite academic rationale was combined with financial imperatives, as occurred in ITE. The introduction of technological universities is potentially the most significant reform since the diversification of the system in the mid 1900s: the real institutional and political backing for regionally based TUs should not be discounted, although the outcomes are likely to vary widely by region and institution. The ambitious project of institutional restructuring through regional clusters, initially a flagship project for the HEA, has achieved minimal outcomes and its prospects are tenuous at best. The most significant pressure for rationalisation came not from any government initiative, but from the economic crisis and severe reduction in public financing of higher education.

Notes

1. OECD, *Higher Education in Ireland*, 19.
2. Skilbeck, *Towards an Integrated System of Tertiary Education*, 14–16.
3. Vaira, 'Globalisation and Higher Education,' *Higher Education* 48 (2004): 484.
4. Simon Marginson and Gary Rhoades, 'Beyond Nation States, Markets and Systems of Higher Education: A Glonacal Agency Heuristic,' *Higher Education* 43 (2002): 288.
5. Ibid.; Olssen and Peters, 'Neoliberalism, Higher Education and the Knowledge Economy: From the Free Market to Knowledge Capitalism,' *Journal of Education Policy* 20, no. 3 (2005): 313–14.
6. Vaira, 'Globalisation and Higher Education,' *Higher Education* 48 (2004): 484.
7. Marginson and Rhoades, 'Beyond Nation States, Markets and Systems of Higher Education: A Glonacal Agency Heuristic,' *Higher Education* 43 (2002): 289–92.
8. Ibid., 288.
9. Vaira, 'Globalisation and Higher Education,' *Higher Education* 48 (2004): 491.
10. Ferlie et al., 'The Steering of Higher Education Systems: A Public Management Perspective,' *Higher Education* 56, no. 3 (2009): 325–48. NPM was considered in more detail above.

11. Ibid., 337.
12. Ibid., 339.
13. John Walsh and Andrew Loxley, "The Hunt Report and Higher Education Policy in the Republic of Ireland: 'An International Solution to an Irish Problem?,'" *Studies in Higher Education* 40, no. 6 (2015): 1128–45. https://doi.org/10.1080/03075079.2014.881350. This paper gives a more detailed evaluation of the narratives outlined by Ferlie et al. and their application to the Irish context.
14. Highman, 'A Case Study on Differentiation,' 65.
15. See pp. 393–99 'Teaching and Learning.'
16. European Parliament, Lisbon European Council, Presidency Conclusions, 23–24 March 2000. Accessed 1 December 2017. http://www.europarl.europa.eu/summits/lis1_en.htm.
17. Ibid.
18. 'The Lisbon Strategy in Short.' Accessed 1 December 2017. https://portal.cor.europa.eu/europe2020/Profiles/Pages/TheLisbon Strategyinshort.aspx.
19. Highman, 'A Case Study on Differentiation,' 135–7.
20. Commission of the European Communities, *Communication from the Commission: The Role of the Universities in the Europe of Knowledge*, 5 February 2003, 5–6.
21. Ibid., 19.
22. Ibid., 18.
23. Highman, 'A Case Study on Differentiation,' 136–7.
24. Hazelkorn et al., 'From Massification to Globalisation,' in *The State in Transition*, ed. Rafter and O'Brien, 237–8.
25. Ibid., 256.
26. Department of Education and Skills, *National Strategy for Higher Education to 2030—Report of the Strategy Group* (Dublin: DES, 2011), 9.
27. Damian Murchan, 'Changing Curriculum and Assessment Mindsets in Higher Education,' in *Higher Education in Ireland: Practices, Policies and Possibilities*, ed. Loxley et al. (Basingstoke: Palgrave Macmillan, 2014), 192–3.
28. Department of Education, *Education for a Changing World*, 185–6.
29. Jim Gleeson, 'The European Credit Transfer System and Curriculum Design: Product Before Process?' *Studies in Higher Education* 38, no. 6 (2013): 921–38. Accessed 16 October 2013. https://doi.org/10.10

80/03075079.2011.610101. Murchan, 'Changing Curriculum and Assessment Mindsets in Higher Education,' 192–3.

30. Murchan, 'Changing Curriculum and Assessment Mindsets in Higher Education,' 193.

31. Frank McMahon, 'Bologna: Consonance or Dissonance,' in *Higher Education in Ireland: Practices, Policies and Possibilities*, ed. Loxley et al. (Basingstoke: Palgrave Macmillan, 2014), 179–80.

32. Ibid., 180.

33. Ibid.

34. Ibid.

35. Gleeson, 'The European Credit Transfer System and Curriculum Design: Product Before Process?' *Studies in Higher Education* 38, no. 6 (2013): 921–38. Accessed 16 October 2013. https://doi.org/10.1080/03075079.2011.610101.

36. Murchan, 'Changing Curriculum and Assessment Mindsets in Higher Education,' 193–4.

37. Gleeson, 'The European Credit Transfer System and Curriculum Design: Product Before Process?' *Studies in Higher Education* 38, no. 6 (2013): 921–38. https://doi.org/10.1080/03075079.2011.610101. Accessed 16 October 2013.

38. This was certainly the author's experience of programme development in both a university and non-university institution in 2010–2012.

39. Ciara O'Farrell, 'Challenges and Opportunities for Teaching and Learning,' in *Higher Education in Ireland: Practices, Policies and Possibilities*, ed. Loxley et al. (Basingstoke: Palgrave Macmillan, 2014), 237.

40. Murchan, 'Changing Curriculum and Assessment Mindsets in Higher Education,' 194.

41. Clancy, *Irish Higher Education*, 152.

42. O'Farrell, 'Challenges and Opportunities for Teaching and Learning,' 235.

43. Clancy, *Irish Higher Education*, 153.

44. Ernest Boyer, *Scholarship Reconsidered: Priorities of the Professoriate a Special Report for the Carnegie Foundation* (Princeton: Carnegie Foundation, 1990), 23–4.

45. http://www.aishe.org/. Accessed 1 November 2017; http://www.edin.ie/. Accessed 1 November 2017.

46. O'Farrell, 'Challenges and Opportunities for Teaching and Learning,' 234.

47. https://www.teachingandlearning.ie/about/. Accessed 1 November 2017.
48. Clancy, *Irish Higher Education*, 153.
49. National Forum, *National Professional Development Framework for All Staff Who Work in Higher Education*, August 2016. Accessed 1 November 2017. https://www.teachingandlearning.ie/wp-content/uploads/2016/09/PD-Framework-FINAL-1.pdf.
50. Personal information given to the author.
51. Clancy, *Irish Higher Education*, 155.
52. Department of Education, *Education for a Changing World*, 196.
53. Clancy, *Irish Higher Education*, 156.
54. Hedley, 'Managerialism in Irish Universities,' *Irish Journal of Legal Studies* 1, no. 1 (2010): 117–41.
55. Ibid., 152.
56. Oireachtas Éireann, No. 26 of 1999.
57. Ibid.
58. Ibid.
59. Clancy, *Irish Higher Education*, 156.
60. Ibid., 158.
61. McMahon, 'Bologna: Consonance or Dissonance,' 180.
62. Clancy, *Irish Higher Education*, 156.
63. Oireachtas Éireann, *Qualification and Quality Assurance (Education and Training Act) 2012*, No. 28 of 2012, 51.
64. Ibid., 22; Murchan, 'Changing Curriculum and Assessment Mindsets in Higher Education,' 192.
65. Oireachtas Éireann, No. 28 of 2012, 22.
66. Quality and Qualifications Ireland (QQI), *Strategy Statement 2016–18* (Dublin: QQI, 2015), 2.
67. Ibid., 6.
68. Hazelkorn et al., 'From Massification to Globalisation: Reflections on the Transformation of Irish Higher Education,' 250.
69. Andrew Loxley, 'Knowledge Production and Higher Education in the Irish Context,' in *Higher Education in Ireland: Practices, Policies and Possibilities*, ed. Loxley et al. (Basingstoke: Palgrave Macmillan, 2014), 55–85.
70. Ibid., 81.
71. Ibid., 63.

72. Tierney et al., *Science Technology and Innovation Advisory Council Report* (Dublin: Forfas, 1995), 12.
73. Ibid., 12–13.
74. Ibid., 18–19.
75. PA Consulting, *Ten Years On: Confirming Impacts from Research Investment* (Dublin: PA, 2011), 14; CIRCA, *A Comparative International Assessment of the Organisation, Management and Funding of University Research in Ireland and Europe* (HEA, 1996), IV; and Loxley, 'Knowledge Production and Higher Education in the Irish Context,' in *Higher Education in Ireland*, ed. Loxley et al., 64.
76. White, *Investing in People*, 201–2.
77. HEA, *Financial Management and Governance in HEIs—Ireland, OECD IMHE/HEFCE Project on International Comparative Higher Education Financial Management and Governance* (Dublin: HEA, 2004), 42.
78. PA Consulting, *Ten Years On*, 14.
79. Ibid., 5.
80. Loxley, 'Knowledge Production and Higher Education in the Irish Context,' in *Higher Education in Ireland*, ed. Loxley et al., 74–5.
81. PA Consulting, *Ten Years On*, 16–17.
82. Ibid., 1.
83. Gary Rhoades and Sheila Slaughter, 'Academic Capitalism in the new economy: challenges and choices', *American Academic* 1 (2004): 37–59.
84. PA Consulting, *Ten Years On*, 16–17; The five thematic areas were bioscience and biomedical; environment and marine; platform technologies and materials; ICT and advanced technology; social science and humanities.
85. Ibid., 16–17.
86. Ibid., 15.
87. OECD, *Review of Higher Education in Ireland*, 16.
88. Loxley, 'Knowledge Production,' in *Higher Education in Ireland*, ed. Loxley et al., 65.
89. Irish Council for Science Technology and Innovation, *Technology Foresight Ireland: An ICSTI Overview* (Dublin: Forfas, 1998), 4.
90. Ibid., 5.
91. Ibid., 4.
92. Ibid., 7.

93. Loxley, 'Knowledge Production,' in *Higher Education in Ireland*, ed. Loxley et al., 65.

94. CHIU Submission, *Technology Foresight and the University Sector* (Dublin: CHIU, 1998), 2–3.

95. Clancy, *Irish Higher Education*, 260.

96. PA Consulting, *Ten Years On*, 16.

97. Ibid., 36–7.

98. Ibid., 53–4.

99. Coolahan, 'The NUI,' 277.

100. Seán Ó Riain, 'The University and the Public Sphere After the Celtic Tiger,' in Maynooth Philosophical Papers (2006). Accessed 15 July 2017. http://eprints.maynoothuniversity.ie/555/.

101. Department of Jobs, Enterprise and Innovation, *Report of the Research Prioritisation Steering Group* (Dublin: Forfas, 2011), 9–11.

102. Ibid., 9.

103. HEA, *Higher Education System Performance 2014–16*, 44.

104. Ibid.

105. Loxley, 'Knowledge Production,' in *Higher Education in Ireland*, ed. Loxley et al., 67–8.

106. Ibid.

107. Government of Ireland, Inter-departmental Committee, *Strategy for Science Technology and Innovation 2007–13* (Dublin: Forfas, 2006).

108. PA Consulting, *Ten Years On*, 40.

109. Ibid.; Loxley, 'Knowledge Production,' in *Higher Education in Ireland*, ed. Loxley et al., 77–8.

110. *Irish Times*, 'Dismay of Researchers at Funds Being Put On Hold,' 8 April 2003.

111. *Irish Times*, 'University Heads Warn Staff Cuts Are Inevitable,' 16 November 2003.

112. Seán Ó Riain, 'The University and the Public Sphere After the Celtic Tiger,' in Maynooth Philosophical Papers (2006). Accessed 15 July 2017. http://eprints.maynoothuniversity.ie/555/.

113. *Irish Times*, 'New Third-Level Funding Scheme,' 29 April 2005; Clancy, *Irish Higher Education*, 238.

114. *Irish Times*, 'Hanafin to Allocate €510 Million After University Heads Protest,' 19 February 2008.

115. Steve Hedley, 'Managerialism in Irish Universities,' *Irish Journal of Legal Studies* 1, no. 1 (2010): 117.

116. Ibid., 119.

117. Ferlie et al., 'The Steering of Higher Education Systems: A Public Management Perspective,' *Higher Education* 56, no. 3 (2009): 325–48.
118. Hedley, 'Managerialism in Irish Universities,' *Irish Journal of Legal Studies* 1, no. 1 (2010): 128–9.
119. Ibid., 129.
120. Ibid., 122.
121. Clancy, *Irish Higher Education*, 244.
122. *Irish Times*, 'Fear and Loathing in UCC,' 28 September 2004; 'Radical Changes Planned for Cork University,' 12 May 2005.
123. *Irish Times*, 'UCC Stays Strong Despite Internal Strife,' 2 December 2003 (the author was Sean Flynn, the long serving education editor).
124. Ibid.; *Irish Times*, 'Fear and Loathing in UCC,' 28 September 2004; Clancy, *Irish Higher Education*, 244.
125. *Irish Times*, 'UCC Head to Resign Post After Turbulent Reign,' 30 May 2006; *Irish Times*, 'Board Calls for End to Bitter Exchange at UCC,' 18 November 2006.
126. *Irish Times*, 'Protests at One-Year Terms for Senior UCD Posts,' 2 June 2004.
127. Clancy, *Irish Higher Education*, 260.
128. *Irish Times*, 'Report into Reform Process at UCD,' 16 October 2007.
129. *Irish Times*, 'TCD Provost Attempt to Win Support for College Shake-Up,' 17 May 2004.
130. *Irish Times*, 'TCD Law Department Rejects Plans for College Restructure,' 28 October 2004; Sean Barrett, 'Provost's Plans for TCD,' 1 November 2004; *Irish Times*, 'Provost to Consider TCD Plan Options,' 26 January 2005.
131. Tom Garvin, 'A Confederacy of Dunces: The Assault on Higher Education in Ireland,' in *Degrees of Nonsense the Demise of the University in Ireland*, ed. Brendan Walsh (Dublin: Glasnevin Press, 2012), 67.
132. *Irish Times*, 'University Restructuring Has Done More Harm Than Good,' 17 October 2006.
133. Ibid.
134. Clancy, *Irish Higher Education*, 261.
135. HEA, *National Plan for Equity of Access to Higher Education 2008–13* (Dublin: HEA, 2008), 59–61.
136. Ibid.

137. Ibid., 65.
138. Ibid., 58.
139. HEA, *Higher Education System Performance 2014–16*, 28; More recent HEA reports have compiled participation data by dividing the number of first year undergraduate new entrants (aged 18–20) by the average of the 17–19 year old cohort in the national population from the 2011 census. Earlier studies used a different baseline for age in determining the age participation.
140. Clancy and Benson, *Higher Education in Dublin*, 17–18.
141. HEA, *National Plan for Equity of Access to Higher Education 2015–19* (Dublin: HEA, 2015), 44–5; This data was based on the estimated participation rate within the 18–20 year old age groups in different counties and postal districts in Dublin.
142. Selina McCoy, Emer Smyth, Dorothy Watson, and Merike Darmody, *Leaving School in Ireland: A Longitudinal Study of Post-school Transitions* (Dublin: ESRI, 2014), xv.
143. Ibid.
144. Delma Byrne and Selina McCoy, 'Effectively Maintained Inequality in Educational Transitions in the Republic of Ireland,' *American Behavioural Scientist* 61, no. 1 (2017): 50.
145. Ibid., 49–73.
146. Ibid., 65–70.
147. Ibid., 69–70.
148. Loxley et al., 'Access and Widening Participation: Stories from the Policy Domain,' 21.
149. HEA, *Higher Education System Performance 2014–16*, 28.
150. Ibid.
151. Ibid.
152. HEA, *National Plan 2008–13*, 30.
153. Clancy, *Irish Higher Education*, 79.
154. Loxley et al., 'Routes In: Access Categories, Mechanisms and Processes,' in *Access and Participation in Irish Higher Education*, ed. Fleming et al. (London: Palgrave Macmillan, 2017), 93–4.
155. HEA, *National Plan 2015–19*, 42.
156. Clancy, *Irish Higher Education*, 97.
157. HEA, *Consultation Paper* (Dublin: HEA, 2014), 6.
158. Ibid.; HEA, *National Plan 2008–13*, 34.

159. Loxley et al., 'Access and Widening Participation: Stories from the Policy Domain,' 75.
160. HEA, *National Plan 2008–13*, 15.
161. Ibid., 16.
162. Ibid.
163. Ibid., 21; Loxley et al., 'Access and Widening Participation: Stories from the Policy Domain,' 76.
164. Clancy, *Irish Higher Education*, 69–77.
165. Loxley et al., 'Access and Widening Participation: Stories from the Policy Domain,' 64.
166. Loxley et al., 'Access and Widening Participation: Stories from the Policy Domain,' 71.
167. *Irish Times*, 'UCD Group Accuses College of Bias Against Women,' 23 June 1998; UCD Governors Back Promotions Despite Discrimination Protest,' 24 June 1998; and *Irish Times*, 'Equality Agency Claims Women Face Bias in UCD Jobs,' 25 September 1998.
168. *Irish Times*, 'Robinson Tells TCD to End Honours Gender Imbalance,' 21 January 2002.
169. *Irish Times*, 'Academic Women Angry at Being Kept Out,' 27 June 1998.
170. *Irish Independent*, 'Four Female Lecturers at NUI Galway Initiate High Court Case Against College,' 30 April 2015; *Irish Times*, 'Micheline Sheehy Skeffington,' 6 December 2014.
171. *Irish Independent*, 'Four Female Lecturers at NUI Galway Initiate High Court Case Against College,' 30 April 2015.
172. Susan Parkes, 'A Hundred Years On,' in *A Danger to the Men*, ed. Parkes (Dublin: Lilliput Press, 2004), 296.
173. https://www.siliconrepublic.com/careers/marion-coy-institutes-of-technology-ireland-ioti. Accessed 1 September 2017.
174. https://www.timeshighereducation.com/news/glyndwr-names-maria-hinfelaar-next-v-c. Accessed 1 September 2017.
175. HEA, *Higher Education Institutional Staff Profiles by Gender* (Dublin: HEA, 2017), 5.
176. Ibid., 3.
177. Ibid., 5.
178. Ibid., 4; The three colleges included were NCAD, MIC and St. Angela's College, Sligo. Including MIE, which was funded by the DES, would have raised the ratio of female presidents to 50%.

179. Pat O'Connor, 'Gender and Organisational Culture at Senior Management Level: Limits and Possibilities for Change,' in *Have Women Made a Difference*, ed. Harford and Rush (Oxford: Peter Lang, 2010), 141.
180. Ibid., 157.
181. Ibid., 157–8.
182. Ibid., 151.
183. HEA, *Higher Education Institutional Staff Profiles by Gender*, 3–5.
184. Ibid., 3.
185. Ibid., 5.
186. Ibid., 4.
187. Ibid., 5.
188. Ibid., 3; The corresponding proportion for the IoTs was 82%.
189. *Irish Times*, "Third Level Fees May Return 'for Those Who Can Afford It,'" 24 September 2002; *Irish Times*, 'Dempsey Defers Decision on Reinstating Third Level Fees,' 17 April 2003.
190. OECD, *Review of Higher Education in Ireland*, 68.
191. Ibid.
192. Ibid., 69.
193. Ibid., 2.
194. Ibid., 7.
195. Ibid., 60.
196. Ibid., 62.
197. Hazelkorn et al., 'From Massification to Globalisation,' in *The State in Transition*, ed. Rafter and O'Brien, 235.
198. OECD, *Review of Higher Education in Ireland*, 61.
199. Ibid.
200. Government of Ireland, Inter-departmental Committee, *Strategy for Science Technology and Innovation 2007–13* (Dublin: Forfas, 2006).
201. OECD, *Review of Higher Education in Ireland*, 63.
202. Ibid., 60.
203. Ibid., 60.
204. Ibid., 63.
205. Ibid., 61–2.
206. Ibid., 64.
207. Ibid., 61.
208. Ibid., 31.
209. Ibid.

210. Ibid., 56–8.
211. Ibid., 59.
212. Oireachtas Éireann, No. 25 of 2006.
213. Ibid.
214. Ibid.
215. Department of Education and Skills, *National Strategy for Higher Education to 2030*, 19–21.
216. *Irish Times*, 'College Charges Set to Increase by Almost 70%,' 19 July 2002.
217. DES, *National Strategy*, 43.
218. Clancy, *Irish Higher Education*, 243.
219. Department of Education and Science, *Statistical Report 1997–98* (Dublin: Stationery Office, 1999), 83; *Statistical Report 2005–06* (Dublin: Stationery Office, 2008), 83.
220. *Irish Times*, "Third Level 'Facing into Competitive Era,'" 16 September 2002.
221. Department of Education and Science, *Statistical Report 2008–09* (Dublin: DES, 2010), 83.
222. Clancy, *Irish Higher Education*, 236.
223. HEA, *Interim Report by the Independent Expert Panel for the HEA, Review of the Allocation Model for Funding Higher Education Institutions* (Dublin: HEA, 2017), 31.
224. Ibid., 32.
225. Ibid.
226. Ibid., 34.
227. Clancy, *Irish Higher Education*, 239.
228. HEA, *Review of Allocation Model*, 31.
229. Ibid., 34.
230. Clancy, *Irish Higher Education*, 238.
231. Ibid.
232. HEA, *Review of the Allocation Model*, 35.
233. Ibid., see 'Contemporary Initiatives' below for a fuller discussion on the mission based compacts.
234. HEA, *Review of the Allocation Model*, 21.
235. HEA, *Higher Education System Performance 2014–16*, 72.
236. Ibid., 67.
237. Clancy, *Irish Higher Education*, 297.
238. HEA, *Higher Education System Performance 2014–16*, 17.

239. Clancy, *Irish Higher Education*, 297.
240. Report of the Expert Group, *Investing in National Ambition* (Dublin: DES, 2016), 65.
241. Clancy, *Irish Higher Education*, 244.
242. Report of the Expert Group, *Investing in National Ambition*, 65.
243. Ibid.
244. Ibid., 69.
245. Ibid., 19.
246. Ibid., 68.
247. Ibid., 19; HEA, *Higher Education System Performance 2014–16*, 71.
248. Interview with Ruairi Quinn TD, 23 December 2015.
249. Mike Jennings, IFUT Statement, October 2016.
250. HEA, *Higher Education System Performance 2014–16*, 71.
251. Ibid.
252. Ibid., 72.
253. Clancy, *Irish Higher Education*, 32.
254. Luce, *Trinity College Dublin*, 146.
255. Daniel C. Levy, *Higher Education and the State in Latin America: Private Challenges to Public Dominance* (Chicago: University of Chicago Press, 1986), 27.
256. Ibid., 37–45.
257. R. L. Geiger, *Private Sectors in Higher Education: Structure, Function and Change in Eight Countries* (Ann Arbor: University of Michigan, 1986), 157–60.
258. Andrew Gibson, 'Private Higher Education in Ireland,' forthcoming (2018).
259. Mark Duncan et al., *National College of Ireland: Past, Present and Future* (Dublin: NCI, 2007), 50.
260. Ibid., 65.
261. Clancy, *Irish Higher Education*, 32; David Limond, 'Prospects for a For-Profit, Private and Indigenous University in Dublin,' in *Higher Education in Ireland: Practices, Policies and Possibilities*, ed. Andrew Loxley et al. (Basingstoke: Palgrave Macmillan, 2014), 116.
262. Clancy, *Irish Higher Education*, 29.
263. http://www.dbs.ie/about-dbs/history-of-dbs. Accessed 1 September 2017.
264. White, *Investing in People*, 221–22.

265. http://www.dbs.ie/about-dbs/history-of-dbs. Accessed 1 September 2017.
266. White, *Investing in People*, 221–2.
267. https://www.griffith.ie/about-griffith/background/our-history. Accessed 1 September 2017.
268. Limond, 'Prospects for a For-Profit, Private and Indigenous University in Dublin,' in *Higher Education in Ireland*, ed. Loxley et al., 116.
269. Clancy, *Irish Higher Education*, 82.
270. *Irish Times*, 'Teacher Training Colleges Worried by Privately Run Internet Course,' 10 October 2003.
271. *Irish Times*, 'College Subjected to "Abuse",' November 2003.
272. Limond, 'Prospects for a For-Profit, Private and Indigenous University in Dublin,' in *Higher Education in Ireland*, ed. Andrew Loxley et al., 116–17.
273. Clancy, *Irish Higher Education*, 29.
274. Department of Education, *Charting Our Education Future*, 107.
275. *Irish Times*, 'Private Colleges Respond on the Bonding Issue,' 19 August 1998.
276. Department of Education, *Charting Our Education Future*, 107.
277. *Irish Times*, 'Private Colleges Respond on the Bonding Issue,' 19 August 1998.
278. Dáil Debates, vol. 507, no. 4, 18 May 1999, col. 1286–7.
279. Clancy, *Irish Higher Education*, 30.
280. *Irish Times*, 'Colleges' Welcome for New Legislation,' 18 August 1999.
281. http://www.dbs.ie/about-dbs/history-of-dbs. Accessed 1 September 2017.
282. http://www.heca.ie/about-us/. Accessed 16 September 2017.
283. http://www.heca.ie/about-us/. Accessed 16 September 2017.
284. Report of the Expert Group, *Investing in National Ambition*, 65.
285. Ibid.
286. Geiger, *Private Sectors in Higher Education*, 157–60.
287. DES, *National Strategy for Higher Education to 2030* (Dublin: DES, 2011), 51.
288. Department of Finance. Accessed 31 July 2017. http://www.finance.gov.ie/news-centre/press-releases/appointment-colin-hunt-special-adviser-department-finance.
289. Interviewee B, May 2018.

290. DES, *National Strategy*, 51.
291. *Irish Times*, 'Goodbye to All That—My Heroes and Villains of 2010,' 14 December 2010.
292. DES, *National Strategy*, 29; John Walsh and Andrew Loxley, "The Hunt Report and Higher Education Policy in the Republic of Ireland: 'An International Solution to an Irish Problem?'" *Studies in Higher Education* 40, no. 6 (2015): 1128–45. https://doi.org/10.1080/0307 5079.2014.881350. This section draws on a previous paper published by the author, jointly with Andrew Loxley, in 2015 and also incorporates more recent research.
293. DES, *National Strategy*, 29.
294. Ibid.
295. Ibid., 33.
296. Ibid., 35–7.
297. Walsh and Loxley, 'The Hunt Report,' *Studies in Higher Education* 40, no. 6 (2015): 1128–45. https://doi.org/10.1080/03075079.2014.881350.
298. DES, *National Strategy*, 87.
299. Ibid., 19.
300. Ibid., 97–9.
301. Ibid., 105.
302. Ibid., 102–3.
303. Walsh and Loxley, 'The Hunt Report,' *Studies in Higher Education* 40, no. 6 (2015): 1128–45. https://doi.org/10.1080/03075079.2014.881350.
304. DES, *National Strategy*, 42.
305. Walsh and Loxley, 'The Hunt Report,' *Studies in Higher Education* 40, no. 6 (2015): 1128–45.
306. Ibid.
307. DES, *National Strategy*, 91.
308. Ibid., 41.
309. Ibid., 98.
310. Clancy, *Irish Higher Education*, 268.
311. Ibid.
312. Government of Ireland, *Investment in Education*; see Chapter 7 above.
313. Interviewee B, May 2018.
314. Interviewee A, July 2016.
315. Interviewee B, May 2018.
316. Interviewee A, July 2016.

317. St. Aubyn et al., *Study on the Efficiency and Effectiveness of Public Spending on Tertiary Education* (ECOFIN, 2009), 66; HEA, *Towards a Future Higher Education Landscape* (Dublin: HEA, 2012), 2.
318. Interviewee A, 2016.
319. DES, *National Strategy*, 93.
320. Ferlie et al., 'The Steering of Higher Education Systems: A Public Management Perspective,' *Higher Education* 56, no. 3 (2009): 325–48.
321. Walsh and Loxley, 'The Hunt Report,' *Studies in Higher Education* 40, no. 6 (2015): 1128–45.
322. DES, *National Strategy*, 116.
323. Ferlie et al., 'The Steering of Higher Education Systems: A Public Management Perspective,' *Higher Education* 56, no. 3 (2009): 325–48.
324. Ibid.
325. Walsh and Loxley, 'The Hunt Report,' *Studies in Higher Education* 40, no. 6 (2015): 1128–45.
326. Ibid.
327. HEA, *Report to the Minister for Education and Skills on System Reconfiguration, Inter-institutional Collaboration and System Governance in Irish Higher Education* (Dublin: HEA, 2013), 13.
328. Ibid., 13–14.
329. Ibid., 13.
330. Olssen and Peters, 'Neoliberalism, Higher Education and the Knowledge Economy,' *Journal of Education Policy* 20, no. 3 (2005): 313.
331. DES, *National Strategy*, 91.
332. Ibid., 39.
333. Walsh and Loxley, 'The Hunt Report,' *Studies in Higher Education* 40, no. 6 (2015): 14.
334. DES, *National Strategy*, 108.
335. Walsh and Loxley, 'The Hunt Report,' *Studies in Higher Education* 40, no. 6 (2015): 14.
336. Ibid., 12.
337. Ibid.
338. Ibid., 15.
339. Ruairi Quinn, 'Delivering the Strategy for Higher Education,' Address by the Minister for Education and Skills to the Royal Irish Academy, 30 May 2011: copy from Mr. Ruairi Quinn.
340. Quinn Interview, 23 December 2015.
341. DES, *National Strategy*, 89.

342. HEA, *Consultation on Implementation of National Strategy for Higher Education to 2030* (Dublin: HEA, 2011).
343. HEA, *Guidelines on Regional Clusters* (Dublin: HEA, 2012), 19; while regional clusters would not impinge on the independent legal status of existing HEIs, this was not necessarily true of 'thematic clusters', at least in teacher education.
344. HEA, *Report to the Minister for Education and Skills on System Reconfiguration*, 16.
345. Ibid., 14.
346. Ibid., 17.
347. Ibid.
348. HEA, *Towards a Future Higher Education Landscape* (Dublin: HEA, 2012).
349. Ibid., 3.
350. HEA, *Report to the Minister for Education and Skills on System Reconfiguration, Inter-institutional Collaboration and System Governance in Irish Higher Education* (Dublin: HEA, 2013), 5.
351. HEA, *Towards a Future Higher Education Landscape*, 6.
352. Ibid.
353. Ibid., 7.
354. HEA, *Report to the Minister for Education and Skills on System Reconfiguration*, 9.
355. Ibid.
356. Ibid., 8.
357. Ibid., 12.
358. Ibid., 25–6.
359. Clancy, *Irish Higher Education*, 268.
360. Rahm Emanuel made the comment during his term as chief of staff to President Barack Obama (2009–2011).
361. DES, *National Strategy*, 89.
362. Clancy, *Irish Higher Education*, 262.
363. Ibid., 264.
364. HEA, *Higher Education System Performance, Institutional and Sectoral Profiles 2013/14* (Dublin: HEA, 2016); This was the fourth report launched in July 2016.
365. DES, *National Strategy*, 89; Clancy, *Irish Higher Education*, 262.
366. HEA, *Report to the Minister for Education and Skills on System Reconfiguration*, 8.

367. O'Donoghue et al., *Teacher Preparation in Ireland*, 179.
368. Ibid., 182–3; Paul Conway and Rosaleen Murphy, 'A Rising Tide Meets a Perfect Storm: New Accountabilities in Teaching and Teacher Education in Ireland,' *Irish Educational Studies* 32, no. 1 (March 2013): 11–36. https://doi.org/10.1080/03323315.2013 .773227; Steffi Smyth, 'Teachers' Perceptions of the Literacy and Numeracy Strategy Within the Primary Curriculum: Challenges and Implications,' M.Ed. diss., TCD, 2015.
369. Department of Education and Skills, *Literacy and Numeracy for Learning and Life: The National Strategy to Improve Literacy and Numeracy Among Children and Young People* (Dublin: DES, 2011), 34.
370. Ibid., 34–5.
371. Ibid., 34–5; Teaching Council Act, 2001, No. 8 of 2001, 8–9. Accessed 1 March 2018. http://www.irishstatutebook.ie/eli/2001/act/8/enacted/en/pdf.
372. O'Donoghue et al., *Teacher Preparation in Ireland*, 186.
373. Sahlberg et al., *Report of the International Review Panel on the Structure of Initial Teacher Education in Ireland* (Dublin: DES, 2012), 25.
374. HEA, *Towards a Future Higher Education Landscape*, 9.
375. Sahlberg et al., *Report of the International Review Panel*, 26.
376. Ibid., 24.
377. Ibid., 29; O'Donoghue et al., *Teacher Preparation in Ireland*, 201.
378. Sahlberg et al., *Report of the International Review Panel*, 27.
379. John Walshe, *An Education: How an Outsider Became an Insider—And Learned What Really Goes on in Irish government* (Dublin: Penguin, 2014), 143.
380. *Irish Times*, 'Church and TCD in Row Over Teacher Training,' 7 December 2012.
381. John Walshe, *An Education*, 143.
382. Ibid., 144.
383. HEA, *Higher Education System Performance 2014–16*, 62; Clancy, *Irish Higher Education*, 275; and O'Donoghue et al., *Teacher Preparation in Ireland*, 201.
384. HEA, *Higher Education System Performance 2014–16*, 62; IFUT, *Report to Annual Delegate Conference 2017*.
385. O'Donoghue et al., *Teacher Preparation in Ireland*, 201.
386. Sahlberg et al., *Report of the International Review Panel*, 28.
387. HEA, *Higher Education System Performance 2014–16*, 62.

388. Ibid., 30.
389. *Irish Times*, 'Training Teachers the Catholic Way,' 24 April 2012.
390. *Irish Times*, 'Priest Who Played Significant Role in Teacher Training: Obituary—Michael A. Hayes,' 29 April 2017.
391. Ibid.
392. *Irish Times*, 'Training Teachers the Catholic Way,' 24 April 2012.
393. O'Donoghue et al., *Teacher Preparation in Ireland*, 205.
394. Frans Van Vught et al., *A Proposed Reconfiguration of the Irish System of Higher Education—Report Prepared by an International Expert Panel for the Higher Education Authority of Ireland* (HEA: 2012), 19.
395. Ibid., 19–21.
396. Ibid., 23–5.
397. Ibid., 22–3.
398. *Irish Times*, 'Trinity Merger with UCD Not "Desirable; Says Minister",' 26 September 2012.
399. Interviewee B, May 2018.
400. *Irish Times*, 'A Radical Vision for Third Level?' 26 September 2012; 'Quinn Should Tackle HEA on University Report,' 26 September 2012.
401. HEA, *Guidelines on Regional Clusters*, 20–1.
402. HEA, *Report to the Minister for Education and Skills on System Reconfiguration*, 14.
403. Clancy, *Irish Higher Education*, 280.
404. Ibid., 275.
405. HEA, *Report to the Minister for Education and Skills on System Reconfiguration*, 20–1. The remaining clusters were: South—UCC, Cork IT, Tralee IT, Waterford IT and Carlow IT. Mid-West—UL, Mary Immaculate College, Limerick IT. West—NUIG, Galway-Mayo, Sligo and Letterkenny ITs.
406. Ibid., 21.
407. Ibid.
408. HEA, *Higher Education System Performance 2014–16*, 65.
409. Ibid.
410. Interviewee B, May 2018.
411. Interview with Ruairi Quinn TD, 23 December 2015.
412. Interviewee B, May 2018.
413. HEA, *Process and Criteria for Designation as a Technological University* (Dublin: HEA, 2012), 1–7.
414. Ibid., 2.

415. Interview with Ruairi Quinn TD, 23 December 2015.

416. HEA, *Higher Education System Performance 2014–16*, 64.

417. Ibid.; HEA, *Report to the Minister for Education and Skills on System Reconfiguration*, 24.

418. HEA, *Higher Education System Performance 2014–16*, 64.

419. *Irish Examiner*, 'Lecturers Vote Clears Way for Laws to Create Technological Universities,' 15 June 2017; Walshe, *An Education*, 141–2.

420. TUI Press Statement, 11 January 2016. Accessed 31 July 2017. https://www.tui.ie/press-releases/technological-universities-bill-must-be-amended-to-protect-sector-.7925.html.

421. *Irish Examiner*, 'Lecturers Vote Clears Way for Laws to Create Technological Universities,' 15 June 2017.

422. Clancy, *Irish Higher Education*, 291; *Irish Times*, 'A Radical Vision for Third Level?' 26 September 2012.

10

Higher Education in the Twenty First Century

Higher education was on the periphery of the dominant ideological narratives which informed public policy and debate in the new Irish state. The hallmark of state policies towards higher education during the first generation of the independent state was benign neglect. Most public figures, civil servants and university leaders associated higher education almost exclusively with the universities, while political and administrative elites until the 1950s explicitly accepted a limited vision of the university as a narrowly defined elite institution geared towards education for the professions. The resilience of this traditionalist world view explains why university education remained an underdeveloped elite sector well into the middle of twentieth century. Even more striking was the neglect of technical education, which occupied an ambivalent, if not explicitly inferior, position on the margins of the second and third level sectors for a generation after 1922. Primary teacher training was positioned by the new nationalist elites mainly as a channel for the achievement of cherished cultural objectives, notably the cultural crusade to restore the Irish language and was subject to a much greater level of direction by central political and administrative institutions than other sectors of higher education.

© The Author(s) 2018
J. Walsh, *Higher Education in Ireland, 1922–2016*,
https://doi.org/10.1057/978-1-137-44673-2_10

If Burton Clark's conceptualisation of forces of coordination may be revisited, a more appropriate 'triangle of coordination'[1] in Ireland from 1922 to the 1970s would have been the state, academic oligarchy and the churches. The complex interaction between politicians, academic organisations and church leaders of various denominations was a distinctive feature in Irish higher education policy and institutional development in the early to mid 1900s. The enduring strength of religious influences and institutions, exemplified particularly by integralist Catholicism, was a constant factor in Irish higher education until the final quarter of the twentieth century. The power of the Catholic church was exercised in part through explicitly denominational educational institutions, notably the teacher training colleges, but this represented only the formal institutional footprint of the church, which greatly understated its actual influence. Despite the non-denominational statutory basis of the universities, ecclesiastical power remained a major factor during the early to mid twentieth century in a triangular relationship between academic institutions and the state. The NUI owed its foundation in 1909 to a pragmatic accommodation between the Catholic bishops led by William Walsh and British ministers. A half a century later, Archbishop McQuaid was an indispensable ally to O'Malley in the launch of the university merger and sought, albeit unsuccessfully, to use the merger to absorb Trinity College into a merged university acting as a bulwark of Catholicism against secularist and atheistic influences. Integralist Catholicism permeated the culture and institutional life of the NUI, while the long-term ecclesiastical 'ban' on Trinity College did much to establish Trinity's defensive, semi-detached status during the first generation of the independent state. Ecclesiastical power began to wane only from the 1960s when long-term denominational divisions in university education were eroded by a combination of a gradual cultural modernisation and educational policy changes.

The traditional universities which commanded the largest share of enrolments, professionally oriented teacher training institutions and the urban technical colleges operated separately in a fragmented post-compulsory, post-primary space. There was no recognised higher technological sector up to the 1950s, any more than there was a coherent system of higher education. The first genuine signs of diversification in terms of institutions and courses appeared in the decade following the second world war. The VEC colleges were expanding during the 1950s both in terms of student enrolments and the type of courses offered, testifying to the resilience of the colleges and public demand for an emergent technical sector at higher level. Teacher training colleges had a very different tradition rooted in prestigious religious institutions and a distinctive function in professional formation which was valued by both church and state. This was arguably a mixed blessing for the academic leaders and staff in these institutions, who were subject to a higher level of control than most third-level educators. The technical schools/institutes and training colleges emerged from very different traditions and cultures, one predominantly secular and vocationally oriented and the other religious and shaped by the dominant ideologies of the period and operated within very different institutional and governance structures. Yet developments in both sectors during the early postwar period indicated the potential for diversification of the third-level space, even if this was not yet conceptualised by policy-makers in a coherent way.

The radical policy changes which followed in the later twentieth century built upon on earlier, more incremental initiatives, but also responded to a growing sense of crisis, affecting both university education and teacher training, following the second world war. Longer term planning remained a distant aspiration in this period, as government initiatives were uneven, piecemeal and often driven by short-term crisis management. Yet the origins of far-reaching policy change emerged in the early postwar era, as growing societal demand for education, coupled with the consequences of long-term political and administrative neglect, increasingly forced a re-appraisal of traditionalist policies and understandings of higher education.

The emergence of economic imperatives in educational policy, closely linked to human capital ideas adopted by Irish domestic elites, exerted a key influence on the development of a recognisable higher education system for the first time. International influences were often mediated through the OECD, which was instrumental in disseminating human capital perspectives on education within the Irish public sphere through the *Investment* study and the review of technical education.[2] The central place of higher education in economic development became an article of faith among policy-makers from the late 1960s through to the first decades of the twenty-first century. Yet economics alone did not explain the transformation of policy, structures and institutions which took place in the mid to late twentieth century. Economic imperatives co-existed with an increased salience for social justice concerns in public debate, allied to a dramatic increase in social demand for higher level courses. The shift to expansionist policies was facilitated by a political context which was receptive to egalitarian appeals for equality of educational opportunity. Government policies were designed to fulfil labour market demands for a more highly skilled work force and achieve knowledge transfer with a pronounced utilitarian emphasis, but also to satisfy unprecedented societal demand for higher education. Politicians, civil servants and most expert advisers saw no contradiction between economic and social priorities, while the OECD in the postwar era of Keynesian economics emphasised both the social and economic benefits of increased participation. The transformation of government policies underpinned an extraordinary expansion of full-time participation particularly among the school leaving age cohort, allied to a diversification of the newly conceptualised HE system through the upgrading and repositioning of higher technical education. A fragmented post-compulsory space dominated by an elite university sector gave way to a diversified, sectorally differentiated binary system encompassing universities, higher technical colleges and colleges of education, which facilitated 'mass' participation while allowing established institutions to adapt gradually to policy and institutional change.

White suggests that since the 1960s at least the key relationship and site of potential conflict was between academic institutions and the state.[3] Certainly a powerful state, which operated on a centralised model conceding very limited authority to local government, was the key interlocutor for higher education institutions from independence. The exercise of power by the political and administrative centre impinged very differently on different sectors or institutions and for a long period involved a laissez-faire approach to the university sector. The major policy changes in the 1960s were driven by an interventionist state, signalling a fundamental policy departure from the traditionalist ideological framework of the previous generation. The emergence of a more authoritative and engaged political centre led first to the creation of a greatly expanded and reconfigured non-university sector but later impinged increasingly on the mission and activity of universities.

The emergence of the modern Irish higher education system was associated with a widening of policy debate to include interests which had previously had little influence on the key relationships between church, state and university leaders. Student militancy failed to achieve many of its objectives, but gave rise to new forms of student activism and organisation which became part of the institutional fabric in the late 1900s. Trade unions such as IFUT and the TUI emerged as a significant force in negotiations with government and national debates over HE. A more vociferous public sphere gave scope to a wider cast of non-university institutional leaders, trade unions and student representatives to impinge on policy formation.

Private industry hardly featured at all in policy or institutional decisions in higher education until the reforms of the 1960s. Subsequently the influence of industry was largely mediated through state agencies, such as the IDA, in the late 1900s.[4] The diversification of HE to create a non-university sector with a strong vocational mission was closely linked to human capital considerations, but also reflected a wider cultural and political break with a traditionalist consensus and was informed by a mixture of labour market and egalitarian influences rooted in societal transformation. Government initiatives to encourage greater engagement with the market, at least by the universities, were selective and focused largely on meeting specific skills shortages up to the 1990s. It was only at the turn of the millennium, with the ambitious repositioning of higher education research on a 'triple helix' model that market mechanisms began to play a more direct role in the activity of HEIs. Yet even in the early 2000s, this effort to mobilise market resources to enhance human capital formation was not wholly successful, as business funding of HERD remained relatively low.

Much of the scholarship on the history of higher education indicates a shift in policy in the late twentieth century involving a reintepretation of the state's role in HE, associated with the triumph of neoliberalism

in the UK and USA during the 1980s.[5] Yet policy and institutional
structure in Ireland showed a high level of continuity in the generation
following the emergence of the modern HE system in the 1960s. The
significant legislative and institutional reforms in the late twentieth century were shaped more by existing ideological and policy frameworks
rather than being reproduced from a neoliberal script imported from
other English-speaking countries. Economic and social priorities co-
existed in policy formation and implementation throughout the late
twentieth century. Indeed egalitarian priorities in some ways became
more influential in the 1990s, as widening participation came to the fore
as a key focus of policy following the Steering Committee report in 1995.
Policy-making in a democratic state was complex rather than mono-
lithic: government initiatives did not always follow a particular ideological script in a period of creative policy formulation, featured conflict
between different actors within the policy system and were open to
amendment by effective interest groups. Different ministers sometimes
had different priorities—the Green Paper promoted by Seamus Brennan
was more market oriented in some respects than the White Paper
authorised by Niamh Bhreathnach. The HEA and government departments often diverged on the scope of regulation, as the authority still
played the role of an influential 'buffer' agency in this period.[6] Certainly
a key turning point was the adoption of universities legislation in 1997,
but the sometimes acrimonious debate and prolonged legislative process
testified to a wide spectrum of attitudes among both government and
academic actors on the type and scope of regulation. The resistance of
institutional leaders and a wider academic lobby to more extreme ver-
sions of an official accountability regime proved effective, not least due
to their ability to mobilise wider political support. Ultimately the legislation was a compromise between academic and managerialist understandings of the university.

A more significant transition in the attitudes of political and official
elites, government policy formation and to a considerable extent the
institutional strategies of HEIs themselves occurred in the early 2000s.
While the utilitarian orientation of government policy was not a new
phenomenon, the more systematic way in which official objectives have
been pursued in the last two decades, allied to reduced public resources

and more intensive pressure to engage with private enterprise, represents a strategic reorientation in contemporary educational policy. The most notable policy changes since the late 1990s have been the repositioning of higher education to prioritise more intensive engagement with industry and deployment of market mechanisms on a large scale for the first time to achieve national objectives. The surge in funding for higher education research at the end of the twentieth century was underpinned by a shift in government policy to prioritise knowledge generation within HEIs. This involved a sustained attempt to achieve the reorientation of HE to serve the requirements of a knowledge-based economy, through commercialisation, competitive allocation of research funding and a 'managerial reform' agenda to transform the internal functioning of the universities.

Globalisation was the most profound and disruptive influence on Irish higher education in the early 2000s, driving the most far-reaching reshaping of policy and institutional patterns since the opening up of the system to mass participation half a century earlier.[7] The intergovernmental Bologna process was crucial in underpinning major curriculum reform, notably the shift to outcomes based programme development and assessment and informed the emergence of national quality assurance systems. The OECD was again influential as an 'institutional carrier', setting the context for acceptable policies and practice and playing a major role in defining specific strategies and 'archetypes' for higher education policy and organisation.[8] The OECD shaped policy formation in various ways, through its periodic publications, contacts with government officials and especially through the review of higher education in 2003–04. The review itself reflected a shared consensus between the OECD, European Commission and national elites on the crucial contribution of higher education in developing a knowledge-based economy. The review's proposals on system structure and institutional reform proved influential, especially in shaping the Hunt Report. Irish ministers were more cautious in responding to the alternative policy choices proposed by the examiners to build greater equity into expansionist policies.

The EU was also a significant player and its role in higher education has been underestimated due to its lack of formal competence in

university education until the 1990s and continuing rhetorical deference to member states. Perhaps the most notable contribution of the
EU institutions was to disseminate a discourse around research concentration, differentiation and critical mass to meet global competition,
which was echoed by national policy-makers in the Hunt report—an
unacknowledged example of 'policy borrowing' shaped by the logic
of globalisation.[9] There were limits to the influence of supranational
agencies. Irish policy-makers were cautious in managing the politically
sensitive issue of tuition fees and slow to acknowledge EU influence
explicitly. Yet the period since 2000 saw a high level of policy, institutional and curriculum change, shaped by discourses derived from the
logic of globalisation and mediated through supranational agencies.

The economic crash in 2008 acclerated the ongoing reappraisal of
HE policies. Higher education was positioned as a key determinant
of national economic salvation in the Hunt report, which adopted
a narrow conceptualisation of human capital theory and abandoned
the more sophisticated explanatory frameworks advanced by a series
of expert group reports from *Investment in Education* to the Steering
Committee. HE was valued almost exclusively for human capital considerations linked to upskilling of the labour force and knowledge generation. Even the traditional emphases on widening participation and
meeting societal demand were reinterpreted in terms of their contribution to the labour market.[10] Yet the rhetorical emphasis on higher education in terms of knowledge based economic renewal was combined
with a sharp reduction in public funding and injunctions to do 'more
with less'.

The harsh winds of economic catastrophe drove a more intensive
assertion of authority over HEIs by government departments and agencies, through increased regulation, revised funding instruments and
a structural rationalisation agenda. Among the key outcomes of this
process are the increased governance and regulatory power of the HEA
and the employment of an eclectic combination of bureaucratic, net-
working and market mechanisms to promote consolidation of smaller
institutions and collaborative clusters. But perhaps the most effective instrument of official policy was also the most traditional—a dramatic reduction in public resourcing of HE, forcing institutions to rely

more on private fund-raising and commercialisation. The effects of this assertion of power are uneven and still uncertain, but the most recent phase of development saw the adoption by Irish political elites, executive agencies and even institutional leaders of a dominant paradigm marked by managerialism, commercialisation and rationalisation, which demanded internal reform within HEIs and ultimately external reconfiguration to create a more globally competitive higher education sector.

Yet Irish higher education is not a neat case study for the triumph of neoliberal ideology: even in its most recent phase higher education policy has not embraced marketisation as a governing principle and the national strategy was far from being a charter for a Thatcherite reconstruction of the higher education system.[11] The Hunt report in terms of content and ideology was not particularly radical, instead representing an explicit reinforcement and clarification of policy frameworks which showed a strong international imprint, influenced by the OECD review, EU university modernisation agenda and the impact of the economic crisis.[12] As Fleming et al. note, Irish political and cultural norms 'did not lend themselves to the founding of a Hayekian-Friedman paradise.'[13] It will be no surprise that Irish policy-makers do not give a high value to ideological consistency—indeed the HEA explicitly referenced pragmatism as a key operational principle of its reform agenda. Most policy-makers in the early 2000s have been firmly supportive of corporate, managerial reform in pursuit of economic imperatives, employing various mechanisms with a definite NPM imprint. Yet a very similar cast of politicians, officials and expert advisors have been notably wary of simply importing solutions from Ireland's nearest neighbour, whose HE system has served as a laboratory for market-oriented policy experiments for over two decades. Irish policy-makers have been more willing to embrace economically 'rational' policies, such as incremental raising of university fees, advocated by the influential OECD and elements of the universities modernisation agenda promoted by the EU Commission. The structural rationalisation and managerial 'reform' agendas owe an ideological debt to NPM, but also draw upon on other public service reform narratives, notably the network governance approach and the more traditional but still robust bureaucratic norms which have shaped government interactions with the academy since the 1920s.

The enduring influence of bureaucratic norms in the Irish system should not be underestimated. Policy change in higher education has often taken the form of increased bureaucratic authority, exercised through the DES and more recently the HEA, or of state-led efforts to mobilise collaborative networks to serve objectives defined by politicians and officials. While HEIs are much more engaged with the market through commercialisation and more dependent on private contributions than a decade ago, this has not led to any reduction in the authority of the state. The decline in public funding has, paradoxically, coincided with an increase in bureaucratic power and the advance of an interventionist state. The Irish system has not experienced large-scale marketisation on the English model, witnessing instead an increase in bureaucratic and regulatory authority, somewhat ironically justified in the name of greater efficiency, responsiveness and flexibility.

Yet if the Irish HE system does not fit neatly within theories of NPM and neoliberalism and has sometimes benefited from the pragmatism of key political actors, this should not be a defence of the current brand of narrowly focused, economically driven utilitarianism. The most significant withdrawal of resources from higher education since the advent of mass education two generations ago underlined in an unmistakable fashion that the contemporary repositioning of the sector in line with a narrow conceptualisation of human capital was linked to an undermining of political and official support for investment in HE. This exposes a central contradiction in current government policies, namely that HE has apparently never been more important to knowledge based economic development, but the sector is in the midst of a profound crisis of funding and sustainability.

The ideological underpinnings of government policy where the contribution of HE is identified almost exclusively with human capital formation contrast sharply with the more diverse policy and ideological assumptions that held sway in the second half of the twentieth century. The human capital paradigm was crucial in stimulating a break from traditionalist cultural understandings of higher education in the 1960s and functioned admirably as a key institutional rationale for investment in higher education in the mid to late twentieth century.[14] But during this period economic value was rarely if ever invoked as the main legitimating factor for the expansion of the HE sector: wider societal considerations linked to egalitarian ideas and assumptions performed much of this legitimating function, as the HEA explicitly acknowledged in 1995.[15] This did not mean that policy was universally enlightened or even consistent in the mid to late 1900s. Yet whatever its shortcomings the impact of policy change can hardly be disputed—a combination of economic and societal rationales offered a compelling ideological and practical justification for expansion, reform and diversification, which led to the creation of the modern system of higher education in Ireland. The transformation of higher education in Ireland was underpinned by a fundamental policy departure in the role of the state during the middle decades of the twentieth century. A similar reorientation involving a reduction in public investment and enhanced role for competitive market forces in the early 2000s has contributed to a contemporary crisis in higher education.

Despite lip service to a wider array of objectives, a narrow economic utilitarianism has emerged as the decisive institutional rationale for investment and reform in HE and it has failed to offer a convincing justification to policy-makers in funding the system adequately, private enterprise in offering additional finance or even academic stakeholders in embracing institutional reform. It is possible to advocate many different paths out of the contemporary impasse and it is beyond the scope of this work to assess in detail the viability of the different financing models proposed by the Cassells report in 2016.[16] Yet an essential starting point is surely to recognise that higher education performs a multiplicity of valuable functions, most of which have a strong historical and philosophical basis and that its intrinsic value to individuals and wider contribution to society cannot be measured primarily in economic terms. If this appears simply to be a statement of the obvious, recent evidence of the interaction between state, the market and academia would suggest the opposite.

Notes

1. Clark, *The Higher Education System,* 142–3.
2. Aidan Seery, John Walsh, and Andrew Loxley, 'Investment: The Tests of Time,' *Irish Educational Studies* 33, no. 2 (2014): 173–91.

3. White, *Investing in People*, 257–8.
4. Ibid.
5. Ó Buachalla, 'Self-Regulation and the Emergence of the Evaluative State: Trends in Irish Educational Policy, 1987–92,' *European Journal of Education* 27, no. 1/2 (1992): 69–78; White, *Investing in People*, 256.
6. White, *Investing in People*, 229.
7. See above pp. 390–414.
8. Massimiliano Vaira, 'Globalisation and Higher Education: A Framework for Analysis,' *Higher Education* 48 (2004): 489
9. Ibid.; Highman, 'A Case Study on Differentiation,' 290–1.
10. See above pp. 441–44.
11. Walsh and Loxley, 'The Hunt Report,' *Studies in Higher Education* 40, no. 6 (2015): 1128–45. https://doi.org/10.1080/03075079.201 4.881350.
12. Ibid.; Clancy, *Irish Higher Education*, 268.
13. Fleming et al., *Access and Participation in Irish Higher Education*, 9.
14. O'Sullivan, *Cultural Politics*, 142–3.
15. See above p. 307.
16. Report of the Expert Group, *Investing in National Ambition*, 7–9.

Bibliography

Archival Sources

Department of Taoiseach (TSCH). National Archives of Ireland (NAI): 1923–1986.

Department of Finance (D/FIN). National Archives of Ireland (NAI): 1961–1962.

Department of Foreign Affairs (DFA). National Archives of Ireland (NAI): 1957–1972.

Papers of Dr. Paul Cullen, Archbishop of Dublin. Dublin Diocesan Archives: 1873.

Papers of Dr. William Walsh, Archbishop of Dublin. Dublin Diocesan Archives: 1908–1921.

Papers of Dr. John Charles McQuaid, Archbishop of Dublin. Dublin Diocesan Archives: 1940–1972.

Eamon de Valera Papers. UCD Archives.

Patrick Hillery Papers. UCD Archives.

Cabinet Minutes.

Minutes of the Board of Trinity College Dublin (MUN/V). Trinity College Dublin: 1908–1977.

Minutes of the Senate of the National University of Ireland. National University of Ireland: 1908–1997.

© The Editor(s) (if applicable) and The Author(s) 2018
J. Walsh, *Higher Education in Ireland, 1922–2016*,
https://doi.org/10.1057/978-1-137-44673-2

Minutes of the Senate of Queen's University, Belfast. Queen's University, Belfast: 1910–1918.
Irish Universities Act, 1908.
St. Patrick's College Archive (SPCA).

Official Publications and Reports

Commission of the European Communities. *Communication from the Commission: The Role of the Universities in the Europe of Knowledge.* Brussels: European Union, 2003.
Dáil Debates 1922–1999.
Department of Education. *Reports of the Department of Education 1923–2009.* Dublin: Stationery Office, 1923–2009.
Department of Education. *Programme for Action in Education.* Dublin: Stationery Office, 1984.
Department of Education. *Education for a Changing World: Green Paper on Education.* Dublin: Stationery Office, 1992.
Department of Education. *Position Paper on University Legislation.* Dublin: Stationery Office, 1995.
Department of Education. *Charting Our Education Future: White Paper on Education.* Dublin: Stationery Office, 1995.
Department of Education and Science. *Report of the Action Group on Access to Third Level Education.* Dublin: DES, 2001.
Department of Education and Skills. *National Strategy for Higher Education to 2030—Report of the Strategy Group.* Dublin: DES, 2011.
Department of Jobs, Enterprise and Innovation. *Report of the Research Prioritisation Steering Group.* Dublin: Forfas, 2011.
European Parliament. Lisbon European Council, Presidency Conclusions, 23–24 March 2000. Accessed 1 December 2017. http://www.europarl.europa.eu/summits/lis1_en.html.
Government of Ireland. *Commission on Technical Education, Report.* Dublin: Stationery Office, 1927.
Government of Ireland. *Report of the Commission on Accommodation Needs of the Constituent Colleges of the National University of Ireland.* Dublin: Stationery Office, 1959.
Government of Ireland. *Second Programme for Economic Expansion, Part 2, Laid by the Government Before Each House of the Oireachtas,* August 1963. Dublin: Stationery Office, 1964.

Government of Ireland. *Investment in Education Report of the Survey Team Appointed by the Minister for Education in October 1962*. Dublin: Stationery Office, 1965.

Government of Ireland. *Report of the Commission on Higher Education 1960–67*. Dublin: Stationery Office, 1967.

Government of Ireland. *Steering Committee on Technical Education, Report to the Minister for Education on Regional Technical Colleges*. Dublin: Stationery Office, 1969.

Government of Ireland. *White Paper on Educational Development*. Dublin: Stationery Office, 1980.

Government of Ireland. *Strategy for Science Technology and Innovation 2007–13 (SSTI)*. Dublin: Forfas, 2006.

Hansard 1845–1922.

HEA. *First Report 1968–69*. Dublin: HEA, 1969.

HEA. *Report to the Minister for Education on Teacher Education*. Dublin: HEA, 1970.

HEA. *Report on the Ballymun Project*. Dublin: HEA, 1972.

HEA. *Report to the Minister for Education on University Reorganisation with Special Reference to the Projected Formation of a Single University of Dublin and to the Alternative Solution Put Forward Jointly by the National University of Ireland and Trinity College, Dublin*. Dublin: HEA, 1972.

HEA. *Progress Report 1974*. Dublin: HEA, 1974.

HEA. *General Report 1974–84*. Dublin: HEA, 1985.

HEA. *Women Academics in Ireland: Report of the Committee on the Position of Women Academics in Third Level Education in Ireland*. Dublin: HEA, 1987.

HEA. *Interim Report of the Steering Committee's Technical Working Group*. Dublin: HEA, 1995.

HEA. *Report of the Steering Committee on the Future Development of Higher Education (based on a study of needs to the year 2015)*. Dublin: HEA, 1995.

HEA. *Financial Management and Governance in HEIs—Ireland, OECD IMHE/ HEFCE Project on International Comparative Higher Education Financial Management and Governance*. Dublin: HEA, 2004.

HEA. *National Plan for Equity of Access to Higher Education 2008–13*. Dublin: HEA, 2008.

HEA. *Consultation on Implementation of National Strategy for Higher Education to 2030*. Dublin: HEA, 2011.

HEA. *Guidelines on Regional Clusters*. Dublin: HEA, 2011.

HEA. *Towards a Future Higher Education Landscape.* Dublin: HEA, 2012.

HEA. *Report to the Minister for Education and Skills on System Reconfiguration, Inter-Institutional Collaboration and System Governance in Irish Higher Education.* Dublin: HEA, 2013.

HEA. *Process and Criteria for Designation as a Technological University.* Dublin: HEA, 2012.

HEA. *Higher Education System Performance, Institutional and Sectoral Profiles 2013/14.* Dublin: HEA, 2016.

HEA. *Higher Education 2015–16—Key Facts and Figures.* Dublin: HEA, 2016.

HEA. *Higher Education System Performance 2014–16—Second Report of the HEA to the Minister for Education and Skills.* Dublin: HEA, 2016.

HEA. *National Plan for Equity of Access to Higher Education 2015–19.* Dublin: HEA, 2015.

HEA. *Higher Education Institutional Staff Profiles by Gender.* Dublin: HEA, 2017.

HEA. *Interim Report by the Independent Expert Panel for the HEA, Review of the Allocation Model for Funding Higher Education Institutions.* Dublin: HEA, 2017.

ICSTI. *Technology Foresight Ireland: An ICSTI Overview.* Dublin: Forfas, 1998.

National Forum for the Enhancement of Teaching and Learning. *National Professional Development Framework for All Staff Who Work in Higher Education*, August 2016. https://www.teachingandlearning.ie/wp-content/uploads/2016/09/PD-Framework-FINAL-1.pdf. Accessed 1 November 2017.

NCEA. *First Annual Report 1972–73.* Dublin: NCEA, 1973.

OECD. *Reviews of National Policies for Science and Education, Training of Technicians in Ireland.* Paris: OECD, 1964.

OECD. *Review of National Policies for Education: Review of Higher Education in Ireland.* Paris: OECD, 2004.

Oireachtas Éireann. No. 15 of 1992.

Oireachtas Éireann. No. 16 of 1992.

Oireachtas Éireann. Universities Act (No. 24 of 1997).

Oireachtas Éireann. No. 26 of 1999.

Oireachtas Éireann. No. 1 of 2000.

Oireachtas Éireann. Teaching Council Act (No. 8 of 2001).

Oireachtas Éireann. No. 25 of 2006.

Oireachtas Éireann. No. 28 of 2012.

PA Consulting. *Ten Years On: Confirming Impacts from Research Investment.* Dublin: PA, 2011.

QQI. *Strategy Statement 2016–18.* Dublin: QQI, 2015.

Report of the Expert Group on Future Funding for Higher Education. *Investing in National Ambition: A Strategy for Funding Higher Education.* Dublin: Department of Education and Skills, 2016.

Report of the Public Accounts Committee. *Appropriation Accounts.* Dublin: Stationery Office, 1923–1981.

Royal Commission on University Education in Ireland. Final Report of the Commissioners. Dublin: His Majesty's Stationery Office, 1903.

Royal Commission on Trinity College, Dublin and the University of Dublin. Appendix to the First Report, Statements and Returns Furnished to the Commissioners in July and August 1906. Dublin: His Majesty's Stationery Office, 1906.

Sahlberg, Pasi, John Furlong, and Pamela Munn. *Report of the International Review Panel on the Structure of Initial Teacher Education in Ireland.* Dublin: DES, 2012.

Seanad Debates 1922–99.

Van Vught, Frans, Vin Massaro, Eva Egron-Polak, Michael Gallagher, Lauritz Holm-Nielsen, and John Randall. *A Proposed Reconfiguration of the Irish System of Higher Education—Report Prepared by an International Expert Panel for the Higher Education Authority of Ireland,* 9 August 2012. Dublin: HEA, 2012.

Books and Journal Articles

Barry, Frank. 'Outward Economic Development and the Irish Education System.' *Irish Educational Studies* 33, no. 2 (2014): 213–223.

Blake, Donal S. *St. Mary's Marino Generalate and Teacher College Century of Educational Leadership, 1904–2004.* Dublin: Marino Institute of Education, 2005.

Boyer, Ernest. *Scholarship Reconsidered: Priorities of the Professoriate, A Special Report for the Carnegie Foundation.* Princeton: Carnegie Foundation for the Advancement of Teaching, 1990.

Burke, Mary Rose. 'Women Staff in the RTC Sector.' In *HEEU Conference Proceedings,* 22–23 September 1995. Accessed 1 September 2017. https://www.ucc.ie/publications/heeu/womenstf/2_burke.htm#top.

Byrne, Delma, and Selina McCoy. 'Effectively Maintained Inequality in Educational Transitions in the Republic of Ireland.' *American Behavioural Scientist* 61, no. 1 (2017): 49–73.

CIRCA. *A Comparative International Assessment of the Organisation, Management and Funding of University Research in Ireland and Europe.* HEA, 1996.

Clark, Burton. *The Higher Education System Academic Organisation in Cross-National Perspective.* Berkeley: University of California Press, 1983.

Clarke, Marie. 'The Development of Vocational and Technical Education in Ireland, 1930–2015.' In *Essays in the History of Irish Education*, edited by Brendan Walsh, 297–319. London: Palgrave Macmillan, 2016.

Clancy, Patrick, and Ciaran Benson. *Higher Education in Dublin a Study of Some Emerging Trends.* Dublin: HEA, 1979.

Clancy, Patrick. *Who Goes to College: A Second National Survey of Participation in Higher Education.* Dublin: HEA, 1988.

Clancy, Patrick. 'The Evolution of Policy in Third-Level Education.' In *Irish Educational Policy: Process and Substance*, edited by D. G. Mulcahy and Denis O'Sullivan, 99–132. Dublin: IPA, 1989.

Clancy, Patrick. *Irish Higher Education a Comparative Perspective.* Dublin: IPA, 2015.

Coleman, Marie. *IFUT—A History 1963–1999.* Dublin: IFUT, 2000.

Conway, Paul, and Rosaleen Murphy. 'A Rising Tide Meets a Perfect Storm: New Accountabilities in Teaching and Teacher Education in Ireland.' *Irish Educational Studies* 32, no. 1 (March 2013): 11–36.

Cooke, Jim. *A History of the Irish Vocational Education Association 1902–2002.* Dublin: IVEA, 2009.

Coolahan, John. 'From Royal University to National University.' In *The National University of Ireland 1908–2008 Centenary Essays*, edited by Tom Dunne, John Coolahan, Maurice Manning, and Gearóid Ó Tuathaigh, 3–18. Dublin: UCD Press, 2008.

Coolahan, John. *Towards the Era of Lifelong Learning A History of Irish Education, 1800–2016.* Dublin: IPA, 2017.

Coolahan, John. 'The NUI and the Changing Structure of Higher Education.' In *The National University of Ireland 1908–2008 Centenary Essays*, edited by Tom Dunne, John Coolahan, Maurice Manning, and Gearóid Ó Tuathaigh, 261–79. Dublin: UCD Press, 2008.

Coolahan, John. 'Higher Education in Ireland.' In *A New History of Ireland, 1921–84*, vol. 7, edited by J. R. Hill, 757–795. Oxford: Oxford University Press, 2003.

Duff, Thomas, Joe Hegarty, and Matthew Hussey, eds. *The Story of the Dublin Institute of Technology.* Dublin: Book Gallery, 2000. Accessed 1 February 2016. http://arrow.dit.ie/ditpress/1.

Duncan, Mark, Eoin Kinsella, and Paul Rouse. *National College of Ireland: Past, Present, Future*. Dublin: The Liffey Press, 2007.

Fahey, Tony, and John FitzGerald. 'The Educational Revolution and Demographic Change.' In *Medium Term Review 1997–2003*, edited by David Duffy, John FitzGerald, Ide Kearney, and Fergal Shortall, 7–33. Dublin: ESRI, 1997.

Fanning, Ronan. 'T.K. Whitaker 1976–96.' In *The National University of Ireland 1908–2008 Centenary Essays*, edited by Tom Dunne, John Coolahan, Maurice Manning, and Gearóid Ó Tuathaigh, 146–62. Dublin: UCD Press, 2008.

Ferlie, Ewan, Christine Musselin, and Gianluca Andresani. 'The Steering of Higher Education Systems: A Public Management Perspective.' *Higher Education* 56, no. 3 (2009): 325–348.

Ferriter, Diarmaid. *The Transformation of Ireland 1900–2000*. London: Profile, 2004.

Ferriter, Diarmuid. *Ambiguous Republic: Ireland in the 1970s*. London: Profile, 2012.

Ferriter, Diarmuid. '"For God's Sake Send Me a Few Packets of Fags": The College, 1922–45." In *St. Patrick's College Drumcondra 1875–2000 a History*, edited by James Kelly, 133–57. Dublin: Four Courts Press, 2006.

FitzGerald, Garret. *All in a Life*. Dublin: Gill and Macmillan, 1991.

FitzGerald, John, Ide Kearney, Edgar Morgenroth, and Diarmuid Smyth. *National Investment Priorities for the Period 2000 to 2006*. Dublin: ESRI, 1999.

Fleming, Ted, Andrew Loxley, and Fergal Finnegan, eds. *Access and Participation in Irish Higher Education*. London: Palgrave Macmillan, 2017.

Fuller, Louise. *Irish Catholicism Since 1950: The Undoing of a Culture*. Dublin: Gill and Macmillan, 2002.

Garvin, Tom. 'A Confederacy of Dunces: The Assault on Higher Education in Ireland.' In *Degrees of Nonsense the Demise of the University in Ireland*, edited by Brendan Walsh, 65–87. Dublin: Glasnevin Press, 2012.

Geiger, R. L. *Private Sectors in Higher Education: Structure, Function and Change in Eight Countries*. Ann Arbor: University of Michigan, 1986.

Gleeson, Jim. 'The European Credit Transfer System and Curriculum Design: Product Before Process?' *Studies in Higher Education* 38, no. 6 (2013): 921–38. Accessed 16 October 2013. https://doi.org/10.1080/03075079.2011.610101.

Harford, Judith. 'Women and the Irish University Question.' In *Have Women Made a Difference? Women in Irish Universities, 1850–2010*, edited by Judith Harford and Claire Rush, 7–24. Oxford: Peter Lang, 2010.

Hazelkorn, Ellen, Andrew Gibson, and Siobhán Harkin. 'From Massification to Globalisation: Reflections on the Transformation of Irish Higher Education.' In *The State in Transition: Essays in Honour of John Horgan*, edited by Kevin Rafter and Mark O'Brien, 235–60. Dublin: New Island, 2015.

Hazelkorn, Ellen. *Rankings and the Reshaping of Higher Education: The Battle for World Class Excellence*. Basingstoke: Palgrave Macmillan, 2015.

Hedley, Steve. 'Managerialism in Irish Universities.' *Irish Journal of Legal Studies* 1, no. 1 (2010): 117–141.

Highman, Ludovic. 'A Case Study on Differentiation in the Mission and Role of Higher Education Institutions in Ireland.' Ph.D. diss., TCD, 2015.

Hussey, Gemma. *At the Cutting Edge, Cabinet Diaries 1982–87.* Dublin: Gill and Macmillan, 1990.

Hyland, Áine, and Kenneth Milne, ed. *Irish Educational Documents*, 2. Dublin: CICE, 1992.

Irish, Tomás. *Trinity in War and Revolution 1912–23.* Dublin: RIA, 2015.

Jones, Valerie. 'Coláiste Moibhi: The Last Preparatory College.' *Irish Educational Studies* 15, no. 1 (1996): 101–11.

Kelham, Brian. 'The Royal College of Science for Ireland (1867–1926).' *Studies: An Irish Quarterly Review* 56, no. 223 (Autumn 1967): 297–309. http://www.jstor.org/stable/30087833.

Keogh, Dáire. 'William J. Walsh.' In *The National University of Ireland 1908–2008 Centenary Essays*, edited by Tom Dunne, John Coolahan, Maurice Manning, and Gearóid Ó Tuathaigh, 121–34. Dublin: UCD Press, 2008.

King, Carla. 'The Early Years of the College, 1875–1921.' In *St. Patrick's College Drumcondra 1875–2000 a History*, edited by James Kelly, 91–129. Dublin: Four Courts Press, 2006.

Leahy, Mary, and Mary Muldowney. 'Catering and Cleaning Workers in a University Environment.' In *HEEU Conference Proceedings*, 22–23 September 1995. Accessed 1 September 2017.https://www.ucc.ie/publications/heeu/womenstf/5_leahy.htm#top.

Lee, Joseph. *Ireland 1912–1985: Politics and Society.* Cambridge: Cambridge University Press, 1988.

Levy, Daniel C. *Higher Education and the State in Latin America: Private Challenges to Public Dominance.* Chicago: University of Chicago Press, 1986.

Limond, David. 'Prospects for a For-Profit, Private and Indigenous University in Dublin.' In *Higher Education in Ireland: Practices, Policies and Possibilities*, edited by Andrew Loxley, Aidan Seery, and John Walsh, 110–22. Basingstoke: Palgrave Macmillan, 2014.

Limond, David. 'Advanced Education for Working People: The Catholic Workers' College, a Case Study.' In *Essays in the History of Irish Education*, edited by Brendan Walsh, 339–58. Dublin: Palgrave Macmillan, 2016.

Loxley, Andrew. 'From Seaweed and Peat to Pills and Very Small Things: Knowledge Production and Higher Education in the Irish Context.' In *Higher Education in Ireland: Practices, Policies and Possibilities*, edited by Andrew Loxley, Aidan Seery, and John Walsh, 55–85. Basingstoke: Palgrave Macmillan, 2014.

Loxley, Andrew, Aidan Seery, and John Walsh, eds. *Higher Education in Ireland: Practices, Policies and Possibilities*. Basingstoke: Palgrave Macmillan, 2014.

Loxley, Andrew, Fergal Finnegan, and Ted Fleming. 'Routes in: Access Categories, Mechanisms and Processes.' In *Access and Participation in Irish Higher Education*, edited by Ted Fleming, Andrew Loxley, and Fergal Finnegan, 87–106. London: Palgrave Macmillan, 2017.

Loxley, Andrew, Fergal Finnegan, and Ted Fleming. 'Access and Widening Participation: Stories from the Policy Domain.' In *Access and Participation in Irish Higher Education*, edited by Ted Fleming, Andrew Loxley, and Fergal Finnegan, 45–85. London: Palgrave Macmillan, 2017.

Luce, John V. *Trinity College Dublin: The First 400 Years*. Dublin: Trinity College Dublin Press, 1992.

Lydon, James. 'The Silent Sister: Trinity College and Catholic Ireland.' In *Trinity College Dublin and the Idea of a University*, edited by C. H. Holland. Dublin: Trinity College Dublin Press, 1992.

Lyons, FSL. *Ireland Since the Famine*. London: Fontana, 1973.

Mac Mathúna, Séamus. 'National University of Ireland, Galway.' In *The National University of Ireland 1908–2008 Centenary Essays*, edited by Tom Dunne, John Coolahan, Maurice Manning, and Gearóid Ó Tuathaigh, 63–86. Dublin: UCD Press, 2008.

McCartney, Donal. *The National University of Ireland and Eamon de Valera*. Dublin: University Press of Ireland, 1983.

McCartney, Donal. *UCD—A National Idea: The History of University College Dublin*. Dublin: Gill and Macmillan, 1999.

McCoy, Selina, Emer Smyth, Dorothy Watson, and Merike Darmody. *Leaving School in Ireland: A Longitudinal Study of Post-school Transitions*. Dublin: ESRI, 2014.

McDowell, R. B., and D. A. Webb. *Trinity College Dublin 1592–1992 an Academic History*. Cambridge: Cambridge University Press, 1982.

McGrath, Fergal. *Newman's University: Idea and Reality.* Dublin: Browne and Nolan, 1951.

MacHale, J. P. 'The University Merger.' *Studies* 56, no. 2 (1967): 122–9.

McMahon, Frank. 'Bologna: Consonance or Dissonance.' In *Higher Education in Ireland: Practices, Policies and Possibilities,* edited by Andrew Loxley, Aidan Seery, and John Walsh, 172–85. Basingstoke: Palgrave Macmillan, 2014.

McManus, Antonia. 'The Transformation of Irish Education: The Ministerial Legacy, 1919–1999.' In *Essays in the History of Irish Education,* edited by Brendan Walsh, 267–96. London: Palgrave Macmillan, 2016.

McQuaid, John Charles. *Higher Education for Catholics.* Dublin: McGill & Son, 1961.

Mayes, Elizabeth. 'The 1960s and '70s: Decades of Change.' In *A Danger to the Men,* edited by Susan Parkes, 202–19. Dublin: Lilliput Press, 2004.

Marginson, Simon, and Gary Rhoades. 'Beyond Nation States, Markets and Systems of Higher Education: A Glonacal Agency Heuristic.' *Higher Education* 43 (2002): 281–309.

Meenan, James. 'The University in Dublin.' *Studies* 57, no. 3 (1968): 314–20.

Moody, T. W. 'The Irish University Question of the Nineteenth Century.' *History* 43 (1958): 90–109.

Moody, T. W. 'The University Merger.' *Studies* 56, no. 2 (1967): 173–5.

Moody, T. W., and J. C. Beckett. *Queen's Belfast 1845–1949: The History of a University,* vol. 1. London: Faber & Faber, 1959.

Morrissey, Thomas J. *Towards a National University, William Delany S.J. 1835–1924.* Dublin: Wolfhound, 1983.

Murchan, Damian. 'Changing Curriculum and Assessment Mindsets in Higher Education.' In *Higher Education in Ireland: Practices, Policies and Possibilities,* edited by Andrew Loxley, Aidan Seery, and John Walsh, 186–97. Basingstoke: Palgrave Macmillan, 2014.

Murphy, Gary. *In Pursuit of the Promised Land, the Politics of Post-War Ireland, 1945–61.* Dublin: Mercier Press, 2009.

Murphy, John A. *The College a History of Queen's/University College Cork, 1845–1995.* Cork: Cork University Press, 1995.

Neave, Guy. 'Academic Drift: Some Views from Europe.' *Studies in Higher Education* 4, no. 2 (1979): 143–59. Accessed 1 February 2015. https://doi.org/10.1080/03075077912331376927.

Neave, Guy. 'The Changing Boundary Between the State and Higher Education.' *European Journal of Education* 17, no. 2 (1982): 231–41.

Newman, John Henry. *Discourses on the Scope and Nature of University Education: Addressed to the Catholics of Dublin.* Dublin: James Duffy, 1852.

Nolan, Ann, and John Walsh. "'In What Orbit We Shall Find Ourselves, No One Could Predict': Institutional Reform, the University Merger and Ecclesiastical Influence on Irish Higher Education in the 1960s." *Irish Historical Studies* 41, no. 159 (2017): 77–96. https://doi.org/10.1017/ihs.2017.7.

Nolan, John. 'The Recognised Colleges.' In *The National University of Ireland 1908–2008 Centenary Essays*, edited by Tom Dunne, John Coolahan, Maurice Manning, and Gearóid Ó Tuathaigh, 192–227. Dublin: UCD Press, 2008.

Ó Broin, Léon. *The Chief Secretary: Augustine Birrell in Ireland.* London: Chatto & Windus, 1969.

Ó Buachalla, Séamus. 'Policy and Structural Developments in Irish Higher Education.' *European Journal of Education* 19, no. 2 (1984): 165–171.

Ó Buachalla, Séamus. *Education Policy in Twentieth Century Ireland.* Dublin: Wolfhound, 1988.

Ó Buachalla, Séamus. 'Self-Regulation and the Emergence of the Evaluative State: Trends in Irish Higher Education Policy, 1987–92.' *European Journal of Education* 27, no. 1–2 (1992): 69–78.

Ó Cathail, Séamus. 'Ireland: The University and the State.' *Cre-Information* 58, no. 2 (1982): 44–55.

Ó Ceallaigh, Tadhg. *Coláiste Phádraig: St. Patrick's College, Centenary Booklet, 1875–1975.* Dublin: St. Patrick's College, 1975.

O'Connor, Loreto. *Passing on the Torch a History of Mary Immaculate College, 1898–1998.* Dublin: Mary Immaculate College, 1998.

O'Connor, Pat. 'Gender and Organisational Culture at Senior Management Level: Limits and Possibilities for Change.' In *Have Women Made a Difference? Women in Irish Universities, 1850–2010*, edited by Judith Harford and Claire Rush, 139–60. Oxford: Peter Lang, 2010.

O'Connor, Seán. *A Troubled Sky: Reflections on the Irish Education Scene, 1957–68.* Dublin: Educational Research Centre, 1986.

O'Connor, Tom. 'Natural Philosophy/Physics.' In *From Queen's College to National University Essays on the Academic History of QCG/UCG/NUI Galway*, edited by Tadhg Foley, 184–217. Dublin: Four Courts Press, 1999.

O'Donoghue, Tom, Judith Harford, and Teresa O'Doherty. *Teacher Preparation in Ireland: History, Policy and Future Directions.* Bingley: Emerald Publishing, 2017.

O'Farrell, Ciara. 'Challenges and Opportunities for Teaching and Learning.' In *Higher Education in Ireland: Practices, Policies and Possibilities*, edited by Andrew Loxley, Aidan Seery, and John Walsh, 233–52. Basingstoke: Palgrave Macmillan, 2014.

O'Flynn, Paddy. *A Question of Identity: The Great Trinity and UCD Merger Plan of the 1960s*. Dublin: Farmar, 2012.

O'Meara, J. J. *Reform in Education*. Dublin: Mount Salus Press, 1958.

O'Malley, Donogh. 'University Education in Dublin: Statement of Minister for Education—18 April 1967.' *Studies* 56, no. 2 (1967): 113–21.

Ó Riain, Seán. 'The University and the Public Sphere After the Celtic Tiger.' Unpublished collection, Maynooth Philosophical Papers (2006). Accessed 15 July 2017. http://eprints.maynoothuniversity.ie/555/.

O'Rourke, Mary. *Just Mary: A Memoir*. Dublin: Gill and Macmillan, 2012.

O'Sullivan, Denis. *Cultural Politics and Irish Education Since the 1950s: Policy, Paradigms and Power*. Dublin: IPA, 2005.

O'Sullivan, Irene. 'Administrative Staff in a University Environment.' In *HEEU Conference Proceedings*, 22–23 September 1995. Accessed 1 September 2017. https://www.ucc.ie/publications/heeu/womenstf/6_sullivan.htm#top.

O'Sullivan, Rory. "From the 'Cinderella' to 'the Fourth Pillar' of the Irish Education System—A Critical Analysis of the Evolution of Further Education and Training in Ireland." Ph.D. diss., TCD, 2018.

Olssen, Mark, and Michael Peters. 'Neoliberalism, Higher Education and the Knowledge Economy: From the Free Market to Knowledge Capitalism.' *Journal of Education Policy* 20, no. 3 (2005): 313–45.

Our Lady of Mercy College, Carysfort Park. *Centenary 1877/1977 Our Lady of Mercy College Carysfort Park, Blackrock, Co. Dublin*. Dublin: Carysfort College, 1977.

Parkes, Susan. *Kildare Place: The History of Church of Ireland Training College and College of Education 1811–2010*. Dublin: CICE Publications, 2011.

Parkes, Susan. 'The First Decade, 1904–14: A Quiet Revolution.' In *A Danger to the Men*, edited by Susan Parkes, 55–86. Dublin: Lilliput Press, 2004.

Parkes, Susan. "The 'Steamboat Ladies': The First World War and After." In *A Danger to the Men*, edited by Susan Parkes, 87–112. Dublin: Lilliput Press, 2004.

Parkes, Susan. 'The 1930s: Consolidation but Still Discrimination.' In *A Danger to the Men*, edited by Susan Parkes, 113–41. Dublin: Lilliput Press, 2004.

Parkes, Susan. 'A Hundred Years On.' In *A Danger to the Men*, edited by Susan Parkes, 296–302. Dublin: Lilliput Press, 2004.

Parkes, Susan. '"An Essential Service": The National Board and Teacher Education." In *Essays in the History of Irish Education*, edited by Brendan Walsh, 45–82. Dublin: Palgrave Macmillan, 2016.

Paseta, Senia. 'Achieving Equality: Women and the Foundation of the University.' In *The National University of Ireland 1908–2008 Centenary Essays*, edited by Tom Dunne, John Coolahan, Maurice Manning, and Gearóid Ó Tuathaigh, 19–32. Dublin: UCD Press, 2008.

Pekin, Harold. 'The Historical Perspective.' In *Perspectives on Higher Education Eight Disciplinary and Comparative Views*, edited by Burton Clark. Berkeley: University of California Press, 1984.

Quinn, Ruairi. 'Delivering the Strategy for Higher Education.' Address by the Minister for Education and Skills to the Royal Irish Academy. Dublin: DES, 30 May 2011.

Raftery, Adrian, and Michael Hout. 'Maximally Maintained Inequality: Expansion, Reform and Opportunity in Irish Education, 1921–75.' *Sociology of Education* 66, no. 1 (1993): 41–62.

Randles, Eileen. *Post-primary Education in Ireland 1957–70*. Dublin: Veritas Publications, 1975.

Relihan, Martina. 'The Church of Ireland, the State and Education in Irish Language and Irish History, 1920s–1950s.' In *Educating Ireland, Schooling and Social Change, 1700–2000*, edited by Deirdre Raftery and Karin Fischer, 147–72. Kildare: Irish Academic Press, 2014.

Rhoades, Gary, and Sheila Slaughter. 'Academic Capitalism in the New Economy: Challenges and Choices.' *American Academic* 1 (2004): 37–59.

Rigney, William J. 'Bartholomew Woodlock and the Catholic University of Ireland 1861–79.' Ph.D. diss., UCD, 1995.

Seery, Aidan, John Walsh, and Andrew Loxley. 'Investment: The Tests of Time.' *Irish Educational Studies* 33, no. 2 (2014): 173–91.

Skilbeck, Malcolm. *Towards an Integrated System of Tertiary Education: A Discussion Paper*. Dublin: DIT, 2003. Accessed 1 September 2013. https://dit.ie/media/newsdocuments/2003/Skilbeckdiscussionpaper_march2003.pdf.

Smyth, Ailbhe. 'Reviewing Breaking the Circle: A Pilot Project.' In *HEEU Conference Proceedings*, 22–23 September 1995. Accessed 1 September 2017. https://www.ucc.ie/publications/heeu/womenstf/1_smyth.htm#top.

Smyth, Séamus. 'National University of Ireland, Maynooth.' In *The National University of Ireland 1908–2008 Centenary Essays*, edited by Tom Dunne, John Coolahan, Maurice Manning, and Gearóid Ó Tuathaigh, 100–6. Dublin: UCD Press, 2008.

Smyth, Steffi. 'Teachers' Perceptions of the Literacy and Numeracy Strategy Within the Primary Curriculum: Challenges and Implications.' M.Ed. diss., TCD, 2015.

Sugrue, Ciarán. 'Three Decades of College Life, 1973–1999: The Old Order Changeth?' In *St. Patrick's College Drumcondra 1875–2000 A History*, edited by James Kelly, 225–65. Dublin: Four Courts Press, 2006.

St. Aubyn, Miguel, Alvaro Pina, Filomena Garcia, and Joana Pais. 'Study on the Efficiency and Effectiveness of Public Spending on Tertiary Education.' *Economic Papers* 390 (November 2009). Brussels: European Commission, 2009.

Teichler, Ulrich. 'Changing Structures of the Higher Education Systems: The Increasing Complexity of the Underlying Forces.' In *Diversification of Higher Education and the Changing Role of Knowledge and Research*, UNESCO Forum Occasional Paper Series no. 6, 3–16. Paris: UNESCO, 2004.

Tierney, Dan, et al. *Science Technology and Innovation Advisory Council Report*. Dublin: Forfas, 1995.

Trow, Martin. *Problems in the Transition from Elite to Mass Higher Education*. California: Carnegie Commission, 1973.

Trow, Martin. 'Reflections on the Transition from Elite to Mass to Universal Access: Forms and Phases of Higher Education in Modern Societies Since WWII.' Working Papers. Berkeley: University of California, 2005. Accessed 1 December 2015. https://escholarship.org/uc/item/96p3s213.

Vaira, Massimiliano. 'Globalisation and Higher Education: A Framework for Analysis.' *Higher Education* 48 (2004): 483–510.

Valiulis, Maryann. 'The Establishment of the Centre for Gender and Women's Studies.' In *A Danger to the Men*, edited by Susan Parkes, 220–36. Dublin: Lilliput Press, 2004.

Von Humboldt, Wilhelm. 'On the Spirit and the Organisational Framework of Intellectual Institutions in Berlin.' *Minerva: A Review of Science, Learning and Policy* 8, no. 2 (April 1970): 242–50.

Walshe, John. *A New Partnership in Education: From Consultation to Legislation in the Nineties*. Dublin: IPA, 1999.

Walshe, John. *An Education: How an Outsider Became an Insider—And Learned What Really Goes on in Irish government*. Dublin: Penguin, 2014.

Walsh, John. 'An Era of Expansion, 1945–75.' In *St. Patrick's College Drumcondra 1875–2000: A History*, edited by James Kelly, 158–83. Dublin: Four Courts Press, 2006.

Walsh, John. 'Eamon de Valera, 1921–75'. In *The National University of Ireland 1908–2008 Centenary Essays*, edited by Tom Dunne, John Coolahan, Maurice Manning, and Gearóid Ó Tuathaigh, 135–45. Dublin: UCD Press, 2008.

Walsh, John. *The Politics of Expansion: The Transformation of Educational Policy in the Republic of Ireland, 1957–72*. Manchester: Manchester University Press, 2009.

Walsh, John. 'International Influence, Domestic Elites and the Transformation of Higher Technical Education in Ireland.' *Irish Educational Studies* 30, no. 3 (September 2011): 365–81.

Walsh, John. 'The Transformation of Higher Education in Ireland.' In *Higher Education in Ireland: Practices, Policies and Possibilities*, edited by Andrew Loxley et al., 5–32. Basingstoke: Palgrave Macmillan, 2014.

Walsh, John. '"The Problem of Trinity College Dublin": A Historical Perspective on Rationalisation in Higher Education in Ireland." *Irish Educational Studies* 33, no. 1 (2014): 1–16. https://doi.org/10.1080/03323 315.2013.867095.

Walsh, John, and Andrew Loxley. "The Hunt Report and Higher Education Policy in the Republic of Ireland: 'An International Solution to an Irish problem?'" *Studies in Higher Education* 40, no. 6 (2015): 1128–45. https://doi.org/10.1080/03075079.2014.881350.

Walsh, John. 'Creating a Modern Educational System: International Influence, Domestic Elites and the Transformation of the Irish Educational Sector, 1950–75.' In *Essays in the History of Irish Education*, edited by Brendan Walsh, 235–60. Dublin: Palgrave Macmillan, 2016.

Walsh, Tom. 'The National System of Education.' In *Essays in the History of Irish Education*, edited by Brendan Walsh, 7–43. Dublin: Palgrave Macmillan, 2016.

White, Tony. *Investing in People: Higher Education in Ireland from 1960 to 2000*. Dublin: IPA, 2001.

Whyte, J. H. *Church and State in Modern Ireland 1923–1979*. Dublin: Gill and Macmillan, 1980.

Williams, T. Desmond. 'The College and the Nation.' In *Struggle with Fortune: A Miscellany for the Centenary of the Catholic University of Ireland 1854–1954*, edited by Michael Tierney, 166–92. Dublin: UCD, 1954.

Newspapers

Belfast Newsletter
Evening Herald
Limerick Leader
Irish Examiner
Irish Independent
Irish Press
Irish Times
Spectator
Silicon Republic
Sunday Chronicle
Times Higher Education
University Observer

Online Sources

http://www.aishe.org/. Accessed 1 November 2017.
http://www.dbs.ie/about-dbs/history-of-dbs. Accessed 16 September 2017.
http://www.edin.ie/. Accessed 1 November 2017.
'The Lisbon strategy in short.' https://portal.cor.europa.eu/europe2020/Profiles/Pages/TheLisbonStrategyinshort.aspx. Accessed 1 December 2017.
https://www.griffith.ie/about-griffith/background/our-history. Accessed 16 September 2017.
http://www.heca.ie/about-us/. Accessed 16 September 2017.
http://www.finance.gov.ie/news-centre/press-releases/appointment-colin-hunt-special-adviser-department-finance. Accessed 31 July 2017.
http://www.jesuit.ie/news/jesuits-teaching-the-teachers/downloaded. Accessed 15 November 2015.

Other Reports and Statements

IFUT. Report to Annual Delegate Conference 2017. IFUT: 2017.
IFUT. Press Statement by Mike Jennings, 11 October 2016.
INTO. Annual Report of the CEC 1968–69. INTO: 1969.

TUI Press Statement. Accessed 11 January 2016 and 31 July 2017. https://
www.tui.ie/press-releases/technological-universities-bill-must-be-amend-
ed-to-protect-sector-.7925.html.

Note on Interviews

The interviews fell into two distinct categories. A number of interviews were
conducted with recent participants in the policy-making process who discussed their recollections on the basis of anonymity and confidentiality.
These interviews have been anonymised and these interviewees are identified only by pseudonym (for example, Interviewee A): the data has been
kept confidential and is being used only for the purpose of this study.

Interviews were also conducted with retired politicians, civil servants and academics, where it was not possible to achieve anonymity: in this instance no
guarantee of anonymity was given. All interviews were conducted in accordance with the terms of the approval granted for this research project by the
School of Education Research Ethics Committee, Trinity College Dublin.

List of Interviewees

Prof. John Coolahan

Mr. James Dukes

Dr. Patrick Hillery

Mr. Tony Ó Dálaigh

Prof. Martin O'Donoghue

Mr. Ruairi Quinn TD

Gary Rhoades and Sheila Slaughter. 'Academic Capitalism in the new economy: challenges and choices.' American Academic 1 (2004): 37-59.

Walshe, John. An Education: How an Outsider Became an Insider—And
Learned What Really Goes on in Irish government. Dublin: Penguin, 2014.

Index

academic freedom 3, 4, 27, 68, 137,
 244, 345, 414
 Hunt Report 448
 Institutes of Technology Act,
  2006 428
 Universities Act, 1997 367, 368,
  370, 409
academic governance. *See* governance
  and leadership; managerial
  reform
academic salaries 207
 DIAS 78, 81–2
 NUI colleges 191, 192, 193, 194
  pay cuts protest 66–70
  UCG 36, 37, 41, 193, 196
  upgrading 195–6, 223
 TCD 49, 51, 197, 198, 208, 209
academic staff

gender equality. *See* gender disparities; women's participation
 Irish language requirement in
  UCG 41
 pay. *See* academic salaries
 professional development 346,
  395–6
 promotions disputes 420–1
 tenure 338, 409, 427
access and participation 354–7, 368,
 414–19. *See also* elite system
 action group 355–6, 418
 core funding for access performance 431
 disabilities, students with 414–15,
  417, 418
 effectively maintained inequality
  (EMI) 416
 equality agenda 419, 428, 488

© The Editor(s) (if applicable) and The Author(s) 2018
J. Walsh, *Higher Education in Ireland, 1922–2016*,
https://doi.org/10.1057/978-1-137-44673-2

Lightning Source UK Ltd.
Milton Keynes UK
UKHW020635151220
375092UK00003B/373

9 781137 446725